The Migration Acquis Handbook

THE FOUNDATION FOR A COMMON EUROPEAN MIGRATION POLICY

The Migration Acquis Handbook

THE FOUNDATION FOR A COMMON
EUROPEAN MIGRATION POLICY

edited by

Peter J. van Krieken

T·M·C·ASSER PRESS
The Hague

Published by T.M.C. ASSER PRESS,
P.O.Box 16163, 2500 BD The Hague, The Netherlands

Sold and distributed in North, Central and South America
by Kluwer Law International,
675 Massachusetts Avenue, Cambridge, MA 02139, U.S.A.

In all other countries, sold and distributed
by Kluwer Law International, Distribution Centre,
P.O.Box 322, 3300 AH Dordrecht, The Netherlands

to be cited as:
P.J. van Krieken (ed.), *The Migration Acquis Handbook* (The Hague, 2001)

ISBN 90-6704-130-0

PREFACE

During the past two decades, industrialized countries, as well as countries in the South with higher and middle levels of income and economic growth, have witnessed record numbers of immigrants. Sustained poverty imbalances, population growth in developing countries combined with dramatic unemployment levels in these countries, ongoing conflict situations, easier communication and access to transport, as well as certain disruptive effects of new globalization policies, are among the key factors that will contribute to ongoing levels of increased migration. In recent years, growing proportions of migrants have been moving irregularly and without authorization to enter. Others have been having recourse to asylum procedures, without fulfilling the conditions for refugee status or other forms of protection. In addition, migrant trafficking, which highlights the growing link between irregular migration and international crime, constitutes a further significant challenge to States.

Increasingly, migration, in particular irregular migration that occurs outside State control, represents an emotionally-charged issue. Touching upon the core fabric of our societies, it has become a priority issue on political agendas, and also tends to be debated in a polarized manner where extreme positions often dominate.

From this perspective, the need for governments to re-establish a more orderly process concerning migration is recognized as a major challenge for all affected countries. Addressing the highly complex migration equation in a comprehensive, innovative and long-term approach is thus imperative, based on considerations related to clear immigration, admission and integration criteria; foreign labour requirements; protection of individual rights of both refugees and other migrants; control, prevention and return; dialogue and co-operation between receiving and sending countries; and longer-term efforts for improving economic and political conditions in migrant source countries.

The European Union, in recent years, has made significant progress in approaching migration issues in a concerted and co-ordinated manner. Until 1992, migration and refugee matters fell squarely within the sovereign realm of Member States. Since then, however, with the Maastricht Treaty, and in particular with the entry into force of the Amsterdam Treaty on 1 May 1999, the policy on asylum, the free movement of persons, visa policy, rules governing the crossing of the EU's external borders, immigration policy and the rights of nationals of third countries, have all become full Community responsibility. Building on the impetus of the Amsterdam Treaty, the special meeting of the European Council in Tampere, Finland, in October 1999 agreed that 'the separate but closely related issues of asylum and migration call for the development of a common EU policy'; it discussed the establishment of an Area of Freedom, Security and Justice; and elaborated the political guidelines for the coming years, including in the field of asylum and immigration. In Tampere, it was thus recognized that the EU needed a common migration policy based on a comprehensive approach to migration that would also address political, human rights and development issues in countries of origin and transit. This policy would be composed of the following elements: partnerships with countries of origin; a common European asylum system; fair treatment of third country nationals; and an effective management of migration flows.

Various factors are contributing to the construction of a common EU migration policy. A first element is the increasing recognition among migrant sending and receiving countries alike of the link between migration and conditions in countries of origin. Taking economic, demographic, social, political and human rights situations in the countries of origin into account represents an essential element for tackling present and future migration challenges. By moving closer to a partnership approach in which European states work alongside countries of origin, migration concerns in both sending and receiving states are more likely to be addressed with a view to long-term solutions.

A second element is the incremental progress made in establishing a common European asylum system. Asylum constitutes a sub-element of the larger migration debate, as asylum claims are often made within the framework of migration movements. While the concepts of migration and asylum are separate and distinct and consequently entail different responses, developments in the area of asylum within the EU have quite naturally expanded the focus to the wider consideration of a common EU migration policy.

Third, in the early stages of the European Community, the construction of a common border led to the recognition of the need to co-ordinate entry rules ranging from border controls to visa requirements. The Schengen Convention (1990) and subsequent agreements on entry procedures and regulations have served to benefit EU signatory states but have also highlighted deficiencies in migration management and border control particularly with respect to illegal migration and, increasingly, concerning migrant trafficking rings.

Fourth, perhaps the component of a common migration policy that remains most elusive is that of the rights of migrants. Despite the drafting of a Charter of Fundamental Rights of the European Union which touches only briefly on the rights of nationals of third countries legally resident in the territory of a Member State, little headway has been made with respect to the rights (and obligations) of third country nationals within the EU. Incidences of social unrest and xenophobia also point to the link between integration and migration. Concrete steps towards an effective integration policy are set out in the Tampere Declaration that states: 'A more vigorous integration policy should aim at granting (third country nationals) rights and obligations comparable to those of EU citizens. It should also enhance non-discrimination in economic, social and cultural life and develop measures against racism and xenophobia'. Antonio Vitorino, the Commissioner for Justice and Home Affairs, goes further in a communication dated 22 November 2000, suggesting that: 'The Charter of Fundamental Rights could provide a reference for the development of the concept of civic citizenship in a particular Member State (comprising a common set of core rights and obligations) for third country nationals. Enabling migrants to acquire such a citizenship after a minimum period of years might be a sufficient guarantee for many migrants to settle successfully into society or be a first step in the process of acquiring the nationality of the Member State concerned'.

Fifth, despite the fact that a clear desire exists to restrict immigration; to control who enters the EU; and to mitigate large migration flows, contemporary demographic figures point to an alarming decrease in the active European population in coming decades with a concomitant decline in the potential support ratio (PSR). This trend has in turn reoriented the immigration debate from one of restrictionism to one of guarded overture in order to meet labour force shortages and potentially to compensate for low fertility rates and population decrease. Whether approaching this demographic challenge solely by way of immigration rather than by placing emphasis on other means such as to ensure that an older European population remains active in the workforce, is a contemporary source of debate and reflection.

Finally, enlargement of the EU inevitably broaches the issue of migration both from the perspective of Candidate Countries, but also concerning what the blueprint of an expansive EU migration policy might look like. Efforts are focusing on controlling migration into the EU and on harmonizing Candidate Countries' migration policies and practice with that of EU states. By extension, these initiatives have called for a clearer vision of a comprehensive policy and more concrete migration objectives within the Union itself.

It is at this timely juncture and with the backdrop of sweeping developments in migration practice and policy over the last decade, that this *'Migration Acquis Handbook'* has been compiled. Constituting a complementary effort to the *Asylum Acquis Handbook* published in the Spring of 2000, it makes available relevant documentation relating to migration in Europe and reflects underpinning discussion and developments concerning a common European migration policy. It does so by incorporating commentaries on the greatest areas of concern affecting Europe in matters of migration today, namely, ageing and demography; globalization; illegal migration; trafficking; and family reunification, in addition to providing a compilation of EC/EU and international instruments relating to migration.

This *Migration Acquis Handbook* will serve as a most useful tool for government migration practitioners and policy makers, relevant international and national institutions, as well as academia and migration experts. We believe that it will significantly contribute to supporting and clarifying the ongoing debate on migration as Europe moves forward with the establishment of a common migration policy, based on co-operation and partnership with migrant source countries, equitable protection and treatment of third-country nationals, a common approach to asylum, and best practices in migration management. We also believe that the Handbook will contribute to a better overall understanding of the migration challenges at hand, and the gradual development of a 'common language in migration' among those who, from often differing perspectives, deal with the matter in sending, transit and receiving countries.

We wish to express our appreciation to the Editor of the Handbook, Dr. Peter van Krieken, and all the other partners who have contributed to this effort.

Dr. R.K. Jenny
Director
The International
Migration Policy Programme (IMP)
UNITAR Senior Special Fellow

ACKNOWLEDGEMENTS

This Handbook is the logical follow-up to the *Asylum Acquis Handbook* which was published last year by the same publisher. Attention in Europe tends to focus on asylum rather than migration as such, and voices can often be heard that Europe should start formulating a proper and appropriate migration policy. It should, however, come as no surprise – to citizens, students, policy makers and the media in the European Union or in the Candidate Countries – that a great many instruments and documents are already available, indicating that the discussion on this issue is by no means a recent one.

The main impetus for this Handbook comes from the Netherlands Chapter of the Society for International Development, their international and multidisciplinary project on the future of asylum and migration in particular. But also the IMP and ICMPD – which gave me the opportunity to embark and elaborate on the various themes contained in this Handbook in far-away places – have been instrumental, as was the Röling Foundation. All these organizations deserve proper thanks.

Additional thanks go first of all to Dr. Rolf Jenny, IMP's inspiring Director who also provided the Preface. Next come Ms Lisa Batey (Chapter 5), and Ms Sabrina van Miltenburg who greatly assisted in the process of creating a sense-making structure for this Handbook and who edited Chapter 3 on EC/EU instruments, as well as Messr. Abella, Chiswick, Garson and Ghosh, excerpts of whose, often unpublished, papers have been kindly incorporated in Chapter 2. Moreover, I owe the team of T. M. C. Asser Press and Mr Peter Morris, the language editor, special thanks for their efficient and supportive roles. But the bouquet of (red) roses goes to Juliette Pieters without whom this and similar 'enterprises' would have been bound to fail.

TABLE OF CONTENTS

INTRODUCTION

(motto: machines were mice and men were lions,
once upon a time, but now that it's the opposite,
it's twice upon a time[1])

The first decade of the new millennium confronts Europe with challenges relating
to five subjects in particular:
- the urge to provide a sustainable basis for employment and growth;
- the need to create an area of freedom, security and justice;
- the enlargement of the Union with the candidate countries from Eastern and
  Central Europe;
- the commitment to strive for a common foreign and security policy, and
- the decision to agree on a common asylum and migration policy.

It could be argued that these five subjects are interrelated: the enlargement might
result in migratory flows, albeit within the Union as such and not necessarily involving third-country nationals. Sustainable growth may bring about the need for
labour immigration. Foreign policy may wish to focus on globalization, and the
latter may result in the abolition of agricultural subsidies, which in turn may have
an impact on the need for foreign labour.

It is quite probable that migration, employment and sustainable growth are
part and parcel of the same equation. Many submit that in order to ensure growth,
an active migration policy would be a prerequisite, whereas others state that migration denies the unemployed the possibility to (re-)enter the labour market and
that migration may make it more difficult for the countries of origin to bridge income gaps. Moreover, it is submitted, generous migration frustrates and delays
the integration of the migrants who have hitherto arrived.

On yet another level, the concern about the changing structure of society, in
particular the divide between the young and the elderly, forces migration to come
to the fore. The payment of pensions is believed to reach a level which should be
considered an insurmountable burden for the young if they are indeed to cater for
the elderly. This will be witnessed for the first time when the baby-boomers reach
retirement age around the year 2015, but might increase until a new balance

---

[1] Moondog, 1968.

P.J. van Krieken (Ed.), The Migration Acquis Handbook
© *2001, T.M.C.Asser Press, The Hague, the Röling Foundation and the authors*

could be found around 2060. The retirement-age discussion is hence believed to be of great importance in and for the migration debate.

Of relevance is also the fact that by now most members of the Union have a population of which some 10% made up of newcomers, and that it is believed that this percentage will increase considerably over the next decade. Big cities in particular are supposed to absorb those newcomers resulting in such cities having 33-50% inhabitants with roots outside the Union. Related to this fact is the conclusion that many of the newcomers might not necessarily be prepared/educated to play an active role in an IT and service-oriented economy. Many of the newcomers are bound to become marginalized, and may add to the submission that through migration poverty is being imported. Any utilitarian approach – the selection of migrants on their skills and the Union's needs – will be 'frustrated' by family reunification and family formation, adding to the adagium that migration generates migration.

DEBATE

The debate is a difficult one, as it is bound to touch upon issues which for quite a while were believed to fall within the realm of what is considered politically incorrect. In the early 1990s a text from the 1975 Preamble of a relevant ILO Convention would certainly have been considered as 'not done': '... *emphasizing the need to avoid the excessive and uncontrolled or unassisted increase of migratory movements because of their negative social and human consequences ...*'[2] Yet, by now, this opinion is no longer disregarded as utter nonsense, although most observers would rather agree with statements like the following one from the IOM: '... *The continuation of international migration both reflects and contributes to the intensification of international and global communication networks that connect European societies with the rest of the world and suggests that it will remain an enduring and, in most respects, enriching aspect of social, political, and economic life in the region for a long time to come ...*'[3]

For many Europeans a generous approach to migration is also a way to try and improve the world at large. It is often submitted that Europe should share its wealth with those who, often after a long and enduring journey, reach their shores. Of course, migration contains both humanitarian and utilitarian aspects. Many leave their country of origin to improve their personal economic status. Many Europeans welcome their arrival, as it solves some of the pressures on the labour market. But, as it were, if 'globalization' would be allowed to enter the equation, non-migration would probably have a more positive impact, as the brain drain would be avoided and as marginal industries would either be forced to

---

[2] ILO C143, 1975; included in full in this Handbook in Chapter 4.4.2.
[3] IOM, *World Migration Report 2000*, p. 213.

introduce innovations and/or to shift activities to lower-wage countries, thereby creating win/win situations.

The issue of migration and globalization also touches upon one of the more sensitive issues in the Union, that of the agricultural subsidies and other protective measures. The fact is often neglected that the total amount of the EU development aid (Brussels and the respective capitals together[4]) is less than what we pay in the Union on agricultural subsidies. As the forthcoming enlargement of the Union forces a rethink of agricultural subsidies in general (as the total bill would become insurmountable if farmers in the candidate countries would have access to similar generous subsidies as their peers in the present Union), the enlargement as such may have an impact on the formulation of a third-country migration policy as well.

FABRIC

Migration is not only about the importation of labour. It is about welcoming new members to a society. It is about solidarity and common values. It is in this respect of the utmost importance to realize that the melting-pot model, like the one applied and promoted in the USA, is melting away. Whereas some ten years ago newcomers would be frustrated if they would not be allowed to enter the mainstream, they now protest if they are forced to enter the mainstream.[5] Migrants no longer necessarily subscribe to the need and logic of becoming members of a new society, as transnationalism allows them to live and work in one place, and to focus their ideas, ideals and concerns on another. Likewise, many of the newcomers can perfectly survive in their own community, speaking the language of the country of origin, using their own banks, their own travel offices, retaining their own norms and values, without the need to communicate with and/or to integrate into the host community. Dishes and cheap charters are symbolic for such an approach.

Related to attitudes, approaches and the issue of integration in general, the notion is gaining attention, particularly now that the lessons of trafficking and smuggling are becoming clear, that the difficult question needs to be asked whether persons who enter a new society by hook or by crook can be expected to change behaviour and attitudes once they have obtained their short-term goal, a (de-facto) residence permit. It should not be denied that abuse takes place by either the newcomers or the scrupulous employers who by hiring e.g. irregular or undocumented migrants falsify market mechanisms and place a bomb under the social security system in its present form. *Already in 1981, the US Select Com-*

---

[4] It should be emphasized that, in conformity with OECD rules, (part of) the cost of e.g. catering for and processing asylum seekers in Europe may be set against ODA, the official development aid.

[5] See e.g. Huntington, the Erosion of American National Interests, *Foreign Affairs*, September/October 1997, pp. 28-49 on p. 33.

mission on Immigration and Refugee Policy argued 'Illegal migration (if un-checked) will continue to undermine the most valued ideals of this nation – the integrity of the law and the fundamental dignity of the individual'.[6] This argument remains equally valid today, as Ghosh, one of the leading experts in this field, submits.[7]

EUROPE

Europe is finally waking up to the challenges. With the Treaty of Amsterdam, the subject of migration is being moved from the Third Pillar to the First Pillar, meaning that it is now part and parcel of the TEC (Treaty establishing the European Community) rather than of the TEU (Treaty of the European Union). This *prima facie* subtle difference carries tremendous weight: by falling under the TEC, 'Brussels' will play the central and paramount role; TEU matters will continue to be mainly decided upon in the respective capitals.

By 1 May 2004 a European migration policy should be in place. The November 2000 Vitorino Communication (see Chapter 1) is a case in point. The Commission feels that it is essential to discuss the migration issues openly and to try and reach a consensus on the objectives of the policy to be formulated and to be followed. Both Article 63 of the EC Treaty (TEC) and the Tampere conclusions ('milestones') call for a common EU immigration policy. To reach this goal, the Commission submits, it is essential to coordinate and to ensure transparency.

It is with this in mind that it should be considered of paramount importance to realize what Europe has already produced and/or agreed upon in this very field. A Migration Acquis as such could be considered to be already in existence, a Union Acquis that is, rather than a Community Acquis. The 'Acquis' concerned is part of the enlargement process (through e.g. the TAIEX list) and deserves to be studied and elaborated upon.

This Handbook on the one hand provides flat information on the European Acquis as such, but also contains some documents originating from outside Europe (e.g. the United Nations), as the latter documents and instruments are believed to be of relevance for the European market. 'Views' are presented on some specific issues (ageing, globalization, illegal migration, trafficking and family reunification) with a dual goal: on the one hand, to assist the enlargement process by enabling the candidate countries to have easy access to a variety of documentation and, on the other, to contribute to an indeed badly needed discussion and debate on the theme of migration within the Union itself.

---

[6] Select Commission on Immigration and Refugee Policy, *US Immigration Policy and the National Interest* (Final Report), US Government Printing Office, Washington DC, 1981, p. 560.
[7] Bimal Ghosh, *Social and Economic Consequences of Irregular Migration*, paper 1999.

SOURCES

In order to fully appreciate the contents of the Acquis and the position of the Acquis in a wider context, regard should be had to the various sources.

Within the EC/EU proper, the following would apply:

First, the May 1998 Acquis occupies central stage. That list, after all, is the most authoritative.[8]

Second, the TAIEX list is to be considered to be of the utmost importance. It contains the instruments which the Candidate Countries have to take into account whilst striving to fulfil the conditions for membership of the EU.[9] Most of the EC/EU instruments which have been included carry a [T.x] number, which indeed refers to that TAIEX list.

Third, and basically the *pièce de résistance* of this Handbook, is the Communication On A Community Immigration Policy from Mr. Vitorino, the EU Commissioner responsible for migration (in agreement with Mrs Diamantopoulou, the Commissioner of Employment and Social Affairs) which was issued in late November 2000. This Communication (incorporated in this Handbook in Chapter 1) should, of course, be seen in the context of Title IV of the Consolidated Version of the Treaty Establishing the European Community (TEC), the Vienna Action Plan and the Tampere Milestones (relevant excerpts of the latter documents having been included in Chapter 3). Moreover, the 2000 EU Charter on Fundamental Freedoms also contains some specific references to migrants and migrant workers.

The topic of migration can be easily extended to a great many related fields. Difficult choices had to be made concerning the to inclusion and exclusion of material in this Handbook. A number of subjects, instruments and debates could not be dealt with. For instance, all material relating to Dublin and/or Schengen have **not** been included.[10] The same is true for instruments dealing with extradition and co-operation in criminal matters, except for the Palermo December 2000 trafficking and smuggling instruments (see Chapter 2.4),[11] and for developments on the issue of discrimination, racism and xenophobia.[12]

---

[8] Included in (Van Krieken:) *The Asylum Acquis Handbook* (Asser/Kluwer, The Hague, 2000) but not in this Volume, due to a lack of space.

[9] See Seiffarth in the *Asylum Acquis Handbook*, op. cit., pp. 61-72.

[10] A Schengen and/or Dublin Acquis Handbook is being prepared (Seiffarth, Vienna).

[11] See e.g. European Convention on Extradition (1957), and the K.3 Convention relating to extradition between EU MS (OJ C 313, 23 October 1996), included in the *Asylum Acquis Handbook* (op. cit.) pp. 288-293, as well as (a) Council Act of 10 March 1995 drawing up the Convention on simplified extradition procedure between the Member States of the E.U. and (b) Council Act of 27 September 1996 drawing up the Convention relating to extradition between the the Member States of the E.U. with accompanying Declarations.

[12] See e.g. the amended Proposal for a Council decision establishing a Community Action Programme to combat discrimination 2001-2006, COM(2000) 649 dated 10 October 2000.

Union Member States and the candidate countries are all members of the Council of Europe (CoE), an institution which has also extensively dealt with the theme at stake. A list of Resolutions, Decisions and Recommendations on migration has been included. Including the texts themselves, however, would be a bridge too far, in view of the space available.

On the global level, mention should be made of the United Nations (UN) proper as all European countries (except for Switzerland) are members of that Organization. Within the UN two main institutions/instruments play a role: Charter-based bodies and resolutions/recommendations and reports on the one hand; and Treaty-based bodies and communications on the other. Relevant documents have been duly included. That is particularly true for the 1990 Convention on the Protection of the Rights of All Migrant Workers and Members of Their Families and the 2000 Palermo Organized Transnational Crime Convention and Protocols (on e.g. trafficking, smuggling and return). The most relevant ILO and UN instruments and documents – including the 2000 report of the UN Population Division – have been included in Chapter 4 (International Instruments), and some in Chapter 2 (Views).[13]

As to collections of migration law related instruments regard should first of all be had to Plender's excellent *Basic Documents on International Migration Law,* the companion volume to his *International Migration Law.*[14] 'Plender' contains a wealth of material (900 pages) including internal EU migration, which, of course, falls outside the scope of the present Handbook. For up-to-date developments, mention should be made of Antonio Cruz' *Migration News Sheet*, a monthly mimeographed publication with a wealth of information.[15] Finally, Guild/Niessen's *The Developing Immigration and Asylum Policies of the European Union* (Kluwer 1996), although containing 19 texts only, provides interesting background information and comments.

ACTORS

Other International Organizations also deal with migrants and migration:
– the International Organization for Migration (the intergovernmental body IOM)
– the Organization for Economic Cooperation and Development (OECD)

---

[13] Mention could also be made of UNHCR's efforts to be included in the migration discussion, e.g. through their 'consultations', exemplified by the October 2000 discussion paper 'Reconciling Migration Control And Refugee Protection In The European Union: A UNHCR Perspective'. In the context of this Handbook, however, attention will neither be paid to asylum-related matters nor to UNHCR.

[14] 2nd revised edition, Nijhoff, 1997. See for a review of the first edition: Van Krieken in (36) *Netherlands International Law Review*, 1989/1, pp. 87-90.

[15] Among the many publications now available in this field, special mention should be made of two Quarterlies: (a) International Migration Review and (b) International Migration.

The reports issued by these institutions, OECD in particular, should be considered to be of the utmost relevance.

NGOs also increasingly display various activities in this field, often as solidarity movements, sometimes as think-tanks. Very relevant is the Metropolis process, a yearly meeting between the Executive and Academia, resulting in a wealth of papers.[16]

Special mention should be made of IMP and ICMPD. The International Migration Policy Programme (IMP), based in Geneva, is a global programme whose primary objectives are to strengthen the capacity of governments in different world regions to manage migration flows at national and regional levels, and to foster regional and international co-operation towards orderly migration. The programme is implemented in cooperation with UNFPA, UNITAR, IOM, ILO, UNHCR, ICMPD and IGC.

ICMPD stands for the International Centre for Migration Policy Development and is based in Vienna.[17] It is actively involved in various Odysseus programmes, e.g. in the Former Yugoslavia.

LEGAL STATUS INSTRUMENTS

Many of the original Acquis documents are not binding on the EU members. The instruments concerned carry the title 'decision', 'conclusion', 'recommendation', 'joint-action', 'joint position', 'resolution' and such like, most of which are to be considered soft law. Remarkably, though, these instruments tend to carry greater weight for the Candidate Countries, as they are part and parcel of the enlargement process as a whole.[18] Other Acquis documents, however, have been adopted by the Council as a 'regulation' and are thus binding on the EU members (hard law).

Concerning other international instruments (i.e. the non-EU ones), the following needs to be stressed:
- GA Resolutions are not binding and are considered soft law only
- Many of the relevant Conventions are not yet in force (e.g. the 1990 Migrant Workers Convention) and even when they do enter into force the impact will be very limited, as no, or hardly any European country has signed and/or ratified such Conventions
- This is slightly different for e.g. C143, the most relevant ILO Convention. Although this Convention, in force since 1978, has thus far obtained only 18 ratifications, it should nevertheless be stressed that countries like Italy, Portu-

---

[16] See e.g. the *Metropolis World Bulletin* (since June 2000) and the *Journal of International Migration and Integration* (since 1999).

[17] ICMPD publications focus on the CEECs, the former Yugoslavia and in particular the activities of the Budapest Group. Informative and useful as teaching material is e.g. *Border Management in Europe* and *Future External Borders of the EU*, both from 1999.

[18] For details, see Staples in the *Asylum Acquis Handbook*, op. cit., pp. 37-46.

gal and Sweden are among this select group (as well as some Eastern European countries), which means that its impact and meaning is not to be neglected.

CHOICES

Migration will be a matter which will be dominated as from 1 May 2004 by 'Brussels' rather than by the respective capitals. It is herewith recalled that this transformation has been given a period of five years. During that period, many of the recommendations and resolutions etc. (soft law) will be reformulated and will finally result in regulations and directives (hard law). A nice example is available, namely on this issue of family reunification. The various documents on this issue have been fully included as it provides an insight into the procedures and the decision-making as a whole. Family reunification and family formation is also proof of the fact that migration might generate migration.

Migration could be subdivided as follows: tourism, business, study, family visits, short-term labour migration, long term labour migration, permanent migration, follow-up migration, family reunification, family formation, etc. All these issues will be properly dealt with, not as much as specific categories in this Handbook but rather included in the various documents.

The main division which will be adhered to in e.g. Chapter 3 (containing the relevant EC/EU instruments) is as follows:
– entry
– sojourn
– family
– illegal migration, and
– return.[19]

Moreover, attention will also be paid to training, technical assistance and cooperation in this field.

VIEWS

A special part (Chapter 2) will focus on the issue from a variety of angles. It will put migration in the context of various themes. A decision had to be made as to

[19] Attention could thus also have been paid to the issue of naturalization and citizenship. Although there is a Strasbourg Convention on the Reduction of Cases of Multiple Nationality and on Military Obligations in Cases of Multiple Nationality (1963, plus Protocols of 1977 and 1993), it is, under international law an issue which still almost exclusively falls under the sovereignty of each individual State and is mainly a matter of municipal, i.e. national law, as e.g. confirmed in various Helsinki (CSCE-) based documents (e.g. the 1992 CSCE Helsinki Summit), and which goes back to Art. 1 of the 1930 Hague Convention on Certain Questions relating to the Conflict of Nationality Laws.

which issues are at present the most dire ones in view of the ongoing discussions. Upon due consultation it has been decided to focus on **ageing and demography, globalization, illegal migration, trafficking and family reunification**. It is hoped that not only the humanitarian and the utilitarian aspects will come to the fore, but also the global interdependency and the social and human consequences of migratory movements, be they positive or negative. When it comes to migration, the following question, after all, needs to be asked: who are the machines and who are the mice, who are the lions and who are the men?

COMMISSION COMMUNICATION ON MIGRATION

COMMUNICATION FROM THE COMMISSION TO THE COUNCIL AND THE EUROPEAN PARLIAMENT ON A COMMUNITY IMMIGRATION POLICY[1]

Executive Summary

The Treaty of Amsterdam establishes for the first time Community competence for immigration and asylum. The European Council, at its meeting in Tampere in October 1999, agreed that *'The separate but closely related issues of asylum and migration call for the development of a common EU policy'* and set out the elements which it should include namely partnership with countries of origin, a common European asylum system, fair treatment of third country nationals and management of migration flows. In this framework, the European Council also stressed the need for rapid decisions on *'the approximation of national legislations on the conditions for admission and residence of third country nationals based on a shared assessment of the economic and demographic developments within the Union as well as the situation in the countries of origin'*. It did not, however, give any detailed indications as to how this policy should be developed and implemented. The Commission has already made proposals on the rights and status of third country nationals and to combat racism and xenophobia, and other legislative measures are being prepared according to the programme agreed in Tampere. However, in view of the complex nature of immigration policy and its impact over a wide range of areas, social, economic, legal and cultural, the Commission believes that we cannot rely simply on a piecemeal approach to the legislative programme foreseen in Article 63 of the EC Treaty. This view has been supported by the European Parliament which has called on the Commission to set these measures into an overall framework.

In addition it is clear from an analysis of the economic and demographic context of the Union and of the countries of origin, that there is a growing recognition that the

---

[1] Brussels, 22 November, 2000, COM(2000) 757 final. Footnotes and references to annexes have been deleted. However, Annex 1, on the demographic and economic context, has been included in full in Chapter 2.1, Ageing and demography; Annex 2, an overview of recent or planned Commission proposals relating to immigration policy has been included in the introduction to Chapter 3, the EC/EU instruments.

'zero' immigration policies of the past 30 years are no longer appropriate. On the one hand large numbers of third country nationals have entered the Union in recent years and these migratory pressures are continuing with an accompanying increase in illegal immigration, smuggling and trafficking. On the other hand, as a result of growing shortages of labour at both skilled and unskilled levels, a number of Member States have already begun to actively recruit third country nationals from outside the Union. In this situation a choice must be made between maintaining the view that the Union can continue to resist migratory pressures and accepting that immigration will continue and should be properly regulated, and working together to try to maximise its positive effects on the Union, for the migrants themselves and for the countries of origin.

In this new situation, the Commission believes that channels for legal immigration to the Union should now be made available for labour migrants. However, in view of the strongly divergent views in the Member States on the admission and integration of third country nationals, the Commission feels that it is essential to discuss these issues openly and to try to reach a consensus on the objectives of the policy to be followed.

The purpose of this Communication is to stimulate this debate, taking into account the essential structural reforms the EU economy is undergoing in the framework of the European Employment Strategy and which are now showing the expected benefits. The admission of labour migrants can make a contribution to this strategy, but, because of the very important human issues involved, one on which there should be a clear understanding between the member States on its role and contribution. Both Article 63 of the EC Treaty and the Tampere conclusions call for a common EU immigration policy. To reach this goal it is essential to co-ordinate and to ensure the transparency, within a Community framework, of actions which at the moment are carried out at Member State level since they have an effect on other areas of EU policy, e.g. abolition of controls at internal borders, Community commitments at international level under the GATS agreement and the European Employment strategy.

This will provide a background for the formulation of commonly agreed objectives for channels of legal immigration which could underpin the detailed legislative proposals concerning migrants which the Council called for in Tampere. These concern not only the conditions for the admission and residence of third country nationals for employment and other reasons, but also standards and procedures for the issue of long-term visas and residence permits, the definition of a set of uniform rights for third country nationals and the criteria and conditions under which third country nationals might be allowed to settle and work in any Member State (see Annex 2) together with the Charter of Fundamental Rights. At the same time, the procedure put in place for the monitoring of migration flows will provide a framework for consultation between the Member States on migration issues, for the co-ordination of policy, for setting common objectives and for developing accompanying measures with respect to the integration of migrants. This mechanism is designed to enable the Community to provide a co-ordinated reaction both to fluctuations in migratory pressures and to changes in the economic and demographic situation in the Union.

1. WHY A NEW APPROACH TO IMMIGRATION?

With the coming into force of the Treaty of Amsterdam, Community competence was firmly established in the areas of immigration and asylum. From being a matter for inter-governmental co-ordination under the 'third pillar' arrangements, responsibility for developing policy was moved to the '1st pillar' with a programme of action to be adopted by the Council in order to establish progressively an area of freedom, security and justice (Articles 61-63). Accordingly, in October 1999, the elements of a common EU asylum and immigration policy were agreed by the European Council in the Tampere Conclusions 1 which, together with the Action Plan which had been approved by the Council in Vienna in 1998, now form the basis of a work programme for the Commission and the Member States that is being made operational in a 'scoreboard'. The present Communication is being issued as part of this programme but in a context which, in a number of respects, is very different from the situation of the Union in 1993-94. On the one hand there is now a more acute recognition than a few years ago of the importance of immigration and asylum matters at the EU level as well as of the necessity for a common approach to them. This is emphasised by the fact that these areas are now the subjects of specific Community policies and no longer simply complementary to those related to the free movement of persons within the Union. On the other hand – and this is a direct consequence – by adopting the conclusions of Tampere, the Heads of State and Government, have defined clearly the political framework in which they wish to see a common EU asylum and immigration policy developed.

This new Commission Communication fits firmly within this framework. It con-stitutes above all a first response to the specific request of the European Council for a clear definition of the conditions of admission and of residence of third country nationals. This, it was agreed, should be based on a common assessment of the economic and demographic development of the Union and of the situation in the countries of origin, and take account of the capacity of reception of each Member State as well as of their historical and cultural links with the countries of origin. In addition, it is not possible to develop an integrated approach to immigration without considering the impact of migration policies on the host society and on migrants themselves. The social conditions which migrants face, the attitudes of the host population and the presentation by political leaders of the benefits of diversity and of pluralistic societies are all vital to the success of immigration policies. Therefore, and the two aspects are intrinsically linked, this Communication will also touch on integration policy in the context set out in Tampere, namely fair treatment of third country nationals residing legally in the Union and the promotion of diversity. In this context the impact of the Charter of Fundamental Rights will also be reviewed. However, with a view to maintaining the coherent approach agreed in Tampere, the Commission also intends to clarify the way in which the other components of an overall immigration policy must be taken into consideration. These include the fight against illegal immigration, relations with countries of origin and of transit and, especially, the humanitarian dimension – asylum policy – the importance of which has been repeatedly emphasised in recent years and which will be the subject of a separate Communication which is being presented jointly with this one. It also includes the reinforcement of integration policies so as to provide the necessary means for a rapid integration of the migrant population into European society and aiming at combating racism and xenophobia.

Finally, this Communication comes at a time when the question of the role of the EU with respect to immigration is of particular pertinence for a number of reasons. The projected decline in population in the EU over the next few decades has caught the attention of public opinion. At the same time labour shortages in some sectors are creating difficulties in a number of countries. There is a growing recognition that, in this new economic and demographic context, the existing 'zero' immigration policies which have dominated thinking over the past 30 years are no longer appropriate. Programmes to regularise the position of illegal migrants, which often give rise to difficult internal political debates, are developing in a number of Member States. Tragic incidents, such as the one in Dover in July 2000 in which 58 Chinese nationals trying to enter illegally into the United Kingdom lost their lives, which are taking place in almost all Member States, point not only to the importance of the fight against the trafficking of human beings, but also to the existence of a demand for clandestine manpower and of the exploitation of such undocumented migrants. The Commission has also taken account of the debates initiated under the French Presidency, notably the discussions at the informal ministerial meeting in Marseilles in July 2000 and at three conferences

– on Co-development and Migrants (6-7 July);
– on Illegal Migration networks (20-21 July); and
– on the Integration of Immigrants (5-6 October 2000).

In the light of these changing circumstances and bearing in mind the emergence of different political points of view and of the divergent reactions and growing concerns of the public which have been expressed in all Member States in recent months, the Commission believes that it is timely to contribute to this debate and to take a fresh look at how immigration policy should be developed within the Tampere mandate. In particular the Commission proposes to examine how the complex issues related to the admission of economic migrants, which were only touched on briefly in the Tampere Council, should be developed within a Community immigration policy. This will provide a background for the formulation of commonly agreed objectives for channels of legal immigration which would underpin the detailed proposals for the admission and residence of third country nationals which the Council called for in Tampere. Furthermore, it will be of equal importance to develop adequate policies aiming at promoting the integration of migrants, including those already living in the EU, and supporting the fight against the phenomena of racism and xenophobia.

2.   THE TAMPERE FRAMEWORK FOR A COMMON EU ASYLUM AND IMMIGRATION POLICY

The European Council in Tampere agreed on a number of milestones to realise an area of freedom, security and justice. One of these was the development of a common

EU asylum and immigration policy and progress with its implementation is set out below.

2.1 Partnership with countries of origin

The Member States at the Tampere Council acknowledged the principle that an EU asylum and immigration policy must necessarily involve cooperation with the countries of origin and transit of migrants. The Council recognised that developing a comprehensive approach to immigration also involves addressing political, and human rights issues in partnership with these countries. With such programmes as TACIS and PHARE, the Commission has developed strategies which address not only the need to reduce push factors, primarily through economic development in countries of origin and transit, but also support such activities as legislative reform, law enforcement capabilities and modern border management systems. A new integrated approach has also begun through the work of the High Level Group on Asylum and Migration. Six action plans, each based on a coherent programme of co-operation and development involving dialogue with the countries concerned, have been drawn up for specific countries or regions and it is expected that financial resources will be made available in the near future for community action to contribute to the implementation of the plans.

In future, while developing measures to understand and try to influence the reasons which cause migration, the EU must, therefore, also examine and take a responsible attitude towards the effects of emigration on the countries of origin taking into account the very different economic, demographic, social, political and human rights situations in each one which cause the migratory flows. Not only does this reflect European values but is also in the interests both of the EU and of the countries themselves.

In most cases the situation is complex and there are both positive and negative impacts of migration. During the initial period of settlement in the host country remittances sent home by migrants can become an important part of the national budget. Transfers on a large scale can be a disincentive for the sending country to cooperate in controlling emigration. For the receiving families remittances can bring significant improvements in standards of living and contribute to the development of the local economy although there is some evidence to suggest that it is the larger towns which benefit most perhaps to the detriment of other areas. On the negative side there can be less favourable impacts on the local economy when it is the most highly skilled and the most entrepreneurial sections of the population who emigrate. The brain drain is of particular concern for developing countries who can least afford to lose the investments which they have made in education and training particularly of those who benefited from tertiary education. The scale of this problem is increasing for a number of countries, notably in Africa and in India, and is likely to grow as shortages in Europe and other parts of the developed world in certain highly skilled sectors, together with important wage differentials, continue to attract qualified people from the developing world to emigrate.

With today's increasingly mixed flows of migrants caused by economic and other reasons and with populations straddling two cultures as part of survivals strategies it is possible to develop policies which use migration to the mutual benefit of the country of origin and the receiving country. In this way the effects of the brain drain can be mitigated and the benefits of remittances can be maximised. Since the issues of immigration and asylum have become matters of Community competence they will, where possible, be incorporated more specifically into Community programmes with third-countries, both in the area of trade and of development. This is particularly true for the TACIS, PHARE and MEDA programmes and migration issues must increasingly form part of the dialogue which takes place within the framework of the Partnership and Co-operation Agreements, the Common Strategies of the EU on Russia, the Ukraine and the Mediterranean region and the discussions with the African, Caribbean and Pacific (ACP) countries.

The partnership approach should provide a framework for dealing flexibly with new trends in migration which are now developing in the world, with the concept of migration as a *pattern of mobility* which encourages migrants tomaintain and develop their links with their countries of origin. This includes ensuring that the legal framework does not cut migrants off from their country of origin e.g. that they have possibilities to visit without losing their status in their host country, and of moving on or going back as the situation develops in the country of origin and elsewhere in the world. Such a concept would encourage migrants to participate in the economic development of their country of origin not only through remittances to family members, but also through supporting development projects, business ventures etc. Such action can lead in some cases to their voluntary return within a supported reintegration framework. The fact that at present in many Member States, visa policies and other legislation, restrict the possibility for migrants to move freely between their country of residence and their country of origin even when retired, creates a barrier to such developments. Co-operation between countries of origin and residence of migrants must be based on dialogue with governments and with the migrants themselves and their associations to ensure that migratory movements are taken into account in developmental, economic and social strategies of the countries concerned (e.g. by promoting more efficient public and financial institutions, training and manpower-skilling programmes as well as the inflow of foreign capital to projects (including those carried out by emigrants in their countries of origin)). In this way it can help to mitigate the effects of the brain drain and the loss of the most entrepreneurial members of society and contribute to the sustainable development of the country of origin which in the long term could reduce the incentive to emigrate. It should be recognised, however, that the partnership approach to managing migrant flows should be seen as part of a medium to long-term strategy and that the impact will vary depending on the situation in the countries of origin.

2.2 A common European asylum system

The Tampere Council reiterated that **the right to seek asylum** must continue to be guaranteed as the cornerstone of EU policy. The objective of a common European asylum system must be to ensure the full application of the Geneva Convention on refugees and that nobody is sent back to persecution. The Treaty of Amsterdam requires the enactment of common measures.

The Commission tabled in May 2000 a proposal on temporary protection in case of mass influx of displaced persons and in September 2000 put forward a proposal on procedures in Member States for granting and withdrawing refugee status. Early in 2001, proposals will be made on reception conditions for asylum seekers and on a system for the clear and workable determination of the State responsible for the examination of an asylum application. The preparation for the setting up of the EURODAC system is ongoing. Further proposals will be made on the approximation of rules on the recognition and content of refugee status and also on subsidiary forms of protection offering an appropriate status to any person in need of such protection. In addition, the Council adopted in September 2000 the Commission's proposal for the establishment of a European Refugee Fund to promote a balance of effort between Member States in receiving refugees and displaced persons.

At the request of the Tampere Council, further proposals for the development of Community rules leading to a common asylum procedure and a uniform status for those who are granted asylum valid throughout the Union are being made in a separate Communication which is being presented jointly with this one and which aims at providing a clear picture of the method and content of the measures to be taken from 2004 under the humanitarian heading.

2.3 Fair treatment of third country nationals

A key element of the development of the European Union as an area of freedom, security and justice agreed in Tampere is ensuring fair treatment of third country nationals residing legally in the territories of the Member States through an integration policy aimed at granting them rights and obligations comparable to those of EU citizens.

With respect to the setting up a legislative framework for the integration of those already resident on the territory of the Member States, the Commission has already proposed the extension of Community co-ordination of social security schemes, as laid down in Regulation EEC No. 1408/71 to employed persons and self-employed persons who are insured in a Member State and who are third country nationals. The Commission has also put forward a proposal to modify regulation 1612/68 aimed at enhancing the legal status of third country national family members of EU workers. These proposals are still, however, under consideration in the Council. In line with the Tampere mandate, further proposals concerning the status of third country nationals who are long-term residents will be made. These will include the rights to be granted, the conditions under which the status may be lost, protection against expulsion and the right to reside in another Member State. The right of abode in another Member State for long-term residents could be an important factor of mobility within the labour market of the Union. In this connection the Commission has already presented two proposals concerning the rights of third country workers and independent operators already legally established in a Member State to provide services in other Member States.

The Commission submitted in November 1999 a package of proposals to combat discrimination. On 29 June 2000 the Council adopted the first of the package's three elements, the proposal for a Directive combating discrimination on grounds of racial or ethnic origin, which will apply in the fields of employment, training, social protection (including health and social security), education and the supply of goods and services, including housing.

Political agreement on the second element, the Commission's proposal for an anti-discrimination action programme, was reached in the Council on 17 October 2000 . The programme is to run for six years from 1 January 2001, and will have a budget of almost M.100 for activities combating discrimination on the grounds of race or ethnic origin, religion or belief, disability, age or sexual orientation. The activities are to be focused on

(i)   analysing discrimination in the Member States and evaluating methods of combating it,

(ii)   strengthening the capacity of organisations combating discrimination via transnational exchanges and the core-funding of NGOs, and

(iii) promoting awareness of discrimination and the measures to combat it in the EU. The Council also reached agreement on the third part of the anti-discrimination package, the Commission's proposal for a framework directive on discrimination in employment on the grounds of religion or belief, disability, age or sexual orientation.

The Amsterdam Treaty, in its provisions on police and judicial co-operation in criminal matters, expressly states that the Union will take steps to prevent and combat racism and xenophobia as one of the prime objectives of its efforts to create an area of freedom, security and justice. In 1996 the Council adopted a Joint Action to facilitate effective judicial co-operation between the Member States to prevent perpetrators of racism and xenophobia from taking advantage of differences in legislation within the Union in order to escape justice. In the light of an evaluation of the Joint Action to be submitted at the end of 2000, the Commission will present a framework decision under Article 29 of the Treaty to enhance judicial co-operation in the fight against racism. This initiative will cover, among other things, the spread of this type of crime on the Internet. In the area of conditions of admission and residence, the first initiative of the Commission since the entry into force of the Treaty of Amsterdam has been a draft Directive on the right to family reunification. This is justified for several reasons: firstly, family reunification is not simply regulated by national laws since many international and regional instruments lay down rules or principles on this issue; secondly, family reunification has been one of the main vectors of immigration over the last twenty years; thirdly, it is an essential element in the integration of persons already admitted and finally, this subject has been a priority for the Council since 1991. This reflects the Commission's view that successful integration of third country nationals to maintain economic and social cohesion is one of the major challenges which the EU faces with respect to immigration policy. The establishment of stable family communities ensures that migrants are able to contribute fully to their new societies. The proposal establishes a conditional right to family reunification on the part of third country nationals. It would allow third country nationals meeting certain criteria to be reunited with the members of their nuclear family, or even, in strictly defined cases, with other members of their wider family. The proposal also defines a number of rights which should be granted to family members. After receiving the opinion of the European Parliament, the Commission has adopted an amended proposal which is currently under consideration in the Council.

Finally, the proposed Charter of Fundamental Rights which should be adopted in December 2000, sets out a number of principles which, because of the universality of certain rights, will apply to third country nationals. This will be particularly important with respect to a number of social rights such as protection against unjustified dismissal and the application of national and Community laws concerning working conditions. The Charter also includes the possibility, on the conditions set out in the Amsterdam Treaty, of free movement and stay for third country nationals legally resident in a Member State.

2.4 **Management of migration flows**

The European Council at Tampere stressed the need to take a comprehensive approach to the management or regulation of migrant flows including political, human rights and development issues and to involve the countries of origin and of transit.

The Council stressed that regulating migration flows includes intensive dialogue between reception countries, transit countries, countries of origin and migrants themselves. A key element should be information campaigns by which potential migrants can be informed about legal possibilities for migration and what they may expect in the destination country and of the dangers of illegal migration and trafficking. The Council requested that steps to develop a common visa policy for the EU be intensified, combined with measures against forgery and the fraudulent use of travel documents. Efficient management of migration flows requires monitoring and must be accompanied by measures to regulate movements. This requires action at all phases of movement of persons, in order both to safeguard legal channels for admission of migrants and for those who seek protection on humanitarian grounds while at the same time combating illegal immigration. A coherent and co-ordinated approach to illegal immigration will be an essential part of a more open immigration policy at the European level. The phenomenon of illegal immigration consists of a number of interlinked phases and each has to be tackled systematically with specific measures. These include action in source and transit countries, police co-operation to pool knowledge of trafficking operations which by their nature are international, action at the point of entry including border controls and visa policies, legislation against traffickers, help for victims and their humane repatriation.

One element in the regulatory process to which greater priority must be given is the voluntary return of persons who are refused admission to a Member State or who have no longer the right to remain in the EU. In cases when calls for voluntary return have no effect, the integrity of the European immigration policy has to be guaranteed in the end by forced return. The most valuable instrument to facilitate returns is by means of readmission agreements. In addition the Commission will be bringing forward proposals for the development of common standards for expulsion decisions, detention and deportation, which should be both efficient and humane.

3.   TOWARDS A COMMUNITY IMMIGRATION POLICY

3.1 Impact of existing immigration policies

Immigration to the EU falls into three broad categories, namely that based on humanitarian considerations, family reunion and then immigration which can be generally described as driven by economic and market forces. Under the **humanitarian heading**, all Member States are signatories to the 1951 Geneva Convention relating to the status of refugees and adhere to its principles. The Convention provides for access to work as a direct individual right stemming from the status of refugee and cannot be made dependent on an economic needs test. A programme for the co-ordination of the EU approach to humanitarian immigration was agreed at the Tampere Council and this will be pursued as outlined in the Scoreboard.

With respect to **family reunion**, all Member States allow, though using a variety of different criteria, family members to join migrants already legally resident on their territory. A Directive to co-ordinate national legislation in this area is now under discussion in the Council (see section 2.3 above). This Communication concerns primarily the third category; **economic migration** which has been said to be close to zero since the 1970's and which, given the economic opportunities now available in the EU, no longer seems appropriate. Many economic migrants have been driven either to seek entry through asylum procedures or to enter illegally. This allows for no adequate response to labour market needs and plays into the hands of well organised traffickers and unscrupulous employers. In addition, there is substantial illegal immigration into the EU which Europol estimates at 500.000 people per annum, many of these being employed as undeclared workers. Given such numbers and the practical difficulties of returning people to the countries from which they came, several Member States have resorted to regularisation or amnesty measures and the total number of those permitted to stay legally as a result is estimated at approximately 1,8 million since the 1970's. While procedures are already in place at EU level to co-ordinate policies in a number of areas to facilitate the operation of the Single Market, notably the free movement of goods, capital, services and EU workers and other citizens, sufficient attention has not yet been given to the role of third country nationals in the EU labour market nor to the need for accompanying measures in support of the integration of existing and prospective migrants.

3.2 Developing a new approach to immigration

The analysis of the current situation with respect to migration flows in the EU suggests that a different, more flexible approach common to all Member States on the issue of legal immigration now needs to be taken. Such a proactive immigration policy should be based on the recognition that migratory pressures will continue and that there are benefits that orderly immigration can bring to the EU, to the migrants themselves and to their countries of origin. The opening up of channels for immigration for economic purposes to meet urgent needs for both skilled and unskilled workers has already begun in a number of Member States. Given the present economic and labour market situation the Commission believes that it is now time to review longer term needs for the EU as a whole, to estimate how far these can be met from existing resources and to define a medium-term policy for the admission of third country nationals to fill those gaps which are identified in a gradual and controlled way. Many of the elements of such a policy were already put forward in the 1994 Communication on Immigration and Asylum Policies but the approach now should also take into account the changing nature of migration itself which has become a much more flexible process of movement between countries rather than simply a one-way flow. Globally, migratory movements change direction, rise and fall depending on the evolution of the economic and demographic situations both in receiving and sending countries. In order to regulate migrant flows successfully, therefore, and to reduce illegal immigration, the EU needs to adopt a co-ordinated approach which takes into account all the various interlinked aspects of the migratory system and to work in close partnership with the countries of origin and transit.

The benefits of a more open and transparent policy on migration movements, together with the co-ordination of policies designed to reduce push factors in countries of origin and greater efforts to enforce labour legislation in the Member States, could also help to reduce illegal immigration, in particular the worst forms of smuggling and trafficking. Member States will be in a better position to address the problem of irregular migration if they are equipped with a broad range of migration management policies going beyond measures to curb the perceived or real misuse of their asylum systems. Opening up legal admission policies for labour migration will not completely prevent this, however, and they should be accompanied by both appropriate anti-smuggling measures and effective asylum adjudication systems which are capable of identifying refugees expeditiously and accurately thereby balancing refugee protection with immigration control. It should be stressed that such strategies do not constitute the adoption of a policy of replacement migration as proposed in the UN report on Replacement Migration as a possible scenario to counteract demographic decline. Rather they make up a controlled approach which is based on a common assessment of the economic and demographic development of the Union, and of the situation in the countries of origin, and takes account of its capacity of reception. Bringing the issue of labour migration into the discussion on the development of economic and social policy for the EU, would also provide an opportunity to reinforce policies to combat irregular work and the economic exploitation of migrants which are at present fuelling unfair competition in the Union. A corollary of an economic immigration policy must be a greater effort in ensuring compliance with existing labour legislation by employers for third country nationals. Equality with respect to wages and working conditions is not only in the interests of the migrants, but of society itself which then both benefits fully from the contribution migrants make to economic and social life.

Given the differences between Member States with respect to links to countries of origin, the capacity of reception, the development of integration policies and labour market needs the Commission proposes that the best way to achieve a regulated immigration policy is to establish an overall framework at EU level, with common standards and procedures and a mechanism for setting objectives and indicative targets, within which Member States would develop and implement national policies.

3.3 Framework for an EU immigration policy

Any EU immigration policy needs to take into account migration of all types – humanitarian, family reunion and economic – and to deal with the impact on the sending and receiving countries as a whole. It will need to respond to the difficult political debates taking place in some countries and will require strong political leadership to help shape public opinion. In dealing with all types of migration, it should present an integrated approach, taking account of thebenefits of diversity in society, the need for a balanced framework of rights and obligations for third country nationals resident in the Union, the importance of developing support for integration and the effects on the labour market. The policy should be developed under a new framework for co-operation at Community level, which would be based on co-operation, exchange of information, and reporting and would be co-ordinated by the Commission.

Admission to the EU for humanitarian reasons would continue in full recognition of member States international obligations to provide protection for refugees, asylum seekers and those in need of temporary protection. The programme to develop a common European asylum system as set out in Section 2.2 above will be pursued. While many people admitted to the EU for humanitarian reasons do return to their countries of origin when the situation there changes, the discussion on the number of economic migrants needed in different sectors should take into account the numbers of persons under international protection, since better use of their skills could also be made, and of family members admitted to the EU who will also be entering the labour market.

Admission for economic migrants should clearly address the needs of the market place particularly for the very highly skilled, or for lesser or unskilled workers or for seasonal labour. Admission policies for economic migrants must enable the EU to respond quickly and efficiently to labour market requirements at national, regional and local level, recognising the complex and rapidly changing nature of these requirements and consequently of the need for greater mobility between Member States for incoming migrants. Such policies must also respect relevant provisions of existing Community law and bilateral and multilateral agreements already in force between the Community, or the Community and its Member States, on the one hand, and third countries on the other hand.

The underlying principle of an EU immigration policy must be for different purposes, that persons admitted should enjoy broadly the same **rights and responsibilities** as EU nationals but that these may be incremental and related to the length of stay provided for in their entry conditions.15 The Commission has already tabled proposals on rights to service provision within the EU for third country nationals legally established in a Member State. 16 The measures under article 13 of the Treaty of Amsterdam to counteract racism and xenophobia must be vigorously pursued and **action to integrate migrants** into our societies must therefore be seen as the essential corollary of the admission policy. At the same time the fight against **illegal immigration** should be intensified with priority to combating trafficking and smuggling. Finally the policy must be developed and implemented in **partnership with countries of origin** and transit.

3.4   Admission of migrants

3.4.1   *Assessing appropriate immigration levels*

Given the difficulties of assessing economic needs it would not be the intention to set detailed European targets. The responsibility for deciding on the needs for different categories of migrant labour must remain with the Member States. However, a new process would be established based on co-operation, exchange of information, and reporting.

Under such a scenario, Member States could be asked to prepare periodic reports in two parts. The first would review the development and overall impact of their immigration policy over the previous period, including the numbers of third country nationals admitted under the various categories and their situation in the labour market. The second would set out the Member States' future intentions on immigration, including a projection of labour migrants they would wish to admit with an indication of skills levels. The need for a flexible approach to changing economic needs would suggest that quotas are impracticable and that an appropriate system of indicative targets would be preferable. This would be closely related to labour market needs but would also take into consideration agreements in place with countries of origin and a range of other factors (e.g. public acceptance of additional migrant workers in the country concerned, resources available for reception and integration, the possibilities for social and cultural adaptation etc). In compiling these reports Member States would need to consult widely and to work closely with the social partners and also with regional and local authorities and all the other actors concerned with the integration of migrants. The reports would follow a commonly agreed structure so as to enable the Commission to prepare a synthesis which would be presented to the Council. Following discussion, the Council would then lay down the principles of the common approach to be implemented in the next period. In this process, the Commission and the Council should take account of the progress made in the implementation of the European Employment Strategy and its impact on labour-market conditions in the Union. The Commission would ensure the monitoring and evaluation of the policy, including its impact on countries of origin, on a regular basis.

3.4.2 *Defining a common legal framework for admission*

As already announced in the Scoreboard, the Commission will be adopting early next year proposals for Directives dealing with the conditions of entry and residence to the EU of third country nationals for the exercise of employment, self-employment or unpaid activities and for study or vocational training. The Commission has already funded comparative studies on the conditions of admission and residence of third country nationals which provide an overall view of the legislation and practice of the Member States. In presenting its proposals, the Commission intends to establish a coherent legal framework which will take into account concepts which have already been successfully applied in the Member States. The framework would determine the basic conditions and procedures to be applied whilst leaving it up to each Member State to adopt *national measures* on the admission of third country nationals based on the criteria set out in the Directives. Preliminary consultation with the Member States, the social partners, and non-governmental organisations will precede the adoption of the proposals by the Commission. This framework approach would be based on the following principles:

– **Transparency and rationality:** laying down clearly the conditions under which third country nationals may enter and stay in the EU as employed or self-employed workers, setting out their rights and obligations and ensuring that they have access to this information and that there are mechanisms in place to see that it is applied fairly. This could imply, amongst others, provisions to facilitate the swift adoption of decisions on individual applications for admission both in the interest of the applicant and of the enterprise seeking to recruit, on the basis of objective and verifiable criteria. A general provision on *access to information* would greatly enhance transparency.

– **Differentiating rights according to length of stay:** The principle that the length of residence has an influence on the rights of the person concerned has a long tradition in the Member States and this is referred to in the Tampere conclusions. In addition, responding to labour market needs means that admission must be facilitated for a wide range of workers, both skilled and unskilled, and ensure a rapid and flexible response. The case of students could be considered separately with special arrangements for third country nationals who have studied for several years in the EU, to provide for easier access to the EU labour market. However, it is clear that a hard-core of rights should be available to migrants on their arrival, in order to promote their successful integration into society. The Community should explore how this core of rights might be extended with the length of stay with a view to coming to broadly comparable arrangements across the Union.

EU legislation should therefore provide for a **flexible** overall scheme based on a limited number of statuses designed so as to **facilitate** rather than create barriers to the admission of economic migrants. The aim should be to give a secure legal status for temporary workers who intend to return to their countries of origin, while at the same time providing a pathway leading eventually to a permanent status for those who wish to stay and who meet certain criteria. One option would be to start with a temporary work permit – with special arrangements for certain types of workers e.g.

seasonal workers, transfrontier workers, intra-corporate transferees. This permit could be renewable and would then be followed by a permanent work permit, after a number of years to be determined, with the possibility of long-term residence status after a certain period. Agreement would be needed on the rights and obligations to be provided for at each stage, based on the principle of equal treatment with nationals, and these should be cumulative leading to those of long term residents. Based on a 'best practice' approach the details of the scheme would be worked out in close consultation with Member States who would be responsible for implementing national admissions policies within the general framework.

 – **Application and assessment procedures:** Application procedures should be clear and **simple**. Initiating them in the country of origin in co-operation with governments, international bodies, NGOs, regional and local authorities could improve the effectiveness of monitoring procedures, the transparency of the procedures and the information available for potential migrants while at the same time respecting the employer's right to choose. However it is recognised that many potential labour migrants will present themselves for employment having already been admitted to a Member State for another reason and the provision of a job-seeker visa could help to regulate and monitor this practice. To facilitate the **availability of information** more extensive use of new communications technology could be used to provide information on job opportunities, conditions of work etc.

A European information point (e.g. a website) could be created and maintained which contains a complete set of information relating to the admission of third country nationals to each Member State and giving contact details of national authorities competent to receive applications for permits in accordance with the Directives. The establishment of a special visa for job seekers from third countries could also be considered. In order to allow European industry, particularly small and medium sized industries, to recruit – in cases of real need – successfully and quickly from third countries, employers need a practical tool for demonstrating that there is a concrete shortage on the EU labour market. One way of tackling this problem would be to foresee that the 'economic needs test' is deemed to be fulfilled if a specific job vacancy has been made public via the employment services of several Member States for a certain period (e.g. by means of the European Employment Services (EURES) network) and no suitable candidate from EU applicants (or certain persons privileged under international agreements) has been received.

3.5 Integration of third country nationals

The importance of the fair treatment of third country nationals was underlined by the European Council in Tampere and an EU immigration policy must, therefore, incorporate steps to ensure that migrants benefit from comparable living and working conditions to those of nationals. Failure to provide the resources necessary to ensure the successful integration of such migrants and their families will in the longer term exacerbate social problems which may lead to exclusion and related problems such as delinquency and criminality. While many legally resident migrants have integrated successfully and make an important contribution to the economic and social

development of their host countries, social exclusion affects migrants dispro-
portionately and they are often the victims of racism and xenophobia. The legal
framework and other actions being proposed by the Commission to fight
discrimination and xenophobia will need to be complemented by specific integration
programmes at national, regional and local level. In its proposals for 2001, the
Commission in its new employment guideline 7 already invites Member States to
meet the needs of disadvantaged groups, including migrant workers already resident
in the Union, as regards their integration into the labour market and to set national
targets for this purpose in accordance with the national situation. However, it is also
essential to create a welcoming society and to recognise that integration is a two-way
process involving adaptation on the part of both the immigrant and of the host
society. The European Union is by its very nature a pluralistic society enriched by a
variety of cultural and social traditions, which will in the future become even more
diverse. There must, therefore be respect for cultural and social differences but also of
our fundamental shared principles and values: respect for human rights and human
dignity, appreciation of the value of pluralism and the recognition that membership of
society is based on a series of rights but brings with it a number of responsibilities for
all of its members be they nationals or migrants. The provision of equality with
respect to conditions of work and access to services, together with the granting of
civic and political rights to longer-term migrant residents brings with it such
responsibilities and promotes integration. By co-ordinating their efforts to ensure that
employers respect the provisions of labour law in the case of third country nationals,
Member States would greatly contribute to the integration process, which will be
particularly important in attracting migrants to highly skilled jobs for which there is
world-wide competition. In this connection the Commission has already tabled
proposals concerning the rights of third country national workers and independent
operators legally established in one Member State to the free provision of services
within the EU. The Charter of Fundamental Rights could provide a reference for the
development of the concept of civic citizenship in a particular Member State
(comprising a common set of core rights and obligations) for third country nationals.
Enabling migrants to acquire such a citizenship after a minimum period of years
might be a sufficient guarantee for many migrants to settle successfully into society
or be a first step in the process of acquiring the nationality of the Member State
concerned. Successful integration policies need to start as soon as possible after
admission and rely heavily on partnership between the migrants and the host society.
Political leaders need to create the environment necessary for the acceptance of
diversity within which integration policies must be anchored. In order to promote
integration, settlement packages could be developed for all new migrants tailored to
their individual needs (these could include language training, information on political
and social structures, accessing services etc with special attention to the needs of
migrant women and children). It must be recognised, however, that integration is a
long-term process and special attention needs to be paid to second generation
migrants, including those born in the EU, to ensure that problems do not lead to
social exclusion and criminality. In this context, women and the family should be an
important focus of integration policies.

While integration is primarily the role of Member States, governments should share this responsibility with civil society notably at the local level where integration measures must be implemented. The key to success is the establishment of micro-level actions based on partnerships between all the many actors who need to be involved: regional and local authorities and their political leaders, especially those of the larger towns where many migrants settle, providers of education, healthcare, social welfare, the police, the media, the social partners, non-governmental organisations and migrants themselves and their associations. Each has a part to play in the design and implementation of integration programmes, which will need to be properly resourced. Such a horizontal approach requires co-ordination at national and local level and the EU could contribute by developing a pedagogical strategy, promoting the exchange of information and good practice, especially at local level and the development of guidelines or common standards for integration measures. A Community Action Programme to promote the integration of third country nationals could be developed aimed at improving the understanding of the issues concerned through evaluation of practices, developing benchmarks and other indicators, promoting dialogue between the actors concerned and supporting European networks and the promotion of awareness raising activities.

3.6 Information, research and monitoring

More information is needed about migration flows and patterns of migration into and out of the EU, including illegal immigration, the role of migrants in the labour market and the overall impact of migration (including its social, cultural and political aspects) on the EU and on the countries of origin and transit. The EU immigration policy itself must be closely monitored and evaluated. Efforts to improve the comparability of migration statistics and to support comparative research on migration should be continued. As suggested already by the European Parliament consideration should be given to reinforcing the work of existing research and data networks and by providing a European focus. Such a European network could co-ordinate current activities in different Member States and promote new research both in the EU and in the countries of origin. The Commission is aware of the need to improve the collection and analysis of statistics on migration and asylum and will participate actively in the on-going debate as to how this can best be done. In this context consideration will be given to the establishment of a legal basis for the collection and analysis of statistical data in these fields.

4. CONCLUSIONS AND FOLLOW UP

Implementing the Tampere mandate implies making an assessment of present and future migration flows to the EU within the context of developing a common policy on asylum and immigration taking into account demographic changes, the situation of the labour market and migration pressures from countries and regions of origin of migrants.

In the light of demographic decline which will become increasingly important in the EU over the next 25 years and of the current strong economic prospects and growing skills shortages in the labour market, it advocates the development of a common policy for the controlled admission of economic migrants to the EU as part of an overall immigration and asylum policy for the Union. Without prejudice to the pursuit of structural reforms through the European Employment Strategy, and within the context of a policy strategy aiming at higher growth, higher employment and a more cohesive society, the Commission believes that, while immigration will never be a solution in itself to the problems of the labour market, migrants can make a positive contribution to make to the labour market, to economic growth and to the sustainability of social protection systems. It must be borne in mind, however, that immigration is a multi-dimensional phenomena which has legal, social and cultural as well as economic impacts. Developing a common policy therefore implies defining an appropriate policy mix. The Communication sets out a framework within which such a common policy might be regulated and managed. Within this framework the Commission proposes a procedure for co-ordination at Community level, based on an assessment by the Member States, in consultation with the social partners and those involved in the integration of migrants, with the provision of periodic reports from which an overall policy for the EU for the admission of new migrants would be agreed by the Council. This open approach is justified by the fact that effective migration management must be based on partnership since a horizontal approach to the various elements is essential.

Such a policy must be accompanied by long-term, comprehensive integration programmes developed through partnerships involving national, regional and local authorities and civil society in order to maximise the positive effects in terms of employment, economic performance and social cohesion within a clear framework of rights and obligations. In this context concerted use of available Community policy instruments should be made (e.g. the anti-discrimination and social inclusion measures introduced under Articles 13 and 137 of the Amsterdam Treaty, the employment strategy, the European Social Fund and other Community initiatives such as EQUAL and URBAN). In order to support this policy, the Commission should play a role in encouraging action at local and national level and the exchange of good practice.

A shift to a proactive immigration policy will require strong political leadership and a clear commitment to the promotion of pluralistic societies and a condemnation of racism and xenophobia. It will be necessary to emphasise the benefits of immigration and of cultural diversity and, in commenting on issues related to immigration and asylum, avoid language which could incite racism or aggravate tensions between communities. They will need to demonstrate support for measures to promote the integration of newly arrived migrants and their families, and promote the recognition and acceptance of cultural differences within a clear framework of rights and obligations. The media also has considerable responsibility in this respect in its role as an educator of public opinion.

The Commission proposes that a common legal framework for admission of third country nationals should be developed, in consultation with the Member States, which would be based on the principles of transparency, rationality and flexibility. The legal status granted to third country nationals would be based on the principle of providing sets of rights and responsibilities on a basis of equality with those of nationals but differentiated according to the length of stay while providing for progression to permanent status. In the longer term this could extend to offering a form of civic citizenship, based on the EC Treaty and inspired by the Charter of Fundamental Rights, consisting of a set of rights and duties offered to third country nationals. Partnership with countries of origin and transit is considered crucial to ensure the regulation of migration flows. The development of differentiated co-operation policies with the various types of countries of origin (e.g. applicant countries, countries parties to regional programmes funded by the Community, other countries) will be necessary. In the longer term, such partnerships should also help to mitigate the effects of emigration by co-ordinated efforts to promote development in the countries concerned, particularly by mobilising migrants themselves in this process. They would provide support for the new patterns of mobility which are developing and facilitate migrants' contacts with their countries of origin as well as their participation in the development of these countries. This more open and transparent immigration policy would be accompanied by a strengthening of efforts to combat illegal immigration and especially smuggling and trafficking, not only through increased co-operation and strengthening of border controls but also by ensuring the application of labour legislation with respect to third country nationals.

Given the complex nature of the issues involved and the need to ensure the participation of a wide range of actors in the implementation of such a policy, the Commission proposes to forward this Communication to the European Parliament, the Committee of the Regions and the Economic and Social Committee for their opinion and to distribute it widely for debate to national and regional authorities, the social partners, the economic and industrial world, and international and non-governmental organisations concerned with migration and migrant associations. It is proposed that the results of this debate be discussed at a conference to be held under the Belgian Presidency in the second half of 2001 and that the conclusions of this conference be presented for discussion to the Council at its meeting in Brussels at the end of 2001 which will also be considering a mid-term review of the implementation of the Tampere programme.[2]

---

[2] The Council which took place in Brussels, 30 November-1 December 2000 focusing on JHA-related matters, took note of the Commission communication on immigration policy presented by Commissioner Vitorino. In the light of the Ministers' comments, the Presidency asked the Member States to submit proposals in writing on the aspects of the communication which concerned them more closely with a view to better preparation for future Council proceedings on the matter. Both Article 63 of the Treaty and the Tampere Conclusions stressed the need to develop a common European policy on immigration. This need is all the more keenly felt since the massive influx of immigrants leaving their country for humanitarian or economic reasons or for family reunification to enter the Union, legally or illegally, is a major problem now faced by all Member States. Forecasts of demographic trends in the countries of origin show that the influx of immigrants is likely to grow in the future, forcing us to give immediate consideration to taking practical measures at Community

level so as to manage the phenomenon effectively. In its communication the Commission sets out the broad lines of an integrated approach to immigration and identifies the following priorities: (a) consolidating partnership with countries of origin; (b) establishing a common European asylum system; (c) defining the conditions necessary to ensure fair treatment of third-country nationals; and (d) effective and coordinated management of migration flows. The communication also outlines a two-pronged framework for immigration policy: (aa) admission for humanitarian reasons, and

(bb) admission of economic migrants.

With regard to the category of economic migrants, the communication proposes an open coordination procedure to assess labour market needs based on annual reports prepared by the Member States in collaboration with the social partners and those dealing with the integration of immigrants. Finally, the communication outlines a common legal framework for the admission of immigrants. To this end, the Commission plans to submit proposals for legislative instruments on: (aaa) the conditions of admission and residence for third-country nationals for the purpose of exercising a professional activity, on an employed or self-employed basis, or an unpaid activity, (bbb) the conditions of admission and residence for third-country nationals for the purpose of study or vocational training, (ccc) standards and procedures for visas and long-term residence permits, (ddd) defining a set of uniform rights for third-country nationals, and (eee) the criteria and conditions to be applied to allow third-country nationals to reside and work in a Member State.

VIEWS

Ageing and Demography

> (motto: '... immigration is no long-term answer: immigrants' birth rates generally fall, often in less than a generation, to match that of their host country ...'[1]

In January 2001 The New York Times 'instructed' the Europeans that higher levels of legal immigration would certainly help the challenges which Europe is about to

---

[1] *The Economist*, December 21st, 2000, in an article called 'the empty nursery.' It is *inter alia* stated: We are seeing what Ron Lestaeghe, a Belgian demographer, calls the 'second demographic transition'. During the first transition, rapidly taking place in many developing countries today, women reduce the number of children they have later in life. They have two, or three, or four, and stop. Families like that of Elizabeth's grandmother all but disappear: most mothers have all the children they want in their 20s. In today's second transition, women postpone having their first baby. In the United States, 27% of all women in their early 30s (and indeed 30% of white non-Hispanic ones) have not yet had a child. In Britain, 7% of births are now to mothers aged 35 or over. This kind of shift in timing is muddling for demographers. They measure total fertility rates by projecting, from the number of children a woman has at any given age, the number that, on average, she will have overall. But how can they tell babies postponed from babies forgone, and so avoid wrongly predicting a fall in family size? It has been a big question for them in recent years. And the moment women postpone a bit less, life grows harder still: it may look as though fertility has suddenly started to rise – yet in the end women may have no more children than before. (...) No wonder either, then, that the UN, even while it notes a rising total world population, is beginning to fret about population decline in parts of the world. But is the decline really here to stay? Or will babies one day come back into fashion? After all, between the two world wars, some countries' birth rates fell so drastically that pessimists predicted that the human race was on the road to extinction. Yet birth rates soared (especially in the United States) in the 1950s, the decade when today's baby boomers were born. Undoubtedly the decline in fertility rates will not continue indefinitely. In many countries, it has stopped already. In 14 out of 18 West European countries, says David Coleman, a demographer at Oxford University, the birth rate rose between 1998 and 1999. One school of thought, led by John Bongaarts, vice-president of the Population Council, a New York think-tank, argues that the apparent fall in fertility rates has reached a plateau – inevitably, as the age to which childbearing was being postponed stopped rising so fast. Europe's true fertility rate, says Mr Bongaarts, is almost certainly under replacement rate, but maybe 1.7 or 1.8 children per woman, rather than below 1.5, as some of the more alarming estimates suggest. (...) In future, only and first-born offspring between

P.J. van Krieken (Ed.), The Migration Acquis Handbook
© 2001, T.M.C.Asser Press, The Hague, the Röling Foundation and the authors

face (small numbers of workers supporting a large pool of retired persones). The newspaper, in an editorial, stated that Europe needs people:[2]

> European leaders know that their nations' plummeting birth-rates and ageing populations cry out for a major change in immigration policy. But they are unwilling or unable to sell the need for greater levels of immigration to a public that does not share Americans' more welcoming spirit. Their failure could imperil Europe's economic vitality. The combined population of the 15 nations of the European Union was larger in 1995 than that of the United States, by 105 million, but by 2050 it could be smaller by 18 million. Spain and Italy will see their populations shrink by more than a quarter in that period. These declining birth-rates translate into ageing populations. European policymakers are grappling with the implications for social welfare programs. There is widespread concern, for example, over the future of the social security pension system, as there is in the United States – how to sustain a pay-as-you-go system with an ever smaller number of workers supporting an ever larger pool of retirees. But in Europe the numbers are a lot starker, with retirees projected to outnumber workers by 2050. As a result, late last year the Organization for Economic Co-operation and Development [OECD] warned that many of its member states might be unable to finance their public pension systems in just a few years. In Germany, Chancellor Gerhard Schröder's government is negotiating with unions and employer groups to reform the current pension system in response to the nation's ageing population. Higher levels of legal immigration would certainly help, easing labour shortages and increasing the number of taxpayers propping up pension systems. According to some estimates, the European Union will need as many as 75 million immigrants over the next half-century. But there is no political will to translate this awareness into an overhaul of restrictive immigration policies. Distressingly, too many politicians are willing to capitalize on anti-immigrant sentiments. The result is a cynical, unacknowledged dependence on foreign labour that is not formally welcome. Turkish immigrants in Germany have been referred to as 'guest workers' for a whole generation. A more recent reliance on illegal immigrants only deprives workers across Europe of basic rights. The European Union's

---

them will probably account for a majority of the human race. Such a world of destined high achievers may be an alarming prospect for the second – or still later born rest of humanity. But, if the world's human numbers do indeed decline, we maybe will need all the high achievers we can get.

On growing demographic imbalances and immigration as a solution, David Coleman, a demographer from Oxford University, stated that this trend is caused by structural changes – a declining birth rate and increased life expectancy – which cannot be addressed through inward migration, unless the migration takes place on a massive and perpetual basis. And although migration can provide some temporary relief, a more effective long-term solution to the skills-shortage problem would be to improve training and educational opportunities at home. What is more, the government's selective emphasis on importing skilled labour, whilst it may be politically understandable, could be misplaced. The Economist (after the flood), September 9th, 2000.

[2] From the *International Herald Tribune*, 8 January 2001.

policy-making bodies are prodding member states to take the lead in fighting racism and xenophobia. Late last year the European Commission issued a policy paper stressing the need for more 'proactive' immigration to ensure Europe's future economic growth and the viability of its social welfare systems. It is time for the national governments to pay heed.

This NYT editorial refers to an OECD report, which in fact tends to be far more 'neutral' than what the NYT suggests:

In spring 1998 the OECD published a report on ageing populations, *Maintaining Prosperity in an Ageing Society*. This report highlights the prospects of rising shares of the elderly in the population and falling shares of the population in employment to support pension and health systems. The report states that therefore policy choices have to be made for the medium-long term in order to meet this demographic challenge. Policies aiming to raise fertility rates or encourage greater immigration are those most frequently mentioned.

More recently, in March 2000, the Population Division of the United Nations published a report entitled *Replacement Migration: Is it a Solution to Declining and Ageing Populations?* This report, which starts from the premise that several OECD and non-OECD countries will face a population decline by 2050, sought to estimate the population flows necessary to maintain demographic equilibria according to various scenarios. The figures at which the authors arrive are considerably greater than the average migration flows calculated by e.g. the OECD from the data available for the 1990s[3] and clearly indicate the highly improbable nature of a purely migration-based remedy for the problems of demographic decline. The work currently being undertaken by the OECD aims to shed some light on the role that international migration might play in moderating the effects of population ageing.

The UN report concerned was indeed received with some dismay, particularly as the assumption that a population decline should be prevented is not properly addressed; many experts are of the opinion that a decline would have a great many positive effects, e.g. on the environment, the quality of life and such like. Yet, it is worth summarizing the findings by citing the relevant press release on this 'UN March 2000 Report on replacement Migration (UN Population Division of the Department of Economic and Social Affairs (DESA).'[4]

---

[3] See e.g. OECD's *Trends in International Migration,* 1998.
[4] Press Release DEV/2234 POP/735, 17 March 2000. The report may be accessed on the internet site of the UN Population Division (http://www.un.org/esa/population/unpop.htm). Further information may be obtained from the office of Joseph Chamie, Director, Population Division, United Nations, New York, NY, 10017, USA; tel. 1-212-963-3179; fax 1-212-963-2147.

Replacement migration refers to the international migration that a country would need to prevent population decline and population ageing resulting from low fertility and mortality rates.

United Nations projections indicate that between 1995 and 2050, the population of Japan and virtually all countries of Europe will most likely decline. In a number of cases, including Estonia, Bulgaria and Italy, countries would lose between one quarter and one third of their population. Population ageing will be pervasive, bringing the median age of population to historically unprecedented high levels. For instance, in Italy, the median age will rise from 41 years in 2000 to 53 years in 2050. The potential support ratio – i.e., the number of persons of working age (15-64 years) per older person – will often be halved, from 4 or 5 to 2.

Focusing on these two striking and critical trends, the report examines in detail the case of eight low-fertility countries (France, Germany, Italy, Japan, Republic of Korea, Russian Federation, United Kingdom and United States) and two regions (Europe and the European Union). In each case, alternative scenarios for the period 1995-2050 are considered, highlighting the impact that various levels of immigration would have on population size and population ageing.
Major findings of this report include:

– In the next 50 years, the populations of most developed countries are projected to become smaller and older as a result of low fertility and increased longevity. In contrast, the population of the United States is projected to increase by almost a quarter. Among the countries studied in the report, Italy is projected to register the largest population decline in relative terms, losing 28 per cent of its population between 1995 and 2050, according to the United Nations medium variant projections. The population of the European Union, which in 1995 was larger than that of the United States by 105 million, in 2050, will become smaller by 18 million.

– Population decline is inevitable in the absence of replacement migration. Fertility may rebound in the coming decades, but few believe that it will recover sufficiently in most countries to reach replacement level in the foreseeable future.

– Some immigration is needed to prevent population decline in all countries and regions examined in the report. However, the level of immigration in relation to past experience varies greatly. For the European Union, a continuation of the immigration levels observed in the 1990s would roughly suffice to prevent total population from declining, while for Europe as a whole, immigration would need to double. The Republic of Korea would need a relatively modest net inflow of migrants – a major change, however, for a country which has been a net sender until now. Italy and Japan would need to register notable increases in net immigration. In contrast, France, the United Kingdom and the United States would be able to maintain their total population with fewer immigrants than observed in recent years.

– The numbers of immigrants needed to prevent the decline of the total population are considerably larger than those envisioned by the United Nations projections. The only exception is the United States.

– The numbers of immigrants needed to prevent declines in the working-age population are larger than hose needed to prevent declines in total population. In some cases, such as the Republic of Korea, France, the United Kingdom or the United States, they are several times larger. If such flows were to occur, post-1995 immigrants and their descendants would represent a strikingly large share of the total population in 2050 (between 30 and 39 per cent in the case of Japan, Germany and Italy).

– Relative to their population size, Italy and Germany would need the largest number of migrants to maintain the size of their working-age populations. Italy would require 6,500 migrants per million inhabitants annually and Germany, 6,000. The United States would require the smallest number – 1,300 migrants per million inhabitants per year.

– The levels of migration needed to prevent population ageing are many times larger than the migration streams needed to prevent population decline. Maintaining potential support ratios would in all cases entail volumes of immigration entirely out of line with both past experience and reasonable expectations.

– In the absence of immigration, the potential support ratios could be maintained at current levels by increasing the upper limit of the working-age population to roughly 75 years of age.

The new challenges of declining and ageing populations will require a comprehensive reassessment of many established policies and programmes, with a long-term perspective. Critical issues that need to be addressed include: (a) the appropriate ages for retirement; (b) the levels, types and nature of retirement and health care benefits for the elderly; (c) labour force participation; (d) the assessed amounts of contributions from workers and employers to support retirement and health care benefits for the elderly population; and (e) policies and programmes relating to international migration, in particular, replacement migration and the integration of large numbers of recent migrants and their descendants.

The UN report itself concluded:

The present study focuses on the question of whether replacement migration is a solution to population decline and population ageing. Replacement migration refers to the international migration that would be needed to offset declines in the size of a population, declines in the population of working age as well as to offset the overall ageing of a population.

This replacement migration study focuses its investigation on the possible effects of international migration on the population size and age structure of a range of countries that have in common a fertility pattern below the replacement level. In the absence of migration, all countries with fertility below placement level will see their population size start declining at some point of time in the near future, if it is not already the case today. In some countries, the projected declines in population size during the first half of the 21st century are as high as a quarter or a third of the entire population of the country.

In addition, the lower the levels of fertility decline, the more pronounced will be the aging of the population of the country. One of the major consequences of population aging is the reduction in the ratio between the population in working-age group 15-64 years and the population 65 years or older, i.e., the potential support ratio (PSR). Everything else being equal, a lower potential support ratio means that it is much more onerous for the working-age population to support the needs of the older retired population.

While to some extent an increase in the proportion of elderly persons aged 65 years or older is accompanied by a decrease in the proportion of children under 15 years of age, the two age groups are not directly comparable. Some studies have estimated that for an industrialized country, on average, the cost to support a person aged 65 years and over is substantially greater than the cost to support a young person less than 20 years old. A number of researchers (...) report that when considering the public provision of programs or taking into account private non-medical expenses, public education expenses and medical care, the costs are roughly two and a half times greater to support an older person (aged 65 or older) than to support a young person (under 20 years of age).

While below-replacement fertility is the major cause of population decline and population ageing, even a sudden sharp increase in fertility in the short to medium term would not substantially alter the situation regarding the potential support ratios. Of course, as was shown earlier in this report, the potential support ratios could be maintained at current levels by increasing the upper limit to the working-age population. In most cases, the upper limit would need to be raised to roughly 75 years. However, if retirement ages remain essentially where they are today, increasing the size of the working-age population through international migration is the only option in the short to medium term to reduce the declines in the potential support ratio.

The present study considers countries where current fertility ranges from 1.2 to 2.0 children per woman. For France, United Kingdom, the United States and the European Union, the number of migrants needed to offset population decline are less than or comparable to recent past experience. While this is also the case for Germany and the Russian Federation, their migration flows in the 1990s were relatively large due to reunification and dissolution, respectively. In contrast, for Italy, Japan, the Republic of Korea and Europe, a level of immigration much higher than experienced in the recent past would be needed to offset population decline. This higher level of immigration for Italy, Japan and Europe would result in 18 to 29 per cent of the 2050 population being post-1995 immigrants and their descendants; for the Republic of Korea the comparable figure is 3 per cent.

In the absence of migration, the size of the working-age population declines faster than the overall population. As a result of this faster rate of decline, the amount of migration needed to prevent a decline in the working-age population is larger than that for the overall population. In the four countries where fertility levels are close to the replacement level, the resultant population in 2050 would have 8 to 14 per cent being post-1995 migrants and their descendants. In the other six countries and regions, the post-1995 migrants and their descendants would be between 26 and 39 per cent of the 2050 population.

While some of these numbers may appear to be high, they remain within the range of migration experienced in the recent past in some industrialized countries. For example, in 1990, 16 per cent of the population of Canada and Switzerland, and 23 per cent of the population of Australia, were foreign-born.

In contrast to the migration streams needed to offset total or working-age population decline, the levels of migration that would be needed to prevent the countries from ageing are of substantially larger magnitudes. By 2050, these larger migration flows would result in populations where the proportion of post-1995 migrants and their descendants would range between 59 per cent and 99 per cent. Such high levels of migration have not been observed in the past for any of these countries or regions. Moreover, it seems extremely unlikely that such flows could happen in these countries in the foreseeable future.

Therefore, it appears inevitable that the populations of the low-fertility countries will age rapidly in the 21st century. The consequences of a much older population age-structure than in the past are numerous and far-reaching. One important consideration that has been examined in this study is the potential support ratio (PSR). The current system of providing income and health services for older no-longer-working persons has been based, by and large, on an age structure with a potential support ratio of 4 to 5 persons in working-age for each older person aged 65 years or older. If the current age at retirement does not change, the PSR is projected to decline to about 2.

A decline of the PSR from 4 or 5 to 2 would certainly create the need to reconsider seriously the modalities of the present system of pensions and health care for the elderly. Theoretically, as noted above, a possible option would be to increase the upper limit of the working age sufficiently to attain a sustainable PSR. Such an option would simultaneously increase the numbers of working-age people and reduce the number of non-working older persons. Other possible options that may need to be examined thoroughly include adjusting economic measures, such as increased labour-force participation, higher contributions from workers and employers and lower benefits provided to retirees. Certainly, increased productivity in the future may increase the available resources from the working-age population.

However, it is also possible that increased productivity may lead to increased aspirations and demands from both the working-age and the retired populations. During the second half of the 20th century, the industrialized countries have benefited from population sizes and population age-structures that were the result of a history of moderate levels of fertility and low mortality. These favourable demographic circumstances made possible, to a large extent, the provision of relatively generous benefits to retirees at comparatively low costs to workers and employers. However, these age-structures were not permanent, but merely transitional.

During the first half of the 21st century, the populations of most industrialized countries are projected to become smaller and older in response to below-replacement fertility as well as increased longevity. The consequences of significant population decline and population ageing are not well understood as they are new demographic experiences for countries. Keeping retirement and health-care systems for older persons solvent in the face of declining and ageing populations, for example, constitutes a new situation that poses serious challenges for Governments and civil society.

The new challenges being brought about by declining and ageing populations will require objective, thorough and comprehensive reassessments of many established economic, social and political policies and programmes. Such reassessments will need to incorporate a long-term perspective. Critical issues to be addressed in those reassessments would include:

(a) the appropriate ages for retirement;
(b) the levels, types and nature of retirement and health-care benefits for the elderly;
(c) the labour-force participation;
(d) the assessed amounts of contributions from workers and employers to support retirement and health-care benefits for the increasing elderly population; and
(e) policies and programmes relating to international migration, in particular replacement migration, and the integration of large numbers of recent migrants and their descendants.

The EUROPEAN COMMISSION, through the 22 November 2000 Communication, also paid attention to this subject. In Annex 1 to this Communication[5] (covering the demographic and economic context), the following can be read:

The demographic context

During the 1990's the world's population increased more rapidly than ever before to reach 6 billion in 1999 and the UN estimates that about 150 million people (or some 2.5% of the total world population) now live outside of their country of origin. The world population increase is expected to continue at least in the short term and it is also estimated that improvements in communication, combined with the persistence of economic disparities, conflict and ecological factors, will ensure that migratory movements continue to ebb and flow during the 21st century.

The demographic situation in the EU has also been changing significantly, but in contrast to the overall world situation, two trends are particularly striking: a slowdown in population growth and a marked rise in the average age of the population. Figures prepared by Eurostat show that between 1975 and 1995, the population of the EU grew from 349 to 372 million people, and the proportion of the elderly (aged 65 and over) rose from 13% to 15.4%. Between 1995 and 2025 Eurostat estimates that the population of EU15 will grow more slowly (from 372 to 386 million) and will then begin to decline. However, the working age population (those aged 20-64) will begin to decline within the next 10 years (from 225m in 1995 to an estimated 223m in 2025), while the over-65 age group will

---

[5] COM(2000) 757 final. Due to lack of space, most footnotes had to be deleted.

continue to rise and is expected to reach 22.4% of the population in 2025.

The general trend among all the Central and Eastern European countries is one of even slower population growth than that of the EU15 for the first quarter of this century. Overall, the accession states will experience a similar ageing of the population to that of EU15. The expected fall in their working-age population will raise, in most of these States, similar challenges to those faced by EU15. However, the implications of the demographic trends will also depend upon the speed of the economic recovery and the labour market conditions in these countries. Regional disparities between urban and rural areas will be particularly pronounced in certain of them. Such disparities are also a feature of EU15 where some (D, I, S) have already entered negative natural growth (births minus deaths), while others (FIN, F, IRL, NL) ill continue to experience relatively high natural growth for some years. However across the EU as a whole, it is net migration that has become the principal component of population growth.

Eurostat figures show that net migration to the EU declined rapidly over the last decade after peaking in the early 1990s at over 1 million per year before starting to climb again and reaching just over 700.000 in 1999. On average for the years 1990-98 the net migration rate for the EU was 2.2 per 1.000 population against 3 for the USA, 6 for Canada and close to 0 for Japan. The flows are now composed of a mix of people: asylum seekers, displaced persons and those seeking temporary protection, family members coming to join migrants already settled in the EU, labour migrants and growing numbers of business migrants. Family reunion and the existence of ethnic communities from the countries of origin in a particular host country have become important factors in their size and direction. The flows have become more flexible – in particular there has been an increase in short-term and cross-border movements – with a complex pattern of people entering but also leaving the Union.

A recent report by the UN, based purely on demographic considerations, suggested that replacement migration could be an important factor in solving the problems caused by the declining and ageing populations in Europe. The Commission believes that, while increased legal immigration in itself cannot be considered in the long term as an effective way to offset demographic changes, since migrants once settled tend to adopt the fertility patterns of the host country, it could, in the short term, be an important element in population growth which could accompany other responses to demographic change, such as more friendly family policies. Equally, increased immigration will not, of itself, be an effective long-term way to deal with labour market imbalances, including skill shortages, which should be addressed by an overall strategy of structural policies in the field of employment and human resources development. However, controlled immigration may help to alleviate shortages provided it takes place within the context of an overall structural strategy.

The economic context and the situation of the EU labour market

The macro-economic prospects for the EU are currently the best for some years with low inflation and interest rates, reduced public sector deficits and a healthy balance of payments. The benefits to the economy of the introduction of the Euro and the completion of the internal market are leading to improved growth and job creation with a consequent drop in unemployment.

The process initiated by the European Council in Luxembourg in 1997 has established an ambitious framework for policy co-ordination in the EU in the area of employment. According to Article 126 of the Amsterdam Treaty, Member States implement their employment policies in a way which is consistent with the employment guidelines and the broad economic policy guidelines drawn up each year by the Council. In the light of these guidelines, Member States prepare National Action Plans whose implementation is monitored on a regular basis by the Commission and the Council.

A number of weaknesses in the EU economy were highlighted at the Lisbon European Council in March 2000, notably the high number of people still unemployed, which although the unemployment rate has fallen to an average of 9.2% in 1999, remains at over 15 million.[6] The labour market is characterised by the insufficient participation of women and older people in the work force and by long-term structural unemployment, with marked regional differences. The European Council emphasised the problems caused by the under-development of the services sector, especially in the areas of telecommunications and the Internet and the widening skills gap, especially in information technology where increasing numbers of jobs remain unfilled. It also drew attention to the need to modernise social protection systems and in particular to secure their sustainability in the face of an ageing population.[7] Adaptation of pension schemes both to encourage more gradual forms of retirement with flexible forms of work and leisure for older age groups would also encourage people, who today are generally in better health and have easier working conditions than their grandparents, to work longer. Making pension schemes less sensitive to demographic changes through sharing responsibility more broadly between government, the social partners and the individual would also reduce the dependency on the working age population. The European Employment Strategy is beginning to tackle these problems.

In Lisbon the Council set a new strategic goal for the EU for the next decade namely that it should become the most competitive and dynamic knowledge-based economy able to sustain economic growth and create more and better jobs with greater social cohesion. An overall strategy was adopted in order to achieve this

---

[6] The rate has continued to fall during 2000 and is currently at 8.4% or just over 14 million unemployed.

[7] *The future evolution of social protection froma long-term point of view: safe and sustainable pensions* (COM (2000) 622)

with the objective of raising the employment rate overall from an average of 61% in 2000 to near 70% in 2010 and for women from 51% to over 60% in this period. This would also reinforce the sustainability of existing social protection systems. The Commission believes that the strategies now in place will reduce the effects of the ageing population in the EU and the level of dependency between those in work and those who have retired.

The Joint Employment Report 2000[8] charts the progress which has been made in raising the employment rate which reached 62.2% in 1999. It also highlights the areas where further efforts are needed and reports on a worrying growth in skills shortages and miss-matches in supply and demand for labour. While this is becoming acute in relation to some sectors employing the highly skilled who are essential to the development of a knowledge-based economy, shortages in the traditional low-skilled areas, such as agriculture and tourism, are continuing even where there are high levels of unemployment in spite of the efforts being made to combat this phenomena. These shortages could threaten the EU's competitivity in the global economy.

In fact, the ability of different countries and regions in the EU to compensate for demographic effects and to mobilise unused labour resources varies considerably and immigration, therefore, will have a contribution to make in offsetting these problems in some countries as an element in the overall strategy to promote growth and reduce unemployment. While procedures are already in place at EU level to co-ordinate policies in a number of areas to facilitate the operation of the Single Market, notably the free movement of goods, capital, services and EU workers and other citizens, sufficient attention has not yet been given to the role of third country nationals in the EU labour market which, given its increasing importance, is an issue which now needs to be addressed.

The situation of migrants in the EU labour market

Reviewing the situation of migrants in the EU labour market there has been, since the mid 1980's, an increasing polarisation between the situations of skilled and unskilled migrants. The number of migrants in the labour force with low or no qualifications has been increasing since 1992 where they are meeting a demand e.g. in agriculture, construction, domestic and personal services and seasonal work in tourism (hotel and catering industry) as well as in some manufacturing sectors. With respect to skilled workers, there is now a new willingness to recruit migrants with special skills into the labour market to meet demands which cannot be met by the existing work force, even in areas of high unemployment. At the same time global competition for such skilled personnel is becoming fiercer (e.g. in the IT sector).

Although data on newly arrived migrants is not comprehensive, partly due to the large numbers of irregular and clandestine workers thought to be working in a

---

[8] COM(2000) 551 (final).

number of Member States, official data (European labour force survey) suggests that employment rate patterns are generally worse for first generation migrants – especially for women – than for the population as a whole. Recent studies by the ILO on ethnic discrimination in the labour market have revealed statistically significant levels of discrimination in a number of Member States. Moreover, migrant populations often show a higher rate of school drop-out than indigenous populations. This may often reflect language difficulties, especially among newcomers, but also problems associated with assimilation into the school system.

Over the past few years a number of studies have tried to assess the economic impact of legal immigration in different Member States notably Germany, Denmark and Austria. These indicate that, while there are both positive and negative effects, especially at local level, these tend to balance out and that overall, migrants generally have a positive effect on economic growth, and do not place a burden on the welfare state. The perception that immigration contributes to unemployment is not borne out in these studies which show, on the contrary, that migrants generally take jobs which have remained unfilled even where there is high unemployment in the local population. This reflects earlier work in the USA, Canada and Australia where it has provided a justification for continuing immigration policies, which seek to attract annual quotas of migrants to specific sectors. It is, of course difficult to evaluate the impact of irregular migrants working in the EU since their number and whereabouts cannot be estimated with any precision. Although they, and in many areas also low-skilled legal migrants, undoubtedly make a contribution to the economy in the short-term, their presence may also hinder the implementation of structural changes which are necessary for long-term growth.

Economic benefits may be more positive with respect to highly qualified migrants who are meeting skills needs, than for the low qualified who may, in some cases, be competing with national workers for jobs. It is in the lower skilled sectors (e.g. agriculture and related industries, catering, cleaning) where the largest numbers of undocumented migrants tend to find employment, often receiving wages which undercut the local workforce and sometimes in conditions which may lead to exploitation and to social unrest. On the other hand, the regional and sectoral concentration of migrants can mean that they represent an important force in the local economy. While difficulties in some of the sectors which have traditionally attracted migrants (notably construction, mining and manufacturing) have contributed to higher levels of unemployment among migrants than nationals in some countries, there is also evidence that migrants have proved more flexible in dealing with such problems in recent years, in particular by moving into the service sector and by setting up their own small businesses. It is also the case that there are often overall productivity gains in sectors employing migrants and in related industries. In agriculture, some manufacturing industries and some business services it is estimated that a shortage of migrants would have negative consequences on the sector concerned.

With respect to social security systems the presence of legal labour migrants and their families may, in the short term at least, be a positive factor in face of an ageing and declining population although there may be initial settlement costs. The availability of effective integration measures for third country nationals ensuring them decent living and working conditions reinforces their socio-economic contribution to their host society. The absence of such policies, leading to discrimination and social exclusion, may result in the end in greater long-term costs to society.

In the above Vitoríno Communication reference was made to the Lisbon European Council (2000) at which a strategy was agreed upon which is aimed at increasing labour market participation, productivity and mobility (the latter assumed to mean social mobility[9] and geographic mobility within the Member States and/or within the Union as a whole). The 2001 Stockholm European Council will also focus on demographic change.

In this context, due attention should be paid to the following characteristics of changing societies:
- Europe has successfully transformed itself from a society based on agriculture and later manufacturing into a service and knowledge-based one. The economics of scale would indicate that this trend is bound to continue;
- Production per labourer has increased consistently over the last 500 years or so, and there is no reason to doubt that this trend will continue;
- The elderly are increasingly able to perform in a constructive and productive manner well beyond retirement age (and may hence be invited to continue to offer their services);[10]
- Europe is still confronted with an unemployment rate of well above 9% (as per 1 January 2001), a figure which is not expected to fall below the 8% range within the next 10 years or so;
- The trend of raising the retirement age started in Iceland in 1999 and is bound to spread all over Europe.[11]

It is with this in mind that the following excerpts from a paper published by the OECD in the context of a project/report on the theme 'Maintaining Prosperity In An Ageing Society: the OECD study on the policy implications of ageing'[12] should be included in this Chapter:

---

[9] One of the main issues is to address social mobility, i.e. not only the upward one, but also the downward one. In order to keep the elderly 'on board' one should include an increased awareness for the added value of the more experienced employees combined with a new assessment of their strength and input. That may indeed result in new tasks, new positions and amended salaries.

[10] The USA may serve as an example in view of the many interesting and successful efforts to keep the elderly 'on board'.

[11] French reactions, January 2001, to a proposal to raise the retirement age were traditional (massive strikes), but were also accompanied by in-depth studies in the various newspapers (including the leftist 'Libération') which would appear to indicate that such a rise is unavoidable.

[12] *Work Force Ageing: Consequences and Policy Responses*; working paper AWP 4.1.
In 1998, the OECD published *Maintaining Prosperity in an Ageing Society* (031998051ᴱ1; see also the policy brief on this subject, October 1999), which reported on its work on the policy implica-

Expanding the range and quality of employment opportunities available to older workers will become increasingly important as populations age in OECD

tions of ageing. This work was 'horizontal' in the sense that a number of OECD directorates with both social and economic mandates were heavily involved. The analysis that was undertaken built on a number of existing OECD studies, on reviews of the literature and on original research conducted internally and by consultants. In 2000, the OECD published *Reforms for an Ageing Society*, which reports on national progress in implementing the policy principles set out in *Maintaining Prosperity in an Ageing Society*. A questionnaire was sent to Member countries in 1999 asking them to report on recent reforms. A benchmarking device was used whereby countries were asked to compare actual reforms against a set of ambitious, hypothetical reforms that were described in the questionnaire. Countries were also asked to identify lessons arising from these reforms that could be shared with other countries. *Reforms for an Ageing Society* describes the many reforms and lessons that were provided by countries, and sets them in the context of recent trends. OECD publications on this theme include a great many relevant papers, e.g.:

On the economics of ageing
AWP 1.1 The macroeconomics of ageing, pensions and savings: a survey
AWP 1.2 The macroeconomic implications of ageing in a global context
AWP 1.3 Macroeconomic effects of pension reforms in the context of ageing populations: OLG sumulations for seven OECD countries
AWP 1.4 The retirement decision in OECD countries
AWP 1.5 Microeconomic analysis of the retirement decision: United States
AWP 1.6 Microeconomic analysis of the retirement decision: Germany
AWP 1.7 Microeconomic analysis of the retirement decision: Italy
AWP 1.8 Microeconomic analysis of the retirement decision: United Kingdom
AWP 1.9 Microeconomic analysis of the retirement decision: the Netherlands
On financial markets and pension regulation
AWP 2.1 Ageing populations and the role of the financial market systems in the provision of retirement income in the OECD area
AWP 2.2 Private pensions systems: regulatory policies
On pensions in general
AWP 3.1 Adequacy and social security principles in pension reform
AWP 3.2 Adequacy and poverty among the retired
AWP 3.3 Incentives and disincentives to early and late retirement[2]
AWP 3.4 Retirement income systems: the reform process across OECD Countries
AWP 3.5 Predictability of individual pensions
AWP 3.6 Comprehensive quantitative modelling for a better pension strategy
AWP 3.7 Retirement income: level, risk and substitution among income components
AWP 3.8 Retirement income systems for different economic, demographic and political environments
On social, labour market and care-giving dimensions
AWP 4.1 Work-force ageing: consequences and policy responses
AWP 4.2 Long term care services to older people: a perspective on future needs
AWP 4.2 Resources during retirement
(covering the non-OECD world)
AWP 5.1 Do funded pensions contribute to higher aggregate savings? A cross country analysis
AWP 5.2 Fiscal alternatives of moving from unfunded to funded pensions
AWP 5.3 Liberalizing foreign investments by pension funds: positive and normative aspects
AWP 5.4 The second-second generation pension reforms in Latin America
AWP 5.5 A Simulation Model of Global Pension Investment
AWP 5.6 The Chilean Pension System
On other dimensions
AWP 6.1 The capacity for long-term decision making in seven OECD countries: the case of ageing
AWP 6.2 Ageing and technology
AWP 6.3 The Basic Demography

countries. Accordingly, there is a need to understand better the capacity of labour markets to adapt to ageing work forces, including how it can be enhanced.

Both the supply and demand sides of the labour market will be important. It is likely that pension programmes and social security systems in many OECD countries will be reformed so that existing incentives for early retirement will be reduced or eliminated. Strengthening financial incentives to extend working life, together with a large increase in the older population and improvements in their health, means that the supply of older workers will increase sharply in the coming decades. The *demand* for older workers, along with the efficacy of labour markets in matching supply and demand, will determine their employment and earnings prospects, as well as the impact of work-force ageing on aggregate productivity and income.

[This study also] assesses how the supply of older workers is likely to change over the next several decades, confirming that significant labour-force ageing is in prospect. A conceptual framework for analysing the implications of this for employment and earnings [will be presented]. The empirical relationships between compensation and age, and productivity and age are taken up [and the next part] then analyses mobility patterns among older workers. The final section presents some concluding remarks.

Main findings

Labour force ageing in OECD countries is likely to be substantial over the next several decades. In many countries, labour force growth will also slow and educational attainment among older workers will rise rapidly. Pension policy changes designed to raise the *effective* retirement age will magnify labour force ageing, but offset part of the projected fall in labour force growth.

OECD labour markets have adapted to significant shifts in the age structure of the labour force in the past. However, the ageing projected over the next several decades is outside the range of recent historical experience. Hence, it is uncertain how easily such a large increase in the supply of older workers can be accommodated, including the implications for the earnings and employment of older workers.

There is only weak evidence that the earnings of older workers are lower relative to younger workers in countries where older workers represent a larger share of total employment. This may indicate that workers of different ages are close substitutes in production, so that an increased supply of older workers can be employed without a significant fall in their relative wages. However, a number of factors affect the demand for older workers at any given relative wage and greater relative wage flexibility may sometimes be an important component of an overall programme to adapt to work-force ageing.

Improved job skills and access to training could help reduce the risks of unemployment and low pay for older workers. Work-force ageing also means that OECD countries will have to rely increasingly on mid- and late-career workers to meet emerging skill demands. This heightens the importance of improving the opportunities of older workers to develop new skills and to renew and re-deploy old skills. The limited evidence currently available suggests that older workers with adequate educational attainment and a history of participation in on-the-job training appear to be good training prospects, and training rates do not fall off strongly until workers approach conventional retirement ages.

However, older workers do encounter significant difficulties if they lose their job, as reflected in a high incidence of long-term unemployment and the large earnings losses experienced by older displaced workers, when they do find a new job. If their labour market mobility remains limited, these problems could increase as the work-force ages, since it is likely that increasing numbers of older workers will experience lay-offs.

Firms' pay, training, recruiting and other personnel practices will be key factors in determining the employment and earnings opportunities of older workers. Furthermore, proactive strategies, emphasising the skill base with which workers enter the later stages of their careers, are likely to be more effective than remedial measures after older workers have encountered employment problems. Thus, the training and other personnel practices of employers, as well as the career planning of workers, need to begin now to adapt to the prospect of work-force ageing. Governments have an important educational and co-ordinating role to play in facilitating these adjustments.

Comparing the two scenarios confirms that the extent to which the labour force will age will be strongly influenced by trends in retirement patterns. The OECD average share of workers aged 60 years and older in 2030 is 9 per cent under the baseline assumption, but rises to 17 per cent if retirement patterns return to those of 1970. Policy measures to encourage delayed retirement imply substantial shifts in the age composition of the work force that lie considerably outside the range of recent historical experience. Conversely, a continued trend toward earlier retirement could off-set the direct effect of the changing age structure of the population on the age composition of the labour force.

However, large reductions in participation rates generally would be required, implying undesirable and, possibly, unsustainable increases in retirement dependency ratios.

Scale of the required adjustments

This sub-section uses recent historical experience to provide a qualitative assessment of the scale of the adjustments required. Some indication of the capacity of OECD labour markets to adapt to these projected changes can be made by comparing the labour market performance of countries whose labour supply trends have differed in the past. This requires a summary index of the rate of change in the age structure. (...)

Several lessons emerge. First, OECD labour markets have faced considerable changes in the age structure in recent decades. lit is possible that the rate of change will actually decelerate (yielding a ratio below 1.0) in many countries under the baseline scenario. Second, there are large cross-country differences. Italy, Mexico and Turkey stand out for the extent to which labour markets will likely need to accommodate a sharp acceleration in the rate of change. Third, the later-retirement scenario shows that reversing the trend toward earlier retirement will significantly increase the rate of change in age composition in all countries compared with the trend over the period *1970-1995*. Finally, there are important qualitative differences between the forecast changes in age composition and the changes already experienced, which the summary index does not capture. Between 1970 and 1995, most countries experienced the labour market entry and initial ageing of the baby-boom generation, and a strong trend toward earlier retirement. By contrast, 1995-2020 will be characterised by increases in the shares of older workers.

There has not been a strong association in the past between these two types of labour supply changes and unemployment. Consistent with this finding, labour supply growth was positively correlated with employment growth. Strong conclusions cannot be drawn from these simple correlations, since no attempt was made to control for other determinants of labour market performance. Nonetheless, they provide a useful reminder that modern economies appear to have considerable capacity to adapt to different demographic conditions.

Several caveats to this optimistic appraisal are required. The demographic changes that will characterise labour supply in the next several decades are qualitatively different from past changes. Also, the fact that different national economies have accommodated quite different demographic environments in the past need not imply that abrupt *changes* in demographic trends will not require a difficult transition period. Finally, even if the macro indices of employment and unemployment examined here should not be greatly affected by work-force ageing, older workers could encounter increased employment difficulties.

The changing educational profile of older workers

The cohort **of workers aged 45-64 years in 2015** will be better educated than their counterparts today. The share not having completed upper secondary schooling is likely to fall by over one-third (the unweighted OECD average falls from about 44 to 27 per cent). This trend is likely for all OECD member countries, although large international differences in the distribution of education levels will persist.

Rising educational attainment should ease the absorption of larger groups of older workers. Recent decades have witnessed a strong increase in the demand for more educated workers and a concomitant deterioration in the opportunities for less-educated workers. Poorly-educated youths, particularly men, appear to have been most disadvantaged. However, older workers have also been negatively affected. Older workers displaced from production jobs, a group with low educational attainment on average, are at a high risk of remaining jobless for an extended period of time and typically experience large earnings losses if they do become re-employed.

The forecast improvement in educational attainment of older workers is good news, perhaps especially for men, but a word of caution is in order. A 'prediction' that the rapid increase in the educational levels of older workers is likely to expand their employment opportunities is potentially subject to a fallacy of composition. For a given cohort, more educated workers fare better on average than less educated ones. If this is due to so-called 'screening' by employers, then it need not follow that an upwards shift in the amount of schooling received by a cohort will result in improved employment prospects for the cohort as a whole.(...)

Economic theory provides a useful framework for analysing the earnings and employment consequences of work-force ageing. This section, therefore, reviews economic models relevant for analysing, in turn, the labour market effects of *individual* ageing *(i.e.* individual employment histories and how they would change if workers desired to delay retirement) and *group* ageing (i.e. a shift in the age distribution of the work force, whether due to population ageing or an rise in the effective age of retirement). Subsequently, the determinants of the age at which workers wish to retire are reviewed.

Individual ageing

The basic model of competitive labour markets implies that, at any point in time, workers' wages reflect their productivity. Human capital theory reconciles this equilibrium condition with the empirical tendency for earnings to rise over a large portion of most careers by positing that workers and their employers invest in on-the-job training that enhances future productivity. When the model is extended to incorporate the depreciation of skills and/or an eventual decline in productivity associated with biological ageing, it can generate realistically shaped age-earnings profiles: initially rapid earnings growth gradually slows, potentially even turning negative beyond a certain age. When this is combined with a rising disutility of working beyond a certain age, it creates an incentive for workers eventually to retire. So long as wages adjust to equal productivity at all ages, employers will find it profitable to employ older workers.

Analysing training choices as an optimal investment problem reveals incentives to concentrate training investments early in a workers' career. Both the shorter time horizon remaining for an older worker to employ any newly acquired skills and any age-related diminution in the ability to learn new skills would reduce the economic returns to training. However, the returns to training older workers may be enhanced by other factors. If firms finance training or it imparts *specific* skills *(i.e.* skills that enhance productivity with the current firm, but would not do so in other firms), the time horizon over which the profitability of training is assessed is the worker's expected remaining tenure with that employer, which may be much shorter than their total expected remaining working life, especially for young workers. In these circumstances, the lower quit rate of older workers would raise the expected returns to training them, relative to that for younger workers. Similarly, rapidly changing skill requirements would reduce the importance of a long pay-back period to the selection of trainees, but magnify the importance of any age-related decline in the ability to learn new skills.

The distinction between general and specific skills has two additional implications for ageing. As workers age, skills learned on the job become more important relative to skills learned in school. On-the-job training tends to impart less general skills than formal education, however, implying that the human capital of older workers is less 'portable' and they, therefore, risk large earnings losses if they change employers. Second, firms may under-invest in general skills because some of the returns accrue to other firms, who have an incentive to recruit workers after they have received general training from their current employers. This potential market failure has implications for workers of all ages, but could particularly disadvantage older workers by discouraging employers from investing to maintain the 'trainability' of workers as they age, or providing them with skill credentials that are recognised in the external labour market.

Long-duration employment relations may facilitate investments in on-the-job training, but may also change how compensation varies with age. Many workers stay with the same employer for long periods and firms may prefer to pay these workers wages that do *not* correspond to their productive contributions at all points during their careers. A 'back-loaded' compensation structure, in which pay is lower than productivity for junior workers, but rises more steeply and eventually surpasses productivity, potentially increases economic efficiency by strengthening incentives for workers to work more diligently, to remain with the same firm or to invest in firm-specific skills. Clearly, older workers generally are not disadvantaged by implicit contracts of this type, since both life-time and current earnings are increased. However, difficulties could arise for older workers attempting to delay retirement or to change jobs because:

– employers will only find it profitable to enter into back-loaded pay schemes if a predetermined maximum retirement age prevails, which limits the period of time during which compensation exceeds productivity. Accordingly, the existence of such incentive schemes could create employment difficulties if future cohorts of older workers should desire to work beyond the retirement age targeted by employers. If pension reforms and related policies cause many mid-and late-career workers to revise upwards their desired age of retirement, it might prove difficult – at that late point – to modify the implicit contract with their employer. Reforms announced sufficiently in advance would be more easily accommodated, because wage profiles could be reconfigured to a later retirement age; and

– employers who use back-loaded compensation schemes may prefer not to hire older job seekers, either because it is infeasible to offer an array of seniority pay schedules that are tailored to workers entering the firm at different ages or because this type of implicit contract creates a fixed cost of hiring and, hence, an incentive to hire younger workers whose expected future tenure with the employer is greater.

The argument that fixed hiring costs may disadvantage older job seekers is more general. The bias could also result from the costs of recruiting new employees or of providing initial job training. Fixed hiring costs typically may increase the job security of older workers who are already employed, since the firm will want to amortize that investment over as many years as possible. However, firms may have a preference to shed their oldest workers when downsizing, because the 'match capital' lost when a worker leaves the firm is larger the longer the worker would be expected to remain with the firm. This time horizon effect may be one reason that early retirement schemes are frequently used as a way to accommodate structural change.

Older workers may also face pay and employment disadvantages that result from *age discrimination,* defined as lesser opportunities of older workers that do not reflect lower productivity. Negative age stereotypes might particularly disadvantage older job seekers, since prospective employers may have difficulty assessing their past job performance or other credentials. As with gender and ethnic discrimination, it has proven difficult to find direct measures of age discrimination and most empirical estimates are based upon residual intergroup differences in pay or employment, after taking account of other explanations. Such estimates are inherently fragile, however, because it is never certain that all other factors have been adequately accounted for. This difficulty is particularly severe in the case of age discrimination, because the relationships between age, productivity and earnings are so complex.

Group ageing

The theory of factor demand with heterogeneous labour has been used to assess the quantitative implications of changes in the age structure of the work force for the employment and earnings levels of workers of different ages. The starting point for this analysis is a production function summarising how much output can be produced for different combinations of factor inputs, including workers of different ages. Intuitively, a high degree of substitutability between workers of different ages would imply that firms could accommodate large shifts in the age mix of their work force with little effect on overall productivity and, hence, that relatively small adjustments in relative wages would be sufficient to maintain labour market equilibrium. If substitutability is more limited, expansion of the relative number of older workers would significantly reduce their marginal product, implying that their relative wage would need to fall considerably if they are not to be at an increased risk of unemployment.

The econometric evidence on substitution patterns for workers of different ages is limited to a few countries and is neither entirely consistent nor easily extrapolated to the future. Overall, this evidence suggests that workers of different ages are quite good substitutes in production. To the extent this finding is reliable, it suggests that modest declines in the relative earnings of older workers would be sufficient to secure their employment in the future. Any such changes in the wage structure would also provide an incentive for employers to adjust recruitment and training practices so as to take fuller advantage of the potential contribution of older workers. However, this research provides little guidance about how efficiently the human resource practices of firms will respond to the market signals created by working-force ageing, or whether public policies can facilitate those adjustments.

The production function approach adopts a static notion of skill requirements that side-steps the difficult issue of whether an older work force will be less adaptable. While future skill needs cannot be forecast with precision, it is virtually certain that the introduction of new technologies and the constant flux of product market competition will create an ongoing need for workers to learn new skills and to move from declining to growing firms. The models of human capital, implicit contracts and fixed hiring costs discussed above suggest that older workers, being more heavily invested in their current jobs and specific skills than younger workers, find it more costly to make these sorts of adjustments. Therefore, younger and low-tenure workers provide a disproportionate share of the work force's overall adaptability. As the share of younger workers falls, it is likely that older workers will have to provide more of these adjustments. If there are age-related disadvantages in adaptability, access to training or job search, they may have increasingly adverse consequences for the employment and earnings security of older workers, and for the overall adaptability of the economy.

Desired age of retirement

A large literature applying the theory of labour/leisure choices to retirement has clarified how economic incentives affect labour supply near the end of the working life. One of the key empirical findings is the importance of pensions for the timing of retirement. Public and private pensions often create strong incentives for workers to retire at the age of first benefit entitlement, because of high effective tax rates on earnings. In some OECD countries, unemployment and disability benefit systems, or special early retirement programmes, also create strong incentives for workers to withdraw from the labour force in advance of conventional retirement ages. Past increases in the generosity of these income transfers and, especially, the extension of eligibility to younger workers appear to explain an important share of the secular trend toward earlier retirement in most countries. Estimates of the effect of pension systems on the age at which workers retire vary considerably, however, and some studies conclude that other factors, such as the secular rise in wage levels, changes in preferences, or shifts in the job structure towards sectors where earlier retirement is typical, account for the majority of the reduction in effective age of retirement. Another complicating factor in assessing the independent impact of expanded pension benefits on lowering the effective age of retirement is that the expansion of benefits has sometimes been a response to the employment difficulties of some groups of older workers.

The empirical research suggests that much of the recent trend toward earlier retirement is potentially reversible. Changes to public pensions or other social security programmes that either reduce the income support provided for early retirement or provide financial incentives for later retirement probably would cause many workers to prefer to retire somewhat later or more gradually. It is more difficult to assess how readily firms would accommodate such a reversal. It is clear, however, that changes would not occur overnight. The theories of on-the-job training and implicit contracts imply that the *anticipated* age of retirement affects recruitment, training and pay practices throughout a career. Mistaken expectations about the timing of retirement could be costly and governments may be able to facilitate the labour market adjustment to work-force ageing by providing timely information to workers and employers that help them anticipate the implications of demographic trends and policy changes for the timing of retirement.

As noted [above] compensation is a potentially key factor affecting the employability of older workers. (...) Whether higher earnings of older, relative to younger, workers reduces the employment opportunities of older workers is an important and complicated issue. There is no significant cross-country correlation between the earnings premium of older relative to younger workers, and the share of older workers in total employment. However, these correlations are always negative. There is also a positive correlation between the earnings of workers aged 45 to 54 years relative to those aged 25 to 29 and the risk of a layoff leading to joblessness for the older group. Consistent with earlier research on substitutability in production, these simple correlations provide, at best, weak evidence that cross-country differences in the relative earnings of older workers have been associated with greater employment difficulties, despite quite large cross-country differences in the relative earnings of older workers.

Low-paid employment

Like unemployment or involuntary retirement, low earnings when employed is also a potential threat to the living standards of older workers and their families. Flexibility in the level and composition of the compensation received by older workers – including possible reductions in earnings towards the end of the working life – might help labour markets to employ an ageing labour force, but could also increase the risk of earnings levels too low to meet family income needs. (...) Labour force ageing will probably tend to increase the risk of low-paid employment among older worker unless off-set by other factors. The increased supply of older workers may generate market pressures for their relative earnings to fall. If older workers also change jobs more frequently, the risk of downwards earnings mobility may also increase. Thus, the incidence of low-paid employment among older workers may well rise and it is probable that older workers, once low paid, would continue to have relatively poor upward mobility prospects. (...)

Training practices will have to adapt in order to minimise any adverse effects of ageing on overall productivity, while also accommodating any preference of older workers to delay retirement. The analysis of training rates by age suggests that firms' training investments reflect their predictions about the time of retirement. As an important complement of pension reforms designed to encourage later retirement, governments may have an important role to play in informing both firms and workers to anticipate such a shift and to begin as soon as possible to adapt training practices. By increasing the perceived pay-back period for investments in older workers, this information – if credible – could raise the age threshold beyond which training rates start to fall in anticipation of retirement.

Even if firms look more favourably on investing in training older workers, they may still be unwilling to invest much in those with low educational attainment. These individuals may become increasingly vulnerable to skill obsolescence, especially if they attempt to delay retirement, and the market incentives for firms to address this risk may be quite weak. Rising educational attainment among future cohorts of older workers should be a positive factor mitigating this risk, but it seems probable that low-skilled older workers will represent a major challenge for labour market programmes.

Mobility of older workers

This section considers whether the mobility of older workers is a problem in the context of work-force ageing. The extent to which limited mobility currently is a cause of long-duration joblessness is first examined. Empirical evidence on hiring patterns are then examined in order to assess whether older job seekers are disadvantaged in competing for jobs. Finally, attention turns to whether older workers may have to change employers more frequently in the future.

It appears likely that work-force ageing will create an increased need for older workers to change jobs because more will be laid-off. Layoffs occur when firms' downsizing needs cannot be met by voluntary attrition. Job losses due to downsizing and firm closure are relatively high in most OECD countries, in the range of 10 per cent of total employment annually, and show no downward or upward trend. By contrast, work-force ageing may cause voluntary attrition to fall, since voluntary quits are relatively infrequent among older workers. The combination of stable job loss rates and falling attrition implies a tendency for layoffs to rise, and the falling share of younger workers over the next few decades suggests that it will become more difficult for employers to protect older workers from these layoffs.

If more older workers do experience job loss, the economic costs resulting from their limited mobility would tend to increase. Greater proactive training investments to maintain trainability and acquire general skills probably could improve the mobility of older job changers. However, little is known about what sort of training would generate the highest returns and market incentives may be inadequate to induce the desired response.

Conclusions

OECD labour forces will become significantly older over the next several decades. The work-force ageing due to population ageing will be strongly amplified to the extent that the trend toward earlier retirement reverses. Such a reversal would limit the growth in the number of retirees relative to the number of active workers, which is one of the keys to avoiding the potentially negative impact of population

ageing on living standards. Reforms to pension and other social security programmes that reduce significantly or eliminate existing incentives for early
retirement probably would generate a significant increase in labour supply at older
ages. However, the full potential benefits of such policies will only be realised if
labour markets are able to generate enough good jobs for an unprecedentedly large
number of older workers.

Proactive measures by workers, employers and governments to enhance the
employability of older workers will be an essential complement to pension reform.

There is a striking disproportion between the importance of the challenge to
expand the employment opportunities of older workers and the limited success of
economic research at providing guidance for policy making. A number of
important relationships between ageing and recruitment, training and pay have
been identified, including potentially important equity and efficiency concerns.
However, relatively little is known about the actual magnitudes of these potential
problems nor about the best policies to redress them. The relationship between age
and job performance, including how it is shaped by training practices, appears to
be critical, but is not well understood. Limited mobility also appears to be an
important concern, but the extent and causes of the apparent disadvantage of older
job seekers are not well understand either. Further research on these and related
topics deserves high priority.

Even with the present limited state of knowledge, several preliminary
judgements appear justified. First, the preponderance of the evidence on ageing
and productivity suggests that most workers have the potential to remain
productive up to and beyond currently standard retirement ages, provided they
receive adequate training. Second, although the market signals created by work-
force ageing will tend to cause recruitment, training and pay practices to adapt in
desirable ways, these adjustments may well not go as far, or proceed as rapidly, as
desirable. In particular, there is a danger that insufficient investments will be made
in maintaining the trainability and mobility of workers as they age. Finally, even if
firms and workers make all desirable provisions for ageing, it will remain true that
older workers face elevated risks of skill obsolescence and poor health. Advocates
of reforming pensions so as to encourage later retirement have rightly emphasised
that unemployment and disability benefit programs need to be tightly regulated, to
ensure that they do not become substitute sources of *de facto* early retirement
benefits. It should be understood, however, that raising the age of pension
eligibility will expand the legitimate demand for these benefits.

Globalization   2.2

(motto: '... the twain will never meet ...')

Globalization is and will remain a hotly debated issue during the forthcoming decade and beyond. The main question to be asked and to be researched is whether 'globalization' as such will create a win/win situation, meaning that all parties involved will benefit.

If globalization were to be defined as opening borders and ensuring free flows and economic integration (including economic liberalization and privatization), global economic imbalances are then supposed to decrease. The main question in this respect is, of course, whether globalization would and/or should also include the free movement of 'labour' or should rather be limited to the free movement of the other factors of production (goods and capital) and services. On the other hand, it is worth studying whether globalization would increase or rather decrease migratory movements.

As for including free movement of labour as a pre-condition for successful globalization, it could be argued that equating labour (i.e. human beings) to goods, services and capital is an affront to mankind in general, and that hence any focus on the latter three is justified and to be preferred.

Such a choice could already be based on the very fact that most migration scholars tend to overlook the general 80/20 rule which in this case means that labour migrants – like everyone duly employed, foreign and local alike – spend only 20% of their time actually doing what labour migration is principally meant for: work.[1] Quite remarkable is also the text of the preambule of the 1975 ILO Convention on Migrant Labour (C143):

---

[1] This statement is by no means indicative of 'ethos' as such: based on 48 weeks'work annually and a 40-hour working-week, the 1800 hours involved amount to almost exactly 20% of the (365x24=) 8,760 hrs a year. That, indeed, means that the other 80% is spent on a) 30% sleep (365x7.5) and b) 50% eating, travel to and fro, recreation, etc. In fact, in major immigration countries, the newly arrived spend up to 25% of their time working.

P.J. van Krieken (Ed.), The Migration Acquis Handbook
© 2001, T.M.C.Asser Press, The Hague, the Röling Foundation and the authors

'... emphasizing the need to avoid the excessive and uncontrolled or unassisted increase of migratory movements because of their negative social and human consequences, and considering that in order to overcome underdevelopment and structural and chronic unemployment, the governments of many countries increasingly stress the desirability of encouraging the transfer of capital and technology rather than the transfer of workers in accordance with the needs and requests of these countries in the reciprocal interest of the countries of origin and the countries of employment ...'

The issue to be raised in the context of a Migration Acquis Handbook is hence how to look upon globalization and whether globalization has to include labour migration. The submission that non-migration would create winners rather than losers will also be touched upon.

GLOBALIZATION

As The Economist stated in a Leader in a September 2000 issue:[2]

The anti-capitalist protesters who wrecked the Seattle trade talks [1999], and who hope to make a great nuisance of themselves in Prague [September 2000] when the city hosts this year's annual meeting of the World Bank and the International Monetary Fund, are wrong about most things. However, they are right on two matters, and the importance of these points would be difficult to exaggerate. The protesters are right that the most pressing moral, political and economic issue of our time is third-world poverty. And they are right that the tide of 'globalisation', powerful as the engines driving it may be, can be turned back. The fact that both these things are true is what makes the protesters – and, crucially, the strand of popular opinion that sympathises with them – so terribly dangerous.

International economic integration is not an ineluctable process, as many of its most enthusiastic advocates appear to believe. It is only one, the best, of many possible futures for the world economy; others may be chosen, and are even coming to seem more likely. Governments, and through them their electorates, will have a far bigger say in deciding this future than most people appear to think. The protesters are right that governments and companies – if only they can be moved by force of argument, or just by force – have it within their power to slow and even reverse the economic trends of the past 20 years.

Now this would not be, as the protesters and their tacit supporters must reckon, a victory for the poor or for the human spirit. It would be just the opposite: an unparalleled catastrophe for the planet's most desperate people, and something that could be achieved, by the way, only by trampling down individual liberty on a daunting scale. Yet none of this means it could never happen. The danger that it will come to pass deserves to be taken much more seriously than it has been so far.

---

[2] The case for globalisation, September 23rd, 2000.

The mighty forces driving globalisation are surely, you might think, impervious to the petty aggravation of street protesters wearing silly costumes. Certainly, one would have hoped so, but it is proving otherwise. Street protests did in fact succeed in shutting down the Seattle trade talks last year. More generally, governments and their international agencies – which means the IMF and the World Bank, among others – are these days mindful that public opinion is anything but squarely behind them. They are not merely listening to the activists but increasingly are pandering to them, adjusting both their policies and the way these policies are presented to the public at large. Companies too are bending to the pressure, modest as it might seem, and are conceding to the anti-capitalists not just specific changes in corporate policy but also large parts of the dissenters' specious argument.

These outbreaks of anti-capitalist sentiment are meeting next to no intellectual resistance from official quarters. Governments are apologising for globalisation and promising to civilise it. Instead, if they had any regard for the plight of the poor, they would be accelerating it, celebrating it, exulting in it – and if all that were too much for the public they would at least be trying to explain it.

Lately, technology has been the main driver of globalisation. The advances achieved in computing and telecommunications in the West offer enormous, indeed unprecedented, scope for raising living standards in the third world. New technologies promise not just big improvements in local efficiency, but also the further and potentially bigger gains that flow from an infinitely denser network of connections, electronic and otherwise, with the developed world.

The 'gains' just referred to are not, or not only, the profits of western and third-world corporations but productive employment and higher incomes for the world's poor. That is what growth-through-integration has meant for all the developing countries that have achieved it so far. In terms of relieving want, 'globalisation' is the difference between South Korea and North Korea, between Malaysia and Myanmar, even (switching time-span) between Europe and Africa. It is in fact the difference between North and South. Globalisation is a moral issue, all right.

If technological progress were the only driver of global integration, the anti-capitalist threat would be less worrying. Technological progress, and (it should follow) increasing global integration, are in some ways natural and self-fuelling processes, depending chiefly on human ingenuity and ambition: it would be hard (though, as history shows, not impossible) to call a halt to innovation. But it is easier to block the effects of technological progress on economic integration, because integration also requires economic freedom.

The state of the developing countries is itself proof of this. The world is still very far from being a single economy. Even the rich industrialised economies, taken as a group, by no means function as an integrated whole. And this is chiefly because governments have arranged things that way. Economic opportunities in the third world would be far greater, and poverty therefore vastly reduced, right now except for barriers to trade – that is, restrictions on economic freedom – erected by rich- and poor-country governments alike. Again, the protesters are absolutely right: governments are not powerless. Raising new barriers is as easy as lowering existing ones. Trade ministers threaten to do so on an almost daily basis.

The likelihood of further restrictions has increased markedly of late. Rich-country governments have all but decided that rules ostensibly to protect labour and the environment will be added to the international trading regime. If this comes about, it will be over the objections of developing-country governments – because most such governments have come round to the idea that trade (read globalisation) is good. Europe and the United States are saying, in effect, that now that the poor countries have decided they would like to reduce poverty as quickly as possible, they can't be allowed to, because this will inconvenience the West.

If that reason were true, it would be a crime to act on it. But it isn't true, or even all that plausible. Rich-country governments know very well that the supposed 'adjustment problems' of expanded trade are greatly exaggerated: how convincing is it to blame accelerating globalisation for the migration of jobs from North to South, when America has an unemployment rate of less than 4% and real wages are growing right across the spectrum? Yet even under these wonderful circumstances, politicians in Europe and America (leftists, conservatives, Democrats and Republicans alike) are wringing their hands about the perils of globalisation, abdicating their duty to explain the facts to voters, and equipping the anti-capitalists with weapons to use in the next fight.

It would be naive to think that governments could let integration proceed mainly under its own steam, trusting to technological progress and economic freedom, desirable as that would be. Politics could never be like that. But is defending globalisation boldly on its merits as a truly moral cause – against a mere rabble of exuberant irrationalists on the streets, and in the face of a mild public scepticism that is open to persuasion – entirely out of the question? If it is, as it seems to be, that is dismal news for the world's poor.

CRITICISM AND VIEWS

The DAVOS 2001 World Economic Forum paid ample attention to both the critics and proponents. It was *inter alia* stated that globalization will deliver benefits to developing countries only if there is 'sufficient and sustained will among industrialized nations and multilateral institutions' to enable developing countries to build the capacity to compete.[3]

The following comment as it appeared on the relevant web-site at that time would appear to summarize the main ideas and concerns:

The past few years have seen a sharp rise in public protests against economic globalization, the most notable of which took place at the 1999 World Trade Organization meeting in Seattle, Washington, which was disrupted by an

---

[3] Benjamin Mkaba, President of Tanzania, IHT, 27-28 January 2001.

estimated 30,000 demonstrators. Public opposition to globalization defines a new and important political divide and cannot be disregarded.

The opposition to globalization brings together labour interests that are concerned about the flight of jobs to low-paying countries, human rights groups that want employees to be paid fairly and treated humanely, environmental groups that are concerned that globalization encourages companies to site plants in countries with the most lax (and low-cost) environmental standards, and all-purpose populists who feel globalization is denying them control over their lives. But a single, broader theme unites these groups: outrage at what they perceive to be the chronic abuse of power by people in high and distant places. A large and growing percentage of the public, as evidenced by the protests, believes that globalization has its own intrinsically harmful momentum, and that our established institutions of governance are unwilling or unable to check its forward movement.

Proponents of globalization believe that economic prosperity is the key to protecting the environment and the rights of workers, and that globalization offers the fastest – and perhaps only – route to prosperity. From their perspective, multinational corporations bring the blessings of technology, know-how and capital to the places where they do business. Often, they bring superior environmental standards, too; many multinational corporations apply the environmental standards of their home country to all their facilities throughout the world.

Ultimately, public concern about globalization will be addressed by action, not argument. Pro-globalization institutions need to develop policies that alleviate public concern about the impact of globalization on environmental health, employee rights and cultural diversity. More broadly still, they must confront the reality of widespread and growing public anxiety about the powerlessness of people in the face of a globalized economy.

This process has begun. The corporate citizenship movement is building. Companies are starting to turn their innovative genius to developing appropriate products for the world's four billion poverty-stricken citizens. They are also placing increasing emphasis on information transparency, a key to building trust, as epitomized by the rapid growth of the Global Reporting Initiative, an international voluntary standard for environmental and social reporting.

MIGRATION AS AN INHERENT PART OF GLOBALIZATION

Part of the Barcelona process, which aims to create an environment for fruitful co-operation among the countries around the Mediterranean, is the issue whether access to each other's markets would or should involve labour migration.

It should be quite obvious that, for example, Northern African countries have an interest in exporting 'labour', particularly as those countries are as yet unable to offer sufficient employment opportunities:

- population growth is decreasing but still around 2.8% (which means that an economic growth of 7% is needed just to offset the growth in population);[4]
- it will prove and has proven impossible to create jobs for the new generation(s);
- high unemployment may threaten political stability;
- by 'exporting' the young (preferably the unskilled) that country may create a win/ win situation, as those who will find a job may start sending home funds ('remittances') which will assist the local economy.

One of the main questions to be posed when it comes to analyzing the relationship between globalization and migration is whether labour should move to where the capital (and hence production) is, or whether capital should move to where the labour is available.[5]

It goes without saying that a major part of the literature concerned is focused on the positive impact of migration on the local economy and whenever possible on the global economy. Stalker submits:

'... Even if the arrival of large numbers of immigrants does not appear to have an immediate effect on income for national workers, there is also the possibility that they will affect long-term growth (...) [T]his will be positive if immigrants are meeting acute labour shortages. (...) however, it could also be argued that an alternative to immigration, particularly of the low-skilled, is to increase levels of technology and make production more capital-intensive. Immigration could inhibit this process, effectively "diluting" the capital-to-labour ration, leading to a drop in productivity. On the other hand, if immigration of low-paid workers leads to increased profits, this could finance greater capital investment. (...) Most historical research suggests, in fact, that immigration has improved total [i.e. local] growth, even if the contribution is slight ...'[6]

Although some figures are available on the long-term impact of migration on the sending countries, these concern mainly the loss of skills and the brain-drain, on the one hand, and the effect of remittances on sending countries on the other. It is herewith submitted, however, that the relationship is a more complex one, as it should include the losses incurred due to a delay of transferring 'marginal' industries to developing countries. This can be explained as follows: in the case of an industry (agricultural, manufacturing and service industries alike) having problems running at

---

[4] Economists have indicated that an economic growth of 8% is needed to offset a population increase of 3% (which, based on the famous '72-rule' means that the population doubles in a mere (72/3=) 24 years, or: just one generation). The 8% is needed mainly in infrastructure: housing, roads, health and education so as to provide the additional population with the same services that the rest of the population already enjoys. Only economic growth over and above this 8% mark can be considered real, objective growth.

[5] This could be paraphrased by e.g. 'sending goods instead of people' (Stalker), or 'workers to work or work to the workers' (Abella).

[6] Peter Stalker, *Workers Without Frontiers,* ILO, 2000, p. 90. This publication with the subtitle 'the impact of globalization on international migration' is strongly recommended. (It could be combined with Starker's 1994 survey of international labour migration, *The Work Of Strangers,* ILO 1994, 2nd edition 1997.)

a profit, a solution is often believed to be found in importing labour. This import, however, frustrates the market mechanisms of the country to where labour is to be imported: the demand/supply balance is falsified, as salaries for scarce labour will not have to be increased, thereby denying a possible 'profit' for the local labourers available (or in fact resulting in a market-based move of labour from one industry to another, preferably by using the existing labour reserve, particularly as unemployment in the Union is still around 9%). Moreover, the import of (cheap) labour delays the need to replace labour by capital, and indeed frustrates innovation and technical developments (new machinery, streamlined production).[7] Most serious, though, is the fact that the import of labour delays the shifting of the industry concerned to a cheap-labour country, and that it thus has a negative impact on globalization as a whole. It could thus be submitted that migration per se is contrary to the idea of globalization, apart from the ethical discourse on moving capital v. moving human beings.

DEMAND AND SUPPLY

The above is clearly based on market mechanisms such as demand and supply. In fact, the supply of foreign labour may result in increased demands, but should above all be seen as a result of demands. The demand for cheap labour (legal or illegal) will always persist. Illegal migration in particular is hence very much linked to control and enforcement of rules relating to the hiring of irregular foreigners. The level and intensity of control, combined with the penalties involved will undoubtedly have an impact. This is not only true for professional football clubs hiring Brazilians with false Portuguese passports, but also for the small restaurants hiring illegal dish-washers or the small-scale agricultural industries using the services of Brussels sprout pickers.

Part of the equation is to be found in the mobility dilemma. With some 9% of the total workforce unemployed, it is of relevance to rethink social mobility. Most countries of the Union do not necessarily expect the unemployed to take new jobs below the 'social' level they may have obtained in their career. Yet the question should be asked why social mobility should only be upwards, and whether the relationship between the tax payer and the receiver of social benefits should include

---

[7] Chiswick, in his paper *The Economics of Illegal Migration for the Host Country* (see elsewhere in this Handbook), provides the following illustration: 'When asked recently what I would do if illegal alien gardeners disappeared from the Chicago labour market I replied that there would be a variety of responses: paying higher wages to attract similarly skilled or higher-skilled native-born workers, switch from labour intensive flower beds to less labour intensive grass lawns, plant slower growing varieties of grass, brick over part or all of the garden, prefer a house with a smaller lawn, and let the grass grow longer, among other alternatives. Thus, substitutions come in the form of using different types of labour inputs, substitution of capital for labour, use of a different technology, and substitution among consumption goods. Similar substitution possibilities exist for other market goods and services.'

such a notion. The same is true for geographic mobility, as many jobs may be available in one part of the country, whereas the unemployed may concentrate themselves in another part (e.g. as a result of a major labour-intensive manufacturing plant closing down. Last but not least, is the issue related to minimum salaries as compared to the unemployment hand-outs: in some of the EU countries the latter hand-outs, particularly combined with related fringe benefits, are higher than the minimum salaries, which obviously has a negative impact on the unemployed re-entering the labour market.

AGRICULTURAL SUBSIDIES

Only very few Europeans are aware of the fact that the Union spends each and every day E 125 million on agricultural subsidies. This is particularly relevant in view of the question whether developing countries should export tomato pickers, or whether they would be allowed to export their tomatoes. Although the subsidies may have strategic value (we should be able to produce at least some of our own food and not become dependent on OPEC-like powers), true globalization would appear to dictate that tariffs and subsidies should disappear. Again, the subsidies frustrate the labour demand/supply mechanisms, make it possible to deny the need for technical innovations, and delay the transfer of that industry, or at least of parts of that industry, to other parts of the world or, in the short-term, to Eastern Europe in particular. It is quite illustrative that the very issue of agricultural subsidies has such an impact on the enlargement schedule, as it is not difficult to understand that if the new EU members were to enjoy the same level of subsidies, the total bill (now E 45 billion) would become too expensive to pay. It is true that under the Lomé Conventions a number of countries have been given the possibility to export their agricultural products, but the idea of protectionism still stands in no uncertain terms. What is needed is to link the subsidies issue with the topic of migration, an issue too often and too conveniently neglected.

Would the abolition of agricultural subsidies result in an immediate collapse of the agricultural industry as a whole? The flower business would appear to indicate that this will not be the case (flowers not being the subject of subsidies). Flowers tend to be a fairly labour-intensive product, not forming part of the daily needs, and hence uncertain of market developments. Yet, increased prices have not deterred consumers, and, more importantly, part of the production now takes place in countries like Kenya, often with new, technically advanced methods, without having had a negative impact on European monetary flows.

STERN, SEN AND PROTECTIONISM[8]

Nick Stern is the new Chief Economist of the World Bank (IBRD). He focuses on opportunity, empowerment and security. These, he argues will help to reduce poverty. Mr Stern is believed to be a 'fan' of the Nobel prize-winning economist and philosopher Amartya Sen. The latter calls protectionism 'a rip-off of the rich consumers, a rip-off of rich-country taxpayers, and intensely damaging to the poor of the world.' Mr. Stern believes in opening up markets, and wants to see a new group of developing countries like Argentina, Brazil, India, Indonesia and South Africa 'blaze a trail' in multilateral issues. The key task in development, in Mr. Stern's opinion, is to open up the markets of the main economic powers (Northern America, Europe, Japan). To cut some of the steepest tariffs that the poorest countries face (tariffs that are close to 100% on manufacturing and agricultural products) will not necessarily solve the problem, since non-tariff barriers can be just as harmful. The challenge, Mr. Stern submits, is a political one: to disabuse the rich-world foes of liberalization, the benefits of trade must be patiently explained.

Scrapping peak tariffs could lead to an increase of E 2.5 billion in exports from the least developed countries, hardly enough to make competitors in the North blink, but resulting in an 11% improvement for the exporting countries. Adding in the rest of the world, and considering other barriers such as excessively rigid country of origin rules (mostly applied to textiles), the potential gains could be E 100 billion a year.

NUMBERS & NAFTA

That brings us to the numbers game. A gain of E 100 billion with a fairly simple and basic liberalization should be seen in the light of remittances and development aid.

Currently, OECD countries spend some E 50 billion per year on Official Development Assistance (ODA).[9] It could thus be submitted that development aid covers a maximum 50% of the losses incurred because developing countries are not able or allowed to export their products to the North. A tremendous win/win situation could thus be created by abolishing agricultural subsidies, by foregoing major parts of the development aid programmes and by opening up the markets of the North to products from the South.

Of course, regard should also be had to remittances as a whole, the total of which is now believed to amount to some E 70 billion yearly. The question is whether such 'remittances' consist solely of transfers of migrants to their families back home. This is not the case, as it also involves investments from which the investor and their families alike may profit. Much of the remittances is based on economically sound

---

[8] Based on an article in The Economist, January 20th, 2001.
[9] This number may include costs incurred for asylum-seekers having come to Europe.

calculations which would indicate that such 'remittances' will continue to flow, disguised as 'investments'.[10]

As to North America and NAFTA, and the relationship between migration and international trade in general, the following remarks by Stalker are illuminating:[11]

The prospect of millions more uninvited immigrants arriving on their doorsteps has prompted many Western countries to ask how these people might be persuaded to stay at home – how the pressure to emigrate might be reduced. The United States, with a 2,000-mile southern frontier, and a seemingly limitless pool of labour on the other side, has posed the question most directly. The 1986 Immigration Reform and Control Act set up a Presidential Commission to examine the issue. and to see what might be done on the other side of the border to give potential migrants an incentive to stay at home. Its 1990 report. *Unauthorized migration. An economic development response.* confirmed what has become clear from evidence in the Americas and elsewhere; the only answer is sustained economic development in the sending countries – even though, paradoxically, in the short term this is likely to increase migration rather than reduce it. Other countries, including Switzerland and Sweden. have also been examining this issue. In 1990 the German cabinet called for a review of development co-operation with the Third World and also proposed the use of economic assistance to counter emigration pressure from countries to the east.

One should always be sceptical about the degree to which public policy is capable of affecting individual decisions. People have always moved from one country to another, and doubtless many will choose to do so regardless of what governments say or do. A more limited objective of public policy should perhaps be to try and make sure that people do have an option about whether to migrate or not, to ensure that they are not forced by economic circumstances into an agonizing decision to uproot themselves and their families for the uncertainties of life in another country.

One of the most fundamental reasons for such decisions is the contrast in wages between sending and receiving countries. Between the United States and Mexico this ratio is as much as 10 to 1. Between Bangladesh and Japan, it is more like 80 to 1. Eliminating these gaps altogether would be a daunting task. But past experience suggests that this need not be necessary: the ratios do not need to be 1 to 1 before migration is substantially reduced. A decade ago in Europe, the wage ratios between then richer countries in the north such as France and Germany and the poorer ones in the south such as Spain. Portugal and Greece were something like 7 to 1 and migrants flocked from south to north to take advantage of them. Nowadays the ratio is more like 4 to 1 and relatively few people migrate – even

---

[10] For details: see Stalker, op.cit., pp. 79-82. Stalker describers the differences between workers' remittances, compensation incomes and migrants' transfers. He also indicates that the main recipient countries are Mexico, Egypt, the Philippines, France and Portugal (!). Included in the calculations is also the fact that many of the transfers take place through informal systems.

[11] Stalker, *The Work of Strangers,* ILO 1994 (1997), pp. 155-158.

though it is now much easier for EU nationals to work in other EU countries. On the other hand, people still migrate in other parts of the world when the differentials are much smaller. For example, in the 1970s the differential between Venezuela and Colombia was only 3 to 1, yet there was still a strong migration flow.

Clearly there are other factors at play here besides wages. And it may be that *future* prospects rather than immediate benefits weigh most heavily, particularly for younger people considering migration as a permanent option. The young in Spain and Greece. for whatever reason, seem to consider that life in their own country is likely to improve in the years ahead. while those in Colombia may be more pessimistic.

How can these prospects be changed? Trade offers one opportunity. If people were free to work for reasonable rewards in their native country and export their production to foreign countries, they would not feel such a strong need to work abroad. Trade could substitute for migration. Classical economic theory positing perfect markets and a free flow of the 'factors of production – goods. capital and labour – across national frontiers suggests that all global economic imbalances should eventually even out of their own accord.

But the world is no more perfect in its markets than in anything else. The developed countries seem as stubbornly determined to keep out not just workers but also goods. Of the 24 industrialized countries', 20 are more protectionist now than they were ten years ago, and the effective rate of protection against exports from developing countries is considerably higher than the rate against exports from industrialized countries. This costs developing countries at least $40 billion per year in forgone exports of goods and services. As Mexico's President has observed, the United States does not want to import Mexican tomato pickers, but it seems to want Mexican tomatoes even less.

Barriers to the flow of goods take a number of forms. The main obstacles are now 'non-tariff' barriers, such as quotas, export restraints, and measures against dumping. The Multi-Fibre Agreement, for example, on exports of textiles and clothing costs developing countries an estimated $24 billion per year in lost export earnings. And tariff systems are also designed to discourage producers of primary commodities from employing people to convert raw materials to manufactured goods: the average tariff on processed cocoa, for example, is more than twice that on raw cocoa – to reduce the developing countries' incentive to make and export chocolate.

The industrialized countries do agree to allow *some* developing countries preferential access to *some* of their markets. One of the most comprehensive of these agreements is the Lomé Convention, of which the fourth was signed in 1989 to run for ten years [and the fifth agreed upon early 2000]. This is an agreement between the countries of the EU and 69 developing countries of Africa, the Caribbean and the Pacific; it offers access for products such as rice, bananas and beef. The United States has a more limited relationship with its neighbouring developing countries through the Caribbean Basin Initiative which, since 1984, has offered unilateral trade preferences to the countries of the Caribbean basin and Central America (but not Mexico).

Unfortunately these agreements tend to stop short in precisely those areas where developing countries might make significant inroads into industrialized country markets – notably in labour-intensive manufactured goods and some key agricultural commodities. One of the more bizarre instances of protectionism relates to sugar. One year after the United States introduced the Caribbean Basin Initiative it also introduced formal quotas for sugar to protect American sugar producers. As a result, Caribbean sugar- producing countries saw their exports fall from $544 million in 1981 to only $97 million by 1988, and the region lost 400,000 jobs. One might assume that this has at least provided a similar number of jobs for American workers, but this is not the case. Most American workers refuse to cut sugar cane (one of the most gruelling of all agricultural tasks) so the American sugar companies have to import thousands of seasonal workers – from the Caribbean.

Flo-Sun, for example, is one of the largest United States sugar producers supplying around 15 per cent of the country's sugar. But it can only do so by bringing in *4,500* Caribbean workers each year to its Florida plantations. By Caribbean standards, these workers are well paid. But American standards are rather higher and the company has frequently been cited for violating minimum wage and other labour laws. In 1988, according to the Federal Election Commission, the company made donations to political action committees and political campaigns (of both parties) of $286,900. It receives price support payments annually of up to $90 million.

Similar protectionist issues are arising between Eastern and Western Europe. With the collapse of trade within the former area, Eastern European countries are desperately in need of markets elsewhere. Hungary, for one, has been having some success: between 1988 and the first half of 1991, the proportion of its exports taken by the EC had risen from 23 to 39 per cent. But the prospects for further increases are dimmed by EC protectionism. In 1991, the EC signed agreements with Poland, Hungary and the then Czechoslovakia, but offered only restricted access for steel, coal, textiles and agricultural products – even though the production of these items accounts for one-third of employment in the four countries and has the greatest potential for inhibiting emigration

The trade agreement most likely to have an impact on migration is the North American Free Trade Agreement (NAFTA). In 1992, a draft accord was signed between the United States, Canada and Mexico which would steadily lower the tariffs between the three countries. Just who will benefit most from this remains to be seen. NAFTA arose out of a Mexican initiative and the Mexican Government remains enthusiastic about the potential – despite the risk that opening the border to a giant competitor might, in the short term at least, also cost Mexico thousands of jobs. Many people have already become unemployed as a result of recent trade liberalization in Mexico. After Mexico joined GATT in 1987, its average tariff on imports dropped from 45 to 9 per cent and between 1986 and 1991 merchandise imports from the United States increased by 20 per cent per year and caused large numbers of casualties – 500 engineering firms in Mexico City alone have gone bankrupt. But the Mexicans are confident that NAFTA will benefit them in the long term. Since the world seemed to be moving towards a system of trading blocs, Mexico has concluded that it has no choice but to throw in its lot with Canada and the United States.

Opinion in the United States is rather more polarized on this issue and it remains to be seen if, and how, the Clinton administration will amend the agreement – particularly on the requirements to raise Mexico's environmental and labour standards closer to those in the United States. US unions fear that NAFTA will cause the export of jobs similar to those in the *maquiladora* plants where wages and working conditions are inferior to those in the United States. Canada, which hitherto has very little trade with Mexico, has proved the least enthusiastic participant: many Canadians believe that the previous free trade agreement signed with the United States in 1989 has already cost Canada many jobs.

A number of calculations have been made on the likely job implications of NAFTA for the United States and for Mexico. A study carried out for the US Department of Labour, for example, has estimated that, by 1995, NAFTA would destroy 150,000 jobs in the United States but also create 325,000 new ones – a net gain of 175,000. Since the American economy typically adds up to 200,000 new jobs per month, this will not be that significant. The effect is likely to be relatively greater in Mexico. Most economic models for Mexico predict that NAFTA will add around 300,000 jobs, but even this must be set against Mexico's need to create 1 million jobs annually just to employ the new entrants to its labour market.

One of the immediate effects of NAFTA is likely to be substantial sales of American agricultural produce to Mexico – causing extensive job losses in Mexico's inefficient agricultural sector (agriculture employs 23 per cent of Mexicans, yet in 1991 contributed only 7 per cent of GNP) and thus a corresponding rise in emigration. One possible response for Mexican agriculture is to move into sugar production. Unsurprisingly, the United States sugar industry is a fierce opponent of NAFTA.

SOLUTIONS?

It would be too simple to submit that globalization will keep everyone at home. Differences are bound to remain, certain twains will never meet, and the urge for personal gain will always pressure people to move in search of greener pastures. However, one needs funds to move, and the truly poor are unable to consider migration, particularly the irregular alternative. This also means that once transportation costs decrease further, and once funds are available – for instance thanks to an improved local economy – the migration pressure is bound to increase, rather than decrease. Only when local conditions are truly satisfying, may patterns change.

As Stalker put it in the concluding chapter of his 'Workers without Frontiers':
Industrial countries are always likely to want cheap immigrant labour to do the

jobs that national workers refuse. But the supply could dry up if closer and deeper integration of economies promotes economic development in poorer countries that eventually blunts the incentive to emigrate. (...) Neither trade nor investment at their current levels will be sufficient to absorb the [50 percent] expansion [of the labour force of low-income countries between 1995 and 2025]. Globalization may help indirectly (...).

If globalization is to have a greater impact on immigration, it will have to proceed in a more even and egalitarian. Thus far, it has been very lopsided – with the greatest benefits going to countries already ahead in the race. Many poor countries have, for example, so far seen very little of the expansion of world trade. The least-developed countries with 10 percent of the world population, have only 0.3 percent of world trade – and that is half the proportion of two decades ago. Similar imbalances are evident in the flows of foreign direct investment. These are concentrated in industrial countries and faster-growing parts of the developing world: 70 percent of the world's population gets only 10 percent of global investment (...).

Globalization may in the end not flatten international disparities but merely re-sort countries into new categories of rich and poor. Sub-Saharan African countries, for example, have yet to feature very strongly on international migration trails, but the exodus toward South Africa and the flows of Africans moving through the fairly relaxed border controls of Eastern Europe, could be a harbinger of things to come.

Moreover, even if globalization does make some countries as a whole richer, it could heighten interbal disparities. India, say, or China, which between them have the majority of the world's poor people, might become much more integrated into the global economy. This could still leave vast number sof their people marginalized – but with sufficient resources to travel overseas in search of work.

Finally, there is the question of time. Even given the most optimistic assumptions, there is little doubt that as development proceeds, migration pressure will rise in the decades ahead. This additional flow of emigrants might represent a temporary hump – as history would suggest. But there is no guarantee that history will repeat itself. Posterity may have other ideas. The poorest developing countries are trying to industrialize in a fiercely competitive environment. In a world of winners and losers, the losers do not simply disappear, they seek somewhere else to go. What could be a temporary hump could develop instead into a steep and relentless ascent.[12]

The conclusion may thus have to be drawn that the situation is more complex than one might have hoped, but simpler than one might have feared. The statement that globalization by definition includes a liberal and generous migration policy could be dismissed as harmful. Migration per se may have a negative impact on the country of origin, the migrant him/herself, as well as the country of destination. Migration

---

[12] Stalker (2000, op. cit.), pp 139-140.

almost always involves a loss of human capital in that many MDs, technicians and other professionals from Third World countries have first to work on a much lower level than they were accustomed to do, whilst studying for the necessary examinations (bar exams, medical school) before they are allowed to perform as the professional they were in the country of origin, whereby substantial labour years become lost. Moreover, as migration does not assist towards bridging gaps, but rather increases those gaps (as the immigration countries will focus on skilled labour rather than unskilled labour) the statement that migration generates migration can thus be upheld: the twain will probably never meet.

Illegal Migration 2.3

(motto: The social consequences of irregular migration can be particularly harmful to both the receiving society and the migrants themselves (...). In these types of situations, exploitation of labour, the loss of public receipts, erosion of respect for the law, and weakening of ethical standards of business go hand in hand. Already in 1981, the US Select Commission on Immigration and Refugee Policy argued: 'Illegal migration (if unchecked) will continue to undermine the most valued ideals of this nation – the integrity of the law and the fundamental dignity of the individual.'[1] This argument remains equally valid today.[2])

The world-wide growth in international migration in recent decades has been accompanied by an increase in what is variously called 'irregular migration,' 'undocumented migration' or 'illegal migration.' That is, there has been an increase in the number of people living in the higher-income countries who have either entered the country in violation of that country's laws or who have done something to violate a condition for legal entry. The latter may arise from staying longer than permitted or from working in spite of a visa that prohibits or limits working, such as a tourist, student or temporary worker visa. In Europe, illegal migration is to a great extent the result of not leaving upon the rejection of an asylum application.[3] The increase in illegal migration has occurred in countries that have generous legal

---

[1] Select Commission on Immigration and Refugee Policy, *US Immigration Policy and the National Interest* (Final Report), US Government Printing Office, Washington DC, 1981, p. 560.

[2] Bimal Ghosh, *Social and Economic Consequences of Irregular Migration (1999).* This paper is largely based on the presentation made at the Conference on Migration in Vienna, 25-27 November 1998 and draws on his book *Huddled Masses and Uncertain Shores: Insights into Irregular Migration,* (Kluwer, 1998).

[3] The Economist (February 10th, 2001) indicated that the (estimated) number of illegal immigrants entering the EU has risen from below 50,000 in 1993 to 500,000 in 1999 ('whoosh'), a tenfold increase in a mere seven years.

P.J. van Krieken (Ed.), The Migration Acquis Handbook
© 2001, T.M.C.Asser Press, The Hague, the Röling Foundation and the authors

immigration programmes, such as the United States which accepts nearly one million legal immigrants each year. It has also occurred in island countries that have virtually no legal migration, such as Japan.[4]

Unofficial figures for the USA – and informally confirmed by the authorities – indicate that no less than 4 million foreigners are believed to reside there illegally. If one takes into account the way one is scrutinized when entering the USA, and the way the control of the Southern border with Mexico is being implemented, one could easily argue that the number of illegals in the European Union should also be considered to amount to at least 3 to 4 million. Given the fact that some 15-20% of the total EU GDP is unaccounted for, indicating that this is money changing hands on the so-called VAT-free black market, one can imagine that illegals may have access to paid employment, and find ways and means to survive.[5]

As indicated elsewhere in this Handbook, illegal migration in particular has a negative impact on the regularized labour market and the inherent demand and supply balances, avoids technical innovations (replacing labour by capital), and more seriously – keeping in mind the interests of the countries of origin – delays the transfer of certain industries to low-income countries. Illegal migration is hence at best a mixed blessing.

Various efforts are now being undertaken to contain illegal migration. Following the fall of the Berlin Wall, it is unthinkable that Europe would become involved in building a true wall, or even to adopt Rio Grande type methods of border control. It should thus be concluded that borders are to a great extent illusionary, irrespective of the need to try and control external borders to the greatest extent possible.

It has been submitted that Europe's real borders are to be found in the Social Welfare Office, meaning that the deciding factor is whether the foreigner has access to public services (health, social security, higher education) or not. This would indeed nevertheless mean that 3 to 4 million illegals in Europe have found jobs or are otherwise supported through informal, or somewhat fraudulent, networks or illegal activities. That again imposes the conclusion that the control on hiring illegals is insufficient (based on the simple equation that most illegals with a job need to be matched with an employer who has taken that person on board.[6]

---

[4] Barry R. Chiswick, *The Economics of Illegal Migration for the Host Economy*, June 1999.

[5] The Economist (February 3rd, 2001) seems to confirm this number: Criminal and other unmeasured economic activity equalled 29% of Greece's GDP in 1999 (...). The shadow economy ranges from markets such as prostitution to the unreported income of self-employed workers. [Of the OECD countries], Switzerland has the smallest underground economy, equal to only 8% of GDP. Such activities are by nature hard to measure. The shadow economy's share of national output grew in every OECD country from 1989 to 1999. Even a country like Sweden is estimated to reach a 19% figure.

[6] There is often a large financial incentive for employers to hire irregular immigrants. For example, in the Netherlands in 1991, the 373 convicted employers who had hired irregular immigrants made a gain of E 365,000 even after paying their fines and out of court financial settlements (source: Ghosh, op. cit.).

As to the economics of illegal migration, regard should be had to Chiswick who submits:[7]

> The demand by employers for illegal alien workers arises from the difference in wages that are paid in the labor market to legal workers and the reservation wage of illegal aliens, the lowest wage needed to induce them to migrate illegally. The demand for illegal alien workers can be reduced by lowering their productivity or by raising the cost of hiring illegal alien workers. Penalties against employers who 'knowingly' hire illegal aliens, referred to as 'employer sanctions,' are a mechanism to reduce illegal alien employment by raising the hiring costs to employers.
>
> The obvious question that arises is: Why are there barriers to the free movement of people for employment across international boundaries? This question becomes increasingly relevant as international barriers to the free trade in market goods and capital have been declining.[8] There are several reasons why nation-states limit the free movement of people.
>
> While it is recognized that individuals have a human right to emigrate from their country of origin, it is also recognized that there is no right to immigrate into any particular country. That is, countries have the right to regulate the number and characteristics of international migrants that enter their country. Governments do this, in part, to influence the impact of migration on the host country's culture and demographic characteristics. Some countries have ideologies or mythologies that emphasize diversity or heterogeneity (such as the United States), while others have ideologies or mythologies that emphasize homogeneity (such as Japan). Many immigrant receiving countries give preference to immigrants with a similar linguistic, cultural, historical, or ancestral background as the dominant population of the host country. This is done because it facilitates economic and social integration, to assist culturally close individuals in danger, as a mechanism for preserving or maintaining the host country culture, or for broader cultural or ideological reasons.
>
> There are, however, political and economic reasons as well for nations to control who enters and for what purposes. On the political side, immigrants may change the political balance of power, and thereby explicitly change the distribution of property rights and the distribution of income by aligning themselves with what would otherwise be a minority of the population. To oversimplify, imported goods do not vote, but 'imported' people do vote, or at least have politically influence. There are also economic arguments for restrictions on immigration into high income countries. One issue is the 'absorptive capacity' of the economy. To what extent does immigration impose externalities on the host

---

[7] Op. cit. (see note 3).

[8] It should be noted that barriers to international migration have decreased in some regions. The free mobility of labour among citizens of the member states within the European Union is one such example.

population? Consider, for example, a situation in which immigrants add to congestion and, thereby, impose costs on others that the immigrants themselves do not pay. These costs may be simple congestion costs (e.g., crowded streets and highways slowing down traffic) or the costs of more pollution and fewer trees, or they may involve the rising marginal cost of adding on to the increased social overhead capital needed by a larger population. These costs may outweigh the benefits from the larger labour force that pushes outward the country's production possibility frontier.

Other economic costs may arise if immigrants, or subsets of immigrants, make use of public income transfers that raise their total income (transfers plus labour market earnings) above their level of productivity. This is more likely to occur for low-skilled immigrants. This would tend to reduce the income of the native population of the immigrant receiving country.

Finally, political and economic factors are intertwined. Migrants may have positive effects on some segments of the population and negative effects on others. For example, low-skilled immigration would change the distribution of income by lowering the wages of all low-skilled workers and raising the earnings of high-skilled workers and the return to the owners of land and capital. If the gainers are diffused, but the losers are concentrated, or have political power, the latter may be more effective politically, and pressure the political process to reduce migration. If the gainers are concentrated or otherwise have political power which the losers lack, there would be political pressure to increase migration, whether legal or illegal. (...)

The low skill levels of illegal migrants have implications for their impact in the labour market. They compete with low-skilled native-born workers for the lower-skilled jobs and compete with low-income native-born families in the low-income housing market and for public income transfers. The larger the stock of illegal migrants in the destination, the greater is the intensity of this competition in the labour market, the housing market and the market for public income transfers, and hence the lower the level of economic well-being among the native-born poor. It is the low-income native-born (and legal immigrant) population that pays the highest economic price from low-skilled illegal migration. (...)

It is often said that one of the benefits of illegal migrant workers is that they will do the jobs that native workers will not do. These are the dirty, dangerous, dull and difficult low-skilled jobs. (...)

If employers have to pay the cost of attracting native-born workers to the less desirable jobs, they will have an incentive to invest in making these jobs less undesirable. A cleaner, safer, more pleasant workplace would emerge. Moreover, employers will invest in substituting capital for the now more expensive labour to reduce the employer's demand for labour in these jobs. Finally, some of these jobs will disappear from the destination labour market, either not be done at all or to be exported to other countries. The goods and services that are worth producing will be produced, even if production methods and market baskets differ due to the higher cost of low-skilled labour. (...)

One extreme policy is to remove illegal migrants from the country, that is, to have wide-scale round-ups and deportations of illegal migrants. This would have a favourable effect on the low-income native-born population, but raises a whole host of civil liberties issues. There are some things that governments in liberal democracies cannot do politically, and one of these is draconian measures toward deporting illegal migrants.

Another extreme policy, at the other end of the spectrum, is to grant illegal migrants legal status through an amnesty program. This policy is also not without its problems. Workers whose presence was not desired in the first place find their status regularized. This does not solve the problem that their presence in the labour market was not wanted. Moreover, it does not deter the inflow of illegal migrants after the amnesty is granted. Once an amnesty is granted it creates expectations that if the illegal migrant pressures once more become intense amnesties will be given again in the future. This lowers the cost or increases the benefits of illegal migration, encouraging additional illegal flows.

Furthermore, with legal status the former illegal migrant has new rights to income transfers, is more likely to bring dependent family members to the destination, and is less likely to return to the origin if and when employment opportunities decrease in the destination due to seasonal, cyclical or other, perhaps random, reasons. In addition, the availability of these benefits tends to decrease the incentives for working, and hence reduces the supply of labour from the beneficiaries of amnesty. Then, the low-skilled illegal migrant worker who contributed more to the public treasury than he or she took out in benefits may become a net cost when these same low-skilled migrants are given legal status.

It is perhaps because the two extremes of 'deportation' and 'amnesty' have such undesirable implications that a middle ground 'solution' is often grudgingly tolerated. Under this approach there is strict enforcement of immigration law at the border, but minimal enforcement in the interior – neither massive deportations nor formal amnesties. (...)

The emergence of a legal population of the same ethnic origin as streams of illegal migrants makes it more difficult to control illegal migration. First, it makes it easier for illegal migrants to mask their illegal identity. They have an enclave that makes it easier to live and work while avoiding detection. Second, as a result of kinship ties, ethnic solidarity and ethnic politics, a vigorous enforcement of immigration law at the border and in the interior becomes politically that much more difficult. The legal population becomes a political advocate for reduced enforcement and for the awarding of amnesty.

Illegal migration flows are seductive. The low-skilled workers come providing 'needed' labour services for employers unwilling or unable to offer higher wages and more attractive job opportunities to those with legal rights to work or to reduce their demand for low-skilled labour. Although initially illegal migrants seem like unsanctioned temporary or guest workers, with the passage of time their attachment increases and their use of government transfers and services also increases. They compete with low-skilled native-born workers in the labour market, the housing market and for public income transfers. It is the low-income native-born population that pays the greatest price for the presence of illegal migrants. With the passage of time measures to combat their presence become more difficult to implement, particularly if a significant legal population of the same ethnicity develops. Some processes are much easier to stop or reverse in their early stages before they have become established, and this is an important characteristic of illegal migration.[9]

Bimal Ghosh, a prolific author and one of the foremost experts in this field has delivered some intriguing remarks on the effects of irregular migration on the welfare system. He states *inter alia*:[10]

Even when irregular immigrants neither receive or pay into the social security and public welfare system, they influence the system and cause important distributional effects. For example, in situations when they compete with local workers and take away their jobs, the financial burden on the legally employed increases. If, on the other hand, irregular immigrants are complementary to the skilled national workers and fill only unskilled and low-skilled positions, the skilled workers would benefit from a higher productivity level. This may act as a possible compensation for the burden of higher taxes. However, the assumption that irregular workers neither pay to nor receive benefits from the welfare schemes does not necessarily hold due, for example, to the fact that irregular immigrants, in some cases, do submit, or are encouraged to submit, fraudulent claims for welfare benefits.

The increasing controversy in both the United States and Western Europe about the fiscal burden of all immigrants, but especially irregulars, on the receiving society is widely known. Several studies have been conducted in order to shed light on the situation, but they often reach drastically different conclusions. For instance, a study completed by the Rice University demonstrated that regular and irregular immigrants who arrived since 1970 cost the United States $42.5 billion in 1992.[11] On the other hand, a more recent study at the Urban Institute in Washington showed that instead of a net cost of $42 billion there was a net benefit of $29 billion on account of the immigrants who arrived in the United States since 1970.[12] (...)

---

[9] Ed.: reference should also be made to Georges Tapinos' contribution to the Sopemi 1999 edition (*Trends in International Migration*), OECD 1999, pp. 229-251: Clandestine Immigration: economic and political issues.

[10] Based on his paper *Social and Economic Consequences of Irregular Migration (1998/1999)*.

[11] Donald Huddle, *The Net Costs of Immigration to California*, Rice University, Houston, 1993; see also 'Immigration: Stem the Flow, Savings Will Follow', *International Herald Tribune, op. cit.* In a more recent study, Huddle estimated that immigration costs the US a net amount of $65 billion, including $15 billion for indirect worker displacement costs in the form, for example, of unemployment benefits. *The Net Costs of Immigration; the Facts, the Trends and Their Critics,* Carrying Capacity Network, Washington DC, 1996.

[12] Donald Huddle, *The Net Costs of Immigration to California*, op. cit. and Michael Fix and Jeff Passel, *Immigration and Immigrants: Setting the Record Straight,* The Urban Institute, Washington DC, May 1994.

From an economic point of view, a serious negative effect of irregular immigration is its contribution to the segmentation and dysfunctioning of the labour market. In addition, it can inhibit restructuring and upgrading of the economy in the destination country. For example, non-competitive firms, which often operate in the informal or underground sector, have little pressure to increase productivity since they can depend on low cost, docile irregular workers while lobbying for trade protection.[13] Once segmentation of the labour market is in place, the secondary labour market tends to attract new irregular immigrants thus propelling the cycle. In this manner, irregular immigration becomes linked to low productivity and trade protectionism. Consumers suffer and a vicious circle is created which impedes economic, technological and social progress.

Particularly disturbing is that in recent years, structural and fiscal distortions, especially in Western Europe, have led to an unprecedented expansion of the underground or black economy in potential receiving countries. This in turn has created a high demand for docile and easily exploited irregular migrant workers, opening up a lucrative market for traffickers. The black economy now accounts for 16% of the European Union's GDP compared to 5% in 1970. It provides between 10 and 20 million jobs (which corresponds to between 7% and 19% of declared employment;) and a high proportion of these jobs, though not all, are occupied by irregular migrants. What is more disquieting in Europe is that even well-known reputed firms are taking advantage of the black economy through sub contracting arrangements. (...)

The negative effects of irregular migration are not limited to the receiving countries. Developing/sending countries also suffer since the industrial countries' reliance on trade barriers and use of irregular immigrant labour denies the developing countries the possibility of expanding their exports through the dynamic use of the comparative advantage of their low-cost labour. While outflows of irregular immigrants can provide the sending country with some temporary economic and social relief, in most cases they are too small to have any major effect. If, however, they are substantial enough to provide relief, this may

---

[13] The general argument is that a large supply of unskilled foreign workers allows firms to expand output and exports at stable wages with current technologies, but it also dampens the employers' urge to search for productivity-increasing technologies. Since improved productivity is the basis of economic and wage growth, cheap foreign labour can be counter-productive in the long run. Some economists (e.g. Lutz, 1963) have further argued that as immigrants, initially confined to the low-wage sector, move into the high-wage sector which employs mostly national workers, the relative wage gains to nationals diminishes. This eventually depresses wage increases for all workers and reduces the short-term benefit of cheap goods for national workers. Whatever may be the general merits of this argument, it is certainly less valid for low-skilled irregular immigrants, most of whom, as discussed in this Chapter, continue to be employed in the low-wage sector because of the segmented labour market and their limited occupational mobility.

Linda Weiss, 'Explaining the Underground Economy: State and Social Structure', *The British Journal of Sociology,* 1987, 38:216-233; see also Bruno Contini, *The Second Economy in Italy* in Vito Tanzi (ed.) *The Underground Economy in the United States and Abroad,* D.C. Heathe and Co., Boston, 1982, pp. 199-208.

induce the sending country to avoid or postpone policy changes needed to address the root causes of these irregular movements.

If indeed irregular migration has so many negative effects on, as we saw above, all the parties involved (the sending country, the receiving country and the irregular migrant him/herself) the legitimate question is then what options do societies and the global community in general have to control the flow, the exodus and the influx. In other words, what policies and measures are available and which ones are feasible.[14]

Abella (ILO) in an unpublished paper[15] stated:

While one may draw useful lessons from the experience of other countries, it is important not to lose sight of the fact that the effectiveness of state policies on

---

[14] As to the EC/EU, reference is made to, for instance, the instruments included hereinbelow, Chapter 3.5. Most recently, 1 December 2000, the Council, in its conclusions, invited the Member States, on the basis of the preliminary conclusions of the proceedings of CIREFI, to:
– make as much use as possible of the early warning system, entrusting to the Presidency of the Council of the European Union the task of taking steps to facilitate consultation among the Member States in the most appropriate forum;
– consider the subsequent development of the early warning system, in particular investigating both the extent to which the system should be reinforced and the use of higher performance means of communication (secure electronic means);
– improve cooperation between liaison officers operating in the same immigration source country or in the same region of the world, which could lead to mutual and reciprocal assistance or even complementarity in carrying out tasks, bearing in mind in particular the proceedings of the seminar held in Madeira from 9 to 11 November 2000;
– examine means of establishing new procedures to enable certain officers to represent other States in source countries of common interest;
The Council also requested each Presidency of the Council of the European Union to ensure that the outcome of CIREFI proceedings (particularly information exchanges) is regularly passed on – through the Strategic Committee on Immigration, Frontiers and Asylum [SCIFA] – to other bodies of the Union which might find it useful, and particularly:
– the High-level Working Group on Asylum and Migration, which is working on the main source countries for immigration to Europe;
– the Article 36 Committee;
– the Chief Police Officers Task Force, which at its meeting on 15 and 16 September 2000 asked for an intensification of work by the Union in these areas;
– Europol, which has powers to act against illegal immigration networks;
– the Working Party on Schengen Evaluation, which could be asked to contribute to the early warning system through its analyses;
And finally, the Council asked future Presidencies and the Commission to take whatever steps are appropriate to strengthen solidarity and operational cooperation between Member States, including regionally, in order to curb illegal immigration flows. With the agreement of the parties concerned, consideration will be given to the possibility of making technical equipment and/or specialist staff available to the Member States in order to improve the effectiveness of surveillance and control arrangements at the Union's external borders most susceptible to illegal immigration.
[15] Manolo Abella, *Policies and Measures to Deal with Illegal Migration and Employment of Undocumented Workers (some views)*, Geneva 1998.

migration cannot be viewed separately from the specific context of a country's history, social and political institutions, the limits imposed by geography, and the pressures unleashed by changing conditions of its economy. Where geography allows more control of one's borders the need for internal controls may be modest. Public attitudes to state regulation are shaped by history. In Europe, state interventions in the labour market may be accepted to an extent unknown in North America. Economic conditions such as periods of full employment may also make it more difficult to enforce sanctions against the employment of undocumented aliens. In the following we review the major policy instruments used by states to curb the employment of undocumented foreign workers.

Internal controls and employer sanctions
With the rise of undocumented migration problems a large number of internal measures, or those taken to control the employment and stay of foreigners after they have already gained entry into the country, have been adopted including: monitoring of their activities; mandatory registration of all non-nationals with local authorities; information drives and campaigns aimed at employers; work permit requirements; work place inspections by immigration, labour ministry, or police agents; sanctions against the worker, the recruiter, and the employers; additional sanctions against employers such as withdrawal of business license in the case of repeated offences and exclusion from public contracts; and various tax rebates or exemptions from social charges when employers hire documented foreign workers in certain industries or occupations.

There has not been enough documentation and research to permit an assessment of each of these measures. What is clear from experience is that illegal migration has grown in all parts of the world, particularly in countries with robust economies. However, the growth of illegal migration has varied among countries reflecting perhaps the difference that internal and external measures make to having some control over the phenomenon. It is clear that consistent policies backed up by strong political will and efficient administration are necessary ingredients to success. In the following we look specifically at some of these measures.

Employer sanctions are the fines and penalties imposed on employers who are caught with undocumented workers. Sanctions raise the *cost of hiring* workers in two ways. One is the expected loss in production time if the undocumented workers are discovered. The other consists of the financial penalties that the employer must pay if they are found guilty of violating the law. Both are supposed to discourage employers from hiring the undocumented unless they are able to pass them on to the undocumented alien worker in terms of lower wages. In evaluating the value of employer sanctions in controlling irregular migration it is helpful to find answers to four key questions: Would sanctions neutralize the 'pull' factor in the labour market? Would they lead to the departure of illegals? Are they likely to lead to discrimination against some ethnic groups? Would they worsen tendencies of employers to use labour contractors? Do they lead to reducing the *demand* for foreign labour?

The answer would depend in the first instance on how effectively they serve as a *deterrent*. In principle, the deterrent power of employer sanctions depends on two features of the policy. One is the probability of being caught. The other is the severity of the penalty if one is caught relative to the benefits that would be foregone if one does not employ illegal foreign workers

Probability of being caught: A cursory survey of some countries that have adopted employers' sanctions suggests that they have seldom been rigorously enforced. In Switzerland, officials look the other way if irregular-status aliens perform work considered necessary. Sanctions were decreed in France as far back as 1946 but there was little effort to enforce them until the 1970s. Some industries with 'well entrenched traditions of utilizing illegal alien labour and with political clout have been exempted from enforcement of employer sanctions'. In the US for the whole of 1998 only 6,500 investigations of employers were completed or about 3 percent of the country's estimated number of employers of unauthorized aliens. Although many are caught, very few actually get prosecuted and fewer still get convicted. How many convictions are won in the courts? Successful prosecution is difficult to obtain because it is hard to establish in court that 'an employer has knowingly offered employment to an illegal alien.' (...) Experience shows that effective enforcement depends on the amount of *resources* devoted to it, the *authority* given to the enforcement agents, the degree of *co-ordination* among various concerned agencies, and the *attitudes* of the national community. where the sympathy of enforcers lie. A low level of enforcement activity could lead employers to discount detection, thus weaken the policy. Inconsistency in policy and tactics create inequities in the treatment of employers.

In the statutes of many countries the penalties usually involve heavy fines, and even imprisonment in case of repeated violations. (...) Criminal penalties are imposed on violators who engage in a 'pattern or practice' of knowing hires of unauthorized aliens. It is also criminal to transport anyone into or within the US with the intention of concealing, harbouring, or shielding them from detection in the US. The impact of the policy is extremely difficult to assess because of doubts everywhere about the seriousness with which it has been enforced in many countries, and because its effects are difficult to separate from those of other measures such as amnesties and regularizations. In the US there is some doubt that sanctions have led to outmigration of the undocumented [In one study it was found] that employers' sanctions appear to have had an effect on the flow of undocumented immigrants to the US but the effect is small (a decline of at most one-fifth). (...) What is also true is that there was little evidence that sanctions have led to a sharp reduction in the availability of undocumented workers. [An] analysis of wage effects shows that regardless of the sample used, wages increased at a slower rate in the cities with large populations of undocumented immigrants than in other cities for all combinations of years and all occupations. (...)

Finally, there has been a notable trend in some countries to address the problem of undocumented workers as one of labour exploitation and to rely on labour standard laws and enforcement machineries to control abuse. Employers of the undocumented can violate minimum wage laws with impunity because they can threaten to report foreign workers to immigration authorities if they complain. In the US [evidence was found] of lower compliance with minimum wages for illegals. The objective of policy is to reduce the economic incentive to employ illegal workers. Because labour ministries undertake inspections of workplaces to check on violations against labour and safety standards one can at the same time pressure enterprises not to rely on cheap undocumented labour. Labour inspectors do not usually check on work permits or immigration documents but it is their business to verify if employers are paying the minimum wage and provide decent working conditions. (...)

Temporary migrant programmes

As the term indicates, temporary foreign labour policies are adopted generally to meet labour shortages without having to make a commitment towards the permanent settlement of the migrants. The specific motivations in any one country may however differ depending on how policy makers perceive migration. Two so-called 'tiger economies', Singapore and Taiwan, assign to temporary foreign labour policy a purely economic objective, that is, to reduce wage pressures during cyclical upswings. The motivations in some European countries like Germany and Switzerland are not qualitatively very different, although they may be tempered by more liberal policies towards eventual longer-term stay and family reunification. In the US, while temporary foreign labour policy is supposed to also meet labour market exigencies, it is recognized widely that the policy is also meant to manage inevitable immigration.

'Guest worker' programmes have everywhere been accompanied by some growth in irregular employment of aliens hence one would be hard put to claim that they serve as instruments for dealing with irregularity. Reflecting on the European and the US experience, [one study] concluded that 'Temporary worker programs are in most countries the source of current illegal immigration problems.' The experience is not wholly confined to Western Europe and North America. Another study, for example, noted that while Malaysia had a well-conceived temporary foreign labour programme, the number of illegal foreign workers reached about a million at the start of the recent financial crisis.

The 'project-tied' temporary foreign labour schemes used widely in the Gulf States during the peak of the oil-boom to complete huge infrastructure modernization programmes did have features which allowed for greater control of irregular migration. One important feature is that the project contractors assumed full responsibility for the return of their foreign workers. The system was designed to insure rotation, and to minimize possible insertion of the foreign workers in the local labour market. Workers were housed in camps and kept a distance from the local community.

J-P Garson (OECD) provided during an April 1999 seminar the following useful overview on policy recommendations:[16]

1) Sanctions against the illegal employment of immigrants must be applied against the main actors involved in the relevant breaches of labour and immigration laws. This list includes not only direct employers, but also indirect employers (subcontractors who outsource segments or phases of their operations to other firms); any persons who actively promote illegal immigration and/or the employment of illegal immigrants, be these persons intermediaries seeking profit by providing lodging, for example, or professional traffickers of illegal labour; and finally, the undocumented workers themselves.

2) Better co-ordination and coherence of administrative measures to tackle the employment of illegal migrants is fundamental, both at the national and local levels. The co-ordination of these measures is important because labour markets and, therefore, illegal hiring practices, have a strong local dimension.

3) A particularly important area of co-operation among agencies is the exchange of information about illegal practices, the measures taken to address them, and their results. This information should be accurate, and the government agencies concerned must have at their disposal effective and accurate methods to evaluate their interventions. However, this information should not be collected at the expense of individual rights to privacy.

4) The difficulties encountered by government inspection agencies in the implementation of measures against the employment of illegal immigrants should be addressed. Participants commented that the jurisdictions and capacities of these agencies are often insufficient, most notably in the case of undocumented work in private residences, to which these agencies have extremely limited access. Participants also observed that fines for illegal employment practices are generally low and were therefore ineffective as deterrents.

5) Several representatives also recommended an awareness-raising programme for the court system personnel, to alert them to the importance of following through with the application of legal sanctions, and ensuring that all imposed fines are paid in full and in a timely manner. This sort of intervention would reinforce and strengthen the role of sanctions in combating illegal hiring practices.

6) The general public must be better informed about the risks and penalties involved in the use of illegal labour; this information should be directed at both employers and workers in industries where these illegal practices are prevalent (e.g. the construction industry and the clothing industry), but they should also be directed at employers that resort to the use of undeclared labour only on an occasional basis.

7) The specific measures adopted in certain OECD Member countries can serve as a model for other nations. Examples of best practices include the requirement to

---

[16] As included in his paper *Combating The Illegal Employment of Foreigners: Some Policy Recommendations.*

notify relevant government agencies prior to a hire being made, fiscal incentives for the employment of legal workers (through the reduction or exemption from social charges and taxes in certain sectors and in certain types of jobs), and the streamlining of contractual and administrative requirements associated with service sector employment (notably as concerns the hiring of domestic help). Another example of a best practice is the forging of partnerships between relevant government agencies on the one hand, and employers and business associations on the other, to promote joint efforts to combat illegal employment.

8) International co-operation to combat the illegal employment of foreigners is very underdeveloped, even if several OECD countries have already co-operated, notably with sending countries. International co-operation, however, is becoming more urgent, in particular to combat labour trafficking networks. European Union members have become aware of this necessity and the Council of the European Union has adopted several recommendations recently concerning the repression of the employment of foreigners in an irregular situation. Likewise, the Commission of the European Union has produced a report on illegal work in general. This report identifies four main groups of participants in the undeclared economy: multiple job holders; the 'economically inactive' population; the unemployed; and third-country nationals illegally resident in the EU. In other OECD member countries, for example in the United States, in Canada and in Mexico, actions for international co-operation, when they exist, are essentially bilateral and often very specific.

9) International co-operation could be further developed by:

– Improvement of the methods of exchange of information between competent administrations.

– Training and exchange of specialized personnel in control and repression, not only at borders but also in the fight against illegal employment.

– Strengthening of co-operation with sending countries: measures to disseminate information to potential migrants regarding the conditions for access to employment and the sanctions that they are likely to face in the receiving country. A productive partnership can be forged with the countries of origin to protect the most vulnerable categories of their nationals, and to inform that they run the risk of becoming victims of trafficking networks.

10) At the same time, there are limits to the benefits which can be expected from greater international co-operation. Democratic societies do not prevent their citizens from emigrating in such a better life for themselves and their families. The individual migrants have, in most cases, a strong self-interest in emigrating, even if this involves them accepting an illegal situation.

AMNESTIES, A USEFUL OR COUNTERPRODUCTIVE TOOL?

Abella, in his above-mentioned paper (see footnote 4), also dwells on the issue of amnesties. He submits:

To reinforce the legal order, to prevent exploitation of alien workers, and to avoid creating a dual labour market, states faced with growing numbers of undocumented immigration undertake amnesties and regularization programmes. Among the most cogent questions that may be asked regarding the effectiveness of these policy instruments in controlling irregular employment of foreign workers are: Do amnesties and regularizations improve wages and working conditions of foreign workers? What is their likely impact on fiscal revenues and expenditures? Do amnesties and regularization undermine long-term immigration policies? Do they have any impact on the inflows of undocumented migrants? What are the essential elements of successful regularization programmes? The assumption is that undocumented foreign workers are stuck in the underground or shadow economy where wages are low and conditions of work are unregulated or unprotected. Regularization opens the way for them to find better-paying jobs and occupations in an open market. There is no question that the workers are better off after being regularized than before, but the impact does not become immediately apparent. In the US most tend to stay in their pre-legalization jobs, receiving the same wages. Occupational mobility depends more on language skills and experience than on legal status. Even the undocumented can be occupationally mobile if they have skills needed in the market. There is evidence however that legal status has enabled many to acquire language proficiency and to avail of opportunities for skills training. [It was] found that there was more than a doubling of the previous rate of human capital accumulation for most origin groups. (...)

'Amnesties' are considered by many to be a useful tool to regularize a situation which is believed to have become too complicated to be solved in any other way. In other words, societies see no other way out, and tend to trust that they will be able, by agreeing on a new policy, to adopt a more stringent implementation in order to avoid a similar situation in the future. How wrong they are, as all studies seem to indicate that amnesties (i.e. regularizing irregular situations) will have a multiplier effect in that new illegals may be lured into the country concerned on the – rightful – assumption that their status too will in due time be legalized. All amnesties, be it in Europe or the USA, have had this result and have thus created an increase in irregular movements rather than a decrease.

As Jean-Pierre Garson (OECD) states in a recent paper:[17]

Amnesties, which can be a long-established and recurrent process (as in France) or the result of a decision taken after lengthy preparations and extensive debate (as in the United States in 1986 or Greece in 1998), have been used repeatedly in recent years in Spain, Italy and Portugal. For the moment, most of the other OECD countries, grappling with illegal migration, do not wish to resort to legalisation

---

[17] Jean-Pierre Garson: *Amnesty Programmes, Recent Lessons* (2000), and drawn from a 1999 paper submitted to the OECD Hague seminar entitled *'preventing and combatting the employment of foreigners in an irregular situation.'*

programmes, although some of them have experimented with such procedures in the past. They are nonetheless paying close attention to the recent amnesties in the six countries mentioned above, as well as to the measures taken in conjunction therewith.

Legalisation programmes are carried out in application of laws or decrees that in some cases have been preceded by vast democratic debates which may call attention to the programmes. Most frequently, lawmakers view them as exceptional, even though over the past fifteen years amnesties have been called on three or four different occasions in Spain and Italy respectively. In the limited framework of this document, the main focus is in the first part on the general information obtained through legalisation programmes and in the second part on the profile of illegal foreign workers and the sectors of activity involved.

Recent amnesties in the United States, France, Italy, Spain, Portugal and Greece all gave rise to legal procedures and the introduction of considerable technical and human resources, distinguishing them from discretionary regularisation. However, the amnesties all took place in different economic and political contexts. For example, the 1981-82 campaign in France was adopted even though new labour immigration had been officially suspended since July 1974. Moreover, the French economy had been characterised by low growth and high unemployment. Conversely, in the United States, the 1986 amnesty took place amidst a context of regular, permanent immigration and an economy that was favourable in terms of growth and employment alike.

Amnesties generally provide the authorities with information on the number of illegal migrants who fulfil the required conditions, on the networks that had enabled them to live illegally, on the industries in which they tended to be employed, and on the workings of the labour market. Data on the number of beneficiaries do not of course provide a precise accounting of the number of illegal immigrants, although they do suggest the magnitude of the phenomenon. Based on recent studies in a number of OECD countries, it can be seen that the figures obtained are far lower than the unrealistic estimations that circulate in public opinion.

But apart from this general information, follow-up on legalisation programmes shows that amnesties uncover situations that governments had not expected. It is sometimes necessary to extend deadlines and/or ease conditions for eligibility. The authorities in charge of implementing amnesties discover that people can find themselves in situations of illegality as a result of administrative dysfunction or gaps in the law, in particular with regard to family members, minor children and special cases of unjustified non-renewal of residence or work permits. Amnesties also reveal categories of illegal immigrants that had been involuntarily excluded or underestimated in the list of prospective amnesties ('itinerant vendors', self-employed persons, retirees, and so forth). For example, the main purpose of the legalisation procedure adopted in France in June 1997 was to rectify certain situations of illegality, primarily affecting migrants' family members, that arose because of successive amendments to the legislation governing the entry and residence of foreigners, or because of certain gaps in the law.

Legalisation programmes also help fulfil public security objectives. Once illegal immigration in a country reaches substantial dimensions and most of the illegal immigrants have jobs, the decision to let this sort of situation be perpetuated and happen again may encourage shameful exploitation of immigrants deprived of any rights, endanger their health and expose some of them to illicit or criminal activities. While public opinion on the whole is not favourably disposed to amnesties, such programmes do tend to limit the frequency of discrimination and racism, which is even more painful when inflicted on immigrants deprived of all rights.

Amnesty programmes, as formulated in a number of OECD countries, have never attempted to cover the entire range of illegal migration. Even after successive amendments, the eligibility conditions make such amnesties selective (e.g. entry prior to a specific cut-off date, employment or possession of a labour contract, proof of direct family ties with citizens or legal aliens, etc.). Notwithstanding, the profile of the illegal immigrant population can be interpreted more reliably if the conditions for legalisation are liberal and the procedure carried out flexibly and with good will, which can sometimes lead to successive modifications.

Amnesty beneficiaries tend to be young workers employed in sectors with a high concentration of foreign labour. Amnesty beneficiaries bring greater flexibility to the productive system

Those granted legal status were found in industries in which legal immigrants were also working (or had been working until only recently). This continuity in the tendency of certain sectors to hire foreign labour might indicate a form of employer preference for immigrant workers, legal or illegal. This continuity may also reflect the fact that illegal immigrants are an integral part of the migratory process as a whole and, as such, get the full benefit of the experience of their elders (home ethnic community and networks of mutual assistance and support), in entering the host country, living there and finding jobs there. Agriculture, manufacturing, construction and public works, and certain categories of services employ the bulk of illegal immigrant workers. Employers are continually on the lookout for workers who are prepared to endure harsh, intensive work.

The use of illegal immigrants reflects a context of systematic attempts to minimise labour costs and maximise labour flexibility. It would seem clear that some employers are reluctant to accept the idea of granting a status that would guarantee elementary rights to immigrant workers. In fact, companies have sought to cushion the impact of the downturn by systematically resorting to subcontracting, and in some cases cascading subcontracting. Given the financial constraints and very short deadlines facing employers, subcontracting prompts them to employ illegal immigrants, among others. The development of subcontracting is part of a process whereby labour management is totally or partially externalised by encouraging salaried workers to acquire self-employed status. In most cases, the self-employed continue to work exclusively for the subcontracting firm, which in some cases actually provides them with essential tools and machinery. This form of concealed dependent employment allows the contracting firm to cut its social insurance contributions and escape the constraints of labour legislation, while leaving the subcontracting firm free to recruit legal or illegal workers – the important thing being to accomplish the subcontracted task. In this context, it is frequently small and medium-sized enterprises that enhance the flexibility of the production system and adjust to economic shifts. In some cases, the adjustments in question are organised and lead to the formation of networks of companies specialising in international labour lending at unbeatable prices, and, under the guise of service contracts[4], it becomes possible to evade national laws restricting the employment of new immigrant workers.

Amnesty beneficiaries come from the same areas as legal immigrants, reflecting two parallel trends: the persistence of traditional areas and the emergence of new nationalities of immigrants

(...) [T]he majority of amnesty beneficiaries come from a limited number of countries. In the case of France and the United States, migrants come, respectively, from Africa and from Mexico and Central America. In Italy and Spain, immigrants from North Africa comprise the largest group, followed by those from the Philippines, in the case of Italy, and from Central and South America, in the case of Spain. In Portugal, most of the beneficiaries of legalisation come from the former Portuguese colonies of Africa. One initial observation is clear: geographical proximity and traditional immigration patterns explain the importance taken on by certain nationalities in the five countries studied. However, and over the course of time, new nationalities are emerging: in Italy, Senegalese, Chinese, Albanians and Romanians; in Spain, Chinese and Poles; and in France, Haitians, Zairians and Chinese.

Recent legalisation programmes in Spain and Italy show that the beneficiaries can slip back into illegality

In 1996, Italy and Spain conducted their third legalisation campaigns for illegal immigrants. While the final results of the two amnesties are not yet available, it is interesting to note that the main beneficiaries of the 1996 programmes were immigrants who were able to have their status legalised in earlier amnesties. This raises the question of what happens to immigrants after they are legalised. An important factor here is the status offered them, and in particular the conditions for renewal of their residence and/or work permits, along with the type of employment (or unemployment) they have after being legalised. Another important question is to determine who replaces the legalised immigrants once they leave the jobs they held at the time of the amnesty but the need for that same labour persists.

The example of Italy clearly shows that it is important to reconsider the issue of illegal immigration, tying it in more closely with the economic and social changes underway in the host countries. The persistence of illegal immigration can be explained in part by the systematic use of undeclared workers. Unless the spread of the underground economy is combated effectively, there is a risk of condemning to illegality (and at times of driving to illicit or criminal activities) most of the immigrants who try to renew their residence permits or to obtain a job in the mainstream labour market.

In the case of the United States, most of the people amnestied obtained resident visas and after four years were able to get permanent immigrant status, which entitles them not only to live permanently in the United States and pursue the occupation of their choice, but also, under certain conditions, to bring in members of their families. The freedom that resident visas confer on amnestied workers enables them to look for jobs in industries other than those in which they were working at the time of the amnesty.

The geographical and occupational mobility of amnestied immigrants will therefore depend on labour market conditions and any qualifications they might have acquired, including those acquired in their home countries. Such mobility is obvious in the case of the United States and was even anticipated by the authorities, who, just after the amnesty, introduced programmes to recruit immigrant workers, especially in the farm sector, to replace amnesty beneficiaries who left the sector. The latter were replaced by 'new' illegal immigrants. In the case of France, a survey carried out one year after the 1981-82 legalisation programme shows that a large number of immigrants changed employers or occupations. In some cases, the authorities had not anticipated this behaviour (immigration of new workers had been officially suspended since 1974), and amnestied immigrants were replaced by 'new' illegal ones.

Longitudinal studies on what becomes of workers whose status has been legalised show that such people behave as suppliers on the labour market, and that the jobs they hold while not yet legal do not necessarily correspond to the full range of their professional experience and qualifications. If new job prospects come their way, they will try to improve their situation and their occupational standing (in the host country or upon return to their country of origin).

Conclusion

The results of the legalisation programmes recently carried out in a number of OECD countries highlight the key labour market role of certain categories of illegal immigrants. This shows that, along with efforts to control flows, there is a need for a clearer understanding of the pressures bearing upon the labour market, mainly flexibility and the adjustment of productive structures to the changes underway. There can be no doubt that the greatest limit on measures taken to combat the hiring of illegal immigrants stems from the fact that whatever is done must address the problem of undeclared work in general and not just the employment of illegal immigrants.

Another major lesson of these legalisation programmes concerns the expectations and the behaviour of migrants in irregular situations. Unlike certain employers who do not hesitate systematically to hire illegal immigrant labour, immigrants tend rather to consider their illegal status as temporary, and as a necessary step on the road to legality, in the hopes of future occupational and/or geographical mobility. Illegality is perceived and envisaged by the migrant as merely a passing phase, whereas it is difficult for certain employers to give up the opportunity of having a workforce composed of illegal immigrants.

Finally, due attention should be paid to efforts undertaken by the Budapest Process, the meetings of Ministers (from Eastern and Western Europe) responsible for matters relating to illegal migration in particular. This process started in the early 1990s and has hitherto continued in a successful way. Whereas early concerns covered illegal migration from East to West, focus has over the years shifted to migration from South to North, often using Eastern Europe as transit. In the context of this sub-chapter on illegal migration, excerpts from the recommendations of the Prague 1997 Conference on the Prevention of Illegal Migration are worth being included:

Underlining that illegal migration and trafficking in aliens constitute a threat to public security and would require concerted action by all States concerned in a spirit of international solidarity and genuine mutual interest, as co-operation on matters relating to internal security reinforces stability at the regional level;

Recognizing that one of the causes of illegal migration is the difference in living standards between regions and that the prevention of illegal migration also presupposes sustainable development in the countries of origin; (...)

Being aware, however, that further measures should be undertaken in this regard and that problems relating to illegal migration and trafficking, and their connection to international organized crime, have changed in character and aggravated;

Recalling that significant institutional developments have occurred since the holding of the last Ministerial conference, notably with regard to the expansion of the membership of the European Union and the Schengen Group, and that ten of the Central and Eastern European States have concluded association agreements with the European Union;

Noting with satisfaction that the European Union has reinforced action to combat illegal migration and trafficking in aliens and other forms of organized crime and is raising these issues in the context of the Structured Dialogue with Associated States, of the Euro-Mediterranean Partnership process, in the framework of the Trans-Atlantic Dialogue, and is planning to do so with the Newly Independent States;

Recognizing that, at the European level, any efforts to counteract illegal migration and trafficking in aliens would have to take into account the relevant activities and co-operation structures of the European Union;

Taking into account recent multilateral action with regard to trafficking in persons for sexual exploitation, notably:

– The Conference on trafficking in women for sexual exploitation held in Vienna 10-11 June 1996 and the Communication of the European Commission on the same subject of 20 November 1996;

– The Declaration and Agenda of the World Congress against commercial and sexual exploitation of children, adopted in Stockholm on 27-31 August 1996;
– The Declaration on European guidelines for effective measures to prevent and combat trafficking in women for the purpose of sexual exploitation, adopted at the Hague Ministerial Conference on 26 April 1997;
– The Joint Action of 21 January 1997 concerning action to combat trafficking in human beings and sexual exploitation of children adopted by the Council of Ministers of the European Union;

Being convinced that consistent strategies are needed to achieve a harmonized approach among all European countries on entry policies, to ensure orderly migration and to ultimately facilitate the freedom to travel throughout Europe;

Being aware that the implementation of relevant measures requires adequate assistance to many States in Central and Eastern Europe, as well as among the Newly Independent States, in terms of legislative development, technical assistance, training and equipment;

Noting that the Budapest Group, in its follow-up of the previous conference of Ministers, has identified the following seven areas as being of major significance in terms of harmonizing and reinforcing relevant policies and measures: (i) harmonization of legislation to combat trafficking in aliens; (ii) pre-entry and entry control, in particular the approximation of visa regimes; (iii) return to the country of origin and readmission agreements; (iv) information exchange on illegal migration; (v) technical and financial assistance to Central and Eastern European States; (vi) linkage between trafficking in aliens and other forms of organized crime and (vii) future co-operation between participating States in the context of the Budapest process; (...)

Emphasizing the need of a collective goal-oriented effort to achieve results in terms of introducing necessary legislation and measures in the coming years;

Being aware that relevant measures should be implemented according to the constitutional provisions and the basic principles of the legal system of each State;

Have adopted the following recommendations:

1.   Harmonization of legislation to combat trafficking in aliens

1.a   *The need for a common understanding of the term 'trafficking in aliens'*

1. Recommend that a common understanding of the term 'trafficking in aliens' should include activities intended deliberately to facilitate the border crossing or residence of an alien in the territory of the State, contrary to the rules and conditions applicable in such a State;

1.b   *The need for criminalizing trafficking in aliens and for applying effective sanctions to trafficking in aliens and related activities*

2. Recommend that participating States, which have not yet done so, adopt natio-

nal legislation which makes it a criminal offence to traffic or to attempt to traffic aliens, and that this should include the instigation and the aiding and abetting of the offence; special consideration should be given to trafficking for the purpose of sexual exploitation;

3. Recommend that participating States examine the possibility of extending the scope of their national legislation on trafficking in aliens so as to make it punishable for their nationals and other persons staying within their territory to facilitate the illegal entry into any state;

4. Recommend that legal and administrative measures in particular be focused on sanctioning organized trafficking in aliens;

5. Recommend that trafficking shall be punishable with effective, proportionate and deterrent penalties which may include imprisonment with a maximum of at least 2 years (under aggravating circumstances 3 years) and that the importance of parallel imposition of fines is recognized;

6. Recommend that it should be possible to confiscate proceeds obtained as a result of trafficking in aliens as well as means of transport such as motor vehicles, ships and aircrafts owned by the traffickers or their accomplices and which are used for trafficking in aliens;

7. Recommend to examine the possibility of imposing appropriate sanctions, in accordance with administrative regulations or criminal law, including the closing of establishments or the suspending of economic activities which continuously provide the basis for committing offences relating to trafficking in aliens;

8. Recommend that illegal border crossing shall in general be dealt with by effective, proportionate and deterrent sanctions which may include fines, and under aggravating circumstances short term imprisonment, taking into account, however, article 31 of the Geneva Convention; and that migrants having entered illegally, lacking grounds for legal stay, should be returned unless there are obstacles hereto based on serious humanitarian considerations or international law;

9. Recommend that measures be taken to ensure appropriate protection for persons trafficked, e.g. for the purpose of sexual exploitation, who provide information concerning the trafficking, and who are available when required by the criminal justice system to give evidence, which may entail the provisional granting of a temporary permit to stay, in appropriate cases; and to ensure necessary discretion for aliens trafficked for sexual exploitation;

10. Recommend that sanctions be introduced, which would punish the production, provision and use of fraudulent documents by effective, proportionate and deterrent penalties which may include imprisonment with a maximum of at least 3 years, fining and confiscation of such documents and the proceeds obtained through these activities;

11. Recommend that employment of illegal migrants shall be dealt with by effective, proportionate and deterrent sanctions which may include imprisonment with a maximum of at least 6 months, fines and confiscation of proceeds obtained as a consequence of the illegal employment;

1.c *The need for accession to and implementation of relevant international instruments*

12. Recommend that participating States, which have not yet done so, accede to and implement the following relevant international instruments:
(i) Instruments safeguarding human rights and the rights of refugees
The 1950 European Convention on Human rights and its eleven additional Protocols;
The 1951 Geneva Convention on the Status of Refugees and the 1967 New York Protocol;
The 1979 Convention on the Elimination of all Forms of Discrimination against Women;
The 1984 Convention against Torture and Other Cruel, Inhuman or Degrading Treatment or Punishment;
The 1989 Convention on the Rights of the Child;
(ii) Instruments improving and facilitating international cooperation
The 1957 European Convention on Extradition and its additional Protocol of 1978;
The 1959 European Convention on Mutual Assistance in Criminal Matters and its 1978 Protocol;
The 1981 European Convention for the Protection of Individuals with regard to Automatic Processing of
Personal Data;
The 1990 Convention on Money Laundering, Search, Seizure and Confiscation of the Proceeds from Crime;

2. **Pre-entry and entry control, in particular the approximation of visa regimes**

13. Recommend the use of information programmes in relevant countries of origin and transit with a view to preventing illegal migration;
14. Recommend that the European Union continues its efforts aimed at informing the Associated and other States about effective practices for controls of persons at external frontiers;
15. Recommend that participating States ensure that satisfactory measures are taken to establish the identity of improperly documented aliens, and that they consider the regulation of the exchange of data in this regard at the international level, which should be in compliance with the 1981 Convention for the Protection of Individuals with regard to Automatic Processing of Personal Data, taking into account also the principles of the recommendation No. 15 of 1987 of the Committee of Ministers of the Council of Europe regulating the use of personal data in the police sector, as well as national legislation on the protection of personal data;
16. Recommend that the ICAO technical standards for the issuing of passports and visas be followed by all participating States and that they introduce systems based

on machine readable passports and visas;

17. Recommend that participating States, taking the Chicago Convention into consideration, develop forms of constructive co-operation with carriers which are conducting transport service, involving assistance and training of personnel to facilitate the identification of improperly documented passengers;

18. Recommend that sanctions be introduced against carriers conducting transport service and failing to identify improperly documented passengers, by fining and holding the carriers liable for the return costs;

19. Recommend that participating States adapt progressively their visa and transit visa regimes, their procedures for issuing visas, as well as their border control practices to the relevant policies and regulations adopted by the European Union;

20. Recommend that the authority to issue visas be restricted to competent authorities which can properly assess whether the granting of a visa will not contribute to illegal activities or would harm the efforts of participating States in controlling irregular migration;

21. Recommend that provisions may be made that visas issued should expire at least 30 days before the expiration of the travel document, if this will help to ensure the return of illegal migrants;

22. Recommend that an expert meeting be held in the context of the Budapest-process in 1998, under the leadership of the Government of Slovenia, to enhance a process of approximation of visa regimes among Central and Eastern European countries, and that the European Commission renders necessary support to this process through an appropriate framework;

23. Recommend to examine how to develop a coherent European system for determining the responsibility for the examination of an asylum application, on the basis of the principles of the Dublin Convention;

3.   Return to the country of origin and readmission agreements

3.a *Return to countries of origin and their obligation to readmit*

24. Recommend that participating States as far as possible give due consideration to the primary option of returning persons concerned directly to their countries of origin, as this in most cases constitutes the appropriate solution;

25. Recommend that participating States co-operate in demanding that the authorities of countries of origin extend their services in ascertaining the identity of undocumented illegal migrants who seemingly are their citizens, and in responding to such readmission requests within reasonable time limits;

26. Recommend that participating States also co-operate in demanding, when the citizenship has been recognized or is evident, that the country of origin issues a consular *laissez-passer* or a document which entitles for readmission at the shortest possible delay, and within the time limits given by national rules for detention on administrative grounds which are valid in the requesting State;

27. Recommend that participating States identify the countries which cause problems in terms of readmitting their own citizens and that they consider taking

joint measures vis-à-vis these countries;

28. Recommend that participating States facilitate the transit of aliens who are being returned to their country of origin, assisting i.a. when transport problems arise and in providing escort, under cost-sharing arrangements, as appropriate;

29. Recommend that participating States agree upon a format for a standard document, similar to the one agreed upon among EU States, to serve as a consular *laissez-passer*, so as to facilitate transfer to the country of destination;

30. Recommend that the authorities of participating States co-operate with those of the countries of origin with a view to facilitating the readmission of persons concerned in their country;

31. Recommend that participating States co-operate in demanding that countries of destination and of origin cooperate in facilitating voluntary return;

32. Recommend that interested States make use of national programmes and/or the services of IOM in enhancing voluntary return directly to the country of origin;

3.b *Readmission agreements*

33. Recommend that participating States continue their efforts to conclude readmission agreements, which should contain clauses on nationals, on citizens of third countries, on transit for the sake of return and on the protection of personal data;

34. Recommend that participating States apply a standard format for readmission agreements, taking into account the specimen bilateral readmission agreement of the European Union or any other model acceptable to all participating States;

35. Recommend that States make use of the most flexible and rapid forms of readmission, i.e. readmission on the basis of a minimum of formalities between competent authorities, determined contact points, standard forms in two languages, simplified recognition of proofs, as well as other measures contributing to the efficiency of the implementation of agreements and to reducing the time in dealing with the cases;

36. Recommend that when participating States consider the abolishment of visa obligations with regard to another State, duly taking into account also the interest of other participating States, they conclude a readmission agreement with the State concerned, as appropriate;

37. Recommend that readmission clauses, relating to both nationals and third country citizens, be inserted in general co-operation agreements with countries which are sources of irregular migration, such as agreements relating to economic or political co-operation;

38. Recommend that the Inter-governmental Consultations continues to maintain an inventory of readmission instruments concluded by European States;

4. Information exchange on illegal migration

39. Recommend that appropriate legislation on the protection of personal data be introduced in all participating States, in accordance with the provisions of international law;

40. Recommend that further measures be undertaken within the European Union to improve the exchange of information with Associated and other States on illegal migration and trafficking;

41. Recommend that participating States take measures to ensure that existing systems for collecting, processing and exchanging information on illegal migration and trafficking are being made compatible, by way of harmonizing definitions and criteria for data collection; to that end criteria developed within the European Union, especially by CIREFI, could usefully be taken into account;

42. Recommend that under the leadership of the Government of Hungary, and with the assistance of the Secretariat of the Budapest Group, the information exchange system between the border guards and other competent services of Central and Eastern European States is being made compatible with systems applied by other participating States, and that a comprehensive European system for the monitoring and analysis of illegal migration be established;

5. Technical and financial assistance to Central and Eastern European States

43. Recommend that Central and Eastern European States make the necessary preparations to present eligible projects for financing via bilateral and multilateral funding schemes, and that in particular Associated States elaborate projects to be funded on the basis of the new orientation of the PHARE programme;

44. Recommend that participating States examine all possibilities to make available the necessary expertise and human resources to assist Central and Eastern European States to implement relevant programmes under development within the PHARE programme;

45. Recommend that the European Commission may pay appropriate attention to the prevention of illegal immigration in preparing Partnership Agreements with the Associated States, which may be decided upon in the framework of a pre-accesion strategy.

46. Recommend that a programme for co-operation in the field of Justice and Home Affairs be established with the Newly Independent States in the framework of TACIS, taking into account the findings of the recent mission of the European Union;

47. Recommend that participating States pursue their co-operation with relevant international organizations, such as the United Nations Commission on Crime Prevention, UNHCR, the Council of Europe, IOM, Interpol and ICMPD with a view to establishing the necessary institutional capacities to facilitate the implementation of the recommendations of the Prague Ministerial Conference;

48. Recommend that participating States and relevant international organizations ensure the co-ordination of measures aiming at assisting Central and Eastern European States in this regard, with a view to avoiding unnecessary overlap and securing an efficient use of the resources available;

49. Recommend that participating States assess whether the co-ordination and implementation at the national level of all measures of relevance to the tackling of illegal migration and trafficking in aliens is optimal;

50. Recommend that participating States set up adequate training and exchange schemes for persons responsible for the fight against trafficking in aliens for sexual exploitation, taking into account the example provided by the STOP programme of the European Union;

6. Linkage between trafficking in aliens and other forms of organized crime

51. Recommend that participating States ensure that their national law enforcement authorities give further consideration to the links between trafficking in aliens and other forms of organized crime;
52. Recommend that participating States facilitate the bilateral and multilateral exchange of experience and information at operational levels in order to improve the knowledge of the methods used in different kinds of trafficking;
53. Recommend that the Budapest Group, in close co-operation with relevant international bodies, ensures the preparation of a study on the extent to which international organized crime is expanding its activities into trafficking in aliens;

7. Further co-operation between participating States

54. Recommend that all participating States actively pursue the implementation of these Recommendations at national and international level, and that the informal working mechanisms of the Budapest process be maintained and strengthened, under the continued leadership of the Government of Hungary;
55. Recommend that the Chairmanship of the Budapest Group, with the assistance of the Secretariat, takes the necessary measures to ensure the follow-up of this Conference, including annual reporting on the implementation of the Recommendations adopted by this Conference. (...)

Trafficking

(motto: '... the end of all our exploring will be to
arrive where we started ...')

Nowadays, migratory movements, in particular the irregular or illegal alternative,
take place with the help of 'travel agents' or traffickers. The money involved now
surmounts the narcotics trade, and is estimated at some E 5 billion a year.

As Gosh submits:[1]
It seems important to make a special reference to migrant trafficking and its various consequences. Once a small part of irregular migration, it has become a source
of major concern, especially since it is now closely intertwined with international
crime and acts of violence. In a growing number of cases in Western Europe, the
same criminal network has been involved in several illicit operations including
trafficking in drugs, smuggling of migrants and money laundering. In Italy for example, recent press reports suggest the involvement of the Mafia in illegal immigration, thus linking it to the world of crime – drugs, arms-trafficking and prostitution.[2] The same trend is discernible elsewhere.

Reliable data on the numbers of irregular migrants who use the services of traffickers, are difficult to come by. Several estimates have been however made on the
basis of indirect evidence. The Vienna-based International Centre for Migration
Policy Development (ICMPD) has calculated that (a) 15-30 per cent of those who
illegally crossed the borders of Western European states for purposes of employment or residence (estimated at between 250,000 and 350,000 in 1993) and (b) 20
to 40 per cent of the non-bon fide asylum seekers (estimated at 300,000) during
the same year used the services of traffickers.[3] An estimate can also be made on

---

[1] Bimal Gosh, *Social and Economic Consequences of Irregular Migration,* a paper largely based
on a November 1998 presentation (Conference on Migration, Vienna), which also draws on Ghosh's
book *Huddled Masses and Uncertain Shores: Insights into Irregular Migration,* Kluwer 1998.

[2] Financial Times, 27 March 1995.

[3] Jonas Widgren, 'Multilateral Cooperation to Combat Trafficking in Migrants and the Role of
International Organizations', ICMPD, Vienna, 1994. Paper presented at the Eleventh IOM Seminar
on Migration, Geneva, October 1994.

P.J. van Krieken (Ed.), The Migration Acquis Handbook
© *2001, T.M.C.Asser Press, The Hague, the Röling Foundation and the authors*

the basis of the assumption that between 20 and 30 per cent of the irregular immigrants moving into Western Europe used the services of traffickers for some parts of the journey and that the total annual flow of such irregular migrants varied between 300,000 and 500,000 in the mid-1990s. This would imply that the flow of trafficked migrants to Western Europe during this period may have been at the level of 100,000 per year.[4] From all indications, the number may well have gone up in more recent years.

As regards trafficking to the United States, the inter-agency working group on trafficking set up by the government has estimated that a total of 100,000 trafficked migrants from 'outside the region' pass through one or more Central American countries on their way to the US each year.

Trafficking in migrants has shown itself to be a particularly lucrative business which yields vast amounts of money. While the financial reward in this thriving multi-billion industry is exceptionally high, the risks involved are relatively low. In contrast to other types of smuggling, trafficking in humans entails relatively lax punishment. As EU Commissioner Anita Gradin stated in October 1998, 'Trafficking in human beings has to be criminalized. It is not acceptable that there are less risks when you traffic in human beings than when you traffic drugs'. While some EU states punish drug dealers with up to 12 years in jail, criminals convicted of forcing women into prostitution may get by with only 1-2 year jail sentences.[5] (...)

[I]n recent years, migrant trafficking has grown to become a multi-billion dollar business yielding vast amounts of money to the traffickers. A study by the University of Bangkok based its estimate on the number of Thai women smuggled each year into Japan, Germany and Taiwan for prostitution and found that the trafficking business yields approximately US$ 3.5 billion per year.[6] The ICMPD speculated that at the global level, the total income derived from global trafficking was between US$ 5-7 billion in 1995. A 1996 US government study estimated that about 50,000 Chinese migrants are smuggled into the US annually – making it a 3.5 billion industry.[7] The indications are that the total income derived from migrant trafficking world wide may well be nearing US$10 billion a year This constitutes an enormous diversion of resources into unproductive and anti-social activities. If we include its multiplier effects on the world economy and add the funds being used by national governments for law enforcement and related punitive measures against human trafficking the diversion of resources seems staggering. (...)

An example of forced migration leading to trafficking relates to the very recent Kosovo crisis. It was reported that 'mafia type groups' have been buying or kid-

---

[4] According to the most recent estimate from the International Center for Migration and Policy Development in Vienna (ICMPD), at least 400,000 people are now smuggled into the EU each year.

[5] Reuters, 1 October 1998.

[6] *Migration News*, Vol. 3, No. 2, February 1996.

[7] *Migration News*, Vol. 5, January1998.

napping Kosovo refugee women and girls from Albanian host families and forcing them into prostitution or turning them over to the rebel Kosovo Liberation Army. The UN High Commissioner for Refugees, Mrs. Sadako Ogata, explained that 'attractive girls are taken away and given to traffickers and then many of them are sent to Italy'. The criminal groups supposedly use threats, bribes and/or force to take the refugees away.[8]

As can be imagined, immigrants who find themselves in the clutches of unscrupulous traffickers undergo exploitation and human rights abuse of alarming proportions. Trafficked migrants may be exploited in several ways such as being charged extortionate prices for the trip, having money and belongings stolen, having their identities taken away (theft of ID cards, passports and other travel documents), and being trapped into bondage. Inhumane conditions and physical abuse sometimes end in death.[9] For example, some migrants die during the journey due to drowning as they travel, either by unsafe fishing boats, or because of suffocation when hiding themselves in the interior of trucks and containers of cargo ships. When detected, traffickers are known to react in exactly the same way as they do when trafficking in drugs – they throw the migrants overboard. In a recent case nearly one thousand emigrants from Africa paid a ship's captain US$ 750 each to be illegally ferried to Italy. On reaching the shore they discovered that they were in the former Yugoslavia. Against an extra payment of US$ 600 each, they were promised to be taken to Austria by bus; in the event they were duped and abandoned in Hungary.[10]

A further negative upshot is that trafficked migrants are in many cases forced to work in legal or illegal enterprises controlled by the traffickers under sub-human conditions or to participate in various activities involving crime and violence. A recent report in the Los Angeles Times illustrated how Mexican drug cartels have taken advantage of irregular immigrants to distribute drugs throughout the mid-west region of the United States.[11] In Spain, trafficked immigrants from China were forced to work in textile factories and restaurants under semi-slavery conditions and received only food and accommodation in return.

As can be surmised from the above, organized migrant trafficking encourages a whole range of other illicit activities, such as clandestine printing of false travel documents, forgery, and bribery including official corruption. Recent cases of corruption have involved immigration officials in a large number of countries including Panama, Belize, Guatemala, Uruguay, Spain, United Kingdom, Belgium, Morocco and the United States.[12]

---

[8] The Washington Times, 6 May 1999.

[9] John Salt and Jeremy Stein, 'Migration as a Business: The Case of Trafficking' in: *International Migration,* Quarterly Review, Vol. 35, No. 4, 1997.

[10] *The Economist*, London, 5-11 August 1995, p. 25.

[11] *Los Angeles Times,* 10 December 1997.

[12] For example, in Panama, Belize and Guatemala, immigration officials were fired in 1995 for accepting bribes from foreign smugglers. (*Migration News,* Vol. 3, No. 1, January 1996) In the United Kingdom an immigration officer was sentenced to two years in prison for having forged visas for irregular immigrants against bribery payments. (*The Independent,* 16 May 1992) Similarly,

Conditions of trafficked women and children can be simply dehumanizing when they are exposed to special forms of exploitation such as prostitution, sexual harassment and other forms of bondage. A disquieting example is the abuse of women and children who are kidnapped from villages by traffickers and brought to larger cities to work as beggars. One case involves children from Cambodia who are brought to Thailand and forced to work on the streets, whereby all the money they manage to pry from kind-hearted tourists goes directly to the traffickers. Since sad and sick children bring in the most money, many of the kidnapped children are handicapped or may even be mutilated by the traffickers on purpose.[13]

Particularly disturbing is the link between trafficking of women and girls and forced prostitution. Thousands of women are lured by advertisements for jobs such as baby-sitters, waitresses, models or dancers and upon arrival find themselves being sold like slaves to pimps and then forced to work as prostitutes. The majority of cases involve women coming from developing and former communist countries. Since 1990 the number of trafficked women from Central and Eastern European countries has more than doubled in Belgium and tripled in the Netherlands.[14] Along the eastern borders of the European Union several cities have become major centers for prostitution. In the Czech Republic the small town of Dubi has an estimated 800 prostitutes within a total population of only 9,000.[15] In Israel, some 2,000 women from the former USSR, and in Spain an equal number of Dominican women have been forced and sometimes tortured into prostitution.[16] Cases such as these are reported almost daily in many other countries, such as Germany, as new networks are being created in this ruthless but lucrative trade. In late 1998 IOM estimated that up to half a million foreign women had fallen victim to forced prostitution in western Europe.[17]

A similar pattern of exploitation of women illegally employed in bars and as prostitutes is found in Japan. Their passports and return tickets are routinely taken away by traffickers, job brokers and club managers and they remain under the constant threat of being reported to the police if they try to run away. In some instances, women have been confined within a single building for months at a time and forced into prostitution; they did not even know where they were.[18] Irregular migration in these situations becomes closely associated with gross violation of

---

the top US immigration officer in Hong Kong was relieved of his duties because of his involvement in the trafficking of Chinese migrants into the United States. (*International Herald Tribune,* 7 April, 1997).

[13] IOM News, no. 2/98.

[14] IOM, *Trafficking and Prostitution: The Growing Exploitation of Migrant Women from Central American and Eastern Europe,* Geneva, 1995, op. cit, p. 8.

[15] '"White meat trade" scars Czech borderland', Reuters News Feature, 4 February 1999.

[16] Jo Strich, 'Women sold into slavery', AFP, 20 January 1999.

[17] Reuters, 1 October 1998.

[18] M. Fukushima, 'Immigrant Asian Workers and Japan: The Reality I Discovered at "HELP"', 1991. Paper presented to the Conference on International Manpower flows and Foreign investment in the Asian Region, Tokyo (mimeo). Peter Stalker: *The Work of Strangers.* op. cit. p. 254.

basic human and workers' rights and tantamounts to some of the worst forms of slavery.

UN activities

It was in, of all places, Palermo where in December 2000 a high-level Conference took place on the UN Convention Against Transnational Organized Crime, aiming at agreement and mutual understanding, culminating in a ceremony during which a maximum of countries would sign the new Convention. The UN provided the following background information:

The United Nations Convention against Transnational Organized Crime, the first international treaty of the twenty-first century and the first legally binding United Nations treaty to fight organized crime, will open for signature at a high-level conference to be held in Palermo, Italy, from 12 to 15 December.

The new treaty, adopted by the General Assembly on 15 November, will enter into force after 40 countries have ratified it. In addition to the Convention, countries will have the opportunity to sign two Protocols, one to prevent, suppress and punish trafficking in persons, especially women and children, and the other against the smuggling of migrants by land, sea and air. Negotiations have been concluded on a third protocol – against trafficking in firearms – but have not yet resulted in a final agreement.

Pino Arlacchi, Executive Director of the United Nations Office for Drug Control and Crime Prevention, has noted that the Convention would go well beyond cooperation on just drug trafficking. 'It will strengthen the hand of governments against all forms of serious crimes', he said, emphasizing that the Convention and the Protocols would provide the basis for stronger common action against money-laundering, greater ease of extradition, measures on the protection of witnesses and enhanced judicial cooperation.

The treaty also marks a new chapter in assistance between developed and developing countries by establishing a funding mechanism to help countries implement the Convention. Under that mechanism, regular voluntary contributions from countries would go to a special account for technical assistance to developing countries and countries with economies in transition.

An important goal of the Convention is to get all countries to harmonize their national laws, so that there can be no uncertainty that a crime in one country is also a crime in another. Furthermore, by passing new or updating existing national legislation on transnational criminal activity, all countries would be in a position to cooperate with each other in the investigation and prosecution of such crimes. Under the treaty, countries must criminalize four types of offences: participation in an organized criminal group; money- laundering; corruption; and obstruction of justice.

The Convention provides a broad definition of transnationality, which will provide law enforcement authorities considerable possibilities in using it to track and apprehend criminals. A crime is considered transnational if it is:

- committed in more than one State;
- takes place in one State but is planned or controlled from another;
- is committed in one State by a criminal group that operates in several countries;
- or if the effects of a crime committed in one country are substantial in another.

A Conference of the Parties to the Convention has been set up to assist governments in combating transnational organized crime and also to promote and monitor implementation of the treaty. To that end, the Conference will meet no later than one year after the treaty has gone into force to agree on various measures, which could include: boosting the exchange of information among nations on patterns and trends in transnational organized crime; cooperating with relevant international and non-governmental organizations; checking periodically on the treaty's implementation; and making recommendations to improve the treaty and its implementation. (...)

The work of the United Nations to strengthen international cooperation to combat organized crime dates back 25 years. In 1992, the Organization intensified its efforts to place action against transnational organized crime high on the international agenda with the establishment of the Commission on Crime Prevention and Criminal Justice.

The General Assembly established an intergovernmental group of experts, which met in Warsaw (February 1998) and elaborated a preliminary draft of a possible convention. Proposals from the Warsaw Intergovernmental Group were submitted to the Commission and led to discussions on a draft resolution. Argentina proposed the drafting of a new convention against trafficking in minors and Austria presented the draft of the convention on illegal trafficking and transport of migrants. Canada and Japan proposed an instrument on firearms.

Upon recommendation by the Commission, the Assembly established in December 1998 an Ad Hoc Committee for the elaboration of the United Nations Convention against Transnational Organized Crime and three additional protocols addressing: trafficking in persons, especially women and children; illegal trafficking in and transporting of migrants; and illicit manufacturing of and trafficking in firearms, their parts, components and ammunition.

The Ad Hoc Committee approved the Convention in July 2000 and the protocols on trafficking in persons and smuggling of migrants in October 2000. They were then formally adopted by the Assembly on 15 November.

The Convention does not stand alone. Two Protocols have been added which would appear to be very relevant indeed. As it was stated by the UN:

Every year hundreds of thousands of men, women and children are trafficked illegally all over the world, with annual earnings from trafficking in 'human cargo' estimated at $7 billion. The Protocol to Prevent, Suppress and Punish Trafficking in Persons, Especially Women and Children sets forth three purposes: to prevent and combat trafficking in persons, paying particular attention to women and children; to protect and assist the victims of such trafficking, with full respect for their human rights; and to promote cooperation among States Parties to meet these objectives.

The Protocol represents a new approach to the problem in several aspects. It defines 'trafficking in persons', a complex and multifaceted problem particularly when considering the involvement of transnational organized criminal groups. It also combines traditional crime control measures for investigating and punishing offenders with measures for protecting trafficked persons. The Protocol will serve as a model for national legislation, detailing provisions on conduct which should be sanctioned, the severity of punishment and effective measures to combat as well as prevent trafficking.

Well-publicized tragedies have prompted the international community to step up the fight against the smuggling of illegal migrants. The Protocol against the Smuggling of Migrants by Land, Sea and Air provides an effective tool to combat and prevent the smuggling of human cargo.

It is designed to fight cross-border crimes by obliging signatories to adopt national legal measures, open up information channels and promote international law enforcement cooperation. However, while they have been created to prevent smuggling, the new laws do not aim to dictate domestic migration policy and migration flow. They recognize that migration in itself is not a crime and, therefore, not liable to criminal prosecution. Migrants are victims in need of protection. Thus, emphasis is placed on the criminalization of the smugglers and the organized criminal groups behind them.

The 2000 Palermo Conference and Convention had been preceded by a December 1999 GA Resolution, GARES 54/129, High-level Political Signing Conference for the United Nations Convention against Transnational Organized Crime:

The General Assembly,
Recalling its resolution 53/111 of 9 December 1998, in which it decided to establish an open-ended intergovernmental ad hoc committee for the purpose of elaborating a comprehensive international convention against transnational organized crime and of discussing the elaboration, as appropriate, of international instruments addressing trafficking in women and children, combating the illicit manufacturing of and trafficking in firearms, their parts and components and ammunition, and illegal trafficking in and transporting of migrants, including by sea,
Bearing in mind that in resolution 54/126 of 17 December 1999 it requested the Ad Hoc Committee on the Elaboration of a Convention against Transnational Organized Crime to schedule sufficient time, subject to the availability of funds from the regular budget or from extrabudgetary resources, for the negotiation of the draft protocols addressing trafficking in persons, especially women and children, the illicit manufacturing of and trafficking in firearms, their parts and components and ammunition, and smuggling of migrants by land, air and sea, in order to enhance the possibility of their completion at the same time as the draft Convention,
Acknowledging the progress made thus far by the Ad Hoc Committee towards the

goal of completing negotiations in 2000, *Mindful* that substantive negotiations on the Convention and the protocols thereto continue in Vienna in accordance with General Assembly resolutions 40/243 of 18 December 1985 and 53/111 and 53/114 of 9 December 1998,

Recalling that in its resolution 54/126 it decided that the Ad Hoc Committee should submit the final text of the Convention and the protocols thereto to the General Assembly for early adoption prior to a high-level signing conference,

Recalling also the Naples Political Declaration and Global Action Plan against Organized Transnational Crime, adopted by the World Ministerial Conference on Organized Transnational Crime, held in Naples, Italy, from 21 to 23 November 1994, 1 in which the Commission on Crime Prevention and Criminal Justice was requested to initiate the process of elaborating international instruments, such as a convention or conventions against organized transnational crime,

Recognizing the initiating role and the contribution of the Government of Poland to the development of a draft convention against transnational organized crime,

Recognizing also the historic and symbolic importance of associating the first international convention against transnational organized crime with the city of Palermo, Italy,

1. *Accepts with appreciation* the offer of the Government of Italy to host a high-level political signing conference in Palermo for the purpose of signing the United Nations Convention against Transnational Organized Crime (Palermo Convention) and the protocols thereto;

2. *Decides* to convene the High-level Political Signing Conference in Palermo;

3. *Requests* the Secretary-General to schedule the Conference for a period of up to one week before the end of the Millennium Assembly in 2000, with the Conference to be organized in accordance with resolution 40/243;

4. *Requests* the Centre for International Crime Prevention of the Office for Drug Control and Crime Prevention of the Secretariat to work with the Government of Italy, in consultation with Member States, to propose the agenda for and the organization of the Conference, including opportunities for high-level delegates to discuss matters related to the Convention and the protocols thereto, in particular the follow-up activities, for their effective implementation and future work;

5. *Invites* all States to be represented at the High-level Political Signing Conference at the highest possible levels of government.

In the Autumn of 2000, the General Assembly adopted the Convention and Protocols concerned:

The General Assembly this morning adopted the United Nations Convention against Transnational Organized Crime, the Protocol to Prevent, Suppress and Punish Trafficking in Persons, Especially Women and Children, and the Protocol against the Smuggling of Migrants by Land, Sea and Air, and opened them for signature at the high-level political signing conference to be held in Palermo, Italy, from 12 to 15 December. It did so by adopting, without a vote, a related draft resolution.

By the terms of that resolution, the Assembly urged all States and regional economic organizations to sign and ratify the United Nations Convention against Transnational Organized Crime and the protocols thereto as soon as possible, in order to ensure the speedy entry into force of the Convention and protocols. It called upon all States to recognize the links between transnational organized criminal activities and acts of terrorism, and to apply the United Nations Convention against Transnational Organized Crime in combating all forms of criminal activity. [19]

Luigi Lauriola, Chairman of the Ad Hoc Committee on the Elaboration of a Convention against Transnational Organized Crime, introducing the Convention and its two additional protocols, said the Convention provided a framework and tools for better international cooperation against organized crime without borders. What was critical, however, would be its implementation. The dangers posed by organized crime to the individual citizen and to the international community had rightly risen to the top of the agenda. The first steps had been taken, but there was still a long way to go. He regretted that the Ad Hoc Committee had been unable to complete its deliberation on a Protocol against illicit manufacturing and trafficking in firearms, their parts and components, and ammunition, in time for submission to the Assembly.[20]

---

[19] The Assembly also decided that, until the Conference of the Parties to the Convention established pursuant to the United Nations Convention against Transnational Organized Crime decides otherwise, the account referred to in article 30 of the Convention will be operated within the United Nations Crime Prevention and Criminal Justice Fund. It encourages Member States to begin making adequate voluntary contributions to the above-mentioned account in order to provide developing countries and countries with economies in transition with the technical assistance they might require for implementation of the Convention and the protocols thereto.

The Assembly requested the Secretary-General to designate the Centre for International Crime Prevention of the Office for Drug Control and Crime Prevention to serve as the secretariat for and under the direction of the Conference of the Parties to the Convention.

[20] Luigi Lauriola, Chairman of the Ad Hoc Committee on the Elaboration of a Convention against Transnational Organized Crime, introduced the Convention and its two additional protocols: one on illicit trafficking in persons, especially women and children; the other on illegal trafficking and transporting of migrants. He said that those texts had been finalized and unanimously agreed upon in less than two years. The idea of preparing a United Nations Convention against Transnational Organized Crime had been first formally raised at the World Ministerial Conference on Organized Transnational Crime in November 1994. Little by little, the political will of the participants, driven by newspaper headlines and public opinion, gave decisive impulse to the search for a global response to global organized crime. Countries which had been opposed even to the idea of discussing the possibility of an international instrument had become some of the Convention's strongest supporters. Other countries, like Italy, Poland and Argentina, had supported the process from the very beginning. The Convention, he continued, provided a framework and tools for better international cooperation against organized crime without borders. But it was implementation of the Convention that would be critical. He recalled that the mandate given to the Ad Hoc Committee also included the elaboration of a Protocol against illicit manufacturing and trafficking in firearms, their parts and components, and ammunition. He regretted that the Ad Hoc Committee had been unable to complete its deliberations on that protocol in time for submission to the Assembly. Accordingly, the Committee requested that it be allowed to continue its work in conformity with resolutions 53/111,

At the Palermo Conference itself, various substantial and interesting statements were given.

Speaking on behalf of the European Community, Antonio Vitorino said:

53/114 and 54/126, so that it might have an opportunity to finalize its work in the near future. The dangers posed by organized crime to the individual citizen and to the international community had rightly risen to the top of the agenda. The first steps had been taken, but there was still a long way to go. Yves Doutriaux (France), speaking on behalf of the European Union and associated States, stated that the growth of transnational organized crime was a major challenge facing the international community. The phenomenon represented one of the major non-military threats to the security of the individual, the stability of societies, the sovereignty of States, and the development and continuance of democracy. His Government believed that, in light of its universal mission, the United Nations was the forum for devising legislative tools to combat transnational organized crime. A period of less than two years had been set aside by the General Assembly for negotiating a Convention against such crime, which was a sign of the urgency attached to the matter by the Member States. The European Union considered the Convention to be an exemplary set of provisions. Moreover, it was the first global legal instrument devised to combat transnational organized crime, introducing essential innovations in law and in the procedures for cooperation among States parties. The Union was pleased that, for the first time, the Convention offered the international community universally recognized definitions of several fundamental concepts of criminal law linked to organized crime, such as 'organized criminal group', 'serious offence' and 'the proceeds of crime'. It was also important that the Convention broached the subject of approximating national criminal legislation by establishing criminal offences of a universal nature (participation in an organized criminal group, money laundering, obstruction of the course of justice, corruption) and by obliging the States parties to transpose them into their domestic criminal law. In regard to the two related Protocols adopted in parallel with the Convention itself, the European Union considered them to be essential complementary tools, especially the Protocol designed to prevent, suppress and punish trafficking in persons, including women and children, thereby providing a legal definition of trafficking in persons. The Union believed that the completion of negotiations on the Convention and two of its related Protocols was a remarkable result, and looked forward to the Signing Conference in Palermo, Italy, this coming December. The European Union called upon all Member States to sign the Convention and its Protocols at the Palermo Conference. Janusz Rydzkowski (Poland) said his country had initiated the practical work on the Convention in terms of concept and implementation. Following that initiative, the Polish Government had invited a group of international experts to Warsaw, in February 1998, to start preliminary discussion on the Convention. The Warsaw meeting marked an important breakthrough in two respects. First and foremost, the issue of drafting such a multilateral convention was no longer addressed in 'whether or not' terms but became a question of 'how and when' instead. Secondly, more than 50 States had agreed unanimously to develop an effective tool to combat transnational organized crime in its most dangerous transnational dimension. In the preparatory stages, delegations had focused on identifying areas of emerging consensus.The new legal instrument was of a unique character, because, for the first time, it delivered a precise definition of the phenomenon of transnational organized crime, and defined the instruments for an effective fight against uncivil society. Adoption of the Convention and its two additional protocols after only three and a half years of work was a significant achievement, and reflected the political will of the international community to combat the increased threat posed by organized crime. However, from a practical point of view, the adoption of a legal instrument was only the beginning. Ahead was the signing ceremony in Palermo, the difficult process of national ratification and implementation on international and national levels. It was important to stress that full implementation of the Convention was possible only when it was carried out on a universal basis – which meant that resources would be necessary to assist States unable to fight organized crime by themselves.

.

Holding the Conference in Palermo is a way of tribute to a community which has not given up the fight against organized crime and has often paid for it with the loss of life. Today, on behalf of the European Community, I had the honour to sign the Convention and its protocols. We are talking about a serious commitment that has been undertaken by the 15-member Community. This commitment can be justified by what is at stake, namely the international cooperation vital for fighting criminal activities. To counter the threats and dangers, we have to make sure we work together and that perpetrators of crimes can find no safe haven.

The results achieved in Vienna are significant. The Convention is the first international legal instrument to fight and prevent organized crime, which provides for common legal standards. Fighting money-laundering, which the Community views as an essential pillar in fighting organized crime, and preventing trafficking have to be strengthened through these instruments. The Community is heartened by the progress attained by its member States with regard to police cooperation, particularly through Interpol. It is well aware that technical cooperation will be crucial at the international level. The Community will continue to help the international community through already existing instruments as well as future ones, such as the convention on corruption. We must ensure a culture of prevention, which is necessary for peace and stability at the global level.

The Minister of Justice of Sweden, Thomas Bodstrom added:

Crime and criminal justice issues cannot be addressed solely at the national level. To successfully meet the challenges from organized crime, we must be prepared to fully cooperate on all fronts and at all levels, bilaterally as well as regionally and globally. It is a shared responsibility and we must all contribute. We are convinced that the Convention, with its wide scope of application, will make it possible to render effective mutual legal assistance and will thus prove to represent a key milestone for international cooperation in the future. The two related protocols are essential complementary tools to the Convention. While it is certainly important to fight all forms of organized crime, we are particularly concerned with those offences where unscrupulous criminals exploit the suffering of others and derive great profits from it.

Now that we have successfully completed the negotiations on the Convention and its protocols, we must not forget that this is only a first step. The next stage will be their entry into force. In order for the Convention to really become the vital global instrument we all wish it be in our fight against organized crime, it is of vital importance that participating States take the necessary steps to ratify it as soon as possible. Having done that, we must also see to it that the Convention and its protocols are effectively implemented.

The Minister of Justice of Denmark, Frank Jensen elaborated:

The cruellest form of transnational organized crime is the exploitation of human beings. The international community must pay special attention to trafficking in human beings and the smuggling of migrants in order to protect vulnerable victims globally.

The investigation and prosecution of trafficking and smuggling of human beings is complicated and requires close cross-border cooperation between law enforcement authorities. Increased cooperation against trafficking in persons and smuggling of migrants must be based on three principles: First, we have to strengthen cooperation and information exchange between the countries of destination, transit countries and the countries of origin. Second, we must base our efforts on a close analysis of the crime situation and make sure we share our analytical experience with relevant partners. Third, we have to provide special investigative techniques, such as wiretapping and joint investigating teams, which enable police and prosecutors to unravel the criminal networks behind the organized trafficking in human beings and smuggling of illegal migrants.

Whereas the Minister of the Interior of Hungary, Sandor Pinter shared the following views:

Combating transnational organized crime is in the fundamental interest of everyone. Hungary is specially threatened, since its democracy is young and its geopolitical position special. The Government has been making serious efforts in the past two-and-a-half years to improve public safety and security. By way of new legislation and by increasing the severity of punishment for existing acts, it has created the necessary legal framework for combating organized crime. Hungary has also developed law enforcement agencies and organizations. These entities have been restructured, their staff increased and their equipment improved. A new life career system was also elaborated for those working for these organizations, thus ensuring them better moral and material esteem.

Hungary has also intensified its international cooperation and has concluded bilateral agreements with some 30 countries to combat organized crime. It has also ratified numerous related international conventions. In Hungary's view, the Budapest Group, with about 40 member countries and 10 international member organizations, plays a very important role in combating illegal migration. The positive experiences of the past confirm that international training programmes – joint projects – are very important pre-conditions for effective anti-crime operations. Learning about one another's legal practices is of great importance since we all want to harmonize our legal systems.

The documents to be signed will create a new legal foundation for combating international organized crime and for promoting cooperation among the law enforcement agencies and judicial bodies of countries. An important task for the future is to publicize the documents and to implement their contents in practice. The law enforcement agencies of Hungary will spare no effort – in cooperation with other countries – to put a stop to transborder crime.

The Minister of State of the United Kingdom, Barbara Roche was quite straightforward:

The Convention is an impressive achievement in itself. It is made still more impressive by the simultaneous completion of the protocols on trafficking in human beings and smuggling of migrants. Human smuggling and trafficking is now a multi-billion pound trade. Its dramatic rise poses a significant challenge to global stability. A European Union report on migration has found that almost all illegal entrants now make use of criminal gangs to facilitate their travel. We must respond as an international community, which is why these protocols which target the gangs behind human smuggling and trafficking, are urgently required. But they are not a solution in themselves. Like the Convention, their success depends on how widely and how quickly they are adopted and implemented, and on the resources, determination and collective effort which are brought to bear.

It is important to recognize that these protocols deal separately with migrant smuggling and human trafficking. While we must recognize and understand the distinctions, the gangs operating in this field do not. To traffic persons to unfamiliar countries and cultures against their will is the most sinister part of this trade. The victims are often too afraid to cooperate with authorities that seek to prosecute the traffickers. It is important that we provide the right environment to encourage them to speak out and to reassure them that, once they are returned home, they will continue to receive support. The Protocol on Trafficking provides the necessary infrastructure, but it will be up to States parties to ensure that it is properly utilized. The gangs must not be able to place themselves beyond the rule of law through intimidation.

Alojz Nemethy (Slovakia) submitted:

Organized crime has long ago ceased to be a domain reserved for organized mafia-type groups operating under strict rules. Today's organized crime groups use their proceeds and corruption to infiltrate many sectors, including trade and politics, infecting them with cancerous criminal activities. The threat of organized crime is felt especially in the countries whose level of economic development does not enable them to allocate sufficient funds and efforts into an effective fight against organized crime, including its prevention through social, educational and other programmes. It is also a problem for countries in transition, including my own. Even economically developed and politically stable countries are not immune to the negative consequences of organized crime.

In spite of achievements, organized crime, mainly in the economic arena, continues to present a problem that could undermine the economic, social and legal system of the State, if the State fails to take appropriate measures. This problem is due, to a considerable extent, to a non-transparent method of privatization of State property, cronyism, corruption and violations of the law by State authorities. Slovakia's broadly conceived National Programme for the Fight against Corruption and its comprehensive programme to fight crime are aimed at combating these problems. In the process of its accession to the European Union, Slovakia is actively fulfilling its obligations resulting from the pre-accession pact on organized crime. The progress made by Slovakia in countering organized crime would be inconceivable without close international cooperation, the exchange of experiences and assistance from global partners.

At the final session no less than 124 countries signed the new Convention and more than 80 the additional Protocols.[21] The UN, in a relevant press release, stressed that the Convention will enter into force after 40 countries have ratified it. The press release furthermore stated:[22]

During the course of the Conference, representatives from more than 100 countries, including Heads of State and Government, and Ministers of Foreign Affairs and Justice, made statements on the new treaty and its protocols. In his closing

---

[21] Convention: Afghanistan, Albania, Algeria, Angola, Argentina, Australia, Austria, Azerbaijan, Belarus, Belgium, Benin, Bolivia, Bosnia and Herzegovina, Brazil, Bulgaria, Burkina Faso, Burundi, Cameroon, Canada, Cape Verde, Chile, China, Colombia, Congo, Cote d'Ivoire, Croatia, Cuba, Cyprus, Czech Republic, Denmark, Dominican Republic, Ecuador, Egypt, El Salvador, Equatorial Guinea, Estonia, Ethiopia, Finland, France, Gambia, Georgia, Germany, Greece, Guatemala, Guinea-Bissau, Haiti, Honduras, Hungary, Iceland, Indonesia, Iran (Islamic Republic of), Ireland, Israel, Italy, Japan, Kazakhstan, Kuwait, Kyrgyzstan, Latvia, Lesotho, Liechtenstein, Lithuania, Luxembourg, The former Yugoslav Republic of Macedonia, Madagascar, Malawi, Mali, Malta, Mauritius, Mexico, Monaco, Morocco, Mozambique, Namibia, Netherlands, New Zealand, Nicaragua, Nigeria, Norway, Pakistan, Panama, Paraguay, Peru, Philippines, Poland, Portugal, Republic of Korea, Republic of Moldova, Romania, Russian Federation, Rwanda, San Marino, Saudi Arabia, Senegal, Seychelles, Singapore, Slovakia, Slovenia, South Africa, Spain, Sri Lanka, Sudan, Swaziland, Sweden, Switzerland, Syrian Arab Republic, Tajikistan, Thailand, Togo, Tunisia, Turkey, Uganda, Ukraine, United Kingdom, United Republic of Tanzania, United States of America, Uruguay, Uzbekistan, Venezuela, Vietnam, Yemen, Yugoslavia, Zimbabwe, European Community.

Protocol on Trafficking in Persons: Albania, Argentina, Austria, Azerbaijan, Belarus, Belgium, Benin, Bolivia, Bosnia and Herzegovina, Brazil, Bulgaria, Burkina Faso, Burundi, Cameroon, Canada, Cape Verde, Colombia, Congo, Croatia, Cyprus, Denmark, Dominican Republic, Ecuador, Equatorial Guinea, Finland, France, Gambia, Georgia, Germany, Greece, Guinea-Bissau, Haiti, Hungary, Iceland, Indonesia, Ireland, Italy, Kyrgyzstan, Lesotho, Luxembourg, The former Yugoslav Republic of Macedonia, Madagascar, Mali, Malta, Mexico, Monaco, Mozambique, Namibia, Netherlands, New Zealand, Nigeria, Norway, Panama, Paraguay, Peru, Philippines, Portugal, Republic of Korea, Republic of Moldova, Romania, Russian Federation, Rwanda, San Marino, Senegal, Seychelles, South Africa, Spain, Sri Lanka, Sweden, Syria, Togo, Tunisia, Turkey, Uganda, United Kingdom, United Republic of Tanzania, United States of America, Uruguay, Venezuela, Yugoslavia, European Community.

Protocol on Smuggling of Migrants: Albania, Argentina, Austria, Azerbaijan, Belarus, Belgium, Bolivia, Bosnia and Herzegovina, Brazil, Bulgaria, Burkina Faso, Burundi, Cameroon, Canada, Cape Verde, Congo, Croatia, Cyprus, Denmark, Dominican Republic, Ecuador, Equatorial Guinea, Finland, France, Gambia, Georgia, Germany, Greece, Guinea-Bissau, Haiti, Hungary, Iceland, Indonesia, Ireland, Italy, Kyrgyzstan, Lesotho, Luxembourg, The former Yugoslav Republic of Macedonia, Madagascar, Mali, Malta, Mexico, Monaco, Mozambique, Namibia, Netherlands, New Zealand, Nigeria, Norway, Panama, Peru, Philippines, Portugal, Republic of Korea, Republic of Moldova, Romania, Russian Federation, Rwanda, San Marino, Senegal, Seychelles, South Africa, Spain, Sri Lanka, Sweden, Syria, Togo, Tunisia, Turkey, Uganda, United Kingdom, United Republic of Tanzania, United States of America, Uruguay, Venezuela, Yugoslavia, European Community.

[22] Press Release L/T/4359 15 December 2000

statement to the Conference, United Nations Under- Secretary-General and Executive Director of the United Nations Office for Drug Control and Crime Prevention (UNDCCP), Pino Arlacchi, declared that never before had an international convention attracted so many signatures barely four weeks following its adoption by the Assembly. The delegations that had spoken during the Conference had left no one in any doubt that there was a strong and clear international commitment to achieving early ratification of the Convention. 'Let us not lose the momentum we have achieved so far', he said. He invited delegations to join forces to ensure that the Convention and its protocols entered into force within the coming 12 months and offered United Nations support to countries that needed help in translating the new instruments into legislation. He stressed the need to maintain a reasonable yet determined sense of urgency to ensure the security and well-being of all societies. With the adoption of the Convention, he stated, the international community was now well ahead in the construction of an international framework of legal instruments aimed specifically at confronting the most serious threats to human security.

The aims of the Protocol to Prevent, Suppress and Punish Trafficking in Persons, Especially Women and Children are three-fold: to prevent and combat trafficking in persons, particularly women and children; to protect and assist the victims of such trafficking; and to promote cooperation among States parties to meet these objectives. The protocol will serve as a model for national legislation, detailing provisions on conduct which should be sanctioned, the severity of punishment and effective measures to combat as well as prevent trafficking.

The Protocol against the Smuggling of Migrants by Land, Sea and Air provides an effective tool to combat and prevent the smuggling of human cargo. However, while it has been created to prevent smuggling, the new laws do not aim to dictate domestic migration policy and migration flow. They recognize that migration in itself is not a crime and, therefore, not liable to criminal prosecution. Migrants are victims in need of protection. Thus, emphasis is placed on the criminalization of the smugglers and the organized criminal groups behind them.

Following the Palermo success, the Commission has efficiently taken action. A proposal for a Council Framework Decision was submitted in early 2001. In the context of this sub-chapter, it suffices to pay attention to the Explanatory Memorandum as it provides insight into the Commission's way of thinking and planning.

TRAFFICKING AND THE EU[23]

On 24 February 1997 the Council adopted a Joint Action concerning action to combat trafficking in human beings and the sexual exploitation of children. The Joint Action covers a wide range of topics such as definitions (...), jurisdiction,

---

[23] Based on the Explanatory Memorandum re COM (2001/0024 CNS) a proposal for a Council Framework Decision on combating trafficking in human beings. The footnotes in the original document have not been included.

criminal procedure, assistance to victims and police and judicial co-operation. Through the Joint Action, the Member States undertook to review their existing laws with a view to providing that trafficking in human beings and the sexual exploitation of children were criminal offences.

Since the adoption of the Joint Action in 1997, actions and initiatives against trafficking in human beings have developed considerably in number and in substance at the level of the European Union as well as at local, regional and international level in a wider context. That said, the continuing divergence of legal approaches in the Member States clearly demonstrates the need for further action against the menace of trafficking. Furthermore, Article 29 of the Amsterdam Treaty provides an explicit reference to trafficking in human beings. The Vienna Action Plan 2 and the Tampere European Council made a clear call for further legislative action against trafficking. Legislative action is also indicated in the Commission´s Scoreboard. At the wider international level, one of the most significant developments has been the United Nations Convention on Transnational Organised Crime with its two supplementing protocols targeting smuggling of migrants and trafficking in persons. The Commission has participated actively in the elaboration of these instruments and important elements of the protocol on trafficking are reflected in this proposal, albeit taken further.

The specific character of an area of freedom, security and justice to be created within the European Union should enable the Member States to develop a Framework Decision in which certain aspects of criminal law and judicial co-operation are taken further than has been possible through instruments available before the entry into force of the Amsterdam Treaty and instruments developed at a wider international level. A Framework Decision should, for instance, address more precisely, issues such as criminalisation, penalties and other sanctions, aggravating circumstances, jurisdiction and extradition.

In conclusion, the Commission believes that a further response to the issue of trafficking is required at the level of the European Union. Use of a Framework Decision, an instrument introduced by the Amsterdam Treaty, will reinforce a common approach of the European Union in this area and fill gaps in existing legislation. The need for a clear common approach on trafficking should also be viewed against the background of the future enlargement of the European Union. The Commission has therefore, as announced in the Scoreboard, decided to put forward a proposal for a Framework Decision on the approximation of the criminal laws of the Member States, including penalties, concerning trafficking in human beings. (...)

1. Trafficking and smuggling

The Commission is of the view that the division into one United Nations-protocol on trafficking in human beings and one United Nations-protocol on smuggling of migrants highlights the complexity of different forms of criminal movements of people that are operated by international criminal organisations. While smuggling of migrants could be said to constitute a crime against the state and often involves a mutual interest between the smuggler and the smuggled, trafficking in human beings constitute a crime against a person and involves an exploitative purpose.

The Commission is therefore of the view that the French initiatives on facilitation of unauthorised entry, movement and residence are related to smuggling of migrants. This proposal, on the other hand, relates to trafficking in persons with its characteristics. The Commission´s conclusion is that the French initiative on facilitation and this proposal on trafficking complement each other and that they both contribute to a European-wide fight against severe types of criminal activities by international criminal organisations.

2. Legal basis

This proposal for a Framework Decision concerns approximation of the laws and regulations of the Member States in the area of police and judicial co-operation in criminal matters. It also to a substantial part concerns 'minimum rules relating to the constituent elements of criminal acts and to penalties in the field of organised crime'. The legal basis indicated in the preamble of the proposal is therefore Articles 29 with an explicit reference to trafficking in human beings, 31(e) and 34(2)(b) of the Treaty on European Union. The proposal will not entail financial implications for the budget of the European Communities.

3. The various articles

Article 1 (Trafficking in human beings for the purpose of labour exploitation)
Article 1 puts on the Member States an obligation to ensure that trafficking in human beings for the purpose of labour exploitation is punishable.

Trafficking is defined in the Article to include the recruitment, transportation, or transfer of a person, including harbouring and subsequent reception of and the exchange of control over him or her for the purpose of exploiting him or her in the production of goods or provision of services. This definition reflects the key elements of one of the parts constituting the definition of trafficking in the United Nations-protocol on trafficking in human beings.

Labour exploitation is defined in the Article to be an infringement of labour standards governing working conditions, salaries and health and safety. The reference to labour market regulations is in no way intended to affect the labour market regulations of the Member States. It is intended to establish a benchmark on the basis of existing regulations for what is an acceptable standard on the labour market. It should be underlined that this definition must be viewed upon in conjunction with the definition of trafficking and qualifying elements such as coercion. In addition the offence includes a requirement that the fundamental rights of the person have been and continue to be suppressed, for instance the rights of the Charter of Fundamental Rights proclaimed by the Nice European Council. This requirement includes also the perspective of the victim´s fundamental rights and not only the conduct of the perpetrator as in the qualifying elements mentioned below. It also expresses a requirement for a continuing suppression of the fundamental rights of a person. As regards the elements qualifying trafficking a person for the purpose of labour exploitation as a criminal offence, points (a) and (b) corresponds to the UN-protocol on trafficking. Points (c) and (d), which partly corresponds to the United Nations-protocol, cover forms of taking advantage or exercising pressure when a person is trafficked. The objective is to ensure a comprehensive coverage of criminal conduct. This includes practices such as debt bondage in which a person has no choice but to submit to the pressure. It also includes the abuse of the vulnerability of persons, for instance of persons being mentally or physically disabled or of persons illegally remaining on the territory of a Member State who are often in a situation in which they have no choice or perceive to have no choice, but to submit to the exploitation. These latter elements ensures also that the offence take the specific situation of the victim into account and not only the conduct performed by the trafficker. The criminal offence described does not include an explicit requirement for the victim to cross a border. The reasoning here is following the Europol Convention and the United Nations-protocol on trafficking, i.e. the context of trafficking in human beings refers generally to international organised crime, but it is not necessary for the victim itself to cross a border. Moreover, the key elements of the offence of trafficking should focus on the exploitative purpose, rather than on the 'movement' across a border. If the requirement of a cross-border element would be maintained, there would be a paradox in that a European citizen forced into prostitution and trafficked within its own country, would be less protected than citizens from third countries would. The approach not to include a cross-border requirement also means that the proposal cover 're-trafficking' within the country of destination, which in many cases form an integral part of the trafficking chain/operation.

Article 2 (Trafficking in human beings for the purpose of sexual exploitation) (...)

Article 3 (Instigation, aiding, abetting and attempt)
Article 3 puts an obligation on Member States to ensure that instigation of, aiding, abetting and attempt to commit trafficking for the purpose of labour exploitation and trafficking for the purpose of sexual exploitation is punishable.

Article 4 (Penalties and aggravating circumstances) (...)

Article 5 (Liability of legal persons)
It is necessary also to cover the situation in which legal persons are involved in the trafficking. Article 5 therefore provides provisions for holding a legal person liable for the offences envisaged by Articles 1, 2, and 3, committed for their benefit by any person, acting either individually or as a part of the organ of the legal person. The term liability should be construed so as to include either criminal or civil liability (see also Article 6 on sanctions).

In addition, paragraph 2 provides that a legal person can also be held liable when the lack of supervision or control by a person in a position to exercise control, has rendered possible the commission of the offence for its benefit. Paragraph

3 indicates that legal proceedings against a legal person do not preclude parallel legal proceedings against a natural person and paragraph 4 definesa legal person for the purpose of this Framework Decision.

Article 6 (Sanctions on legal persons) (...)

Article 7 (Jurisdiction and prosecution) (...)
The international nature of the trafficking offence implies that an efficient legal response requires procedural provisions on jurisdiction and on extradition which are as clear and as far reaching as national legal systems will allow in order to guard against persons evading prosecution.

   Paragraph 1 establishes a series of criteria conferring jurisdiction on national enforcement and judicial authorities to prosecute and examine cases involving the offences referred to in this Framework Decision. A Member State shall establish its jurisdiction in three situations:
(a) where the offence is committed in whole or in part on its territory, irrespective of the status or the nationality of the person involved (territoriality principle), or
(b) where the offender is a national (active personality principle). The criterion of the status as a national means that jurisdiction can be established regardless of the *lex locus delicti*. It is up to Member States to prosecute for offences committed abroad. This is particularly important for Member States which do not extradite their own nationals, or
(c) where the offence is committed for the benefit of a legal person established in the territory of that Member State.

   However, as not all Member States' legal traditions recognise extraterritorial jurisdiction for all types of criminal offences, Member States may, subject to the obligation under paragraph 1, limit their jurisdiction to the first of these three situations. In addition, if they do not do so, they can still make provisions the applicability of paragraphs 1(b) and 1(c) to cases where the offence has been committed outside the territory of that Member State.

   Paragraph 3 takes account of the fact that some Member States do not extradite their nationals and seeks to ensure that persons suspected of having committed trafficking offences do not evade prosecution because extradition is refused in principle on the grounds that they are nationals of that state. A Member State which does not extradite its own nationals must, in accordance with paragraph 3, take the necessary measures to establish its jurisdiction over and to prosecute, where appropriate, the offences concerned when committed by its own nationals outside its territory. Paragraph 4 says that Member States shall inform the General Secretariat and the Commission where they decide to apply paragraph 2.

Article 8 (Victims)
In the European Union´s approach against trafficking in human beings, special importance has been attached to assistance to the victims. In many cases, victims of trafficking have been severely abused by the trafficker. The Commission is therefore of the view that an Article on victims should be included in this Framework

Decision. Social assistance for children in order to help them overcome the consequences of such events and enable them to reintegrate, inter alia, into the labour market, forms part of the overall policy.

Article 9 (Co-operation between Member States)
The purpose of Article 9 is to take advantage of instruments on international judicial co-operation to which Member States are parties and which should apply to the matters covered in this Framework Decision. For instance, arrangements on mutual legal assistance and extradition are contained in a number of bilateral and multilateral agreements as well as conventions of the European Union. An additional purpose with this Article is to facilitate the exchange of information. (...)

Article 10 (Implementation)
Article 10 concerns the implementation and follow-up of this Framework Decision. It establishes that the Member States shall take the necessary measures to comply with this Framework Decision not later than 31 December 2002. It also establishes that the Member States shall, by the same date, transmit to the General Secretariat of the Council and to the Commission the provisions transposing into their national legislation the obligations imposed on them under this Framework Decision. On the basis of a report established on the basis of this information and on a written report from the Commission, the Council will by 30 June 2004 assess the extent to which Member States have taken the necessary measures to comply with this Framework Decision.

Article 11 (Repeal of the Joint Action of February 1997) (...)

Article 12 (Entry into force)
Article 12 indicates that this Framework Decision will enter into force on the day of its publication in the Official Journal of the European Communities.

From what has been incorporated in this sub-chapter, the conclusion should be drawn that a great many activities have recently been undertaken to try and effectively deal with trafficking and other related criminal activities which have such an impact on migratory movements. All these instruments, documents and notes are proof of and have themselves increased awareness concerning the intrinsic misery of many of those movements.

Family Reunification   2.5

The EU Commissioner for Internal Markets, Mr Frits Bolkestein, in a January 2001 address, stated that if the influx of 'economic asylum seekers' becomes uncontrollable, Europe will be importing poverty. He stressed that a loss/loss situation will be created for both the country of arrival (in this case, the European Union) and the country of origin. He made the point that Europe has to make a choice between becoming a Continent of immigration with strong qualitative demands for the potential immigrants or increasing the labour participation of the now non-active part of Europe's population.[1]

Bolkestein insisted, however, that there should always be room for political refugees. It is now calculated that Europe receives yearly on average some 400,000 asylum seekers, their distribution over the various Member States differing over the years. Some 5-10% are considered to fall within the terms of the 1951 Refugee Convention, whereas some 10-15% are considered to be in need of protection because of war or other forms of violence in the asylum seekers' countries of origin. Another 10% may be allowed to stay for humanitarian reasons. This means that 30% will in one way or another obtain a residence permit, whereas 70% are supposed to return home, or at least to leave the territory of the Union. Many of the latter category will stay on as 'illegals', becoming part of the continuously growing group now believed to consist in the European Union alone of 3 to 4 million illegals/undocumented or irregulars.

Out of the 120,000 or so allowed to stay, many, if not most, will be allowed to bring their families. The same is true for the category of those foreign workers (non-refugees) who have resided for a substantial period of time and have in the meantime obtained a status which allows them to reunify with their families or to take a bride or groom from abroad, in most cases from the country of origin. It is hence submitted that family reunification and family formation has become and will continue to re-

---

[1] Hofstad Lecture, the Hague. Bolkestein preferred the latter alternative. NRC, 27 January, 2001.

P.J. van Krieken (Ed.), The Migration Acquis Handbook
© 2001, T.M.C.Asser Press, The Hague, the Röling Foundation and the authors

main the one single main factor for immigration, a fact which is often overlooked.[2] Concerning the multiplier involved (the factor by which each residence permit results in an additional influx) many conflicting 'guesstimates' can be found. The present author would, therefore, like to work with an average of 2.5, meaning that in the long run, the number of 120,000 foreigners allowed to stay in the Union should rather be read as 300,000 (that is, without calculating the possible results of amnesties regularizing the stay of the illegals, rejectees or overstayers[3]).

The link between family reunification and 'importing poverty' is, of course, to some extent provocative and incorrect: among the newcomers are a great many well-educated persons who perfectly fit into the labour market. Yet, one cannot deny that in most European countries, the bigger cities in particular, literacy rates are declining (Afghans, Moroccans from the Rif mountains, etc.) and that, for example, U5M numbers (the Under Five Mortality rate) are increasing.[4]

It is thus legitimate to try and seek answers to the principles underlying family reunification and family formation, taking Strasbourg case-law on Article 8 of the ECHR duly into account.[5]

POLICY

Policy in the Union has not as yet been harmonized. The most recent Commission Proposal has been included in this Handbook in full (as it also provides an insight into the institutional relationships and decision-making in general). All countries allow wives and husbands to be reunited. Most countries allow children under 18 to be reunited, although some countries insist that it should include the under 16 only. The elderly (over 60, dependent on the children) are often allowed to be reunited as well,

---

[2] The Economist (3 February, 2001) indicated that since the late 1990s immigration has been rising in most OECD countries. The OECD expects that immigration will increase in Europe if the economic recovery lasts. *Although family-linked immigration continues to dominate*, the number of workers migrating to find jobs is rising (emphasis added).

[3] See Chapter 2.3 on Illegal Migration.

[4] See on health-related migration Van Krieken (ed.) *Health, Migration and Return,* (Asser/ Kluwer, The Hague 2001).

[5] ECHR Art. 8 reads as follows: (1) Everyone has the right to respect for his private and family life, his home and his correspondence. (2) There shall be no interference by a public authority with the exercise of this right except such as is in accordance with the law and is necessary in a democratic society in the interests of national security, public safety or the economic well-being of the country, for the prevention of disorder or crime, for the protection of health or morals, or for the protection of the rights and freedoms of others. This article has developed over the years from the principle that the State should abstain from interfering, to the idea that the State should actively protect, including ensuring that families be reunited. Ample case-law is available, with recent years tending towards an approach indicating (a) that the unity of the family is not sacrosanct (persons with a criminal record may be deported in spite of their close family living in a CoE country; e.g in quite some cases concerning persons from the *Maghreb* v. *France*) and (b) that the unity and hence reunification, if so desired, can also, more often than not, be assured in the country of origin (e.g. in re Gül).

and some countries also include brothers and sisters (with their families)[6] in the case of the latter depending on the ones who have in the meantime reached greener pastures.

It is in this respect worth noting that Europeans tend to focus on the dependency relations as they are believed to be valid in non-European countries. It is true that interdependency among family members outside Europe may be of a different nature, but it is often forgotten that an important feature in any society is the change of responsibility characteristics. Children used to be responsible for the well-being of their parents. However, over the years, in particular also following state-involvement through social welfare benefits for the elderly, this responsibility has changed from children/parents to parents/children only, meaning that in a great many societies the parents are responsible for the well-being of their children without the latter assuming a similar responsibility once the parents are in need. Remarkably, this change results in, or develops parallel to, the decreasing number of children being born: with a one-way responsibility only, the urge to have many children becomes less, whereas the increasing costs of educating children has a similar effect.

The belief that Third World societies will continue patterns of responsibility which have changed in Europe some 50 to 75 years ago is naïve and due to mistaken remains of once popular 'cultural relativism'. Urbanization – the biggest trigger and result of migratory movements – normally results in changed patterns of family responsibilities and the number of births. If generosity is based on Third World characteristics, it would be the result of mistaken presumptions.

CHARACTERISTICS

These days, thousands of families are split. Some of them voluntarily, most, however, involuntarily. It often concerns guest-workers with their families staying behind in the country of origin; children at boarding schools with the parents abroad or in rural areas; children living in foster homes, where they may have been placed by the country's authorities; sailors at sea, with the family back home in the harbour town; soldiers and officers, fighting a war far away from home; prison inmates; refugees fleeing from war with their families still in their war-torn country; persons enjoying temporary protection in one country with other members of the family enjoying the same protection in another country; and last but not least, individuals who have been granted asylum e.g. for humanitarian reasons, but who are, as yet, not entitled to family reunification.

Family life can be experienced in different ways. It is definitely not certain that a family should live together day after day. In this respect there is a big difference between nomadic and sedentary people: in nomadic societies, the economic necessities force many families to be separated during the major part of the year; the men wander around with their herds, whereas the women tend to live a more settled life. Hunting

---

[6] See e.g. the new Netherlands Aliens Act, Art. 29.1.f.

in general involves a high level of mobility. And hunting may take the form of trying to capture animals, or the acquisition of contracts and/or profitable deals. Airports are filled with modern-day hunters.

In virtually all societies, families are considered the cornerstone of society, for security, economic and, of course, procreation reasons. In some (mostly experimental) forms, the family is abolished in favour of slightly bigger groups: the labour unit, the kibbutz in its early form, the commune, religious sects. The importance of the family as the basic unit of society has, however, been embedded in virtually all cultures, in traditions, prescriptions, law, legal norms and religious teaching.

In view of the various traditions and regulations, it is therefore not a surprise to see that these views are confirmed in the 1948 Universal Declaration of Human Rights, arts. 10 and 16 in particular. Article 16.3 of this Declaration reads as follows: '... The family is the natural and fundamental group unit of society and is entitled to protection by society and the state ...'

We need to analyze how international instruments have dealt with the family concept, and in particular to describe how the principle of family unity and reunification has been embedded, interpreted and looked upon in this context.

The issue of family unity and reunification is often blurred by related issues like the minimum age for marriage[7], the issue of consent to marriage[8], polygamy[9] and marriage by proxy.[10] Of importance is also that the main texts refer to the principle of

---

[7] Minimum Age: Among the fundamental rights and freedoms included in the Universal Declaration is the right to marry and to found a family. The article refers to men and women of full age. That could mean that there is a minimum age for marriage and that child marriages should be prevented. It is believed, though, that the only limitation is linked to the physical fitness of the prospective spouses, in particular their capability of procreating, rather than to (intellectual) maturity. This issue has been taken up on various occasions, which has resulted in various instruments:
– 1962, Convention on Consent to Marriage, Minimum Age for Marriage and Registration of Marriage;
– 1965, UN General Assembly: Recommendation on Consent to Marriage. The latter instrument specifically provides a minimum age of no less than 15 years.

[8] Consent to Marriage. Involuntary or forced marriage has been defined as slavery-like practice. Instruments like the Supplementary Convention on the Abolition of Slavery, the Slave Trade, and Institutions and Practices Similar to Slavery, and the Convention on the Elimination of All Forms of Discrimination against Women, as well as other instruments mentioned in the text are of relevance. Literature would seem to indicate that marriages as a result of arrangements between the parents (or by the parents of one partner and the prospective partner directly) are to be considered as consenting marriages, as long as the bride and groom are present at the ceremonies.

[9] Polygamy. The main texts seem to avoid the issue of polygamy. However, the principle of equality as guaranteed by Article 23.4 of the relevant 1966 Covenant (CCPR) is at stake. The European Commission of Human Rights has expressly cited monogamy as a possible restriction (for entry or sojourn) in a few cases (Eriksson, *The Right to Marry and to Found a Family (A World-Wide Human Right)*, Uppsala 1990, p. 101). In France the Conseil d'Etat has expressed the view that the authorities are not entitled to issue a deportation order against a polygamous wife solely on the ground of '*ordre public*' (Eriksson 1990, p. 102).

[10] Marriage by proxy. In some countries where e.g. the influence of Islamic law on the legal system is considerable, the proxy has the power to decide if and with whom a marriage can be concluded (Eriksson 1990, p. 92). This, it could be argued, violates the principle of free and full consent

family unity and the respect thereof. Thus, it is the unity of the family which is being referred to, rather than reunification. Only gradually has the concept of reunification come to the surface and is now slowly being codified. Whilst analyzing the various texts and developments, it is worth keeping these differences and the development concerned in mind. Of paramount importance is also the need to differentiate between rights and respect as well as between protection and assistance.

RIGHTS & RESPECT; PROTECTION AND ASSISTANCE

The 1948 Universal Declaration states that the family is entitled to protection. In this respect it is worth noting that the Universal Declaration does not use the term 'right' in the context of the family principle. This might appear somewhat remarkable as virtually all other relevant articles of the Universal Declaration have a formula such as 'everyone has the right to ...' Where it concerns 'right' it has been stated that men and women have the right to marry and to found a family. It does not refer to family life as such, nor to family unity.

In fact, to understand the present (legal) position of the family, family unity and family reunification, we need to pay proper attention to the various formulations used. As we shall see, there is at first sight no consistency in the terminology. It would appear that various concepts are used without any obvious pattern:

Rights
The term 'right' has been used in the context of the 'right to marry' and the 'right to found a family'. Moreover, the relevant 1966 Covenant (ICCPR, Art. 17.2) uses the term 'right to the protection of the law against unlawful interference with the family or unlawful attacks against the family.'

Entitlement
The family is 'entitled to protection by society and the State.'[11] It is believed that the term 'entitlement' does not differ substantially from a right, but, in this very context, 'entitlement to protection' remains fairly vague, as protection is not easily defined in this context.

Protection & Assistance
The concept of 'entitlement to protection' has been used in the Universal Declaration, in the 1966 CCPR, as well as in the 1990 Migrants Convention. In the 1966 CCPR it has in one connection been upgraded to a 'right to protection of the law.' The 1966

---

and/or the principle of presence at the ceremony. Some countries, therefore, find it difficult to pursue family reunification if it concerns a marriage by proxy, (or even 'arranged marriages' for that matter). The Nordics in particular show disagreement with this type of marriage. Yet, many of the former colonial powers are well accustomed to marriage by proxy as it was often a precondition needed for the fiancée to be allowed to join her partner in the colonies.

[11] UDHR Art. 16.3; ICCPR Art. 23.1.

CESCR Covenant (Article 10) has added value, as it introduces the concept 'assistance'; this Covenant goes one step further by stating that: '... the widest possible protection and assistance should be accorded to the family...' Assistance would indicate a slightly more active approach, and thereby goes over and above 'protection', which reflects a more passive attitude. In this respect it should be emphasized that there seems to be a consensus of opinion on the question of safeguarding family unity as an aspect of protection. The 1989 CRC contains in the Preamble a similar formula: 'the family (...) should be afforded the necessary protection and assistance (so that it can fully assume its responsibilities within the community ...'[12]

Respect

The term 'respect', which entails a realistic yet almost passive non-interference approach, has been used in the European Human Rights Convention. This Convention uses both the 'right' and 'respect' elements: everyone has the right to respect for his private and family life; there shall be no interference with the exercise of this right. It is believed that 'respect' is also the essential idea behind the formula used in the 1966 ICCPR Covenant: 'no one shall be subjected to arbitrary or unlawful interference with his family'. Thus most observers seem to agree that the actual wording indicates a respect (combined with protection) for family life, rather than a right to family life.

What we need to acknowledge from the above is that a great many different formulas may have been used, but that apart from the right to marry and to found a family, as well as the respect for family life and the entitlement to protection and assistance, not much has really been codified. However, assistance and protection have been duly agreed upon and thus the principle of family unity has been firmly embedded. It is of importance, though, to acknowledge that the 'right to respect' differs from a straightforward 'right to family life'. One would be forced to conclude (particularly with the abundant, fairly consistent case-law on Article 8 of the European Human Rights Convention in mind) that the obligations which derive from the rights enumerated are limited to respect, protection and non-intervention. These elements focus on action (to be more precise: non-action, abstention) to separate families (cf. decisions to expel just one member of the family), rather than on pro-action towards reunification.

The principle of family unity stands. The right to family unity has, however, not been laid down as clearly as one might have wished. Some learned writers resolve this problem by referring to the right to family unity as part of customary law. I consider this (strategic) move to be rather artificial: the many texts which have been drafted and/or agreed upon would indicate that the right to family unity has not yet reached the level of customary law. The principle of family unity, however, is non-derogatory, and does not need to be discussed. But as so often, the principle has not been interlinked with an absolute right.

---

[12] The Revised European Social Charter (1996, aiming to replace the 1961 European Social Charter) contains an Art. 16 on 'the right of a family to social, legal and economic *protection*'; Art. 19 focuses on 'the right of migrant workers and their families *to protection and assistance*' (emphasis added).

FAMILY

At this juncture it is worth paying some attention to the definition of 'family'. It is of course meant by most to refer to the nuclear family only. The extended family is sometimes promoted as a legal unit. It is, however, herewith submitted that with the ever ongoing urbanization the concept of extended family will slowly disappear. In fact, two divergent developments take place. On the one hand, urbanization with its decreased social control and decreasing family ties, and, on the other, the shift of responsibility, from the emphasis of children looking after their parents to the sole responsibility of parents having to look after the children. Both developments have had and will continue to have an impact on the family structure and presumed dependency patterns.

Elements of contention concern the status of children of, say, 12 or 16 years old, as well as that of married children. The 1990 Migrant Workers Convention gives us some clues. Article 44.2 of this Convention refers to the reunification of the migrant worker with his spouse or person with whom the migrant worker has a relationship that, according to applicable law, produces effects equivalent to marriage, as well as their minor dependent unmarried children. This is a fairly remarkable text, the more so as 'members of the family' have been defined in Article 4 of the same Convention as: '... persons married to the migrant workers or having with them a relationship that, according to applicable law, produces effects equivalent to marriage, as well as their dependent children and other dependent persons who are recognized as members of the family by applicable legislation or applicable bilateral or multilateral agreements between States concerned ....' The latter part can not be retracted to Article 44.2. The difference between 'minor dependent unmarried children' and 'dependent children' is noticeable. Indeed, for the purpose of reunification the 'family' has been limited, understandably in my view, to the nuclear family only.

UNITY / REUNIFICATION

The concept of reunification is a fairly new one. It is believed that the above instruments, without expressly using the term, have agreed on 'unity' as a principle. Unity as a concept has, incidentally, emerged at a fairly early stage in the context of refugees.[13] But, whenever any mention of 'unity' was made, it was often in the context of 'maintaining the unity', by not breaking it up, rather than in the context of 're-unification'.

---

[13] The Conference of Plenipotentiaries which adopted the 1951 Convention Relating to the Status of Refugees refers to the principle of family unity in the Final Act. The principle has not been embedded in the text of the Convention itself nor has it been formulated as a right to family unity and/or family reunification: 'The Conference (...) considering that the unity of family, the natural and fundamental group unit of society, is an essential right of the refugee, and that such unity is constantly threatened; and noting with satisfaction that ... the rights granted to a refugee are extended to members of his family; recommends Governments to take the necessary measures for the protection of the refugee's family, especially with a view to ensuring that the unity of the refugee's family is maintained ...'

Reunification as a concept was introduced at a relatively late stage. I will deal here with the 1989 Convention on the Rights of the Child, the Helsinki process and the 1990 Migrants Convention. The 1994 Cairo Report will be dealt with below.

Convention on the Rights of the Child

The Convention on the Rights of the Child confirms the view of the family as the fundamental group of society '... and the natural environment for the growth and well-being of all its members and particularly children ...'. The family should be accorded '... the necessary protection and assistance so that it can fully assume its responsibilities within the community ...'[14] Articles 9 and 10 of this Convention deal with split families. Article 9.4 focuses on the right of the child who is separated from one or both parents to maintain personal relations and direct contact; '... where such separation results from any action initiated by a State Party, such as detention, imprisonment, exile, deportation or death ... of one or both parents or of the child, that State Party shall, upon request, provide the parents (or) the child ... with the essential information concerning the whereabouts of the absent member(s) of [the] family ....' Article 10.1 then continues by stating that '... applications by a child or his or her parents to enter or to leave a State Party for the purpose of family reunification shall be dealt with by States Parties in a positive, humane and expeditious manner ...'

Of relevance is also Article 22. Therein it is stated, on the one hand, that a refugee child whether accompanied or unaccompanied should receive appropriate protection and humanitarian assistance. On the other hand, it has been carefully formulated that efforts should be supported to trace parents or other members of the family towards reunification: '... States Parties shall provide, as they consider appropriate, co-operation in any effort by the UN and other competent intergovernmental organizations or NGOs to protect and assist such a child and to trace the parents or other members of the family of any refugee child in order to obtain information necessary for reunification with his or her family ...' The fact that this 1989 Convention refers to family reunification and how to deal with it can be considered a very positive step forward. The obligation concerned (Article 10: 'shall') is a strong one, and the words 'positive', 'humane' and 'expeditious' do not leave much room for machination and manipulation. It is, however, to be stressed that it concerns reunification of the child with his/her parents and not necessarily the unification of the father with the mother/child. This has also to be concluded as Article 10.2 refers to children whose parents live in different States (and the right to regular visits).

Helsinki

In the context of the Helsinki Process some references to the subject can be found. Most texts refer to migrant workers (e.g. the aim to facilitate, as far as possible, the reuniting of migrant workers with their families). In fact a whole chapter was dedicated to this issue, but again, no recognition of any right: '... the states will deal in a

---

[14] Quotes from the CRC Preamble.

positive and humanitarian spirit with the applications ...' Of importance, though, is that the term 'reunification' has been introduced.[15]

The Migrants Convention

The December 1990 International Convention on the Protection of the Rights of all Migrant Workers and Members of their Families addresses the issue at stake in a very positive manner, but does not, in my opinion, define the right to family reunification as a human right as such. It takes into account that 'migration is often the cause of serious problems for the members of the families of migrant workers as well as for the workers themselves in particular because of the scattering of the family.' It also recognizes that the family is the natural and fundamental group unit of society and is entitled to protection by society and the state. Article 44.2 states: 'State Parties shall take measures that they deem appropriate and that fall within their competence to facilitate the reunification of migrant workers with their [family] ...' This codification does not amount to a recognition of an (absolute) right to family reunification. Too many careful words have been used: 'shall take measures that they deem appropriate'; 'to facilitate', etc., but the text does not avoid the reunification issue either.[16]

MIGRANTS

In the discussion on the issue concerned, due reference needs to be made to the difference between migrants and refugees. Moreover, dividing lines have been drawn between documented (legal) and undocumented (irregular) migrants. There is also a difference between convention refugees and victims of war. The various instruments do make this differentiation. As we will note, it is quite remarkable that migrants (that is the documented ones) seem to be somewhat better off than refugees, as more formal instruments have been agreed upon concerning the status of migrant workers and their families. On the other hand, instruments on the civilian population in areas of war contain some extremely relevant keys to understanding some of the underlying issues. The convention refugees have been dealt with (as far as unity and reunification is concerned) in the final act of the main instrument (i.e. the 1951 Refugee Convention) and some relevant Conclusions have been agreed upon by the Executive Committee of the UNHCR Programme (ExCom).

By the mid-1970s it became clear that the movements of migrant workers had reached substantial proportions and that migrant workers constitute an important eco-

---

[15] Reference should *inter alia* be made to the Final Act (1975), the Human Dimension Conferences (Copenhagen 1989, Moscow 1990) and in particular the so-called Third basket. The 1983 CSCE Madrid meeting clearly stated that the participating States will favourably deal with applications relating to contacts and regular meetings on the basis of family ties, reunification and marriage of citizens of different States. This statement, however, should be seen in the light of the cold war and the related tension between East and West.

[16] Various other instruments also refer to the issue at stake, e.g. ILO instruments, the European Social Charter 1961, para. 6; the European Convention on the Legal status of Migrant Workers 1977 [in force since 1983]; CoE Res. (78)33, all of which, however, do not significantly differ from the texts included hereinabove.

nomic, social and human factor for host countries as well as for countries of origin. It was realized that most migrant workers had come to stay and could no longer be regarded as a temporary feature. This, of course, had a tremendous impact on the related issue of family reunification. It is, therefore, no suprise to see that virtually all relevant instruments deal with the latter issue in a positive and constructive spirit. However, none of the instruments recognize the right to family reunification as a human right, not even the extremely important December 1990 Migrant Workers Convention, although Perruchoud indicates in this context that recent studies on the matter recognize that the reunification of families is an independent and separate right which is closely linked to the right to leave and return. He admits, however, that the right to leave one's country has not been completed by a right to enter another country, whereby a right to reunification becomes very artificial indeed.[17]

EUROPE

It is no surprise that the European Community/Union has also been dealing with the issue at stake. A resolution on the harmonization of national policies on family reunification was adopted by the 'Ministers of Member States of the European Communities responsible for Immigration' on 1 June 1993. The Resolution covers non-EC immigrant residents in the respective Member States. It does not cover refugees 'for whom some Member States have more favourable policies'. It has been stated that the Member States will normally grant admission to the resident's spouse and children. The term 'resident' refers to non-EC nationals who are lawfully resident within the territory of a Member State on a basis which affords them an expectation of permanent or long-term residence. Polygamous relations are excluded to some extent: 'a wife and her children will not be admitted for the purpose of family reunification if the marriage is polygamous and the resident already has a wife resident in the territory of a Member State.' The maximum age for children should be between 16 and 18 years. 'Member States reserve the right to require non-EC nationals to be lawfully present in their territory for certain periods on time before family members may be reunited with them under the terms of these principles.' 'Member States reserve the right to make the entry and stay of family members conditional upon the availability of adequate accommodation and of sufficient resources to avoid a burden being placed on ... public funds ..., and on the existence of sickness insurance.'

Moreover, the Resolution also contains references to 'a threat to national security or public policy (ordre publique) and public health'. It thus confirms the fact that the right to family reunification in a country of one's choice is far from having been recognized.

Similarly, the 1999 Commission Proposal for a Council Directive as amended following the various procedural moves (October 2000[18]), is far from inclusive: It refers

---

[17] Perruchoud, Family Reunification, in: *Quarterly Review of the Intergovernmental Committee for Migration (IOM)*, December 1989, pp. 507-524, at p. 519.

to TEC Article 63.3.a in that the Council is to adopt measures relating to the conditions of entry and residence and standards on procedures for the issue by member States of long term visas and residence permits, including those for the purpose of family reunification. Those measures must be adopted in conformity with the obligation to protect the family and respect family life. Family reunification is considered a necessary way of making family life possible. It helps to create socio-cultural stability facilitating the integration of third-country nationals, which also serves to promote economic and social cohesion. The proposed Council Directive, however, does not cover family reunification enjoying subsidiary forms of protection. The Proposal on Temporary Protection clearly states in Article 13 that it does not provide for a right to family reunification '...as it is felt that the temporary nature of the situation does not allow for the exercise of this right in the same form ...' [19]

The main Proposal applies to members of the nuclear family (i.e. spouse and minor children) and may also cover unmarried partners, in as far as corresponding legislation in the Member State is concerned. It is then stated that reunification should also apply to children of full age and to relatives in the ascending line where for important, objective reasons, their personal situation prevents them from living, in acceptable conditions and self-sufficiently, separately from their relative, who is a third-country national lawfully residing in a Member State.

Applications shall be submitted when the family members are outside the territory of the Member State (not: outside the Union), but applications shall be examined when the family members are already residing in the territory in exceptional cases or on humanitarian grounds.

REACTIONS

It is now fully acknowledged that by inviting migrants (guest-workers) or by granting asylum (refugees), regard should be had not only to the ones directly involved, but in particular also to subsequent developments regarding the family, marriage etc. Family reunification has been and still is by far the biggest contributor to the net influx of foreigners to the Union. This is in particular the case as second and third-generation members of a group of immigrants may wish to marry partners from the country of the parents' or grandparents' origin, irrespective of whether the citizenship of the country of residence has in the meantime been obtained. Fake marriages (and fake adoptions) took place on a fairly large scale, often only to grant the 'partners' a residence permit. Abuse was widespread and loopholes in the legislation were easily found.

Against this background it comes as no surprise that various European countries continuously elaborate their respective aliens acts, moving in a direction to frustrate marriages of convenience on the one hand, and making genuine family reunification

---

[18] COM(2000) 624 final; 1999/0258 (CNS).
[19] Commission Proposal dated 25 May 2000 (COM)2000.

and/or family formation easier on the other. **Denmark**, for instance, is in the process of developing interesting views, as included in a 2000 draft law:[20]

> The purpose of the Bill is to ensure that spouses are only granted reunification when the spouses or the cohabitants have aggregate ties with Denmark of such strength that they should be reunited in Denmark.
>
> For assessment of the requirement of ties, the period that the resident has lived in Denmark as well as his or her ties with other residents in Denmark, including family resident in Denmark, will be emphasised. It will also be emphasised whether the resident has been educated or trained in Denmark or has a firm attachment to the Danish labour market. Furthermore, the resident's skills in the Danish language and his or her ties with another country will be emphasised.
>
> In addition, the applicant's ties with Denmark must be emphasised. In this connection, the same circumstances as stated above for the resident will be emphasised. Furthermore, the applicant's ties with another country must be emphasised, including whether the applicant has children or other family in another country.
>
> The requirement of ties will usually be satisfied if the resident was born and grew up in Denmark or arrived here as a child.[21]
>
> The legal entitlement to reunification with a spouse that applies to young people under 25 years of age will be repealed. Instead it will become possible to grant young people over 18 years, but under 25 years of age reunification with their spouse if the marriage or the cohabitation must undoubtedly be considered contracted or entered into by the resident's own will.
>
> The purpose of the Bill is to protect young people against contraction of marriages against their own will.[22]

---

[20] Summary of Bill No. L 208 of 29 February 2000 amending the Aliens Act and other Acts (Requirement of own dwelling for family reunification purposes, requirement of ties for reunification with spouse, and efforts against marriages not based on the parties' free will).

[21] In special cases, particular personal circumstances may have the effect that spouses must be granted reunification after all, despite the fact that the spouses or cohabitants have aggregate ties with Denmark that do not at least equal their aggregate ties with another country.

[22] In their assessment of this issue, the immigration authorities have to include all information available in the matter. The authorities can emphasise the circumstances under which the marriage was contracted as well as the spouses' personal contact prior to the marriage. The fact that the marriage was contracted with the assistance of their families does not in itself preclude the authorities from deeming the marriage to have been contracted by the resident's own will. To illustrate the actual facts of the case, the immigration authorities may base their decision on testimony from persons other than the spouses. Even if it is not evident whether a marriage or cohabitation was contracted or entered into by the resident's own will, particular personal circumstances may have the effect that the spouses have to be granted reunification, for example in a case of permanent cohabitation of some duration.

UN, CAIRO 1994[23]

The issue of family unity and family reunification was addressed *inter alia* at the International Conference on Population and Development which was held in Cairo in 1994. The Conference dealt above all with the need to increase awareness of the impact of population growth on development. A hotly debated issue was the paragraph on birth control ('reproductive health'), a topic which will remain on the agenda for a great many years to come.[24]

One of the, at first sight, less popular items dealt with family reunification. Efforts had been undertaken to codify the principle of the right to family reunification. Many observers were ever so slightly disappointed with the outcome. This was particularly the case as there had been a heavy lobby to grant legal migrants the right to family reunification. In fact, a proposal to this effect was duly tabled (by above all Third World countries). Western countries objected to this idea, however.

The increased importance of the subject of international migration had been recognized in ECOSOC Resolution 1991/93 which scheduled the 1994 Cairo International Conference on Population and Development Cairo. 'Population Distribution and Migration' was identified as one of the six issues requiring attention at this conference. The subject of international migration was, quite significantly, sub-divided into:
a) international migration and development;
b) documented migrants;
c) undocumented migrants; and
d) refugees, asylum seekers and displaced persons.

The family reunification issue was above all dealt with under (b) documented migrants. Documented migrants were defined as '... those who satisfy all the legal requirements to enter, stay and, if applicable, hold employment in the country of destination ...' In the proposed text it was stated in the chapter on documented migrants that 'Governments of receiving countries must ensure the protection of migrants and their families, [and recognize the right to family reunification] ...' The part within brackets had been contested and was open to discussion. Many G-77 delegates wanted the brackets removed and to see this right recognized and codified. That was not to be. First and foremost, the Western countries were not able or willing to go that far. Some compromises were proposed, but the Main Committee had to refer this issue to a sub-committee specially set up for the purpose of finding a suitable compromise. After protracted negotiations the Main Committee finally agreed to delete the text within brackets and to add the following sentence: '... consistent with Article 10 of the Convention on the Rights of the Child and all other relevant universally recognized human rights instruments, all Governments, particularly those of receiving

---

[23] This part is based on – and often identical to – my contribution 'Cairo and Family-Reunification' published in *AWR-Bulletin* Vol. 33/42, No. 2-3/1995, pp. 51-65.

[24] See e.g. the January 2001 exchange of letters between the Commission and various EU ministers on the US Administration's stance on assistance to international organizations which might promote abortion.

countries, must recognize the vital importance of family reunification and promote its integration into their national legislation in order to ensure the protection of family unity of the families of documented migrants ...'[25] Moreover, in the next paragraph of this document it was stated that '... governments are urged to promote, through family reunion, the normalization of the family life of legal migrants who have the right to long-term residence ...'

It should be stressed that the following sub-chapters of the Cairo document (on undocumented migrants and refugees etc) do **not** contain any reference to family re-unification or family unity for that matter. Family reunification had also been dealt with in Chapter V of the Conference document, which dealt with 'the family, its roles, rights, composition and structure', (part B on 'socio-economic support to the family', to be more precise), in the context of victimized families. In that context it has been stated that: '... Governments and the international community should give greater attention to, and manifest greater solidarity with, poor families and families that have been victimized by war, drought, famine, natural disasters and racial and ethnic discrimination or violence. Every effort should be made to keep their members together, to reunite them in case of separation and to ensure access to government programmes designed to support and assist those vulnerable families ...'[26] This result is rather meagre. And the present author thus feels forced to submit that the Cairo Conference has indeed contributed a great deal to the issue of family reunification. Not by agreeing on the right hereto, but rather by clearly indicating that the time for a fully-fledged recognition of this right on the global scale has not yet materialized.

DIFFERENTIATION

It is worthwhile to differentiate between migrants, victims of war and convention refugees. It should be realized that they do indeed represent different categories.

While developments concerning the family unity and reunification of migrant workers should be closely scrutinized, it should always be stressed that migrant work-ers are voluntary migrants, whereas victims of war and convention refugees are invol-untary migrants. This should enable all the parties involved to agree that the latter groups should always enjoy a treatment which is at least as favourable as the one granted to migrant workers, if not better. Whenever Helsinki, Strasbourg and UN in-struments talk about the facilitation of the reunification of migrant workers with their families, involuntary migrants deserve the same, if not more and better.

CONCLUSION

A realistic, pragmatic approach is necessary:

– reunification is above all an issue for migrant workers; their status seems to have been fairly well codified, albeit true that the 1990 Migrants Convention has hitherto

---

[25] Ibidem, paragraph 10.12.

[26] Paragraph 5.12 of the Report of the International Conference on Population and Development A/CONF.171/13 dated 18 October 1994, p. 34.

yielded very few ratifications indeed; however, as it concerns voluntary deprivation from family life, a straightforward approach should be considered acceptable; Cairo's outcome (the need to 'recognize the vital importance of family reunification', and to 'promote, through family reunion, the normalization of family life') should hence come as no surprise.

– short-term labour is by definition of a temporary nature; once family unity comes into the equation, experience shows that return becomes increasingly difficult to contemplate and materialize. The Swiss have successfully implemented a short-term labour programme (9 months of work; 3 months in the country of origin), which has been effective also because of the non-reunification. Now that NGOs are starting to question this – in their eyes inhuman – imposition, changes may be imposed. However, such 9/3 schemes are bound to fail if the family would be allowed to join.

– family reunification should not necessarily take place in the country where only one member of the family resides, or which is the furthest away from the country of origin: reunification in the region of origin should be considered a valid option; regard may also have to be had to where the family breadwinner(s) find themselves, as well as to where repatriation could most successfully be implemented from, once that would become a viable option.

– most experts are of the opinion that efforts to agree on the principle of the extended family are not supported by legal texts; although it is surely desirable to take circumstances and traditions in the country of origin into account, efforts to insist on these considerations are at this juncture counterproductive and are bound to be outdated, as the Third World is moving in a direction which will not be too different from developments which occurred elsewhere over the last 100 years or so.

As yet, there is no well-defined right to family reunification, but the proposed Council Directive (see Chapter 3.4.2) has indeed the purpose to establish such a right. Yet, due attention should be paid to the numbers involved as family reunification is the foremost instrument to subscribe to the *adagium* that migration generates migration. There is as yet no right to migration, and the right to family reunification for migrants should hence be looked upon from both the humanitarian and utilitarian angles. After all, the migrant should be considered perfectly able to return to his/her country of origin and to enjoy family life and the desired family unity, if he/she so wishes. If the country where the migrant worker is residing wants him/her to stay, then indeed family reunification in that country should be considered part of the equation.

EC/EU INSTRUMENTS

Introduction and Detailed Contents[1]

WHAT IS THE 'ACQUIS'?[2]

The term Acquis is normally reserved for the Acquis Communautaire; this is the sum of legislation, standards and practices which have been developed within the Community framework (First Pillar), which governs Member State actions in matters within the competence of the Community and which cannot be disassociated from the achievements of the objectives of the Community. The European Court of Justice (ECJ) has jurisdiction over the Acquis Communautaire.

Instruments, standards and practices have also been developed within the framework of the Union, i.e. in the Second and Third Pillars. Here, following the European Council formula, we should use the term 'Acquis of the Union and its Member States', or: 'Third-pillar Acquis'. Often the term 'Union Acquis' is used, which indeed correctly describes what it is all about.

For the purpose of this Handbook, we refer to this wider set of EU instruments and standards. The Union Acquis should be adopted and transposed into policy and practice by each Member State and it must be accepted by candidate countries as a condition for EU membership. Of paramount importance, however, is that the 'Union Acquis' is now being transformed into 'Acquis Communautaire' as a direct result of the Treaty of Amsterdam.

THE EU ACQUIS ON MIGRATION

Prior to the TEU I (Maastricht) migration policy had been handled as a matter of cooperation between Member States outside the European Community institutions, as migration policy was not mentioned in the Treaty on the European Communities.

---

[1] This Chapter has been prepared and edited by Ms Sabrina van Miltenburg, IND Schiphol.

[2] Based on the text prepared under the PHP asylum. See also *The Asylum Acquis Handbook* op. cit. pp. 83 and 115-122, as well *as Practitioner Commentaries on the EU Acquis on Asylum* (Vienna, 2000), pp. 3-39, which, however, focuses solely on the issue of asylum.

P.J. van Krieken (Ed.), The Migration Acquis Handbook
© *2001, T.M.C.Asser Press, The Hague, the Röling Foundation and the authors*

In the TEU I, migration policy became listed with other justice and home affairs areas in Title VI 'Provisions on co-operation in the fields of Justice and Home Affairs' as a 'matter of common interest' for the Member States (Article K.1). Migration was hence a matter of cooperation within the Union, between the Union Members, but continued to fall within the sovereignty of each and every State: the respective capitals remained responsible.

WHAT IS COMMUNITARISATION?

In order for an instrument to be officially considered to be part of the EU Acquis Communautaire, the official decision taking mechanisms involving the main institutions[3] of the EU's First Pillar must be utilised to incorporate the instrument into the body of EC laws and legislation.[4]

TEU II (Amsterdam) allows for the 'communitarisation' of virtually all of the instruments, which today make up the EU Acquis on migration. Once the instruments have been taken into the First Pillar they will form part of the Acquis Communautaire. In a way, 'Brussels' will take over from the respective capitals.

In Article 63 of TEC a 'Five Year Window' (five-year time limit after its ratification by all Member States) for the 'communitarisation' of specified migration measures is formally set out. The 'communitarisation' of such measures will follow the procedure outlined in Article 67. This process should be over by 1 May 2004, five years upon the entering into force of the Treaty of Amsterdam.

TEXTS OF THE EU ACQUIS ON MIGRATION

In May 1998 the Acquis of the Union and of its Member States on Justice and Home Affairs was listed and formally approved by the Committee of Permanent Representatives of the Council Members – Coreper, and in December 1998 an addendum was issued.[5] The EU Acquis on migration contains the instruments relevant for the development of asylum systems in the CEECs.[6]

The relevant documents which make up the EU Acquis on migration are taken from the parts dealing with Migration (III) and Human Rights Related Issues (XII) of the Justice and Home Affairs Acquis which comprises twelve sub-sections.

International conventions, which are regarded as indissociable from the achievements of the objectives of the EU, are considered to be part of the EU Acquis. In mi-

---

[3] The EU Commission, Council of Ministers and European Parliament.

[4] The EU Commission and the EU Member States acting through the Council are responsible for drafting instruments and amending successive drafts. Theoretically, the European Court of Justice has jurisdiction over the interpretation of such instruments.

[5] The complete list can be found in (Van Krieken:) *The Asylum Acquis Handbook* (The Hague 2000, ISBN 90-6704-122-X), Chapter 2. That Chapter (pp. 83-114) contains the original 1998/1999 list, a chronological list, a topical list, and the TAIEX list, but focuses above all on the issue of asylum.

[6] Central and Eastern European Countries with agreements to join the EU.

gration matters these include the European Convention on Human Rights and Fundamental Freedoms (ECHR), the Dublin Convention and its implementing provisions, Joint Actions and Positions adopted by the Council, Resolutions, Decisions and Ministerial Conclusions which have been adopted.

For clarity these documents have been divided into three categories:
1. International conventions to be regarded as indissociable from the achievements of the objectives of the EU related to migration;
2. Instruments adopted by Member States before the entry into force of the TEU I (Maastricht);
3. Instruments adopted by the Council after the entry into force of the TEU I (Maastricht).

INSTRUMENTS ADOPTED BY MEMBER STATES BEFORE THE ENTRY INTO FORCE OF THE TEU I (MAASTRICHT)

A series of instruments have been agreed upon at Ministerial level in order to improve the implementation of the Dublin Convention. These instruments include a standard form for *inter alia* the application of the family reunion criteria.

INSTRUMENTS ADOPTED BY THE COUNCIL AFTER THE ENTRY INTO FORCE OF THE TEU I (MAASTRICHT)

– Council Recommendations concerning readmission agreements (Brussels, 30 November 1994 and 24 July 1995). The Council Recommendations concerning readmission agreements are listed under the EU acquis on migration. They are an important reality as readmission agreements are designed to facilitate the return of asylum applicants rejected on the basis of safe third country grounds or because their claim has been determined to be manifestly unfounded. Two Council Recommendations have been produced, one concerning a specimen bilateral readmission agreement, and the second which sets out the guiding principles to be followed in the drawing up of readmission agreements.

– Council Resolution on Unaccompanied Minors who are Nationals of Third Countries (Brussels, 26 June 1997).[7] This Council Resolution concerns third-country nationals below the age of eighteen who arrive on the territory of a Member State unaccompanied or not awaited upon arrival by an adult responsible for them. It also applies to minors who are left after being brought into the territory of the Member States. The Resolution establishes guidelines for the treatment of unaccompanied minors (UAM) with regard to reception, stay and return conditions and the handling of their applications for asylum, taking into consideration the particular needs of minors and their vulnerable situation. The Resolution also especially recognises the need to provide, as soon as possible, the assistance of a legal guardian, either a specifically appointed adult representative or an institution. The resolution also stresses the im-

---

[7] OJ No. C 221, 19.07.97, p. 23.

portance of making efforts to trace the minor's relatives in order to, whenever possible and in the best interest of the child, reunite him/her with them.

AN OVERVIEW OF RECENT OR PLANNED COMMISSION PROPOSALS RELATING TO IMMIGRATION POLICY[8]

1. Proposal for a Council Regulation amending Regulation (EEC) No. 1408/71 as regards its extension to nationals of third countries (COM (97) 561 final)
2. Proposal for a European Parliament and Council Regulation amending Council Regulation (EEC) No. 1612/68 on freedom of movement for workers within the Community (COM (98) 394 final)
3. Directive implementing the principle of equal treatment between persons irrespective of racial or ethnic origin (Directive 2000/43, OJ 19/7/2000 L 180)
4. Directive on discrimination in employment on the grounds of religion or belief, disability, age or sexual orientation (COM (99) 565 final) (presented in October 1999)
5. Council Decision establishing a Community Action Programme to combat discrimination 2001-2006 (COM (2000) 649) (adopted in October 2000)
6. Directive on the right to family reunification (presented in December 1999) amended version October 2000 Directive concerning the status of third county nationals who are long-term residents in a Member State (February 2001)
7. Directive on the conditions of entry and residence for the purpose of study or vocational training (first half of 2001)
8. Directive on the conditions of entry and residence for the purpose of unpaid activities (first half of 2001)
9. Directive on the conditions of entry and residence for paid employment and self-employed economic activity (first half of 2001). Mobilisation on the collection of statistics relating to migration on the basis of the collection which started in 1998 (first half of 2001) Communication on return policy (first half of 2001)
10. Proposals for a co-ordination and monitoring procedure for the implementation of the Community immigration policy
11. Proposals for a Community Action Programme to promote the integration of third country nationals concerning horizontal measures to support the exchange of experience and the development of good practice.[9]

---

[8] Annex 2 to the 22 November 2000 Migration Communication (see elsewhere in this Handbook: Chapter 2). Reference should also be made to the 'scoreboard', a twice yearly exercise to check the step-by-step approach (e.g. COM(2000) 782 final, 30 November 2000). It is recalled that the Stockholm meeting of February 2001 expressed concern relating to the progress which had been made up to that time. It is herewith submitted, however, that the Art. 63 process as a whole would appear to be on track. One important discussion which is avoided concerns the *minimum* norms versus the need to formulate (absolute) 'norms'. See e.g. Van Krieken in the International Spectator (The Hague), March 2001.
[9] Mention should also be made of some instruments (not included in this Handbook) which have been listed in the Council Proposal on Family Reunification (see Chapter 3.4.2): Council Directive 64/221/EEC of 25 February 1964 on the coordination of special measures concerning the movement

STRUCTURE OF THIS CHAPTER 3

In Part 3.1 the relevant parts of Title IV TEC have been reproduced, as well as from the Vienna Action Plan, the Tampere 'Milestones' and the Nice 2000 Charter of the Fundamental Rights of the EU.

Parts 3.2-3.7 contain virtually all the instruments which are considered to belong to the Migration Acquis and/or on the TAIEX list. They have been completed by recent relevant instruments e.g. the (amended) Commission Proposal for a Council Directive on Family Reunification and the Eurodac Regulation which has been agreed upon in December 2000. The set-up follows a thematic approach:

3.2   Entry
3.3   Sojourn
3.4   Family
3.5   Illegal Migration
3.6   Return
3.7   Training, Assistance and Cooperation

Moreover, part 3.8 contains a list of relevant Council Documents 1998-2001.

This Handbook is fairly up to date, but it is realized that the developments are many, not least because of the debate as launched by Commissioner Vitoríno, which may result in an acceleration of awareness building and decision making. It is believed that this Handbook, this Chapter 3 in particular, will assist in the efforts towards the foundation of a common European migration policy.

---

and residence of foreign nationals which are justified on grounds of public policy, public security or public health; Council Directive 68/360/EEC of 15 October 1968 on the abolition of restrictions on movement and residence within the Community for workers of Member States and their families; Regulation (EEC) No 1251/70 of the Commission of 29 June 1970 on the right of workers to remain in the territory of a Member State after having been employed in that State; Council Directive 73/148/EEC of 21 May 1973 on the abolition of restrictions on movement and residence within the Community for nationals of Member States with regard to establishment and the provision of services; Council Directive 75/34/EEC of 17 December 1974 concerning the right of nationals of a Member State to remain in the territory of another Member State after having pursued therein an activity in a self-employed capacity; Council Directive 90/364/EEC of 28 June 1990 on the right of residence; Council Directive 90/365/EEC of 28 June 1990 on the right of residence for employees and self-employed persons who have ceased their occupational activity; Council Directive 93/96/EEC of 29 October 1993 on the right of residence for students.

CONTENTS CHAPTER 3

---

[10] See also the Council Regulation 574/99 listing which nationals need to apply for visa.OJ L 72, 12 March 1999 (not included in this Handbook).

[11] An asterix (*) indicates that the instrument concerned has been included in this Handbook, but under a different heading; a reference to the relevant number has been duly made: (see…), in this case: document 3.2.12.

[12] See also the Council recommendation on the provision for the detection of falsified documents in the vida departments of representations abroad and in the offices of domestic authorities dealing with the issue or extension of visas (OC J 140, 20 May 1999) (not included in this Handbook).

---

[13] On 24 February 1997 the Council adopted a Joint Action concerning action to combat trafficking in human beings and the sexual exploitation of children. Following the Palermo 2000 UN
Convention and Protocols on inter alia trafficking, the Commission has submitted in early 2001 a
proposal for a Council Framework Decision on combating trafficking in human beings (see the Explanatory Memorandum re COM (2001/0024 CNS). Due attention to this proposal has been paid in
Chapter 2.4, Views on Trafficking.

[14] Reference should also be made to two Council recommendations on false documents: (a) recommendation on the provision of equipment for the detection of false documents at points of entry
in the EU (OJ C 189, 17 June 1998), and (b) recommendation on the provision for the detection of
falsified documents in the vida departments of representations abroad and in the offices of domestic
authorities dealing with the issue or extension of visas (OC J 140, 20 May 1999) (not included in
this Handbook).

---

[15] It could be argued that a reference to the September 2000 Refugee Fund would be relevant.
However, as that Fund covers above all projects in the realm of asylum (including the return of refugees and asylum seekers), it was decided not to include this instrument in this Handbook.

---

[16] Reference should also be made to the 'position commune du 25 octobre 1996 concernant les missions d'assistance et d'information effectuées en amont de la frontière' OJ L 281, 31 October 1996 (not included in this Handbook).

General   3.1

TEC Title IV   3.1.1
(Visas, Asylum, Immigration and Other Policies Related to Free Movement of Persons[1])

Article 61
In order to establish progressively an area of freedom, security and justice, the Council shall adopt:

(a) within a period of five years after the entry into force of the Treaty of Amsterdam[2], measures aimed at ensuring the free movement of persons in accordance with Article 14, in conjunction with directly related flanking measures with respect to external border controls, asylum and immigration in accordance with the provisions of Articles 62(2), 62(3), 63(1)(a) and 63(2)(a) and measures to prevent and combat crime in accordance with the provisions of Article 31(e) of the Treaty on European Union;

(b) other measures in the fields of asylum, immigration and safeguarding the rights of nationals of third countries, in accordance with the provisions of Article 63;

(c) measures in the field of judicial cooperation in civil matters as provided for in Article 65;

(d) appropriate measures to encourage and strengthen administrative cooperation, as provided for in Article 66;

(e) measures in the field of police and judicial cooperation in criminal matters aimed at a high level of security by preventing and combating crime within the Union in accordance with the provisions of the Treaty on European Union.

---

[1] Ed.: It concerns Title IV of the (revised) Consolidated Version of the Treaty Establishing the European Community (TEC).The 1997 Treaty of Amsterdam amended the TEC and TEU, the two major treaties governing European cooperation and integration. We now hence speak of:
1) The Consolidated Version of the Treaty on European Union, which is, in fact, an amendment of the 1991 Maastricht Treaty, and
2) Consolidated Version of the Treaty Establishing the European Community, which, in fact, is an amended version of the, already quite often amended 1957 Rome Treaty.
Concerning this Title, it needs to be stressed that the new Title IV of the EC Treaty is not applicable to the United Kingdom and Ireland, unless they 'opt in' in the manner provided by the Protocol on the position of the United Kingdom and Ireland which is annexed to the Treaties. At the Council meeting (Justice and Home Affairs) on 12 March 1999, these two Member States announced their intention of being fully associated with Community activities in the field of asylum. It will be for them to embark on the appropriate procedure under the Protocol in due course. Title IV of the EC Treaty is likewise not applicable to Denmark, by virtue of the Protocol on the position of Denmark which is annexed to the Treaties. Denmark has so far given no notice of an intention to embark on a procedure to participate in e.g. the Eurodac system or other related instruments/directives.

[2] Ed.: The Treaty of Amsterdam entered into force on 1 May 1999. The period referred to runs, therefore through 30 April 2004. But note the last sentence of this Article, referring to 2(b), 3(a) and 4.

Article 62
The Council, acting in accordance with the procedure referred to in Article 67, shall, within a period of five years after the entry into force of the Treaty of Amsterdam, adopt
(1) measures with a view to ensuring, in compliance with Article 14, the absence of any controls on persons, be they citizens of the Union or nationals of third countries when crossing border;
(2) measures on the crossing of the external borders of the Member States which shall establish:
    (a) standards and procedures to be followed by Member States in carrying out checks on persons at such borders;
    (b) rules on visas for intended stays of no more than three months, including:
        (i) the list of third countries whose nationals must be in possession of visas when crossing the external borders and those whose nationals are exempt from that requirement;
        (ii) the procedures and conditions for issuing visas by Member States;
        (iii) a uniform format for visas;
        (iv) rules on a uniform visa;
(3) measures setting out the conditions under which nationals of third countries shall have the freedom to travel within the territory of the Member States during a period of no more than three months.

Article 63
The Council, acting in accordance with the procedure referred to in Article 67, shall, within a period of five years after the entry into force of the Treaty of Amsterdam, adopt:
(1) measures on asylum, in accordance with the Geneva Convention of 28 July 1951 and the Protocol of 31 January 1967 relating to the status of refugees and other relevant treaties, within the following areas:
    (a) criteria and mechanisms for determining which Member State is responsible for considering an application for asylum submitted by a national of a third country in one of the Member States,
    (b) minimum standards on the reception of asylum seekers in Member States,
    (c) minimum standards with respect to the qualification of nationals of third countries as refugees,
    (d) minimum standards on procedures in Member States for granting or withdrawing refugee status;
(2) measures on refugees and displaced persons within the following areas:
    (a) minimum standards for giving temporary protection to displaced persons from third countries who cannot return to their country of origin and for persons who otherwise need international protection,
    (b) promoting a balance of effort between Member States in receiving and bearing the consequences of receiving refugees and displaced persons;
(3) measures on immigration policy within the following areas:
    (a) conditions of entry and residence, and standards on procedures for the issue by Member States of long term visas and residence permits, including those of family reunion,
    (b) illegal immigration and illegal residence, including repatriation of illegal residents;
(4) measures defining the rights and conditions under which nationals of third countries who are legally resident in a Member State may reside in other Member States.

Measures adopted by the Council pursuant to points 3 and 4 shall not prevent any Member State from maintaining or introducing in the areas concerned national provisions which are compatible with this Treaty and with international agreements

Measures to be adopted pursuant to points 2(b), 3(a) and 4 shall not be subject to the five-year period referred to above.

Article 64

1. This Title shall not affect the exercise of the responsibilities incumbent upon Member States, with regard to the maintenance of law and order and the safeguarding of internal security.

2. In the event of one or more Member States being confronted with an emergency situation characterised by a sudden inflow of nationals of third countries and without prejudice to paragraph 1, the Council may, acting by qualified majority on a proposal from the Commission, adopt provisional measures of a duration not exceeding six months for the benefit of the Member States concerned.

(Ed.: Article 65, on judicial cooperation in civil matters having cross-border implications: not reproduced)

Article 66

The Council, acting in accordance with the procedure referred to in Article 67, shall take measures to ensure cooperation between the relevant departments of the administrations of the Member States in the areas covered by this Title, as well as between those departments and the Commission.

Article 67

1. During a transitional period of five years following the entry into force of the Treaty of Amsterdam, the Council shall act unanimously on a proposal from the Commission or on the initiative of a Member State and after consulting the European Parliament.

2. After this period of five years:
– the Council shall act on proposals from the Commission; the Commission shall examine any request made by a Member State that it submit a proposal to the Council;
– the Council, acting unanimously after consulting the European Parliament, shall take a decision with a view to providing for all or for parts of the areas covered by this Title to be governed by the procedure referred to in Article 251[3] and adapting the provisions relating to the powers of the Court of Justice.

3. By derogation from paragraphs 1 and 2, measures referred to in Article 62(2)(b)(i) and (iii) shall, from the entry into force of the Treaty of Amsterdam, be adopted by the Council acting by a qualified majority on a proposal by the Commission and after consulting the European Parliament.

4. By derogation from paragraph 2, measures referred to in Article 62(2)(b)(ii) and (iv) shall, after a period of five years following the entry into force of the Treaty of Amsterdam, be adopted by the Council in accordance with the procedure referred to in Article 251.

---

[3] Ed.: Art. 251 lays down procedures for adoption of an act (Council, qualified majority; Parliament rejection by an absolute majority; Conciliation Committee, etc).

Article 68

1. Article 234[4] shall apply to this Title under the following circumstances and conditions: where a question on the interpretation of this Title or on the validity or interpretation of acts of the institutions of the Community based on this Title is raised in a case pending before a court or tribunal of a Member State against whose decisions there is no judicial remedy under national law, that court or tribunal shall, if it considers that a decision on the question is necessary to enable it to give judgement, request the Court of Justice to give a ruling thereon.

2. In any event, the Court of Justice shall not have jurisdiction to rule on any measure or decision taken pursuant to Article 62(1) relating to the maintenance of law and order and the safeguarding of internal security.

3. The Council, the Commission, or a Member State may request the Court of Justice to give a ruling on a question of interpretation of this Title or of acts of the institutions of the Community based on this Title. The ruling given by the Court of Justice in response to such a request shall not apply to judgements of courts or tribunals of the Member States which have become res judicata.

Article 69

The application of this Title shall be subject to the provisions of the Protocol on the position of the United Kingdom and Ireland and to the Protocol on the position of Denmark and without prejudice to the Protocol on the application of certain aspects of Article 14 of the Treaty establishing the European Community to the United Kingdom and Ireland.

Vienna Action Plan[5]   3.1.2

Action Plan of the Council and the Commission on how best to implement the provisions of the Treaty of Amsterdam on an area of freedom, security and justice (...).

PART I – INTRODUCTION

1. The European Council, meeting at Cardiff called on the Council and the Commission to submit at its meeting in Vienna an action plan on 'how best to implement the provisions of the Treaty of Amsterdam on an area of freedom, security and justice'.

Heads of State and Government at Pörtschach further confirmed the importance they attach to this subject by agreeing to hold a special European Council in Tampere in October 1999. Under the Amsterdam Treaty, the areas of visa, asylum, immigration and other policies related to free movement of persons, like judicial cooperation in civil matters, are transferred

---

[4] Ed.: Art. 234 indicates on which issues the Court of Justice shall have jurisdiction to give preliminary rulings.

[5] Document submitted to the Vienna European Council: 13844/98; Brussels, 11 December 1998.

from the EU's third pillar to its first pillar (albeit not all of the first pillar procedures will be applicable), whereas provisions on police and judicial cooperation in criminal matters contained in the new Title VI of the TEU remain within the EU's third pillar. In addition to these changes in responsibilities, the Amsterdam Treaty also lays down the broad lines of action in the areas currently assigned to the third pillar. (...)

3. Without underestimating what has already been achieved in this area under the EC Treaty, under the Title VI provisions of the Maastricht Treaty and within Schengen, it is worth recalling the reasons why the new provisions adopted in Amsterdam open up improved possibilities. First, the objective of maintaining and developing the Union as an area of freedom, security and justice is asserted and the various aspects involved are reviewed. Secondly, the Union has been given the necessary framework in which to accommodate it and the instruments required have been strengthened and at the same time, thanks to the enhanced role foreseen for the European Court of Justice and the European Parliament, made subject to tighter judicial and democratic review. The Community method is extended: several of the areas of the current 'third pillar' are brought under Community arrangements and restrictions which used to apply to the Community institutions in the areas of police and criminal justice cooperation have been lifted. Access to the Community budget has been made less cumbersome. Finally, the integration of Schengen recognizes the efforts of the Member States which embarked on this cooperation and gives the Union a base on which to build further. (...)

5. Although any action plan drawn up must, in concrete terms, necessarily reflect the priorities and timetable set out in the Amsterdam Treaty itself, it needs to reflect also the general approach and philosophy inherent in the concept of an 'area of freedom, security and justice'. These three notions are closely interlinked. Freedom loses much of its meaning if it cannot be enjoyed in a secure environment and with the full backing of a system of justice in which all Union citizens and residents can have confidence. These three inseparable concepts have one common denominator – people – and one cannot be achieved in full without the other two. Maintaining the right balance between them must be the guiding thread for Union action. It should be noted in this context that the Treaty instituting the European Communities (Article 61 ex Article 73 I a), makes a direct link between the measures establishing freedom of movement of persons and the specific measures seeking to combat and prevent crime (Article 31 e TEU), thus creating a conditional link between the two areas.

A. **An Area of Freedom**

a) A wider concept of freedom (...)
b) Immigration and asylum policies

8. When looking at the priorities ahead, different considerations must apply to immigration policy on the one hand and asylum policy on the other. Future work in these areas will essentially be determined by the fact that the new Treaty itself contains an obligation to take action within 5 years in a wide range of immigration and asylum-related areas involving both substance and procedure. An impressive amount of work has already been carried out. However, the instruments adopted so far often suffer from two weaknesses: they are frequently based on 'soft law', such as resolutions or recommendations that have no legally binding

effect. And they do not have adequate monitoring arrangements. The commitment in the Amsterdam Treaty to use European Community instruments in the future provides the opportunity to correct where necessary these weaknesses. Particular priority needs to be attached to combating illegal immigration on the one hand, while on the other hand ensuring the integration and rights of those third country nationals legally present in the Union as well as the necessary protection for those in need of it even if they do not meet fully the criteria of the Geneva Convention.

B. **An Area of Security**

9. The full benefits of any area of freedom will never be enjoyed unless they are exercised in an area where people can feel safe and secure.

10. The agreed aim of the Treaty is not to create a European Security area in the sense of a common territory where uniform detection and investigation procedures would be applicable to all law enforcement agencies in Europe in the handling of security matters. Nor do the new provisions affect the exercise of the responsibilities incumbent upon Member States to maintain law and order and safeguard internal security.

11. Amsterdam rather provides an institutional framework to develop common action among the Member States in the indissociable fields of police cooperation and judicial cooperation in criminal matters and thus not only to offer enhanced security to their citizens but also to defend the Union's interests, including its financial interests. The declared objective is to prevent and combat crime at the appropriate level, 'organised or otherwise, in particular terrorism, trafficking in persons and offences against children, illicit drug trafficking and illicit arms trafficking, corruption and fraud'.

a) Organised crime
(...)
b) Drugs
(...)
c) Europol
(...)

C. **An Area of Justice (...)**

D. **Enlargement**

21. There is an important link with the enlargement process, in particular with the pre-accession strategy.
   The countries applying for membership of the European Union are well aware that Justice and Home Affairs will have a special significance for their applications.
However, the JHA acquis is different in nature from other parts of the Union's acquis. Much still needs to be done and the acquis will therefore be developing constantly over the pre-accession years.
   The adoption of the Action Plan will have the additional advantage of setting out for the benefit of the applicant countries a clear and comprehensive statement of the Union's priorities in this area.

E. Relations with Third Countries and International Organisations

22. The advances introduced by the Amsterdam Treaty will also enhance the Union's role as a player and partner on the international stage, both bilaterally and in multilateral fora. As a result, and building on the dialogue that it has already started in Justice and Home Affairs cooperation with an increasing number of third countries and international organisations and bodies (e.g. Interpol, UNHCR, Council of Europe, G8 and the OECD), this external aspect of the Union's action can be expected to take on a new and more demanding dimension. Full use will need to be made of the new instruments available under the Treaty. In particular, the communautarisation of the matters relating to asylum, immigration and judicial cooperation in civil matters permit the Community – to the extent permitted by the established case law of the European Court of Justice related to the external competence of the Community – to exercise its influence internationally in these matters. In those subjects which remain in Title VI of TEU, the Union can also make use of the possibility for the Council to conclude international agreements in matters relating to Title VI of the Treaty, as well as for the Presidency, assisted by the Secretary General of the Council and in full association with the Commission, to represent the Union in these areas.

F. Structure of Work in the Field of Justice and Home Affairs (...)

PART II – PRIORITIES AND MEASURES

II.A. Selection criteria for priorities

24. A number of principles have determined the way in which the Council and the Commission have identified – and intend to implement – the measures listed in this Part:
(i) The Amsterdam Treaty itself has set out some clear guidance on the measures to which priority importance must be attached, particularly during the first five years after its entry into force. The Action Plan must respect this guidance;
(ii) The principle of subsidiarity, which applies to all aspects of the Union's action, is of particular relevance to the creation of an area of freedom, security and justice.
(iii) The principle of solidarity among Member States and between them and the European institutions, should apply in facing the transnational challenges presented by organised crime and migration movements;
(iv) Operational efficiency in implementing the legal framework established by the Treaty is no less important than the legislative framework itself. Measures taken shall meet factual needs and add value In this context, working methods which have proved already their worth, for example in the Schengen context, should find their place in the Union's Action Plan.
(v) Responsibility for safeguarding of internal security rests with Member States. It is therefore important, when developing European cooperation, to take into account national interests and common approaches as well as differences.
(vi) A realistic approach requires, when selecting priorities, the resources and time available to be taken into account.

25. According to Article 2 of the TEU, the Union shall set itself the objective to maintain and develop an area of freedom, security and justice in which the free movement of persons is assured in conjunction with appropriate measures with respect to external borders, asylum, immigration and the prevention and combating of crime. The mutual interdependence between the different aspects of this overall objective is confirmed by Article 61, a) which mentions Article 31(e) of the TEU. It is therefore in the interest of as high level as possible of security for the public that some activities in one area be meshed in timing and substance with those in the other.

26. Integration of the Schengen acquis into the framework of the European Union will have as a consequence that as from the date of entry into force of the Treaty of Amsterdam the objectives of the Community as set out in the entire Article 62 TEC and to a large extent in Article 63(3)(b) of the TEC in their versions of the Treaty of Amsterdam will largely have been realized in respect of 10 Member States, and in respect of 13 Member States as from the date of the decision of the Council referred to in Article 2(2) of the Schengen Protocol. This is to say that much of the substantive work will have been done far in advance of the 5 years time limit set by the Articles concerned. It would permit the Council to concentrate initially particularly on other objectives of the Community and the Union in the field of Justice and Home Affairs for the realization of which a maximum time limit of 5 years has been determined (Article 63(1)) and (2)(a) TEC and Article 30(2) TEU, for example and to deal with matters which would require urgent handling or which become politically important.

In order to put the priorities listed in those Articles into practice, efforts will have to be made to adopt measures detailed in the following sections.

27. In the context of the Treaty requirements, account should also be taken of the position of the United Kingdom and Ireland under the Protocols to the Amsterdam Treaty and, in setting priorities, of existing plans and the need to continue taking forward present medium-term work programmes.

28. In establishing substantive and political priorities, first consideration has had to be given in particular to those projects on which work is already in hand at present or for which work is likely still to be in progress at the time of entry into force of the Amsterdam Treaty. It has basically been attempted here, in fully adjusting to the new environment, to ensure maximum continuity.

29. In legislative work, account has also had to be taken of the existing third-pillar 'acquis'; making it necessary to decide which, if any, of the present provisions should be replaced by more effective ones. Those classifiable as 'soft law' formed the prime candidates for this purpose.

30. The entry into force of the Treaty of Amsterdam is likely to have the effect of increasing the case-load of the European Court of Justice, whereas an Area of freedom, security and justice precisely requires judicial proceedings to be as expedient as possible. It is therefore in the interest of both the Member States and the individuals concerned that priority be given to examining jointly with the Court all possible means to shorten the average length of procedures before the Court, in particular of requests for preliminary rulings under Title VI TEU and Title IV TEC.

31. The levels of priority set out below become effective, logically, upon entry into force of the Amsterdam Treaty. The priority measures are to be found in two categories. On the one hand, the actions and measures for which it is important that they are implemented or adopted within two years from the entry into force of the Treaty of Amsterdam (hereinafter referred to as 'measures to be taken within two years'), and on the other hand the actions and measures which must be adopted or implemented within five years following the entry into force of the Treaty or, at least, to commence elaboration of the actions and measures in the area (hereinafter referred to as 'measures to be taken within five years'). However, a start may have to be made on many activities in the first level of priority without delay upon adoption of this action plan as they require preparatory work, e.g. in technical working parties, which should if possible have been completed by the date of the entry into force. Such particularly urgent measures are specifically indicated below.

II.B. Policies related to free movement of persons

II.B.I. *Measures in the field of asylum, external borders and immigration*

32. The objective is to introduce the area of freedom within the next five years. As a result, to ensure increased security for all European citizens, achieving this objective requires accompanying measures to be drawn up, particularly in the areas of external border controls and the combating of illegal immigration while full account is taken of the principles set out in Article 6 of the TEU and Articles 12 and 13 of the TEC. (...)

33. The measures to be drawn up must take due account of the fact that the areas of asylum and immigration are separate and require separate approaches and solutions.

34. An overall migration strategy should be established in which a system of European solidarity should figure prominently. The experiences gained and progress achieved through cooperation in the Schengen framework should prove particularly pertinent as regards short-term residence (up to three months), the fight against illegal immigration as well as the controls at external borders.

An overall priority should be to improve the exchange of statistics and information on asylum and immigration. This exchange should include statistics on asylum and immigration, information on the status of third country nationals and national legislation and policy on the basis of the Commission's Action Plan.

35. In order to complete the area of free movement, it is crucial for there to be a swift and comprehensive extension of the principles of the free movement of persons in accordance with the Protocol integrating the Schengen acquis into the framework of the EU.

Measures to be taken within two years

36. The following measures should be taken within two years after the entry into force of the Treaty:

a) Measures in the fields of asylum and immigration
Assessment of countries of origin in order to formulate a country specific integrated approach.

b) Measures in the field of asylum
   (...)

c) Measures in the field of immigration
   i) Instrument on the lawful status of legal immigrants.
   ii) Establish a coherent EU policy on readmission and return.
   iii) Combat illegal immigration (Article 63(3)(b) TEC) through, inter alia, information campaigns in transit countries and in the countries of origin.
   In line with the priority to be given to controlling migration flows, practical proposals for combating illegal immigration more effectively need to be brought forward swiftly.

d) Measures in the fields of external borders and free movement of persons:
   i) Procedure and conditions for issuing visas by Member States (resources, guarantees of repatriation or accident and health cover) as well as the drawing up of a list of countries whose nationals are subject to an airport transit visa requirement (abolition of the current grey list).
   ii) Define the rules on a uniform visa (Article 62 (iv) TEC)
   iii) Draw up a Regulation on countries:
      – whose nationals are exempt from any visa requirement in the Member States of the European Union;
      – whose nationals are subject to a visa requirement in the Member States of the European Union (Article 62(2)(b)(i) TEC).
   iv) Further harmonising Member States' laws on carriers' liability.

Measures to be taken as quickly as possible in accordance with the provisions of the Treaty of Amsterdam:

37. (...)

Measures to be taken within five years

38. The following measures should be taken within five years after the entry into force of the Treaty:
a) Measures in the fields of asylum and immigration
Identification and implementation of the measures listed in the European migration strategy
b) Measures in the field of asylum (...)
c) Measures in the field of immigration
   i) Improvement of the possibilities for the removal of persons who have been refused the right to stay through improved EU co-ordination implementation of readmission clauses and development of European official (Embassy) reports on the situation in countries in origin.
   ii) Preparation of rules on the conditions of entry and residence, and standards on procedures for the issue by Member States of long-term visas and residence permits, including those for the purposes of family reunion (Article 63(3)(a) TEC).
   The question of giving third-country nationals holding residence permits the freedom to settle in any Member State of the Union will shortly be discussed by the relevant working party.

iii) Determination of the rights and conditions under which nationals of third countries who are legally resident in a Member State may reside in other Member States (Article 3(4) TEC).

Within the competent Council bodies discussions could be held, taking account of the consequences for social equilibrium and the labour market, on the conditions under which, like Community nationals and their families, third country nationals could be allowed to settle and work in any Member State of the Union.

In these two last fields, although the Amsterdam Treaty does not request action to be accomplished in a five year period, efforts should be made towards an improvement of the situation in due time.

d) Measures in the fields of external borders and free movement of persons:

i) Extension of the Schengen representation mechanisms with regard to visas:

A discussion could be initiated on the possibility of establishing an arrangement between the Member States, which will improve the possibility of preventing visa applicants from abusing the foreign representations of one or more Member States in order to gain access to another Member State, which at the time of application was the actual intended country of destinations.

ii) Attention will be given to new technical developments in order to ensure – as appropriate – an even better security of the uniform format for visas (sticker).

II.B.II. *Judicial cooperation in civil matters* (...)

II.C. **Police and judicial cooperation in criminal matters** (...)

Tampere Milestones[6]   3.1.3

The European Council held a special meeting on 15 and 16 October 1999 in Tampere on the creation of an area of freedom, security and justice in the European Union. At the start of proceedings an exchange of views was conducted with the President of the European Parliament, Mrs Nicole Fontaine, on the main topics of discussion.

The European Council is determined to develop the Union as an area of freedom, security and justice by making full use of the possibilities offered by the Treaty of Amsterdam. The European Council sends a strong political message to reaffirm the importance of this objective and has agreed on a number of policy orientations and priorities, which will speedily make this area a reality.

The European Council will place and maintain this objective at the very top of the political agenda. It will keep under constant review progress made towards implementing the necessary measures and meeting the deadlines set by the Treaty of Amsterdam, the Vienna Action Plan and the present conclusions. The Commission is invited to make a proposal for an appropriate scoreboard to that end. The European Council underlines the importance of ensuring the

---

[6] Presidency Conclusions Tampere European Council 15 and 16 October 1999.

necessary transparency and of keeping the European Parliament regularly informed. It will hold a full debate assessing progress at its December meeting in 2001.

In close connection with the area of freedom, security and justice, the European Council has agreed on the composition, method of work and practical arrangements (attached in the annex) for the body entrusted with drawing up a draft Charter of fundamental rights of the European Union. It invites all parties involved to ensure that work on the Charter can begin rapidly.

(...)

TOWARDS A UNION OF FREEDOM, SECURITY AND JUSTICE: THE TAMPERE MILESTONES

From its very beginning European integration has been firmly rooted in a shared commitment to freedom based on human rights, democratic institutions and the rule of law. These common values have proved necessary for securing peace and developing prosperity in the European Union. They will also serve as a cornerstone for the enlarging Union.

The European Union has already put in place for its citizens the major ingredients of a shared area of prosperity and peace: a single market, economic and monetary union, and the capacity to take on global political and economic challenges. The challenge of the Amsterdam Treaty is now to ensure that freedom, which includes the right to move freely throughout the Union, can be enjoyed in conditions of security and justice accessible to all. It is a project, which responds to the frequently expressed concerns of citizens and has a direct bearing on their daily lives.

This freedom should not, however, be regarded as the exclusive preserve of the Union's own citizens. Its very existence acts as a draw to many others world-wide who cannot enjoy the freedom Union citizens take for granted. It would be in contradiction with Europe's traditions to deny such freedom to those whose circumstances lead them justifiably to seek access to our territory. This in turn requires the Union to develop common policies on asylum and immigration, while taking into account the need for a consistent control of external borders to stop illegal immigration and to combat those who organise it and commit related international crimes. These common policies must be based on principles which are both clear to our own citizens and also offer guarantees to those who seek protection in or access to the European Union. (...)

A common approach must also be developed to ensure the integration into our societies of those third country nationals who are lawfully resident in the Union.

The enjoyment of freedom requires a genuine area of justice, where people can approach courts and authorities in any Member State as easily as in their own. Criminals must find no ways of exploiting differences in the judicial systems of Member States. Judgements and decisions should be respected and enforced throughout the Union, while safeguarding the basic legal certainty of people and economic operators. Better compatibility and more convergence between the legal systems of Member States must be achieved.

People have the right to expect the Union to address the threat to their freedom and legal rights posed by serious crime. To counter these threats a common effort is needed to prevent and fight crime and criminal organisations throughout the Union. The joint mobilisation of police and judicial resources is needed to guarantee that there is no hiding place for criminals or the proceeds of crime within the Union.

The area of freedom, security and justice should be based on the principles of transparency and democratic control. We must develop an open dialogue with civil society on the aims and principles of this area in order to strengthen citizens' acceptance and support. In order to maintain confidence in authorities, common standards on the integrity of authorities should be developed.

The European Council considers it essential that in these areas the Union should also develop a capacity to act and be regarded as a significant partner on the international scene. This requires close cooperation with partner countries and international organisations, in particular the Council of Europe, OSCE, OECD and the United Nations.

The European Council invites the Council and the Commission, in close cooperation with the European Parliament, to promote the full and immediate implementation of the Treaty of Amsterdam on the basis of the Vienna Action Plan and of the following political guidelines and concrete objectives agreed here in Tampere.

A. A Common EU Asylum and Migration Policy

The separate but closely related issues of asylum and migration call for the development of a common EU policy to include the following elements.

I. *Partnership with countries of origin*

The European Union needs a comprehensive approach to migration addressing political, human rights and development issues in countries and regions of origin and transit. This requires combating poverty, improving living conditions and job opportunities, preventing conflicts and consolidating democratic states and ensuring respect for human rights, in particular rights of minorities, women and children. To that end, the Union as well as Member States are invited to contribute, within their respective competence under the Treaties, to a greater coherence of internal and external policies of the Union. Partnership with third countries concerned will also be a key element for the success of such a policy, with a view to promoting co-development.

In this context, the European Council welcomes the report of the High Level Working Group on Asylum and Migration set up by the Council, and agrees on the continuation of its mandate and on the drawing up of further Action Plans. It considers as a useful contribution the first action plans drawn up by that Working Group, and approved by the Council, and invites the Council and the Commission to report back on their implementation to the European Council in December 2000.

II. *A Common European Asylum System (...)*

III. *Fair treatment of third country nationals*

The European Union must ensure fair treatment of third country nationals who reside legally on the territory of its Member States. A more vigorous integration policy should aim at granting them rights and obligations comparable to those of EU citizens. It should also enhance non-discrimination in economic, social and cultural life and develop measures against racism and xenophobia.

Building on the Commission Communication on an Action Plan against Racism, the European Council calls for the fight against racism and xenophobia to be stepped up. The Member States will draw on best practices and experiences. Cooperation with the European Monitoring Centre on Racism and Xenophobia and the Council of Europe will be further strengthened. Moreover, the Commission is invited to come forward as soon as possible with proposals implementing Article 13 of the EC Treaty on the fight against racism and xenophobia. To fight against discrimination more generally the Member States are encouraged to draw up national programmes.

The European Council acknowledges the need for approximation of national legislations on the conditions for admission and residence of third country nationals, based on a shared assessment of the economic and demographic developments within the Union, as well as the situation in the countries of origin. It requests to this end rapid decisions by the Council, on the basis of proposals by the Commission. These decisions should take into account not only the reception capacity of each Member State, but also their historical and cultural links with the countries of origin.

The legal status of third country nationals should be approximated to that of Member States' nationals. A person, who has resided legally in a Member State for a period of time to be determined and who holds a long-term residence permit, should be granted in that Member State a set of uniform rights which are as near as possible to those enjoyed by EU citizens; e.g. the right to reside, receive education, and work as an employee or self-employed person, as well as the principle of non-discrimination vis-à-vis the citizens of the State of residence. The European Council endorses the objective that long-term legally resident third country nationals be offered the opportunity to obtain the nationality of the Member State in which they are resident.

IV. *Management of migration flows*

The European Council stresses the need for more efficient management of migration flows at all their stages. It calls for the development, in close cooperation with countries of origin and transit, of information campaigns on the actual possibilities for legal immigration, and for the prevention of all forms of trafficking in human beings. A common active policy on visas and false documents should be further developed, including closer cooperation between EU consulates in third countries and, where necessary, the establishment of common EU visa issuing offices.

The European Council is determined to tackle at its source illegal immigration, especially by combating those who engage in trafficking in human beings and economic exploitation of migrants. It urges the adoption of legislation foreseeing severe sanctions against this serious crime. The Council is invited to adopt by the end of 2000, on the basis of a proposal by the Commission, legislation to this end. Member States, together with Europol, should direct their efforts to detecting and dismantling the criminal networks involved. The rights of the victims of such activities shall be secured with special emphasis on the problems of women and children.

The European Council calls for closer cooperation and mutual technical assistance between the Member States' border control services, such as exchange programmes and technology transfer, especially on maritime borders, and for the rapid inclusion of the applicant States in this cooperation. In this context, the Council welcomes the memorandum of understanding between Italy and Greece to enhance cooperation between the two countries in the Adriatic and Ionian seas in combating organised crime, smuggling and trafficking of persons.

As a consequence of the integration of the Schengen acquis into the Union, the candidate countries must accept in full that acquis and further measures building upon it. The European Council stresses the importance of the effective control of the Union's future external borders by specialised trained professionals.

The European Council calls for assistance to countries of origin and transit to be developed in order to promote voluntary return as well as to help the authorities of those countries to strengthen their ability to combat effectively trafficking in human beings and to cope with their readmission obligations towards the Union and the Member States.

The Amsterdam Treaty conferred powers on the Community in the field of readmission. The European Council invites the Council to conclude readmission agreements or to include standard clauses in other agreements between the European Community and relevant third countries or groups of countries. Consideration should also be given to rules on internal readmission.

B. A Genuine European Area of Justice

In a genuine European Area of Justice individuals and businesses should not be prevented or discouraged from exercising their rights by the incompatibility or complexity of legal and administrative systems in the Member States.

V. *Better access to justice in Europe* (...)

VI. *Mutual recognition of judicial decisions*

Enhanced mutual recognition of judicial decisions and judgements and the necessary approximation of legislation would facilitate cooperation between authorities and the judicial protection of individual rights. The European Council therefore endorses the principle of mutual recognition which, in its view, should become the cornerstone of judicial cooperation in both civil and criminal matters within the Union. The principle should apply both to judgements and to other decisions of judicial authorities. (...)

C. A Unionwide Fight Against Crime

The European Council is deeply committed to reinforcing the fight against serious organised and transnational crime. The high level of safety in the area of freedom, security and justice presupposes an efficient and comprehensive approach in the fight against all forms of crime. A balanced development of union-wide measures against crime should be achieved while protecting the freedom and legal rights of individuals and economic operators. (...)

Nice Charter 2000   3.1.4
(Charter of the Fundamental Rights of the European Union,
December 2000 (soft law))

Article 34 – Social security and social assistance
1. The Union recognises and respects the entitlement to social security benefits and social services providing protection in cases such as maternity, illness, industrial accidents, dependency or old age, and in the case of loss of employment, in accordance with the procedures laid down by Community law and national laws and practices.
2. Everyone residing and moving legally within the European Union is entitled to social security benefits and social advantages in accordance with Community law and national laws and practices.
3. In order to combat social exclusion and poverty, the Union recognises and respects the right to social and housing assistance so as to ensure a decent existence for all those who lack sufficient resources, in accordance with the procedures laid down by Community law and national laws and practices

Article 45 – Freedom of movement and of residence
1. Every citizen of the Union has the right to move and reside freely within the territory of the Member States.
2. Freedom of movement and residence may be granted, in accordance with the Treaty establishing the European Community, to nationals of third countries legally resident in the territory of a Member State.

Entry   3.2

                                                                         3.2.1

[T.22] Text adopted by Ministers 11 June 1992 on acceptable/ unacceptable travel documents

1. In connection with the preparation of common instructions to consular posts, at their meeting in Lisbon on 11 June 1992 Ministers emphasized the desirability of:
– compiling very swiftly a list of travel documents issued by recognized third states;
– defining the attitude to be adopted towards documents issued by non-recognized bodies.

2. To achieve these objectives in an optimum manner, the Ministers endorsed the following conclusions with a view to eventual approval by the Committee provided for in Article 26:
    (i) the following documents are acceptable for the purposes of Article 19(2) and/or Article 7(1)(a) provided they satisfactorily establish the identity and, in the case of (a) and (b) below, the nationality or citizenship of the holder:

(a) travel documents issued to the standard demanded by international practice by countries or territorial entities recognized by all Member States;

(b) passports or travel documents in which return is guaranteed, even if issued by countries or territorial entities not recognized by all the Member States, provided that the Executive Committee has recognized their validity for the purposes of issuing on them or on a separate sheet a uniform visa, by approving unanimously:

– both the list of such passports or travel documents;

– and the list of the non-recognized countries or entities which issue them;

– however, exceptionally, the Article 26 Committee, acting on a proposal by a Member State, may decide whether, for certain of these non-recognized countries or territorial entities, only a visa with limited territorial validity may be issued;

(c) refugee travel documents issued under the 1951 Convention relating to the Status of Refugees;

(d) stateless person travel documents issued under the 1954 Convention on the Status of Stateless Persons[7].

(ii) in accordance with its duty under Article 26(2) to interpret the terms of the Convention, the Committee provided for in Article 26 declares that the discretion bestowed upon each Member State under Article 12(2) to allow, on humanitarian grounds, persons who are not nationals of Member States and who fail to fulfil the conditions of Article 7(1) to enter its territory includes a discretion to permit entry to its territory to a person who holds a travel document which is not acceptable for the purposes of Article 7(1)(a). Accordingly, such a person who satisfies the other conditions of Article 7(1) may be admitted to the territory of the Member State concerned for a short stay restricted to that Member State.

(iii) the drawing up of the list provided for in these conclusions does not prejudice the question of recognition by the Member States of the non-recognized countries or territorial entities.

3.2.2

[T.18] Council Regulation (EC) of 29 May 1995 laying down a uniform format for visas[8]

THE COUNCIL OF THE EUROPEAN UNION,
Having regard to the Treaty establishing the European Community, in particular Article 100c (3) thereof, Having regard to the proposal from the Commission, Having regard to the opinion of the European Parliament, Whereas Article 100c (3) of the Treaty requires the Council to adopt measures relating to a uniform format for visas before 1 January 1996;

---

[7] The Portuguese delegation said it was giving its agreement subject to ratification by Portugal of the 1954 Convention on the Status of Stateless Persons.

[8] No 1683/95, OJ L164, p. 1, 4 July 1995 (395R1683).

Whereas the introduction of a uniform format for visas is an important step towards the harmonization of visa policy;

Whereas Article 7a of the Treaty stipulates that the internal market shall comprise an area without internal frontiers in which the free movement of persons is ensured in accordance with the provisions of the Treaty;

Whereas this step is also to be regarded as forming a coherent whole with measures falling within Title VI of the Treaty on European Union;

Whereas it is essential that the uniform format for visas should contain all the necessary information and meet very high technical standards, notably as regards safeguards against counterfeiting and falsification;

Whereas it must also be suited to use by all the Member States and bear universally recognizable security features which are clearly visible to the naked eye;

Whereas this Regulation only lays down such specifications as are not secret;

Whereas these specifications need to be supplemented by further specifications which must remain secret in order to prevent counterfeiting and falsification and which may not include personal data or references to such data;

Whereas powers to adopt further specifications should be conferred on the Commission;

Whereas, to ensure that the information referred to is not made available to more persons than necessary, it is also essential that each Member State should designate not more than one body having responsibility for printing the uniform format for visas, with Member States remaining free to change the body, if need be;

Whereas, for security reasons, each Member State must communicate the name of the competent body to the Commission and the other Member States;

Whereas, to be effective, this Regulation should apply to all visas covered by Article 5;

Whereas Member States should be free also to use the uniform visa format for visas which can be used for purposes other than those covered by Article 5 provided differences visible to the naked eye are incorporated to make confusion with the uniform visa impossible;

Whereas, with regard to the personal data to be entered on the uniform format for visas in accordance with the Annex hereto, compliance should be ensured with Member States' data-protection provisions as well as with the relevant Community legislation,

HAS ADOPTED THIS REGULATION:

Article 1
Visas issued by the Member States in conformity with Article 5 shall be produced in the form of a uniform format (sticker). They shall conform to the specifications set out in the Annex.

Article 2
Further technical specifications which render the visa difficult to counterfeit or falsify shall be laid down in accordance with the procedure set out in Article 6.

Article 3
1. The specifications referred to in Article 2 shall be secret and not be published. They shall be made available only to bodies designated by the Member States as responsible for printing and to persons duly authorized by a Member State or the Commission.

2. Each Member State shall designate one body having responsibility for printing visas. It shall communicate the name of that body to the Commission and the other Member States. The same body may be designated by two or more Member States for this purpose. Each Member State shall be entitled to change its designated body. It shall inform the Commission and the other Member States accordingly.

Article 4

1. Without prejudice to the relevant more extensive provisions concerning data protection, an individual to whom a visa is issued shall have the right to verify the personal particulars entered on the visa and, where appropriate, to ask for any corrections or deletions to be made.

2. No information in machine-readable form shall be given on the uniform format for visas unless it also appears in the boxes described in points 6 to 12 of the Annex, or unless it is mentioned in the relevant travel document.

Article 5

For the purposes of this Regulation a 'visa' shall mean an authorization given by or a decision taken by a Member State which is required for entry into its territory with a view to:
- an intended stay in that Member State or in several Member States of no more than three months in all,
- transit through the territory or airport transit zone of that Member State or several Member States.

Article 6

1. Where reference is made to the procedure defined in this Article, the following provisions shall apply.

2. The Commission shall be assisted by a committee composed of the representatives of the Member States and chaired by the representative of the Commission.

The representative of the Commission shall submit to the committee a draft of the measures to be taken. The committee shall deliver its opinion on the draft within a time limit which the chairman may lay down according to the urgency of the matter. The opinion shall be delivered by the majority laid down in Article 148 (2) of the Treaty in the case of decisions which the Council is required to adopt on a proposal from the Commission. The votes of the representatives of the Member States within the committee shall be weighted in the manner set out in that Article. The chairman shall not vote.

3. (a) The Commission shall adopt the measures envisaged if they are in accordance with the opinion of the committee.

(b) If the measures envisaged are not in accordance with the opinion of the committee, or if no opinion is delivered, the Commission shall, without delay, submit to the Council a proposal relating to the measures to be taken. The Council shall act by a qualified majority. If, on the expiry of a period of two months, the Council has not acted, the proposed measures shall be adopted by the Commission, save where the Council has decided against the said measures by a simple majority.

Article 7

Where Member States use the uniform visa format for purposes other than those covered by Article 5, appropriate measures must be taken to ensure that confusion with the visa referred to in Article 5 is not possible.

Article 8

This Regulation shall enter into force on the twentieth day following that of its publication in the Official Journal of the European Communities. Article 1 shall become applicable six months after the adoption of the measures referred to in Article 2.

This Regulation shall be binding in its entirety and directly applicable in all Member States.

ANNEX

Security features

1. A sign consisting of nine ellipses in a fan-shape shall appear in this space.

2. An optically variable mark ('kinegram' or equivalent) shall appear in this space. Depending on the angle of view, 12 stars, the letter 'E' and a globe become visible in various sizes and colours.

3. The logo consisting of a letter or letters indicating the issuing Member State (or 'BNL' in the case of the Benelux countries, namely Belgium, Luxembourg and the Netherlands) with a latent image effect shall appear in this space. This logo shall appear light when held flat and dark when turned by 90 . The following logos shall be used: A for Austria, BNL for Benelux, D for Germany, DK for Denmark, E for Spain, F for France, FIN for Finland, GR for Greece, I for Italy, IRL for Ireland, P for Portugal, S for Sweden, UK for the United Kingdom.

4. The word 'visa' in capital letters shall appear in the middle of this space in optically variable colouring. Depending on the angle of view, it shall appear green or red.

5. This box shall contain the number of the visa, which shall be pre-printed and shall begin with the letter or letters indicating the issuing country as described in point 3 above. A special type shall be used.

Sections to be completed

6. This box shall begin with the words 'valid for'. The issuing authority shall indicate the territory or territories for which the visa is valid.

7. This box shall begin with the word 'from' and the word 'until' shall appear further along the line. The issuing authority shall indicate here the period of validity of the visa.

8. This box shall begin with the words 'number of entries' and further along the line the words 'duration of stay' (i.e. duration of applicants' intended stay) and again 'days' shall appear.

9. This box shall begin with the words 'issued in' and shall be used to indicate the place of issue.

10. This box shall begin with the word 'on' (after which the date of issue shall be filled in by the issuing authority) and further along the line the words 'number of passport' shall appear (after which the holder's passport number shall appear).

11. This box shall begin with the words 'type of visa'. The issuing authority shall indicate the category of visa in conformity with Articles 5 and 7 of this Regulation.

12. This box shall begin with the word 'remarks'. It shall be used by the issuing authority to indicate any further information which is considered necessary, provided that it complies with Article 4 of this Regulation. The following two and a half lines shall be left empty for such remarks.

13. This box shall contain the relevant machine-readable information to facilitate external border controls.

The paper shall be pastel green with red and blue markings. The words designating the boxes shall appear in English and French. The issuing State may add a third official Community language. However, the word 'visa' in the top line may appear in any one official language of the Community.

3.2.3

[T.19] Council Regulation (EC) of 25 September 1995 determining the third countries whose nationals must be in possession of visas when crossing the external borders of the Member States[9]

THE COUNCIL OF THE EUROPEAN UNION,

Having regard to the Treaty establishing the European Community,

Having regard to the proposal from the Commission,[10]

Having regard to the opinion of the European Parliament,[11]

Whereas Article 100c of the Treaty requires the Council to determine the third countries whose nationals must be in possession of a visa when crossing the external borders of the Member States;

Whereas the drawing up of the common list annexed to this Regulation represents an important step towards the harmonization of visa policy;

Whereas the second paragraph of Article 7a of the Treaty stipulates in particular that the internal market shall comprise an area without internal frontiers in which the free movement of persons is ensured in accordance with the Treaty;

Whereas other aspects of the harmonization of visa policy, including the conditions for the issue of visas, are matters to be determined under Title VI of the Treaty on European Union; Whereas risks relating to security and illegal immigration should be given priority consideration when the said common list annexed hereto is drawn up; whereras, in addition, Member States' international relations with third countries also play a role;

Whereas the principle that a Member State may not require a visa from a person wishing to cross its external borders if that person holds a visa issued by another Member State which meets the harmonized conditions governing the issue of visas and is valid throughout the Community or if that person holds an appropriate permit issued by a Member State is a matter that should be determined under Title VI of the Treaty on European Union;

Whereas this Regulation shall not prevent a Member State from deciding under what conditions nationals of third countries lawfully resident within its territory may re-enter it after having left the territory of the Member States of the Union during the period of validity of their permits;

---

[9] No 2317/95, OJ L 234, 3 October 1995, p. 1-3; 395R2317

[10] OJ C11, 15 January 1994, p. 15

[11] OJ C128, 9 May 1994, p. 350

Whereas, in special cases justifying an exemption where visa requirements would in principle exist, Member States may exempt certain categories of person in keeping with international law or custom;

Whereas since national rules differ on stateless persons, recognized refugees and persons who produce passports or travel documents issued by a territorial entity or authority which is not recognized as a State by all Member States, Member States may decide on visa requirements for that group of persons, where that territorial entity or authority is not on the said common list;

Whereas when adding new entities to the list it is necessary to take account of diplomatic implications and guidelines adopted on the matter by the European Union;

Whereas, at all events the inclusion of a third country on the common list is entirely without prejudice to its international status;

Whereas the determination of third countries whose nationals must be in possession of visas when crossing the external borders of the Member States should be achieved gradually;

Whereas Member States will constantly endeavour to harmonize their visa policies with regard to third countries not on the common list;

Whereas the present provisions must not prejudice the achievement of free movement for persons as provided for in Article 7a of the Treaty;

Whereas the Commission should draw up a progress report on harmonization after five years;

Whereas, with a view to ensuring that the system is administered openly and that the persons concerned are informed, Member States must communicate to the other Member States and to the Commission the measures which they take pursuant to this Regulation;

Whereas for the same reasons that information must also be published in the Official Journal of the European Communities;

Whereas the information provided for in Articles 2(4) and 4(2) must be published before the other provisions of this Regulation come into force;

Whereas Articles 2(4) and 4(2) must therefore become applicable one month before the other provisions of the Regulation,

HAS ADOPTED THIS REGULATION:

Article 1

1. Nationals of third countries on the common list in the Annex shall be required to be in possession of visas when crossing the external borders of the Member States.[12]

---

[12] Ed: The Common List referred to in this Article contained the following States:
Afghanistan, Albania, Algeria, Angola, Armenia, Azerbaijan, Bahrain, Bangladesh, Belarus, Benin, Bhutan, Bulgaria, Burkina Faso, Burundi, Cambodia, Cameroon, Cape Verde, Central African Republic, Chad, China, Comorros, Congo, Côte d'Ivoire, Cuba, Djibouti, Dominican Republic, Egypt, Equatorial Guinea, Eritrea, Ethiopia, Fiji, Gabon, the Gambia, Georgia, Ghana, Guinea, Guinea Bissau, Guyana, Haiti, India, Indonesia, Iran, Iraq, Jordan, Kazakstan, Kyrgyzstan, Kuwait, Laos, Lebanon, Liberia, Libya, Madagascar, Maldives, Mali, Mauritania, Mauritius, Moldova, Mongolia, Morocco, Mozambique, Myanmar, Nepal, Niger, Nigeria, North Korea, Oman, Pakistan, Papua New Guinea, Peru, Philippines, Quatar, Romania, Russia, Rwanda, Sao Tomé and Principe, Saudi Arabia, Senegal, Sierra Leone, Somalia, Sri Lanka, Sudan, Suriname, Syria, Tajikistan, Tanzania, Thailand, Togo, Tunisia, Turkey, Turkmenistan, Uganda, United Arab Emirates, Uzbekistan, Vietnam, Yemen, Zaire, Zambia; and the following Entities and Territorial Authorities not recognized as

2. Nationals of countries formerly part of countries on the common list shall be subject to the requirements of paragraph 1 unless and until the Council decides otherwise under the procedure laid down in Article 100c of the Treaty.

Article 2

1. The Member States shall determine the visa requirements for nationals of third countries not on the common list.
2. The Member States shall determine the visa requirements for stateless persons and recognized refugees.
3. The Member States shall determine the visa requirements for persons who produce passports or travel documents issued by a territorial entity or authority which is not recognized as a State by all Member States if that entity or territorial authority is not on the common list.
4. Within ten working days of the entry into force of this paragraph, Member States shall communicate to the other Member States and the Commission the measures they have taken pursuant to paragraphs 1, 2 and 3. Any further measures taken pursuant to paragraph 1 shall be similarly communicated within five working days. The Commission shall publish the measures communicated pursuant to this paragraph and updates thereof in the Official Journal of the European Communities for information.

Article 3

Five years after the entry into force of this Regulation the Commission shall draw up a progress report of the harmonization of Member States' visa policies with regard to third countries not on the common list and, if necessary, submit to the Council proposals for further measures required to achieve the objective of harmonization laid down in Article 100c.

Article 4

1. A Member State may exempt nationals of third countries subject to visa requirements under Article 1(1) and (2) from those requirements. This shall apply in particular to civilian air and sea crew, flight crew and attendants on emergency or rescue flights and other helpers in the event of disaster or accident and holders of diplomatic passports, official duty passports and other official passports.
2. Article 2(4) shall apply mutatis mutandis.

Article 5

For the purposes of this Regulation, 'visa` shall mean an authorization given or a decision taken by a Member State which is required for entry into its territory with a view to:
– an intended stay in that Member State or in several Member States of no more than three months in all,
– transit through the territory of that Member State or several Member States, except for transit through the international zones of airports and transfers between airports in a Member State.

States by all the Member States: Taiwan, Former Yugoslav Republic of Macedonia, and Federal Republic of Yugoslavia (Serbia and Montenegro).

Article 6
This Regulation shall be without prejudice to any further harmonization between individual Member States, going beyond the common list, determining the third countries whose nationals must be in possession of a visa when crossing their external borders.

Article 7
This Regulation shall enter into force six months after its publication in the Official Journal of the European Communities except for Articles 2 (4) and 4 (2) which shall enter into force on the day following publication. This Regulation shall be binding in its entirety and directly applicable in all Member States.

3.2.4
[T.30] Council Recommendation of 4 March 1996 relating to local consular cooperation regarding visas[13]

THE COUNCIL OF THE EUROPEAN UNION,
Having regard to the Treaty on European Union, and in particular Article K.1(3) thereof,
Whereas it is advisable to prepare for greater harmonization in the policy and practice of the issue of visas;
Whereas the issue of visas, pending the possible preparation of joint instructions on the matter, is governed by each Member State's national legislation;
Whereas each Member State, when issuing its own visas, should have the necessary information to take account of the interests of the other Member States, in particular the protection of national security and public order and the prevention of clandestine immigration,

HEREBY RECOMMENDS THAT THE GOVERNMENTS OF THE MEMBER STATES:
in so far as the practical need is felt, take the measures necessary to facilitate that:
1. the Member States' consular services should maintain local cooperation on visas, involving an exchange of information on the criteria for issuing visas and an exchange of information on risks to national security and public order or the risk of clandestine immigration;
2. the Heads of their consular services and their assistants in visa matters should hold meetings for the purposes of exchanging the information referred to in paragraph 1;
3. their consular services should organize mutual visits of officials responsible for issuing visas in order to improve the exchange of information and reciprocal knowledge;
4. at the request of the Council, their consular services should draw up joint reports on local visa issues which are likely to be relevant to the Council's discussions;
5. their consular services should adopt any appropriate joint measures to establish the existence of simultaneous visa applications or a series of applications, and, if need be, to ascertain any earlier visa refusal by another Member State;

---

[13] (96/C 80/01)

6. their consular services should exchange information to help to determine the good faith of visa applicants and their reputation, it being understood that the fact that the applicant has obtained a visa for another Member State does not exempt the authorities of the other Member States from their responsibility to examine individually the visa application and perform the verification required for purposes of security, public order and clandestine immigration control.

The exchange of information provided for in this recommendation must take the relevant data protection rules into account.

3.2.5

[T.24] Council Resolution of 20 June 1994 on limitation of admission of third-country nationals to the territory of the Member States for employment

A. *General considerations on policy*

(i) The Council recalls that, in the report adopted by the European Council held in Maastricht in 1991, priority was given to the harmonization of policies on admission for work as an employed or self-employed person, although it was emphasized that these policies should of necessity be restrictive.

(ii) The Council acknowledges the contribution of migrant workers to the economic development of their respective host countries. At present, however, no Member State is pursuing an active immigration policy. All States have, on the contrary, curtailed the possibility of permanent legal immigration for economic, social and thus political reasons. Admission for temporary employment may therefore be considered only in terms of what is purely exceptional.

(iii) The Council recognizes that the present high levels of unemployment in the Member States increase the need to bring Community employment preference properly into practice by making full use of the Eures system to improve the transparency of the labour markets and facilitate placement within the European Community. The Council further recognizes that the provisions within the European Community. The Council further recognizes that the provisions of the EC Treaty and the EEA Agreement enable job vacancies to be filled as far as possible by nationals of other Member States or of Member States or of EFTA countries which are parties to the EEA Agreement.

(iv) The Council agreed not to regulate via this resolution the issue of third-country nationals lawfully resident on a permanent basis in the territory of a Member State, but who have no right of admission and residence in another Member State.

It agreed to examine the matter at a later date.

(v) Member States reserve the right to allow, in accordance with their national law, the spouse and dependent children to accompany persons admitted in accordance with this resolution.

(vi) In the light of these considerations, the Council resolves that the present restrictive measures should be continued and where necessary reinforced as regards the admission of third-country nationals for employment. To this end, the Council agrees that the national policies of Member States in respect of third-country nationals seeking admission to, or permission to remain in, their territories for employment should be governed by the principles set out below, which may not be relaxed by Member States in their national legislation. It agrees to have regard to these principles in any proposals for the revision of national legislation. The Member States will further endeavour to seek to ensure by 1 January 1996 that national legislation is in conformity with such principles. The principles are not legally binding on the Member States and do not afford a ground for action by individual workers or employers.

B. *Persons to whom this resolution does not apply*
The harmonization principles do not apply to:
– persons who have right of free movement under Community law, i.e. nationals of Member States, nationals of EFTA countries parties to the Agreement on the European Economic Area and members of their families,
– third-country nationals who have been allowed admission for the purpose of family reunification to join nationals of a Member State or of a third country resident in the Member State concerned,
– third-country nationals whose access to employment is covered by rights stemming from agreements governed by Community law concluded with third countries,
– persons undertaking casual work in the course of youth exchange or youth mobility schemes, including 'au pairs',
– persons entering Member States in order to pursue economic activities as self-employed persons or to set up and/or manage a business/undertaking which they effectively control. Such persons will be governed by the principles to be set out in a draft resolution covering the self-employed;
– persons who are lawfully present in a Member State as:
– refugees under the terms of the Geneva Convention,
– applicants for asylum,
– third-country nationals admitted for asylum,
– displaced persons who are temporarily admitted,
– persons exceptionally allowed to stay on humanitarian grounds.

C. *Principles governing Member States' policies*
(i) General criteria
Member States will refuse entry to their territories of third-country nationals for the purpose of employment,
Member States will consider requests for admission to their territories for the purpose of employment only where vacancies in a Member State cannot be filled by national and Community manpower or by non-Community manpower lawfully resident on a permanent basis in that Member State and already forming part of the Member State's regular labour market. In this context they will apply the procedure laid down in Part II of Council Regulation (EEC) No 1612/68 of 15 October 1968 on freedom of movement for workers within the Community (1), in the light of Commission Decision 93/569/EEC (2) on the implementing of the Regulation, in particular with regard to Article 15 (16);

without prejudice to the application of the above two criteria, third-country nationals may, if necessary, be admitted on a temporary basis and for a specific duration to the territory of a Member State for the purpose of employment where:
– such an offer is made to a named worker or named employee of a service provider and is of a special nature in view of the requirement of specialist qualifications (professional qualifications, experience, etc.),
– an employer offers named workers vacancies only where the competent authorities consider, if appropriate, that the grounds adduced by the employer, including the nature of the qualifications required, are justified in view of a temporary manpower shortage on the national or Community labour market which significantly affects the operation of the undertaking or the employer himself,
– vacancies are offered to:
  – seasonal workers, whose numbers are strictly controlled on admission to the territory of the Member States and who undertake well-defined jobs, normally fulfilling a traditional need in the Member State in question. Member States will restrict the admission of these workers to cases where there is no reason to believe that the persons concerned will seek to stay within their territory on a permanent basis,
  – trainees,
  – frontier workers,
– the persons concerned are intra-corporate transferees being transferred temporarily by the company as key personnel.

(ii) Procedure for admission employment
A third-country national will not be admitted for employment unless prior authorization has been given for him to take up employment in the territory of the Member State concerned. Such prior authorization may be in the form of a work permit issued either to the employer or to the employee. In addition, third-county nationals must also be in possession of any necessary visa or, if the Member State concerned so requires, of a residence permit.

(iii) Restrictions as to the scope of employment
Initial authorization for employment will normally be restricted to employment in a specific job with a specified employer.

(iv) Restrictions as to the period of admission for employment
A seasonal worker will be admitted for a maximum of six months in any 12-month period, and must remain outside the territories of the Member States for a period of at least six months before being readmitted for employment.
Trainees will be admitted for a maximum period of one year in the first instance. This period may be fixed at more than a year and extended exclusively for the time needed to obtain a professional qualification recognized by the Member State concerned in the sphere of their activity. Other third-country nationals admitted to the territories of the Member States for employment will only be admitted for a period not exceeding four years in the first instance.

(v) Applications to extend a stay for the purpose of employment
A person already present in the territory of a Member State as a visitor or student will not in principle be permitted to extend his stay for the purpose of taking or seeking employment. Such persons must return to their own countries on conclusion of their visit or studies. In principle, a person admitted as a trainee or service provider or employee of a service provider will not be permitted to extend his stay in authorized employment except in order to complete the training or activity under contract for which he was admitted.
A seasonal worker will not be permitted to extend his stay for the purpose of taking employ-

ment of a different type. An extension of the period of his stay may be authorized to allow him to complete the work for which the original authorization was granted. However, the total length of his stay may not exceed six months in any 12-month period. Other workers may be permitted to extend their period to stay in authorized employment, but only if the criteria originally applied to the decision on whether to admit them for authorized employment continue to be met, in any event when the first extension is granted.

The Member States will examine the desirability of issuing a permanent residence permit to third-country nationals who have had restrictions on their employment lifted.

(vi) Business visitors

Nothing in these principles prevents a Member State from admitting as workers third-country nationals not residing in the territory of a Member State who are seeking entry in particular to:

− negotiate for the supply of goods or services,
− deliver goods or assemble machinery manufactured in a third country as part of a supply contract, provided that such persons will be dealing only with businesses in the territory of the Member State and not with the general public and that any one visit and possibly the work permit do not exceed six months.

(vii) Third countries with close links with a Member State

Nothing in these principles prevents a Member State from continuing to admit third-country nationals to its territory for the purpose of employment pursuant to arrangements concluded by that Member State by the date of adoption of this resolution for nationals of a third country with which it has especially close links.

The Member States will undertake as soon as possible to renegotiate such arrangements in accordance with the terms of this resolution. Where these arrangements concern the employees of a service provider, the Member States undertake to examine them in the spirit of this resolution within a reasonable period of time not exceeding three years, and to arrive at an assessment.

When this examination is carried out, account should be taken of the economic development of the States with which the Member States concluded the agreements in question.

The above provisions do not apply to arrangements covering employment of persons for instruction and vocational training purposes.

ANNEX: Definitions

'*Trainees*' means workers whose presence in the territory of a Member State is strictly limited in duration and closely connected with increasing their skills and qualifications in their chosen profession before returning to their own countries to pursue their careers.

'*Seasonal workers*' means workers who are resident in a third country but are employed in an activity dependent on the rhythm of the seasons in the territory of a Member State on the basis of a contract for a specified period and for specific employment.

'*Frontier workers*' means workers who are employed in the frontier zone of a Member State but who return each day or at least once a week to the frontier zone of a neighbouring country in which they reside and of which they are nationals.

'*Intra-corporate transferee*' means a natural person working within a legal person, other than a non-profit making organization, established in the territory of a WTO member, and being temporarily transferred in the context of the provision of a service through commercial presence in the territory of a Member State of the Community; the legal persons concerned must have their principal place of business in the territory of a WTO member other than the Community and its Member States and the transfer must be to an establishment (office, branch or subsidiary) of that legal person, effectively providing like services in the territory of a Member State to which the EC Treaty applies. In Italy, 'intra-corporate transferee' is defined as a natural person working within a legal person constituted as a SPA (joint stock company) or an SRL (capital stock company with limited responsibility).

3.2.6

[T.25] Council Resolution of 30 November 1994 relating to the limitation of the admission of third-country nationals to the territory of the Member States for the purpose of pursuing activities as self-employed persons

THE COUNCIL OF THE EUROPEAN UNION,
Having regard to the Treaty on European Union, and in particular Article K.1 thereof,
HEREBY ADOPTS THIS RESOLUTION:

A. *General considerations on policy*
1. The Council recalls that, in the report on immigration and asylum policy by the Ministers responsible for immigration adopted by the European Council held in Maastricht in 1991, priority was given to the harmonization of policies on admission for the purposes of pursuing self-employed occupation. In principle, these policies are restrictive. In any case, existing obligations and future developments for example in GATT, GATS and OECD agreements must be taken into account.
2. The Council notes that the 1994 programme of priority work in the field of justice and home affairs, adopted by the Council at its meeting in Brussels on 29 and 30 November 1993, included, as a priority measure, a decision to conclude work in the field of the admission of self-employed persons.
3. The Council welcomes the progress achieved as a result of the signing of the final act and agreements under the Uruguay Round in Marrakesh on 15 April 1994 towards free international trade for the promotion of investment and the creation of jobs.
4. The Council takes the view that, to a certain extent, the question of the admission of persons for the purposes of pursuing a salaried activity and that of the admission of self-employed persons can be treated distinctly. The admission of persons for the purpose of an independent economic activity who add value (investment, innovation, transfer of technology, job creation) to the economy of the host country is of benefit. Artists exercising an independent activity of significance may also be admitted.
5. The Council considers that third-country nationals should not be admitted to a Member State for the purposes of pursuing an independent economic activity when the latter is of no economic benefit to that State or any of its regions.
6. The Council considers it necessary to ensure that persons who are attempting to find employment in a dependent working relationship are not admitted as self-employed persons.

7. The Council also considers that it is necessary to avoid persons establishing themselves and embarking on a self-employed occupation without having the appropriate qualifications and/or financial means and to avoid their entering into a dependent working relationship.

8. The Council agrees not to deal in this resolution with the question of third-country nationals legally resident on a permanent basis in the territory of a Member State although they do not have the right to admission or residence in another Member State. It agrees to examine this question at a later date.

9. The Council accordingly agrees that the national policies of Member States in respect of third-country nationals seeking admission to, or permission to remain in, their territories in order to engage in a self-employed occupation should be governed by the principles set out below, which may not be relaxed by Member States in their national legislation. It agrees to have regard to these principles in any proposals for the revision of national legislation. The Member States will further endeavour to seek to ensure by 1 January 1996 that national legislation is in conformity with such principles. The principles are not legally binding on Member States and do not afford a ground for action by individuals.

10. The Council agrees that there shall be a regular review of the transposition of this resolution and of the need for amendments to it.

11. The Council also confirms that the application of these principles is no bar to the application of national rules on law and order, public health and national security.

B. *Persons to whom this resolution does not apply*
The harmonization principles do not apply to:
– persons who have right of free movement under Community law, i. e. nationals of Member States, nationals of EFTA countries parties to the Agreement on the European Economic Area and members of their families,
– third-country nationals who have been allowed admission for the purpose of family reunification to join nationals of a Member State or a third-country resident in the Member State concerned,
– third-country nationals whose access to employment is covered by rights stemming from agreements concluded with third countries which are governed by Community law and by bilateral and multilateral agreements, such as GATT, GATS or OECD agreements,
– third-country nationals entering the Member States in order to engage in paid employment. Such persons are covered by the principles set out in the resolution on limitations on admissions of third-country nationals to the Member States for employment adopted by the Council on 20 and 21 June 1994,
– third-country nationals entering the Member States for study purposes. Such persons are covered by the principles to be set out in the resolution on the admission of third-country nationals to the Member States for study purposes.

C. *General principles*
Point 1
1. This Resolution concerns only individuals and does not affect the setting up of firms.
2. 'Activity as a self-employed person' means any activity carried out in a personal capacity or in the legal form of a company or firm within the meaning of the second paragraph of Article 58 of the EC Treaty without being answerable to an employer in either case.
3. Only those associates actively involved and whose presence is necessary in pursuing the company's or firm's aims and in its management may be authorized to establish themselves in the host Member State's territory. In cases where those associates do not have a majority

or substantial shareholding in the company or firm, Member States may reserve the right not to admit them except in the case of salaried persons when they have received authorization to work.

Point 2

1. Member States may allow third-Country nationals wishing to pursue activities as self-employed persons to enter their territory where it has been duly established that that activity will produce the benefits referred to in Section A(4) or corresponds to the activity referred to in the last sentence of Section A(4) as required by each Member State and that general legal provisions governing entry and residence have been complied with.

2. The admission procedure should ensure that persons who quite obviously wish to engage in paid employment or whose partnership or directorship amounts to disguised paid employment are not admitted as self-employed persons. Without prejudice to the application of point 8(2), once admitted, the admission to activities as a self-employed person does not extend to looking for or accepting a job on the labour market.

Point 3

1. Requests for admission must be submitted to the authorities of the host Member State which are competent under national law through the consular or diplomatic representation of the State or through another national competent authority designated for this purpose in the home country or the country of origin of the person seeking admission to pursue activities as a self-employed person.

2. Requests for admission must be accompanied by information which can be used to assess whether the planned activity meets the preconditions referred to under point 2, and also by documentary evidence that the activity will be carried out in accordance with the relevant national legislation.

3. The following could, for example, be required for assessing the preconditions referred to under point 2 in accordance with national legislation:
– documents indicating the nature, scale and duration of the activity in which the person wishes to engage,
– documents indicating the number of staff likely to be required,
– a description of the premises where the activity will be carried out, which should be appropriate for it,
– evidence of the funds available for the intended purpose.

4. The following could for example be required for assessing compliance with legislation in force, in accordance with national legislation:
– proof that the self-employed person meets the conditions of the host Member State regarding professional qualifications and access to the occupation,
– in the case of companies or firms, the instrument of incorporation, evidence of publication or registration thereof, and the names of the directors and managerial staff and of the associates authorized to act on their behalf,
– proof such as police documentation or similar documents, showing the integrity of the person concerned.

Point 4

1. Authorization to engage in a self-employed occupation will be granted in accordance with the provisions of national aliens' legislation and in writing, for example in the form of

a passport stamp or other document. Such authorization will be personal and non-transferable.
2. The validity of the initial authorization may be limited in time. Upon application, it may be extended for a further period and/or be of unlimited validity, if the conditions for access continue to obtain as provided for in national legislation.

Point 5
1. All requests for renewal must, where so required under Member States' national legislation, be accompanied by documentary evidence that the self-employed person offers guarantees for the continued orderly pursuit of his occupation.
2. At least at the time when any renewal application referred to under point 4(2) is submitted, a check may be made on the bona fide nature of the activity engaged in, whether it still corresponds to the activity for which authorization was given, the ability of the person concerned to support himself by the income from that activity and its continuing compliance with the preconditions referred to under point 2(1).
3. Any further checks which Member States may make thereafter could in principle be limited.

Point 6
1. Under the conditions laid down by national law, Member States may grant third-country nationals wishing to provide a service, leave to enter their territory with authorization to carry out the relevant work for the performance of the service.
2. 'Service provider' means a self-employed person (residing abroad) whose services are sought by a person residing in a Member State in order to carry out, against remuneration, a specific task over a specific period.

Point 7
Persons already present in the territory of a Member State as students, trainees, seasonal workers, service providers, contract workers or for other reasons will not as a general rule be permitted to extend their stay for the purpose of establishing themselves as self-employed persons. Such persons must leave the country once the purpose of stay on the basis of which they were given leave to enter the country has ceased to apply.

Point 8
1. In principle, care must be taken to ensure that persons admitted to pursue activities as self-employed persons do not eventually enter into a paid employment relationship.
2. Member States may allow self-employed persons who have acquired the right to long-term/permanent residence to seek where appropriate a work permit in order to obtain paid employment.

Point 9
The spouse and unmarried children under a maximum age, varying between 16 and 18 years depending on the Member State concerned, of a self-employed person will in principle be admitted to join that person, subject to the conditions set out in the resolution concerning family reunification adopted by the Ministers responsible for immigration questions of the European Union on 1 June 1993.

Point 10

1. Member States' arrangements enabling them to refuse admission on grounds of public security and public order shall not be affected by this resolution.

2. The provisions of this resolution shall not affect Member States' provisions governing trades and professions or arrangements concerning the mutual recognition of vocational qualifications.

Point 11

Nothing in this resolution prevents a Member State from reserving the right to admit, subject to its national law, third-country nationals who make very substantial investments in the commerce and industry of that Member State where there are strong economic reasons justifying exemption from those principles in this resolution that limit the business activities in which the third-country national is engaged.

3.2.7

[T.26] Council Resolution of 30 November 1994 on the admission of third-country nationals to the territory of the Member States for study purposes

THE COUNCIL OF THE EUROPEAN UNION,
Having regard to the Treaty on European Union, and in particular Article K.1 thereof,
HEREBY ADOPTS THIS RESOLUTION:

A. *General considerations*

1. The Council recalls that, in the report adopted by the Maastricht European Council (December 1991) from the Ministers responsible for immigration and asylum policy, priority was given to the harmonization of rules for the admission of students from third countries. In the 1994 programme of work on justice and home affairs, which the Council approved at its meeting on 29 and 30 November 1993 in Brussels, the completion of work on the admission of students was also given priority status.

2. The Council confirms that the international exchange of students and academics is desirable; it acknowledges that the education of students and the exchange of academics have positive implications for relations between the Member States and the States of origin.

3. The Council agrees that, at the end of their studies, students must in principle return to their countries of origin so that the knowledge and skills they have acquired are made available to those countries.

4. The Council considers it is important to ensure that the admission of third-country nationals to study in the Member States for a limited period in principle does not turn into permanent immigration. Similarly, the Council considers it is necessary to devise suitable systems to prevent those who are mainly seeking employment from receiving authorization to stay on as students.

5. The Council agrees not to regulate via this resolution the issue of third-country nationals lawfully resident on a permanent basis in the territory of a Member State, but who have no right of admission and residence in another Member State.

This does not affect the position of third-country nationals who are already covered or who may, in the future, be covered by bilateral agreements between the Member States regarding the cooperation between institutions of higher education.

6. The Council agrees that the national policies of Member States in respect of the admission of third-country nationals for study purposes should be governed by the principles set out below, which may not be relaxed by Member States in their national legislation. The Council agrees to have regard to these principles in any proposals for the revision of national legislation.

The Member States will further endeavour to seek to ensure by 1 January 1996 that national legislation is in conformity with such principles. The principles are not legally binding on Member States and do not afford a ground for action by individuals.

7. The Council agrees that there shall be a regular review of the transposition of this resolution and of the need for amendments to it.

8. The Member States should facilitate the admission and residence of students from third countries within the framework of special cooperation programmes, the financing of which is secured at national or Community level.

9. Application of the said principles does not prevent application of national rules on public policy, public health or safety.

B. *Persons exempt from the scope of this resolution*
The principles of harmonization will not apply to:
– individuals who enjoy the right of freedom of movement under Community law, i.e. nationals of the Member States, nationals of the EFTA countries which are parties to the Agreement on the European Economic Area and members of their families,
– third-country nationals who have been admitted for the purposes of family reunification to take up residence with nationals of a Member State or third country who reside in the Member State in question.

C. *Principles by which the policies of the Member States will be guided*
1. General criteria
Within the meaning of these principles, a student is a national of a third country admitted by a State or State-recognized higher education institution or a comparable institution in a Member State in order to:
– take up a course of study,
– study for a doctorate, or
– pursue academic activity following a course of higher education within the framework of further study or training, where the earning of income is not the principal aim.
It should also be noted that for the purposes of this resolution school pupils and apprentices are not included.
For the purpose of this resolution, a person who participates in a course aimed at preparing for a specific course of university studies (e.g. providing language training) shall also be deemed to be a student.

2. Requirements for admission

A national of a third country who requests admission as a student will have to prove to the competent authorities of the Member State that he/she:
–   fulfils all the requirements applicable to foreigners as regards entry and stay in the territory of the Member State,
–   has a firm offer of admission to a State or State-recognized higher education institution or a comparable institution appropriate to his/her studies for a course of study as a main activity and is so required by national legislation that this offer concurs with requirements made by the competent immigration authorities. Member States may also request proof of continuity between previous studies and studies to be undertaken in the host country,
–   has the financial means required to support the cost of his/her studies and subsistence for himself/herself so that during his/her stay the student does not need to claim social assistance in the host Member State and the earning of an income is not the principal aim,
–   if required by national legislation, has health cover for all risks in the host Member State.

A Member State may also require the student to satisfy the immigration authorities that he/she would return to his/her own country on completion of studies.

A Member State may permit persons to enter who are interested in preparing their application for studies in the respective State or who can demonstrate a genuine and realistic plan for undertaking a course of study. It may be permitted for the person concerned not to have to leave the country in order to obtain an extension of his/her authorization to stay. Nationals of third countries who entered the Member State with the aim of working there in an employed or self-employed capacity shall on the basis of this resolution not be admitted in principle to engage in study as a main activity.

3. Authorization to reside

The duration of residence is limited to the length of the course. The length of the course is dictated by the duration of studies in the chosen subject. At the end of the course of study, or if the student abandons his/her studies, authorization to reside expires. Any change in subject will involve a change in the reason for residence which, as a rule, argues against a fresh authorization or an extension of the existing one if it does not take place within the initial phase of the studies. Proof of authorization to reside will take the form of an entry in the student's passport or a particular personal identity card. If the period of study is longer than one year, the authorization can initially be limited to a one-year period; in that case it can be renewed on a yearly basis. Renewal will depend on the student's ability to prove that he/she fulfils the requirements for its original issue and that he/she has passed any tests or examinations set by the institution in which he/she is studying.

At the end of his/her course of study, or if the student abandons his/her studies, a national of a third country will in principle have to leave the territory of the Member State; if he/she wishes to return to that country he/she will have to re-apply for authorization to re-enter.

4. Employment authorization

In principle a national of a third country who is studying in the territory of a Member State may not engage in gainful employment, either in a self-employed or employed capacity. Member States may allow short-term or subsidiary jobs. Such jobs must not affect the continuation of his/her studies; neither must they, in principle, represent an income vital for the subsistence of the student.

5. Admission of family members

National provisions will apply as regards the possible admission of family members and the taking-up of employment or study by the spouse. Once the third country national has ended his/her studies, the spouse and children to whom authorization to stay was granted are also required to leave the territory of the Member State if they have no other authorization to remain.

[T.28] Decision of 22 December 1995 on monitoring the implementation of instruments already adopted concerning admission of third-country nationals[14]

THE COUNCIL OF THE EUROPEAN UNION,

Having regard to Article K.3(2)(a) of the Treaty on European Union, Having regard to the priority work programme adopted by the Council on 30 November 1993 in Brussels, calling in particular for the preparation of an annual report on achievements in the field of justice and home affairs, Whereas Article K.1(3)(a) of the Treaty on European Union states that Member States shall regard conditions of entry by nationals of third countries on the territory of Member States as a matter of common interest;

Whereas the instruments adopted by the Council concerning the admission of third-country nationals express a common political will;

Whereas monitoring of the implementation of the provisions contained in these instruments will reveal the practical effect of the Council's work in this matter and provide useful lessons for its future work;

Whereas Member States consequently intend to agree on practical arrangements for such monitoring,

HAS DECIDED AS FOLLOWS:

Article 1 – Preparation of a questionnaire

Each year, the Presidency shall forward to the Member States a questionnaire designed to show how they have implemented the resolutions and acts already adopted by the Council concerning the admission of third-country nationals.

Article 2 – Content of the questionnaire

The questionnaire shall refer to the following:
– provisions adopted during the preceding year by the Member States in any of the areas referred to by the instruments already adopted,
– difficulties in adopting those provisions,
– the possibility of any provision on those areas being adopted in the near future,

---

[14] OJ C 11 of 16 January 1996, p. 1 (396Y0116(01))

– application in practice of the instruments, irrespective of the adoption of internal provisions where appropriate.

Article 3 – Evaluation of the replies
A report on the application of the instruments referred to in Article 1 shall be drawn up on the basis of the replies from the Member States and shall be submitted to the Council.

Article 4 – Implementation
The first questionnaire shall be sent to the Member States in the first half of 1996.

3.2.9
Proposal for a Council Act establishing the Convention on rules for the admission of third-country nationals to the Member States[15]

THE COUNCIL OF THE EUROPEAN UNION,
Having regard to the Treaty on European Union, and in particular Article K.3(2), first indent, point (c) thereof,
Having regard to the proposal from the Commission,
Having regard to the opinion of the European Parliament,
Considering that for the purposes of achieving the objectives of the European Union, the Member States regard immigration policy and in particular the conditions of residence by third-country nationals on the territory of the Member States, including family reunification and access to employment, as a matter of common interest falling within the scope of cooperation as laid down in Title IV of the Treaty;
HAS DECIDED to establish the Convention the text of which is attached, signed this day by the Representatives of the Governments of the Member States of the European Union;
RECOMMENDS its adoption by the Member States in accordance with their respective constitutional rules.

CONVENTION on rules for the admission of third-country nationals to the Member States of the European Union
THE HIGH CONTRACTING PARTIES to this Convention, Member States of the European Union,
REFERRING to the Act of the Council of the European Union of...;
1. CONSIDERING that (....) immigration policy and in particular the conditions of residence by third-country nationals on the territory of the Member States, including family reunion and access to employment, are a matter of common interest falling within the scope of cooperation as laid down in Title VI of the Treaty;

---

[15] (97/C 337/03)(Text with EEA relevance) COM(97) 387 final – 97/0227 (CNS); submitted by the Commission pursuant to Article K.3(2)(c) of the Treaty on European Union on 30 July 1997.

2. CONSIDERING that rules governing the conditions of residence and access to employment for citizens of the Union and other persons covered by Community law fall under the Treaty establishing the European Community;

Whereas this Convention lays down rules applicable to persons not covered by Community law;

3. CONSIDERING that resolutions on rules of admission and on the status of third-country nationals residing in the Member States on a long-term basis have already been adopted;

Whereas this established policy approach may usefully be enhanced by closer cooperation leading to the laying-down of common legal rules governing immigration policy, subject to the requirements of law and order and of public security;

4. CONSIDERING that those rules should, in particular, lay down conditions of admission for the purposes of paid employment and the pursuit of independent economic activities, taking due account of the interests of all the Member States;

5. CONSIDERING that the rules laid down are also intended to underpin the Member States' openness to the rest of the world and their level of exchanges with other countries, especially in the cultural, scientific and economic spheres, through common provisions on admission for the purposes of education and vocational training;

6. CONSIDERING that those rules should allow families to exercise their right to live together, by laying down arrangements for families to be reunited;

7. CONSIDERING that the common rules should also define the rights of third-country nationals residing legally in a Member State, especially those who are resident on a long-term basis, and the conditions under which they may enjoy those rights in a Member State other than the Member State where they have acquired the status of long-term residents;

8. CONSIDERING that these common rules should accord with their common international undertakings, in particular the [1950 ECHR and the 1951 Refugee Convention], and with more favourable constitutional provisions on asylum;

9. CONSIDERING that these common rules on admission, with the exception of the rules concerning family reunification together with those applying to persons recognized as long-term residents, confer no right of residence and that the Member States retain their discretionary powers to take actual decisions as to the admission of nationals of non-member countries,

HAVE AGREED AS FOLLOWS:

CHAPTER I – DEFINITIONS AND SCOPE

Article 1 – Definitions
For the purposes of this Convention:
(a) 'admission' means permission for a third-country national to enter the territory of a Member State in order to reside there for longer than three months;
(b) 'residence authorization' means decision taken by a Member State in whatever form is provided by its own legislation to permit a person to reside in its territory for a period of more than three months; this does not include temporary authorizations which may be issued by Member States in certain cases.

Article 2 – Scope
1. The provisions of this Convention shall apply to nationals of third countries, except where more favourable provisions apply under:

(a) bilateral or multilateral agreements concluded between the Community, or the Community and its Member States, of the one part, and third States of the other part, which entered into force before this Convention was signed;

(b) agreements concluded between one or more Member States and third countries which entered into force before this Convention was signed.

It shall not apply to:

(a) persons who have applied in a Member State for recognition of refugee status under the terms of the 1951 Geneva Convention;

(b) displaced persons granted admission to stay for temporary protection in a Member State;

(c) persons granted exceptional authorization to stay in the territory of a Member State, particularly on humanitarian grounds.

2. The provisions of this Convention shall not apply to citizens of the Union or to nationals of third countries enjoying a right of residence in a Member State by virtue of Community law.

CHAPTER II – GENERAL RULES

Article 3 – Examination of initial applications for admission

1. An initial application by a third-country national for admission to a Member State may be considered by the competent authorities only if the applicant is outside the territory of the Member States when the application is made and remains so until notified of the decision reached.

2. The Member State to which application is made shall examine applications carefully, having regard among other things to considerations of public policy, public security and health. Common rules on the examination of applications shall be laid down in accordance with the procedure under Article 36.

Article 4 – Travel documents

Third-country nationals must have the necessary travel documents in order to enter the territory of the Member State to which they have been granted admission. The Member State shall issue any visas required.

Other Member States shall issue any transit visas necessary to enable such third-country nationals to travel to the Member State to which they have been granted admission.

Article 5 – Permitted absences

1. Third-country nationals admitted to a Member State shall be permitted to leave that Member State for reasons other than those for which they were admitted to it, for a period not exceeding 13 full weeks in any full calendar year plus statutory holidays.

Where the absence is for the same reasons as those which justified their admission, the limit as to duration contained in the first subparagraph shall not apply.

2. By way of derogation from paragraph 1, third-country nationals recognized as long-term residents in accordance with Articles 32 and 33 may leave the Member State where they have been recognized as long-term residents for a period not exceeding 26 consecutive weeks. This period may be exceeded where they leave the Member State to change their Member State of residence in accordance with Article 35.

3. Longer authorized periods of absence than those provided for by paragraphs 1 and 2 may be permitted:

(a) provided that a request based on cogent grounds is submitted by the person concerned before leaving and receives approval;

(b) provided that a request based on exceptional grounds is submitted by the person concerned after leaving and receives approval.

A list of such grounds shall be defined in accordance with the procedure laid down in Article 36.

Article 6 – Renewal of residence authorization

1. Without prejudice to the provisions of the 1951 Geneva Convention, third-country nationals may, when their authorized period of residence expires, apply locally for the renewal of their residence authorization if the conditions which justified the granting of admission are still met.

2. Without prejudice to the provisions of Article 31, third-country nationals may only submit an application for admission on a different ground from that on which admission was previously granted if they are outside the territory of the Member States. Fresh applications of this kind may be considered only if the applicant is staying outside the territory of the Member States when the application is made and remains so until notified of the decision reached.

3. By way of derogation from paragraph 2, applications for admission made locally on a different ground from that on which admission was previously granted shall be permitted, but only in circumstances strictly set out in accordance with the procedure under Article 36, for the following persons:

(a) persons admitted pursuant to Article 7 or 8 and wishing to reside pursuant to Chapter IV;

(b) persons admitted pursuant to Chapter IV and wishing to reside pursuant to Article 7 or 8.

4. By way of derogation from paragraphs 2 and 3, third-country nationals who have been recognized as long-term residents under Articles 32 and 33 shall not be required to leave the territory of the Member States in order to submit an application for renewal of their residence authorization.

CHAPTER III – ADMISSION FOR THE PURPOSES OF PAID EMPLOYMENT

Article 7 – Principles

1. A third-country national may be granted admission to the territory of a Member State for the purposes of paid employment where a job vacancy in a Member State cannot be filled in the short term:

(a) by citizens of the Union; or

(b) by a third-country national who is legally resident in the Member State and already forms part of the regular labour market in that Member State; or

(c) by a third-country national who has been recognized as a long-term resident.

2. Measures for the implementation of paragraph 1 shall be adopted under the procedure laid down in Article 36.

Article 8 – Conditions of admission

1. On their initial admission for the purposes of paid employment, third-country nationals must already have obtained a work contract of not less than one year's duration and

authorization to take up that employment in the territory of the Member State concerned. Once these conditions are satisfied, and admission is granted, third-country nationals shall be issued with a residence authorization for a period at least equivalent to the duration of the work contract. The first residence authorization, however, is limited to a period of four years.

2. A residence authorization granted for the purposes of paid employment may be renewed if the conditions of Article 7(1) are still satisfied when the application for renewal is made.

3. Measures for the implementation of paragraph 2 shall be adopted under the procedure laid down in Article 36.

Article 9 – Seasonal workers

1. For the purposes of this Convention 'seasonal workers' means third-country nationals who retain their legal domicile in a third country but are employed in the territory of a Member State in a sector of activity dependent on the passing of the seasons, under a fixed-term contract for a specific job.

2. Third-country nationals may be admitted as seasonal workers for up to six months in any calendar year, after which they must return to a third country.

3. Where residence authorization has been granted for less than six months, this may be extended at the place of employment to allow seasonal workers to complete the work for which they were originally granted admission. The employer must submit the extension request, duly substantiated, at least one month before expiry of the initial authorization.

4. In admitting seasonal workers, a Member State shall give third-country nationals who have previously performed seasonal work in that State preference over third-country nationals making their first application for admission for the purposes of seasonal work.

Article 10 – Transfrontier workers

1. For the purposes of this Convention, 'transfrontier workers` means third-country nationals resident in the frontier zone of a third country who are employed in the frontier zone of an adjacent Member State and who return to the frontier zone of that third country each day or at least once a week.

2. Transfrontier workers who are nationals of third countries may be admitted for the purposes of paid employment in the frontier zone of an adjacent Member State notwithstanding the principles set out in Article 7 of this Convention

CHAPTER IV – ADMISSION FOR THE PURPOSES OF PURSUING AN INDEPENDENT ECONOMIC ACTIVITY

Article 11 – Definition

For the purposes of this Convention, 'admission for the purposes of pursuing an independent economic activity` means the entry into the territory of a Member State of a natural person who is a third-country national in order to pursue in that Member State an economic activity involving no subordinate relationship to an employer.

Article 12 – Conditions of admission

Third-country nationals wishing to establish themselves in a Member State in order to pursue an independent economic activity may be admitted to the territory of that Member State on condition that they comply with the rules governing the exercise of the activity concerned, namely if:

(a) they have sufficient resources to undertake, in the relevant Member State, the activity for which they submit their admission application; and

(b) the business generated by the person admitted will have, during the period of validity of the initial residence authorization, a beneficial effect on employment in the Member State in which he resides.

Measures for the implementation of the first paragraph shall be adopted in accordance with the procedure laid down in Article 36.

Article 13 – Residence authorization

1. The residence authorization granted to third-country nationals to pursue an independent economic activity referred to in Article 12 shall be issued for at least two years.

2. Applications for renewal may be made in the host Member State for the same activity as that for which initial authorization was given or for an activity which is a continuation or development of it.

When the application for renewal is submitted, third-country nationals must:

(a) have actually pursued the activity for which admission was authorized;

(b) be able to guarantee that they can continue to pursue that activity lawfully and regularly;

(c) satisfy the conditions set out in point (b) of Article 12.

Article 14 – Provision of services

The admission of third-country nationals to the Member States to pursue activities involving the supply of services shall, without prejudice to Community law, be governed by the procedure laid down in Article 36.

CHAPTER V – ADMISSION FOR THE PURPOSES OF STUDY AND VOCATIONAL TRAINING

Article 15 – Admission for study purposes

Third-country nationals may be granted admission to the territory of a Member State for study purposes if they have been admitted to a State or State-recognized establishment of higher education in order to:

(a) attend preparatory courses for a specific course of study in higher education;

(b) pursue a course of study;

(c) prepare a doctoral thesis;

(d) pursue research activity as part of a basic or advanced vocational education after obtaining a degree or higher education diploma, where that activity is not primarily intended to secure an income.

Article 16 – Residence authorization

1. The period of residence shall be limited to the length of the course of study chosen. The duration of the residence authorization issued shall be the same as the duration of enrolment at the establishment attended.

2. Residence authorizations may be renewed annually. They shall be renewed if the applicants produce evidence that they continue to satisfy the requirements set for the issuance of the initial authorization and that they have taken any tests required by the higher education establishment which they attend.

3. Students may not change their course of study after the first year. If they do change course after that time, they shall make a fresh admission application for study purposes.

4. Measures for the implementation of paragraphs 1, 2 and 3 shall be adopted in accordance with the procedure laid down in Article 36.

Article 17 – Employment authorization for students
Third-country nationals admitted to the territory of a Member State for study purposes are not authorized to engage in a gainful occupation, whether in paid employment or in a self-employed capacity. Subsidiary or short-term work such as, by way of derogation from Article 9, seasonal work shall continue to be open to them provided that this does not interfere with their studies.

Article 18 – Completion of study
1. Third-country nationals who have completed one of the categories of study as defined in Article 15, and who wish to continue studying under another category, may apply for a new authorization in the host Member State.
2. Third-country nationals who wish to remain in a Member State for another purpose after completing their studies must go through the initial admission procedure.

Article 19 – Trainees
1. For the purposes of this Convention, 'trainees` means workers whose presence in the territory of a Member State is closely linked to their wish to improve their skills and qualifications in their chosen occupation in order to pursue it in a third country.
2. Third-country nationals seeking admission to the territory of a Member State as trainees must satisfy the following requirements:
(a) they shall hold a training agreement with a host establishment, guaranteeing them sufficient remuneration to support themselves; and
(b) they shall enjoy social security cover for risks that may arise in the host Member State.
3. Residence authorization granted to trainees shall be limited to one year. If the time required to obtain a vocational qualification is more than one year, the authorization may be extended annually. In no circumstances may an extension be granted to allow the person concerned to take up employment.

Article 20 – Specific programmes
Member States shall facilitate the admission of third-country nationals as students, trainees or researchers, under cooperation programmes that receive Community funding.
To that end, implementing measures shall be laid down in accordance with the procedure under Article 36.

Article 21 – Limits of scope
The provisions of this chapter shall not apply to:
(a) pupils in primary and secondary education;
(b) apprentices.

CHAPTER VI – ADMISSION FOR OTHER PURPOSES

Article 22 – Conditions of admission
Third-country nationals to whom the provisions of Chapters III, IV, V or VII do not apply may be granted admission to the territory of a Member State if they satisfy the following requirements:

(a) they shall have sufficient means to support themselves without engaging in any of the gainful activities referred to in Chapters III and IV; and
(b) they shall enjoy social security cover that is valid in the Member State to which they are seeking admission; and
(c) they shall be able to show the lawful origin of their means of support; and
(d) they shall have accommodation in the Member State to which application is made.
Measures for the implementation of the first paragraph shall be adopted in accordance with the procedure laid down in Article 36.

Article 23 – Residence authorization
1. The initial residence authorization granted to a third-country national shall be issued for at least one year.
2. Residence authorizations may be extended for at least one year. Third-country nationals must show that they continue to satisfy the requirements laid down in Article 22 when they apply for an extension.

CHAPTER VII – ADMISSION FOR THE PURPOSES OF FAMILY REUNIFICATION

Article 24 Principles
1. Third-country nationals may exercise their right to family reunification provided that they have been legally resident in a Member State for at least one year and have the right of residence in that Member State for at least one year on the date when they submit the application provided for in Article 28.
2. By way of derogation from paragraph 1, third-country nationals enjoying the provisions of Article 15 may submit the application provided for in Article 28 when they have been legally resident in a Member State for at least two years and have the right of residence in that Member State for one more year.

Article 25 – Members of families of Union citizens not exercising the right to freedom of movement
By way of derogation from this chapter, family reunification of nationals of non-member countries who are members of the family of a Union citizen who resides in the Member State of which he is a national shall be subject to the same conditions as are imposed by Articles 10, 11 and 12 of Council Regulation (EEC) No 1612/68 of 15 October 1968 on freedom of movement for workers within the Community (1) and by all other relevant provisions of Community law.

Article 26 – Categories of persons entitled to be reunited
1. The following persons shall be admitted for the purposes of family reunification, provided that the marriage is compatible with the fundamental principles of the law of the Member State:
(a) the resident's spouse;
(b) children of the resident and his or her spouse, including children adopted in accordance with a decision by the authority responsible in the Member State or a decision recognized by that authority;
(c) children, including adopted children, of the resident or his or her spouse where one or other of them has sole parental authority over those children, has been given custody of them, and is de facto responsible for them.

2. To qualify for admission for the purposes of family reunification, children shall be below the age of legal majority in the Member State concerned and shall be unmarried.

3. Member States shall give favourable consideration to family reunification involving dependent relatives in the ascending line as well as other dependent relatives in the descending line, provided that the conditions laid down in Article 28 are met.

Article 27 – Fraud

1. Member States may refuse to admit a spouse or a child for the purposes of family reunification, or shall withdraw their residence authorization, if it is found that fraud or forgery has been used.

2. Member States shall refuse to admit a spouse or an adopted child for the purposes of family reunification or may withdraw their residence authorization, if it is found that the sole purpose of the marriage or adoption was to enable such person to be admitted to a Member State.

Article 28 – Accommodation and means of support

1. To exercise their right to family reunification, a third-country national shall submit an application in the Member State where he is resident and at the same time furnish proof that he has suitable accommodation and adequate means to support his family when reunited. This application may be submitted six months after his entry into the Member State where he is resident.

2. The conditions of paragraph 1 shall be laid down in detail by implementing measures adopted in accordance with the procedure provided for in Article 36.

Article 29 – Residence authorization

Once a Member State has approved an application for family reunification, it shall issue residence authorizations to the family members to be reunited, which shall be valid for the remaining duration of the current residence authorization of the person with whom they are being reunited.

Article 30 – Employment of persons admitted for the purposes of family reunification

1. Persons admitted for the purposes of family reunification shall not be authorized to take up employment or pursue an independent economic activity until a period of six months from the date of their arrival has elapsed.

2. By way of derogation from paragraph 1, the six-month period shall not be mandatory where there are unforeseen changes in the composition or income of the family that generate a need for the persons admitted for the purposes of family reunification to be allowed to pursue an activity.

Article 31 – Acquisition of separate status by persons admitted for the purposes of family reunification

1. Where persons admitted for the purposes of family reunification are widowed, divorced or legally separated, lose their parents through death or reach the age of majority, they may submit an application for residence authorization in another capacity. This application shall be examined in the Member State to which they were admitted.

2. The persons concerned must submit their application no later than three months before their residence authorization expires. However, if the residence authorization expires less

than three months after the circumstances justifying admission have ceased to apply, this deadline shall be extended to a total of three months.

Where necessary, the Member State concerned shall issue them with a provisional residence authorization for the period during which their application is being considered until they are notified of the decision reached.

CHAPTER VIII – THIRD-COUNTRY NATIONALS WHO ARE LONG-TERM RESIDENTS

Article 32 – Definition
Third-country nationals shall be recognized as long-term residents in a Member State if they satisfy the following requirements:
(a) they shall have been legally resident on a regular basis in a Member State for at least five years; and
(b) they shall hold an authorization which permits residence for a total period of at least 10 years from their first admission.

Article 33 – Residence authorization
1. Once third-country nationals acquire recognition as long-term residents, this shall be shown by a specific entry on their residence authorization document.
2. When their residence authorization referred to in point (b) of Article 32 expires, third-country nationals who are long-term residents shall be entitled to a residence authorization for the maximum period allowed in the Member State where they reside, and in any event for not less than 10 years.

Article 34 – Rights in the Member State of residence
1. In the Member State in which they are long-term residents and without prejudice to Community law, third-country nationals recognized as long-term residents shall:
(a) have access to the entire territory of that Member State;
(b) be authorized to exercise all activities referred to in Chapters III, IV and V;
(c) be authorized to reside for all the purposes referred to in Chapters VI and VII;
(d) be afforded increased protection against expulsion, subject to the requirements of law and order and of internal security;
(e) enjoy the same treatment as citizens of the Union with regard to: (i) access to employment or self-employment; (ii) vocational training; (iii) trade union rights; (iv) the right of association; (v) access to housing, whether in the private, public or para-Statal sector; (vi) social welfare; (vii) schooling.
2. Measures for the implementation of paragraph 1 shall be defined in accordance with the procedure laid down by Article 36.

Article 35 – Rights in other Member States
1. A third-country national recognized as a long-term resident may:
(a) apply for employment in another Member State by answering a vacancy known to him, subject to compliance with the principles laid down in Article 7;
(b) apply to pursue a course of study as defined in Article 15 in another Member State.
In the cases shown in the first subparagraph, if the person obtains a work contract or enrolment in an establishment of higher education, the Member State concerned shall admit the third-

country national concerned and shall issue him with the necessary authorizations, including those relating to residence.

2. A third-country national settled in accordance with paragraph 1 in a Member State other than that which has recognized him as a long-term resident shall be recognized as such likewise in his new Member State of residence, after a period of two years' residence. This shall be shown by the issue of a residence authorization for a period equal to that which enabled him to be recognized as a long-term resident in his previous Member State of residence.

3. A third-country national recognized as a long-term resident of a Member State shall cease to be recognized as such in that Member State once he is recognized as a long-term resident of another Member State in accordance with paragraph 2.

CHAPTER IX – FINAL PROVISIONS

Article 36 – Procedure for the adoption of implementing measures

1. Subject to paragraphs 2 and 3, implementing measures provided for in this Convention shall be adopted within the Council by a two-thirds majority of the High Contracting Parties.

2. The implementing measures referred to in Articles 6(3), 7(2), 8(3), 12, and 34 shall be adopted by common accord amongst the High Contracting Parties within two years of publication of the act establishing this Convention in the Official Journal of the European Communities.

After the period set out in the first subparagraph, the implementing measures shall be adopted in accordance with paragraph 1.

3. The implementing measures referred to in Articles 14 and 22 and any implementing measures not expressly provided for in this Convention shall be adopted by common accord amongst the High Contracting Parties.

4. The implementing measures referred to in paragraphs 1, 2 and 3 shall be published in the Official Journal of the European Communities.

Article 37 – Jurisdiction of the Court of Justice of the European Communities

1. Any dispute between Member States or between a Member State and the Commission as to the interpretation or application of this Convention shall first be considered by the Council with a view to reaching a settlement. If no solution is found within six months, the matter shall be referred to the Court of Justice of the European Communities by any party to the dispute.

2. The Court of Justice shall have jurisdiction to give preliminary rulings on the interpretation of this Convention. Any court or tribunal of a Member State against whose decisions there is no judicial remedy under national law shall request the Court of Justice to give a preliminary ruling on a question raised in a case pending before it concerning the interpretation of this Convention, if it considers that a decision on that question is necessary to enable it to give judgment.

Article 38 – Relations with third countries

Any Member State which intends to conduct negotiations with a third country to lay down more favourable rules for the admission of nationals of that State shall inform the other Member States and the Commission in good time.

No Member State may conclude such agreements with one or more third countries without the prior approval of the Council.

Article 39 – Safeguard clause
The provisions of this Convention shall not preclude derogations from its clauses by a Member State under the provisions of Article K.2(2) of the Treaty on European Union. Such derogations may be made only in exceptional cases and shall be confined to such period as is strictly necessary.
A Member State availing itself of this option shall, in so doing, take into account the interests of the other Member States and keep both they and the Commission closely informed.

Article 40 – Reservations
Reservations shall not be permissible in respect of this Convention.

Article 41 – Adoption and entry into force (...)

Article 42 – Amendment of the Convention (...)

Article 43 – Accession by new Member States
1. This Convention shall be open to accession by any State that becomes a member of the European Union.
2. The text of this Convention in the language or languages of the acceding State, drawn up by the Council, shall be authentic.
3. Instruments of accession shall be deposited with the depositary.
4. This Convention shall enter into force with respect to any State that accedes to it on the first day of the month following the expiry of a two-month period following the date of deposit of its instrument of accession or on the date of entry into force of the Convention if it has not already entered into force at the time of expiry of the said period.

Article 44 – Depositary (...)

3.2.10

[T.21] Joint Action of 16 December 1996 concerning a uniform format for residence permits[16]

THE COUNCIL OF THE EUROPEAN UNION,
Having regard to the Treaty on European Union, and in particular Article K.3 (2)(b) thereof,
Whereas Article K.1 (3) of the Treaty provides that immigration policy and policy regarding nationals of third countries constitute a matter of common interest;
Whereas it is desirable to harmonize the format of residence permits issued by Member States to third country nationals;

---

[16] OJ L 7 of 10 January 1997, (497X0011).

Whereas it is essential that the uniform format for residence permits should contain all the necessary information and meet very high technical standards, in particular as regards safeguards against counterfeiting and falsification;

Whereas it must also be suited to use by all the Member States and bear universally recognizable security features which are clearly visible to the naked eye;

Whereas this Joint Action only lays down such specifications as are not secret;

Whereas these specifications need to be supplemented by further specifications which are to remain secret in order to prevent counterfeiting and falsifications and which may not include personal data or references to such data;

Whereas the Council should lay down these supplementary specifications;

Whereas, to ensure that the information referred to is not made available to more persons than necessary, it is also essential that each Member State should designate not more than one body having responsibility for printing the uniform format for residence permits, with Member States remaining free to change the body, if need be;

Whereas, for security reasons, each Member State must communicate the name of the competent body to the Council and the Commission;

Whereas, with regard to the personal data to be entered on the uniform format for residence permits in accordance with the Annex hereto, compliance should be ensured with applicable data-protection provisions,

HAS ADOPTED THIS JOINT ACTION:

Article 1

Residence permits issued by Member States to third country nationals shall be in a uniform format and provide space for the information set out in the Annex hereto.

The uniform format can be used as a sticker or a stand-alone document. Each Member State may add in the relevant space of the uniform format any information of importance regarding the nature of the permit and the person concerned, including information as to whether or not the person is permitted to work.

Article 2

1. The technical specifications for incorporating the information set out in the Annex on the uniform format for residence permits shall be laid down by the Council without delay.

Further technical specifications which render the residence permit difficult to counterfeit or falsify shall also be laid down by the Council without delay. These specifications shall be secret and shall not be published. They shall be made available only to bodies designated by the Member States as responsible for printing and to persons duly authorized by a Member State.

2. Each Member State shall designate one body having responsibility for printing residence permits. It shall communicate the name of that body to the Council and the Commission. The same body may be designated by two or more Member States for this purpose. Each Member State shall be entitled to change its designated body. It shall inform the Council and the Commission accordingly.

3. Each Member State shall inform the Council and the Commission of the competent authority or authorities for issuing residence permits.

Article 3

1. Without prejudice to any more extensive provisions applicable concerning data protection, an individual to whom a residence permit is issued shall have the right to verify the personal particulars entered on the residence permit and, where appropriate, to ask for any corrections or deletions to be made.

2. No information in machine-readable form shall be given on the uniform format for residence permits unless it also appears in the boxes described in points 10 and 11 of the Annex, or unless it is mentioned in the relevant travel document.

Article 4

For the purpose of this Joint Action, 'residence permit' shall mean any authorization issued by the authorities of a Member State allowing a third country national to stay legally on its territory, with the exception of:
– visas,
– permits issued for a stay whose duration is determined by national law but which may not exceed six months,
– permits issued pending examination of an application for a residence permit or for asylum.

Article 5

Where Member States use the uniform format for residence permits for purposes other than those covered by Article 4, appropriate measures must be taken to ensure that confusion with the residence permit referred to in Article 4 is not possible.

Article 6

This Joint Action applies to residence permits issued to third country nationals, with the exception of:
– members of the families of citizens of the Union exercising their right to free movement,
– nationals of Member States of the European Free Trade Association party to the Agreement on the European Economic Area and members of their families exercising their right to free movement.

Article 7

This Joint Action shall be published in the Official Journal, and shall enter into force the day after that of its publication. The Member States shall apply Article 1 no later than five years after the adoption of the measures referred to in Article 2 (1). However, the validity of authorizations granted in documents already issued shall not be affected by the introduction of the uniform format for residence permits, unless the Member State concerned decides otherwise.

ANNEX

Description

The document will be produced either as a sticker, if possible in ID 2 format, or as a stand-alone document.

1. The title of the document (Residence permit) shall appear in this space in the language(s) of the issuing Member State.

2. The document number – with special security features and preceded by an identification letter – shall appear in this space.

The section to be completed has nine sub-sections:

3. first sub-section

Name: this sub-section shall contain surname and forename(s) in that order.

4. second sub-section

Valid until: this sub-section shall indicate the relevant expiry date, or, where appropriate, a word to indicate unlimited validity.

5. third sub-section

Place/date of issue: this sub-section shall indicate the place and date of issue of the residence permit.

6. fourth sub-section

Type of permit: this sub-section shall indicate the specific type of residence permit issued to the third country national by the Member State.

7. fifth to ninth sub-section

Remarks: in the fifth to ninth sub-sections Member States may enter details and indications for national use necessary with regard to their rules on third country nationals including indications relating to any permission to work.

8. Date/Signature/Authorization: here – if necessary – the signature and seal of the issuing authority and/or the holder may appear.

9. In this space the printed area shall contain the national emblem of the Member State to distinguish the residence permit and provide a safeguard of its national origin.

10. This box shall be reserved for the machine-readable area. The machine-readable area shall conform to ICAO guidelines.

11. The printed text of this box shall contain a character indicating exclusively the respective Member State. This character may not affect the technical features of the machine-readable zone.

12. This space shall contain a metallized latent image effect including the country code of the Member State.

13. This space shall contain an OVD (kinegram or equivalent sign).

14. If the residence permit is produced as a stand-alone document, an identity photograph shall be affixed in this space and secured with OVD film (kinefilm or equivalent security laminate).

15. The following additional information boxes shall be provided on the back in the case of a stand-alone document:

date/place of birth, nationality, sex, remarks.

The address of the permit holder may also be indicated. (...)

3.2.11

[T.32/1/C] Council Decision of 3 December 1998 on common standards relating to filling in the uniform format for residence permits[17]

THE COUNCIL OF THE EUROPEAN UNION,

Having regard to Joint Action 97/11/JHA of 16 December 1996 concerning a uniform format for residence permits, and in particular Article 2(1) thereof,

Whereas it is necessary to establish common standards relating to filling in the said format, so as to ensure the uniform aspect thereof;

Whereas this Decision does not affect the competence of Member States relating to the recognition of States and territorial entities, as well as of passports and travel documents issued by these States or entities;

Whereas the attribution of the codes in the Appendix to this Decision is of a purely administrative nature and is without prejudice to the determination of the nationality of third country residents,

HAS DECIDED AS FOLLOWS:

Article 1

The uniform format for residence permits shall be filled in in accordance with the procedures contained in the Annex hereto.

Article 2

The Council shall examine, at least once a year, the procedures and codes contained in the Annex and the Appendix hereto with a view to adapting them.

Article 3

This Decision shall enter into force on the day following its publication in the Official Journal of the European Communities.

ANNEX

I. PROCEDURES FOR COMPLETION OF THE COMMON REFERENCE AREA OF THE STICKER IN THE UNIFORM FORMAT OF THE RESIDENCE PERMIT

The format adopted for the sticker is in ID2 format (conforming with the dimensions for the ID2 type card (ISO7810)).

There are eight spaces to be completed in accordance with the technical specifications, where appropriate, as follows:

1. Permit No: The number of the document shall appear in this space (protected by special security features and preceded by a letter code), in accordance with part one paragraph 3.7 (initial letter(s) as detailed in paragraph 3.2) of the technical specifications.

2. Name:The surname(s) and first name(s) shall be inserted here in order. The surname(s) and first name(s) on the document to which the sticker is attached must be exactly the same as those on the sticker.

---

[17] OJ L 333, 9 December (1998) p 8-16; (398D0701).

3. 'Valid until' space: The relevant date of expiry shall be entered in this space or, if necessary, a word or a code indicating unlimited validity. Member States shall forward to the General Secretariat of the Council the various words or codes referred to in the previous subparagraph, to enable the Secretariat to draw up a list for distribution to all Member States. Such a list could also be used as an additional device for discovering falsifications.

Where an expiry date is entered, the date must be entered by means of three groups of two figures in the following order, two for the day, two for the month and two for the year, to be separated by a hyphen, and the first figure shall be a nought where the number is lower than 10 (e.g. 15-01-96: 15 January 1996).

4. Place/date of issue: This space shall indicate the place and date of issue of the residence permit.

The date of issue shall be entered by means of three groups of two figures in the order laid down in the third subparagraph of point 3.

5. Type of permit: This space shall show the specific type of the residence permit issued by the Member State to the national of a third country. This space should not be harmonised because of disparities between the laws of the Member States. However, Member States will forward to the General Secretariat of the Council the various references they include in this space to enable the Secretariat to draw up a list for distribution to all Member States. Such a list could also be used as an additional device for discovering falsifications.

6. Remarks: Member States may enter in this space information and remarks for national use which are required by national provisions concerning nationals from third countries, including information on authorisation to work and passport number. Member States will forward to the General Secretariat of the Council the various permanent references they include in this space to enable the Secretariat to draw up a list for distribution to all Member States. Such a list could also be used as an additional device for discovering falsifications.

7. Date/signature/authorisation: Where necessary, the issuing authority may affix here its signature and its stamp and/or require the holder to affix his signature. If this space is used, the date should be entered by means of three groups of two figures in the order laid down in the third subparagraph of point 3. Where the Member State's legislation or practices require the affixing of an issuing-office stamp, the stamp should be located in the rectangle bounded on the right by the right edge of the sticker, on the left by the 'Remarks' box, above by the emblem of the Member State and below by the machine-readable area. It is also desirable that the stamp consist of a rectangle 1 cm high + 2,5 cm wide showing the name of the authority issuing the residence permit and the signature and/or the date. The signature and/or the date should be framed on each side by three parallel horizontal lines, the middle one being half as long as the other two.

8. Machine-readable area: The area reserved for machine reading (including codes indicating nationality or other status) shall be completed in accordance with the standards of the International Civil Aviation Organisation (ICAO), as set out in the technical specification. On the second line, either the number of the permit or the passport number shall be recorded. The three codes relating to the nationality or status of the permit holder shall be entered in accordance with the list in the Appendix.

Member States shall notify the General Secretariat of the Council whether they intend to record the permit or the passport number. The Secretariat will circulate this information to all Member States.

II. PROCEDURES FOR COMPLETION OF THE COMMON REFERENCE AREA OF
THE STAND-ALONE DOCUMENT IN THE UNIFORM FORMAT OF THE RESIDENCE
PERMIT.

The format adopted for the stand-alone document is either the ID1 or ID2 format in accordance with ISO standard 7810.1995. In both formats there are 12 boxes to be completed in accordance with the technical specifications where appropriate.

A. FRONT

1. Permit No: The number of the document shall appear in this space preceded by a letter code, in accordance with Part 2 of paragraph 3.2 (initial letter(s) as detailed in Part I, paragraph 3.2) of the technical specifications.

2. Name: The surname(s) and first name(s) shall be inserted here in order.

3. 'Valid until' space: The corresponding date of expiry shall be entered in this space or, if necessary, a word or a code indicating unlimited validity. Member States shall forward to the General Secretariat of the Council the various words or codes referred to in the previous subparagraph, to enable the Secretariat to draw up a list for distribution to all Member States. Such a list could also be used as an additional device for discovering falsifications. Where an expiry date is entered, the date must be entered by means of three groups of two figures in the following order, two for the day, two for the month and two for the year, to be separated by a hyphen, and the first figure shall be a nought where the number is lower than 10 (e.g. 15-01-96: 15 January 1996).

4. Place/date of issue: This space shall indicate the place and date of issue of the residence permit.

The date of issue shall be entered by means of three groups of two figures in the order laid down in the third subparagraph of point 3.

5. Type of permit: This space shall show the specific type of the residence permit issued by the Member State to the national of a third country. This space should not be harmonised because of disparities between the laws of the Member States. However, Member States will forward to the General Secretariat of the Council the various references they include in this space to enable the Secretariat to draw up a list for distribution to all Member States. Such a list could also be used as an additional device for discovering falsifications.

6. Remarks: Member States may enter in this space information and remarks for national use which are required by national provisions concerning nationals from third countries, including information on authorisation to work. Member States will forward to the General Secretariat of the Council the various permanent references they include in this space to enable the Secretariat to draw up a list for distribution to all Member States. Such a list could also be used as an additional device for discovering falsifications.

7. Date/signature/authorisation: Where necessary, the issuing authority may affix here its signature and its stamp and/or require the holder to affix his signature. If this space is used, the date should be entered by means of three groups of two figures in the order laid down in the third subparagraph of point 3. Where the Member State's legislation or practices require the affixing of an issuing-office stamp, the stamp could be located in the rectangle bounded on the right by the right edge of the stand- alone document, on the left by the 'Remarks' box, above by the emblem of the Member State and below by the base of the card in the ID1 format, or by the machine-readable area in the ID2 format. It is also desirable that the stamp consist of a rectangle 1 cm high + 2,5 cm (1) wide showing the name of the authority issuing the residence permit and the signature and/or the date; the signature and/or the date should

be framed on each side by three parallel horizontal lines, the middle one being half as long as the other two.

B. BACK

Where there is a stand-alone document, the following additional references shall appear on the back.

8. Date and place of birth: Reference to the place and date of birth of the holder of the residence permit shall be entered here. The place of birth shall be the name of the city, if known, as well as the country where the holder of the permit was born. Reference to the country of birth must be given since the holder's nationality may be different from the country of his birth. The date of birth shall be entered by means of three groups of two figures in the order laid down in the third subparagraph of point 3.

9. Nationality: The nationality or any other status of the holder of the residence permit shall be entered here.

Reference to the nationality shall be by reference to the name of the country of which the foreigner is a national, or to any other relevant status, e.g. Colombia.

10. Sex: The sex of the holder of the residence permit shall be entered here in accordance with ICAO standards for the machine-readable zone. Member States will forward to the General Secretariat of the Council the various references they include in this box to enable the Secretariat to draw up a list for distribution to all Member States. Such a list could also be used as an additional device for discovering falsifications.

11. Remarks: Member States may enter in this box information and remarks for national use which are required by national provisions concerning nationals from third countries, for example the holder's address.

Member States will forward to the General Secretariat of the Council the various references they include in this box to enable the Secretariat to draw up a list for distribution to all Member States. Such a list could also be used as an additional device for discovering falsifications.

12. Machine-readable area: (on reverse side of the document in ID1 format and on the front of the document in ID2 format). The area reserved for machine reading (including codes indicating nationality or other status) shall be completed in accordance with the standards of the International Civil Aviation Organisation (ICAO), as set out in the technical specification. The three codes relating to the nationality or status of the permit holder shall be entered in accordance with the list in the Appendix (For ID1 format, these dimensions should be reduced by half).

3.2.12

[T.16] Joint Action of 4 March 1996 on airport transit arrangements[18]

THE COUNCIL OF THE EUROPEAN UNION,

Having regard to the Treaty on European Union, and in particular Article K.3(2)(b) thereof,

Having regard to the initiative of 23 February 1995 from the French Republic,

Whereas the determination of the conditions of entry and movement by nationals of third countries into and within the territory of Member States, and combating unauthorized immigration by nationals of third countries, are matters of common interest under Article K.1(3)(a) and (c) respectively of the Treaty;

Whereas the air route, particularly when it involves applications for entry or de facto entry, in the course of airport transit, represents a significant way in with a view in particular to illegally taking up residence within the territory of the Member States;

Whereas improvements should be sought in controlling that route;

Whereas Annex 9 to the Chicago Convention on International Civil Aviation establishes the principle of free transit passage through the international areas of airports;

Whereas States may nevertheless make exceptions to this general principle by notifying the International Civil Aviation Organization (ICAO) and requiring an airport transit visa;

Whereas this possibility should be limited as far as possible to avoid any unnecessary constraint on the development of air transport;

Whereas the harmonization of Member States' policies in this field is an accordance with the objectives of security and control of illegal immigration of the Treaty, while contributing to harmonizing the conditions of competition between airlines and airports in the Member States;

Whereas this matter does not concern visas required when crossing the external borders of the Member States and is therefore not covered by Article 100c(1) of the Treaty establishing the European Community;

Whereas it is nevertheless of common interest and could be more effectively dealt with by means of joint action;

Whereas the Member States that do not have airport visa arrangements should be allowed sufficient time to draw up such arrangements,

HAS ADOPTED THIS JOINT ACTION:

Article 1

For the purposes of this joint action, 'airport transit visa (ATV)' shall mean the authorization to which nationals of certain third countries are subject, as an exception to the principle of free transit laid down in Annex 9 to the Chicago Convention on International Civil Aviation, for transit through the international areas of the airports of Member States.

---

[18] 96/197/JHA; OJ L 06, 13 March 1996, p. 8-9 [EUDOR] 496X0197.

Article 2

1. The airport transit visa shall be issued by the consular services of the Member States.

2. The conditions of issue of airport transit visas shall be determined by each Member State subject to adoption by the Council of criteria to the preliminaries for and issue of visas. In all cases, the consular services must ascertain that there is no security risk or risk of illegal immigration. They must above all be satisfied that the application for an airport transit visa is justified on the basis of the documents submitted by the applicant, and that as far as possible these documents guarantee entry into the country of final destination, in particular by presentation of a visa where so required.

3. With effect from the entry into force of the provisions contained in Council Regulation (EC) No 1683/95 of 29 May 1995 laying down a uniform format for visas,[19] Member States shall issue airport transit visas using the uniform visa format laid down in that Regulation.

Article 3

Each Member State shall require and airport transit visa of nationals of third countries included on the joint list annexed hereto who do not already hold an entry or transit visa for the Member State in question when passing through the international areas of airports situated within its territory.

Article 4

A Member State may provide for exceptions to the requirement for an airport transit visa in respect of nationals of third countries included on the joint list annexed hereto, in particular for:

– crew member of aircraft and ships,
– holders of diplomatic, official or service passports,
– holders of residence permits or equivalent documents issued by a Member State,
– holders of visas issued by a Member State, or by a State which is a party to the Agreement on the European Economic Area.

Article 5

Each Member State shall decide whether an airport transit visa should be required of nationals of countries not included on the joint list annexed hereto.

Article 6

Each Member State shall determine the airport transit arrangements applicable to statutory stateless persons and refugees.

Article 7

Within 10 working days of the entry into force of this joint action, Member States shall notify the other Member States and the General Secretariat of the Council of the measures taken pursuant to Articles 4, 5 and 6. Those measures shall be published, for information, in the Official Journal.

---

[19] OJ L 164, 14 July 1995, p. 1.

Article 8
Each year the Council Presidency shall draw up a report on progress in the harmonization of airport transit arrangements within the Union. The Council shall examine any proposal for amending the list annexed hereto.

Article 9
This joint action shall not prevent closer airport-transit harmonization between some Member States, extending in scope beyond the joint list annexed hereto.

Article 10
This joint action shall enter into force on the first day of the sixth month following its publication in the Official Journal. However, in the case of Denmark, Finland and Sweden, it shall enter into force on the first day of the 18th month following its publication in the Official Journal.

3.2.13

[T.31] Resolution of 26 June 1997 on unaccompanied minors who are nationals of third countries[20]

THE COUNCIL OF THE EUROPEAN UNION,
Having regard to the Treaty on European Union, and in particular Article K.1 thereof,
Whereas, pursuant to Article K.1(3)(a), (b) and (c) of the Treaty, the conditions of entry of, and residence by, nationals of third countries on the territory of Member States and measures to combat unauthorized immigration and residence by nationals of third countries on the territory of Member States constitute matters of common interest;
Whereas Article K.1(1) of the Treaty provides that asylum policy is to be regarded as a matter of common interest for the Member States;
Whereas third-country minors sometimes enter and stay in the territory of member States without being accompanied by a responsible person and without obtaining the necessary authorization;
Whereas unaccompanied minors who are nationals of third countries can be the victims of facilitators, and it is important for Member States to co-operate in combating such form of facilitating;
Whereas unaccompanied minors who are nationals of third countries generally are in a vulnerable situation requiring special safeguards and care;
Whereas recognition of the vulnerable situation of unaccompanied minors in the territory of Member States justifies the laying down of common principles for dealing with such situations;
Whereas, in accordance with Article K.2(1) of the Treaty, this Resolution is without prejudice to the international commitments entered into by the Member States pursuant to the European

---

[20] OJ L 63 of 13 March 1996, p. 8 (496X0197).

Convention for the Protection of Human Rights and Fundamental Freedoms of 4 November 1950;

Whereas this Resolution is without prejudice to the international commitments entered into by the Member States pursuant to the United Nations Convention on the Rights of the Child, 1989;

Whereas, pursuant to Article 2 of that Convention, States Parties shall respect the rights set forth in the Convention without discrimination;

Whereas, pursuant to Article 3 of that Convention, in all actions concerning children, the best interests of the child shall be a primary consideration;

Whereas Article 22 of that Convention aims to protect and assist minors who seek refugee status or who are regarded as refugees;

Whereas it is of great importance for the Member States, true to their common humanitarian tradition and in accordance with the provisions of the Geneva Convention of 28 July 1951 relating to the Status of Refugees, as amended by the New York Protocol of 31 January 1967, to grant refugees appropriate protection;

Whereas on 20 June 1995 the Council adopted a Resolution on minimum guarantees for asylum procedures;

Whereas this Resolution is without prejudice to the Strasbourg Convention of 28 January 1981 of the Council of Europe for the Protection of Individuals with regard to Automatic Processing of Personal Data;

Whereas the unauthorized presence in the territory of Member States of unaccompanied minors who are not regarded as refugees must be temporary, with Member States endeavouring to co-operate among themselves and with the third countries of origin to return the minor to his country of origin or to a third country prepared to accept him, without jeopardizing his safety, in order to find, whenever possible, the persons responsible for the minor, and to reunite him with such persons;

Whereas the application of such principles should not interfere with the application of national laws on public policy, public health or public security,

HEREBY ADOPTS THIS RESOLUTION:

Article 1 – Scope and purpose

1. This Resolution concerns third-country nationals below the age of eighteen, who arrive on the territory of the Member States unaccompanied by an adult responsible for them whether by law or custom, and for as long as they are not effectively in the care of such a person. This Resolution can also be applied to minors who are nationals of third countries and who are left unaccompanied after they have entered the territory of the Member States. The persons covered by the previous two sentences shall be referred to herein as 'unaccompanied minors`.

2. This Resolution shall not apply to third-country nationals who are members of the family of nationals of a Member State of the European Union, nor to nationals of a Member State of the European Free Trade Association party to the Agreement on the European Economic Area and the members of their family, whatever the latter's nationality may be, where, pursuant to the Treaty establishing the European Community or the Agreement on the European Economic Area respectively, rights to freedom of movement are being exercised.

3. The purpose of this Resolution is to establish guidelines for the treatment for unaccompanied minors, with regard to matters such as the conditions for their reception, stay and return and, in the case of asylum seekers, the handling of applicable procedures.

4. This Resolution shall be without prejudice to more favourable provisions of national law.

5. The following guidelines are to be notified to the competent authorities responsible for matters covered by this Resolution, and such authorities shall take them into consideration in their action. Implementation of these guidelines is not to be subject to any form of discrimination.

Article 2 – Admission

1. Member States may, in accordance with their national legislation and practice, refuse admission at the frontier to unaccompanied minors in particular if they are without the required documentation and authorizations. However, in case of unaccompanied minors who apply for asylum, the Resolution on Minimum Guarantees for Asylum Procedures is applicable, in particular the principles set out in paragraphs 23 to 25 thereof.

2. In this connection, Member States should take appropriate measures, in accordance with their national legislation, to prevent the unauthorized entry of unaccompanied minors and should co-operate to prevent illegal entry and illegal residence of unaccompanied minors on their territory.

3. Unaccompanied minors who, pursuant to national provisions, must remain at the border until a decision has been taken on their admission to the territory or on their return, should receive all necessary material support and care to satisfy their basic needs, such as food, accommodation suitable for their age, sanitary facilities and medical care.

Article 3 – Minimum guarantees for all unaccompanied minors

1. Member States should endeavour to establish a minor's identity as soon as possible after arrival, and also the fact that he or she is unaccompanied. Information on the minor's identity and situation can be obtained by various means, in particular by means of an appropriate interview, which should be conducted as soon as possible and in a manner in keeping with his age. The information obtained should be effectively documented. In requesting, receiving, forwarding and storing information obtained, particular care and confidentiality should be exercised, in particular in the case of asylum seekers in order to protect both the minor and the members of his family. This early information may in particular enhance the prospects of reunification of the minor with his family in the country of origin or a third country.

2. Irrespective of their legal status, unaccompanied minors should be entitled to the necessary protection and basic care in accordance with the provisions of national law.

3. Member States should, with a view to reunification, endeavour to trace the members of the family of an unaccompanied minor as soon as possible, or to identify the place of residence of the members of the family, regardless of their legal status and without prejudging the merits of any application for residence.

Unaccompanied minors may also be encouraged and assisted in contacting the International Committee of the Red Cross, national Red Cross organizations, or other organizations for the purpose of tracing their family members. Particularly, in the case of asylum seekers, whenever contracts are made in the context of tracing family members, confidentiality should be duly respected in order to protect both the minor and the members of his family.

4. For the purposes of applying this Resolution, Member States should provide as soon as possible for the necessary representation of the minor by:

(a) legal guardianship, or

(b) representation by a (national) organization which is responsible for the care and well-being of the minor, or

(c) other appropriate representation.

5. Where a guardian is appointed for an unaccompanied minor, the guardian should ensure, in accordance with national law, that the minor's needs (for example, legal, social, medical or psychological) are duly met.

6. When it can be assumed that an unaccompanied minor of school age will be staying in a Member State for a prolonged period, the minor should have access to general education facilities on the same basis as nationals of the host Member State or alternatively, appropriate special facilities should be offered to him.

7. Unaccompanied minors should receive appropriate medical treatment to meet immediate needs. Special medical or other assistance should be provided for minors who have suffered any form of neglect, exploitation, or abuse, torture or any other form of cruel, inhuman or degrading treatment or punishment, or armed conflicts.

Article 4 – Asylum procedure (...)

Article 5 – Return of unaccompanied minors

1. Where a minor is not allowed to prolong his stay in a Member State, the Member State concerned may only return the minor to his country of origin or a third country prepared to accept him, if on arrival therein – depending on his needs in the light of age and degree of independence – adequate reception and care are available. This can be provided by parents or other adults who take care of the child, or by governmental or non-governmental bodies.

2. As long as return under these conditions is not possible, Member States should in principle make it possible for the minor to remain in their territory.

3. The competent authorities of the Member States should, with a view to a minor's return, co-operate:

(a) in re-uniting unaccompanied minors with other members of their family, either in the minor's country of origin or in the country where those family members are staying;

(b) with the authorities of the minor's country of origin or with those of another country, with a view to finding an appropriate durable solution;

(c) with international organizations such as UNHCR or UNICEF, which already take an active part in advising governments on guidelines for dealing with unaccompanied minors, in particular asylum-seekers;

(d) where appropriate, with non-governmental organizations in order to ascertain the availability of reception and care facilities in the country to which the minor will be returned.

4. In any case, a minor may not be returned to a third country where this return would be contrary to the Convention relating to the status of refugees, the European Convention on Human Rights and Fundamental Freedoms or the Convention against Torture and other Cruel, Inhuman or Degrading treatment or Punishment or the Convention on the Rights of the Child, without prejudice to any reservations which Member States may have tabled when ratifying it, or the Protocols to these Conventions.

Article 6 – Final provisions

1. Member States should take account of these guidelines in the case of all proposals for changes to their national legislations. In addition, Member States should strive to bring their national legislations into line with these guidelines before 1 January 1999.

2. Member States shall remain free to allow for more favourable conditions for unaccompanied minors.

3. The Council, in conjunction with the Commission and in consultation with UNHCR in the framework of its competences, shall review the application of the above guidelines once

a year, commencing on 1 January 1999, and if appropriate adapt them to developments in asylum and migration policy.

ANNEX

MEASURES TO COMBAT TRAFFICKING IN MINORS
Member States, mindful of the particular vulnerability of minors, should take all measures to prevent and combat the trafficking and exploitation of minors, and co-operate in this regard.

MEASURES TO PREVENT ILLEGAL ENTRY
Measures which Member States may take to prevent the unauthorized arrival in the territory of the Member States of unaccompanied minors who are nationals of third countries may include:
(i) collaboration with competent authorities and bodies including airline companies in the countries of departure, in particular through the use of liaison officers;
(ii) observation at airports of arrival of flights from sensitive countries;
(iii) consequent application of international obligations including carriers' liability legislation where unaccompanied minors who are nationals of third countries arrive without the appropriate documentation.

Sojourn   3.3

3.3.1

[T.20] Joint Action of 30 November 1994 concerning travel facilities for school pupils from third countries resident in a Member State[21]

THE COUNCIL OF THE EUROPEAN UNION, (...)
HAS DECIDED AS FOLLOWS:

Article 1
1. A Member State shall not require a visa of a school pupil who is not a national of a Member State but who is legally resident in another Member State and who seeks to enter its territory either for a short stay or transit if:
(a) in the framework of a school excursion, the school pupil is travelling as a member of a group of school pupils from a general education school;
(b) the group is accompanied by a teacher from the school in question who is able to present a list of the schoolchildren he or she is accompanying, issued by the school in question on

---

[21] OJ L 327 of 19 December 1994, p. 1; (494D0795).

the common form contained in the Annex:
– identifying the school pupils being accompanied;
– documenting the purpose and circumstances of the intended stay or transit;
(c) the school pupil presents a travel document valid for crossing the border in question, except in cases covered by
Article 2.
2. A Member State may refuse entry of a school pupil if he or she does not fulfil the other relevant national immigration conditions. (...)

3.3.2

[T.29] Resolution of 4 March 1996 on the status of third-country nationals residing on a long-term basis in the territory of the Member States[22]

THE COUNCIL OF THE EUROPEAN UNION,

Whereas under Article K.1(3)(b) of the Treaty on European Union the conditions of residence by nationals of third countries on the territory of Member States are regarded as a matter of common interest;
Whereas the Member States must make progress in the adoption of measures to facilitate the integration into the host society of third-country nationals settled in their territory as long-term residents;
Whereas the integration of long term residents contributes to greater security and stability, both in daily life and in work, and to social peace in the various Member States;
Whereas, in order to make progress in the integration of long-term residents in the territory of the State in which they reside, a number of principles common to the Member States should be defined;
Whereas the application of such principles should not interfere with the application of national laws on public policy, public health or public security,
HEREBY ADOPTS THIS RESOLUTION:

I
The Council calls upon the Member States to take account in their policies on integration of the persons referred to in II (1) below of the principles defined in this resolution.

II
1. This resolution shall apply to third-country nationals residing on a long-term basis in the territory of Member States (hereinafter 'long-term residents').
2. This resolution shall not apply to:

---

[22] (96/C 80/02), OJ C 80 of 18 March 1996, p. 2; 396Y0318(02).

(a) the following persons, where their right to freedom of movement is exercised pursuant to the Treaty establishing the European Community or the Agreement on the European Economic Area:
– members of the families of a citizen of the European Union,
– nationals of the Member States of the European Free Trade Association party to the Agreement on the European Economic Area, and members of their families;
(b) nationals of third States whose status is governed by agreements concluded by the European Community and its Member States with third countries, inasmuch as such agreements contain more favourable provisions;
(c) nationals of third States who have been admitted to a Member State for the purposes of study or research.
3. This resolution shall not affect the rights of:
– members of the family of a citizen of the European Union residing with the latter in the Member State of which he is a national where the legislation of that Member State grants them, with respect to residence, in situations where Community law does not apply, the same rights as are granted to persons to whom Community law applies,
– nationals of third countries legally resident in a Member State as refugees within the meaning of the Geneva Convention on the status of refugees of 28 July 1951,
– nationals of a third country with which the Member State concerned has concluded a bilateral agreement governing the conditions of entry, residence or employment.
4. For the purposes of paragraphs 2 and 3, the term 'family members' shall be construed in accordance with Community legislation.

III
1. Without prejudice to the provisions of Point IV, the following third-country nationals should be recognized in each Member State, as long-term residents:
– those who provide proof that they have resided legally and without interruption in the territory of the Member State concerned for a period specified in the legislation of that Member State and, in any event, after 10 years' legal residence,
– those who, under the legislation of the Member State concerned, are granted the same residence conditions as the category of persons referred to in the first indent.
2. In accordance with their national laws, Member States should grant a residence authorization for at least 10 years, or for a period corresponding to the longest period of validity under their national law, which should tend to be of equivalent length, or an unlimited residence authorization, to persons recognized as being long-term residents in accordance with paragraph 1.

IV
1. In any event, the granting of a residence authorization is subject to there being no public policy or national security reasons for not so doing.
2. Where a person makes an application for a residence authorization on grounds of prior lawful, uninterrupted residence in the Member State concerned, it should be possible for the factors determining whether the authorization is to be granted to include the level and stability of the means of existence which the applicant demonstrates, in particular whether he has health insurance, and the conditions for exercising an occupation.

V

1. A long-term resident and the members of his family should, in accordance with the legislation of the Member State in which they reside, have access to the entire territory of that Member State.

2. A long-term resident and the members of his family legally resident with him should enjoy no less favourable treatment than is enjoyed, in accordance with the legislation of the Member State concerned, by nationals of that Member State with regard to: working conditions, membership of trade unions, public policy in the sector of housing, social security, in accordance with, in addition to the national legislation of the Member State concerned, the international agreements on the matter, emergency health care, and compulsory schooling.

3. In accordance with the legislation of the Member State concerned, it should be possible for the long-term resident and the members of his family legally resident with him to be granted non-contributory benefits.

VI

It should be possible for a residence authorization granted to a long-term resident to be cancelled or not renewed on one of the following grounds:

– the fact that an expulsion measure has been issued against the long-term resident in accordance with the provisions of the legislation of the Member State concerned, on the understanding that such resident enjoys, with respect to the expulsion measure taken concerning him, the maximum legal protection provided for in the legislation of the said Member State, in accordance with procedures guaranteeing that due account is taken of the length of his period of legal residence (where the expulsion measure was adopted for reasons of public policy, these should be based on the personal behaviour of the long-term resident involving a sufficiently serious threat to public policy, or to national security),

– the long-term resident has definitively left the territory of the Member State concerned,

– the long-term resident has been absent from the territory of the Member State concerned for a period to be determined by that Member State's legislation, which should in no case be less than six consecutive months,

– the residence authorization has proved to have been obtained by means of fraud.

VII

Long-term residents in the territory of the Member State concerned should be able to obtain authorization to engage in gainful activities, in accordance with the provisions of that Member State's legislation.

VIII

1. The Council calls upon the Member States to notify it, by 1 January 1997, of the changes in their national law in the area covered by this resolution.

2. This resolution is without prejudice to the option open to a Member State to grant a more favourable legal status to third-country nationals residing permanently on its territory.[23]

---

[23] Ed.: The discussion and norm-setting relating to the status of third-country nationals residing on a long-term basis is an important one. On 1 December 2000 the Council concluded that the establishment of a status of long-term resident in Member States, as provided for by Article 63 of the Treaty establishing the European Community, as amended by the Treaty of Amsterdam, and envisaged by the European Council in Tampere, forms a key part of the integration of third-country na-

Family   **3.4**

                                                                                    3.4.1

[T.23] Resolution of 1 June 1993 on Harmonization of Family Reunification[24]

Ministers (...) responsible for Immigration adopted the following Resolution (...)

The question of family reunification is already to some extent governed by international Conventions (...)

On the other hand, there is also a need to control migration flows into the territories of the Member States. This is considered to be one of the factors for the successful integration of immigrants who are lawfully resident within the territories of Member States.

With these considerations in mind, [the] Ministers resolved that the national policies (...) should be governed by the principles set out below. (...) The principles are not legally binding on the Member States and do not afford a ground of action by individuals.

The harmonization efforts are confined at this stage (...) to persons who are not nationals of a Member State but who are lawfully resident (...) on a basis which affords them an expectation of permanent or long-term residence. (...)

This Resolution does [not] cover family reunification in respect of persons who have been granted refugee status, for whom some Member States have more favourable policies.

The harmonization of policy in respect of the families of persons in [this category] will be further examined in the course of considering admission policies in respect of them.

Principles Governing Member States' Policies on family Reunification

(1. Non-Community nationals to whom the Principles relate)

---

tionals into the European Union. The Commission plans to submit a proposal for a Directive on the subject in 2001. The Presidency organised a seminar in Paris on 5 and 6 October 2000 concerning the integration of foreign nationals settling in Member States on a long-term basis. The seminar showed that, while national laws have their own specific features stemming from the different legal traditions found in Europe, they nevertheless share a good deal of common ground, particularly in all making allowance for the length of standing and closeness of ties established in the host country. Following the seminar, the French Presidency submitted a set of draft Council conclusions on conditions for harmonising the status of third-country nationals residing on a long-term basis. Initial discussions among experts in working parties revealed Member States' interest in the draft, although it did not prove possible to reach agreement, mainly for reasons of timing. However, it seems important to ask Ministers for their views on the policy guidelines on which the future long-term resident status to be put to the Council by the Commission early next year could be based. There appear to be four basic points: (1) access to the status in accordance with three criteria (length of presence, integration and private family life); (2) substance of the status (guaranteed residence – economic and social rights); (3) entitlement to freedom of residence (the principle of long-term residents' freedom to live in a Member State other than the one which granted them such status should be established); (4) the need for collateral policies (integration, combating discrimination) and for interchange at European level.

[24] (WGI 1497 REV 1).

2. The Member States will normally grant admission, under the conditions set out in the remainder of this Resolution, to
– the resident's spouse (that is, a person bound to him or her in a marriage recognized by the host Member State)
– the children, other than adopted children, of the resident and his or her spouse,
– children adopted by both the resident and his or her spouse while they were resident together in a third country, in accordance with a decision taken by the competent administrative authority or court of that state and which is recognized and accepted by the Member State of residence, and where the adopted children have the same rights and obligations as the other children and there has been a definitive break with the family of origin.
The spouse and the children may be admitted only for the purpose of living together with the resident.
3. Member States reserve the right to require non-EC nationals to be lawfully present in their territory for certain periods of time before family members may be reunited with them under the terms of these principles.
4. Member States reserve the right to determine whether a marriage was contracted solely or principally for the purpose of enabling the spouse to enter and take up residence in a Member State and to refuse permission to enter and stay accordingly.
5. A wife and her children will not be admitted for the purpose of family reunification if the marriage is polygamous and the resident already has a wife resident in the territory of a Member State.
6. Member States reserve the option of admitting a child (including an adopted child) where the child is the offspring of the resident or of his/her spouse, but not of the couple involved (... parental authority ... custody ... effectively in their charge)
7. Member States reserve the possibility of admitting a child adopted by both the resident and his or her spouse while one or both were resident in a Member State (...)
8. In order to qualify for admission for the purpose of family reunification children must be below a maximum age, which the Member State agree should be between 16 and 18 years, and must not have married or have formed an independent family unit or be leading an independent life.
9. Member States will consider whether and adoption has been arranged solely or principally for the purpose of enabling the child to enter and take up residence in a Member State, and whether to refuse permission to enter and stay accordingly.
10. Member States reserve the possibility of permitting the entry and stay of family members, other than those envisaged in paragraphs 2, 6 and 7 of this Resolution, for compelling reasons which justify the presence of the person concerned.
11. An authorization to stay on the basis of family reunification may, for such a period as the Member State concerned determines, be conditional upon the continued fulfilment of the criteria for admission.
12. Within a reasonable period of time following their admission, family members, in accordance with the national legislation in each Member State, may be authorized to stay on a personal basis independently from the person whom they joined on the basis of family reunification, and, if appropriate, be authorized to work.
13. The authorization to stay granted to a family member may be terminated at any time if there are grounds for presuming that it was obtained by means of fraud or forgery.
14. A person will normally not be admitted to the territory of a Member State for the purpose of family reunification without a visa or other prior written authorization for that purpose,

issued by the Member State in which the family intends to reside. The application must normally be made whilst the family member concerned is outside the territory of the Member State concerned. A visa or prior written authorization will not be issued unless the applicant meets all the criteria for entry and stay in the territory of the Member State concerned as set out in these principles.

15. Family members must also, in principle, be in possession of valid travel documents, which are recognized by the Member State in which the family intends to reside.

16. Member States reserve the right to make the entry and stay of family members conditional upon the availability of adequate accommodation and of sufficient resources to avoid a burden being placed on the public funds of the Member State concerned, and on the existence of sickness insurance.

17. Member States will normally refuse entry and stay to a family member if his presence would constitute a threat to national security or public policy ('ordre publique'). They reserve the right to refuse entry and stay on grounds of public health.

3.4.2

Amended Proposal for a Council Directive on the Right to Family Reunification[25]

EXPLANATORY MEMORANDUM

1. BACKGROUND

On 1 December 1999 the Commission adopted a proposal for a Council Directive on the right to family reunification (COM(1999) 638 final – 1999/0258 (CNS)). The proposed directive is based on Article 63 of the EC Treaty and introduces a right to family reunification for third-country nationals legally residing on the territory of a Member State. It lays down the conditions for exercising this right to obtain authorisation for the entry and residence of family members who are nationals of third countries. The proposal was sent to the Council, the European Parliament, the Economic and Social Committee and the Committee of the Regions. The Economic and Social Committee was consulted by the Council on 10 February 2000 and delivered its Opinion on 25 May 2000. By letter dated 11 February 2000, the Council consulted Parliament in accordance with Article 67 of the EC Treaty. Parliament referred the proposal to its Committee on Citizens' Freedoms and Rights, Justice and Home Affairs for an in-depth examination and to its Committee on Legal Affairs and the Internal Market for an opinion. The Committee on Citizens' Freedoms and Rights, Justice and Home Affairs, after receiving and examining the Legal Committee's opinion adopted on 17 April 2000, adopted its own report on 13 July 2000. On 6 September 2000, Parliament adopted its Opinion 2 in plenary, approving the Commission proposal subject to amendments and calling

---

[25] Presented by the Commission pursuant to Article 250(2) of the EC Treaty, Brussels, 10.10.2000, COM(2000) 624 final [1999/0258 (CNS)]. This document has been included *in toto* as it clearly indicates the results of the various procedures as described in part 1. Bold text has been adopted at a later stage, whereas text that has been deleted has been indicated as such.

on the Commission to amend its proposal accordingly, in accordance with Article 250(2) of the EC Treaty.

2. THE AMENDED PROPOSAL

Parliament supports the general thrust and main objectives of the Commission's proposal, in particular the introduction of a right to family reunification for third-country nationals who are already resident. It adopted 17 amendments. The Commission can accept most of them in full or in part or, in some cases, subject to a change of wording. The amendments are completely in line with the Commission's approach and complement and enrich the directive. One amendment restricts the scope of the directive. It excludes persons enjoying a subsidiary form of protection and calls for the adoption without delay of a proposal on their admission and residence. The Commission accepts this amendment and has changed the relevant Articles accordingly. It considers that persons in this category must have the right to family reunification and need protection; however, it recognises that the absence of a harmonised concept of subsidiary protection at Community level constitutes an obstacle to their inclusion in the proposed directive.

The Conclusions of the Tampere European Council of 15 and 16 October 1999 specify that '[refugee status] should also be completed with measures on subsidiary forms of protection offering an appropriate status to any person in need of such protection'. To that end, the Scoreboard presented by the Commission in March 2000 and endorsed by the Council envisages the adoption before 2004 of a proposal on the status of persons enjoying subsidiary forms of protection. The Commission intends to make such a proposal next year, which could also cover family reunification for this category of third-country nationals.

2.1. **Amendments accepted in full or in part**

2.1.1. *The recitals*

Recital 1 (new): this new recital incorporates Amendment 1 and places the directive proposed by the Commission in the context of the progressive establishment of an area of freedom, security and justice.

Recital 2 (formerly recital 1): in line with Amendment 2, the original wording has been changed so as to cite Article 63(3)(a) of the EC Treaty in its entirety.

Recital 5 (new): in the spirit of Amendment 3, the Commission refers in this new recital to its need to have access to statistical data and information in order to be able to evaluate migration flows.

Recital 8 (formerly recital 6): in line with Amendment 4, the original wording incorporates clarification that family reunification helps to create socio-cultural stability; the part which defined integration has not been included, since it contains considerations that go beyond the purpose of the proposed directive.

Recital 11 (new): the Commission has inserted this new recital in order to take account of Amendment 19, which excludes persons enjoying a subsidiary form of protection from the scope of the proposed directive and calls for the adoption of a directive to govern the absorption of persons in this category.

Recital 14 (formerly recital 11): the recital has been amended in accordance with Amendment 5 and now specifies the nature of the dependence on the applicant of relatives in the ascending line and children of full age.

Recital 15 (formerly recital 12): this recital has been amended in order to take account of Amendment 6 and now specifies that procedures must be manageable for national administrations and transparent, so as to ensure legal certainty for the people concerned.

Recital 17 (formerly recital 14): in line with Amendment 8, the original wording has been improved in order to emphasise prevention of breaches of procedure.

2.1.2. *The Articles*

Article 2(c), Article 3(2)(c), Article 5(4), Article 7(4), Article 9(3) and Article 10(2)

As a consequence of Amendment 19, persons enjoying subsidiary forms of protection are excluded from the scope of the directive. They will be covered by another proposal from the Commission, which the Scoreboard schedules for adoption before 2004 and which will deal with family reunification.

Article 7(1), Article 8 and Article 11(1)

The changes to these Articles incorporate Amendments 10 (2nd part), 11 (1st part) and 15 and specify, in the spirit of the original proposal, that applicants may simultaneously make several applications for several members of their families.

Article 9(1)(a)

The changes are designed to simplify what is said on the quality of the accommodation, in accordance with Amendment 12. The Article has also been amended in order to establish an objective and precise criterion for the assessment of the accommodation, in the spirit of Parliament's amendment calling for the assessment to be made on the basis of objective, measurable criteria.

Article 9(1)(c)

In line with Amendment 13, the original wording regarding the evidence of resources that the applicant may be required to provide has been simplified.

Article 12(2)

Amendment 16 proposes removing the prohibition on access to employment and vocational training by relatives in the ascending line or the children of full age covered by Article 5(1)(e). Since such persons are dependent on the applicant at the time of their admission, the Commission has not taken over the entire amendment, but has changed the wording to make it more flexible and to give Member States the option of allowing them access to these activities.

2.2. **Amendments that cannot be accepted**

Amendment 9

The Commission cannot accept this amendment introducing a standstill clause and allowing more favourable arrangements to be maintained since it is not compatible with the objective of aligning national legislation. A number of the directive's provisions already offer a considerable degree of flexibility.

Amendments 11(2nd part) and 28

The Commission shares the concern expressed in this amendment, but the obligation to give reasons for a decision rejecting an application on whatever ground is already laid down in Article 7(3) and it is unnecessary to repeat it here.

Amendment 25

This amendment broadens the concept of dependence applied to relatives in the ascending line. The Commission cannot accept it, since it wants admission of relatives in the ascending line for the purposes of family reunification to be subject to strict rules.

Amendment 50 (2nd part)

Issuing a renewable residence permit ensures a certain degree of legal certainty for family members who are admitted; removing the obligation to provide one would place them in a more precarious situation.

Amended proposal for a Council Directive on the right to family reunification
THE COUNCIL OF THE EUROPEAN UNION,

Having regard to the Treaty establishing the European Community, and in particular Article 63 thereof,

Having regard to the proposal from the Commission,

Having regard to the Opinion of the European Parliament,

Having regard to the Opinion of the Economic and Social Committee,

Whereas:

(1) With a view to the progressive establishment of an area of freedom, security and justice, the Treaty establishing the European Community provides both for the adoption of measures aimed at ensuring the free movement of persons, in conjunction with flanking measures relating to external border controls, asylum and immigration, and for the adoption of measures relating to asylum, immigration and safeguarding the rights of third-country nationals.

(2) Article 63(3) of the Treaty provides that the Council is to adopt measures on immigration policy. Article 63(3)(a) provides, in particular, that the Council is to adopt measures relating to the conditions of entry and residence, **and standards on procedures for the issue by Member States of long term visas and residence permits, including those for the purpose of family reunification.** ~~and specifically refers to entry and residence for the purpose of family reunion.~~

(3) Measures concerning family reunification must be adopted in conformity with the obligation to protect the family and respect family life which is laid down in a variety of international legal instruments, including the European Convention for the Protection of Human Rights and Fundamental Freedoms, signed in Rome on 4

November 1950. The Union respects the fundamental rights secured by that Convention by virtue of Article 6(2) of the Treaty on European Union.

(4) The European Council, at its special meeting in Tampere on 15 and 16 October 1999, acknowledged the need for harmonisation of national legislation on the conditions for admission and residence of third-country nationals, to be based on a common evaluation both of economic and demographic trends within the Union and of the situation in countries of origin. The European Council accordingly asked the Council rapidly to adopt decisions on the basis of Commission proposals. Those decisions were to take account not only of the absorption capacity of each Member State but also their historical and cultural links with countries of origin.

(5) In order to evaluate migration flows and to prepare for the adoption of measures by the Council, the Commission needs to have access to statistical data and information on the legal immigration of third-country nationals in each Member State, and in particular on the number of permits issued, and on their type and validity; to this end, Member States must regularly and rapidly make the necessary data and information available to the Commission.

(6) The European Council, at its special meeting in Tampere, stated that the European Union should ensure fair treatment of third-country nationals residing lawfully on the territory of the Member States and that a more vigorous integration policy should aim at granting them rights and obligations comparable to those of citizens of the European Union.

(7) In accordance with the Council and Commission Plan of Action of 3 December 1998, an instrument on the legal status of legal immigrants should be adopted within two years of the entry into force of the Amsterdam Treaty, and rules on the conditions of entry and residence, and standards on procedures for the issue by Member States of long-term visas and residence permits, including those for the purposes of family reunification, should be prepared within five years.

(8) Family reunification is a necessary way of making family life possible. It helps to create a socio-cultural ~~environment~~ **stability** facilitating the integration of third-country nationals in the Member State, which also serves to promote economic and social cohesion, a fundamental Community objective stated in Article 2 and Article 3(1)(k) of the EC-Treaty.

(9) To ensure protection of the family and the preservation or formation of family life, a right to family reunification should be established and recognised by the Member States. The practical conditions for the exercise of that right should be determined on the basis of common criteria.

(10) Special attention should be paid to the situation of refugees ~~and persons enjoying subsidiary protection~~ on account of the reasons, which obliged them to flee their country and prevent them from leading a normal family life there. More favourable conditions should therefore be laid down for the exercise of their right to family reunification.

(11) The scope of this Directive does not extend to family reunification for persons enjoying a subsidiary form of protection; a directive on the rules for admission of persons in this category, which should also cover their right to family reunification, should be adopted as soon as possible.

(12) To avoid discriminating between citizens of the Union who exercise their right to free movement and those who do not, provision should be made for the family reunification of citizens of the Union residing in countries of which they are nationals to be governed by the rules of Community law relating to free movement.

(13) Family reunification applies to members of the nuclear family, that is to say the spouse and the minor children. However, if the situation of unmarried couples is treated as corresponding to that of married couples in a Member State, the principle of equal treatment should be respected and provision should be made for unmarried partners to be eligible for reunification.

(14) Family reunification should also apply to children of full age and to relatives in the ascending line where, ~~in view of~~ **for important objective reasons, their personal situation,** ~~there are for not separating them from the~~ **prevents their living, in acceptable conditions and self-sufficiently, separately from their relative, a** third-country national residing lawfully in a Member State.

(15) A set of rules governing the procedures for examination of applications for family reunification and for entry and residence of family members should be laid down. Those procedures should be effective **and manageable, taking account of the normal workload of the Member States' administrations, as well as transparent** and fair, ~~and~~ **in order to** offer appropriate **legal certainty** ~~protection~~ to those concerned.

(16) The integration of family members should be promoted. To that end, they should be granted a status independent of that of the applicant after a period of residence in the Member State. They should have access to education, employment and vocational training.

(17) Effective, proportionate and dissuasive measures should be taken to avoid prevent and penalise breaches of the rules and procedures relating to family reunification.

(18) In accordance with the principles of subsidiarity and proportionality as set out in Article 5 of the Treaty, the objectives of the proposed action, namely the establishment of a right to family reunification for third-country nationals to be exercised in accordance with common rules, cannot be sufficiently achieved by the Member States and can therefore, by reason of the scale and impact of the action, be better achieved by the Community. This Directive confines itself to the minimum required to achieve those objectives and does not go beyond what is necessary for that purpose,

HAS ADOPTED THIS DIRECTIVE:
Chapter I
General provisions

Article 1
The purpose of this Directive is to establish a right to family reunification for the benefit of third-country nationals residing lawfully in the territory of the Member States and citizens of the Union who do not exercise their right to free movement. This right shall be exercised in the manner prescribed by this Directive.

Article 2
For the purposes of this Directive:
(a) *'third-country national'* means any person who is not a citizen of the Union within the meaning of Article 17(1) of the Treaty establishing the European Community;
(b) *'refugee'* means any third-country national or stateless person enjoying refugee status within the meaning of the Convention on the Status of Refugees of 28 July 1951, as amended by the Protocol signed in New York on 31 January 1967;
~~(c) 'person enjoying subsidiary protection' means any third country national or stateless person authorised to reside in a Member State pursuant to a subsidiary form of protection in accordance with international law, national legislation or the practice of the Member States;~~
(c) *'applicant for reunification'* or *'applicant'* means **either** a third-country national residing lawfully in a Member State or a citizen of the Union ~~and~~ applying to be joined by members of his family;
(d) *'family reunification'* means the entry into and residence in a Member State by family members of a citizen of the Union or of a third-country national residing lawfully in that Member State in order to form or preserve the family unit, whether the family relationship arose before or after the resident's entry;

(e) *'residence permit'* means a permit or authorisation issued by the authorities of a Member State in accordance with its legislation allowing a third-country national to reside in its territory, with the exception of provisional authorisations pending examination of an application for asylum.

Article 3
1. This Directive applies where the applicant for reunification is:
(a) a third-country national residing lawfully in a Member State and holding a residence permit issued by that Member State for a period of at least one year;
(b) a refugee, irrespective of the duration of his residence permit;
(c) a citizen of the Union not exercising his right to free movement, if the applicant's family members are third-country nationals, irrespective of their legal status.

2. This Directive shall not apply where the applicant for reunification is:
(a) a third-country national applying for recognition of refugee status whose application has not yet given rise to a final decision;
(b) a third-country national authorised to reside in a Member State on the basis of temporary protection or applying for authorisation to reside on that basis and awaiting a decision on his status.
(c) a third-country national authorised to reside in a Member State on the basis of a subsidiary form of protection in accordance with international obligations, national legislation or the practice of the Member States or applying for authorisation to reside on that basis and awaiting a decision on his status.

3. This Directive shall not apply to family members of citizens of the Union exercising their right to free movement of persons.

4. This Directive is without prejudice to more favourable provisions of:
(a) bilateral and multilateral agreements between the Community or the Community and its Member States, on the one hand, and third countries, on the other, which entered into force before the date of entry into force of this
Directive;
(b) the European Social Charter of 18 October 1961 and the European Convention on the Legal Status of Migrant Workers of 24 November 1977.

Article 4
By way of derogation from this Directive, the family reunification of third-country nationals who are family members of a citizen of the Union residing in the Member State of which he is a national and who has not exercised his right to free movement of persons, is governed mutatis mutandis by Articles 10, 11 and 12 of Council Regulation (EEC) No 1612/68 5 and by the other provisions of Community law listed in the Annex.

Chapter II
Family members
Article 5
1. The Member States shall authorise the entry and residence, pursuant to this Directive and subject to compliance with the conditions laid down in Chapter IV, of the following family members:

(a) the applicant's spouse, or an unmarried partner living in a durable relationship with the applicant, if the legislation of the Member State concerned treats the situation of unmarried couples as corresponding to that of married couples;

(b) the minor children of the applicant and of his spouse or unmarried partner, including children adopted in accordance with a decision taken by the competent authority in the Member State concerned or a decision recognised by that authority;

(c) the minor children including adopted children of the applicant or his spouse or unmarried partner, where one of them has custody and the children are dependent on him or her; where custody is shared, the agreement of the other parent shall be required;

(d) the relatives in the ascending line of the applicant or his spouse or unmarried partner who are dependent on them and have no other means of family support in the country of origin;

(e) children of the applicant or his spouse or unmarried partner, being of full age, who are objectively unable to satisfy their needs by reason of their state of health.

2. In the event of a polygamous marriage, where the applicant already has a spouse living with him in the territory of a Member State, the Member State concerned shall not authorise the entry and residence of a further spouse, nor the children of such spouse; the entry and residence of children of another spouse shall be authorised if the best interests of the child so require.

3. The minor children referred to in points (b) and (c) of paragraph 1 must be below the age of majority set by the law of the Member State concerned and must not be married.

4. Where the applicant is a refugee or a person enjoying subsidiary protection, the Member States shall facilitate the reunification of other family members not referred to in paragraph 1, if they are dependent on the applicant.

5. Third-country nationals residing in a Member State for the purpose of study may not be joined by the relatives in the ascending line as defined in point (d) of paragraph 1.

Article 6
If the refugee is an unaccompanied minor, the Member States may:
(a) authorise the entry and residence for the purposes of family reunification of his relatives in the ascending line without applying the conditions laid down in Article 5(1)(d);
(b) authorise the entry and residence for the purposes of family reunification of other family members not referred to in Article 5, where the minor has no relatives in the ascending line or such relatives cannot be traced.

Chapter III
Submission and examination of the application
Article 7
1. In order to exercise his right to family reunification, the applicant shall submit an application for entry and residence of a one or more members of his family to the competent authorities of the Member State where he resides. The application shall be accompanied by documentary evidence of the family relationship and of compliance with the conditions laid down in Articles 5, 8 and, where applicable, 9 and 10. The application shall be submitted when the family members is are outside the territory of the Member State.

2. By way of derogation from paragraph 1, the Member State concerned shall examine an application submitted when the family members is **are** already residing in its territory, in exceptional circumstances or on humanitarian grounds.

3. After examining the application, the competent authorities of the Member State shall give the applicant written notification of the decision within a period, which may not exceed six months. Reasons shall be given for the decision rejecting the application.

4. If the applicant is a refugee or a person enjoying subsidiary protection and cannot provide documentary evidence of the family relationship, the Member States shall have regard to other evidence of the existence of the family relationship. A decision rejecting an application may not be based solely on the fact that documentary evidence is lacking.

5. When examining an application, the Member States shall have due regard to the best interests of minor children.

Chapter IV
Practical conditions for the exercise of the right to family reunification
Article 8
1. The Member States may refuse to allow the entry and residence of a family members on grounds of public policy, domestic security or public health.

2. The grounds of public policy or domestic security must be based exclusively on the personal conduct of the family member concerned.

3. Renewal of the residence permit may not be withheld and removal from the territory may not be ordered by the competent authority of the Member State concerned on the sole ground of illness or disability suffered after the issue of the residence permit.

Article 9
1. When the application for family reunification is submitted, the Member State concerned may ask the applicant to provide evidence that he has:
(a) adequate accommodation, **which is at least equivalent in size to that provided as social housing and which meets general health and safety standards in force in the Member State concerned;** that is to say accommodation that would be regarded as normal for a comparable family living in the same region of the Member State concerned;
(b) sickness insurance in respect of all risks in the Member State concerned for himself and the members of his family;
(c) stable and sufficient resources, that is to say resources which are higher than or equal to the level of resources below which the Member State concerned may grant social assistance; Where the first subparagraph cannot be applied, resources shall **must** be deemed sufficient if they are equal to or higher than **or at least equal to** the level of the minimum social security pension paid by the Member State.

2. The conditions relating to accommodation, sickness insurance and resources provided for by paragraph 1 may be set by the Member States only in order to ensure that the applicant for family reunification will be able to satisfy the needs of his reunified family members

without further recourse to public funds. They may not have the effect of discriminating between nationals of the Member State and third-country nationals.

3. Paragraph 1 shall not apply if the applicant is a refugee ~~or a person enjoying subsidiary~~ protection.

Article 10
1. The Member States may require the applicant to have resided lawfully in their territory for a period not exceeding one year, before having his family members join him.
2. Paragraph 1 shall not apply if the applicant is a refugee ~~or a person enjoying subsidiary protection~~.

Chapter V
Entry and residence of family members
Article 11
1. As soon as the application for family reunification has been accepted, the Member State concerned shall authorise the entry of the family member **or members**. The Member States shall grant such persons every facility for obtaining the requisite visas, including transit visas where required. Such visas shall be issued without charge.

2. The Member State concerned shall grant the family members a renewable residence permit of the same duration as that held by the applicant. If the applicant's residence permit is permanent or for an unlimited duration, the Member States may limit the duration of the family members' first residence permits to one year.

Article 12
1. The applicant's family members shall be entitled, in the same way as citizens of the Union, to:
(a) access to education;
(b) access to employment and self-employed activity;
(c) access to vocational guidance, initial and further training and retraining.

2. ~~Points (b) and (c) of paragraph 1 shall not apply to relatives in the ascending line or to children of full age~~ **Member States may restrict access to employment or self-employed activity by relatives in the ascending line or children of full age** to whom Article 5(1)(d) and (e) applies.

Article 13
1. At the latest after four years of residence, and provided the family relationship still exists, the spouse or unmarried partner and a child who has reached majority shall be entitled to an autonomous residence permit, independent of that of the applicant.
2. The Member States may issue an autonomous residence permit to children of full age and to relatives in the ascending line to whom Article 5(1)(d) and (e) applies.
3. In the event of widowhood, divorce, separation or death of relatives in the ascending or descending line, persons who have entered by virtue of family reunification and have been resident for at least one year, may apply for an autonomous residence permit. Where necessary by reason of particularly difficult situations, Member States shall accept such applications.

Chapter VI
Penalties and redress
Article 14
1. Member States may reject an application for entry and residence for the purpose of family reunification, or withdraw or refuse to renew a residence permit, where it is shown that:
(a) entry and/or residence was obtained by means of falsified documents or fraud;
(b) the marriage or adoption was contracted for the sole purpose of enabling the person concerned to enter or reside in a Member State.

2. Member States shall undertake specific checks where there are grounds for suspicion.

Article 15
Member States shall have proper regard for the nature and solidity of the person's family relationships and the duration of his residence in the Member State and to the existence of family, cultural and social ties with his country of origin where they withdraw or refuse to renew a residence permit or decide to order the removal of the applicant or members of his family.

Article 16
Where an application for family reunification is rejected or a residence permit is either not renewed or is withdrawn or removal is ordered, the applicant and the members of his family have the right to apply to the courts of the Member State concerned.

Article 17
The Member States shall lay down the rules on penalties applicable to infringements of the national provisions adopted pursuant to this Directive and shall take all measures necessary to ensure that they are implemented. The Member States shall notify those provisions to the Commission by the date specified in Article 19 at the latest and shall notify it without delay of any subsequent amendment affecting them.

Chapter VII
Final provisions
Article 18
No later than two years after the deadline set by Article 19 the Commission shall report to the European Parliament and the Council on the application of this Directive in the Member States and shall propose such amendments as may appear necessary.

Article 19
Member States shall bring into force the laws, regulations and administrative provisions necessary to comply with this Directive by 31 December 2002 at the latest. They shall forthwith inform the Commission thereof. When Member States adopt those provisions, they shall contain a reference to this Directive or be accompanied by such a reference on the occasion of their official publication. Member States shall determine how such reference is to be made.

Article 20
This Directive shall enter into force on the twentieth day following that of its publication in the *Official Journal of the European Communities*.

Article 21
This Directive is addressed to the Member States.

[T.32] Resolution of 4 December 1997 on marriages of convenience[26]

THE COUNCIL OF THE EUROPEAN UNION,

Having regard to Article K.1 (3) of the Treaty on European Union, Bearing in mind the provisions of the resolution on the harmonization of national policies on family reunification (Copenhagen conclusions of 1 June 1993),

Whereas the right to marry and to found a family is recognized by Article 12 of the European Convention on Human Rights and by Article 16 of the Universal Declaration of Human Rights, and whereas the right to respect for family life is recognized by Article 8 of the European Convention on Human Rights, Noting that marriages of convenience constitute a means of circumventing the rules on entry and residence of third-country nationals, Convinced that the Member States should adopt or continue to adopt equivalent measures to combat the phenomenon;

Whereas the objective of this resolution is not to introduce systematic checks on all marriages with third-country nationals, but whereas checks will be carried out where there are well-founded suspicions;

Whereas this resolution is without prejudice to the possibility of Member States checking before a marriage is performed whether it is one of convenience;

Whereas this resolution is without prejudice to Community law,

HEREBY ADOPTS THIS RESOLUTION:

1. For the purposes of this resolution, a 'marriage of convenience' means a marriage concluded between a national of a Member State or a third-country national legally resident in a Member State and a third-country national, with the sole aim of circumventing the rules on entry and residence of third-country nationals and obtaining for the third-country national a residence permit or authority to reside in a Member State.

2. Factors which may provide grounds for believing that a marriage is one of convenience are in particular:
– the fact that matrimonial cohabitation is not maintained,
– the lack of an appropriate contribution to the responsibilities arising from the marriage,
– the spouses have never met before their marriage,
– the spouses are inconsistent about their respective personal details (name, address, nationality and job), about the circumstances of their first meeting, or about other important personal information concerning them,

---

[26] OJ C 328 of 16 December 1997; (397Y1216(01)).

– the spouses do not speak a language understood by both,

– a sum of money has been handed over in order for the marriage to be contracted (with the exception of money given in the form of a dowry in the case of nationals of countries where the provision of a dowry is common practice),

– the past history of one or both of the spouses contains evidence of previous marriages of convenience or residence anomalies.

In this context, such information may result from:

– statements by those concerned or by third parties,

– information from written documentation, or

– information obtained from inquiries carried out.

3. Where there are factors which support suspicions for believing that a marriage is one of convenience, Member States shall issue a residence permit or an authority to reside to the third-country national on the basis of the marriage only after the authorities competent under national law have checked that the marriage is not one of convenience, and that the other conditions relating to entry and residence have been fulfilled. Such checking may involve a separate interview with each of the two spouses.

4. Should the authorities competent under national law find the marriage to be one of convenience, the residence permit or authority to reside granted on the basis of the third-country national's marriage shall as a general rule be withdrawn, revoked or not renewed.

5. The third-country national shall have an opportunity to contest or to have reviewed, as provided for by national law, either before a court or before a competent administrative authority, a decision to refuse, withdraw, revoke or not renew a residence permit or authority to reside.

6. Member States shall have regard to this resolution in any proposals to amend their national legislation. They shall furthermore endeavour to bring their national legislation into line with this resolution by 1 January 1999. The Council shall review the implementation of this resolution once a year, starting from 1 January 1999.

Illegal Migration 3.5

3.5.1

[T35] Recommendation of 1 June 1993 concerning checks on and expulsion of third-country nationals residing or working without authorization[27]

MINISTERS OF THE MEMBER STATES OF THE EUROPEAN COMMUNITIES, RESPONSIBLE FOR IMMIGRATION

HAVING REGARD to the high priority given to promoting a common approach to the question of illegal immigration adopted by the Ministers responsible for Immigration and by the European Council at Maastricht;

HAVING REGARD to the need to reinforce common endeavours to combat illegal immigration reiterated by the European Council at Edinburgh;

HAVING REGARD to the fact that this objective presupposes the improvement of means for checking and expelling third-country nationals who are in an irregular situation;

HAVING REGARD to the recommendation regarding practices followed by Member States on expulsion adopted by Immigration Ministers in London (WG....);

NOTING that it is fundamental to expulsion practices that there should also be effective means of identifying and apprehending those to be expelled;

NOTING that the implementation of the measures outlined in this recommendation will need to take account of the nature and extent of illegal immigration to be combated in particular Member States;

STRESSING that, in the light of the recommendation adopted at the Ministerial Conference held in Budapest on the implementation of measures to deal with uncontrolled migration, measures should be taken to combat the employment of those known to have entered or remained illegally or those whose immigration status does not allow them to work;

NOTING that this recommendation is without prejudice to Community law and also takes into account other relevant international instruments including the 1950 Convention for the protection of human rights and fundamental freedoms, the 1951 Geneva Convention relating to the status of refugees and 1967 New York Protocol;

NOTING in particular that this recommendation excludes from its scope:

– nationals of some EFTA countries who will have rights of free movement when the Agreement on the European Economic Area comes into force;

– family members of nationals of Member States and of some EFTA countries entering or residing in the territories of Member States in accordance with Community law and the EEA Agreement;

NOTING that checks and controls on the residence and employment of third country nationals shall be decided upon and carried out by those authorities which are empowered to do so under national legislation,

---

[27] WGI 1516.

ADOPTED THE FOLLOWING RECOMMENDATION:

1. Measures should be taken with a view to ensuring that third-country nationals do not remain beyond the period for which they have been admitted or given permission to remain and that they do not work without authority to do so. The general rule should be that persons not entitled to free movement in conformity with Community legislation and found:
    (i)   to have entered or remained unlawfully in Member States (where their stay has not been regularized);
    (ii) to be liable to expulsion on grounds of public policy or national security; or
    (iii) to have failed definitively in an application for asylum and to have no other claim to remain, should be expelled, unless there are compelling reasons, normally of a humanitarian nature, for allowing them to remain.

2. In addition, Member States may expel persons who have been working in breach of immigration/aliens or related provisions. In this context, under the same conditions, they may also expel those people who are subject to immigration/aliens provisions who have been involved in the facilitation, harbouring or employment of illegal immigrants.

3. Checks should, in particular, be carried out in respect of persons who are known or suspected of staying or working without authority, including persons whose request for asylum has been rejected. Member States shall examine the types of checks which would be most appropriate to introduce with a view to detecting third-country nationals who are residing or working illegally, including those persons whose application for asylum has been rejected.

4. Checks should be conducted to ensure that third-country nationals not entitled to free movement in conformity with Community legislation and who have received authorization for residence and, as the case may be, for employment for a limited period of time continue to fulfil the relevant conditions. To this end, in appropriate circumstances Member States should consider undertaking checks, inter alia, in the following situations:
    (i)   persons who have received authorization for residence but not for employment;
    (ii) persons who have received a residence permit, but whose work permit is of a limited nature;
    (iii) persons who work without authorization after being admitted as short-term visitors or tourists.
    Furthermore, to the extent that this is necessary, Member States should consider undertaking checks in view of detecting abuse, inter alia on:
    (i)   persons who have been authorized to be reunited with their family with a view to living together;
    (ii) persons who have received a residence/work permit on the basis of their marriage to a person president in the Member State.

5. The decision as to whether checks should be conducted depends on the circumstances in any given case. Exchanges of information between Member States on the type of checks and control procedures together with related legislation should be carried out within CIREFI.

6. Checks on persons suspected of residing or working illegally in Member States are to be carried out in conformity with national legislation and should be aimed at reinforcing common endeavours to combat illegal immigration to the Community.

3.5.2

[T.37] Recommendation of 22 December 1995 on harmonizing means of combating illegal immigration and illegal employment and improving the relevant means of control[28]

THE COUNCIL OF THE EUROPEAN UNION,

Having regard to the Treaty on European Union, and in particular K.3 (2) thereof,

Having regard to the initiative submitted by the French Republic on 22 December 1994,

Having regard to the recommendation of the Ministers of the Member States of the European Communities with responsibility for immigration of 1 June 1993 concerning checks on, and expulsion of, third-country nationals residing or working without authorization,

Having regard to the recommendation of the Ministers of the Member States of the European Communities with responsibility for immigration of 30 November 1992 regarding practices followed by Member States on expulsion,

Whereas, pursuant to Article K.1 (2) and (3) of the EC Treaty, policy regarding nationals of third countries and in particular combating unauthorized immigration, residence and work are matters of common interest and therefore fall within the areas for cooperation between Member States referred to in Title VI of the Treaty;

Whereas the Member States, faced with an increase in illegal immigration, have already adopted specific measures to ensure better control of population flows and to avoid the continued unlawful presence in their territories of foreign nationals who have entered or are residing without authorization;

Whereas, however, the efficiency of that action implies the implementation of co-ordinated and consistent measures;

Whereas, although recommendations laying down guiding principles for practice with regard to expulsion have already been adopted, that effort at alignment needs to be reinforced by recommending Member States to comply with a number of principles designed to ensure a better check on the situation of foreign nationals present within their territories;

Whereas this recommendation is in keeping with Community legislation, the Convention for the Protection of Human Rights and Fundamental Freedoms of 4 November 1950, and in particular Articles 3 and 14 thereof, and the Geneva Convention of 28 July 1951 relating to the Status of Refugees, as amended by the New York Protocol of 31 January 1967,

HEREBY RECOMMENDS Member States to harmonize further the means for checking on foreign nationals to verify that they fulfil the conditions laid down by the rules applicable to entry, residence and employment on the basis of the following guidelines:

---

[28] OJ C 005, 10 January 1996, p. 1-3 [EUDOR] 396Y0110(01).

1. This recommendation does not extend to citizens of the European Union or to nationals of EFTA member countries party to the Agreement on the European Economic Area, or to members of their families entitled under Community law.
2. Where an identity check is carried out on a foreigner in accordance with national law, at least where a person appears to be residing in the country unlawfully, his residence situation should be verified. This may apply in particular in the following cases:
    –   identity checks in connection with the investigation or prosecution of offences,
    –   identity checks to ward off threats to public order or security,
    –   identity checks in order to combat illegal entry or residence in certain areas (e.g. frontier areas and ports, airports and railways stations handling international traffic), without prejudice to border controls.
3. Third-country nationals should be in a position, according to national law, to present to the competent authorities confirmation, for example by way of papers or documents by virtue of which they are so authorized, of their authority to reside within the territory of the Member State where they are.
4. Where national law regards the residence or employment situation as a prerequisite for foreign nationals to qualify for benefits provided by a public service of a Member State in particular in the area of health, retirement, family or work, that condition cannot be met until it has been verified that the residence and employment situation of the person concerned and his or her family does not disqualify them from the benefit. Verification of residence or employment status is not required where intervention by a public authority is necessary on overriding humanitarian grounds.

    Such verifications are carried out by the services providing the benefits, with the assistance, if necessary, of the authorities responsible in particular for issuing residence or work permits, in accordance with national law relating, in particular, to data protection. Member States should inform the central or local authorities responsible for dispensing benefits to foreign nationals of the importance of combating illegal immigration in order to encourage them to report to the competent authorities, in accordance with national law, such cases of breaches of the residence rules as they may detect in the course of their work.

    The attention of the authorities responsible for issuing residence permits should also be drawn to the risk of marriages of convenience.
5. Employers wishing to recruit foreign nationals should be encouraged to verify that their residence or employment situations are in order by requiring them to present the document(s) by virtue of which they are authorized to reside and work in the Member State concerned. Member States could stipulate that employers may, if necessary, under the conditions laid down by national law relating, in particular, to data protection, check with the authorities responsible in particular for issuing residence and work permits; the said authorities may communicate the relevant information under procedures which guarantee confidentiality in the transmission of individual data.
6. Any person who is considered, under the national law of the Member State concerned, to be employing a foreign national who does not have authorization should be made subject to appropriate penalties.
7. The authorities competent to authorize residence should be empowered to take measures to check that persons who have been refused authorization to reside within the territory of the Member State have left that territory of their own accord.
8. Each Member State should consider setting up a central file of foreign nationals containing information on the administrative situation of foreign nationals with regard

to residence, including any refusal of authorization to reside and any expulsion measures. Any file thus set up will operate in compliance with the standards laid down in Council of Europe Convention 108 of 28 January 1981 for the Protection of Individuals with regard to Automatic Processing of Personal Data.

9. Member States should satisfy themselves that residence documents issued to foreign nationals are adequately secured against forgery and fraudulent use – particularly by colour photocopying – and, should, if necessary, amend them accordingly.

10. Member States should take the measures necessary to reinforce and improve means of identifying foreign nationals who are not in a lawful position and who have no travel documents or other documents by which they can be identified. Where a foreign national who is not in a lawful position is, or is likely to be, detained under the circumstances provided for in Chapter II of the recommendation of 30 November 1992 of the Ministers of the Member States of the European Communities with responsibility for immigration regarding practices followed by Member States on expulsion, the period of detention should be used in particular to obtain the necessary travel documents for expelling foreign nationals who have no documents. The consular authorities of the country of origin or the country of the nationality of the foreign national concerned should be encouraged to make additional identification efforts to obtain travel documents. Foreign nationals who have deliberately brought about their illegal position, particularly by refusing to supply travel documents, should be subject to penalties. In appropriate cases, such penalties may fall under criminal law. Member States will review the follow-up to Chapter III.2 of the recommendation of 30 November 1992 of the Ministers of the Member States of the European Communities with responsibility for immigration regarding practices followed by Member States on expulsion. The Council will review regularly, for example once a year, the progress made on harmonization in the fields covered by this recommendation.

3.5.3

[T.39] Recommendation of 27 September 1996 on combating the illegal employment of third-country nationals[29]

THE COUNCIL OF THE EUROPEAN UNION,

Having regard to the Treaty on European Union, and in particular Articles K.1 and K.2 thereof,

Having regard to the Council Recommendation of 22 December 1995 on harmonizing means of combating illegal immigration and illegal employment and improving the relevant means of control, Having regard to the Resolution of the Council of 20 June 1994 on limitations on admission of non-EC nationals to Member States for employment, Whereas Article K.1(3)(c) lays down that combating unauthorized immigration, residence and work by nationals of third countries on the territory of Member States constitutes a matter of common interest;

---

[29] OJ C 5, 10 January 1996, p. 1. (496Y1014(01)).

Whereas measures to combat the illegal employment and exploitation of third-country nationals should be complemented by measures to promote the integration of foreign workers lawfully established and legally employed in the territory of the Member States, guaranteeing them appropriate conditions of access to vocational training;

Whereas illegal employment may distort the conditions of free competition in the internal market by reducing social costs or giving employers other advantages and by lowering levels of social protection;

Whereas this Recommendation is aimed at strengthening cooperation between Member States on immigration policies in relation to third countries,

RECOMMENDS THAT the governments of the Member States apply the principles set out below with a view to combating illegal employment of third-country nationals:

I. Scope

This Recommendation applies to third-country nationals, with the exception of: members of the families of citizens of the Union exercising their right to free movement, nationals of Member States of the European Free Trade Association party to the Agreement on the European Economic Area and members of their families exercising their right to free movement. This Recommendation does not apply to third-country nationals to the extent that they are in a situation covered by Community law. This Recommendation is without prejudice to the rights of third-country nationals whose status is covered by agreements concluded with third countries by the Community, by the Community and its Member States or by one or more Member States, where such agreements contain more favourable provisions relating to employment.

II. Authorization to reside and to work

1.   Third-country nationals wishing to work in the territory of a Member State must be in possession of the authorizations to reside and to work required by the law of the Member State concerned.
2.   The activity carried out, the post and its location and duration must, in accordance with the law in force, effectively correspond to the content of the authorization granted by the Member State concerned.

III. Penalties for employing persons without authorization

1.   The employment of third-country nationals who do not possess the necessary authorization is prohibited and should give rise to the imposition of criminal and/or administrative penalties in accordance with the provisions of the law of the Member State concerned.
2.   The penalties referred to in paragraph 1 should be imposed in accordance with the provisions of the law of the Member State concerned upon those who employ illegal workers and those who encourage, facilitate or promote illegal employment.
3.   Illegal trafficking in labour organized by persons acting on their own or in networks should constitute a criminal offence and incur criminal and/or administrative penalties in accordance with the law of the Member State concerned.
4.   The procedures for punishing the employment of workers who do not possess the necessary authorization could:

– allow the application of penalties which are effective, dissuasive, appropriate and proportionate to the seriousness of the offences committed,
– permit the elimination of added profits or other advantages obtained by employers as a result of the offences committed in particular as regards the wages and charges imposed by the relevant provisions in each Member State.
The said procedures must provide for appropriate mechanisms and procedures for judicial control.

IV. Co-ordination and collaboration between enforcement agencies Member States should adopt the measures necessary to coordinate the activities of the competent services or authorities with the aim of combating the illegal employment and the exploitation of third-country nationals, given that the specialization in separate areas of control should be supplemented by the necessary coordination and collaboration in the activities of the services concerned.
The co-ordination could be put into practice through the preparation of joint operations to be defined by sectors of productive activity, geographical areas and periods of time in which non-compliance with the rules on the employment of third-country nationals appears to be concentrated.
The collaboration might take the form of:
–   support, at the request of one of the competent services, for preventive action, such as inspection visits to places of work where there is hard evidence that the activities of those services could be obstructed or nullified or could involve any type of risk,
–   support during inspections where the work of the competent services is seriously impeded in their investigations into the hidden economy, - prompt support where assistance is requested by the competent services in emergency situations.

V. Exchange of information
Member States should exchange information, both bilaterally and within the Council, regarding the fight against the illegal employment of third-country nationals and organized networks trafficking in labour.

VI. Monitoring of compliance with the Recommendation
The Council will examine the progress of compliance with the principles of this Recommendation periodically, and for the first time one year after its adoption.

3.5.4

[T.40] Decision of 16 December 1996 on monitoring the implementation of instruments adopted by the Council concerning illegal immigration, readmission, the unlawful employment of third country nationals and cooperation in the implementation of expulsion orders[30]

THE COUNCIL OF THE EUROPEAN UNION,
Having regard to the Treaty on European Union and in particular Article K.3(2)(a) thereof,
Having regard to the priority work programme adopted by the Council on 30 November 1993 in Brussels, calling in particular for the preparation of an annual report on achievements in the field of justice and home affairs and to the Council resolution on 14 October 1996, laying down the priorities for cooperation in the field of justice and home affairs for the period from 1 July 1996 to 30 June 1998.
Whereas Article K.1(3)(c) of the Treaty states that Member States shall regard the combating of unauthorized immigration, residence and work by nationals of third countries on the territory of Member States as a matter of common interest;
Whereas monitoring the implementation by Member States of the instruments adopted by the Council in this area will reveal the practical effect of the Council's work in this matter and provide useful lessons for its future work,

HAS DECIDED AS FOLLOWS:

Article 1 – Preparation of a questionnaire
Each year, the Presidency shall forward to the Member States a questionnaire designed to show how they have implemented the instruments adopted by the Council concerning illegal immigration, readmission, the unlawful employment of third country nationals and cooperation in the implementation of expulsion orders.

Article 2 – Content of the questionnaire
The questionnaire shall refer to the following matters:
– provisions adopted during the preceding year by the Member States in any of the areas covered by the instruments referred to in Article 1,
– any difficulties encountered in adopting such provisions,
– the likelihood of provisions in the areas referred to in the first indent being adopted in the near future,
– practical application of the aforementioned instruments and provisions.

Article 3 – Evaluation of the replies
A report shall be drawn up by the General Secretariat of the Council on the basis of the replies received from the Member States and shall be submitted to the Council.

---

[30] OJ L 342, 31 December 1996 p. 5 [EUDOR] 396D0749.

Article 4 – Implementation for the first time
The first questionnaire shall be sent to the Member States no later than 30 June 1997 and shall cover the period since the entry into force of the Treaty on European Union.

Return 3.6

3.6.1

[T.33] Recommendation of 30 November 1992 regarding practices followed by Member States on expulsion[31]

MINISTERS OF THE MEMBER STATES OF THE EUROPEAN COMMUNITIES RESPONSIBLE FOR IMMIGRATION, MEETING IN LONDON ON 30 NOVEMBER AND 1 DECEMBER 1992

With a view to reflecting the best practices existing in Member States and to meeting the requirements of speed, efficiency, effectiveness and economy with regard to expulsion;
Taking account of the need for effective means to identify, apprehend and expel those who are required to leave the territory of the Member States;
Noting that this Recommendation does not affect the provisions of international conventions currently in force on extradition;
Noting that this Recommendation is without prejudice to Community law;
Noting that this Recommendation does not apply to people refused entry at the border or who are identified attempting to cross the border illegally;

ADOPTED THE FOLLOWING RECOMMENDATION

I – GENERAL POLICY
1. Member States will ensure that without prejudice to Community law, their policies and practice with regard to expulsion are fully consistent with their obligations under the 1951 Geneva Convention relating to the Status of Refugees and the 1967 New York Protocol. Account should also be taken of other relevant international instruments, including the 1950 Convention for the Protection of Human Rights and Fundamental Freedoms.
2. Subject to the above, the general rule should be that people found:
– to have entered or remained unlawfully in Member States (where their stay has not been regularised);
– to be liable to expulsion on grounds of public policy or national security; or
– to have failed definitively in an application for asylum and to have no other claim to remain, should be expelled, unless there are compelling reasons, normally of a humanitarian nature, for allowing them to remain. In addition, consideration should be

---

[31] ESN 4678192 WGI 1266.

given to the question whether, in appropriate circumstances, a person who has been working in breach of immigration/aliens or related provisions should be expelled.

3. In accordance with Article 15(2) of the draft External Frontiers. Convention expulsion should be to the country of origin or to any other country to which the individual may be admitted. Where a person is being expelled on public policy or national security grounds this should not be to another Member State unless the individual has a right of residence there.

4. There should be provision for expulsion under either criminal or administrative law.

5. People being expelled should be notified in an appropriate manner of the reasons for the decision unless the interests of national security make such notification undesirable.

6. Whenever there is any doubt about a person's ability to understand the language in which an interview is being conducted, consideration should be given to the provision of an interpreter.

7. There should be a right to be represented and an appropriate means to challenge expulsion decisions.

8. Expulsion should take place as soon as possible after the decision to expel the individual has been taken.

II – RESTRICTIONS ON PERSONAL LIBERTY

1. There should be power in appropriate circumstances to restrict the personal liberty of people liable to expulsion.

2. Any restriction on liberty should be limited to the period necessary to effect expulsion, including identification, the making of any necessary arrangements and the provision of tickets, travel documents and escorts.

3. Appropriate places of custody should be available, where possible providing accommodation separate from that used by prisoners.

4. People in custody with a view to expulsion should have reasonable access to legal advisers and others in accordance with the general rules relating to the place of custody.

III – DOCUMENTATION

1. Any necessary arrangements for the identification and documentation of the individual should be made at the earliest possible opportunity.

2. Insofar as legislation does not already so permit consideration should be given to the introduction of laws to allow the fingerprinting of those to be expelled, to assist identification.

3. With a view to minimising delays in obtaining necessary travel documents and/or visas, early contact should be established with the Embassy or Consular authorities of States to which expulsion is to be effected and/or through which transit will be necessary.

4. Where a travel document is not held and cannot be arranged within a reasonable period, consideration should be given to the use of a 'one-way' document similar to that referred to in paragraph 3.38 and Appendix 8 of Annex 9 to the Chicago Convention.

IV – READMISSION AGREEMENTS

1. Insofar as re-admission agreements do not already exist, consideration should be given to establishing them with appropriate States. Where possible, such agreements should be multilateral, but where this is not possible bilateral agreements should be considered. Consideration should be given to preparing agreements in a standard format and, in the case of multilateral agreements, these might be along the lines of that between Poland and the

Schengen States, with such adaptations as appear necessary to take account of national situations and practical experience of that agreement.

2. When readmission agreements have been concluded Member States should communicate details of them to Community partners.

3. Specific measures should be adopted bilaterally or multilaterally as required with a view to improving existing arrangements among Member States for re-admission.

V – PROSECUTION OF FACILITATORS OF ILLEGAL ENTRANTS AND THOSE WHO HARBOUR PEOPLE WHO HAVE ENTERED OR REMAINED UNLAWFULLY AND ACTION AGAINST THOSE WHO EMPLOY ILLEGAL ENTRANTS

1. Insofar as legislation does not already exist, Member States should consider the introduction of laws which would provide for the prosecution of people who knowingly facilitate or attempt to facilitate the entry or transit of illegal entrants, and, subject to appropriate safeguards, of those who knowingly harbour those who have entered or remained unlawfully. It will be particularly appropriate to provide for the prosecution of those who commit such acts for reward or in an organized way. It is also recommended that appropriate measures should be taken to combat the employment of those known to have entered or remained in breach of the immigration or aliens provisions or who are not authorised to work under immigration aliens or related provisions.

2. Consideration should also be given to the question whether it would be appropriate to have power to expel people subject to immigration/aliens provisions who have been involved in the facilitation, harbouring or employment of illegal immigrants.

3. The European Convention on Mutual Assistance in Criminal Matters provides a cooperative framework between countries enabling those signatory to it to obtain and supply evidence for use in criminal proceedings, both in their own country and in others, and to facilitate the appearance of individuals from one country, in criminal proceedings to another. Insofar as national policy permits, Member States are encouraged to enter into arrangements which would enable them to assist their Community partners, for example in obtaining evidence, or service of summonses or other judicial documents on suspects or witnesses.

VI – CONFISCATION OF MODES OF TRANSPORT USED BY THOSE WHO FACILITATE ILLEGAL ENTRANTS

Insofar as legislation does not already exist, Member States should consider the introduction of laws which would permit a court, which had convicted a person of knowingly facilitating or attempting to facilitate unlawful entry, to order that the vehicle, ship or aircraft used should be forfeited. However, such legislation might specify limits on the exercise of the power to order confiscation, relating, for example, to the knowledge of the owners and to the size and nature of the vehicle, ship or aircraft involved.

VII – TRANSIT DUPING THE COURSE OF EXPULSION

Where a person who is being expelled cannot be sent direct to his point of destination, arrangements for the expulsion should be in accordance with the guidelines set out in WGI 1110.

VIII – ESCORTS

In order to ensure that a person being expelled reaches the intended destination, consideration should always be given to the question whether an escort is required. Escorts may be necessary either for those who require assistance or those who are likely to resist expulsion and may be a potential danger to themselves or others. Early consultation with the carrier is recommended in cases in which an escort may be necessary.

IX – SELECTION, TRAINING AND EQUIPMENT OF THOSE INVOLVED IN EXPULSION

1. All staff charged with the duty of expulsion should be appointed for the purpose and should receive appropriate training.

2. Staff should be properly trained and equipped to tackle the problems of illegal immigration and traffickers. In considering Forgery Detection Training it will be particularly appropriate to take account of the evaluation of the Pilot Course for Training Instructors from Member States.

3. Bearing in mind that costs of investigation, detention and removal can be reduced if illegal immigrants can be prevented from entering Member States, there are benefits to be gained from providing appropriate technical equipment, for example for the detection of forged and falsified documents.

X – EXCHANGES OF INFORMATION

1. With a view to combating the unlawful trafficking of illegal immigrants, Member States should arrange for appropriate exchange of information with their Community partners, perhaps through CIREFI, if established.

2. With a view to encouraging appropriate exchanges of information the principles set out in the Appendix to this paper are commended to Member States.

3. It is acknowledged that in considering the exchange of personal information States will have to take account of relevant national Data Protection legislation. It is noted that the need for an international agreement containing an appropriate standard for data protection should be considered.

4. Subject to the need to comply with national legislation and data protection requirements, where fingerprints have been taken for the purpose of documenting a person liable to be expelled, Member States should be prepared to make them available to another Member State, if this will assist in making arrangements for expulsion and the individual does not have an acceptable travel document.

APPENDIX
EXCHANGES OF INFORMATION

1. Contacts for Exchange of Information

1.1 It is desirable to have broad exchanges of information, which might involve exchanges of operation experience. These present an opportunity for discovering the practices used by traffickers of illegal immigrants and to take action to prevent them.

1.2 In addition, there is value in having personal contacts for the exchange of information, and the value of such contacts could be increased by countries exchanging officers for training or other purposes. This is relevant not only in neighbouring countries but elsewhere also.

1.3 The Presidency proposes to circulate a questionnaire designed to supplement and up-date existing information about useful points of contact in other Member States.

2. Exchange of Non-personal Information

2.1 Exchanges of non-personal factual information have a most important part to play in combating illegal immigration. These exchanges might be of both an informal, albeit structured nature, and of a formal nature.

2.2 The speed of exchanging information is most important.

2.3 Information should be exchanged about the routes and the methods of illegal entry that were used; about the transit points that illegal entrants and their traffickers used; about the nationalities involved; and in particular about emerging trends concerning those nationalities.

2.4 It is also important to have information about the main types of vehicle used and to consider what could be done to deter people from trying to travel illegally, for example by the use of publicity when traffickers are caught and in particular when traffickers are sentenced to imprisonment or are otherwise punished, for example by confiscation of the ship, aircraft or vehicle used.

2.5 Account should be taken of arrangements already in force, for example those which have been reached within groups such as the Schengen Group and TREVI, in order that those planning exchanges of information might benefit from the experience already gained.

3. Exchange of Personal Information

Arrangements for the exchange of information about those known or suspected of involvement in organized illegal entry may assist considerably in combating it. It is of particular importance that the information passed should be sufficient to enable the individual to be readily identified, and that it should be passed speedily to the competent authorities in other Member Sates.

3.6.2

[T.34] Recommendation of 30 November 1992 concerning transit for the purpose of expulsion[32]

The Ministers with responsibility for immigration,

CONSIDERING Member States' practices regarding transit for the purposes of expulsion;

WHEREAS it is appropriate to standardize such practices with a view to their harmonization;

WHEREAS the measures to be applied should meet the criteria of speed, efficiency and economy,

RECOMMEND that the following guidelines be applied:

I – For the purposes of this recommendation 'transit` means the transit of a person who is not a national of a Member State through the territory or the transit zone of a port or airport of a Member State.

---

[32] Approved by the Ministers on 30 November 1992.

II – A Member State which has decided to expel a third-country national
–   to a third country should in principle do so without the person transiting through the territory of another Member State,
–   to another Member State should in principle do so without the person transiting through the territory of a third Member State.

III – Where there are special reasons to justify this and, in particular, in the interests of efficiency, speed and economy, Member States may ask another Member State to authorize entry into its territory or transit through its territory of third-country nationals who are the subject of an expulsion measure.
1.   The State which has adopted the expulsion measure shall prove, before such a request is made, that the expellee's right to continue his journey and to enter the country of destination are guaranteed in the normal way.
2.   The State to which the request is made shall deal with it without prejudice to the cases referred to in section VI.

IV – The State taking the expulsion measure shall notify the transit State whether the person being expelled needs to be escorted. The transit State may:
–   authorize the State which adopted the expulsion measure to provide the escort itself,
–   decide to provide the escort itself, or
–   decide to provide the escort in cooperation with the State which adopted the expulsion measure.

V – Requests for transit for purposes of expulsion must include information concerning:
–   the identity of the third-country national being expelled,
–   the State of final destination,
–   the nature and date of the expulsion decision, and the authority which took the decision,
–   factors enabling a judgement to be made as to whether the third-country national can be admitted to the country of final destination or the second transit country,
–   the travel documents or other personal documents in the possession of the person concerned,
–   the identification of the department making the request,
–   the conditions of transit through the requested State (timetable, route, means of transport, etc.),
–   whether an escort is required, and the details thereof.
     Requests for transit for expulsion purposes must be submitted as soon as possible in accordance with the domestic legislation of the requested State to the authorities responsible for expulsion, who must reply to the request at the earliest opportunity.
     The transit State may request information, particularly concerning the need for transit.

VI – Cases in which transit for expulsion purposes may be refused:
–   where the third-country national who is the subject of a request for overland transit constitutes a threat to public order, national security or the international relations of the transit State,
–   where the information referred to in Section V(3) is not considered satisfactory.

VII – If for some reason the expulsion measure cannot be carried out, the State through which transit is to take place may return the expellee, without any formalities, to the territory of the requesting State.

VIII – Where expulsion cannot be carried out at the expense of the third-country national or a third party, the requesting State shall be liable for:
–   travel and other expenses, including escort costs, up until the departure from the territory of the Member State of transit of a third-country national whose transit has been authorized
–   the costs involved in any return.

IX – These recommendations shall not preclude closer cooperation between two or more Member States.

X – Member States which propose to conduct negotiations with another Member State or with a third State on transit for purposes of expulsion shall inform the other Member States in due time.

XI – This recommendation shall not contravene the provisions of the European Convention for the Protection of Human Rights and Fundamental Freedoms of 4 November 1950, nor those of the Convention on the Status of Refugees of 28 July 1951. This recommendation shall not contravene the provisions of international conventions currently in force concerning extradition and extradition in transit. This recommendation shall not replace extradition and transit extradition procedures by the transit procedure for expulsion purposes.

ADDENDUM to the recommendation concerning transit for the purposes of expulsion (approved by the Ministers on 1 and 2 June 1993)
1.   With a view to meeting the criteria of efficiency, speed and economy in connection with transit for purposes of expulsion a distinction may be made between the different expulsion measures, by air, sea or land, applied by the Member States.
2.   Expulsion by air accompanied by transit through the transit zone of an airport should be excluded from the provisions requiring an entry and transit authorization (see Section III of the recommendation), so that in such cases it will be sufficient to notify the country of transit.
3.   Notification of transit for expulsion purposes by air should contain the information required for transit requests indicated in Section V of the recommendation.
4.   In the case of expulsion by land or sea, requests for and notifications of entry into the territory of a State or transit through that State shall be addressed to a central contact body designated by the transit State, in accordance with the recommendations set out in the recommendation.
5.   If, in the case of expulsion by air, the transit State does not grant permission, that information must be communicated to the requesting State within 24 hours of the notification of transit.
6.   Member States shall draw up a joint list of contact bodies. In the case of expulsion by air, it would be desirable to contact directly the competent official(s) of the transit airport concerned or, in accordance with national procedures, any other competent official, provided that the 24-hour rule is observed (see point 4 above).

3.6.3

[T.36] Recommendation of 30 November 1994 concerning the adoption of a standard travel document for the removal/expulsion of third-country nationals[33]

THE COUNCIL OF THE EUROPEAN UNION,

Having regard to the Treaty on European Union, and in particular Article K.1(3)(c) thereof,

Whereas combating unauthorized immigration, residence and work by nationals of third countries on the territory of Member States is regarded as a matter of common interest;

Noting that consultation and cooperation on the execution of expulsion measures is considered a priority action in the 1994 work programme;

Acknowledging that a recent seminar on expulsion measures showed that the great majority of Member States experience difficulties in cases of third-country nationals possessing no travel documents who are required to be expelled from their territory;

Desirous of improving the efficiency with which expulsion measures are executed,

HEREBY RECOMMENDS THAT:

– with effect from 1 January 1995 the attached standard travel document valid for a single journey shall be used as appropriate by all Member States in the case of third-country nationals being expelled from the territory of the Union,

– the document shall be established in the language of the Member State executing the expulsion order,

– the document, where appropriate, shall be translated into both French and English.

MEMBER STATE:
Reg. No:
Doc. No:
No d'enregistrement No doc.:
Valid for one journey from:
Valable pour un seul voyage de to:
Name:
Nom Forename:
Prénom Date of birth:
Date de naissance Height:
Taille Distinguishing marks:
Signes particuliers Nationality:
Nationalité PHOTO Photo Address in home country (if known):
Adresse dans le pays d'origine (si connu) Seal/Stamp Sceau:Cachet Issuing authority:
Autorité de délivrance Issued at:
Lieu de délivrance Issued on:
Date de délivrance Signature:
Signature Remarks/Observations:

---

[33] OJ C 274, 19 October 1996, p. 18-19 [EUDOR] 396Y0919(06).

3.6.4

[T.38] Recommendation of 22 December 1995 on concerted action and cooperation in carrying out expulsion measures[34]

THE COUNCIL OF THE EUROPEAN UNION,

Having regard to the recommendation of the Ministers of the Member States of the European Communities responsible for immigration of 30 November 1992 concerning transit for the purposes of expulsion and the addendum thereto of 1 and 2 June 1993,

Whereas Article K.1 (3)(c) of the Treaty on European Union stipulates that combating unauthorized immigration, residence and work by nationals of third countries on the territory of Member States are matters of common interest;

Whereas the Council has already adopted specific measures to secure better control of migratory flows and to prevent third-country nationals entering Member States' territory unauthorized and remaining there illegally;

Whereas expulsion measures in respect of third-country nationals whose presence is unauthorized cannot be carried out owing to the absence of travel or identity documents;

Whereas, in order to achieve the effective carrying-out of expulsion measures, recommendations addressed to the Member States of the European Union and aimed at better co-ordination of those measures should be adopted at Council level;

Whereas the provisions of this recommendation are without prejudice to the European Convention for the Protection of Human Rights and Fundamental Freedoms of 4 November 1950 of to the Geneva Convention of 28 July 1951 relating to the Status of Refugees, as amended by the New York Protocol of 31 January 1967,

HEREBY RECOMMENDS MEMBER STATES' GOVERNMENTS:

to apply the principles set out below:

With a view to cooperation in the procurement of the necessary documentation

1. to implement specific mechanisms to improve the procurement of the necessary documentation from the consular authorities of the third State to which third-country nationals are to be expelled when they lack travel or identity documents;
2. where Member States experience repeated difficulties with certain third States in the matter of procuring documentation:
    (a) to make a particular effort to arrange for persons to be expelled to be identified by the consular authorities;
    (b) to issue repeated invitations to consular authorities to visit centres in which third-country nationals are being held, where appropriate, in order to identify them for the purpose of providing documentation;
    (c) to urge the same authorities to issue travel documents with a period of validity sufficient for expulsion to be carried out;
3. in the first instance to make use of the provisions on presumption of nationality of the standard readmission agreement adopted by the Council on 30 November 1994;

---

[34] OJ C 5 of 10 January 1996, p. 3-7; (396Y0110(02)).

4.   to issue, where it is not possible to obtain the necessary travel documents by using the above means, the standard travel document adopted by the Council on 30 November 1994;

With a view to cooperation in carrying out transit for expulsion purposes

5.   to co-operate to facilitate transit for expulsion purposes when the decision has been adopted by another Member State on the basis of the principles set out herein:

(a) In accordance with the Ministers' recommendation of 30 November 1992 concerning transit for the purposes of expulsion and the addendum thereto of 1 and 2 June 1993, which are annexed hereto, any Member State may, at the request of another Member State, authorize the transit of a third-country national across its territory for expulsion purposes.

(b) The Member State requesting the transit shall notify the requested State whether it considers it essential for the person being expelled to have an escort.

(c) The requested State shall be free to decide on the transit procedures; whether the escort is to be provided by the Member State which decided on the expulsion, whether it will provide the escort itself during transit or whether escort during transit will be arranged jointly with the State which decided on the expulsion.

(d) In the case of unescorted transit, the Member State which adopted the expulsion measure may, giving sufficient notice, request the State which has authorized transit to take the necessary measures in order to ensure departure to the place of destination.

(e) In the event of a third-country national's refusal to embark in the transit Member State, the Member States concerned may consider, in accordance with their laws and lest expulsion prove impossible to carry out, the possibility of availing themselves of, or seeking to establish, the appropriate legal machinery for enforcing expulsion.

(f) The transit Member State may return the third-country national to the territory of the Member State which adopted the expulsion measure if, for any reason whatsoever, the expulsion measure cannot be carried out.

(g) Member States may determine bilaterally the circumstances in which it may be possible to forego the refunding of costs on a case-by-case basis and replace it with an annual settlement of expenses occasioned by expulsion operations at either party's request;

With a view to concerted action in carrying out expulsions

6.   to carry out expulsions, in appropriate instances, as a concerted effort with other Member States on the basis of the following principles:

(a) the Member State which adopts the expulsion measure shall assume responsibility for carrying out measures for the expulsion of a third-country national it has itself adopted and shall use the resources available on the air transport market or, if necessary, resources it has organized itself.

(b) The Member State which adopts the expulsion measure may request cooperation from another Member State to locate seats available to carry out the expulsion by air.

(c) The Member State whose cooperation has been requested for carrying out an expulsion measure by air shall be entitled to refuse to allow expulsion to be carried out from its territory.

(d) With a view to co-ordinating the carrying-out of expulsion measures, each Member State shall inform other Member States which authority in its territory shall be responsible for:

- centralizing information on seats available on flights for expulsion purposes,
- contacting the competent authorities in the other Member States with a view to using seats available on flights,
- requesting authorization from other Member States to use seats available on flights departing from them,
- exchanging information with the authorities in other Member States in relation to carrying out expulsions by air,

With a view to monitoring the implementation of this recommendation the Council shall regularly review the progress achieved in relation to the practical application of the cooperation and concerted action measures covered by this recommendation.

ADDENDUM to the recommendation concerning transit for the purposes of expulsion (approved by the Ministers on 1 and 2 June 1993)
1. With a view to meeting the criteria of efficiency, speed and economy in connection with transit for purposes of expulsion a distinction may be made between the different expulsion measures, by air, sea or land, applied by the Member States.
2. Expulsion by air accompanied by transit through the transit zone of an airport should be excluded from the provisions requiring an entry and transit authorization (see Section III of the recommendation), so that in
such cases it will be sufficient to notify the country of transit.
3. Notification of transit for expulsion purposes by air should contain the information required for transit requests indicated in Section V of the recommendation.
4. In the case of expulsion by land or sea, requests for and notifications of entry into the territory of a State or transit through that State shall be addressed to a central contact body designated by the transit State, in accordance with the recommendations set out in the recommendation.
If, in the case of expulsion by air, the transit State does not grant permission, that information must be communicated to the requesting State within 24 hours of the notification of transit.
5. Member States shall draw up a joint list of contact bodies. In the case of expulsion by air, it would be desirable to contact directly the competent official(s) of the transit airport concerned or, in accordance with national procedures, any other competent official, provided that the 24-hour rule is observed (see point 4 above).

3.6.5

Note on Proposed Council Directive on Mutual Recognition of Decisions on the Expulsion of Third Country Nationals, 18 October 2000[35]

COUNCIL DIRECTIVE 2000/ /EC (...) on the mutual recognition of decisions on the expulsion of third country nationals

THE COUNCIL OF THE EUROPEAN UNION,

Having regard to the Treaty establishing the European Community, and in particular Article 63(3) thereof,

Having regard to the initiative by the French Republic,

Having regard to the Opinion of the European Parliament,

Whereas:

(1)   The Treaty stipulates that the Council is to adopt measures on immigration policy within areas comprising conditions of entry and residence as well as illegal immigration and illegal residence.

(2)   The Tampere European Council on 15 and 16 October 1999 reaffirmed its resolve to create an area of freedom, security and justice. For that purpose, a common European policy on asylum and migration should aim both at fair treatment of third country nationals and better management of migration flows.

(3)   The need to ensure greater effectiveness in enforcing expulsion decisions and better cooperation between Member States entails mutual recognition of expulsion decisions.

(4)   Decisions on the expulsion of third country nationals have to be adopted in accordance with fundamental rights, as safeguarded by the European Convention for the Protection of Human Rights and Fundamental Freedoms of 4 November 1950, in particular Articles 3 and 8 thereof, and the Geneva Convention relating to the Status of Refugees of 28 July 1951 and as they result from the constitutional principles common to the Member States.

(5)   In accordance with the principles of subsidiarity and proportionality, the objective of the proposed action, namely cooperation between Member States on expulsion of third country nationals, cannot be sufficiently achieved by the Member States and can therefore, by reason of the effects of the action, be better achieved by the Community. This Directive does not go beyond what is necessary to achieve that objective.

(6)   In accordance with Article 3 of the Protocol on the position of the United Kingdom and Ireland annexed to the Treaty on European Union and the Treaty establishing the European Community, the United Kingdom has given notice by letter of 18 October 2000 of its wish to take part in the adoption and application of this Directive.

---

[35] Text of the initiative as revised by the *Presidency* following the meetings of the *Working Party on Migration and Expulsion* on 11 October 2000 and of the Strategic Committee on Immigration, Frontiers and Asylum on 16 October 2000 (Migr 74, 11384/00, dd 18 October 2000).

(7)   In accordance with Articles 1 and 2 of the Protocol on the position of Denmark annexed to the Treaty on European Union and the Treaty establishing the European Community, Denmark is not participating in the adoption of this Directive, and is therefore not bound by it or subject to its application. Given that this instrument aims to build upon the Schengen acquis under the provisions of Title IV of the Treaty establishing the European Community, in accordance with Article 5 of the abovementioned Protocol, Denmark shall decide within a period of 6 months after the Council has decided on a proposal or initiative whether it will implement this decision in its national law.

(8)   As regards the Republic of Iceland and the Kingdom of Norway, this Directive constitutes a development of the Schengen acquis within the meaning of the agreement concluded on 18 May 1999 by the Council of the European Union and those two States. As a result of the procedures laid down in the agreement, the rights and obligations arising from this Directive shall also apply to those two States and in relations between those two States and the Member States of the European Community to which this Directive is addressed.

HAS ADOPTED THIS DIRECTIVE:
Article 1
1. Without prejudice to the obligations arising from Article 23 of the Convention implementing the Schengen agreement of 14 June 1985, signed at Schengen on 19 June 1990, the purpose of this Directive is to make possible the recognition of an expulsion decision issued by a competent authority in one Member State, hereinafter referred to as the 'issuing Member State', against a third country national present within the territory of another Member State, hereinafter referred to as the 'enforcing Member State'.
2. Any decision taken pursuant to paragraph 1 shall be implemented according to the applicable legislation of the enforcing Member State.
3. This Directive shall not apply to family members of citizens of the Union who have exercised their right of free movement.

Article 2
For the purposes of this Directive,
(a)   'third country national' shall mean anyone who is not a national of any of the Member States;
(b)   'expulsion decision' shall mean any decision which orders an expulsion taken by a competent administrative authority of an issuing Member State;
(c)   'enforcement measure' shall mean any measure taken by the enforcing Member State with a view to implementing an expulsion decision.

Article 3
1. The expulsion referred to in Article 1 shall be carried out in the following cases:
(a)   a third country national is the subject of an expulsion decision based on a serious and present threat to public order or to national security and safety, taken in the following cases:
        –   conviction of a third country national by the issuing Member State for an offence punishable by a penalty involving deprivation of liberty of at least one year;
        –   the existence of serious grounds for believing that a third country national has

committed serious criminal offences or the existence of solid evidence of his intention to commit such offences within the territory of a Member State.

If the person concerned holds a residence permit issued by the enforcing Member State or by another Member State, the enforcing State shall consult the issuing State and, where appropriate, the State which issued the permit. The existence of an expulsion decision taken under this point shall be regarded as sufficient motive for withdrawing the residence permit if the national legislation of the State which issued the permit so allows.

(b)   a third country national is the subject of an expulsion decision based on failure to comply with national rules on the entry or residence of aliens.

In the two cases mentioned in (a) and (b), the expulsion decision must not have been rescinded or suspended by the issuing Member State.

2. The expulsion decision and the enforcement measure must comply with the European Convention for the Protection of Human Rights and Fundamental Freedoms and other applicable international instruments.

3. This Directive shall be applied without prejudice to the provisions of the Dublin Convention and readmission agreements between Member States.

Article 4

The authorities of the issuing Member State and of the enforcing Member State shall make use of all appropriate means of cooperation to implement this Directive.

The issuing Member State shall provide the enforcing Member State with all documents needed to certify the continued enforceability of the decision by the fastest appropriate means. The enforcing Member State shall first examine the situation of the person concerned to ensure that neither the relevant international instruments nor the national rules applicable conflict with the enforcement of the expulsion decision.

After implementation of the enforcement measure, the enforcing Member State shall inform the issuing Member State.

Article 5

The Member States shall ensure that the third country national concerned may, in accordance with the enforcing Member State's legislation, bring proceedings for a remedy against any measure referred to in Article 1(2).

Article 6

Protection of personal data and data security shall be ensured in accordance with Directive 95/46/EC of the European Parliament and of the Council of 24 October 1995 on the protection of individuals with regard to the processing of personal data and on the free movement of such data.

Personal data files may be used in the context of this Directive only for the purposes laid down therein.

Article 7

Member States shall compensate each other for any financial imbalances which may result from application of this Directive where expulsion cannot be effected at the expense of the national(s) of the third country concerned.

In order to enable this Directive to be implemented, the Council, acting on a proposal from the Commission, shall adopt appropriate criteria and practical arrangements before the date mentioned in the first subparagraph of Article 8(1). These criteria and practical arrangements shall also apply to the implementation of Article 24 of the Convention implementing the Schengen Agreement.

Article 8
1. Member States shall bring into force the laws, regulations and administrative provisions necessary to comply with this Directive not later than [Eighteen months after the entry into force of this Directive]. They shall forthwith inform the Commission thereof. When Member States adopt these measures, they shall contain a reference to this Directive or shall be accompanied by such reference on the occasion of their official publication. The methods of making such reference shall be laid down by Member States.
2. Member States shall communicate to the Commission the text of the main provisions of domestic law which they adopt in the field governed by this Directive.

Article 9
This Directive is addressed to the Member States, in accordance with the Treaty establishing the European Community.

Article 10
This Directive shall enter into force on the day of its publication in the Official Journal of the European Communities.

3.6.6

[T.41] Decision of 26 May 1997 on the exchange of information concerning assistance for the voluntary repatriation of third-country nationals[36]

THE COUNCIL OF THE EUROPEAN UNION,
Having regard to the Treaty on European Union, and in particular Article K.3 (2)(a) thereof,
Whereas Article K.1 (3) of the Treaty on European Union states that the Member States shall regard immigration policy and policy regarding nationals of third countries as matters of common interest;
Whereas point 111 of the Communication by the Commission dated 23 February 1994 on immigration and asylum policy suggests that Member States' policies on the voluntary return of third-country nationals be approximated;

---

[36] OJ L 147, 5 June 1997, p. 3 - 4 [EUDOR] 397D0340.

Whereas a number of Member States have established programmes to support the voluntary return of legally as well as illegally resident third-country nationals;

Whereas, in the case of legally resident third-country nationals, Member States' policies should aim at their integration into society and whereas assistance for voluntary return should not be interpreted as reflecting a policy of actively encouraging such return, but is purely designed to facilitate return of those who have taken a decision of their own free will to this effect;

Whereas assistance for the voluntary return of illegally resident third-country nationals is in line with the European humanitarian tradition and may contribute to finding a dignified solution to reducing the number of illegally resident third-country nationals in the Member States;

Whereas it should be avoided that such assistance leads to undesired incentive effects;

Whereas this Decision is without prejudice to the provisions of the European Convention for the Protection of Human Rights and Fundamental Freedoms of 4 November 1950 and the Geneva Convention of 28 July 1951 relating to the Status of Refugees, as amended by the New York Protocol of 31 January 1967,

HAS DECIDED AS FOLLOWS:

Article 1 – Information exchange

1. Those Member States which have taken steps to develop programmes to support the voluntary return of third-country nationals to their country of origin shall report annually on them to the General Secretariat of the Council. The General Secretariat shall circulate such information to all Member States and the Commission.

2. Information on these national return programmes shall, in particular, include the following information:
    – the authorities responsible for carrying out the programme, i.e. non-governmental and/or international organizations;
    – the scope of the programme in terms of the persons covered;
    – any further requirements to be met by individual returnees in order to be considered for assistance under the programme;
    – any requirements to be met by the country of origin under the programme;
    – the type and level of assistance granted (e.g. travel expenses for the returnee and his/ her family, removal costs, repatriation allowance);
    – estimate of the effects of the programme, including the number of beneficiaries and the occurrence of any incentive effects.

Article 2 – Analysis

1. The General Secretariat of the Council shall make available annually to Member States and the Commission a draft report on the information received on the basis of Article 1. This report shall be exhaustive in nature and shall contain specific information on each of the points listed in Article 1(2).

2. The draft report referred to in paragraph 1 shall be examined by the Member States concerned and the Commission and adjusted if necessary.

Article 3 – Co-ordination

1. On the basis of the draft report referred to in Article 2(1), Member States concerned and

the Commission shall, within the Council, exchange their views on the programmes referred to in Article 1. In so doing, they shall, in particular, compare the scope, conditions and effects of those programmes with a view to their possible approximation.

2.   The Member States concerned which have not introduced these programmes shall examine the results and usefulness thereof.

Article 4
1.   This Decision shall be published in the Official Journal.
2.   The Member States concerned shall draw up the report mentioned in Article 1 for the first time within six months of the publication of this Decision in the Official Journal.

3.6.7

Conclusions on Conditions for the Readmission of Persons Who Are Illegally Resident in a Member State But Who Hold a Residence Permit for Another Member State 1994[37]

CROSSING EXTERNAL FRONTIERS
The Council adopted the following conclusions on conditions for the readmission of persons who are illegally resident in a Member State but who hold a residence permit for another Member State (Article 8(3) of the draft External Frontiers Convention):

Conclusion 1: Scope
The provisions on taking back pursuant to Article 8(3) are applicable to persons who are not nationals of a Member State, who hold a valid residence permit or valid provisional residence permit within the meaning of Article 8(1) and (2) and who are illegally resident in the territory of another Member State.
The provisions do not affect Member States' obligations under the Dublin Asylum Convention to take back applicants for asylum who are illegally resident in another Member State.

Conclusion 2: Voluntary Departure or Return to the Member State Which Issued a Valid Residence Permit or Valid Provisional Residence Permit
Where a person covered by conclusion 1 entered a Member State from another Member State without a visa for the purposes of a short stay or transit, under Article 8 (1) or (2), and is illegally resident there, that person must go without delay to the Member State for which he holds a residence permit unless he is authorized to go to another country to which he is certain to be admitted, in accordance with Article 15 (1).
If a foreign national wishes to go to another country, he must provide documentary evidence that he may be admitted to that country, e.g. in the form of an entry permit or valid visa, and

---

[37] EU Council of General Affairs Ministers, Luxembourg, 31 October 1994, Press Release 10314194 (Presse 219-G).

that he is in possession of the necessary resources, e.g. in the form of a ticket or other documentation that allows him to travel, and cash or a bank deposit in order to secure his transportation and his residence in the country to which he may be admitted.

If the person has provided documentary evidence that he may be admitted to another country and that he is in possession of the necessary resources to travel to and take up residence in that country; his wishes should normally be accepted.

Conclusion 3: Member State Which is Required to Take Back the Person if He Does Not Leave Voluntarily

If a person who is not a national of a Member State and who is illegal resident in the territory of a Member State refuses to leave voluntarily, Member States are required to take him back in accordance with the guidelines set out below.

a. Persons Holding a Valid Residence Permit or Valid Provisional Residence Permit for Another Member State

If the person holds a valid residence permit or valid provisional residence permit for another Member State, the Member State which issued the valid residence permit or valid provisional residence permit is required to take him back.

If the person holds more than one valid residence permit or provisional residence permit issued by different Member States, the Member State required to take him back is:

a) the State which issued the residence permit or provisional residence permit allowing the longest period of residence: or

b) where the residence permits allow the same period of residence, the State which issued the residence permit or provisional residence permit with the latest expiry date.

b. Persons Holding an Expired Residence Permit for Another Member State

In case the person concerned holds a residence permit or a provisional residence permit the validity of which has expired by no more than two months, the Member State which has issued the residence permit will take back the person, provided that the requesting State:

– has discovered the illegal presence of that person in its territory within this period; and

– has lodged the request for taking him back within a period of an additional month at the latest.

If the person holds more than one residence permit, the validity of which has been expired by no more than a period of 2 months, the Member State required to take him back is:

a) the State which issued the residence permit which had allowed the longest period of residence; or

b) where the residence permits allowed the same period of residence, the State which issued the residence permit with the latest expiry date.

Conclusion 4: Taking Back

The person is to be taken back after a request has been made by the competent authorities in the requesting State establishing that the person in question holds a valid residence permit or provisional residence permit for the taking back Member State.

The request must be accompanied by a copy of the administrative act establishing the person's unlawful presence in the Member State in question and stating, inter alia, when and where he was found to be unlawfully present.

A Member State receiving a request in accordance with conclusion 3 must reply to the request within 8 days. If the member State does not respond within that time, it will be deemed to have agreed to taking back, unless it has expressly requested a one-week extension of that time limit. The Member State to which the request was addressed is required to take in, within a month at the most, the person it has agreed to take back. That time limit may be extended by agreement between the two Member States concerned, upon submission by the requesting Member State of an explicit and justified application.

Member States are to exchange lists of competent authorities to consider requests for taking back and of points at borders where the taking back can take place.

Conclusion 5: Costs for Taking Back

The financial costs entailed by the taking back are to be met by the person concerned. Where the person is unable to meet the expenses, the expenses up to the point of taking back are as a rule to be met by the State requesting the taking back.

3.6.8

[T.42] Recommendation of 30 November 1994 concerning a specimen bilateral readmission agreement between a Member State of the European Union and a third country[38]

THE COUNCIL OF THE EUROPEAN UNION,

Having regard to the Treaty on European Union, and in particular Article K.1(3) thereof,

Recalling that these policies are regarded as matters of common interest under the Treaty,

Determined to combat unauthorized immigration to the Member States,

Noting that the laying down of principles which must appear in bilateral and multilateral readmission agreements appears in the action plan in the field of justice and home affairs which was approved by the Council and endorsed by the European Council in December 1993,

Recalling that these principles were approved by the Council in May 1994 and that it was agreed to devise a specimen readmission agreement on the basis of these principles at a later date,

Whereas the specimen readmission agreement is to be used flexibly by the Member States and that it may be adapted to the particular needs of the Contracting Parties;

Hereby RECOMMENDS that with effect from 1 January 1995 the specimen agreement attached should be used by the Member States as a basis for negotiation with third countries on the conclusion of readmission agreements.

---

[38] OJ C 274, 19 September 1996, p. 20-24 [EUDOR] 396Y0919(07).

ANNEX

SPECIMEN AGREEMENT

between the Government of (... Member State...) and the Government of (... third country...) on the readmission of persons residing without authorization

(Readmission Agreement)

THE GOVERNMENT OF (... MEMBER STATE...) and THE GOVERNMENT OF (... THIRD COUNTRY...),

hereinafter referred to as the 'Contracting Parties`, desirous of facilitating the readmission of persons staying illegally on the territory of the other Contracting Party, i.e. persons who do not, or who no longer, fulfil the conditions in force for entry or residence, and of facilitating the transit of persons in a spirit of cooperation and on the basis of reciprocity,

HAVE AGREED AS FOLLOWS:

Article 1 – Readmission of own nationals

1.   Each Contracting Party shall readmit at the request of the other Contracting Party and without any formality persons who do not, or who no longer, fulfil the conditions in force for entry or residence on the territory of the requesting Contracting Party provided that it is proved or may be validly assumed that they possess the nationality of the requested Contracting Party. The same shall apply to persons who have been deprived of the nationality of the requested Contracting Party since entering the territory of the requesting Contracting Party without at least having been promised naturalization by the requesting Contracting Party.

2.   Upon application by the requesting Contracting Party, the requested Contracting Party shall without delay issue the persons to be readmitted with the travel documents required for their repatriation.

3.   The requesting Contracting Party shall readmit such persons again under the same conditions if checks reveal that they where not in possession of the nationality of the requested Contracting Party when they departed from the territory of the requesting Contracting Party. This shall not apply if the readmission obligation is based on the fact that the requested Contracting Party deprived the person in question of its nationality after that person had entered the territory of the requesting Contracting Party without that person at least having been promised naturalization by the requesting Contracting Party.

Article 2 – Readmission in the case of third-country nationals who entered via the external frontier

1.   The Contracting Party via whose external frontier a person can be proved, or validly assumed, to have entered who does not meet, or who no longer meets, the conditions in force for entry or residence on the territory of the requesting Contracting Party shall readmit the person at the request of that Contracting Party and without any formality.

2.   For the purposes of this Article, the external frontier shall be deemed to be the first frontier to have been crossed which is not a frontier common to the Contracting Parties.

3.   The readmission obligation pursuant to paragraph 1 shall not apply in respect of a person who was in possession of a valid residence permit issued by the requesting Contracting Party when the person entered the territory of that Contracting Party or who was issued with a residence permit by that Contracting Party after entering its territory.

4.   The Contracting Parties shall make every effort to give priority to deporting nationals of an adjacent State to their country of origin.

Article 3 – Readmission of nationals of third countries by the Contracting Party responsible for the entry
1.   If a person who has arrived in the territory of the requesting Contracting Party does not fulfil the conditions in force for entry or residence and if that person is in possession of a valid visa issued by the other Contracting Party or a valid residence permit issued by the requested party, that Contracting Party shall readmit the person without any formality upon application by the requesting Contracting Party.
2.   If both Contracting Parties issued a visa or a residence permit, responsibility shall reside with the Contracting Party whose visa or residence permit expires last.
3.   Paragraphs 1 and 2 shall not apply where a transit visa was issued.

Article 4 – Residence permits
A residence permit pursuant to Article 2(3) and Article 3 means an authorization of any type issued by one Contracting Party, entitling the person to reside on the territory of that Contracting Party. This shall not include temporary permission to reside on the territory of one of the Contracting Parties in connection with the processing of an asylum application.

Article 5 – Time limits
1.   The requested Contracting Party shall reply to readmission requests addressed to it without delay, and in any event within a maximum of 15 days.
2.   The requested Contracting Party shall take charge of persons whose readmission has been agreed to without delay, and in any event, within a maximum of one month. Upon application by the requesting Contracting Party, this time limit may be extended by the time taken to deal with legal or practical obstacles.

Article 6 – Time limit after which the readmission obligation will lapse
The application for readmission must be submitted within a maximum of one year of the Contracting Party noting the illegal entry and presence of the said national of a third country on its territory.

Article 7 – Transit
1.   Without prejudice to Article 11, the Contracting Parties shall allow third-country nationals to pass through their territory in transit if the other Contracting Party so requests and if admission to other possible States of transit and to the State of destination is assured.
2.   It shall not be essential for the requested Contracting Party to issue a transit visa.
3.   Notwithstanding any authorization issued, persons taken in charge for transit purposes may be returned to the other Contracting Party if circumstances within the meaning of Article 11 subsequently arise or come to light which stand in the way of a transit operation or if the onward journey or admission by the State of destination is no longer assured.
4.   The Contracting Parties shall endeavour to restrict transit operations to aliens who cannot be returned to their States of origin directly.

Article 8 – Data protection
In so far as personal data have to be communicated in order to implement this Agreement, such information may concern only the following:

1. the particulars of the person to be transferred and, where necessary, of the members of the person's family (surname, forename, any previous names, nicknames or pseudonyms, aliases, date and place of birth, sex, current and any previous nationality);
2. passport, identity card and other identity and travel documents and laissez-passer (number, period of validity, date of issue, issuing authority, place of issue, etc.);
3. other details needed to identify the persons to be transferred;
4. stopping places and itineraries;
5. residence permits or visas issued by one of the Contracting Parties;
6. in the cases covered by Article 7, the place where the asylum application was submitted and the date of submission of any previous asylum application, the date of submission of the present asylum application, the present stage of the procedure and the content of any decision taken.

Article 9 – Costs
1. The costs of transporting persons taken in charge pursuant to Articles 1, 2 and 3 shall be borne by the requesting Contracting Party as far as the border of the requested party.
2. The costs of transit as far as the border of the State of destination, and, where necessary, the costs arising from return transport, shall be borne by the requesting Contracting Party in accordance with Article 7.

Article 10 – Committee of Experts
1. The Contracting Parties shall provide each other with mutual assistance in the application and interpretation of this Agreement. To this end, they shall set up a Committee of Experts to:
   (a) monitor application of this Agreement;
   (b) submit proposals for resolving problems associated with the application of this Agreement;
   (c) propose amendments and additions to this Agreement;
   (d) prepare and recommend appropriate measures for combating illegal immigration.
2. The Contracting Parties shall reserve the right to agree to the proposals and measures or not to do so.
3. The Committee shall be composed of three representatives of each Contracting Party. The Contracting Parties shall appoint the chairman and his deputies from among them, and shall also appoint alternate members. Additional experts may be associated with the consultations.
4. The Committee shall meet at the initiative of one of the chairmen and at least once a year.

Article 11 – Clause stipulating that international agreements/conventions shall not be affected
These agreements shall not affect the Contracting Parties' obligations arising from:
1. the Convention of 28 July 1951 on the Status of Refugees as amended by the Protocol of 31 January 1967 on the Status of Refugees;
2. international conventions on extradition and transit;
3. the Convention of 4 November 1950 for the Protection of Human Rights and Fundamental Freedoms;
4. international conventions on asylum, in particular under the Dublin Convention of 15 June 1990 determining the State responsible for examining applications for asylum lodged in a Member State of the European Community;

5.   international conventions and agreements on the readmission of foreign nationals.

Article 12 – Entry into force
This Agreement shall enter into force on the first day of the second month following its signature. It shall not be applied until the date agreed upon by the Contracting Parties in an exchange of notes.

Article 13 – Suspension, termination
1.   This Agreement is concluded for an indefinite period.
2.   After informing the other Contracting Party each Contracting Party may suspend this Agreement by giving notification on important grounds, in particular on the grounds of the protection of State security, public order or public health. The Contracting Parties shall notify each other of the cancellation of any such measure without delay via diplomatic channels.
3.   After informing the other Contracting Party, each Contracting Party may terminate this Agreement on important grounds by giving notification.
4.   The suspension or termination of this Agreement shall become effective on the first day of the month following the month in which notification was received by the other Contracting Party.

3.6.9
[T.43] Recommendation of 24 July 1995 on the Principles for the Drafting of Protocols on the Implementation of Readmission Agreements[39]

THE COUNCIL OF THE EUROPEAN UNION,
Having regard to the Treaty on European Union, and in particular Article K.1 (3) thereof,
Recalling that the Council has adopted a recommendation concerning a specimen bilateral readmission agreement between a Member State and a third Country,
Whereas such readmission agreements are often accompanied by protocols laying down certain technical details for their implementation;
Whereas a series of guiding principles should therefore be adopted for Member States to use as a basis when negotiating such protocols;

RECOMMENDS that, as from 1 July 1995, the Member States should use the following guiding principles as a basis for negotiations with third countries when drawing up protocols on implementing readmission agreements.

---

[39] OJ C274, 19 September 1996, p. 25-33

I – Readmission procedures

1. Common forms
For the return/readmission of persons residing without authorization, it is recommended that provision be made for the Contracting Parties to use common forms. The forms concerned are as follows:
– record of the return/readmission of a person under the simplified procedure,
– request for the readmission/transit of a person,
– record of the return/readmission of a person.
Member States could use the three documents annexed hereto as a basis for drawing up such forms, incorporating the relevant headings from them according to the specific nature of relations with the third country party to the agreement and the resulting information requirements. The need for simplicity and speed should be the prime concern.

2. Return/readmission under the simplified procedure
Persons apprehended in a border area are to be returned/readmitted under the simplified procedure. A provision allowing this should therefore be included in the protocol. The Contracting Parties will determine the total time taken by the simplified readmission procedure (comprising the submission and answering of all requests), which should in any event be very short. Member States may take as a basis agreements already signed by some of them in which that time does not exceed 48 hours. Formalities for the return of a person should be simplified in the case of this procedure. Notification of the return would be given in any form (by telephone, fax, telex or orally) and it would be carried out directly by the local border authorities. If necessary, a record (see I.1) may be drawn up.

3. Return/readmission under the normal procedure
This procedure is applicable where a person cannot be returned or readmitted under the simplified procedure. The readmission request should be made and the answer given in writing. The Parties could take as a basis the document annexed hereto. Answers should be compulsory and be given within a short time determined by the Parties. In accordance with the specimen draft bilateral agreement, the time in question must not exceed 15 days. However, it would be desirable for Member States to take as a basis agreements already signed in which this time is shorter.

II – Means of identifying persons to be readmitted

1. Effect of proof or a presumption
Proof produced of nationality and entry should have to be accepted by the Parties without further investigation. A presumption established of nationality and entry should be deemed accepted by the Parties unless the requested party proves otherwise.

2. Proof or a presumption of nationality or of entry via an external frontier
The protocol should clearly lay down the means of proving or establishing a presumption of nationality. Nationality may be proved by means of:
– nationality papers which can be definitely ascribed to a particular person,
– any type of passport (national, diplomatic or official duty passport or officially issued passport substitutes with a photograph) or any other travel document indicating nationality,
– consular registration cards,

– identity cards (even if provisional or temporary),
– a minor's travel document in lieu of passport,
– provisional identity papers,
– service record books and military passes.

A presumption of nationality may be established in particular by means of:
– specific information from the official authorities,
– an official service pass,
– a company pass,
– a driving license,
– an extract from register office records,
– a seaman's book,
– a bargeman's identity document,
– photocopies of any of the above documents,
– statements by witnesses,
– particulars supplied by the person concerned,
– the language of the person concerned.
The protocol should also clearly lay down the means of proving or establishing a presumption of entry via an external frontier, under Article 2 of the specimen readmission agreement.

Entry via an external frontier may be proved by means of:
– an entry stamp or equivalent entry in a travel document,
– an exit stamp of a State adjacent to a Member State, taking into account the travel route and the date of the frontier crossing,
– an entry stamp in a false or falsified passport,
– travel tickets which can formally establish entry across an external frontier,
– fingerprints taken by authorities at the time of crossing an external frontier.

A presumption of entry via an external frontier may be established in particular by means of:
– statements by the person to be transferred,
– statements by officials and other persons,
– fingerprints other than those taken by the authorities at the time of crossing an external frontier,
– travel tickets,
– hotel bills,
– cards for access to public or private amenities in the Member States,
– appointment cards for doctors, dentists etc.,
– data showing that the person to be transferred has used the services of a facilitator or travel agency.

III – Designation of the competent authorities
The protocol should stipulate that Ministers with responsibility for border controls are to designate the border posts which may be used for aliens' readmission and entry in transit and the central or local authorities competent to deal with readmission and transit requests. The choice should be geared to efficiency and speed.

IV – Conditions for transit of third-country nationals under escort
In their relations with third-country Contracting Parties, Member States could make provision for the use of a readmission/transit form for requests for transit under escort in accordance with Article 7 of the specimen readmission agreement. They could use the appropriate form annexed hereto as a basis. However, the parties could dispense with such formalities for the transit of a third-country national being repatriated by one of the Contracting Parties via an airport in the other Contracting Party. In that event, the competent authority of the requesting party would notify the competent authority of the other party in good time of the intended repatriation, informing it of the identity of the person concerned, the flight details and the particulars of any official escorts.

V. Data protection
An Article on data protection could be inserted; its content will largely depend on the legislation in force within Member States. It should in any event be stipulated that information must be supplied only for the purposes for which the agreement has been concluded.

VI – Conditions of applicability of the protocol
It should be stipulated that the protocol is to enter into force at the same time as the readmission agreement, that its application is to be suspended upon suspension of the agreement's application and that it will cease to be applicable once the agreement is no longer applicable.

3.6.10
Conséquences de l'entrée en vigueur du traité d'Amsterdam sur les clauses de réadmission dans les accords communautaires et dans les accords entre la Communauté européenne, ses Etats membres et des pays tiers (accords mixtes) – Adoption d'une décision du Conseil

1. A la fin de 1995, le Conseil a établi un lien entre le rapatriement de personnes qui se trouvent en séjour irrégulier sur le territoire d'un Etat membre et la conclusion d'accords européens d'association et de coopération, et il s'est mis d'accord sur des clauses de réadmission pour les accords communautaires et les accords mixtes (doc. 12509/95 RELEX 45 pour les accords communautaires et doc. 4272/96 ASIM 6 + COR 1 (gr, p, s) pour les accords mixtes).

2. Selon le traité d'Amsterdam, le rapatriement des personnes en séjour irrégulier dans un Etat membre est un des objectifs communautaires de la politique d'immigration (Article 63, point 3 du traité instituant la Communauté européenne). La Communauté européenne a ainsi le pouvoir de conclure des accords de réadmission avec des Etats tiers.

3. Il convient donc d'adapter les clauses types adoptées par le Conseil pour les directives de négociation d'accords mixtes.

4. Lors de sa réunion du 24 novembre 1999, le Comité des représentants permanents est parvenu à un accord sur le texte, qui figure en annexe, de la décision relative à l'insertion de clauses de réadmission types dans les accords de la Communauté et dans les accords entre la Communauté européenne, ses Etats membres et des pays tiers. Le Comité des représentants permanents est convenu de proposer au Conseil d'adopter la décision en question comme point «A» de l'ordre du jour d'une de ses prochaines sessions.

ANNEXE

Décision du Conseil relative à l'insertion de clauses de réadmission types dans les accords de la Communauté et dans les accords entre la Communauté européenne, ses Etats membres et des pays tiers.
Le Conseil de l'Union européenne a décidé que les clauses types définies ci-dessous devraient être insérées, à l'avenir, dans tous les accords de la Communauté et dans tous les accords entre la Communauté européenne, ses Etats membres et des pays tiers.

Article A
La Communauté européenne et l'Etat X décident de coopérer afin de prévenir et de contrôler l'immigration illégale. A cette fin
– l'Etat X accepte de réadmettre ses ressortissants présents illégalement sur le territoire d'un Etat membre de l'Union européenne, à la demande de ce dernier et sans autres formalités;
– et chaque Etat membre de l'Union européenne accepte de réadmettre ses ressortissants, définis comme tels aux fins poursuivies par la Communauté, présents illégalement sur le territoire de l'Etat X, à la demande de ce dernier et sans autres formalités.
Les Etats membres de l'Union européenne et l'Etat X fourniront également à leurs ressortissants les documents d'identité nécessaires à cette fin.

Article B
Les parties conviennent de conclure, à la demande de l'une d'entre elles, un accord entre l'Etat X et la Communauté européenne régissant les obligations spécifiques incombant à l'Etat X et aux Etats membres de la Communauté européenne en matière de réadmission, y compris une obligation de réadmission des ressortissants d'autres pays et des apatrides.

Article C
Sous réserve de la conclusion de l'accord avec la Communauté mentionné à l'Article B, l'Etat X accepte de conclure avec tel ou tel Etat membre de la Communauté européenne, à la demande d'un Etat membre, des accords bilatéraux régissant les obligations spécifiques incombant à l'Etat X et aux Etats membres de la Communauté européenne en matière de réadmission, y compris une obligation de réadmission des ressortissants d'autres pays et des apatrides.

Article D
Le Conseil de coopération examine les autres efforts conjoints susceptibles d'être déployés en vue de prévenir et de contrôler l'immigration illégale.

Training, Assistance and Cooperation   **3.7**

3.7.1

Commission Decision 88/384/EEC of 8 June 1988 Setting Up a Prior Communication and Consultation Procedure on Migration Policies in Relation to Non-Member Countries[40]

THE COMMISSION OF THE EUROPEAN COMMUNITIES

Having regard to the Treaty establishing the European Economic Community and in particular Article 118 thereof,

Whereas the foreign populations in the Community and the changes which have taken place in their composition are important demographic factors, more especially by virtue of the permanent nature of their presence, the reuniting of families and the fact of their high birth rate;

Whereas there are problems linked with their integration into the workforce and society and, more particularly, those encountered in the education, training and employment of the second generation;

Whereas it is important to ensure that the migration policies of Member States in relation to non-member countries take into account both common policies and the actions taken at Community level, particularly within the framework of Community labour market policy, in order not to jeopardize the results;

Whereas it is necessary to facilitate the exchange of information and views in these areas with a view to adopting common propositions, and it is therefore important to organize a consultation procedure ensuring the participation of all Member States;

Whereas, moreover, the Council in its resolution of 9 February 1976 concerning an action programme in favour of migrant workers and members of their families and in its resolution of 27 June 1980 concerning orientation towards a Community labour market policy, underlined the importance of undertaking appropriate consultation on migration policies in relation to non-member countries, and whereas integration of the Community labour market should be favoured in the framework of free movement of the labour force within the Community, in particular by appropriate consultation on these policies, in accordance with the conclusions which the Council adopted on 22 November 1979 on this subject;

Whereas its resolution of 16 July 1985 on guidelines for a Community policy on migration reaffirmed the need for such consultation;

Whereas, moreover, the final communiqué of the Conference of Heads of State or of Government of 9 and 10 December 1974 in Paris recommends, in point 10, the stage-by-stage harmonization of legislation concerning foreigners;

Whereas the European Council on 25 and 26 June 1984 adopted conclusions on social policy;

Whereas in a declaration annexed to the Final Act of the Single European Act, the Intergovernmental Conference expressed the will of the Member States to co-operate without

---

[40] OJ 1988 L183/35.

prejudice to the powers of the Community, in particular as regards the entry movement and residence of nationals of third countries;

Whereas in its resolution of 9 June 1983 concerning, inter alia, the passport union and the suppression of individual controls at Community frontiers, the European Parliament urged the Council and the Commission to make further proposals particularly with a view to harmonization of visa policies and legislation concerning foreigners;

Whereas the role of the Commission, in view of the powers conferred on it by the Treaty, is to promote cooperation between Member States in the field of social policy, in particular in the different areas mentioned above, and to organize appropriate consultations to this end;

Whereas, to this end, the Commission adopted Decision 85/381/EEC setting up a prior communication and consultation procedure on migration policies in relation to non-member countries;

Whereas in its judgement of 9 July 1987 handed down in joined cases 281, 283, 284, 285 and 287/85 (*Federal Republic of Germany, French Republic, Kingdom of the Netherlands, Kingdom of Denmark, United Kingdom* v *Commission*), the Court of Justice ruled that cooperation between Member States in the social field, provided for in the first paragraph of Article 118 of the Treaty, extends to migration policies in relation to non-member countries in that the power to arrange consultation granted to the Commission under the second paragraph of Article 118 authorizes it to adopt rules of a binding nature;

Whereas this Decision reproduces the content of Decision 85/381/EEC with the amendments dictated by the above-mentioned judgement of 9 July 1987,

HAS ADOPTED THIS DECISION:

Article 1

1. The Member States shall give the Commission and the other Member States in good time, and at the latest at the moment they are made public, advance information of:
- Draft measures which they intend to take with regard to third country workers and members of their families, in the areas of entry, residence and employment, including illegal entry, residence and employment, as well as the realization of equality of treatment in living and working conditions, wages and economic rights, the promotion of integration into the workforce and society, and the voluntary return of such persons to their countries of origin,
- Draft agreements relating to the abovementioned matters, as well as draft cooperation agreements which they intend to negotiate or renegotiate with third countries, when these agreements involve provisions relating to the abovementioned matters,
- Draft agreements relating to conditions of residence and employment of their nationals working in third countries and members of their families, which they intend to negotiate or renegotiate with those countries.

2. Member States shall communicate to the Commission and to the other Member States, in the areas mentioned in paragraph 1, the texts of provisions laid down by law, regulation or administrative action already in force, and also the texts of agreements made with third countries.

Article 2

1. If, within the space of two weeks from the date of receipt of the documents mentioned in Article 1, a Member State so requests, or if the Commission so decides on its own initiative,

the Commission shall proceed with the consultation with the Member States on those documents within six weeks of their receipt.

The Commission shall proceed with this consultation immediately, if a Member State requests it to do so as a matter of urgency.

2. The Commission may at any time, at the request of a Member State or on its own initiative, arrange a consultation on the draft provisions and agreements referred to in Article 1, except in the case of questions upon which consultation has already taken place and concerning which no new developments have arisen.

Article 3

The objectives of the consultation procedure provided for in Article 2(1) shall be, inter alia:

a) to facilitate the mutual exchange of information and the identification of problems of common interest and, in relation to those problems, to facilitate the adoption of a common policy by the Member. States particularly as regards international instruments relating to migration;

b) to examine the possibility of measures, which might be taken by the Community or Member States in the fields referred to in Article 1, aimed at achieving progress towards the harmonization of national legislation on foreigners, promoting the inclusion of a maximum of common provisions in bilateral agreements, and improving the protection of Community nationals working and living in third countries.

Article 4

1. Consultation shall be arranged by the Commission. Meetings shall be chaired by the Commission, which shall also provide the Secretariat.

2. The consultation procedure established by this Decision shall not affect the responsibilities of committees already in existence, in particular those of the Advisory and Technical Committee, as determined by Council Regulation (EEC) No. 1612/68.

3. Member States shall take all necessary steps to ensure the proper functioning of the consultation procedure, and in particular, where necessary, to safeguard the confidential nature of the information which will be made available to them in that connection.

Article 5

This Decision is addressed to the Member States.

Decision setting up a centre for information, discussion and exchange on the crossing of borders and immigration (CIREFI), London, 30 November 1992[41]

1. At their meeting in Lisbon on 11 and 12 July 1992, the Ministers with responsibility for immigration called upon the ad hoc Group on Immigration to submit a feasibility study for the establishment of a Centre for Information, Discussion and Exchange (Clearing House) for their meeting in December 1992. The ad hoc Group on Immigration hereby submits to Ministers its conclusions on this matter.

2. The ad hoc Group considers that the setting up of such a centre for information concerning the crossing of borders and immigration (CIREFI) would be beneficial.

Reasons for the establishment of CIREFI

3. The immigration work programme endorsed by Ministers of Maastricht in December 1991 (WGI 930) encompasses a wide range of topics – admission policies, common approaches to the problems of illegal immigration, analysis of the causes of immigration pressure – on which close and detailed cooperation between Member States is called for. Successful developments in these areas will require reliable data and information flows.

4. Information on a number of issues is already made available and exchanged between Member States on an ad hoc basis as required on any particular occasion. Experience has, however, shown that the exchange and collation of information have not always been particularly effective or rapid; questionnaires tend to be given low priority and need to be carefully drafted to elicit appropriate information. The ad hoc Group considers that there would be benefit in having a permanent mechanism for the regular exchange of information, supported, as the equivalent clearing house on asylum (CIREA) already is, by staff from the General Secretariat of the Council of the European Communities.

5. Unlike the current Sub-Groups, which under the arrangements contemplated for the implementation of the Maastricht Treaty are intended to be temporary and to be disbanded

---

[41] Ed.: Apart from CIREFI, other working groups and committees are also active and effective in the Brussels arena. Special mention should be made of the HLWG, the High Level Working Group, as it tries to combine cross-pillar views and activities. At its 1 December 2000 meeting, the Council took note of the information supplied by the Presidency regarding the report to the European Council by the High-level Working Group on Asylum and Migration to be submitted to the General Affairs Council on 4 December 2000 for adoption and forwarding to the Nice European Council. The report gives an evaluation of activities since 'Tampere' regarding asylum and migration issues and the prospects for future proceedings. In this context, the Group took stock of measures taken in the year 2000 to implement the Action Plans. The High-level Working Group on Asylum and Migration, set up by the General Affairs Council in December 1998, was given a brief to prepare cross-pillar Action Plans for the countries of origin and transit of asylum seekers and migrants. Five Action Plans, one each on Afghanistan and region, Iraq, Morocco, Somalia and Sri Lanka, were adopted by the Council in October 1999 and approved by the Tampere European Council. A sixth Action Plan, on Albania and region (mainly Kosovo), was adopted by the Council in June 2000, as the situation in Kosovo in 1999 had prevented the High-level Working Group from finalizing a definitive Action Plan in time for the Tampere European Council.

once they have fulfilled their mandate, such a body would provide a regular, permanent vehicle for the exchange of information, with a dedicated staff. Under the Maastricht Treaty arrangements this would be the primary institutional arrangement for exchange of information on an ongoing basis between Member States.

Recommendation
6. The ad hoc Working Group on Immigration accordingly invites Ministers responsible for immigration to endorse the establishment of such a Centre for Information, Discussion and Exchange on the crossing of Borders and Immigration (CIREFI), as a forum for exchanges of information and consultations, during the first half of 1993. Ministers are also invited to endorse the following broad tasks and operating methods for the Centre.

Functions
7. The function of the clearing house would be to gather, exchange and disseminate information and compile documentation on matters relating to immigration and the crossing of borders, with a view to the development of greater informal consultation, close cooperation and consultation of competent bodies and increased dissemination of information to Member States. It would aid the rapid exchange of practical information between officials, responsible for controls at the external borders for the purpose of combating illegal immigration. If agreed, the clearing house will, in due course, provide a focal point under the institutional arrangements established by the Maastricht Treaty for information on matters taken under consideration in the course of implementing the work programme adopted by Ministers. It will also serve as the mechanism for consultation and collaboration on practical matters between the relevant departments of the Member States.
8. The clearing house will not seek to duplicate or replace other arrangements which are already in place for cooperation between the Member States. In particular, it will not seek to assume the role or functions of the Rapid Consultation Centre, established following an informal Ministerial meeting held in March 1991, or to duplicate work undertaken by the Centre for Information, Discussion and Exchange on Asylum (CIREA). It may, however, work in conjunction with the Asylum Clearing House on matters which fall within the sphere of interest of both.

Gathering of Information
9. Information on the following matters would be exchanged within the clearing house:
– authorised immigration flows;
– unlawful immigration flows (country of origin, routes, means of transport);
– unlawful immigration methods (with a view to preventing and halting attempts at unlawful immigration);
– genuine, forged or falsified travel documents;
– control procedures;
– legislation bearing on immigration control procedures, and information on immigration policies generally;
– the question of rejected asylum applicants and illegal immigrants who abuse the asylum procedure, in conjunction with the clearing house on asylum (CIREA);
– information on the expulsion of illegally present third country nationals;
– information on carriers' liability legislation and practice, including data on inadmissible passenger arrivals and routings; and
– statistics.

10. The clearing house would also have, as one of its functions, practical cooperation by experts on operational matters, including in the field of forged documents, and would supersede the existing forged documents Sub-Group as the forum for such work. Such cooperation might include the organisation and oversight of relevant training seminars.

Access to Information

11. The clearing house would report to the ad hoc Working Group on Immigration and to its Sub-Groups (or to the successor bodies under the Union Treaty arrangements) on any matter on which its assistance was required or which it felt should be brought to notice.

12. Ministers, national authorities participating in the work of the clearing house, their officials (including officials responsible for border control) and the Commission would also have access to the information held by the clearing house.

Constitution

13. The clearing house would operate under the direction of the ad hoe Working Group on Immigration or its successor body. It would not itself have any decision-making powers, but could draw attention to specific problems and make proposals.

14. The Member States would designate to participate in the clearing house appropriate national experts, who might be officials responsible in the Member States for implementing laws and regulations on those matters set out above, together with other suitable individuals whose particular experience or expertise (e.g., statisticians) might be beneficial.

15. The clearing house would be supported by suitably qualified staff of the General Secretariat of the Council. In all probability, and in order to avoid unnecessary bureaucracy, such staff would be those also employed in connection with the clearing house dealing with asylum matters (CIREA).

The details of the organisation of CIREFI are to be discussed by the Sub-Group 'External Frontiers' on the basis of WGI 1240 and in the light of proposals submitted by the German delegation. Detailed proposals should be submitted to the ad hoe Group on Immigration as quickly as possible.

3.7.3

[T.27] Conclusions of 30 November 1994 on the organisation and development of the Centre for Information, Discussion and Exchange on the Crossing of Frontiers and Immigration (CIREFI)[42]

THE COUNCIL OF THE EUROPEAN UNION,

RECALLS the decision taken by the Ministers responsible for immigration on 30 November and 1 December 1992 to establish a Centre for information, discussion and exchange on the crossing of frontiers and immigration (Cirefi) and NOTES that in the 1994 priority work

---

[42] OJ C 274 of 19 September 1996, p. 50-51, (396Y0919(15)).

programme in the field of justice and home affairs which it adopted in November 1993, Cirefi was requested to continue its work;

EMPHASIZES the urgent problems arising from illegal immigration and unlawful residence by nationals of third countries in the Member States and considers that only concerted action by the Member States on a basis of solidarity can stem or reduce the flow of unauthorized immigration;

UNDERLINES the need for all Member States to combat criminal illegal immigration networks and make it impossible for them to arrange or assist large scale illegal immigration flows;

Given that further progress in cooperation between Member States requires improved exchanges of information and uniform situation assessments in order to improve coordination on a Union-wide basis in the areas of illegal immigration and expulsion,

CONSIDERS AND DECIDES that Cirefi should be, as a further step, progressively developed in the following way:

1.   Cirefi will assist the Member States in effectively studying legal immigration preventing illegal immigration and unlawful residence, in effectively combating immigration crime, in better detecting forged documents and in improving expulsion practice.

2.   Cirefi shall meet on a regular basis and shall consist of expert representatives of the Member States (Standing Conference) with logistical back-up from the General Secretariat of the Council.

3.   Without prejudice to the other tasks included in the Decision taken by the Ministers responsible for immigration on 30 November and 1 December 1992, the specific tasks of Cirefi shall be to:

3.1. collate, using standard forms, statistical information concerning:

(a) legal immigration;

(b) illegal immigration and unlawful residence;

(c) facilitating of illegal immigration;

(d) use of false or falsified travel documents;

(e) measures taken by competent authorities, and draw up regular and occasional situation reports on this basis commenting on trends, developments and changes;

3.2. analyse the information compiled, draw conclusions and, when appropriate, give advice;

3.3. conduct exchanges of information on expulsion matters, particularly in respect of countries of destination, airports of departure or arrival, carriers, flight routes, fares, reservation possibilities, conditions of carriage, escort requirements and charter possibilities as well as on problems in obtaining repatriation travel documents. Cirefi will submit an annual report on its activities, and any additional reports on request, to the Council (JHA).

Personal data may not be processed and, in particular, may not be communicated by or to Cirefi.

Cirefi will not be empowered to give instructions to Member States' authorities.

The activities of Cirefi will not affect closer cooperation between Member States.

4.   Cirefi, in the form of the Standing Conference as defined in paragraph 2, will meet regularly or as circumstances require; as a general rule this should be once a month.

Where possible, discussions adequately prepared in advance should be structured around a particular current item of common interest to permit an efficient exchange of information. The relevant bodies of the Council will determine priorities for Cirefi's ongoing work within the framework of the tasks assigned to it under paragraph 3.

The logistical back-up at the General Secretariat of the Council will provide Cirefi with the necessary administrative and organizational assistance and will contribute to prior and subsequent processing of agendas for Cirefi's meetings. The General Secretariat of the Council will, within its budgetary constraints, ensure provision of the staff and equipment required for Cirefi to perform its tasks.

5. The Council also notes that during the time between meetings of Cirefi as a Standing Conference as defined in paragraph 2, the national central units of the Member States concerned will exchange information directly at a multilateral or bilateral level in cases requiring immediate action. Information will be exchanged as far as possible using standard forms or as events dictate using an agreed layout.

Costs incurred by national central units, including the cost of communicating with other national central units, will be borne by the Member State concerned.

6. The Council considers that Cirefi may begin to carry out its work as defined in these conclusions from 1 January 1995.

3.7.4

[T.17] Joint Position of 25 October 1996 on pre-frontier assistance and training assignments[43]

THE COUNCIL OF THE EUROPEAN UNION,

Having regard to the Treaty on European Union, and in particular Article K.3(2)(a) thereof,

Whereas checks carried out on embarkation on to flights to Member States of the European Union are a useful contribution to the aim of combating unauthorized immigration by nationals of third countries, which, pursuant to Article K.1(3)(c) of the Treaty, is regarded as a matter of common interest;

Whereas the posting to airports of departure of Member States' officers who are specialized in such checks, to assist the officers who carry out checks on departure locally on behalf of the local authorities or on behalf of the airlines, is a means of helping to improve those checks, as is also the organizing of training assignments aimed at airline staff;

Whereas these matters could be dealt with more effectively by a joint position;

Whereas the terms of such a position should therefore be established,

---

[43] OJ L 281 of 31 October 1996, p. 1; (496X0622).

HAS DEFINED THIS JOINT POSITION:

Article 1 – Assistance assignments

1. The joint organization of assistance assignments at third-country airports shall be carried out within the Council with full use being made of the possibilities for cooperation offered.

2. Assistance assignments shall have as their objective the provision of assistance to officers locally responsible for checks either on behalf of the local authorities or on behalf of the airlines.

3. Assistance assignments shall be carried out in agreement with the competent authorities of the third country concerned.

4. Assistance assignments may be of varying duration. For this purpose, a list of airports at which joint assignments could be carried out on a temporary or permanent basis shall be drawn up.

Article 2 – Training assignments

1. The joint organization of training assignments for airline staff shall be carried out within the Council.

2. The purpose of joint training assignments shall be among other things to describe Member States' document and visa requirements and the methods by which the validity of documents and visas may be checked.

3. For this purpose, the following shall be drawn up:

– a list of airports at which joint training assignments could be carried out,

– a six-monthly programme of joint training assignments,

– a collection of information of use to airlines,

– a collection of travel documents and visas of use to airlines.

4. Assignments shall be carried out in agreement with the competent authorities and the airlines concerned.

Article 3 – Common provisions

1. Joint assistance or training assignments shall be carried out by specialist officers designated by the Member States and forming part of a joint assignment.

2. Member States shall inform each other if they wish to participate in an assignment covered by this joint action.

3. In so far as the costs incurred by the officers designated by a Member State are not borne by the third country and/or airline concerned, such costs shall be borne by the Member State concerned.

4. The embassies of the Member States present in the country in which the assignment is carried out shall be informed by the Presidency of the Council in time to enable them to lend any assistance.

5. The Member States shall inform each other within the Council of any assistance or training measures which they conduct outside the framework of this joint position.

6. Each year the General Secretariat of the Council shall draw up a report on the activities carried out under this joint position.

7. Subject to the necessary adjustments, the assignments provided for in this joint position may also be carried out at sea ports.

8. The Member States shall take all necessary steps to implement this joint position without prejudice to any cooperation organized bilaterally or in the framework of other organizations; in this context there shall be the widest possible coordination between the Member States.

Article 4
This joint position shall be published in the Official Journal.

Joint Action adopted by the Council on the basis of Article K 3 of the Treaty on European Union, introducing a programme of training, exchanges and cooperation in the field of asylum, immigration and crossing of external borders (Odysseus programme) 24 February 1998

THE COUNCIL OF THE EUROPEAN UNION,
Having regard to the Treaty on European Union, and in particular Articles K.3(2)(b) and K.8(2) thereof,
Having regard to the proposal from the Commission,
Whereas the Member States consider as matters of common interest:
– asylum policy;
– the rules governing the crossing by persons of external borders of the Member States and the exercise of controls thereon, including matters concerning the security of identity documents; and
– immigration policy and policy regarding nationals of third countries;
Whereas the establishment of a framework for training, information, study and exchange activities will serve to improve the effectiveness of cooperation between the administrations of the Member States in the above areas;
Whereas incorporating the Sherlock programme into the Odysseus programme will make it possible to coordinate cooperation in the areas concerned more closely and to achieve economies of scale in the running of the two programmes without impairing the Sherlock programme;
Whereas this programme contributes to a better understanding of the instruments of the European Union in the fields of asylum, immigration and the crossing of external borders on the part of the officials responsible for implementing the detailed rules in this connection;
Whereas extension of the cooperation between the Member States and the third States which are applying for accession as a measure to prepare for their accession will help the applicant countries to attain the Union's standards in the fields covered by the programme;
Whereas, thanks to the economies of scale and cumulative effects implicit in the intended measures, these objectives can be achieved more effectively at Union level than at the level of the individual Member States;
Whereas this Joint Action is without prejudice to the powers of the Community and will therefore not detract from the conduct of the PHARE programme nor from the Community measures taken in implementation of vocational training policy, in particular the Leonardo da Vinci programme;
Whereas action under this programme is to be complementary to and coordinated with the other training measures financed in accordance with Community law;

Whereas future developments in Community law may require this programme to be adapted; Whereas the Presidency has consulted the European Parliament in accordance with Article K.6 of the Treaty on European Union,

HAS ADOPTED THIS JOINT ACTION

CHAPTER I: GENERAL

Article 1 – Principle and objectives
1. A programme (the 'Odysseus programme') of training, exchanges and cooperation, within the meaning of the definitions in Article 3, which shall qualify for Community financial support, is hereby established for the period from 1998 to 2002. This programme shall concern the field of asylum, immigration and the crossing of external borders.
2. For the purposes of setting priorities in the annual programming of measures, account shall be taken of:
– Article K.3(1) of the Treaty;
– the existence of Community or Union legislation already in force;
– the existence of proposals for legislation already under discussion, to anticipate their entry into force by means of cooperation between administrations;
– priorities set by the Council for cooperation in the fields of justice and home affairs;
– any other cooperation required for the purposes of Article K.3(1) of the Treaty.
3. Without prejudice to the powers of the Community, the general objective of the Odysseus programme shall be to extend and strengthen existing cooperation in the matter of asylum, immigration, the crossing of external borders and the security of identity documents, and cooperation in these same areas with States applying for accession, by means of multiannual programming.

Article 2
The financial reference amount for the implementation of the programme for the period mentioned in Article 1(1) shall be ECU 12 million. The annual appropriations shall be authorized by the budget authority within the limits of the financial perspective.

Article 3 – Definitions
1. For the purposes of the Odysseus programme the following definitions shall apply to the measures referred to in Article 1(2):
– training measures: organization of practical training courses focusing on theoretical and practical knowledge;
– exchange measures: period spent by officials, magistrates or other servants empowered by the Member States in a Member State other than their own for the purpose of comparing their practice with that of their counterparts there, in compliance with the data-protection requirements laid down in that State;
– studies and research: work of an educational nature involving the design, development and dissemination of teaching materials, or other documents such as databases and directories.
2. For the purposes of the Odysseus programme, 'identity documents' shall be taken to mean the documents issued by the Member States and third countries, principally to enable the holders thereof to prove their identity and to cross an external border, if need be.

Article 4 – Training
In the field of training, the Odysseus programme shall focus on:
- training for instructors;
- specialist training, in particular advanced courses for decision-makers, officials responsible for preparing administrative decisions, judges and courses designed for those in charge of training;
- the exchange of information and expertise between national authorities.

Article 5 – Exchanges
Exchanges under the Odysseus programme shall take the form in particular of placements of limited duration within the national administrative departments responsible for the matters to which the programme relates.

Article 6 – Studies and research
1. The Odysseus programme shall comprise:
- the design, production and dissemination of teaching materials to enhance the effectiveness of training schemes;
- ways of improving the circulation of information in the areas to which the programme relates;
- analyses and reports on subject areas connected with this programme and compatible with its objectives.

CHAPTER II: STRUCTURE

Article 7 – Asylum
(...)

Article 8 – Immigration
Projects may be taken into consideration under the heading of measures in the field of immigration of nationals of third countries, if they are concerned with the following areas:
- admission of third country nationals, and in particular conditions for entry, conditions for travel within the Union, residence rules, family unification, access to employment and to activity as self-employed persons, whether or not salaried;
- combating illegal immigration, and in particular combating illegal entry, residence and employment, and the organization of the expulsion and repatriation of illegal immigrants, as well as combating trafficking in human beings and those responsible for organizing it.

Article 9 – Crossing of external borders
Projects may be taken into consideration under the heading of measures to monitor the crossing of external borders if they are concerned with organizing the practicalities of controls, including matters concerning the security of identity documents. Special attention will be paid to addressing problems on a thematic basis (in particular by type of border) or on a geographical basis.

Article 10 – Cooperation with applicant countries
Specific subprogrammes in the areas listed in Articles 7 to 9 shall be set up in each annual programme to prepare the applicant countries for accession in those areas. Special attention

shall be paid to transposal into national law and application by civil servants on the ground.

Within the framework of cooperation with the applicant States, measures shall be targeted on:
- improving knowledge of the Union acquis in order to help the applicant States to take the measures needed to enable their services to work in line with Union standards and rules,
- exchange information on the legal and administrative institutional systems of the Member States and the applicant States.

CHAPTER III: FINANCIAL PROVISIONS

Article 11 – Financing criteria
To qualify for Community finance, projects must be of demonstrable interest to the Union and involve at least two Member States. Projects may involve States applying for accession where the aim is to prepare for their accession and may involve other third countries where this would be useful for the purpose of the projects.

Article 12 – Financial control
The financing decisions and the contracts arising therefrom shall provide in particular for monitoring and financial control by the Commission and audits by the Court of Auditors, the results of which shall be forwarded to the budget authority.

Article 13 – Level of Community finance
1. All types of expenditure which are directly chargeable to the implementation of the measure and have been incurred over a specific, contractually defined period shall be eligible, up to the ceiling of appropriations authorized under the annual budgetary procedure.
2. The proportion of financial support from the Community budget shall be 60% of the total cost of the programme save in exceptional cases where, subject to the procedures laid down in Chapter IV, it shall not exceed 80%.
3. Translation and interpreting costs, computing costs and expenditure on durables or consumables shall not be considered unless they are essential for the realization of the project and shall be financed only up to a limit of 50% of the grant, or 80% in cases where the nature of the project makes them indispensable.
4. Expenditure relating to premises, collective facilities and the salaries of officials of the State and public bodies shall be eligible only if it corresponds to postings and tasks not connected with national use or function but specifically connected with the implementation of this Joint Action.

Article 14 – Rules of procedure
1. Measures incorporated in the programme and financed by the general budget of the European Communities shall be managed by the Commission in accordance with the Financial Regulation of 21 December 1977 applicable to the general budget of the European Communities.
2. When presenting financing proposals, the Commission shall take account of the principles of sound financial management and in particular of economy and cost-effectiveness as required by Article 2 of the Financial Regulation.

CHAPTER IV: MANAGEMENT AND MONITORING

Article 15 – Devising of the programme
1. The Commission shall be responsible for managing and monitoring the programme and shall take such measures as are necessary to that end.
2. The Commission shall draw up a draft annual programme comprising a breakdown of the appropriations available and based on thematic priorities corresponding to the structure, content and objectives of the programme. The annual programme shall cover the three areas referred to in Articles 7, 8 and 9, but may give preference to one of these if required to meet the needs of the national administrations.
To that end, the Commission shall scrutinize the projects submitted to it in the light of the criteria specified in Article 1(2), taking due account of the innovative character of the proposed measure and of the overall consistency of the programme.

Article 16 – Annual implementation of the programme
1. The Commission shall be assisted by a committee consisting of a representative of each Member State and chaired by a representative of the Commission.
2. The Commission shall submit to the Committee the draft annual programme, together with a plan for the allocation of the available appropriations to the various areas of the programme and proposals for implementing rules and evaluations. The Committee shall deliver its opinion unanimously within two months. This period may be reduced by the Chairman for reasons of urgency. The Chairman shall not vote.

If a favourable opinion is not given within the time limit, the Commission shall either withdraw its proposal or present a proposal to the Council, which shall decide unanimously within two months.
3. Once the programme has been agreed, it will be forwarded to the European Parliament; the Commission will keep the Committee informed of the views of the European Parliament.

Article 17 – Management of the programme
1. As from the second financial year, projects for which finance is requested shall be submitted to the Commission for scrutiny before 31 March of the budgetary year to which they are to be charged.
2. Where the financing requested is less than ECU 50 000, the Commission representative shall submit a draft to the Committee referred to in Article 16(1). The Committee, acting by the majority provided for in the second subparagraph of Article K.4(3) of the Treaty, shall deliver its opinion on this draft within a time limit which the Chairman may lay down according to the urgency of the matter. The Chairman shall not vote. The opinion shall be recorded in the Committee's minutes; each Member State shall have the right to ask that its position be recorded in the minutes. The Commission shall take full account of the opinion delivered by the Committee. It shall inform the Committee of how it has done so.
3. Where the financing requested exceeds ECU 50,000, the Commission shall submit to the Committee referred to in Article 16(1) a list of the projects submitted to it under the annual programme. The Commission shall indicate the projects it selects and shall give reasons for its selection. The Committee, acting by the majority provided for in the second subparagraph of Article K.4(3) of the Treaty, shall deliver its opinion on the various projects within

a period of two months. The Chairman shall not vote. If a favourable opinion is not delivered within the time limit, the Commission shall either withdraw the project(s) concerned or submit it (them), with any opinion from the Committee, to the Council which, acting by the majority provided for in the second subparagraph of Article K.4(3) of the Treaty, shall take a decision within two months.

4. Notwithstanding paragraphs 2 and 3, a Member State may, at any time before the Committee has given its opinion, request that, for important and stated reasons of national policy, a project concerning the crossing of external borders be submitted to the Council.

If such a request has been made, the Commission shall forthwith submit a proposal to the Council, which shall decide unanimously within two months.

Article 18 – Evaluation (...)

Article 19 (...)

Article 20
This Joint Action shall enter into force on the day of its adoption.

3.7.6

[T17/1/A] Joint Action of 3 December 1998 adopted by the Council on the basis of Article K.3 of the Treaty on European Union concerning the setting up of a European Image Archiving System (FADO)[44]

THE COUNCIL OF THE EUROPEAN UNION,
Having regard to the Treaty on European Union, and in particular Article K.3(2)(b) thereof,
Whereas Article K.1(3) of the Treaty provides that immigration policy and policy regarding nationals of third countries are matters of common interest;
Whereas the fight against false documents is an area covered by immigration policy and police cooperation;
Whereas the proliferation of genuine and false documents necessitates frequent updating;
Whereas the fact that the techniques used to produce genuine documents and their counterfeits are increasingly sophisticated also necessitates a high-quality medium;
Whereas the European Fraud Bulletin and the Handbook of Genuine Documents do not fully meet the requirements of speed and accuracy of reproduction, which is why the use of a computerised image archiving system, with proper training for the staff concerned, is a key element in any overall strategy designed to meet the needs of the Member States;
Whereas several Member States have computerised image archiving systems which they are in the process of putting into operation;

---

[44] (98/700/JHA), OJ L 333, 9 December 1998, p. 4-7 (498X0700).

Whereas, in order to ensure a high level of control by the Member States, it would be useful to introduce a computerised image archiving system providing access to document checkers in the Member States;

Whereas this system should enable users to have at their disposal information on any new forgery methods that are detected and on the new genuine documents that are in circulation;

Whereas, in order to ensure that the information in the system is compatible and uniform, it is necessary to draw up procedures for the preparation of Member States' contributions for inclusion in the system and procedures for controlling and verifying such contributions;

Whereas this Joint Action does not affect the competence of the Member States relating to the recognition of passports, travel documents, visas, or other identity documents,

HAS ADOPTED THIS JOINT ACTION:

Article 1

1. A European image archiving system shall be set up for the purpose of exchanging, by computerised means and within very short periods of time, information which the Member States possess concerning genuine and false documents that have been recorded in accordance with the procedures set out in the Annex to this Joint Action.

2. This system shall not replace or eliminate ordinary exchanges on paper until all the Member States are in a position to use the computerised system.

Article 2

The database of the system shall contain, among other things, the following information:
(a) images of false and forged documents;
(b) images of genuine documents;
(c) summary information on forgery techniques;
(d) summary information on security techniques.

Article 3

The setting up of the European system shall not prevent each Member State from developing and using its own national system corresponding to the requirements of the national border services and the internal services responsible for the verification of documents.

Article 4

The Council shall adopt without delay the technical specifications relating to compatibility with existing systems, to the entering of information in the system and to the procedures for controlling and verifying such information.

Article 5

This Joint Action shall be published in the Official Journal and enter into force on the day following that of its publication. Article 1 shall apply no later than 12 months after the measures referred to in Article 4 are adopted.

ANNEX
EUROPEAN IMAGE ARCHIVING SYSTEM

A computerised system shall be created within the General Secretariat of the Council, which shall contain genuine documents, together with false and forged documents.

The name of the European system is FADO (False and Authentic Documents).

1. Description of the system
- the system shall be read from one central service located in each Member State,
- the system shall be based on the Internet technology. The system shall ensure that the information can be transmitted quickly to the national central services. As soon as the information has been given to the General Secretariat of the Council, it shall be entered as quickly as possible into the FADO system. Each Member State shall be responsible for adding these data to its own national system or copy of the FADO system,
- the system shall be multilingual,
- the system shall be 'user-friendly',
- the system shall be based on a very strict codification. The security of the information contained in the computerised system shall be guaranteed,
- The system shall use special data lines between the General Secretariat of the Council and the central services located in the Member States,
- within each Member State, the system shall be read through a secure internet from a central service. The Member State may use the same system internally on its own territory (which means connecting different stations at its various border control posts or other competent authorities). There shall be no direct link between a workstation, other than a national central service, and the central point in the General Secretariat. A mechanism shall be created to duplicate and update the system located in the Member States from the FADO system (tape, removable discs, CD-ROM etc.),
- each Member State shall be free to develop its own national secure system for internal data transmission,
- the FADO system shall work through a network between the central point within the General Secretariat and the central services located in each Member State, which will allow for the rapid exchange of information, - as documents will be sent electronically to enable them to be entered in the existing national systems, the format used for the images shall be a standard one (JPEG, TIFF, BMP, etc.). The image quality shall be the best one possible, but there shall also be a proper balance between the image quality, the size and the compression,
- zoomed images shall, if necessary, be available for the important parts of the image,
- the system shall allow for a comparison on the screen between the original document and a false or forged document,
- the system shall provide explanations on different forgery techniques and on security techniques,
- cross-references shall be necessary in order to enable the users to find all the information about a document very quickly,
- first priority shall be given to the documents of the Member States, as well as to the documents of third countries from where there are regular immigration flows to the Member States. The information in the system shall be extended and updated to include all other documents, making it as complete as possible,
- the system shall introduce a 'flash' which would entail sending a warning to all Member States about a particular false document via e-mail, - the system shall have more than one level. The possibility of developing an additional level of query, in order to include more detailed information for experts, shall be borne in mind from the outset,
- the system shall contain a special zone for the inclusion of documents which are not recognised by one or more Member States.

2. Costs of the system

The costs relating to the setting up and running of the FADO system will consist of the acquisition of technical equipment and staffing costs. Since the FADO system is designed purely for the electronic archiving and transmission of documents, which is currently done in hard-copy form, such costs will constitute administrative expenditure for the Council, within the meaning of Article K.8(2), first sentence of the Treaty on European Union.

3.7.7
[T32/1/B] Joint Principles for the exchange of data in CIREFI[45]

INTRODUCTION

1. CIREFI exists as a co-ordinating body for the exchange between Member States of information on the crossing of frontiers and illegal immigration. One of CIREFI's key tools in meeting this objective should be the collection and analysis of statistics. CIREFI has identified the following areas of concern with which statistics may assist in providing insight:
a. the migration pressure on the EU as a whole and on individual Member States;
b. travel routes to the EU;
c. the nature and extent of traffic in illegal immigrants, with respect to both the immigrants and the smugglers;
d. the return of illegally present third country nationals to their countries of origin.

2. It has been recognised that the practical arrangements for the collection and processing of data have been capable of some improvement. It was agreed at the Justice and Home Affairs Council on 19 March 1998 that the Commission's statistical service, EUROSTAT should be invited to take responsibility for the gathering and processing of data on behalf of CIREFI. At the same time it was agreed that national experts from interested Member States, together with the Commission, should meet to examine within the Council the method of collecting data to improve its comparability as regards both content and frequency. This document reports the findings and recommendations of that experts meeting.

3. This document is to be regarded as a statement of CIREFI's working method in relation to statistics and its contents must necessarily be taken into account in the framing of subsequent proposals relating to the gathering, processing and any preliminary analysis of such data on behalf of CIREFI by EUROSTAT. At the same time this document provides guidelines for the future interpretation and analysis of such data by national experts in the context of CIREFI.

4. It is also clear that CIREFI's arrangements and methods in relation to statistics will inevitably need improvement or refinement in response to future priorities. The conclusions of this document must therefore be open to future review.

---

[45] Doc 8927 CIREFI 35.

A. Categories and definitions

5. The following section sets out the categories of statistical data which CIREFI has identified as relevant to its work, the definitions which CIREFI has agreed are to be employed and, in relation to each, further specifications as to the data to be supplied by Member States.

I. Category: Refused aliens;
Definition:
'Persons not covered by Community law who are refused entry at the border owing to:
– a lack of, or counterfeit/falsified, border documents
– an existing entry or residence prohibition
– other grounds for refusal'.

Specification
6. The purpose of this category is to record figures for third country nationals who are formally refused permission to enter the territory of a Member State. For most Member States such data will be generated only at the external border but where Member States do not, or are not able to make a distinction, data should relate to refusals of entry at any border post where such a control is exercised. Figures submitted for this category should, where national arrangements allow, relate to the actual number of decisions taken to refuse entry irrespective of whether those decisions necessarily resulted in removals. Furthermore, where Member States have administrative procedures which allow a decision whether to give formal permission to enter to be taken some time after the arrival of the third country national, such cases should be included in the figures for this category provided no more than three months has elapsed between arrival and the decision.

7. Member States should, where possible, provide a breakdown of data in this category by air, land and sea borders. With regard to figures for land borders it is also open to those Member States which are in a position to do so to provide data for the number of refusals of entry at specific external borders but this should be provided as a separate return and possibly on an annual, rather than quarterly basis.

II. Category: Illegal presence of aliens
Definition:
'Persons other than those entitled under Community law who are officially found to be on the territory of a Member State having either entered:
– without being in possession of the requisite border documents (passport, residence permit, visa); or
– despite the fact that they were refused entry at the border; or
– despite the fact that they are subject to an entry or residence prohibition;
    or, having been given permisson to enter, have become liable to expulsion on the grounds of their remaining illegally'.

Specification
8. This purpose of category is to provide for the recording of data in relation to third country nationals who are detected by Member States' authorities and have been determined to be illegally present. The category covers those who have been found to have entered illegally

(whether this be by avoiding immigration controls altogether, by employing some sort of deception, such as the use of a fraudulent document, in order to gain entry or by failing to comply with a decision to refuse or prohibit the subject's entry) and those who may have entered legitimately but have subsequently remained on an illegal basis (by, for example, overstaying their permission to remain or by taking unauthorised employment). It is a composite category in order to reflect the fact that not all Member States, for the purposes of collecting such data, distinguish illegal entry cases from other third country nationals found to be illegally present. Where Member States are able to do so they should, in a separate column, provide figures relating specifically to illegal entry.

9. Figures submitted for this category should not relate to persons who are detected as having overstayed when they leave the territory of a Member State. The data should relate only to detections which have occurred during the reporting period.

10. As with category I data should, where possible, be broken down to indicate whether the person found to be illegally present arrived via an air, land, or sea border. Again the provision of a separate return relating the data to specific external land borders is optional.

III. Category: Facilitators
Definition:
'Persons intercepted on the territory of the Member States who have intentionally assisted the unauthorised entry of persons other than those entitled under community law'.

Specification
11. Data submitted for this category, which may derive from intelligence records rather than statistics derived from formal decisions, should relate to those apprehended and/or charged with an offence of this nature rather than those convicted. While this may result in the recording of some cases that are not pursued or proved, such an approach has the merit of relating the incidence of cases directly to the period for which data is collected. As defined, data should relate only to the facilitation of illegal entry and not assistance with the illegal stay of a third country national. Data for this category will include, but not solely relate to, traffickers.

IV. Category: Facilitated aliens
Definition:
'Persons other than those entitled under Community law whose illegal entry and/or presence is found to have been assisted'.

Specification
12. The purpose of this category is to provide information as to both the numbers and nationalities of third country nationals who have been found to have received help to evade a Member State's immigration controls. Data for this category is likely to derive from intelligence sources rather than statistics arising from formal administrative decisions. Data recorded for this category will include, but not solely relate to, those who have been trafficked.

13. The definition, which is similar to that employed by the IGC, covers facilitation in relation both to entry and presence. It is desirable that Member States provide distinct figures

for each. The interpretation of the term 'assisted' will be in part determined by individual Member States' legislation and practice but the term should, at the minimum, relate to activity of a third party which has the specific purpose of helping a third country national to evade or fraudulently satisfy the requirements of a Member State's immigration controls. In the case of facilitated entry such cases would, for example, include those who are:
- provided with fraudulent documents;
- provided with a guide in order to evade border controls;
- provided with some means of concealment in order to evade border controls;
- transported to a Member State's borders with a deliberate lack of regard for carriers liability or visa regulations.

In the case of facilitated presence such cases might include those who are:
- provided with fraudulent documents;
- knowingly assisted in obtaining a residence or work permit under false pretences (for example, sham marriages);
- those employed illegally where there is systematic activity on the part of the employer (use of concealment, restrictions on freedom of movement, etc) to ensure that immigration controls are avoided.

14. Member States should as far as possible, in relation to facilitated entry figures, provide a breakdown as to whether the facilitated entry took place by air, sea or land.

V. Category: Removed aliens
Definition:
'Persons other than those entitled under Community law who, having entered the country illegally, having resided in the country illegally or for other reasons, are returned to a third country'.

Specification
15. The purpose of this category is to record figures for the number of third country nationals who are actually removed to a third country. Removals to another Member State (for example, Dublin Convention cases) are not to be included. Figures should relate to those who are expelled having been found to be liable for removal within the meaning of Category II. The definition does, however, include those removed 'for other reasons' in recognition that expulsion may take place for reasons (criminal activity, security reasons) not directly related to a person's immigration status. Figures for this category may include voluntary departure where such a departure takes place in order to comply with a formal order to leave. Statistics for removals may, where possible, be broken down according to whether removal took place by land, sea or air.

B. Interpretation of data

a. Possibilities
16. CIREFI statistics have not to date been subject to any rigorous processing or analysis and it is early to state what possibilities exist for the interpretation of data supplied by the 15 Member States. It is not possible for this document, in anticipation of the data to be yielded, to prescribe comprehensively the insights which that data will be expected to deliver. Nevertheless it should be possible for these statistics to provide information as to:

–   nationalities which present an immigration problem;
–   the extent to which such problems are increasing or decreasing;
–   the extent to which such problems are common to some or all Member States;
–   nationalities which are encountered as illegally present but prove difficult to remove;
–   nationalities which resort to facilitation.

b. Limitations

17. It is necessary to acknowledge that there are a number of obstacles to the proper interpretation of statistics yielded by these definitions. Above all it must be recalled that the 15. Member States have separate and distinct immigration regimes and that the statistics generated by the operation of these regimes are inevitably going to reflect how these controls work as much as they reflect the problems they are intended to observe. Insofar as CIREFI's statistics are generated by administrative actions and decisions they may in fact be influenced as much by the enforcement effort deployed by a Member State as they are by the real incidence of immigration problems (to the extent that a high figure may be both an indication of success in combatting illegal immigration as well as a cause for concern).

18. It will therefore be necessary, in preparing any analysis of this data, to be aware of the need to put the raw data in perspective. The following are merely examples:
–   figures for refused aliens do not take account of the total number of persons of that nationality arriving at the border nor do they indicate the extent to which pre-border control arrangements (visa regimes, carriers liability legislation) prevent nationals of countries of real migratory risk arriving;
–   those refused entry will not always be prospective migrants;
–   the classification of those illegally present and/or facilitated may be influenced by the accounts given by third country nationals themselves: these are not necessarily reliable;
–   those whose arrival is facilitated will not necessarily join the population of those illegally present (they may, for example, join the population of asylum seekers); figures for removed aliens are not set directly against a figure for persons liable for removal (although the relationship between Categories II and V may provide opportunities in this direction).

19. These points underline the importance of Member States providing information as to how their statistics are compiled and any additional information which serves to put their data in context. They also underline the importance of keeping CIREFI's methodology under continuous review.

c. Technical issues[46]

20. The sections above have set out CIREFI's views on the nature of the data to be collected and the parameters for the interpretation of that data. It is also, however, clear that existing practical arrangements for the submission, collation and circulation of data can be improved considerably. Present arrangements, which rely on the submission of data on diskette and the circulation of collated data by means of a bulky paper document are not ideal.

---

[46] EUROSTAT will propose solutions to the technical aspects of data transfer.

21. The following arrangements are to be regarded as a minimum requirement:

i. for each category data should be supplied by each Member State, [insofar as they are able to collect such data centrally] the format for tables should allow the submission of all the data identified in Section A above;

ii. for each category data should be submitted, by the most appropriate means of transmission, to the central unit[47] within two months of the end of the relevant reporting period;

iii. the central unit will, within three months of the end of the reporting period and by the most effective means of transmission, provide Member States with an updated copy of collated data for that reporting period.[48]

iv. in submitting the data referred to at (i) above Member States may consider that some explanation or commentary upon figures provided is necessary or would be helpful. The format for the submission of data should permit the inclusion of any commentary and the central unit should provide for the filing of such material in the database;

v. use should be made of a commonly agreed list of nationality codes.[49]

22. With regard to (ii) and (iii) above the current means of transmission is either by diskette or by paper. CIREFI's view is that the electronic, 'on-line' transmission of data both to and from the central unit would be more efficient in terms of speed, ensuring that data is received, and in terms of improving the accessibility and opportunities for use of the data by national units. Nevertheless, while considering that such arrangements should be the objective of any future development of the system, it is nevertheless noted that not all Member States are, in the short term, able to comply with such a requirement. It is also noted that any system for the electronic transmission of such data would need to be secure.

---

[47] At present the central unit is the Council Secretariat. It has been agreed that in due course EUROSTAT will assume this role

[48] National units may wish to maintain a complete local database of CIREFI statistics but the Central Unit will, in any event, provide summary tables and respond to data requests against the complete database when information or statistical data is required

[49] A list was annexed to this document and has – as per the annex – been compiled from the ISO code list (using both Alpha-2 and Alpha-3 Codes). It is not a prescriptive list and the intention behind is only to assist data providers in the Member States in completing the templates, in addition to helping the Commission to provide data which are as harmonised as possible. In the cases where citizenships which no longer exist in the ISO list, but which do exist in reality for those people who have passports or other documents, Member States are invited to use either: the full name of the citizenship for those from national states which no longer exist, or, the codes currently used by Eurostat for those citizenships. The proposal is to use this list only for the country of citizenship. The full ISO code list should be used for country of previous/next residence and country of birth information. [Full list not included]

3.7.8

Council Regulation (EC) concerning the establishment of 'Eurodac' for the comparison of the fingerprints of applicants for asylum and certain other aliens[50]

THE COUNCIL OF THE EUROPEAN UNION,

Having regard to the Treaty establishing the European Community, and in particular Article 63(1)(a) thereof,

Having regard to the proposal from the Commission (...)

Having regard to the opinion of the European Parliament (...),

Whereas:

(1) Member States have concluded the Dublin Convention determining the State responsible for examining applications for asylum lodged in one of the Member States of the European Communities, signed in Dublin on 15 June 1990 (hereinafter referred to as 'the Dublin Convention')(OJ C 254, 19.8.1997, p. 1).

(2) For the purposes of applying the Dublin Convention, it is necessary to establish the identity of applicants for asylum and of persons apprehended in connection with the unlawful crossing of the external borders of the Community. It is also desirable in order to effectively apply the Dublin Convention, and in particular points (c) and (e) of Article 10(1) thereof, to allow each Member State to check whether an alien found illegally present on its territory has applied for asylum in another Member State.

---

[50] 14 December 2000 OJ L 316, 15 December 2000 (12314/00, 12186/00) 'Adoption du règlement du Conseil concernant la création du système 'Eurodac' pour la comparaison des empreintes digitales aux fins de l'application efficace de la Convention de Dublin'. Ed.: This text is based on Document 599PC0260. Since the acts drawing up the draft Eurodac Convention and draft Eurodac Protocol [see for details: *The Asylum Acquis Handbook* (The Hague 2000) on pp. 310-343] were not formally adopted and the Convention and Protocol were not signed, their provisions are clearly not applicable. The Council (Justice and Home Affairs) decided at its meetings on 3-4 December 1998 and 12 March 1999 to 'freeze' the texts of the Convention and the Protocol, and invited the Commission to put forward a proposal for a Community legal instrument after the entry into force of the Treaty of Amsterdam. The purpose of the proposal was to assist in determining the Member State which is responsible pursuant to the Dublin Convention for examining an application for asylum lodged in a Member State and otherwise to facilitate the application of the Dublin Convention under the conditions set out in the proposal. The proposal had been made in order to facilitate the ongoing work of the institutions following the entry into force of the Treaty of Amsterdam. The subject matter should be viewed in the context of the broader work programme set out in new Title IV of the Treaty establishing the European Community, and in particular in Article 63 paragraphs (1) and (2). A full account of this work programme is contained in section B of the Commission Working Document 'Towards common standards on asylum procedures', Brussels, 3.3.1999, SEC(1999) 271 final.

The form chosen for the instrument – a Regulation – is warranted in view of the need to apply strictly defined and harmonised rules in relation to the storage, comparison and erasure of fingerprints, for otherwise the system would not work. These rules constitute a set of precise, unconditional provisions that are directly and uniformly applicable in a mandatory way and, by their very nature, require no action by the Member States to transpose them into national law.

(3) Fingerprints constitute an important element in establishing the exact identity of such persons;

Whereas it is necessary to set up a system for the comparison of their fingerprints.

(4) To this end, it is necessary to set up a system known as 'Eurodac', consisting of a Central Unit, to be established within the Commission and which will operate a computerized central database of fingerprints, as well as of the electronic means of transmission between the Member States and the central database.

(5) It is also necessary to require the Member States promptly to take fingerprints of every applicant for asylum and of every alien who is apprehended in connection with the irregular crossing of an external Community border, if they are at least 14 years of age.

(6) It is necessary to lay down precise rules on the transmission of such fingerprint data to the Central Unit, the recording of such fingerprint data and other relevant data in the central database, their storage, their comparison with other fingerprint data, the transmission of the results of such comparison and the blocking and erasure of the recorded data; such rules may be different for, and should be specifically adapted to, the situation of different categories of aliens.

(7) Aliens who have requested asylum in one Member State may have the option of requesting asylum in another Member State for many years to come;

Whereas, therefore, the maximum period during which fingerprint data should be kept by the Central Unit should be of considerable length;

Whereas, given that most aliens who have stayed in the Community for several years will have obtained a settled status or even citizenship of the Union after that period, a period of 10 years should be considered a reasonable period for the conservation of fingerprint data.

(8) The conservation period should be shorter in certain special situations where there is no need to keep fingerprint data for that length of time: fingerprint data should be erased immediately once aliens obtain Union citizenship.

(9) It is necessary to lay down clearly the respective responsibilities of the Commission, in respect of the Central Unit, and of the Member States, as regards data use, data security, access to and correction of recorded data.

(10) While the non-contractual liability of the Community in connection with the operation of the Eurodac system will be governed by the relevant provisions of the Treaty, it is necessary to lay down specific rules for the non-contractual liability of the Member States in connection with the operation of the system.

(11) Directive 95/46/EC of the European Parliament and of the Council of 24 October 1995 on the protection of individuals with regard to the processing of personal data and on the free movement of such data (OJ L 281, 23.11.1995, p. 31) applies to the processing of personal data by the Member States within the framework of the Eurodac system.

(12) In accordance with the principles of subsidiarity and proportionality as set out in Article 5 of the Treaty, the objective of the proposed measures, namely the creation within the Commission of a system for the comparison of fingerprints to assist the implementation of the Community's asylum policy, cannot, by its very nature, be sufficiently achieved by the Member States and can therefore be better achieved by the Community: this Regulation confines itself to the minimum required in order to achieve those objectives and does not go beyond what is necessary for that purpose.

(13) By virtue of Article 286 of the Treaty, Directive 95/46/EC also applies to the Community institutions and bodies;

Whereas, the Central Unit being established within the Commission, that Directive applies to the processing of personal data by that Unit.

(14) The principles set out in Directive 95/46/EC regarding the protection of the rights and freedoms of individuals, notably their right to privacy, with regard to the processing of personal data should be supplemented or clarified, in particular as far as certain sectors are concerned.

(15) It is appropriate to monitor and evaluate the performance of Eurodac.

(16) Member States should provide for a system of sanctions for infringements of this Regualtion.

(17) It is appropriate to restrict the territorial scope of this Regulation so as to align it on the territorial scope of the Dublin Convention.

(18) This Regulation should enter into force on the day of its publication in the Official Journal of the European Communities in order to serve as legal basis for the implementing rules which, with a view to its rapid application, are required for the establishment of the necessary technical arrangements by the Member States and the Commission; the Commission should therefore be charged with verifying that those conditions are fulfilled.

HAS ADOPTED THIS REGULATION:

Chapter I – General provisions

Article 1 – Purpose of 'Eurodac'[51]

1. A system known as 'Eurodac' is hereby established, the purpose of which shall be to assist in determining which Member State is to be responsible pursuant to the Dublin Convention for examining an application for asylum lodged in a Member State, and otherwise to facilitate the application of the Dublin Convention under the conditions set out in this Regulation.

2. Eurodac shall consist of:

(a) the Central Unit referred to in Article 3,

(b) a computerized central database in which the data referred to in Article 5(1), Article 8(2) and Article 11(2) are processed for the purpose of comparing the fingerprints of applicants for asylum and certain other aliens,

(c) means of data transmission between the Member States and the central database.

The rules governing Eurodac shall also apply to operations effected by the Member States as

---

[51] Ed.: This Article sets out the nature and purpose of the Eurodac system. Paragraph 1 establishes a direct and exclusive link with the Convention determining the State responsible for examining an application for asylum lodged in one of the Member States of the European Communities (the 'Dublin Convention').

Paragraph 2 provides that Eurodac consists of the Central Unit, a computerised central database for recording and storing fingerprints, and the means of transmission between the Member States and the central database. This paragraph also specifies that Eurodac's rules shall apply to operations carried out in the Member State from the point when data is transmitted to the Central Unit until the point where use is made of the results of the comparison.

Paragraph 3 provides that processing of fingerprints and other data in Eurodac may only be for the purposes set out in Article 15(1) of the Dublin Convention. These purposes are: determining the Member State which is responsible for examining the application for asylum; examining the application for asylum; and implementing any obligation arising under the Dublin Convention. Under paragraph 3, the fingerprints which a Member State takes and communicates to the Eurodac central unit may also be used in databases set up under that Member State's national law for another purpose.

from the transmission of data to the Central Unit until use is made of the results of the comparison.

3. Without prejudice to the use of data intended for Eurodac by the Member State of origin in databases set up under the latter's national law, fingerprints and other personal data may be processed in Eurodac only for the purposes set out in Article 15(1) of the Dublin Convention.

Article 2 – Definitions

1. For the purposes of this Regulation:

(a) 'The Dublin Convention' means the Convention determining the State responsible for examining applications for asylum lodged in one of the Member States of the European Communities, signed at Dublin on 15 June 1990.

(b) An 'applicant for asylum' means an alien who has made an application for asylum or on whose behalf such an application has been made.

(c) 'Personal data' means any information relating to an identified or identifiable natural person ('data subject'); an identifiable person is one who can be identified, directly or indirectly, in particular by reference to an identification number or to one or more factors specific to his physical, physiological, mental, economic, cultural or social identity.

(d) 'Processing of personal data' ('processing') means any operation or set of operations which is performed on personal data, whether or not by automatic means, such as collection, recording, organisation, storage, adaptation or alteration, retrieval, consultation, use, disclosure by transmission, dissemination or otherwise making available, alignment or combination, blocking, erasure or destruction.

(e) 'Transmission of data' means:

(i) communication of personal data from Member States to the Central Unit for recording in the central database and communication to Member States of the results of the comparison made by the Central Unit; and

(ii) recording of personal data directly by Member States in the central database and direct communication of the results of the comparison to such Member States.

(f) 'Member State of origin' means:

(i) in relation to an applicant for asylum or a person covered by Article 11, the Member State which transmits the personal data to the Central Unit and receives the results of the comparison;

(ii) in relation to a person covered by Article 8, the Member State which communicates such data to the Central Unit.

(g) 'Refugee' means a person who has been recognised as a refugee in accordance with the Geneva Convention on Refugees of 28 July 1951, as amended by the New York Protocol of 31 January 1967.

2. Unless stated otherwise, the terms defined in Article 1 of the Dublin Convention shall have the same meaning in this Regulation.

Article 3 – Central Unit

1. A Central Unit shall be established within the Commission which shall be responsible for operating the central database of fingerprints on behalf of the Member States. The Central Unit shall be equipped with a computerized fingerprint recognition system.

2. Data on applicants for asylum, persons covered by Article 8 and persons covered by Article 11 which are processed at the Central Unit shall be processed on behalf of the Member State of origin.

3. Pursuant to the procedure laid down in Article 22, the Central Unit may be charged with carrying out certain statistical tasks on the basis of the data processed at the Unit.

Chapter II – Applicants for asylum

Article 4 – Collection, transmission and comparison of fingerprints
1. Each Member State shall promptly take the fingerprints of every applicant for asylum of at least 14 years of age and shall promptly transmit the data referred to in points (a) to (f) of Article 5(1) to the Central Unit. The procedure for taking fingerprints shall be determined in accordance with the national practice of the Member State concerned.
2. The data referred to in Article 5(1) shall be immediately recorded in the central database by the Central Unit, or, provided that the technical conditions for such purposes are met, directly by the Member State of origin.
3. Fingerprint data within the meaning of point (b) of Article 5(1), transmitted by any Member State, shall be compared by the Central Unit with the fingerprint data transmitted by other Member States and already stored in the central database.
4. The Central Unit shall ensure, on the request of a Member State, that the comparison referred to in paragraph 3 covers the fingerprint data previously transmitted by that Member State, in addition to the data from other Member States.
5. The Central Unit shall forthwith communicate the results of the comparison to the Member State of origin, together with the data referred to in Article 5(1) relating to those fingerprints which, in the opinion of the Central Unit, are so similar as to be regarded as matching the fingerprints which were transmitted by that Member State.
Direct transmission to the Member State of origin of the results of the comparison shall be permissible where the technical conditions for such purpose are met.
6. The results of the comparison shall be immediately checked in the Member State of origin. Final identification shall be made by the Member State of origin in cooperation with the Member States concerned, pursuant to Article 15 of the Dublin Convention.
Information received from the Central Unit relating to any data mismatch or other data found to be unreliable shall be erased by the Member State of origin as soon as the mismatch or unreliability of the data is established.
7. The implementing rules setting out the procedures necessary for the application of paragraphs 1 to 6 shall be adopted in accordance with the procedure laid down in Article 22.

Article 5 – Recording of data
1. Only the following data shall be recorded in the central database:
(a) Member State of origin, place and date of the application for asylum;
(b) fingerprints;
(c) sex;
(d) reference number used by the Member State of origin;
(e) date on which the fingerprints were taken;
(f) date on which the data were transmitted to the Central Unit;
(g) date on which the data were entered in the central database;
(h) details in respect of the recipient(s) of the data transmitted and the date(s) of transmission(s).
2. After recording the data in the central database, the Central Unit shall destroy the media used for transmitting the data, unless the Member State of origin has requested their return.

Article 6 – Data storage
Each set of data, as referred to in Article 5(1), shall be stored in the central database for ten years from the date on which the fingerprints were taken.
Upon expiry of this period, the Central Unit shall automatically erase the data from the central database.

Article 7 – Advance data erasure
Data relating to a person who has acquired citizenship of the Union before expiry of the period referred to in Article 6 shall be erased from the central database, in accordance with Article 15(3) as soon as the Member State of origin becomes aware that the person has acquired citizenship of the Union.

Chapter III – Aliens apprehended in connection with the irregular crossing of an external border[52]

Article 8 – Collection and communication of fingerprint data
1. Each Member State shall promptly take the fingerprints of every alien of at least 14 years of age who is apprehended by the competent control authorities in connection with the irregular crossing by land, sea or air of the border of that Member State having come from a third country and who is not turned back
2. The Member State concerned shall promptly communicate to the Central Unit the following data in relation to any alien as referred to in paragraph 1:
(a) Member State of origin;
(b) fingerprints;
(c) sex;
(d) reference number used by the Member State of origin;
(e) date on which the fingerprints were taken;
(f) date on which the data were communicated to the Central Unit.

Article 9 – Recording of data
1. The data referred to in point (g) of Article 5(1) and in Article 8(2) shall be recorded in the central database.
Without prejudice to Article 3(3), data communicated to the Central Unit pursuant to Article 8(2) shall be recorded for the sole purpose of comparison with data on applicants for asylum transmitted subsequently to the Central Unit.

---

[52] Ed.: Persons apprehended in connection with the irregular crossing of an external border (Articles 8 – 10). The Regulation creates an obligation to take the fingerprints of persons apprehended in connection with the irregular crossing of the external border of the European Union and transmit them to the Central Unit. This data is stored in the Central Unit for a maximum of two years. Fingerprint data on asylum applicants which is subsequently transmitted to the Central Unit under paragraph (a) above is also compared against this data. The detection of a match, indicating that an asylum applicant had previously crossed the external border of the Union irregularly and entered a specified Member State, facilitates the application of Article 6 of the Dublin Convention. The data is erased before the expiry of the two year period if the person in question is granted a residence permit, leaves the territory of the Union, or becomes a citizen of the Union.

The Central Unit shall not compare data communicated to it pursuant to Article 8(2) with any data previously recorded in the central database, nor with data subsequently communicated to the Central Unit pursuant to Article 8(2).

2. The procedures provided for in Article 4(1) to (6) and Article 5(2) as well as the provisions laid down pursuant to Article 4(7) are applicable.

Article 10 – Storage of data

1. Each set of data relating to an alien as referred to in Article 8(1) shall be stored in the central database for two years from the date on which the fingerprints of the alien were taken. Upon expiry of this period, the Central Unit shall automatically erase the data from the central database.

2. The data relating to an alien as referred to in Article 8(1) shall be erased from the central database in accordance with Article 15(3) immediately, if the Member State of origin becomes aware of one of the following circumstances before the two-year period mentioned in paragraph 1 has expired:

(a) the alien has been issued with a residence permit;

(b) the alien has left the territory of the Member States;

(c) the alien has acquired citizenship of the Union.

Chapter IV – Aliens found illegally present in a Member State[53]

Article 11 – Comparison of fingerprints

1. With a view to checking whether an alien found illegally present within its territory has previously lodged an application for asylum in another Member State, each Member State may communicate to the Central Unit any fingerprints which it may have taken of any such alien of at least 14 years of age together with the reference number used by that Member State.

As a general rule there are grounds for checking whether the alien has previously lodged an application for asylum in another Member State where:

(a) the alien declares that he/she has lodged an application for asylum but without indicating the Member State in which he/she made the application;

(b) the alien does not request asylum but objects to being returned to his/her country of origin by claiming that he/she would be in danger, or

(c) the alien otherwise seeks to prevent his/her removal by refusing to cooperate in establishing his/her identity, in particular by showing no, or false, identity papers.

2. The fingerprints of an alien as referred to in paragraph 1 shall be communicated to the Central Unit solely for the purpose of comparison with the fingerprints of applicants for asylum transmitted by other Member States and already recorded in the central database.

---

[53] Ed.: Persons found illegally present within the territory of a Member State (Article 11). The Regulation allows a Member State, if it has fingerprinted a person found illegally present on its territory, to transmit this data to Eurodac in certain circumstances in order to check whether the person concerned has previously claimed asylum in another Member State. In the event that Eurodac identifies a match, the data is transmitted back to the Member State of origin for final checking. The existence of a match can facilitate the application of Articles 10(1)(c) and 10(1)(e) of the Dublin Convention. Data relating to persons found illegally present in a Member State is destroyed as soon as the comparison within Eurodac has been carried out.

The fingerprints of such an alien shall not be stored in the central database, nor shall they be compared with the data communicated to the Central Unit pursuant to Article 8(2).

3. The procedures provided for Article 4(1) to (6) as well as the provisions laid down pursuant to Article 4(7) are applicable.

4. The Central Unit shall destroy the fingerprints communicated to it under paragraph 1 forthwith, once the results of the comparison have been communicated to the Member State of origin.[54]

Chapter V – Recognised refugees

Article 12 – Blocking of data

1. Data relating to a person who has been recognised and admitted as a refugee in a Member State shall be blocked in the central database. Such blocking shall be carried out by the Central Unit on the instructions of the Member State of origin.

---

[54] Ed.: Article 11 is concerned with facilitating the implementation of Articles 10(1)(c) and 10(1)(e) of the Dublin Convention. Article 10(1)(c) provides that the Member State responsible for considering an asylum application under the criteria set out in the Dublin Convention shall be obliged to readmit or take back an applicant whose application is under examination and who is irregularly in another Member State. Article 10(1)(e) provides that the Member State responsible for considering an asylum application under the criteria set out in the Dublin Convention shall be obliged to take back a person whose application it had rejected and who is illegally in another Member State.

Article 11 does not create an obligation or a power in Community legislation for a Member State to fingerprint persons found illegally present within its territory. The Member State in question can only take the fingerprints of the person in question if it is permitted to do so under its national law. The provisions of Article 11 on persons found illegally present within the territory of a Member State differ in this important respect from the provisions of Article 4 on applicants for asylum and the provisions of Article 8 on persons apprehended in connection with the irregular crossing of the external border.

Article 11 creates a facility for Member States to use Eurodac if they wish to do so to check whether a person found illegally present on its territory has previously claimed asylum in another Member State. Paragraph 1 sets out the circumstances in which, as a general rule, there are grounds for carrying out such checks. Three sets of circumstances are specified.

Paragraph 2 sets out the rules for the communication and comparison of fingerprint data relating to persons found illegally present within the territory of a Member State. The data in question can only be compared against data on applicants for asylum which has previously been transmitted to the Central Unit by other Member States and recorded in the central database. The data may not be compared with data on persons apprehended in connection with the irregular crossing of the external border communicated to the Central Unit under Article 8. Nor may the data be stored in the central database. Paragraph 4 provides that the Central Unit must destroy the fingerprints communicated to it under this Article as soon as the results of the comparison have been communicated to the Member State of origin.

Article 11 corresponds to Article 7 of the frozen Protocol text. The use of permissive language in places in the frozen text is, in the Commission's view, unorthodox in relation to a Community Regulation. Adaptation of the text into language which is legally more appropriate language would, however, appear to be incompatible with the compromise found in the Council on this point.

2. Five years after Eurodac starts operations, and on the basis of reliable statistics compiled by the Central Unit on persons who have lodged an application for asylum in a Member State after having been recognised and admitted as refugees in another Member State, a decision shall be taken in accordance with the procedure referred to in Article 67 of the Treaty, as to whether the data relating to persons who have been recognised and admitted as refugees in a Member State should:

(a) be stored in accordance with Article 6 for the purpose of the comparison provided for in Article 4(3); or

(b) be erased in advance once a person has been recognised and admitted as a refugee.

In the case of point (a) of the first subparagraph, the data blocked pursuant to paragraph 1 shall be unblocked and the procedure referred to in that pargraph shall no longer apply.

In the case of point (b) of the first subparagraph:

(a) data which have been blocked in accordance with paragraph 1 shall be erased immediately by the Central Unit; and

(b) data relating to persons who are subsequently recognised and admitted as refugees shall be erased in accordance with Article 15(3), as soon as the Member State of origin becomes aware that the person has been recognised and admitted as a refugee in a Member State.

3. The implementing rules concerning the compilation of the statistics referred to in paragraph 2 shall be adopted in accordance with the procedure laid down in Article 22.

Chapter VI – Data use, data protection, security and liability

Article 13 – Responsibility for data use

1. The Member State of origin shall be responsible for ensuring that:

(a) fingerprints are taken lawfully;

(b) fingerprints and the other data referred to in Article 5(1), Article 8(2) and Article 11(2) are lawfully transmitted to the Central Unit;

(c) data are accurate and up-to-date when they are transmitted to the Central Unit;

(d) without prejudice to the responsibilities of the Commission, data in the central database are lawfully recorded, stored, corrected and erased;

(e) the results of fingerprint comparisons transmitted by the Central Unit are lawfully used.

2. In accordance with Article 14, the Member State of origin shall ensure the security of these data before and during transmission to the Central Unit as well as the security of the data it receives from the Central Unit.

3. The Member State of origin shall be responsible for the final identification of the data pursuant to Article 4(6).

4. The Commission shall ensure that the Central Unit is operated in accordance with the provisions of this Regulation and its implementing rules. In particular, the Commission shall:

(a) adopt measures ensuring that persons working in the Central Unit use the data recorded in the central database only in accordance with the purpose of Eurodac as laid down in Article 1(1);

(b) ensure that persons working in the Central Unit comply with all requests from Member States made pursuant to this Regulation in relation to recording, comparison, correction and erasure of data for which they are responsible;

(c) take the necessary measures to ensure the security of the Central Unit in accordance with Article 14;

(d) ensure that only persons authorised to work in the Central Unit shall have access to data recorded in the central database, without prejudice to Article 20 and the powers of the independent supervisory body which will be established under Article 286(2) of the Treaty. The Commission shall inform the European Parliament and the Council of the measures it takes pursuant to the firs subparagraph.

Article 14 – Security
1. The Member State of origin shall take the necessary measures to:
(a) prevent any unauthorized person from having access to national installations in which the Member State carries out operations in accordance with the aim of Eurodac;
(b) prevent data and data media in Eurodac from being read, copied, modified or erased by unauthorized persons;
(c) guarantee that it is possible to check and establish a posteriori what data have been recorded in Eurodac, when and by whom;
(d) prevent the unauthorized recording of data in Eurodac and any unauthorized modification or erasure of data recorded in Eurodac;
(e) guarantee that, in using Eurodac, authorized persons have access only to data which are within their competence;
(f) guarantee that it is possible to check and establish to which authorities data recorded in Eurodac may be transmitted by data transmission equipment;
(g) prevent the unauthorized reading, copying, modification or erasure of data during both the direct transmission of data to or from the central database and the transport of data media to or from the Central Unit.
2. As regards the operation of the Central Unit, the Commission shall be responsible for applying the measures mentioned under paragraph 1.

Article 15 – Access to and correction or erasure of data recorded in Eurodac
1. The Member State of origin shall have access to data which it has transmitted or communicated and which are recorded in the central database in accordance with the provisions of this Regulation. No Member State may conduct searches in the data transmitted by another Member State, nor may it receive such data apart from data resulting from the comparison referred to in Article 4(5).
2. The authorities of Member States which, pursuant to paragraph 1, have access to data recorded in the central database shall be those designated by each Member State. Each Member State shall communicate to the Commission a list of those authorities.
3. Only the Member State of origin shall have the right to amend the data which it has transmitted to the Central Unit by correcting or supplementing such data, or to erase them, without prejudice to erasure carried out in pursuance of Article 6, Article 10(1) or point (a) of the third subparagraph of Article 12(2)(b). Where the Member State of origin records data directly in the central database, it may amend or erase the data directly. Where the Member State of origin does not record data directly in the central database, the Central Unit shall alter or erase the data at the request of that Member State.
4. If a Member State or the Central Unit has evidence to suggest that data recorded in the central database are factually inaccurate, it shall advise the Member State of origin as soon as possible. If a Member State has evidence to suggest that data were recorded in the central database contrary to this Regulation, it shall similarly advise the Member State of origin as soon as possible. The latter shall check the data concerned and, if necessary, amend or erase them without delay.

Article 16 – Keeping of records by the Central Unit

1. The Central Unit shall keep records of all data processing operations within the Central Unit. These records shall show the purpose of access, the date and time, the data transmitted, the data used for interrogation and the name of both the unit putting in or retrieving the data and the persons responsible.

2. Such records may be used only for the data-protection monitoring of the admissibility of data processing as well as to ensure data security pursuant to Article 14. The records must be protected by appropriate measures against unauthorised access and erased after a period of one year, if they are not required for monitoring procedures which have already begun.

Article 17 – Liability

1. Any person who, or Member State which, has suffered damage, whether physical or moral, as a result of an unlawful processing operation or any act incompatible with the provisions laid down in this Regulation shall be entitled to receive compensation from the Member State responsible for the damage suffered. That State may be exempted from its liability, in whole or in part, if it proves that it is not responsible for the event giving rise to the damage.

2. If failure of a Member State to comply with its obligations under this Regulation causes damage to the central database, that Member State shall be held liable for such damage, unless and insofar as the Commission failed to take reasonable steps to prevent the damage from occurring or to minimise its impact.

3. Claims for compensation against a Member State for the damage referred to in paragraphs 1 and 2 shall be governed by the provisions of national law of the defendant Member State.

Article 18 – Rights of the data subject

1. A person covered by this Regulation shall be informed by the Member State of origin of the following when his/her fingerprints are taken:

(a) the purpose of taking his/her fingerprints;

(b) the transmission or communication to the Central Unit of data referred to in Article 5(1), Article 8(2) or Article 11(2);

(c) the obligation to have his/her fingerprints taken, where applicable;

(d) the existence of the right of access to data concerning him/her and the right to rectify such data.

2. In each Member State any data subject may, in accordance with the laws, regulations and procedures of that State, exercise the rights provided for in Article 12 of Directive 95/46/EC. Without prejudice to the obligation to provide other information in accordance with point (a) of Article 12 of Directive 95/46/EC, the person shall obtain communication of the data relating to him/her recorded in the central database and of the Member State which transmitted them to the Central Unit. Such access to data may be granted only by a Member State.

3. In each Member State, any person may request that data which are factually inaccurate be corrected or that data recorded unlawfully be erased. The correction and erasure shall be carried out by the Member State which transmitted the data, in accordance with its laws, regulations and procedures.

4. If the rights of correction and erasure are exercised in a Member State, or States, other than that, or those, which transmitted the data, the authorities of that Member State shall contact the authorities of the Member State, or States, in question so that the latter may check the accuracy of the data and the lawfulness of their transmission and recording in the central database.

5. If it emerges that data recorded in the central database are factually inaccurate or have been recorded unlawfully, the Member State which transmitted them shall correct or erase the data in accordance with Article 15(3). That Member State shall confirm in writing to the data subject without excessive delay that it has taken action to correct or erase data relating to him/her.

6. If the Member State which transmitted the data does not agree that data recorded in the central database are factually inaccurate or have been recorded unlawfully, it shall explain in writing to the data subject without excessive delay why it is not prepared to correct or erase the data. That Member State shall also provide the data subject with information explaining the steps which he/she can take if he/she does not accept the explanation provided. This shall include information about how to bring an action or, if appropriate, a complaint before the competent authorities or courts of that Member State and any financial or other assistance that is available in accordance with the laws, regulations and procedures of that Member State.

7. Any request under paragraphs 2 and 3 shall contain all the necessary particulars to identify the data subject, including fingerprints. Such data shall be used exclusively to permit the exercise of the rights referred to in paragraphs 2 and 3 and shall be destroyed immediately afterwards.

8. The competent authorities of the Member States shall cooperate actively to enforce promptly the rights laid down in paragraphs 3, 4 and 5.

9. In each Member State, the national supervisory authority shall assist the data subject in accordance with Article 28(4) of Directive 95/46/EC in exercising his/her rights.

10. The national supervisory authority of the Member State which transmitted the data and the national supervisory authority of the Member State in which the data subject is present shall assist and, where requested, advise him/her in exercising his/her right to correct or erase data. Both national supervisory authorities shall cooperate to this end. Requests for such assistance may be made to the national supervisory authority of the Member State in which the data subject is present, which shall transmit the requests to the authority of the Member State which transmitted the data. The data subject may also apply for assistance and advice to the joint supervisory authority set up in Article 20.

11. In each Member State any person may, in accordance with the laws, regulations and procedures of that State, bring an action or, if appropriate, a complaint before the competent authorities or courts of the State if he/she is refused the right of access provided for in paragraph 2.

12. Any person may, in accordance with the laws, regulations and procedures of the Member State which transmitted the data, bring an action or, if appropriate, a complaint before the competent authorities or courts of that State concerning the data relating to him/her recorded in the central database, in order to exercise his/her rights under paragraph 3. The obligation of the national supervisory authorities to assist and, where requested, advise the data subject, in accordance with paragraph 10, shall subsist throughout the proceedings.

Article 19 – National supervisory authority

1. Each Member State shall provide that the national supervisory authority or authorities designated pursuant to Article 28(1) of Directive 95/46/EC shall monitor independently, in accordance with its respective national law, the lawfulness of the processing, in accordance with the provisions of this regulation, of personal data by the Member State in question, including their transmission to the Central Unit.

2. Each Member State shall ensure that its national supervisory authority has access to advice from persons with sufficient knowledge of fingerprint data.

Article 20 – Joint supervisory authority
1. An independent joint supervisory authority shall be set up, consisting of a maximum of two representatives from the supervisory authorities of each Member State. Each delegation shall have one vote.
2. The joint supervisory authority shall have the task of monitoring the activities of the Central Unit to ensure that the rights of data subjects are not violated by the processing or use of the data held by the Central Unit. In addition, it shall monitor the lawfulness of the transmission of personal data to the Member States by the Central Unit.
3. The joint supervisory authority shall be responsible for the examination of implementation problems in connection with the operation of Eurodac, for the examination of possible difficulties during checks by the national supervisory authorities and for drawing up recommendations for common solutions to existing problems.
4. In the performance of its duties, the joint supervisory authority shall, if necessary, be actively supported by the national supervisory authorities.
5. The joint supervisory authority shall have access to advice from persons with sufficient knowledge of fingerprint data.
6. The Commission shall assist the joint supervisory authority in the performance of its tasks. In particular, it shall supply information requested by the joint supervisory body, give it access to all documents and paper files as well as access to the data stored in the system and allow it access to all its premises, at all times.
7. The joint supervisory authority shall unanimously adopt its rules of procedure.
8. Reports drawn up by the joint supervisory authority shall be made public and shall be forwarded to the bodies to which the national supervisory authorities submit their reports, as well as to the European Parliament, the Council and the Commission for information. In addition, the joint supervisory authority may submit comments or proposals for improvement regarding its remit to the European Parliament, the Council and the Commission at any time.
9.   In the performance of their duties, the members of the joint supervisory authority shall not receive instructions from any government or body.
10. The joint supervisory authority shall be consulted on that part of the draft operating budget of the Eurodac Central Unit which concerns it. Its opinion shall be annexed to the draft budget in question.
11. The joint supervisory authority shall be disbanded upon the establishment of the independent supervisory body referred to in Article 286(2) of the Treaty. The independent supervisory body shall replace the joint supervisory authority and shall exercise all the powers conferred on it by virtue of the act under which that body is established.

Chapter VII – Final provisions

Article 21 – Costs
1. The costs incurred by national units and the costs for their connection to the central database shall be borne by each Member State.
2. The costs of transmission or communication of data from the Member State of origin and of the findings of the comparison to that State shall be borne by the State in question.

Article 22 – Committee

The Commission shall be assisted by a committee composed of the representatives of the Member States and chaired by the representative of the Commission. The representative of the Commission shall submit to the committee a draft of the measures to be taken. The committee shall deliver its opinion on the draft within a time limit which the chairman may lay down according to the urgency of the matter. The opinion shall be delivered by the majority laid down in Article 205(2) of the Treaty in the case of decisions which the Council is required to adopt on a proposal from the Commission. The votes of the representatives of the Member States within the committee shall be weighted in the manner set out in that Article. The chairman shall not vote. The Commission shall adopt the measures envisaged if they are in accordance with the opinion of the committee. If the measures envisaged are not in accordance with the opinion of the committee, or if no opinion is delivered, the Commission shall, without delay, submit to the Council a proposal relating to the measures to be taken. The Council shall act by a qualified majority. If, on the expiry of a period of three months from the date of referral to the Council, the Council has not acted, the proposed measures shall be adopted by the Commission.

Article 23 – Annual Report: Monitoring and evaluation

1. The Commission shall submit to the European Parliament and the Council an annual report on the activities of the Central Unit. The annual report shall include information on the management and performance of the system against pre-defined quantitative indicators for the objectives referred to in paragraph 2.

2. The Commission shall ensure that systems are in place to monitor the functioning of the Central Unit against objectives, in terms of outputs, cost-effectiveness and quality of service.

3. The Commission shall regularly evaluate the operation of the Central Unit in order to establish whether its objectives have been attained cost-effectively and with a view to providing guidelines for improving the efficiency of future operations.

4. One year after Eurodac starts operations, the Commission shall produce an evaluation report on the Central Unit, focusing on the level of demand compared with expectation and on operational and management issues in the light of experience, with a view to identifying possible short-term improvements to operational practice.

5. Three years after Eurodac starts operations and every six years thereafter, the Commission shall produce an overall evaluation of Eurodac, examining results achieved against objectives and assessing the continuing validity of the underlying rationale and any implications for future operations.

Article 24 – Penalties

Member States shall lay down the rules on penalties applicable to infringements of the provisions of this Regulation and shall take all measures necessary to ensure that they are implemented. The penalties provided for must be effective, proportionate and dissuasive. Member States shall notify those provisions to the Commission by [...] at the latest and shall notify it without delay of any subsequent amendment affecting them.

Article 25 – Territorial scope

As regards the French Republic, the provisions of this Regulation shall apply only to the European territory of the French Republic.

Article 26 – Entry into force and applicability

1. This Regulation shall enter into force on the day of its publication in the Official Journal of the European Communities.

2. This Regulation shall apply, and Eurodac shall start operations, from the date which the Commission shall publish in the Official Journal of the European Communities, when the following conditions are met:

(a) each Member State has notified the Commission that it has made the necessary technical arrangements to transmit or communicate data to the Central Unit in accordance with the implementing measures adopted under Article 4(7); and

(b) the Commission has made the necessary technical arrangements for the Central Unit to begin operations in accordance with the implementing measures adopted under Article 4(7).

This Regulation shall be binding in its entirety and directly applicable in all Member States.[55]

---

[55] Ed.: See, however, the note under Chapter 4.1.1 on the position of the UK and Denmark.

List of Relevant Council Documents   3.8

Council Documents 1998-2001[56]

Document Information	Title	Date
14265/98	Strategy on migration and asylum policy	21-12-1998
14348/98	Assistance in cases of transit for the purposes of expulsion by air	21-12-1998
10338/1/98 REV 1	Draft Readmission Agreement between the EU Member States, of the one part, and third countries, of the other part	21-12-1998
10338/1/98 REV 1 COR 1	Draft Readmission Agreement between the EU Member States, of the one part, and third countries, of the other part	13-01-1999
11768/2/98 REV 2	Letter to third countries concerning the use of standard travel documents for the expulsion of third-country nationals	12-01-1999
5645/99	Temporary protection of displaced persons and solidarity in matters of admission and residence	29-01-1999
6097/99	Strategy on migration and asylum policy	17-02-1999
6580/99	Letter to third countries concerning the use of standard travel documents for the expulsion of third-country nationals	10-03-1999
6691/99	Strategy on migration and asylum policy	11-03-1999
7298/99	Letter to third countries concerning the use of standard travel documents for the expulsion of third-country nationals	13-04-1999
7665/99	Letter to third countries concerning the use of standard travel documents for the expulsion of third-country nationals	26-04-1999

[56] This list is neither authoritative, nor exhaustive.

<u>**7572/99**</u>	Effects of the entry into force of the Treaty of Amsterdam on future readmission agreements	21-04-1999
<u>**5001/3/99**</u> REV 3	Creation of an early warning system – Draft Resolution	30-03-1999
<u>**7668/99**</u>	Monitoring the implementation of instruments adopted by the Council concerning illegal immigration, re-admission, the unlawful employment of third-country nationals and cooperation in the implementation of expulsion orders – Summary report of the Member States' replies to the questionnaire launched in 1998	27-04-1999
<u>**7707/99**</u>	Analysis of the institute concerning readmission agreements	27-04-1999
<u>**7264/99**</u>	Assistance in cases of transit for the purposes of expulsion by air	12-04-1999
<u>**5001/3/99**</u> REV 3 COR 1	Creation of an early warning system – Draft Resolution	28-04-1999
<u>**6658/99**</u>	Standard Readmission Agreement between the Member States of the European Union, of the one part, and a third country, of the other part	10-03-1999
<u>**10338/2/98**</u> REV 2 COR 1	Draft Readmission Agreement between the EU Member States, of the one part, and third countries, of the other part	30-04-1999
<u>**7609/1/99**</u> REV 1	Summary report of Member States' contributions on readmission questions (see 6933/99 MIGR 15 + ADD 1 and ADD 2)	03-05-1999
<u>**7157/99**</u>	Practical application of the principle of solidarity in burden-sharing with regard to the admission and residence of displaced persons	31-03-1999
<u>**7669/99**</u>	Readmission Agreements concerning third-country nationals	26-04-1999
<u>**7847/99**</u>	UN Convention against transnational organized crime	10-05-1999
<u>**8204/99**</u>	Adoption, in the official languages of the Community, of a Council Resolution on the creation of an early warning system for the transmission of information on illegal immigration and facilitator networks	11-05-1999

7965/99	COUNCIL RESOLUTION of on the creation of an early warning system for the transmission of information on illegal immigration and facilitator networks	11-05-1999
8150/99	Effects of the entry into force of the Treaty of Amsterdam on future re-admission agreements	10-05-1999
8265/99	Effects of the entry into force of the Treaty of Amsterdam on future readmission agreements	18-05-1999
8710/99	Council of Europe European Committee on Migration (CDMG), Strasbourg, 26-28 May 1999	28-05-1999
8131/99	Information campaigns in countries of origin and transit	18-05-1999
9009/99	Comments on migration-related aspects of the draft protocol against the smuggling of migrants by land, air and sea, and the draft protocol against trafficking in women and children, supplementing the United Nations convention against organised crime	07-06-1999
7462/1/99 REV 1	Monitoring the implementation of instruments already adopted concerning admission of third-country nationals – Summary report of the Member States' replies to the questionnaire launched in 1998	11-06-1999
8204/99 ADD 1	Adoption, in the official languages of the Community, of a Council Resolution on the creation of an early warning system for the transmission of information on illegal immigration and facilitator networks	27-05-1999
9009/99 ADD 1	Comments on migration-related aspects of the draft protocol against the smuggling of migrants by land, air and sea, and the draft protocol against trafficking in women and children, supplementing the United Nations convention against organised crime	17-06-1999
7668/1/99 REV 1	Monitoring the implementation of instruments adopted by the Council concerning illegal immigration, re-admission, the unlawful employment of third-country nationals and cooperation in the implementation of expulsion orders – Summary report of the Member States' replies to the questionnaire launched in 1998	14-06-1999
7292/99	Consequences of the Treaty of Amsterdam on readmission clauses in Community agreements and in agreements between the European Community, its Member States and third countries (mixed agreements)	11-05-1999
9781/99	Discussion Paper on Temporary Protection and Solidarity	07-07-1999

9874/99	Updated information on Council decision of 16 December 1996 on monitoring the implementation of instruments adopted by the Council concerning illegal immigration, readmission, the unlawful employment of third-country nationals and cooperation in the implementation of expulsion orders (OJ L 342 of 31.12.96, p. 5)(see Telex No 2371 of 21.5.99)	09-07-1999
7456/99 ADD 1	Compilation of replies to the request from the Greek delegation on legalization of illegal immigrants (see Telex No 93 dated 8.1.99)	12-07-1999
10338/3/98 REV 3	Draft standard readmission agreement between the European Community and a third country	09-07-1999
10338/3/98 REV 3 COR 1	Draft standard readmission agreement between the European Community and a third country	13-07-1999
10176/99	'Schengen Relevancy' in the context of issues to be handled by the Expulsion Working Party	15-07-1999
10208/99	Assistance for Turkey in detecting false or falsified travel documents	26-07-1999
10504/99	Discussion Paper on guidelines concerning readmission between Member States of the European Community	29-07-1999
10795/99	The mandate concerning readmission agreements between the European Community and a third country	09-09-1999
10798/99	EU-Russia Seminar on Migration in Lappeenranta (4-6.7.1999)	09-09-1999
9821/99 ADD 1	Updated information on assistance for the voluntary repatriation of third-country nationals (see Telex No 1859 dated 27.4.99)	14-09-1999
9874/99 ADD 1	Updated information on Council decision of 16 December 1996 on monitoring the implementation of instruments adopted by the Council concerning illegal immigration, readmission, the unlawful employment of third-country nationals and cooperation in the implementation of expulsion orders (OJ L 342 of 31.12.96, p. 5)(see Telex No 2371 of 21.5.99)	14-09-1999
8734/99 ADD 1	Compilation of replies to an earlier survey by the German delegation on immigration rules in other Member States (see SN 1506/99)	14-09-1999

7462/1/99 REV 1 COR 1	Monitoring the implementation of instruments already adopted concerning admission of third-country nationals – Summary report of the Member States' replies to the questionnaire launched in 1998	14-09-1999
11672/99	Discussion paper on a draft Council Directive concerning readmission between Member States of the European Community	11-10-1999
11486/99	Inventory of readmission agreements	18-10-1999
12134/99	Consequences of the Treaty of Amsterdam on readmission clauses in Community agreements and in agreements between the European Community, its Member States and third countries (mixed agreements)	21-10-1999
11486/1/99 REV 1	Inventory of readmission agreements	11-11-1999
13035/99	Initiative of the Republic of Finland with a view to the adoption of a Council Regulation determining obligations as between the Member States for the readmission of third-country nationals	19-11-1999
12488/99	Initiative of the Republic of Finland with a view to the adoption of a Council Regulation determining obligations as between the Member States for the readmission of third-country nationals	22-11-1999
11486/2/99 REV 2	Inventory of readmission agreements	24-11-1999
13409/99	Consequences of the Treaty of Amsterdam on readmission clauses in Community agreements and in agreements between the European Community, its Member States and third countries – Adoption of a Council decision	25-11-1999
12488/99 COR 1	Initiative of the Republic of Finland with a view to the adoption of a Council Regulation determining obligations as between the Member States for the readmission of third-country nationals	26-11-1999
13488/99	Review of the implementation of the Council Resolution of 4 December 1997 on measures to be adopted on the combating of marriages of convenience (OJ C 382 of 16.12.1997, p. 1) – Summary report of the Member States' replies to the 1999 questionnaire (see Telex No 1858 of 22.4.99)	30-11-1999

13757/99	Effects of the entry into force of the Treaty of Amsterdam on the incorporation of readmission clauses in Member States' bilateral agreements	07-12-1999
13758/99	Agreements of 11 October 1999 between the Government of the Federal Republic of Germany and the Macedonian Government on authorising the transit and transit transportation of Yugoslavian nationals to Kosovo in the Federal Republic of Yugoslavia	07-12-1999
5318/00	Draft report on assistance for the voluntary repatriation of third-country nationals (see Telex No 1859 dated 27.4.99)	17-01-2000
5350/00	Assistance for the voluntary return of third-country nationals	17-01-2000
5351/00	Questionnaire on the practices of the Member States of the European Union with regard to transit for the purposes of expulsion by air	17-01-2000
5350/00 COR 1	Assistance for the voluntary return of third-country nationals	19-01-2000
9821/99 ADD 2	Updated information on assistance for the voluntary repatriation of third-country nationals (see Telex No 1859 dated 27.4.99)	21-01-2000
5555/00	Compilation of replies to questionnaire on 'Embassy reporting of migration issues from countries of origin (see Telex No 3556 of 29.7.99)	24-01-2000
5599/00	Initiative of the Republic of Finland with a view to the adoption of a Council Regulation determining the obligations as between Member States for the readmission of third-country nationals	24-01-2000
5396/00	Proposal for a Council Directive on the right to family reunification	24-01-2000
5407/00	Summary report of the Member States' replies to the questionnaire on 'Embassy reporting of migration issues from countries of origin' (see Telex No 3556 of 29.7.99)	25-01-2000
5599/00 COR 1	Initiative of the Republic of Finland with a view to the adoption of a Council Regulation determining the obligations as between Member States for the readmission of third-country nationals	31-01-2000

5774/00	Initiative of the Republic of Finland with a view to the adoption of a Council Regulation determining the obligations as between Member States for the readmission of third-country nationals	31-01-2000
10998/99 COR 1	Compilation of replies to questionnaire concerning Council Resolution of 4 December 1997 on measures to be adopted on the combating of marriages of convenience (OJ C 382 of 16.12.1997, p. 1)(see Telex No 1858 dated 22.4.99)	31-01-2000
13488/99 COR 1	Review of the implementation of the Council Resolution of 4 December 1997 on measures to be adopted on the combating of marriages of convenience (OJ C 382 of 16.12.1997, p. 1) – Summary report of the Member States' replies to the 1999 questionnaire (see Telex No 1858 of 22.4.99)	31-01-2000
10998/99 ADD 1	Compilation of replies to questionnaire concerning Council Resolution of 4 December 1997 on measures to be adopted on the combating of marriages of convenience (OJ C 382 of 16.12.1997, p. 1)(see Telex No 1858 dated 22.4.99)	03-02-2000
9821/99 ADD 3	Updated information on assistance for the voluntary repatriation of third-country nationals (see Telex No 1859 dated 27.4.99)	07-02-2000
10998/99 ADD 2	Compilation of replies to questionnaire concerning Council Resolution of 4 December 1997 on measures to be adopted on the combating of marriages of convenience (OJ C 382 of 16.12.1997, p. 1)(see Telex No 1858 dated 22.4.99)	10-02-2000
5772/00	Proposal for a Council Directive on the right to family reunification	10-02-2000
6030/00	The regularisation operation and the associated temporary reintroduction of border checks pursuant to Article 2 (2) of the Schengen Convention	08-02-2000
6283/00	Draft Council Recommendation on voluntary return	18-02-2000
6720/00	Recommendations for Council Decisions authorising the Commission to negotiate readmission agreements between the European Community and Sri Lanka Morocco Pakistan Russia = 'Schengen Relevancy'	06-03-2000
6504/00	Proposal for a Council Directive on the right to family reunification	16-03-2000

7160/00	Council of Europe – Group of experts on security of residence of long-term immigrants, Strasbourg, 23-24 March 2000	21-03-2000
6283/1/00 REV 1	Draft Council Recommendation on voluntary return	22-03-2000
7131/00	Agreements of 27 January 2000 between the Government of the Federal Republic of Germany and the Government of the Republic of Albania authorising voluntary transit and transit transportation of Yugoslav nationals (Kosovar Albanians) to Kosovo	24-03-2000
7200/00	Compilation of replies to questionnaire concerning the practice of Member States with regard to transit for the purposes of expulsion by air (5351/00 MIGR 4)(see Telex No 0565 of 9-2-2000)	29-03-2000
6465/00	Council of Europe – Group of experts on security of residence of long-term immigrants, Strasbourg, 23-24 March 2000	28-03-2000
10998/99 ADD 3	Compilation of replies to questionnaire concerning Council Resolution of 4 December 1997 on measures to be adopted on the combating of marriages of convenience (OJ C 382 of 16.12.1997, p. 1)(see Telex No 1858 dated 22.4.99)	04-04-2000
13488/1/99 REV 1	Review of the implementation of the Council Resolution of 4 December 1997 on measures to be adopted on the combating of marriages of convenience (OJ C 382 of 16.12.1997, p. 1) – Summary report of the Member States' replies to the 1999 questionnaire (see Telex No 1858 of 22.4.99)	04-04-2000
7675/00	Proposal for a Council Directive on the right to family reunification	07-04-2000
6283/2/00 REV 2	Draft Council Recommendation on voluntary return	10-04-2000
7796/00	Questionnaire on combating crime in connection with illegal immigration networks	13-04-2000
7675/1/00 REV 1	Proposal for a Council Directive on the right to family reunification	10-04-2000
7984/00	European Commission proposal for a Council Directive on the Right to Family Reunification	20-04-2000

7941/00	Analysis of replies to the questionnaire concerning the practice of Member States, including Iceland and Norway, with regard to transit for the purpose of expulsion by air.	04-05-2000
8613/00	Agreement of 21 March 2000 between the Governments of the Republic of Albania, the Federal Republic of Germany, the Italian Republic, the Republic of Croatia, the Republic of Slovenia and the Republic of Hungary, the Council of Ministers of Bosnia and Herzegovina, the Austrian Federal Government and the Swiss Federal Council on authorisation for the transit of Yugoslav nationals for the purpose of return to their country of origin	18-05-2000
9739/00	Proposal for a Council Directive on the right to family reunification	28-06-2000
9738/00	Proposal for a Council Directive on Family Reunification	28-06-2000
10017/00	Action plan to improve the control of immigration	04-07-2000
9896/00	Draft initiative by the French Republic for the adoption of a Council Directive on mutual recognition of decisions concerning expulsion of third-country nationals	30-06-2000
9892/00	Communication from the French Republic – Initiative of the French Republic with a view to the adoption of a framework Decision on strengthening the penal framework for preventing the facilitation of unauthorised entry and residence	30-06-2000
10373/00	Initiative of the French Republic with a view to the adoption of a Council Framework Decision on strengthening the penal framework for preventing the facilitation of unauthorised entry and residence	20-07-2000
10460/00	French Republic's initiative for the adoption of a framework Decision on preventing the facilitation of unauthorised entry and residence	17-07-2000
9892/00 ADD 1	Communication from the French Republic – Initiative of the French Republic with a view to the adoption of a framework Decision on strengthening the penal framework for preventing the facilitation of unauthorised entry and residence	05-07-2000

10130/00	Initiative of the French Republic with a view to the adoption of a Council Directive on mutual recognition of decisions on the expulsion of third country nationals	20-07-2000
10545/00	Initiative of the French Republic with a view to the adoption of a Council Directive on mutual recognition of decisions concerning expulsion of third-country nationals – publication in the Official Journal – consultation of the European Parliament	18-07-2000
10374/00	Initiative of the French Republic with a view to the adoption of a Council Framework Decision on strengthening the penal framework for preventing the facilitation of unauthorised entry and residence – publication in the Official Journal – consultation of the European Parliament	19-07-2000
10130/00 ADD 1	Initiative of the French Republic with a view to the adoption of a Council Directive on mutual recognition of decisions on the expulsion of third-country nationals – Explanatory memorandum	19-07-2000
7507/00	Proposal for a Council Directive on the right to family reunification	28-07-2000
10712/00	Initiative on the part of the French Republic with a view to the adoption of a Framework Decision on the strengthening of the penal framework to prevent the facilitation of unauthorised entry and residence	28-07-2000
10711/00	Initiative on the part of the French Republic with a view to the adoption of a Directive defining the facilitation of unauthorised entry, movement and residence	28-07-2000
10676/00	Initiative of the French Republic with a view to the adoption of a Council Framework Decision on the strengthening of the penal framework to prevent the facilitation of authorised entry and residence	03-08-2000
10675/00	Initiative of the French Republic with a view to the adoption of a Council Directive defining the facilitation of unauthorised entry, movement and residence	03-08-2000
10859/00	Draft Framework Decision on the strengthening of the penal framework to prevent the facilitation of unauthorised entry and residence	08-09-2000
7796/1/00 REV 1	Questionnaire on combating crime in connection with illegal immigration networks	20-09-2000

11122/00	Proposal for a Council Directive on the right to family reunification	20-09-2000
11119/00	Questionnaire on the initiative of the French Republic with a view to the adoption of a Council Directive on mutual recognition of decisions on the expulsion of third country nationals	15-09-2000
11120/00	Initiative of the French Republic with a view to the adoption of a Council Directive on mutual recognition of decisions on the expulsion of third country nationals	15-09-2000
12082/00	Action plan to improve the control of immigration	06-10-2000
12067/00	Barcelona Process: preparation of the meeting at ministerial level	06-10-2000
12323/00	Initiative of the French Republic with a view to the adoption of a Council Directive on mutual recognition of decisions on the expulsion of third country nationals	13-10-2000
7941/00 COR 1	Analysis of replies to the questionnaire concerning the practice of Member States, including Iceland and Norway, with regard to transit for the purpose of expulsion by air.	04-05-2000
12026/00	Draft Council Directive defining the facilitation of unauthorised entry, movement and residence	06-10-2000
11123/00	Amended proposal for a Council Directive on the right to family reunification	16-10-2000
12025/00	Draft Council Framework Decision on the strengthening of the penal framework to prevent the facilitation of unauthorised entry and residence	06-10-2000
12534/00	Proposal for a Council Directive on Mutual Recognition of Decisions on the expulsion of Third Country Nationals	19-10-2000
12351/00	Comments on the French Presidency proposals for a Council Directive and Council Framework Decision on preventing the facilitation of unauthorised entry and residence	16-10-2000
11384/00	Initiative of the French Republic with a view to the adoption of a Council Directive on mutual recognition of decisions on the expulsion of third country nationals	18-10-2000

11384/00 ADD 1	Initiative of the French Republic with a view to the adoption of a Council Directive on mutual recognition of decisions on the expulsion of third country nationals	25-10-2000
11385/00	Conditions for harmonising the status of third-country nationals residing on a long-term basis – Draft conclusions	23-10-2000
12951/00	Proposal for a Council Directive defining the facilitation of unauthorised entry, movement and residence	03-11-2000
12957/00	Initiative of the French Republic with a view to the adoption of a Council Directive on mutual recognition of decisions on the expulsion of third country nationals	03-11-2000
13274/00	Conditions for harmonising the status of third-country nationals residing on a long-term basis – Draft conclusions	14-11-2000
13168/00	Initiative of the French Republic with a view to the adoption of a Council Directive on mutual recognition of decisions on the expulsion of third-country nationals	09-11-2000
12914/1/00 REV 1	Draft Council Framework Decision on the strengthening of the penal framework to prevent the facilitation of unauthorised entry and residence Draft Council Directive defining the facilitation of unauthorised entry, movement and residence	13-11-2000
13095/1/00 REV 1	Initiative of the French Republic with a view to the adoption of a Council Directive on mutual recognition of decisions on the expulsion of third country nationals	17-11-2000
12950/00	Information on illegal migratory flows from Bosnia and Herzegovina and the Federal Republic of Yugoslavia	03-11-2000
13578/00	Draft Council Framework Decision on the strengthening of the penal framework to preventing the facilitation of unauthorised entry and residence Draft Council Directive defining the facilitation of unauthorised entry, movement and residence	20-11-2000
13095/2/00 REV 2	Draft Council Directive on the mutual recognition of decisions on the expulsion of third country nationals	24-11-2000
13739/00	Draft Council Framework Decision on the strengthening of the penal framework to prevent the facilitation of unauthorised entry and residence Draft Council Directive defining the facilitation of unauthorised entry, movement and residence	24-11-2000

11529/00	Communication from the Commission to the Council and the European Parliament on a Community immigration policy	27-11-2000
13968/00	Draft Council Directive on the mutual recognition of decisions on the expulsion of third-country nationals	29-11-2000
13474/00	International Seminar on Liaison Officers dealing with migration	30-11-2000
14276/00	Recommendations of the Expert Meeting on Illegal Immigration via the Balkan route, Ljubljana, 16-17 November 2000	05-12-2000
10120/00	Compilation of replies to questionnaire on 'Financial incentives in voluntary return programmes' (see Telex No 1685 of 7.4.00)	21-12-2000
14404/00	Compilation of replies to questionnaire on the initiative of the French Republic wit a view to the adoption of a Council Directive on mutual recognition of decisions on the expulsion of third country nationals	21-12-2000
14920/00	Draft Council Framework Decision on the strengthening of the penal framework to prevent the facilitation of unauthorised entry and residence Draft Council Directive defining the facilitation of unauthorised entry, movement and residence	22-12-2000
5186/01	Draft Council Framework Decision on the strengthening of the penal framework to prevent the facilitation of unauthorised entry and residence and Draft Council Directive defining the facilitation of unauthorised entry, movement and residence	11-01-2001

INTERNATIONAL INSTRUMENTS

Introduction and Detailed Contents

As indicated in the Introduction, the Migration Acquis, albeit European Union in character, is not complete without proper reference to those regional or global instruments which have, have had, or are expected to have an impact on European policy making and implementation. The Union, after all, is not isolationist.

In this respect regard should be had to:
– the Council of Europe (CoE)
– the International Labour Organization (ILO), and
– the UN (as a source of both charter-based and treaty-based instruments).

Most of the instruments which have been included in this Handbook (Conventions, Resolutions and Reports) belong to soft law. This is in particular true for the 1990 UN Convention on the Protection of the Rights of All Migrant Workers and Members of Their Families, as it has been signed and/or ratified by very few countries indeed, none of them from Europe, except for Bosnia-Herzegovina. Yet, the relevant parts of this Convention too have been included as it is a clear indication of the way some countries and some circles think about the issues at stake. Moreover, it is expected that that Convention may enter into force in/around 2002.

As for the inclusion of instruments in this Chapter, difficult choices had to be made, in view of the limited space at our disposal. None of the CoE instruments, for instance, have been included, in spite of their relevance for the issue at stake. The reason for this omission is that this Handbook may be considered to focus on Third Country nationals coming form outside Europe rather than from the countries which are contracting parties to those instruments. Similarly, *l'embarras de choix* could also be felt as regards the ILO and UN documents.

Yet, the chapters on CoE, ILO and UN instruments are preceded by general overviews on the various instruments and articles dealing with migration (**4.1**) and return (**4.2**).

CoE (4.3)
The Council of Europe documents mainly contain resolutions, recommendations and decisions. None of the texts have been included but a survey of those instruments (listing) was believed to be useful.

P.J. van Krieken (Ed.), The Migration Acquis Handbook
© 2001, T.M.C.Asser Press, The Hague, the Röling Foundation and the authors

Other CoE instruments should also be mentioned, such as the European Convention for the Protection of Human Rights and Fundamental Freedoms 1950 and the various Protocols thereto, as is the official title of what is commonly known as the European Convention on Human Rights (ECHR).[1] The European Conventions on Establishment (1955) and Extradition (1957) should also be considered of relevance. Moreover, the (revised) European Charter (1996 *juncto* 1961), the European Convention on Social and Medical Assistance (1953) and the one on Social Security (1972) should be deemed to be of interest as well. This is particularly true for the European Convention on the Repatriation of Minors (1970) and the European Convention on the Legal Status of Migrant Workers (1977).

The reason for not including these instruments is twofold. On the one hand, a lack of space, but, on the other – and far more relevant – the very fact that virtually all of these instruments refer to rules and regulations valid for subjects from fellow European countries only, or, to be more exact, for nationals from 'another Contracting Party'. In other words, these instruments hardly touch upon Third Country nationals, the subject of this Handbook, with the main exception of Turkish nationals, as Turkey is indeed a Contracting Party to most of the instruments mentioned hereinabove. This is, for instance the case with the Convention on the Legal Status of Migrant Workers (1977, in force since 1983) which, by the end of 1996 had been ratified by 8 countries, 6 of whom are EU MS[2] (plus Norway and Turkey) and signed by 4 countries (all of whom are EU Member States). Yet, candidate countries may wish to consider accession. But even then, this Convention would soon be outmoded, once the candidate countries become fully-fledged members of the Union as at that time the TEC/TEU would apply.

ILO (4.4.1–4.4.3)

Other, often neglected but still very relevant, instruments have been adopted in the realm of the International Labour Organization (ILO) and carry quite some weight, not only because the ILO is the foremost organization dealing with labour and hence with migrant labour. This is also because the ILO as an institution has managed to continuously – that is since 1919 which makes it the oldest still effectively functioning international institution – focus on relevant labour conditions, which includes 'migration for employment', 'equality of treatment in social security', 'migrant workers' and, for example, 'medical care to persons during temporary residence'. It is recalled that the main ILO body consists not only of Government representatives, but also of equal numbers of representatives of Employers' Associations and Trade Unions, which, indeed, makes the ILO instruments so important.

---

[1] Article 8 of the ECHR on the family has been dealt with in Chapter 2.5, Views/Family Reunification.

[2] As of February 2001: eight parties (France, Italy, the Netherlands, Norway, Portugal, Spain, Sweden and Turkey) and four signatories (Belgium, Germany, Greece, Luxembourg); no new signatories since 1989; only one ratification since 1990.

UN (4.5.1–4.5.9)

The topic of migration topic has only recently been given the UN attention which it deserves. On the one hand, it is the negative dimension which migration sometimes carries, trafficking and smuggling in particular, which culminated in the Palermo Protocols of December 2000, and which are duly dealt with in Chapter 2, Views/Trafficking. On the other hand, it is noteworthy that the UN General Assembly adopted at around the same time a Resolution declaring the 18th of December henceforth to be International Migrants' Day. Moreover, in accordance with the Commission on Human Rights Resolution 1999/44, a Special Rapporteur has been appointed on the human rights of migrants. This Rapporteur submitted her first report in January 2000 and it was hence deemed appropriate to include major excerpts of that report in this Handbook.

As to Treaty-based bodies, it goes virtually without saying that the General Comments on the issue of migration, as submitted by the Human Rights Committee (a Committee of 18 independent experts set up under the 1966 International Covenant on Civil and Political Rights), have been incorporated as well.

Other Relevant Texts (4.1–4.2)

As indicated, the above is preceded by a survey of other relevant texts, from Banjul to Bogotá, and from San José to Nice, in order to also provide an impression as to how the various regions try to deal with this subject and how they translate the issues into legal language.

CONTENTS CHAPTER 4

The survey contains a number of texts relating to the issue of migration.[1] In order to appreciate the global interest and the chronological developments the various excerpts have been included in chronological order. One theme has been focused upon, however, namely that of return (see Chapter 4.2). Moreover, some of the texts can also be found elsewhere in this Handbook i.e. in the proper context. One of the purposes of this survey is to emphasize that a right to migration has hitherto not been agreed upon. The right to leave one's country has not been complemented by a right to enter another country, but for the right to seek asylum.[2] As will be shown in Chapter 4.2 the right to return to one's country has, of course, been complemented by the duty of the country of origin/citizenship to accept the 'prodigal son (and daughter)'.

American Declaration of the Rights and Duties of Man, Bogotá, Colombia, 1948
Article VIII – Right to residence and movement
Every person has the right to fix his residence within the territory of the state of which he is a national, to move about freely within such territory, and not to leave it except by his own will.

Universal Declaration of Human Rights, 10 December 1948[3]
Article 13.
(1) Everyone has the right to freedom of movement and residence within the borders of each state.
(2) Everyone has the right to leave any country, including his own, and to return to his country.

Protocol No. 4 to the ECHR, 16 November 1963, in force[4]
Article 2 – Freedom of movement
1. Everyone lawfully within the territory of a State shall, within that territory, have the right to liberty of movement and freedom to choose his residence.
2. Everyone shall be free to leave any country, including his own (...)

---

[1] Please note that it concerns Declarations, Resolutions, Constitutions, Covenants and Conventions, all with a different legal impact (soft, hard, binding, not binding). Moreover, not all of them have entered into force.

[2] It should also once again be emphasized that this survey focuses on migration only, and excludes asylum and asylum-related legal texts.

[3] This UDHR Art. 13 should be seen as part of a triptych, the other two being arts. 14 and 15 (dealing with respectively the right to seek asylum and the right to a nationality). Because of this 'triptych' art. 13 can only be understood to mean that everyone has a right to leave one's own country, but that this right is not complemented by a right to enter another one, the exception being the right to seek asylum in another country. It should hence be concluded that a right to migration has not been established.

[4] ECHR's art. 8 on the protection of the family (unity) can be found in Chapter 2.5, footnote (5).

Article 3 – Prohibition of expulsion of nationals
(2) No one shall be deprived of the right to enter the territory of the state of which he is a national.

International Convention on the Elimination of All Forms of Discrimination, 21 December 1965,
entry into force 4 January 1969
Article 5
In compliance with the fundamental obligations laid down in article 2 of this Convention, States Parties undertake to prohibit and to eliminate racial discrimination in all its forms and to guarantee the right of everyone, without distinction as to race, colour, or national or ethnic origin, to equality before the law, notably in the enjoyment of the following rights: (...)
(d) Other civil rights, in particular:
(i) The right to freedom of movement and residence within the border of the State;
(ii) The right to leave any country, including one's own, and to return to one's country;

International Covenant on Civil and Political Rights, 16 December 1966, *entry into force* 23 March 1976
Article 12
1. Everyone lawfully within the territory of a State shall, within that territory, have the right to liberty of movement and freedom to choose his residence.
2. Everyone shall be free to leave any country, including his own.
3. The above-mentioned rights shall not be subject to any restrictions except those which are provided by law, are necessary to protect national security, public order (*ordre public*), public health or morals or the rights and freedoms of others, and are consistent with the other rights recognized in the present Covenant.
4. No one shall be arbitrarily deprived of the right to enter his own country.

American Convention on Human Rights, Costa Rica, 22 November 1969, *entry into force* 18 July 1978
Article 22 – Freedom of Movement and Residence
1. Every person lawfully in the territory of a State Party has the right to move about in it, and to reside in it subject to the provisions of the law.
2. Every person has the right to leave any country freely, including his own.
3. The exercise of the foregoing rights may be restricted only pursuant to a law to the extent necessary in a democratic society to prevent crime or to protect national security, public safety, public order, public morals, public health, or the rights or freedoms of others.
4. The exercise of the rights recognized in paragraph 1 may also be restricted by law in designated zones for reasons of public interest.
5. No one can be expelled from the territory of the state of which he is a national or be deprived of the right to enter it.
6. An alien lawfully in the territory of a State Party to this Convention may be expelled from it only pursuant to a decision reached in accordance with law.
7. Every person has the right to seek and be granted asylum in a foreign territory, in accordance with the legislation of the state and international conventions, in the event he is being pursued for political offenses or related common crimes.

8. In no case may an alien be deported or returned to a country, regardless of whether or not it is his country of origin, if in that country his right to life or personal freedom is in danger of being violated because of his race, nationality, religion, social status, or political opinions.

9. The collective expulsion of aliens is prohibited.

African [Banjul] Charter on Human and Peoples' Rights, adopted June 27, 1981, *entry into force* 21 October 1986

Article 12

1. Every individual shall have the right to freedom of movement and residence within the borders of a State provided he abides by the law.

2. Every individual shall have the right to leave any country including his own, and to return to his country. This right may only be subject to restrictions, provided for by law for the protection of national security, law and order, public health or morality.

3. Every individual shall have the right, when persecuted, to seek and obtain asylum in other countries in accordance with laws of those countries and international conventions.

4. A non-national legally admitted in a territory of a State Party to the present Charter, may only be expelled from it by virtue of a decision taken in accordance with the law.

5. The mass expulsion of non-nationals shall be prohibited. Mass expulsion shall be that which is aimed at national, racial, ethnic or religious groups.

Declaration on the Human Rights of Individuals Who are not Nationals of the Country in Which They Live (GA Resolution A/RES/40/144), 13 December 1985

Article 1

For the purposes of this Declaration, the term 'alien' shall apply, with due regard to qualifications made in subsequent articles, to any individual who is not a national of the State in which he or she is present.

Article 4

Aliens shall observe the laws of the State in which they reside or are present and regard with respect the customs and traditions of the people of that State.

Article 5

2. Subject to such restrictions as are prescribed by law and which are necessary in a democratic society to protect national security, public safety, public order, public health or morals or the rights and freedoms of others, and which are consistent with the other rights recognized in the relevant international instruments and those set forth in this Declaration, aliens shall enjoy the following rights: (a)The right to leave the country; (...)

3. Subject to the provisions referred to in paragraph 2, aliens lawfully in the territory of a State shall enjoy the right to liberty of movement and freedom to choose their residence within the borders of the State.

4. Subject to national legislation and due authorization, the spouse and minor or dependent children of an alien lawfully residing in the territory of a State shall be admitted to accompany, join and stay with the alien.

International Convention on the Protection of the Rights of All Migrant Workers and Members of Their Families (GA Resolution A/RES/45/158), 18 December 1990 (not yet in force; 16 ratifications as per 1 January 2001)
Article 8
1. Migrant workers and members of their families shall be free to leave any State, including their State of origin. This right shall not be subject to any restrictions except those that are provided by law, are necessary to protect national security, public order (ordre public), public health or morals or the rights and freedoms of others and are consistent with the other rights recognized in the present part of the Convention.
2. Migrant workers and members of their families shall have the right at any time to enter and remain in their State of origin.
Article 39
1. Migrant workers and members of their families shall have the right to liberty of movement in the territory of the State of employment and freedom to choose their residence there.

Cairo Conference on Population and Development, 1994[5]
Chapter X
10.13 States are free to control at will the entry and residence of aliens. The States can regulate access to their territory and adopt policies that respond to and shape immigration flows.
10.15 It is the right of every Nation State to decide who can enter and stay in its territory and under what conditions.

Charter of the Fundamental Rights of the European Union, December 2000 (soft law)
Article 45 – Freedom of movement and of residence
1. Every citizen of the Union has the right to move and reside freely within the territory of the Member States.
2. Freedom of movement and residence may be granted, in accordance with the Treaty establishing the European Community, to nationals of third countries legally resident in the territory of a Member State.

# Legal Texts Return							4.2

A. GENERAL

Universal Declaration of Human Rights 1948
Article 13(2)
Everyone has the right to leave any country, including his own, and to return to his country.

---

[5] See also Chapter 4.5.4 for additional relevant Cairo texts.

Protocol no 4 of the European Convention on Human Rights 1963
Article 3(2)
No one shall be deprived of the right to enter the territory of the State of which he is a national.

International Convention on the Elimination of All Forms of Racial Discrimination 1965
Article 5(dii)
The right to leave any country, including one's own, and to return to one's country.

International Covenant on Civil and Political Rights 1966
Article 12(4)
No one shall be arbitrarily deprived of the right to enter his own country.

American Convention on Human Rights 1969
Article 22(5)
No one can be expelled from the territory of the State of which he is a national or be deprived of the right to enter it.

African Charter on Human and People's Rights 1981
Article 12(2)
Every individual shall have the right to leave any country including his own, and to return to his country.This right may only be subject to restrictions, provided for by law for the protection of national security, law arid order, public health or morality.

The International Convention on the Protection of the Rights of All Migrant Workers and Members of Their Families 1990
Article 67
1. States Parties concerned shall co-operate as appropriate in the adoption of measures regarding the orderly return of migrant workers and members of their families to the State of origin when they decide to return or their authorization of residence or employment expires or when they are in the State of employment in an irregular situation.
2. Concerning migrant workers and members of their families in a regular situation, States Parties concerned shall co-operate as appropriate, on terms agreed upon by those States, with a view to promoting adequate economic conditions for their resettlement and to facilitating their durable social and cultural reintegration in the State of origin.

Cairo Conference on Population and Development 1994
Chapter X
10.2(c) To facilitate the reintegration process of returning migrants
10.5 Governments of countries of origin are urged to facilitate the return of migrants and their reintegration into their home communities, and to advise ways of using their skills.
10.20 Governments of countries of origin of undocumented migrants and persons whose asylum claims have been rejected have the responsibility to accept the return and reintegration of those persons, and should not penalize such persons on their return.

Protocol to Prevent, Suppress and Punish Trafficking in Persons, Especially Women and Children, supplementing the United Nations Convention against Transnational Organized Crime 2000

Article 8: Repatriation of victims of trafficking in persons

1. The State Party of which a victim of trafficking in persons is a national or in which the person had the right of permanent residence at the time of entry into the territory of the receiving State Party shall facilitate and accept, with due regard for the safety of that person, the return of that person without undue or unreasonable delay.

2. When a State Party returns a victim of trafficking in persons to a State Party of which that person is a national or in which he or she had, at the time of entry into the territory of the receiving State Party, the right of permanent residence, such return shall be with due regard for the safety of that person and for the status of any legal proceedings related to the fact that the person is a victim of trafficking and shall preferably be voluntary.

3. At the request of a receiving State Party, a requested State Party shall, without undue or unreasonable delay, verify whether a person who is a victim of trafficking in persons is its national or had the right or permanent residence in its territory at the time of entry into the territory of the receiving State Party.

4. In order to facilitate the return of a victim of trafficking in persons who is without proper documentation, the State Party of which that person is a national or in which he or she had the right of permanent residence at the time of entry into the territory of the receiving State Party shall agree to issue, at the request of the receiving State Party, such travel documents or other authorization as may be necessary to enable the person to travel to and re-enter its territory.

5. This article shall be without prejudice to any right afforded to victims of trafficking in persons by any domestic law of the receiving State Party.

6. This article shall be without prejudice to any applicable bilateral or multilateral agreement or arrangement that governs, in whole or in part, the return of victims of trafficking in persons.

Protocol against Smuggling of Migrants by Land, Air and Sea, supplementing the United Nations Convention against Transnational Organized Crime 2000

Article 18: Return of smuggled migrants

1. Each State Party agrees to facilitate and accept, without undue or unreasonable delay, the return of a person who has been the object of conduct set forth in article 6 of this Protocol and who is its national or who has the right of permanent residence in its territory at the time of return.

2. Each State Party shall consider the possibility of facilitating and accepting the return of a person who has been the object of conduct set forth in article 6 of this Protocol and who had the right of permanent residence in its territory at the time of entry into the receiving State in accordance with its domestic law.

3. At the request of the receiving State Party, a requested State Party shall, without undue or unreasonable delay, verify whether a person who has been the object of conduct set forth in article 6 of this Protocol is its national or has the right of permanent residence in its territory.

4. In order to facilitate the return of a person who has been the object of conduct set forth in article 6 of this Protocol and is without proper documentation, the State Party of which that person is a national or in which he or she has the right of permanent residence shall agree to issue, at the request of the receiving State Party, such travel documents or other

authorization as may be necessary to enable the person to travel to and re-enter its territory.

5. Each State Party involved with the return of a person who has been the object of conduct set forth in article 6 of this Protocol shall take all appropriate measures to carry out the return in an orderly manner and with due regard for the safety and dignity of the person.

6. States Parties may cooperate with relevant international organizations in the implementation of this article.

7. This article shall be without prejudice to any right afforded to persons who have been the object of conduct set forth in article 6 of this Protocol by any domestic law of the receiving State Party.

8. This article shall not affect the obligations entered into under any other applicable treaty, bilateral or multilateral, or any other applicable operational agreement or arrangement that governs, in whole or in part, the return of persons who have been the object of conduct set forth in article 6 of this Protocol.

The General Assembly has underlined state responsibility as it relates to countries of origin, including facilitating the return of their nationals who are not refugees[6]

B. THE PROHIBITION OF COLLECTIVE EXPULSIONS

Protocol no 4 of the European Convention on Human Rights 1963
Article 4
Collective expulsion of aliens is prohibited.

American Convention on Human Rights 1969
Article 22(9)
The collective expulsion of aliens is prohibited.

African Charter on Human and People's Rights 1981
Article 12(5)
The mass expulsion of non-nationals shall be prohibited. Mass expulsion shall be that which is aimed at national, racial, ethnic or religious group.

C. INDIVIDUAL EXPULSION (OF THE LAWFULLY PRESENT)

International Covenant on Civil and Political Rights 1966
Article 13(2)
An alien lawfully in the territory of a state party to the present Covenant may be expelled therefrom only in pursuance of a decision reached in accordance with law and shall, except where compelling reasons of national security otherwise require, be allowed to submit the reasons against his expulsion and to have his case reviewed by, and be represented

---

[6] GA Res 45/150 of 14 December 1990, para 9; GA Res 46/106 of 16 December 1991, para 10; GA Res 47/105 of 16 December 1992, para. 10. Reference could also be made to the 1990 Convention on on the Protection of All Migrant Workers and Members of Their Families (thus far 16 ratifications only) which promotes measures regarding the orderly return of migrants to their country of origin.

for the purpose before, the competent authority or a person or persons especially designated by the competent authority.

Protocol no 7 of the European Convention On Human Rights
Article 1.2
An alien may be expelled before the exercise of his rights under paragraph 1.a, b and c of this article, when such expulsion is necessary in the interests of public order or is grounded on reasons of national security.

American Convention on Human Rights 1969
Article 22(6)
An alien lawfully in the territory of a State party to this Convention may be expelled from it only pursuant to a decision reached in accordance with the law.

D. MOREOVER:

– UNHCR's ExCom Conclusions have been referring to the issue of return since the mid-1990s. At the 48th session of the Executive Committee the following text was adopted:
'... Executive Committee (...) reaffirms the right of all persons to return to their countries, and the responsibility of States to facilitate the return and reintegration of their nationals ...'[7]
– UNHCR's Executive Committee, addressing international cooperation, went even further by stating in their 1998 Conclusion that:
'...The Executive Committee (...) recommends to States that strategies for facilitating the return, in safety and dignity, of persons not in need of international protection be examined within a framework of international cooperation; and encourages UNHCR to continue, in cooperation with other appropriate international organizations, to look into ways in which the return process of individuals, determined through fair and effective procedures not to be in need of international protection, can be facilitated...'
– International cooperation will also have a positive outcome at the regional level. In Europe, under the Treaty of Amsterdam, the Community objectives in the area of immigration policy also include the repatriation of persons illegally resident in a Member State (Article 63(3) of the (consolidated) Treaty establishing the European Community): 'The Council [shall adopt]measures on immigration policy [also within the area of] illegal immigration and illegal residence, including repatriation of illegal residents'[8]

---

[7] ExCom, General Conclusion no. 81 (1997); worth mentioning is also the ExCom Standing Committee document EC/46/SC/CRP.36 of 28 May, 19996, which exclusively focuses on 'return of persons not in need of international protection'. Although this document falls short of clearly addressing the responsibility of countries of origin, it underlines the general principles and indicates that UNHCR 'is willing to support States in their efforts to return categories categories of rejected asylum-seekers'.

[8] For various details, also on readmission agreements, see Van Krieken, Return and Responsibility, *International Migration,* Quarterly Review Vol. 38 No. 4 (2000), pp. 23-40.

Council of Europe Documents   **4.3**

A: RESOLUTIONS

Res(49)31 Convention on Migrant Workers
Date: 11/05/49 Meeting: CM2
Res(50)12 Preparatory Conference on Migration
Date: 01/10/50 Meeting: NA
Res(52)12 European Convention on Extradition
Date: 03/10/52 Meeting: 1
Res(53)4 European Convention on Extradition
Date: 19/03/53 Meeting: 9
Res(53)20 Overseas emigration
Date: 05/07/53 Meeting: CM12
Res(58)16 Reduction of the number of cases of multiple nationality Recommendation 164
Date: 19/09/58 Meeting: 63
Res(68)2 Social services for migrant workers
Date: 26/01/68 Meeting: 167
Res(68)18 Teaching of languages to migrant workers
Date: 28/06/68 Meeting: 172
Res(69)8 Low-cost housing for migrant workers
Date: 03/07/69 Meeting: 178
Res(69)9 Participation of immigrants in the life of the firms in which they work
Date: 03/07/69 Meeting: 178
Res(70)36 Occupational safety of migrant workers
Date: 27/11/70 Meeting: 194
Res(72)1 on the standardisation of the legal concepts of 'domicile' and of 'residence'
Date: 18/01/72 Meeting: 206
Res(72)18 Methods of compiling statistics on international migration of workers
Date: 30/05/72 Meeting: 211
Res(74)14 on the situation of migrant workers and on their families in Europe
Date: 21/05/74 Meeting: 232
Res(74)15 on equal treatment of national and migrant workers in the following sectores:
working conditions, remuneration, dismissal, geographical and occupational mobility
Date: 29/05/74 Meeting: 232
Res(75)12 on the practical application of the European Convention on Extradition
Date: 21/03/75 Meeting: 243
Res(76)11 on equal treatment for national and migrant workers with regard to vocational
guidance, training and retraining
Date: 03/09/76 Meeting: 255
Res(76)25 on the model contract or model contract for the introduction of migrant workers
Date: 13/04/76 Meeting: 256
Res(78)4 on social and economic repercussions on migrant workers of economic recessions or crises
Date: 02/02/78 Meeting: 282

Res(78)33 on the reunion of families of migrant workers in Council of Europe member states
Date: 06/08/78 Meeting: 289
Res(78)44 on clandestine immigration and the illegal employment of foreign workers
Date: 26/10/78 Meeting: 294

B: DECISIONS

615/6.1a European Committee on Migration (CDMG) – Abridged report of the 36th meeting (Strasbourg, 14-17 April 1997) Date: 20/01/98 Meeting: 615
615/6.1b European Committee on Migration (CDMG) – Abridged report of the 37th meeting (Strasbourg, 5-7 November 1997) Date: 20/01/98 Meeting: 615
625/1.6 Follow-up to the Mediterranean Conference on Population, Migration and Development (Palma de Mallorca, 15-17 October 1996) – Parliamentary Assembly Recommendation 1329 (1997) Date: 31/03/98 Meeting: 625
629/2.3 Influx of Migrants – Resumption of the discussion Date: 30/04/98 Meeting: 629
635/6.1 European Committee on Migration (CDMG) – Abridged report of the 38th meeting (Strasbourg, 25-27 March 1998) Date: 09/06/98 Meeting: 635
645/6.5 Activities of the International Organisation for Migration (IOM), 1994-97 – Parliamentary Assembly Recommendation 1370 (1998) Date: 20/10/98 Meeting: 645
645/4.1 Traffic in women and forced prostitution in Council of Europe member States – Parliamentary Assembly Recommendation 1325 (1997) Date: 20/10/98 Meeting: 645
652/6.1 European Committee on Migration (CDMG) Abridged report of the 39th meeting (Strasbourg, 14-16 October 1998) Date: 15/12/98 Meeting: 652
698/41b Steering Committee for Equality between Women and Men (CDEG).- b. Draft Recommendation of the Committee of Ministers to member states on action against trafficking in human beings or the purpose of sexual exploitation. Date: 09/02/00 Meeting: 698
720/6.1b European Committee on Migration – b) Draft Recommendation Rec(2000)... to member states concerning the security of residence of long-term migrants. Date: 13/09/00 Meeting: 720
720/6.1a European Committee on Migration (CDMG) – a) Abridged report of the 42nd meeting (Strasbourg, 3-5 May 2000) Date: 13/09/00 Meeting: 720
730/6.1 European Committee on Migration (CDMG) – Abridged report of the 42nd meeting (Strasbourg, 4-5 May 2000) Date: 22/11/00 Meeting: 730

C: RECOMMENDATIONS

Rec(80)7 concerning the practical application of the European Convention on Extradition
Date: 27/06/80 Meeting: 321
Rec(80)9 concerning extradition to states non party to the European Convention on Human Rights
Date: 27/06/80 Meeting: 321
Rec(80)14 concerning the vocational re-integration of migrant workers who return to their countries of origin
Date: 18/09/80 Meeting: 322

Rec(84)7 on the maintenance of migrants' cultural links with their countries of origin and leisure facilities
Date: 28/02/84 Meeting: 367
Rec(84)9 on second-generation migrants
Date: 20/03/84 Meeting: 368
Rec(86)13 concerning the practical application of the European Convention on extradition in respect of detention pending extradition
Date: 16/09/86 Meeting: 399
Rec(88)14 on migrants' housing
Date: 22/09/88 Meeting: 419
Rec(90)14 on the preparation of an information brochure of the social security rights and obligations of migrant workers and of their families
Date: 18/06/90 Meeting: 442
Rec(96)9 concerning the practical application of the European Convention on Extradition
Date: 05/09/96 Meeting: 572
Rec(97)22 containing guidelines on the application of the safe third country concept
Date: 27/11/97 Meeting: 609
Rec(2000)15 concerning the security of residence of long-term migrants
Date: 13/09/00 Meeting: 720

ILO   4.4

4.4.1

Convention concerning Migration for Employment (Revised 1949)[9] C97

The General Conference of the International Labour Organisation,
Having been convened at Geneva by the Governing Body of the International Labour Office, and having met in its Thirty-second Session on 8 June 1949, and
Having decided upon the adoption of certain proposals with regard to the revision of the Migration for Employment Convention, 1939, adopted by the Conference at its Twenty-fifth Session, which is included in the eleventh item on the agenda of the session, and
Considering that these proposals must take the form of an international Convention,
adopts the first day of July of the year one thousand nine hundred and forty-nine, the following Convention, which may be cited as the Migration for Employment Convention (Revised), 1949:

---

[9] Date of coming into force: 22 January 1952; adopted in Geneva, 1 July 1949; 41 Parties, among whom Belgium, (Bosnia-Herzegovina), France, Germany, Italy, (FYR Macedonia), the Netherlands, (Norway), Portugal, Slovenia, Spain, Sweden, (Yugoslavia), United Kingdom, i.e. 10 from the 25 target countries and four other relevant European countries.

Article 1

Each Member of the International Labour Organisation for which this Convention is in force undertakes to make available on request to the International Labour Office and to other Members:

(a) information on national policies, laws and regulations relating to emigration and immigration;

(b) information on special provisions concerning migration for employment and the conditions of work and livelihood of migrants for employment;

(c) information concerning general agreements and special arrangements on these questions concluded by the Member.

Article 2

Each Member for which this Convention is in force undertakes to maintain, or satisfy itself that there is maintained, an adequate and free service to assist migrants for employment, and in particular to provide them with accurate information.

Article 3

1. Each Member for which this Convention is in force undertakes that it will, so far as national laws and regulations permit, take all appropriate steps against misleading propaganda relating to emigration and immigration.

2. For this purpose, it will where appropriate act in co-operation with other Members concerned.

Article 4

Measures shall be taken as appropriate by each Member, within its jurisdiction, to facilitate the departure, journey and reception of migrants for employment.

Article 5

Each Member for which this Convention is in force undertakes to maintain, within its jurisdiction, appropriate medical services responsible for:

(a) ascertaining, where necessary, both at the time of departure and on arrival, that migrants for employment and the members of their families authorised to accompany or join them are in reasonable health;

(b) ensuring that migrants for employment and members of their families enjoy adequate medical attention and good hygienic conditions at the time of departure, during the journey and on arrival in the territory of destination.

Article 6

1. Each Member for which this Convention is in force undertakes to apply, without discrimination in respect of nationality, race, religion or sex, to immigrants lawfully within its territory, treatment no less favourable than that which it applies to its own nationals in respect of the following matters:

(a) in so far as such matters are regulated by law or regulations, or are subject to the control of administrative authorities

(i) remuneration, including family allowances where these form part of remuneration, hours of work, overtime arrangements, holidays with pay, restrictions on home work, minimum age for employment, apprenticeship and training, women's work and the work of young persons;

    (ii) membership of trade unions and enjoyment of the benefits of collective bargaining;

    (iii) accommodation;

(b) social security (that is to say, legal provision in respect of employment injury, maternity, sickness, invalidity, old age, death, unemployment and family responsibilities, and any other contingency which, according to national laws or regulations, is covered by a social security scheme), subject to the following limitations:

    (i) there may be appropriate arrangements for the maintenance of acquired rights and rights in course of acquisition;

    (ii) national laws or regulations of immigration countries may prescribe special arrangements concerning benefits or portions of benefits which are payable wholly out of public funds, and concerning allowances paid to persons who do not fulfil the contribution conditions prescribed for the award of a normal pension;

(c) employment taxes, dues or contributions payable in respect of the person employed; and

(d) legal proceedings relating to the matters referred to in this Convention.

2. In the case of a federal State the provisions of this Article shall apply in so far as the matters dealt with are regulated by federal law or regulations or are subject to the control of federal administrative authorities. The extent to which and manner in which these provisions shall be applied in respect of matters regulated by the law or regulations of the constituent States, provinces or cantons, or subject to the control of the administrative authorities thereof, shall be determined by each Member. The Member shall indicate in its annual report upon the application of the Convention the extent to which the matters dealt with in this Article are regulated by federal law or regulations or are subject to the control of federal administrative authorities. In respect of matters which are regulated by the law or regulations of the constituent States, provinces or cantons, or are subject to the control of the administrative authorities thereof, the Member shall take the steps provided for in paragraph 7(b) of article 19 of the Constitution of the International Labour Organisation.

Article 7

1. Each Member for which this Convention is in force undertakes that its employment service and other services connected with migration will co-operate in appropriate cases with the corresponding services of other Members.

2. Each Member for which this Convention is in force undertakes to ensure that the services rendered by its public employment service to migrants for employment are rendered free.

Article 8

1. A migrant for employment who has been admitted on a permanent basis and the members of his family who have been authorised to accompany or join him shall not be returned to their territory of origin or the territory from which they emigrated because the migrant is unable to follow his occupation by reason of illness contracted or injury sustained subsequent to entry, unless the person concerned so desires or an international agreement to which the Member is a party so provides.

2. When migrants for employment are admitted on a permanent basis upon arrival in the country of immigration the competent authority of that country may determine that the provisions of paragraph 1 of this Article shall take effect only after a reasonable period which shall in no case exceed five years from the date of admission of such migrants.

Article 9
Each Member for which this Convention is in force undertakes to permit, taking into account the limits allowed by national laws and regulations concerning export and import of currency, the transfer of such part of the earnings and savings of the migrant for employment as the migrant may desire.

Article 10
In cases where the number of migrants going from the territory of one Member to that of another is sufficiently large, the competent authorities of the territories concerned shall, whenever necessary or desirable, enter into agreements for the purpose of regulating matters of common concern arising in connection with the application of the provisions of this Convention.

Article 11
1. For the purpose of this Convention the term *migrant for employment* means a person who migrates from one country to another with a view to being employed otherwise than on his own account and includes any person regularly admitted as a migrant for employment.
2. This Convention does not apply to:
(a) frontier workers;
(b) short-term entry of members of the liberal professions and artistes; and
(c) seamen.

Article 12
The formal ratifications of this Convention shall be communicated to the Director-General of the International Labour Office for registration.

Article 13
1. This Convention shall be binding only upon those Members of the International Labour Organisation whose ratifications have been registered with the Director-General.
2. It shall come into force twelve months after the date on which the ratifications of two Members have been registered with the Director-General.
3. Thereafter, this Convention shall come into force for any Member twelve months after the date on which its ratifications has been registered.

Article 14
1. Each Member ratifying this Convention may, by a declaration appended to its ratification, exclude from its ratification any or all of the Annexes to the Convention.
2. Subject to the terms of any such declaration, the provisions of the Annexes shall have the same effect as the provisions of the Convention.
3. Any Member which makes such a declaration may subsequently by a new declaration notify the Director-General that it accepts any or all of the Annexes mentioned in the declaration; as from the date of the registration of such notification by the Director-General the provisions of such Annexes shall be applicable to the Member in question.
4. While a declaration made under paragraph 1 of this Article remains in force in respect of any Annex, the Member may declare its willingness to accept that Annex as having the force of a Recommendation.

Article 15
(*validity for territories*)

Article 16
(1. *validity for territories*)
2. The Member, Members or international authority concerned may at any time by a subsequent declaration renounce in whole or in part the right to have recourse to any modification indicated in any former declaration.
3. The Member, Members or international authority concerned may, at any time at which the Convention is subject to denunciation in accordance with the provisions of Article 17, communicate to the Director-General a declaration modifying in any other respect the terms of any former declaration and stating the present position in respect of the application of the Convention.

Article 17
1. A Member which has ratified this Convention may denounce it after the expiration of ten years from the date on which the Convention first comes into force, by an Act communicated to the Director-General of the International Labour Office for registration. Such denunciation should not take effect until one year after the date on which it is registered.
2. Each Member which has ratified this Convention and which does not, within the year following the expiration of the period of ten years mentioned in the preceding paragraph, exercise the right of denunciation provided for in this Article, will be bound for another period of ten years and, thereafter, may denounce this Convention at the expiration of each period of ten years under the terms provided for in this Article.
3. At any time at which this Convention is subject to denunciation in accordance with the provisions of the preceding paragraphs any Member which does not so denounce it may communicate to the Director-General a declaration denouncing separately any Annex to the Convention which is in force for that Member.
4. The denunciation of this Convention or of any or all of the Annexes shall not affect the rights granted thereunder to a migrant or to the members of his family if he immigrated while the Convention or the relevant Annex was in force in respect of the territory where the question of the continued validity of these rights arises.

Article 18
(*notification of ratifications*)

Article 19
The Director-General of the International Labour Office shall communicate to the Secretary-General of the United Nations for registration in accordance with Article 102 of the Charter of the United Nations full particulars of all ratifications and acts of denunciation registered by him in accordance with the provisions of the preceding Articles.

Article 20
At the expiration of each period of ten years after the coming into force of this Convention, the Governing Body of the International Labour Office shall present to the General Conference a report on the working of this Convention and shall examine the desirability

of placing on the agenda of the Conference the question of its revision in whole or in part.

Article 21

1. Should the Conference adopt a new Convention revising this Convention in whole or in part, then, unless the new Convention otherwise provides:

a) the ratification by a Member of the new revising Convention shall ipso jure involve the immediate denunciation of this Convention, notwithstanding the provisions of Article 17 above, if and when the new revising Convention shall have come into force;

b) as from the date when the new revising Convention comes into force this Convention shall cease to be open to ratification by the Members.

2. This Convention shall in any case remain in force in its actual form and content for those Members which have ratified it but have not ratified the revising Convention.

Article 22

1. The International Labour Conference may, at any session at which the matter is included in its agenda, adopt by a two-thirds majority a revised text of any one or more of the Annexes to this Convention.

2. Each Member for which this Convention is in force shall, within the period of one year, or, in exceptional circumstances, of eighteen months, from the closing of the session of the Conference, submit any such revised text to the authority or authorities within whose competence the matter lies, for the enactment of legislation or other action.

3. Any such revised text shall become effective for each Member for which this Convention is in force on communication by that Member to the Director-General of the International Labour Office of a declaration notifying its acceptance of the revised text.

4. As from the date of the adoption of the revised text of the Annex by the Conference, only the revised text shall be open to acceptance by Members.

Article 23

The English and French versions of the text of this Convention are equally authoritative.[10]

ANNEX I

Recruitment, placing and conditions of labour of migrants for employment recruited otherwise than under government-sponsored arrangements for group transfer.

Article 1

This Annex applies to migrants for employment who are recruited otherwise than under Government-sponsored arrangements for group transfer.

Article 2

For the purpose of this Annex:

(a) the term *recruitment* means:

---

[10] Cross references: this Convention revises the 1939 Convention on Migration for Employment, and is supplemented by the 1949 recommendation on this same subject..

(i) the engagement of a person in one territory on behalf of an employer in another territory, or

(ii) the giving of an undertaking to a person in one territory to provide him with employment in another territory, together with the making of any arrangements in connection with the operations mentioned in (i) and (ii) including the seeking for and selection of emigrants and the preparation for departure of the emigrants;

(b) the term *introduction* means any operations for ensuring or facilitating the arrival in or admission to a territory of persons who have been recruited within the meaning of paragraph (a) of this Article; and

(c) the term *placing* means any operations for the purpose of ensuring or facilitating the employment of persons who have been introduced within the meaning of paragraph (b) of this Article.

Article 3

1. Each Member for which this Annex is in force, the laws and regulations of which permit the operations of recruitment, introduction and placing as defined in Article 2, shall regulate such of the said operations as are permitted by its laws and regulations in accordance with the provisions of this Article.

2. Subject to the provisions of the following paragraph, the right to engage in the operations of recruitment, introduction and placing shall be restricted to:

(a) public employment offices or other public bodies of the territory in which the operations take place;

(b) public bodies of a territory other than that in which the operations take place which are authorised to operate in that territory by agreement between the Governments concerned;

(c) any body established in accordance with the terms of an international instrument.

3. In so far as national laws and regulations or a bilateral arrangement permit, the operations of recruitment, introduction and placing may be undertaken by:

(a) the prospective employer or a person in his service acting on his behalf, subject, if necessary in the interest of the migrant, to the approval and supervision of the competent authority;

(b) a private agency, if given prior authorisation so to do by the competent authority of the territory where the said operations are to take place, in such cases and under such conditions as may be prescribed by:

(i) the laws and regulations of that territory, or

(ii) agreement between the competent authority of the territory of emigration or any body established in accordance with the terms of an international instrument and the competent authority of the territory of immigration.

4. The competent authority of the territory where the operations take place shall supervise the activities of bodies and persons to whom authorisations have been issued in pursuance of paragraph 3(b), other than any body established in accordance with the terms of an international instrument, the position of which shall continue to be governed by the terms of the said instrument or by any agreement made between the body and the competent authority concerned.

5. Nothing in this Article shall be deemed to permit the acceptance of a migrant for employment for admission to the territory of any Member by any person or body other than the competent authority of the territory of immigration.

Article 4
Each Member for which this Annex is in force undertakes to ensure that the services rendered by its public employment service in connection with the recruitment, introduction or placing of migrants for employment are rendered free.

Article 5
1. Each Member for which this Annex is in force which maintains a system of supervision of contracts of employment between an employer, or a person acting on his behalf, and a migrant for employment undertakes to require:
(a) that a copy of the contract of employment shall be delivered to the migrant before departure or, if the Governments concerned so agree, in a reception centre on arrival in the territory of immigration;
(b) that the contract shall contain provisions indicating the conditions of work and particularly the remuneration offered to the migrant;
(c) that the migrant shall receive in writing before departure, by a document which relates either to him individually or to a group of migrants of which he is a member, information concerning the general conditions of life and work applicable to him in the territory of immigration.
2. Where a copy of the contract is to be delivered to the migrant on arrival in the territory of immigration, he shall be informed in writing before departure, by a document which relates either to him individually or to a group of migrants of which he is a member, of the occupational category for which he is engaged and the other conditions of work, in particular the minimum wage which is guaranteed to him.
3. The competent authority shall ensure that the provisions of the preceding paragraphs are enforced and that appropriate penalties are applied in respect of violations thereof.

Article 6
The measures taken under Article 4 of the Convention shall, as appropriate, include:
(a) the simplification of administrative formalities;
(b) the provision of interpretation services;
(c) any necessary assistance during an initial period in the settlement of the migrants and members of their families authorised to accompany or join them; and
(d) the safeguarding of the welfare, during the journey and in particular on board ship, of migrants and members of their families authorised to accompany or join them.

Article 7
1. In cases where the number of migrants for employment going from the territory of one Member to that of another is sufficiently large, the competent authorities of the territories concerned shall, whenever necessary or desirable, enter into agreements for the purpose of regulating matters of common concern arising in connection with the application of the provisions of this Annex.
2. Where the members maintain a system of supervision over contracts of employment, such agreements shall indicate the methods by which the contractual obligations of the employers shall be enforced.

Article 8
Any person who promotes clandestine or illegal immigration shall be subject to appropriate penalties.

ANNEX II
recruitment, placing and conditions of labour of migrants for employment recruited under government-sponsored arrangements for group transfer

Article 1
This Annex applies to migrants for employment who are recruited under Government-sponsored arrangements for group transfer.

Article 2
For the purpose of this Annex:

(a) the term *recruitment* means:

(i) the engagement of a person in one territory on behalf of an employer in another territory under a Government-sponsored arrangement for group transfer, or

(ii) the giving of an undertaking to a person in one territory to provide him with employment in another territory under a Government-sponsored arrangement for group transfer, together with the making of any arrangements in connection with the operations mentioned in (i) and (ii) including the seeking for and selection of emigrants and the preparation for departure of the emigrants;

(b) the term *introduction* means any operations for ensuring or facilitating the arrival in or admission to a territory of persons who have been recruited under a Government-sponsored arrangement for group transfer within the meaning of subparagraph (a) of this paragraph; and

(c) the term *placing* means any operations for the purpose of ensuring or facilitating the employment of persons who have been introduced under a Government-sponsored arrangement for group transfer within the meaning of subparagraph (b) of this paragraph.

Article 3
1. Each Member for which this Annex is in force, the laws and regulations of which permit the operations of recruitment, introduction and placing as defined in Article 2, shall regulate such of the said operations as are permitted by its laws and regulations in accordance with the provisions of this Article.

2. Subject to the provisions of the following paragraph, the right to engage in the operations of recruitment, introduction and placing shall be restricted to:

(a) public employment offices or other public bodies of the territory in which the operations take place;

(b) public bodies of a territory other than that in which the operations take place which are authorised to operate in that territory by agreement between the Governments concerned;

(c) any body established in accordance with the terms of an international instrument.

3. In so far as national laws and regulations or a bilateral arrangement permit, and subject, if necessary in the interest of the migrant, to the approval and supervision of the competent authority, the operations of recruitment, introduction and placing may be undertaken by:

(a) the prospective employer or a person in his service acting on his behalf;

(b) private agencies.

4. The right to engage in the operations of recruitment, introduction and placing shall be subject to the prior authorisation of the competent authority of the territory where the said operations are to take place in such cases and under such conditions as may be prescribed by:

(a) the laws and regulations of that territory, or

(b) agreement between the competent authority of the territory of emigration or any body established in accordance with the terms of an international instrument and the competent authority of the territory of immigration.

5. The competent authority of the territory where the operations take place shall, in accordance with any agreements made between the competent authorities concerned, supervise the activities of bodies and persons to whom authorisations have been issued in pursuance of the preceding paragraph, other than any body established in accordance with the terms of an international instrument, the position of which shall continue to be governed by the terms of the said instrument or by any agreement made between the body and the competent authority concerned.

6. Before authorising the introduction of migrants for employment the competent authority of the territory of immigration shall ascertain whether there is not a sufficient number of persons already available capable of doing the work in question.

7. Nothing in this Article shall be deemed to permit the acceptance of a migrant for employment for admission to the territory of any Member by any person or body other than the competent authority of the territory of immigration.

Article 4

1. Each Member for which this Annex is in force undertakes to ensure that the services rendered by its public employment service in connection with the recruitment, introduction or placing of migrants for employment are rendered free.

2. The administrative costs of recruitment, introduction and placing shall not be borne by the migrants.

Article 5

In the case of collective transport of migrants from one country to another necessitating passage in transit through a third country, the competent authority of the territory of transit shall take measures for expediting the passage, to avoid delays and administrative difficulties.

Article 6

1. Each Member for which this Annex is in force which maintains a system of supervision of contracts of employment between an employer, or a person acting on his behalf, and a migrant for employment undertakes to require:

(a) that a copy of the contract of employment shall be delivered to the migrant before departure or, if the Governments concerned so agree, in a reception centre on arrival in the territory of immigration;

(b) that the contract shall contain provisions indicating the conditions of work and particularly the remuneration offered to the migrant;

(c) that the migrant shall receive in writing before departure, by a document which relates either to him individually or to a group of migrants of which he is a member, information concerning the general conditions of life and work applicable to him in the territory of immigration.

2. Where a copy of the contract is to be delivered to the migrant on arrival in the territory of immigration, he shall be informed in writing before departure, by a document which relates either to him individually or to a group of migrants of which he is a member, of the

occupational category for which he is engaged and the other conditions of work, in particular the minimum wage which is guaranteed to him.

3. The competent authority shall ensure that the provisions of the preceding paragraphs are enforced and that appropriate penalties are applied in respect of violations thereof.

Article 7

1. The measures taken under Article 4 of this Convention shall, as appropriate, include:

(a) the simplification of administrative formalities;

(b) the provision of interpretation services;

(c) any necessary assistance, during an initial period in the settlement of the migrants and members of their families authorised to accompany or join them;

(d) the safeguarding of the welfare, during the journey and in particular on board ship, of migrants and members of their families authorised to accompany or join them; and

(e) permission for the liquidation and transfer of the property of migrants for employment admitted on a permanent basis.

Article 8

Appropriate measures shall be taken by the competent authority to assist migrants for employment, during an initial period, in regard to matters concerning their conditions of employment; where appropriate, such measures may be taken in co-operation with approved voluntary organisations.

Article 9

If a migrant for employment introduced into the territory of a Member in accordance with the provisions of Article 3 of this Annex fails, for a reason for which he is not responsible, to secure the employment for which he has been recruited or other suitable employment, the cost of his return and that of the members of his family who have been authorised to accompany or join him, including administrative fees, transport and maintenance charges to the final destination, and charges for the transport of household belongings, shall not fall upon the migrant.

Article 10

If the competent authority of the territory of immigration considers that the employment for which a migrant for employment was recruited under Article 3 of this Annex has been found to be unsuitable, it shall take appropriate measures to assist him in finding suitable employment which does not prejudice national workers and shall take such steps as will ensure his maintenance pending placing in such employment, or his return to the area of recruitment if the migrant is willing or agreed to such return at the time of his recruitment, or his resettlement elsewhere.

Article 11

If a migrant for employment who is a refugee or a displaced person and who has entered a territory of immigration in accordance with Article 3 of this Annex becomes redundant in any employment in that territory, the competent authority of that territory shall use its best endeavours to enable him to obtain suitable employment which does not prejudice national workers, and shall take such steps as will ensure his maintenance pending placing in suitable employment or his resettlement elsewhere.

Article 12

1. The competent authorities of the territories concerned shall enter into agreements for the purpose of regulating matters of common concern arising in connection with the application of the provisions of this Annex.

2. Where the Members maintain a system of supervision over contracts of employment, such agreements shall indicate the methods by which the contractual obligations of the employer shall be enforced.

3. Such agreements shall provide, where appropriate, for co-operation between the competent authority of the territory of emigration or a body established in accordance with the terms of an international instrument and the competent authority of the territory of immigration, in respect of the assistance to be given to migrants concerning their conditions of employment in virtue of the provisions of Article 8.

Article 13

Any person who promotes clandestine or illegal immigration shall be subject to appropriate penalties.

ANNEX III

importation of the personal effects, tools and equipment of migrants for employment

Article 1

1. Personal effects belonging to recruited migrants for employment and members of their families who have been authorised to accompany or join them shall be exempt from customs duties on arrival in the territory of immigration.

2. Portable hand-tools and portable equipment of the kind normally owned by workers for the carrying out of their particular trades belonging to recruited migrants for employment and members of their families who have been authorised to accompany or join them shall be exempt from customs duties on arrival in the territory of immigration if such tools and equipment can be shown at the time of importation to be in their actual ownership or possession, to have been in their possession and use for an appreciable time, and to be intended to be used by them in the course of their occupation

Article 2

1. Personal effects belonging to migrants for employment and members of their families who have been authorised to accompany or join them shall be exempt from customs duties on the return of the said persons to their country of origin if such persons have retained the nationality of that country at the time of their return there.

2. Portable hand-tools and portable equipment of the kind normally owned by workers for the carrying out of their particular trades belonging to migrants for employment and members of their families who have been authorised to accompany or join them shall be exempt from customs duties on return of the said persons to their country of origin if such persons have retained the nationality of that country at the time of their return there and if such tools and equipment can be shown at the time of importation to be in their actual ownership or possession, to have been in their possession and use for an appreciable time, and to be intended to be used by them in the course of their occupation.

4.4.2

Migrant Workers Convention (C143) ILO, 1975[11]

The General Conference of the International Labour Organisation (...),

Considering that the Preamble of the Constitution of the International Labour Organisation assigns to it the task of protecting the interests of workers when employed in countries other than their own, and

Considering that the Declaration of Philadelphia reaffirms, among the principles on which the Organisation is based, that labour is not a commodity, and that poverty anywhere constitutes a danger to prosperity everywhere, and recognises the solemn obligation of the ILO to further programmes which will achieve in particular full employment through the transfer of labour, including for employment (...),

Considering the ILO World Employment Programme and the Employment Policy Convention and Recommendation, 1964, and emphasising the need to avoid the excessive and uncontrolled or unassisted increase of migratory movements because of their negative social and human consequences, and

Considering that in order to overcome underdevelopment and structural and chronic unemployment, the governments of many countries increasingly stress the desirability of encouraging the transfer of capital and technology rather than the transfer of workers in accordance with the needs and requests of these countries in the reciprocal interest of the countries of origin and the countries of employment, and

Considering the right of everyone to leave any country, including his own, and to enter his own country, as set forth in the Universal Declaration of Human Rights and the International Covenant on Civil and Political Rights, and

Recalling the provisions contained in the Migration for Employment Convention and Recommendation (Revised), 1949, in the Protection of Migrant Workers (Underdeveloped Countries) Recommendation, 1955, in the Employment Policy Convention and Recommendation, 1964, in the Employment Service Convention and Recommendation, 1948, and in the Fee-Charging Employment Agencies Convention (Revised), 1949, which deal with such matters as the regulation of the recruitment, introduction and placing of migrant workers, the provision of accurate information relating to migration, the minimum conditions to be enjoyed by migrants in transit and on arrival, the adoption of an active employment policy and international collaboration in these matters, and

Considering that the migration of workers due to conditions in labour markets should take place under the responsibility of official agencies for employment or in accordance with the relevant bilateral or multilateral agreements, in particular those permitting free circulation of workers, and

Considering that evidence of the existence of illicit and clandestine trafficking in labour calls for further standards specifically aimed at eliminating these abuses, and

---

[11] Convention concerning Migrations in Abusive Conditions and the Promotion of Equality of Opportunity and Treatment of Migrant Workers (C.143). Date of adoption: 24 June 1975; in force since 9 December 1978; 18 ratifications, among whom: Bosnia and Herzegovina, Cyprus, Italy, FYR Macedonia, Norway, Portugal, San Marino, Slovenia, Sweden and Yugoslavia.

Recalling the provisions of the Migration for Employment Convention (Revised), 1949, which require ratifying Members to apply to immigrants lawfully within their territory treatment not less favourable than that which they apply to their nationals in respect of a variety of matters which it enumerates, in so far as these are regulated by laws or regulations or subject to the control of administrative authorities, and

Recalling that the definition of the term 'discrimination' in the Discrimination (Employment and Occupation) Convention, 1958, does not mandatorily include distinctions on the basis of nationality, and

Considering that further standards, covering also social security, are desirable in order to promote equality of opportunity and treatment of migrant workers and, with regard to matters regulated by laws or regulations or subject to the control of administrative authorities, ensure treatment at least equal to that of nationals, and

Noting that, for the full success of action regarding the very varied problems of migrant workers, it is essential that there be close co-operation with the United Nations and other specialised agencies, and

Noting that, in the framing of the following standards, account has been taken of the work of the United Nations and of other specialised agencies and that, with a view to avoiding duplication and to ensuring appropriate co-ordination, there will be continuing co-operation in promoting and securing the application of the standards, and

Having decided upon the adoption of certain proposals with regard to migrant workers, which is the fifth item on the agenda of the session, and

Having determined that these proposals shall take the form of an international Convention supplementing the Migration for Employment Convention (Revised), 1949, and the Discrimination (Employment and Occupation) Convention, 1958,

Adopts the twenty-fourth day of June of the year one thousand nine hundred and seventy-five, the following Convention, which may be cited as the Migrant Workers (Supplementary Provisions) Convention, 1975:

PART I. MIGRATIONS IN ABUSIVE CONDITIONS

Article 1
Each Member for which this Convention is in force undertakes to respect the basic human rights of all migrant workers.

Article 2
1. Each Member for which this Convention is in force shall systematically seek to determine whether there are illegally employed migrant workers on its territory and whether there depart from, pass through or arrive in its territory any movements of migrants for employment in which the migrants are subjected during their journey, on arrival or during their period of residence and employment to conditions contravening relevant international multilateral or bilateral instruments or agreements, or national laws or regulations.
2. The representative organisations of employers and workers shall be fully consulted and enabled to furnish any information in their possession on this subject.

Article 3
Each Member shall adopt all necessary and appropriate measures, both within its jurisdiction and in collaboration with other Members:

(a) to suppress clandestine movements of migrants for employment and illegal employment of migrants, and

(b) against the organisers of illicit or clandestine movements of migrants for employment departing from, passing through or arriving in its territory, and against those who employ workers who have immigrated in illegal conditions, in order to prevent and to eliminate the abuses referred to in Article 2 of this Convention.

Article 4

In particular, Members shall take such measures as are necessary, at the national and the international level, for systematic contact and exchange of information on the subject with other States, in consultation with representative organisations of employers and workers.

Article 5

One of the purposes of the measures taken under Articles 3 and 4 of this Convention shall be that the authors of manpower trafficking can be prosecuted whatever the country from which they exercise their activities.

Article 6

1. Provision shall be made under national laws or regulations for the effective detection of the illegal employment of migrant workers and for the definition and the application of administrative, civil and penal sanctions, which include imprisonment in their range, in respect of the illegal employment of migrant workers, in respect of the organisation of movements of migrants for employment defined as involving the abuses referred to in Article 2 of this Convention, and in respect of knowing assistance to such movements, whether for profit or otherwise.

2. Where an employer is prosecuted by virtue of the provision made in pursuance of this Article, he shall have the right to furnish proof of his good faith.

Article 7

The representative organisations of employers and workers shall be consulted in regard to the laws and regulations and other measures provided for in this Convention and designed to prevent and eliminate the abuses referred to above, and the possibility of their taking initiatives for this purpose shall be recognised.

Article 8

1. On condition that he has resided legally in the territory for the purpose of employment, the migrant worker shall not be regarded as in an illegal or irregular situation by the mere fact of the loss of his employment, which shall not in itself imply the withdrawal of his authorisation of residence or, as the case may be, work permit.

2. Accordingly, he shall enjoy equality of treatment with nationals in respect in particular of guarantees of security of employment, the provision of alternative employment, relief work and retraining.

Article 9

1. Without prejudice to measures designed to control movements of migrants for employment by ensuring that migrant workers enter national territory and are admitted to employment in conformity with the relevant laws and regulations, the migrant worker shall,

in cases in which these laws and regulations have not been respected and in which his position cannot be regularised, enjoy equality of treatment for himself and his family in respect of rights arising out of past employment as regards remuneration, social security and other benefits.

2. In case of dispute about the rights referred to in the preceding paragraph, the worker shall have the possibility of presenting his case to a competent body, either himself or through a representative.

3. In case of expulsion of the worker or his family, the cost shall not be borne by them.

4. Nothing in this Convention shall prevent Members from giving persons who are illegally residing or working within the country the right to stay and to take up legal employment.

PART II. EQUALITY OF OPPORTUNITY AND TREATMENT

Article 10
Each Member for which the Convention is in force undertakes to declare and pursue a national policy designed to promote and to guarantee, by methods appropriate to national conditions and practice, equality of opportunity and treatment in respect of employment and occupation, of social security, of trade union and cultural rights and of individual and collective freedoms for persons who as migrant workers or as members of their families are lawfully within its territory.

Article 11
1. For the purpose of this Part of this Convention, the term *migrant worker* means a person who migrates or who has migrated from one country to another with a view to being employed otherwise than on his own account and includes any person regularly admitted as a migrant worker.

2. This Part of this Convention does not apply to:
(a) frontier workers;
(b) artistes and members of the liberal professions who have entered the country on a short-term basis;
(c) seamen;
(d) persons coming specifically for purposes of training or education;
(e) employees of organisations or undertakings operating within the territory of a country who have been admitted temporarily to that country at the request of their employer to undertake specific duties or assignments, for a limited and defined period of time, and who are required to leave that country on the completion of their duties or assignments.

Article 12
Each Member shall, by methods appropriate to national conditions and practice:
(a) seek the co-operation of employers' and workers' organisations and other appropriate bodies in promoting the acceptance and observance of the policy provided for in Article 10 of this Convention;
(b) enact such legislation and promote such educational programmes as may be calculated to secure the acceptance and observance of the policy;
(c) take measures, encourage educational programmes and develop other activities aimed at acquainting migrant workers as fully as possible with the policy, with their rights and

obligations and with activities designed to give effective assistance to migrant workers in the exercise of their rights and for their protection;

(d) repeal any statutory provisions and modify any administrative instructions or practices which are inconsistent with the policy;

(e) in consultation with representative organisations of employers and workers, formulate and apply a social policy appropriate to national conditions and practice which enables migrant workers and their families to share in advantages enjoyed by its nationals while taking account, without adversely affecting the principle of equality of opportunity and treatment, of such special needs as they may have until they are adapted to the society of the country of employment;

(f) take all steps to assist and encourage the efforts of migrant workers and their families to preserve their national and ethnic identity and their cultural ties with their country of origin, including the possibility for children to be given some knowledge of their mother tongue;

(g) guarantee equality of treatment, with regard to working conditions, for all migrant workers who perform the same activity whatever might be the particular conditions of their employment.

Article 13

1. A Member may take all necessary measures which fall within its competence and collaborate with other Members to facilitate the reunification of the families of all migrant workers legally residing in its territory.

2. The members of the family of the migrant worker to which this Article applies are the spouse and dependent children, father and mother.

Article 14

A Member may

(a) make the free choice of employment, while assuring migrant workers the right to geographical mobility, subject to the conditions that the migrant worker has resided lawfully in its territory for the purpose of employment for a prescribed period not exceeding two years or, if its laws or regulations provide for contracts for a fixed term of less than two years, that the worker has completed his first work contract;

(b) after appropriate consultation with the representative organisations of employers and workers, make regulations concerning recognition of occupational qualifications acquired outside its territory, including certificates and diplomas;

(c) restrict access to limited categories of employment or functions where this is necessary in the interests of the State.

PART III. FINAL PROVISIONS

Article 15

This Convention does not prevent Members from concluding multilateral or bilateral agreements with a view to resolving problems arising from its application.

Article 16

1. Any Member which ratifies this Convention may, by a declaration appended to its ratification, exclude either Part I or Part II from its acceptance of the Convention.

2. Any Member which has made such a declaration may at any time cancel that declaration by a subsequent declaration.

3. Every Member for which a declaration made under paragraph 1 of this Article is in force shall indicate in its reports upon the application of this Convention the position of its law and practice in regard to the provisions of the Part excluded from its acceptance, the extent to which effect has been given, or is proposed to be given, to the said provision and the reasons for which it has not yet included them in its acceptance of the Convention.

Article 17

The formal ratifications of this Convention shall be communicated to the Director-General of the International Labour Office for registration.

Article 18

1. This Convention shall be binding only upon those Members of the International Labour Organisation whose ratifications have been registered with the Director-General.

2. It shall come into force twelve months after the date on which the ratifications of two Members have been registered with the Director-General.

3. Thereafter, this Convention shall come into force for any Member twelve months after the date on which its ratifications has been registered.

Article 19

1. A Member which has ratified this Convention may denounce it after the expiration of ten years from the date on which the Convention first comes into force, by an Act communicated to the Director-General of the International Labour Office for registration. Such denunciation should not take effect until one year after the date on which it is registered.

2. Each Member which has ratified this Convention and which does not, within the year following the expiration of the period of ten years mentioned in the preceding paragraph, exercise the right of denunciation provided for in this Article, will be bound for another period of ten years and, thereafter, may denounce this Convention at the expiration of each period of ten years under the terms provided for in this Article.

Article 20
(on ratifications)

Article 21
(on ratifications)

Article 22

At such times as may consider necessary the Governing Body of the International Labour Office shall present to the General Conference a report on the working of this Convention and shall examine the desirability of placing on the agenda of the Conference the question of its revision in whole or in part.

Article 23

1. Should the Conference adopt a new Convention revising this Convention in whole or in part, then, unless the new Convention otherwise provides:

a) the ratification by a Member of the new revising Convention shall ipso jure involve the immediate denunciation of this Convention, notwithstanding the provisions of Article 19 above, if and when the new revising Convention shall have come into force;

b) as from the date when the new revising Convention comes into force this Convention shall cease to be open to ratification by the Members.

2. This Convention shall in any case remain in force in its actual form and content for those Members which have ratified it but have not ratified the revising Convention.

Article 24
The English and French versions of the text of this Convention are equally authoritative.

4.4.3
Recommendation Concerning Migrant Workers 1975 (R151)[12]

The General Conference of the International Labour Organisation,

Having been convened at Geneva by the Governing Body of the International Labour Office, and having met in its Sixtieth Session on 4 June 1975, and

Considering that the Preamble of the Constitution of the International Labour Organisation assigns to it the task of protecting the interests of workers when employed in countries other than their own, and

Recalling the provisions contained in the Migration for Employment Convention and Recommendation (Revised), 1949, and in the Protection of Migrant Workers (Underdeveloped Countries) Recommendation, 1955, which deal with such matters as the preparation and organisation of migration, social services to be provided to migrant workers and their families, in particular before their departure and during their journey, equality of treatment as regards a variety of matters which they enumerate, and the regulation of the stay and return of migrant workers and their families, and

Having adopted the Migrant Workers (Supplementary Provisions) Convention, 1975, and

Considering that further standards are desirable as regards equality of opportunity and treatment, social policy in regard to migrants and employment and residence, and

Having decided upon the adoption of certain proposals with regard to migrant workers, which is the fifth item on the agenda of the session, and

Having determined that these proposals shall take the form of a Recommendation,

Adopts this twenty-fourth day of June of the year one thousand nine hundred and seventy-five, the following Recommendation, which may be cited as the Migrant Workers Recommendation, 1975:

---

[12] Adopted on 24 June 1975 in Geneva.

1. Members should apply the provision of this Recommendation within the framework of a coherent policy on international migration for employment. That policy should be based upon the economic and social needs of both countries of origin and countries of employment; it should take account not only of short-term manpower needs and resources but also of the long-term social and economic consequences of migration for migrants as well as for the communities concerned.

I. EQUALITY OF OPPORTUNITY AND TREATMENT

2. Migrant workers and members of their families lawfully within the territory of a Member should enjoy effective equality of opportunity and treatment with nationals of the Member concerned in respect of
(a) access to vocational guidance and placement services;
(b) access to vocational training and employment of their own choice on the basis of individual suitability for such training or employment, account being taken of qualifications acquired outside the territory of and in the country of employment;
(c) advancement in accordance with their individual character, experience, ability and diligence;
(d) security of employment, the provision of alternative employment, relief work and retraining;
(e) remuneration for work of equal value;
(f) conditions of work, including hours of work, rest periods, annual holidays with pay, occupational safety and occupational health measures, as well as social security measures and welfare facilities and benefits provided in connection with employment;
(g) membership of trade unions, exercise of trade union rights and eligibility for office in trade unions and in labour-management relations bodies, including bodies representing workers in undertakings;
(h) rights of full membership in any form of co-operative;
(i) conditions of life, including housing and the benefits of social services and educational and health facilities.

3. Each Member should ensure the application of the principles set forth in Paragraph 2 of this Recommendation in all activities under the control of a public authority and promote its observance in all other activities by methods appropriate to national conditions and practice.

4. Appropriate measures should be taken, with the collaboration of employers' and workers' organisations and other bodies concerned, with a view to
(a) fostering public understanding and acceptance of the above-mentioned principles;
(b) examining complaints that these principles are not being observed and securing the correction, by conciliation of other appropriate means, of any practices regarded as in conflict therewith.

5. Each Member should ensure that national laws and regulations concerning residence in its territory are so applied that the lawful exercise of rights enjoyed in pursuance of these principles cannot be the reason for non-renewal of a residence permit or for expulsion and is not inhibited by the threat of such measures.

6. A Member may

(a) make the free choice of employment, while assuring migrant workers the right to geographical mobility, subject to the conditions that the migrant worker has resided lawfully in its territory for the purpose of employment for a prescribed period not exceeding two years or, if its laws or regulations provide for contracts for a fixed term of less than two years, that the worker has completed his first work contract;

(b) after appropriate consultation with the representative organisations of employers and workers, make regulations concerning recognition of occupational qualifications acquired outside its territory, including certificates and diplomas;

(c) restrict access to limited categories of employment or functions where this is necessary in the interests of the State.

7. (1) In order to enable migrant workers and their families to take full advantage of their rights and opportunities in employment and occupation, such measures as may be necessary should be taken, in consultation with the representative organisations of employers and workers

(a) to inform them, as far as possible in their mother tongue or, if that is not possible, in a language with which they are familiar, of their rights under national law and practice as regards the matters dealt with in Paragraph 2 of this Recommendation;

(b) to advance their knowledge of the language or languages of the country of employment, as far as possible during paid time;

(c) generally, to promote their adaptation to the society of the country of employment and to assist and encourage the efforts of migrant workers and their families to preserve their national and ethnic identity and their cultural ties with their country of origin, including the possibility for children to be given some knowledge of their mother tongue.

(2) Where agreements concerning the collective recruitment of workers have been concluded between Members, they should jointly take the necessary measures before the migrants' departure from their country of origin to introduce them to the language of the country of employment and also to its economic, social and cultural environment.

8. (1) Without prejudice to measures designed to ensure that migrant workers and their families enter national territory and are admitted to employment in conformity with the relevant laws and regulations, a decision should be taken as soon as possible in cases in which these laws and regulations have not been respected so that the migrant worker should know whether his position can be regularised or not.

(2) Migrant workers whose position has been regularised should benefit from all rights which, in accordance with Paragraph 2 of this Recommendation, are provided for migrant workers lawfully within the territory of a Member.

(3) Migrant workers whose position has not been or could not be regularised should enjoy equality of treatment for themselves and their families in respect of rights arising out of present and past employment as regards remuneration, social security and other benefits as well as regards trade union membership and exercise of trade union rights.

(4) In case of dispute about the rights referred to in the preceding sub-paragraphs, the worker should have the possibility of presenting his case to a competent body, either himself or through a representative.

(5) In case of expulsion of the worker or his family, the cost should not be borne by them.

II. SOCIAL POLICY

9. Each Member should, in consultation with representative organisations of employers and workers, formulate and apply a social policy appropriate to national conditions and practice which enables migrant workers and their families to share in advantages enjoyed by its nationals while taking account, without adversely affecting the principle of equality of opportunity and treatment, of such special needs as they may have until they are adapted to the society of the country of employment.

10. With a view to making the policy as responsive as possible to the real needs of migrant workers and their families, it should be based, in particular, on an examination not only of conditions in the territory of the Member but also of those in the countries of origin of the migrants.

11. The policy should take account of the need to spread the social cost of migration as widely and equitably as possible over the entire collectivity of the country of employment, and in particular over those who profit most from the work of migrants.

12. The policy should be periodically reviewed and evaluated and where necessary revised.

II. A. REUNIFICATION OF FAMILIES

13. (1) All possible measures should be taken both by countries of employment and by countries of origin to facilitate the reunification of families of migrant workers as rapidly as possible. These measures should include, as necessary, national laws or regulations and bilateral and multilateral arrangements.
(2) A prerequisite for the reunification of families should be that the worker has, for his family, appropriate accommodation which meets the standards normally applicable to nationals of the country of employment.

14. Representatives of all concerned, and in particular of employers and workers, should be consulted on the measures to be adopted to facilitate the reunification of families and their co-operation sought in giving effect thereto.

15. For the purpose of the provisions of this Recommendation relating to the reunification of families, the family of the migrant worker should include the spouse and dependent children, father and mother.

16. With a view to facilitating the reunification of families as quickly as possible in accordance with Paragraph 13 of this Recommendation, each Member should take full account of the needs of migrant workers and their families in particular in its policy regarding the construction of family housing, assistance in obtaining this housing and the development of appropriate reception services.

17. Where a migrant worker who has been employed for at least one year in a country of employment cannot be joined by his family in that country, he should be entitled:

(a) to visit the country of residence of his family during the paid annual holiday to which he is entitled under the national law and practice of the country of employment without losing during the absence from that country any acquired rights or rights in course of acquisition and, particularly, without having his employment terminated or his right to residence in the country of employment withdrawn during that period; or

(b) to be visited by his family for a period corresponding at least to the annual holiday with pay to which he is entitled.

18. Consideration should be given to the possibility of giving the migrant worker financial assistance towards the cost of the travel envisaged in the preceding Paragraph or a reduction in the normal cost of transport, for instance by the arrangement of group travel.

19. Without prejudice to more favourable provisions which may be applicable to them, persons admitted in pursuance of international arrangements for free movement of labour should have the benefit of the measures provided for in Paragraphs 13 to 18 of this Recommendation.

II. B. PROTECTION OF THE HEALTH OF MIGRANT WORKERS

20. All appropriate measures should be taken to prevent any special health risks to which migrant workers may be exposed.

21. (1) Every effort should be made to ensure that migrant workers receive training and instruction in occupational safety and occupational hygiene in connection with their practical training or other work preparation, and, as far as possible, as part thereof.

(2) In addition, a migrant worker should, during paid working hours and immediately after beginning his employment, be provided with sufficient information in his mother tongue or, if that is not possible, in a language with which he is familiar, on the essential elements of laws and regulations and on provisions of collective agreements concerning the protection of workers and the prevention of accidents as well as on safety regulations and procedures particular to the nature of the work.

22. (1) Employers should take all possible measures so that migrant workers may fully understand instructions, warnings, symbols and other signs relating to safety and health hazards at work.

(2) Where, on account of the migrant workers' lack of familiarity with processes, language difficulties or other reasons, the training or instruction given to other workers is inadequate for them, special measures which ensure their full understanding should be taken.

(3) Members should have laws or regulations applying the principles set out in this Paragraph and provide that where employers or other persons or organisations having responsibility in this regard fail to observe such laws or regulations, administrative, civil and penal sanctions might be imposed.

II. C. SOCIAL SERVICES

23. In accordance with the provisions of Paragraph 2 of this Recommendation, migrant workers and their families should benefit from the activities of social services and have access thereto under the same conditions as nationals of the country of employment.

24. In addition, social services should be provided which perform, in particular, the following functions in relation to migrant workers and their families—
(a) giving migrant workers and their families every assistance in adapting to the economic, social and cultural environment of the country of employment;
(b) helping migrant workers and their families to obtain information and advice from appropriate bodies, for instance by providing interpretation and translation services; to comply with administrative and other formalities; and to make full use of services and facilities provided in such fields as education, vocational training and language training, health services and social security, housing, transport and recreation: Provided that migrant workers and their families should as far as possible have the right to communicate with public authorities in the country of employment in their own language or in a language with which they are familiar, particularly in the context of legal assistance and court proceedings;
(c) assisting authorities and bodies with responsibilities relating to the conditions of life and work of migrant workers and their families in laws and regulations have not been respected so that the migrant worker should know whether his position can be regularised or not. identifying their needs and in adapting thereto;
(d) giving the competent authorities information and, as appropriate, advice regarding the formulation, implementation and evaluation of social policy with respect to migrant workers;
(e) providing information for fellow workers and foremen and supervisors about the situation and the problems of migrant workers.

25. (1) The social services referred to in Paragraph 24 of this Recommendation may be provided, as appropriate to national conditions and practice, by public authorities, by approved non-profit-making organisations or bodies, or by a combination of both. The public authorities should have the over-all responsibility of ensuring that these social services are at the disposal of migrant workers and their families.
(2) Full use should be made of services which are or can be provided by authorities, organisations and bodies serving the nationals of the country of employment, including employers' and workers' organisations.

26. Each Member should take such measures as may be necessary to ensure that sufficient resources and adequately trained staff are available for the social services referred to in Paragraph 24 of this Recommendation.

27. Each Member should promote co-operation and co-ordination between different social services on its territory and, as appropriate, between these services and corresponding services in other countries, without, however, this co-operation and co-ordination relieving the States of their responsibilities in this field.

28. Each Member should organise and encourage the organisation, at the national, regional or local level, or as appropriate in a branch of economic activity employing substantial numbers of migrant workers, of periodic meetings for the exchange of information and experience. Consideration should also be given to the exchange of information and experience with other countries of employment as well as with the countries of origin of migrant workers.

29. Representatives of all concerned and in particular of employers and workers should be consulted on the organisation of the social services in question and their co-operation sought in achieving the purposes aimed at.

III. EMPLOYMENT AND RESIDENCE

30. In pursuance of the provision of Paragraph 18 of the Migration for Employment Recommendation (Revised), 1949, that Members should, as far as possible, refrain from removing from their territory, on account of lack of means or the state of the employment market, a migrant worker regularly admitted thereto, the loss by such migrant worker of his employment should not in itself imply the withdrawal of his authorisation of residence.

31. A migrant who has lost his employment should be allowed sufficient time to find alternative employment, at least for a period corresponding to that during which he may be entitled to unemployment benefit; the authorisation of residence should be extended accordingly.

32. (1) A migrant worker who has lodged an appeal against the termination of his employment, under such procedures as may be available, should be allowed sufficient time to obtain a final decision thereon.
(2) If it is established that the termination of employment was not justified, the migrant worker should be entitled, on the same terms as national workers, to reinstatement, to compensation for loss of wages or of other payment which results from unjustified termination, or to access to a new job with a right to indemnification. If he is not reinstated, he should be allowed sufficient time to find alternative employment.

33. A migrant worker who is the object of an expulsion order should have a right of appeal before an administrative or judicial instance, according to conditions laid down in national laws or regulations. This appeal should stay the execution of the expulsion order, subject to the duly substantiated requirements of national security or public order. The migrant worker should have the same right to legal assistance as national workers and have the possibility of being assisted by an interpreter.

34. (1) A migrant worker who leaves the country of employment should be entitled, irrespective of the legality of his stay therein—
(a) to any outstanding remuneration for work performed, including severance payments normally due;
(b) to benefits which may be due in respect of any employment injury suffered;
(c) in accordance with national practice

(i) to compensation in lieu of any holiday entitlement acquired but not used;

(ii) to reimbursement of any social security contributions which have not given and will not give rise to rights under national laws or regulations or international arrangements: Provided that where social security contributions do not permit entitlement to benefits, every effort should be made with a view to the conclusion of bilateral or multilateral agreements to protect the rights of migrants.

(2) Where any claim covered in subparagraph (1) of this Paragraph is in dispute, the worker should be able to have his interests represented before the competent body and enjoy equal treatment with national workers as regards legal assistance.

UN   4.5

4.5.1

Declaration on the Human Rights of Individuals Who are Not Nationals of the Country in Which They Live[13]

The General Assembly,

Considering that the Charter of the United Nations encourages universal respect for and observance of the human rights and fundamental freedoms of all human beings, without distinction as to race, sex, language or religion,

Considering that the Universal Declaration of Human Rights proclaims that all human beings are born free and equal in dignity and rights and that everyone is entitled to all the rights and freedoms set forth in that Declaration, without distinction of any kind, such as race, colour, sex, language, religion, political or other opinion, national or social origin, property, birth or other status,

Considering that the Universal Declaration of Human Rights proclaims further that everyone has the right to recognition everywhere as a person before the law, that all are equal before the law and entitled without any discrimination to equal protection of the law, and that all are entitled to equal protection against any discrimination in violation of that Declaration and against any incitement to such discrimination,

Being aware that the States parties to the International Covenants on Human Rights undertake to guarantee that the rights enunciated in these Covenants will be exercised without discrimination of any kind as to race, colour, sex, language, religion, political or other opinion, national or social origin, property, birth or other status,

Conscious that, with improving communications and the development of peaceful and friendly relations among countries, individuals increasingly live in countries of which they are not nationals,

Reaffirming the purposes and principles of the Charter of the United Nations,

Recognizing that the protection of human rights and fundamental freedoms provided for

---

[13] A/RES/40/144, 13 December 1985, 116th plenary meeting.

in international instruments should also be ensured for individuals who are not nationals of the country in which they live,
Proclaims this Declaration:

Article 1
For the purposes of this Declaration, the term 'alien' shall apply, with due regard to qualifications made in subsequent articles, to any individual who is not a national of the State in which he or she is present.

Article 2
1. Nothing in this Declaration shall be interpreted as legitimizing the illegal entry into and presence in a State of any alien, nor shall any provision be interpreted as restricting the right of any State to promulgate laws and regulations concerning the entry of aliens and the terms and conditions of their stay or to establish differences between nationals and aliens. However, such laws and regulations shall not be incompatible with the international legal obligations of that State, including those in the field of human rights.
2. This Declaration shall not prejudice the enjoyment of the rights accorded by domestic law and of the rights which under international law a State is obliged to accord to aliens, even where this Declaration does not recognize such rights or recognizes them to a lesser extent.

Article 3
Every State shall make public its national legislation or regulations affecting aliens.

Article 4
Aliens shall observe the laws of the State in which they reside or are present and regard with respect the customs and traditions of the people of that State.

Article 5
1. Aliens shall enjoy, in accordance with domestic law and subject to the relevant international obligations of the State in which they are present, in particular the following rights:
The right to life and security of person; no alien shall be subjected to arbitrary arrest or detention; no alien shall be deprived of his or her liberty except on such grounds and in accordance with such procedures as are established by law;
The right to protection against arbitrary or unlawful interference with privacy, family, home or correspondence;
The right to be equal before the courts, tribunals and all other organs and authorities administering justice and, when necessary, to free assistance of an interpreter in criminal proceedings and, when prescribed by law, other proceedings;
The right to choose a spouse, to marry, to found a family;
The right to freedom of thought, opinion, conscience and religion; the right to manifest their religion or beliefs, subject only to such limitations as are prescribed by law and are necessary to protect public safety, order, health or morals or the fundamental rights and freedoms of others;
The right to retain their own language, culture and tradition;
The right to transfer abroad earnings, savings or other personal monetary assets, subject to domestic currency regulations.

2. Subject to such restrictions as are prescribed by law and which are necessary in a democratic society to protect national security, public safety, public order, public health or morals or the rights and freedoms of others, and which are consistent with the other rights recognized in the relevant international instruments and those set forth in this Declaration, aliens shall enjoy the following rights:

The right to leave the country;

The right to freedom of expression;

The right to peaceful assembly;

The right to own property alone as well as in association with others, subject to domestic law.

3. Subject to the provisions referred to in paragraph 2, aliens lawfully in the territory of a State shall enjoy the right to liberty of movement and freedom to choose their residence within the borders of the State.

4. Subject to national legislation and due authorization, the spouse and minor or dependent children of an alien lawfully residing in the territory of a State shall be admitted to accompany, join and stay with the alien.

Article 6

No alien shall be subjected to torture or to cruel, inhuman or degrading treatment or punishment and, in particular, no alien shall be subjected without his or her free consent to medical or scientific experimentation.

Article 7

An alien lawfully in the territory of a State may be expelled therefrom only in pursuance of a decision reached in accordance with law and shall, except where compelling reasons of national security otherwise require, be allowed to submit the reasons why he or she should not be expelled and to have the case reviewed by, and be represented for the purpose before, the competent authority or a person or persons specially designated by the competent authority. Individual or collective expulsion of such aliens on grounds of race, colour, religion, culture, descent or national or ethnic origin is prohibited.

Article 8

1. Aliens lawfully residing in the territory of a State shall also enjoy, in accordance with the national laws, the following rights, subject to their obligations under article 4:

The right to safe and healthy working conditions, to fair wages and equal remuneration for work of equal value without distinction of any kind, in particular, women being guaranteed conditions of work not inferior to those enjoyed by men, with equal pay for equal work;

The right to join trade unions and other organizations or associations of their choice and to participate in their activities. No restrictions may be placed on the exercise of this right other than those prescribed by law and which are necessary, in a democratic society, in the interests of national security or public order or for the protection of the rights and freedoms of others;

The right to health protection, medical care, social security, social services, education, rest and leisure, provided that they fulfil the requirements under the relevant regulations for participation and that undue strain is not placed on the resources of the State.

2. With a view to protecting the rights of aliens carrying on lawful paid activities in the

country in which they are present, such rights may be specified by the Governments concerned in multilateral or bilateral conventions.

Article 9
No alien shall be arbitrarily deprived of his or her lawfully acquired assets.

Article 10
Any alien shall be free at any time to communicate with the consulate or diplomatic mission of the State of which he or she is a national or, in their absence, with the consulate or diplomatic mission of any other State entrusted with the protection of the interests of the State of which he or she is a national in the State where he or she resides.

4.5.2

Convention on the Protection of the Rights of All Migrant Workers and Members of Their Families, 1990[14]

PREAMBLE

The States Parties to the present Convention,

Taking into account the principles embodied in the basic instruments of the United Nations concerning human rights, in particular the Universal Declaration of Human Rights, the International Covenant on Economic, Social and Cultural Rights, the International Covenant on Civil and Political Rights, the International Convention on the Elimination of All Forms of Racial Discrimination, the Convention on the Elimination of All Forms of Discrimination against Women and the Convention on the Rights of the Child,

Taking into account also the principles and standards set forth in the relevant instruments elaborated within the framework of the International Labour Organisation, especially the Convention concerning Migration for Employment (No. 97), the Convention concerning Migrations in Abusive Conditions and the Promotion of Equality of Opportunity and Treatment of Migrant Workers (No.143), the Recommendation concerning Migration for Employment (No. 86), the Recommendation concerning Migrant Workers (No.151), the Convention concerning Forced or Compulsory Labour (No. 29) and the Convention concerning Abolition of Forced Labour (No. 105),

---

[14] The Convention, which was adopted as an Annex to General Assembly Resolution ARES/45/158 on 18 December 1990 has as yet not entered into force. As per Art. 87, twenty instruments of ratification or accession are needed for this Convention to enter into force. Early January 2001, only fifteen such instrument had been received (among whom Azerbaijan, Bosnia-Herzegovina and Morocco); ten others had signed it (among whom Turkey). It is nevertheless foreseen that by 2002 this Convention may attain the desired official status, albeit only between the Contracting Parties. No EU Member State is expected to sign up and/or to accede. In spite of Europe's 'enthousiasm' it has been decided to include this text in this Handbook *in toto*, as many UN documents and instruments refer to it.

Reaffirming the importance of the principles contained in the Convention against Discrimination in Education of the United Nations Educational, Scientific and Cultural Organization,

Recalling the Convention against Torture and Other Cruel, Inhuman or Degrading Treatment or Punishment, the Declaration of the Fourth United Nations Congress on the Prevention of Crime and the Treatment of Offenders, the Code of Conduct for Law Enforcement Officials, and the Slavery Conventions,

Recalling that one of the objectives of the International Labour Organisation, as stated in its Constitution, is the protection of the interests of workers when employed in countries other than their own, and bearing in mind the expertise and experience of that organization in matters related to migrant workers and members of their families,

Recognizing the importance of the work done in connection with migrant workers and members of their families in various organs of the United Nations, in particular in the Commission on Human Rights and the Commission for Social Development, and in the Food and Agriculture Organization of the United Nations, the United Nations Educational, Scientific and Cultural Organization and the World Health Organization, as well as in other international organizations,

Recognizing also the progress made by certain States on a regional or bilateral basis towards the protection of the rights of migrant workers and members of their families, as well as the importance and usefulness of bilateral and multilateral agreements in this field,

Realizing the importance and extent of the migration phenomenon, which involves millions of people and affects a large number of States in the international community,

Aware of the impact of the flows of migrant workers on States and people concerned, and desiring to establish norms which may contribute to the harmonization of the attitudes of States through the acceptance of basic principles concerning the treatment of migrant workers and members of their families,

Considering the situation of vulnerability in which migrant workers and members of their families frequently-find themselves owing, among other things, to their absence from their State of origin and to the difficulties they may encounter arising from their presence in the State of employment,

Convinced that the rights of migrant workers and members of their families have not been sufficiently recognized everywhere and therefore require appropriate international protection,

Taking into account the fact that migration is often the cause of serious problems for the members of the families of migrant workers as well as for the workers themselves, in particular because of the scattering of the family,

Bearing in mind that the human problems involved in migration are even more serious in the case of irregular migration and convinced therefore that appropriate action should be encouraged in order to prevent and eliminate clandestine movements and trafficking in migrant workers, while at the same time assuring the protection of their fundamental human rights,

Considering that workers who are non-documented or in an irregular situation are frequently employed under less favourable conditions of work than other workers and that certain employers find this an inducement to seek such labour in order to reap the benefits of unfair competition,

Considering also that recourse to the employment of migrant workers who are in an irregular situation will be discouraged if the fundamental human rights of all migrant workers are more widely recognized and, moreover, that granting certain additional rights to migrant workers and members of their families in a regular situation will encourage all migrants and employers to respect and comply with the laws and procedures established by the States concerned,

Convinced, therefore, of the need to bring about the international protection of the rights of all migrant workers and members of their families, reaffirming and establishing basic norms in a comprehensive convention which could be applied universally,

Have agreed as follows:

PART I: SCOPE AND DEFINITIONS

Article 1
1. The present Convention is applicable, except as otherwise provided hereafter, to all migrant workers and members of their families without distinction of any kind such as sex, race, colour, language, religion or conviction, political or other opinion, national, ethnic or social origin, nationality, age, economic position, property, marital status, birth or other status.
2. The present Convention shall apply during the entire migration process of migrant workers and members of their families, which comprises preparation for migration, departure, transit and the entire period of stay and remunerated activity in the State of employment as well as return to the State of origin or the State of habitual residence.

Article 2
For the purposes of the present Convention:
1. The term 'migrant worker' refers to a person who is to be engaged, is engaged or has been engaged in a remunerated activity in a State of which he or she is not a national.
2. (a) The term 'frontier worker' refers to a migrant worker who retains his or her habitual residence in a neighbouring State to which he or she normally returns every day or at least once a week;
(b) The term 'seasonal worker' refers to a migrant worker whose work by its character is dependent on seasonal conditions and is performed only during part of the year;
(c) The term 'seafarer', which includes a fisherman, refers to a migrant worker employed on board a vessel registered in a State of which he or she is not a national;
(d) The term 'worker on an offshore installation' refers to a migrant worker employed on an offshore installation that is under the jurisdiction of a State of which he or she is not a national;
(e) The term 'itinerant worker'' refers to a migrant worker who, having his or her habitual residence in one State, has to travel to another State or States for short periods, owing to the nature of his or her occupation;
(f) The term 'project-tied worker' refers to a migrant worker admitted to a State of employment for a defined period to work solely on a specific project being carried out in that State by his or her employer;
(g) The term 'specified-employment worker' refers to a migrant worker:
(i) Who has been sent by his or her employer for a restricted and defined period of time to a State of employment to undertake a specific assignment or duty; or
(ii) Who engages for a restricted and defined period of time in work that requires professional, commercial, technical or other highly specialized skill; or

(iii) Who, upon the request of his or her employer in the State of employment, engages for a restricted and defined period of time in work whose nature is transitory or brief; and who is required to depart from the State of employment either at the expiration of his or her authorized period of stay, or earlier if he or she no longer undertakes that specific assignment or duty or engages in that work;

(h) The term 'self-employed worker' refers to a migrant worker who is engaged in a remunerated activity otherwise than under acontract of employment and who earns his or her living through this activity normally working alone or together with members of his or her family, and to any other migrant worker recognized as self-employed by applicable legislation of the State of employment or bilateral or multilateral agreements.

Article 3

The present Convention shall not apply to:

(a) Persons sent or employed by international organizations and agencies or persons sent or employed by a State outside its territory to perform official functions, whose admission and status are regulated by general international law or by specific international agreements or conventions;

(b) Persons sent or employed by a State or on its behalf outside its territory who participate in development programmes and other co-operation programmes, whose admission and status are regulated by agreement with the State of employment and who, in accordance with that agreement, are not considered migrant workers;

(c) Persons taking up residence in a State different from their State of origin as investors;

(d) Refugees and stateless persons, unless such application is provided for in the relevant national legislation of, or international instruments in force for, the State Party concerned;

(e) Students and trainees;

(f) Seafarers and workers on an offshore installation who have not been admitted to take up residence and engage in a remunerated activity in the State of employment.

Article 4

For the purposes of the present Convention the term 'members of the family' refers to persons married to migrant workers or having with them a relationship that, according to applicable law, produces effects equivalent to marriage, as well as their dependent children and other dependent persons who are recognized as members of the family by applicable legislation or applicable bilateral or multilateral agreements between the States concerned.

Article 5

For the purposes of the present Convention, migrant workers and members of their families:

(a) Are considered as documented or in a regular situation if they are authorized to enter, to stay and to engage in a remunerated activity in the State of employment pursuant to the law of that State and to international agreements to which that State is a party;

(b) Are considered as non-documented or in an irregular situation if they do not comply with the conditions provided for in subparagraph (a) of the present article.

Article 6

For the purposes of the present Convention:

(a) The term 'State of origin' means the State of which the person concerned is a national;

(b) The term 'State of employment' means a State where the migrant worker is to be engaged, is engaged or has been engaged in a remunerated activity, as the case may be;

(c) The term 'State of transit,' means any State through which the person concerned passes on any journey to the State of employment or from the State of employment to the State of origin or the State of habitual residence.

PART II: NON-DISCRIMINATION WITH RESPECT TO RIGHTS

Article 7

States Parties undertake, in accordance with the international instruments concerning human rights, to respect and to ensure to all migrant workers and members of their families within their territory or subject to their jurisdiction the rights provided for in the present Convention without distinction of any kind such as to sex, race, colour, language, religion or conviction, political or other opinion, national, ethnic or social origin, nationality, age, economic position, property, marital status, birth or other status.

PART III: HUMAN RIGHTS OF ALL MIGRANT WORKERS AND MEMBERS OF THEIR FAMILIES

Article 8

1. Migrant workers and members of their families shall be free to leave any State, including their State of origin. This right shall not be subject to any restrictions except those that are provided by law, are necessary to protect national security, public order (*ordre public*), public health or morals or the rights and freedoms of others and are consistent with the other rights recognized in the present part of the Convention.

2. Migrant workers and members of their families shall have the right at any time to enter and remain in their State of origin.

Article 9

The right to life of migrant workers and members of their families shall be protected by law.

Article 10

No migrant worker or member of his or her family shall be subjected to torture or to cruel, inhuman or degrading treatment or punishment.

Article 11

1. No migrant worker or member of his or her family shall be held in slavery or servitude.

2. No migrant worker or member of his or her family shall be required to perform forced or compulsory labour.

3. Paragraph 2 of the present article shall not be held to preclude, in States where imprisonment with hard labour may be imposed as a punishment for a crime, the performance of hard labour in pursuance of a sentence to such punishment by a competent court.

4. For the purpose of the present article the term 'forced or compulsory labour' shall not include:

(a) Any work or service not referred to in paragraph 3 of the present article normally required of a person who is under detention in consequence of a lawful order of a court or of a person during conditional release from such detention;

(b) Any service exacted in cases of emergency or clamity threatening the life or well-being of the community;

(c) Any work or service that forms part of normal civil obligations so far as it is imposed also on citizens of the State concerned.

Article 12

1. Migrant workers and members of their families shall have the right to freedom of thought, conscience and religion. This right shall include freedom to have or to adopt a religion or belief of their choice and freedom either individually or in community with others and in public or private to manifest their religion or belief in worship, observance, practice and teaching.

2. Migrant workers and members of their families shall not be subject to coercion that would impair their freedom to have or to adopt a religion or belief of their choice.

3. Freedom to manifest one's religion or belief may be subject only to such limitations as are prescribed by law and are necessary to protect public safety, order, health or morals or the fundamental rights and freedoms of others.

4. States Parties to the present Convention undertake to have respect for the liberty of parents, at least one of whom is a migrant worker, and, when applicable, legal guardians to ensure the religious and moral education of their children in conformity with their own convictions.

Article 13

1. Migrant workers and members of their families shall have the right to hold opinions without interference.

2. Migrant workers and members of their families shall have the right to freedom of expression; this right shall include freedom to seek, receive and impart information and ideas of all kinds, regardless of frontiers, either orally, in writing or in print, in the form of art or through any other media of their choice.

3. The exercise of the right provided for in paragraph 2 of the present article carries with it special duties and responsibilities. It may therefore be subject to certain restrictions, but these shall only be such as are provided by law and are necessary:

(a) For respect of the rights or reputation of others;

(b) For the protection of the national security of the States concerned or of public order (ordre public) or of public health or morals;

(c) For the purpose of preventing any propaganda for war;

(d) For the purpose of preventing any advocacy of national, racial or religious hatred that constitutes incitement to discrimination, hostility or violence.

Article 14

No migrant worker or member of his or her family shall be subjected to arbitrary or unlawful interference with his or her privacy, family, home, correspondence or other communications, or to unlawful attacks on his or her honour and reputation. Each migrant worker and member of his or her family shall have the right to the protection of the law against such interference or attacks.

Article 15

No migrant worker or member of his or her family shall be arbitrarily deprived of property, whether owned individually or in association with others. Where, under the legislation in force in the State of employment, the assets of a migrant worker or a member of his or her family are expropriated in whole or in part, the person concerned shall have the right to fair and adequate compensation.

Article 16

1. Migrant workers and members of their families shall have the right to liberty and security of person.

2. Migrant workers and members of their families shall be entitled to effective protection by the State against violence, physical injury, threats and intimidation, whether by public officials or by private individuals, groups or institutions.

3. Any verification by law enforcement officials of the identity of migrant workers or members of their families shall be carried out in accordance with procedure established by law.

4. Migrant workers and members of their families shall not be subjected individually or collectively to arbitrary arrest or detention; they shall not be deprived o their liberty except on such grounds and in accordance with such procedures as are established by law.

5. Migrant workers and members of their families who are arrested shall be informed at the time of arrest as far as possible in a language they understand of the reasons for their arrest and they shall be promptly informed in a language they understand of any charges against them.

6. Migrant workers and members of their families who are arrested or detained on a criminal charge shall be brought promptly before a judge or other officer authorized by law to exercise judicial power and shall be entitled to trial within a reasonable time or to release. It shall not be the general rule that while awaiting trial they shall be detained in custody, but release may be subject to guarantees to appear for trial, at any other stage of the judicial proceedings and, should the occasion arise, for the execution of the judgement.

7. When a migrant worker or a member of his or her family is arrested or committed to prison or custody pending trial or is detained in any other manner:

(a) The consular or diplomatic authorities of his or her State of origin or of a State representing the interests of that State shall, if he or she so requests, be informed without delay of his or her arrest or detention and of the reasons therefor;

(b) The person concerned shall have the right to communicate with the said authorities. Any communication by the person concerned to the said authorities shall be forwarded without delay, and he or she shall also have the right to receive communications sent by the said authorities without delay;

(c) The person concerned shall be informed without delay of this right and of rights deriving from relevant treaties, if any, applicable between the States concerned, to correspond and to meet with representatives of the said authorities and to make arrangements with them for his or her legal representation.

8. Migrant workers and members of their families who are deprived of their liberty by arrest or detention shall be entitled to take proceedings before a court, in order that that court may decide without delay on the lawfulness of their detention and order their release if the detention is not lawful. When they attend such proceedings, they shall have the assistance, if necessary without cost to them, of an interpreter, if they cannot understand or speak the language used.

9. Migrant workers and members of their families who have been victims of unlawful arrest or detention shall have an enforceable right to compensation.

Article 17

1. Migrant workers and members of their families who are deprived of their liberty shall be treated with humanity and with respect for the inherent dignity of the human person and for their cultural identity.

2. Accused migrant workers and members of their families shall, save in exceptional circumstances, be separated from convicted persons and shall be subject to separate treatment appropriate to their status as unconvicted persons. Accused juvenile persons shall be separated from adults and brought as speedily as possible for adjudication.

3. Any migrant worker or member of his or her family who is detained in a State of transit or in a State of employment for violation of provisions relating to migration shall be held, in so far as practicable, separately from convicted persons or persons detained pending trial.

4. During any period of imprisonment in pursuance of a sentence imposed by a court of law, the essential aim of the treatment of a migrant worker or a member of his or her family shall be his or her reformation and social rehabilitation. Juvenile offenders shall be separated from adults and be accorded treatment appropriate to their age and legal status.

5. During detention or imprisonment, migrant workers and members of their families shall enjoy the same rights as nationals to visits by members of their families.

6. Whenever a migrant worker is deprived of his or her liberty, the competent authorities of the State concerned shall pay attention to the problems that may be posed for members of his or her family, in particular for spouses and minor children.

7. Migrant workers and members of their families who are subjected to any form of detention or imprisonment in accordance with the law in force in the State of employment or in the State of transit shall enjoy the same rights as nationals of those States who are in the same situation.

8. If a migrant worker or a member of his or her family is detained for the purpose of verifying any infraction of provisions related to migration, he or she shall not bear any costs arising therefrom.

Article 18

1. Migrant workers and members of their families shall have the right to equality with nationals of the State concerned before the courts and tribunals. In the determination of any criminal charge against them or of their rights and obligations in a suit of law, they shall be entitled to a fair and public hearing by a competent, independent and impartial tribunal established by law.

2. Migrant workers and members of their families who are charged with a criminal offence shall have the right to be presumed innocent until proven guilty according to law.

3. In the determination of any criminal charge against them, migrant workers and members of their families shall be entitled to the following minimum guarantees:

(a) To be informed promptly and in detail in a language they understand of the nature and cause of the charge against them;

(b) To have adequate time and facilities for the preparation of their defence and to communicate with counsel of their own choosing;

(c) To be tried without undue delay;

(d) To be tried in their presence and to defend themselves in person or through legal assistance of their own choosing; to be informed, if they do not have legal assistance, of this right; and to have legal assistance assigned to them, in any case where the interests of jus-

tice so require and without payment by them in any such case if they do not have sufficient means to pay;

(e) To examine or have examined the witnesses against them and to obtain the attendance
and examination of witnesses on their behalf under the same conditions as witnesses
against them;

(f) To have the free assistance of an interpreter if they cannot understand or speak the language used in court;

(g) Not to be compelled to testify against themselves or to confess guilt.

4. In the case of juvenile persons, the procedure shall be such as will take account of their
age and the desirability of promoting their rehabilitation.

5. Migrant workers and members of their families convicted of a crime shall have the
right to their conviction and sentence being reviewed by a higher tribunal according to
law.

6. When a migrant worker or a member of his or her family has, by a final decision, been
convicted of a criminal offence and when subsequently his or her conviction has been reversed or he or she has been pardoned on the ground that a new or newly discovered fact
shows conclusively that there has been a miscarriage of justice, the person who has suffered punishment as a result of such conviction shall be compensated according to law,
unless it is proved that the non-disclosure of the unknown fact in time is wholly or partly
attributable to that person.

7. No migrant worker or member of his or her family shall be liable to be tried or punished again for an offence for which he or she has already been finally convicted or ac-
quitted in accordance with the law and penal procedure of the State concerned.

Article 19

1. No migrant worker or member of his or her family shall be held guilty of any criminal
offence on account of any act or omission that did not constitute a criminal offence under
national or international law at the time when the criminal offence was committed, nor
shall a heavier penalty be imposed than the one that was applicable at the time when it
was committed. If, subsequent to the commission of the offence, provision is made by law
for the imposition of a lighter penalty, he or she shall benefit thereby.

2. Humanitarian considerations related to the status of a migrant worker, in particular with
respect to his or her right of residence or work, should be taken into account in imposing a
sentence for a criminal offence committed by a migrant worker or a member of his or her
family.

Article 20

1. No migrant worker or member of his or her family shall be imprisoned merely on the
ground of failure to fulfil a contractual obligation.

2. No migrant worker or member of his or her family shall be deprived of his or her authorization of residence or work permit or expelled merely on the ground of failure to fulfil an obligation arising out of a work contract unless fulfilment of that obligation constitutes a condition for such authorization or permit.

Article 21

It shall be unlawful for anyone, other than a public official duly authorized by law, to confiscate, destroy or attempt to destroy identity documents, documents authorizing entry to

or stay, residence or establishment in the national territory or work permits. No authorized confiscation of such documents shall take place without delivery of a detailed receipt. In no case shall it be permitted to destroy the passport or equivalent document of a migrant worker or a member of his or her family.

Article 22

1. Migrant workers and members of their families shall not be subject to measures of collective expulsion. Each case of expulsion shall be examined and decided individually.
2. Migrant workers and members of their families may be expelled from the territory of a State Party only in pursuance of a decision taken by the competent authority in accordance with law.
3. The decision shall be communicated to them in a language they understand. Upon their request where not otherwise mandatory, the decision shall be communicated to them in writing and, save in exceptional circumstances on account of national security, the reasons for the decision likewise stated. The persons concerned shall be informed of these rights before or at the latest at the time the decision is rendered.
4. Except where a final decision is pronounced by a judicial authority, the person concerned shall have the right to submit the reason he or she should not be expelled and to have his or her case reviewed by the competent authority, unless compelling reasons of national security require otherwise. Pending such review, the person concerned shall have the right to seek a stay of the decision of expulsion.
5. If a decision of expulsion that has already been executed is subsequently annulled, the person concerned shall have the right to seek compensation according to law and the earlier decision shall not be used to prevent him or her from re-entering the State concerned.
6. In case of expulsion, the person concerned shall have a reasonable opportunity before or after departure to settle any claims for wages and other entitlements due to him or her and any pending liabilities.
7. Without prejudice to the execution of a decision of expulsion, a migrant worker or a member of his or her family who is subject to such a decision may seek entry into a State other than his or her State of origin.
8. In case of expulsion of a migrant worker or a member of his or her family the costs of expulsion shall not be borne by him or her. The person concerned may be required to pay his or her own travel costs.
9. Expulsion from the State of employment shall not in itself prejudice any rights of a migrant worker or a member of his or her family acquired in accordance with the law of that State, including the right to receive wages and other entitlements due to him or her.

Article 23

Migrant workers and members of their families shall have the right to have recourse to the protection and assistance of the consular or diplomatic authorities of their State of origin or of a State representing the interests of that State whenever the rights recognized in the present Convention are impaired. In particular, in case of expulsion, the person concerned shall be informed of this right without delay and the authorities of the expelling State shall facilitate the exercise of such right.

Article 24

Every migrant worker and every member of his or her family shall have the right to recognition everywhere as a person before the law.

Article 25

1. Migrant workers shall enjoy treatment not less favourable than that which applies to nationals of the State of employment in respect of remuneration and:

(a) Other conditions of work, that is to say, overtime, hours of work, weekly rest, holidays with pay, safety, health, termination of the employment relationship and any other conditions of work which, according to national law and practice, are covered by these terms;

(b) Other terms of employment, that is to say, minimum age of employment, restriction on home work and any other matters which, according to national law and practice, are considered a term of employment.

2. It shall not be lawful to derogate in private contracts of employment from the principle of equality of treatment referred to in paragraph 1 of the present article.

3. States Parties shall take all appropriate measures to ensure that migrant workers are not deprived of any rights derived from this principle by reason of any irregularity in their stay or employment. In particular, employers shall not be relieved of any legal or contractual obligations, nor shall their obligations be limited in any manner by reason of such irregularity.

Article 26

1. States Parties recognize the right of migrant workers and members of their families:

(a) To take part in meetings and activities of trade unions and of any other associations established in accordance with law, with a view to protecting their economic, social, cultural and other interests, subject only to the rules of the organization concerned;

(b) To join freely any trade union and any such association as aforesaid, subject only to the rules of the organization concerned;

(c) To seek the aid and assistance of any trade union and of any such association as aforesaid.

2. No restrictions may be placed on the exercise of these rights other than those that are prescribed by law and which are necessary in a democratic society in the interests of national security, public order (ordre public) or the protection of the rights and freedoms of others.

Article 27

1. With respect to social security, migrant workers and members of their families shall enjoy in the State of employment the same treatment granted to nationals in so far as they fulfil the requirements provided for by the applicable legislation of that State and the applicable bilateral and multilateral treaties. The competent authorities of the State of origin and the State of employment can at any time establish the necessary arrangements to determine the modalities of application of this norm.

2. Where the applicable legislation does not allow migrant workers and members of their families a benefit, the States concerned shall examine the possibility of reimbursing interested persons the amount of contributions made by them with respect to that benefit on the basis of the treatment granted to nationals who are in similar circumstances.

Article 28

Migrant workers and members of their families shall have the right to receive any medical care that is urgently required for the preservation of their life or the avoidance of irreparable harm to their health on the basis of equality of treatment with nationals of the State concerned. Such emergency medical care shall not be refused them by reason of any irregularity with regard to stay or employment.

Article 29
Each child of a migrant worker shall have the right to a name, to registration of birth and to a nationality.

Article 30
Each child of a migrant worker shall have the basic right of access to education on the basis of equality of treatment with nationals of the State concerned. Access to public preschool educational institutions or schools shall not be refused or limited by reason of the irregular situation with respect to stay or employment of either parent or by reason of the irregularity of the child's stay in the State of employment.

Article 31
1. States Parties shall ensure respect for the cultural identity of migrant workers and members of their families and shall not prevent them from maintaining their cultural links with their State of origin.
2. States Parties may take appropriate measures to assist and encourage efforts in this respect.

Article 32
Upon the termination of their stay in the State of employment, migrant workers and members of their families shall have the right to transfer their earnings and savings and, in accordance with the applicable legislation of the States concerned, their personal effects and belongings.

Article 33
1. Migrant workers and members of their families shall have the right to be informed by the State of origin, the State of employment or the State of transit as the case may be concerning:
(a) Their rights arising out of the present Convention;
(b) The conditions of their admission, their rights and obligations under the law and practice of the State concerned and such other matters as will enable them to comply with administrative or other formalities in that State.
2. States Parties shall take all measures they deem appropriate to disseminate the said information or to ensure that it is provided by employers, trade unions or other appropriate bodies or institutions. As appropriate, they shall co-operate with other States concerned.
3. Such adequate information shall be provided upon request to migrant workers and members of their families, free of charge, and, as far as possible, in a language they are able to understand.

Article 34
Nothing in the present part of the Convention shall have the effect of relieving migrant workers and the members of their families from either the obligation to comply with the laws and regulations of any State of transit and the State of employment or the obligation to respect the cultural identity of the inhabitants of such States.

Article 35

Nothing in the present part of the Convention shall be interpreted as implying the regularization of the situation of migrant workers or members of their families who are non-documented or in an irregular situation or any right to such regularization of their situation, nor shall it prejudice the measures intended to ensure sound and equitable-conditions for international migration as provided in part VI of the present Convention.

PART IV: OTHER RIGHTS OF MIGRANT WORKERS AND MEMBERS OF THEIR FAMILIES WHO ARE DOCUMENTED OR IN A REGULAR SITUATION

Article 36

Migrant workers and members of their families who are documented or in a regular situation in the State of employment shall enjoy the rights set forth in the present part of the Convention in addition to those set forth in part III.

Article 37

Before their departure, or at the latest at the time of their admission to the State of employment, migrant workers and members of their families shall have the right to be fully informed by the State of origin or the State of employment, as appropriate, of all conditions applicable to their admission and particularly those concerning their stay and the remunerated activities in which they may engage as well as of the requirements they must satisfy in the State of employment and the authority to which they must address themselves for any modification of those conditions.

Article 38

1. States of employment shall make every effort to authorize migrant workers and members of the families to be temporarily absent without effect upon their authorization to stay or to work, as the case may be. In doing so, States of employment shall take into account the special needs and obligations of migrant workers and members of their families, in particular in their States of origin.

2. Migrant workers and members of their families shall have the right to be fully informed of the terms on which such temporary absences are authorized.

Article 39

1. Migrant workers and members of their families shall have the right to liberty of movement in the territory of the State of employment and freedom to choose their residence there.

2. The rights mentioned in paragraph 1 of the present article shall not be subject to any restrictions except those that are provided by law, are necessary to protect national security, public order (ordre public), public health or morals, or the rights and freedoms of others and are consistent with the other rights recognized in the present Convention.

Article 40

1. Migrant workers and members of their families shall have the right to form associations and trade unions in the State of employment for the promotion and protection of their economic, social, cultural and other interests.

2. No restrictions may be placed on the exercise of this right other than those that are pre-scribed by law and are necessary in a democratic society in the interests of national secu-rity, public order (ordre public) or the protection of the rights and freedoms of others.

Article 41
1. Migrant workers and members of their families shall have the right to participate in public affairs of their State of origin and to vote and to be elected at elections of that State, in accordance with its legislation.
2. The States concerned shall, as appropriate and in accordance with their legislation, fa-cilitate the exercise of these rights.

Article 42
1. States Parties shall consider the establishment of procedures or institutions through which account may be taken, both in States of origin and in States of employment, of spe-cial needs, aspirations and obligations of migrant workers and members of their families and shall envisage, as appropriate, the possibility for migrant workers and members of their families to have their freely chosen representatives in those institutions.
2. States of employment shall facilitate, in accordance with their national legislation, the consultation or participation of migrant workers and members of their families in deci-sions concerning the life and administration of local communities.
3. Migrant workers may enjoy political rights in the State of employment if that State, in the exercise of its sovereignty, grants them such rights.

Article 43
1. Migrant workers shall enjoy equality of treatment with nationals of the State of em-ployment in relation to:
(a) Access to educational institutions and services subject to the admission requirements and other regulations of the institutions and services concerned;
(b) Access to vocational guidance and placement services;
(c) Access to vocational training and retraining facilities and institutions;
(d) Access to housing, including social housing schemes, and protection against exploita-tion in respect of rents;
(e) Access to social and health services, provided that the requirements for participation in the respective schemes are met;
(f) Access to co-operatives and self-managed enterprises, which shall not imply a change of their migration status and shall be subject to the rules and regulations of the bodies con-cerned;
(g) Access to and participation in cultural life.
2. States Parties shall promote conditions to ensure effective equality of treatment to en-able migrant workers to enjoy the rights mentioned in paragraph 1 of the present article whenever the terms of their stay, as authorized by the State of employment, meet the ap-propriate requirements.
3. States of employment shall not prevent an employer of migrant workers from establish-ing housing or social or cultural facilities for them. Subject to article 70 of the present Convention, a State of employment may make the establishment of such facilities subject to the requirements generally applied in that State concerning their installation.

Article 44

1. States Parties, recognizing that the family is the natural and fundamental group unit of society and is entitled to protection by society and the State, shall take appropriate measures to ensure the protection of the unity of the families of migrant workers.

2. States Parties shall take measures that they deem appropriate and that fall within their competence to facilitate the reunification of migrant workers with their spouses or persons who have with the migrant worker a relationship that, according to applicable law, produces effects equivalent to marriage, as well as with their minor dependent unmarried children.

3. States of employment, on humanitarian grounds, shall favourably consider granting equal treatment, as set forth in paragraph 2 of the present article, to other family members of migrant workers.

Article 45

1. Members of the families of migrant workers shall, in the State of employment, enjoy equality of treatment with nationals of that State in relation to:

(a) Access to educational institutions and services, subject to the admission requirements and other regulations of the institutions and services concerned;

(b) Access to vocational guidance and training institutions and services, provided that requirements for participation are met;

(c) Access to social and health services, provided that requirements for participation in the respective schemes are met;

(d) Access to and participation in cultural life.

2. States of employment shall pursue a policy, where appropriate in collaboration with the States of origin, aimed at facilitating the integration of children of migrant workers in the local school system, particularly in respect of teaching them the local language.

3. States of employment shall endeavour to facilitate for the children of migrant workers the teaching of their mother tongue and culture and, in this regard, States of origin shall collaborate whenever appropriate.

4. States of employment may provide special schemes of education in the mother tongue of children of migrant workers, if necessary in collaboration with the States of origin.

Article 46

Migrant workers and members of their families shall, subject to the applicable legislation of the States concerned, as well as relevant international agreements and the obligations of the States concerned arising out of their participation in customs unions, enjoy exemption from import and export duties and taxes in respect of their personal and household effects as well as the equipment necessary to engage in the remunerated activity for which they were admitted to the State of employment:

(a) Upon departure from the State of origin or State of habitual residence;

(b) Upon initial admission to the State of employment;

(c) Upon final departure from the State of employment;

(d) Upon final return to the State of origin or State of habitual residence.

Article 47

1. Migrant workers shall have the right to transfer their earnings and savings, in particular those funds necessary for the support of their families, from the State of employment to their State of origin or any other State. Such transfers shall be made in conformity with

procedures established by applicable legislation of the State concerned and in conformity with applicable international agreements.

2. States concerned shall take appropriate measures to facilitate such transfers.

Article 48

1. Without prejudice to applicable double taxation agreements, migrant workers and members of their families shall, in the matter of earnings in the State of employment:

(a) Not be liable to taxes, duties or charges of any description higher or more onerous than those imposed on nationals in similar circumstances;

(b) Be entitled to deductions or exemptions from taxes of any description and to any tax allowances applicable to nationals in similar circumstances, including tax allowances for dependent members of their families.

2. States Parties shall endeavour to adopt appropriate measures to avoid double taxation of the earnings and savings of migrant workers and members of their families.

Article 49

1. Where separate authorizations to reside and to engage in employment are required by national legislation, the States of employment shall issue to migrant workers authorization of residence for at least the same period of time as their authorization to engage in remunerated activity.

2. Migrant workers who in the State of employment are allowed freely to choose their remunerated activity shall neither be regarded as in an irregular situation nor shall they lose their authorization of residence by the mere fact of the termination of their remunerated activity prior to the expiration of their work permits or similar authorizations.

3. In order to allow migrant workers referred to in paragraph 2 of the present article sufficient time to find alternative remunerated activities, the authorization of residence shall not be withdrawn at least for a period corresponding to that during which they may be entitled to unemployment benefits.

Article 50

1. In the case of death of a migrant worker or dissolution of marriage, the State of employment shall favourably consider granting family members of that migrant worker residing in that State on the basis of family reunion an authorization to stay; the State of employment shall take into account the length of time they have already resided in that State.

2. Members of the family to whom such authorization is not granted shall be allowed before departure a reasonable period of time in order to enable them to settle their affairs in the State of employment.

3. The provisions of paragraphs I and 2 of the present article may not be interpreted as adversely affecting any right to stay and work otherwise granted to such family members by the legislation of the State of employment or by bilateral and multilateral treaties applicable to that State.

Article 51

Migrant workers who in the State of employment are not permitted freely to choose their remunerated activity shall neither be regarded as in an irregular situation nor shall they lose their authorization of residence by the mere fact of the termination of their remunerated activity prior to the expiration of their work permit, except where the authorization of residence is expressly dependent upon the specific remunerated activity for which they were admitted. Such migrant workers shall have the right to seek alternative employment, participation in public work schemes and retraining during the remaining period of their authorization to work, subject to such conditions and limitations as are specified in the authorization to work.

Article 52

1. Migrant workers in the State of employment shall have the right freely to choose their remunerated activity, subject to the following restrictions or conditions.

2. For any migrant worker a State of employment may:

(a) Restrict access to limited categories of employment, functions, services or activities where this is necessary in the interests of this State and provided for by national legislation;

(b) Restrict free choice of remunerated activity in accordance with its legislation concerning recognition of occupational qualifications acquired outside its territory. However, States Parties concerned shall endeavour to provide for recognition of such qualifications.

3. For migrant workers whose permission to work is limited in time, a State of employment may also:

(a) Make the right freely to choose their remunerated activities subject to the condition that the migrant worker has resided lawfully in its territory for the purpose of remunerated activity for a period of time prescribed in its national legislation that should not exceed two years;

(b) Limit access by a migrant worker to remunerated activities in pursuance of a policy of granting priority to its nationals or to persons who are assimilated to them for these purposes by virtue of legislation or bilateral or multilateral agreements. Any such limitation shall cease to apply to a migrant worker who has resided lawfully in its territory for the purpose of remunerated activity for a period of time prescribed in its national legislation that should not exceed five years.

4. States of employment shall prescribe the conditions under which a migrant worker who has been admitted to take up employment may be authorized to engage in work on his or her own account. Account shall be taken of the period during which the worker has already been lawfully in the State of employment.

Article 53

1. Members of a migrant worker's family who have themselves an authorization of residence or admission that is without limit of time or is automatically renewable shall be permitted freely to choose their remunerated activity under the same conditions as are applicable to the said migrant worker in accordance with article 52 of the present Convention.

2. With respect to members of a migrant worker's family who are not permitted freely to choose their remunerated activity, States Parties shall consider favourably granting them priority in obtaining permission to engage in a remunerated activity over other workers who seek admission to the State of employment, subject to applicable bilateral and multilateral agreements.

Article 54

1. Without prejudice to the terms of their authorization of residence or their permission to work and the rights provided for in articles 25 and 27 of the present Convention, migrant

workers shall enjoy equality of treatment with nationals of the State of employment in respect of:

(a) Protection against dismissal;

(b) Unemployment benefits;

(c) Access to public work schemes intended to combat unemployment;

(d) Access to alternative employment in the event of loss of work or termination of other remunerated activity, subject to article 52 of the present Convention.

2. If a migrant worker claims that the terms of his or her work contract have been violated by his or her employer, he or she shall have the right to address his or her case to the competent authorities of the State of employment, on terms provided for in article 18, paragraph 1, of the present Convention.

Article 55

Migrant workers who have been granted permission to engage in a remunerated activity, subject to the conditions attached to such permission, shall be entitled to equality of treatment with nationals of the State of employment in the exercise of that remunerated activity.

Article 56

1. Migrant workers and members of their families referred to in the present part of the Convention may not be expelled from a State of employment, except for reasons defined in the national legislation of that State, and subject to the safeguards established in part III.

2. Expulsion shall not be resorted to for the purpose of depriving a migrant worker or a member of his or her family of the rights arising out of the authorization of residence and the work permit.

3. In considering whether to expel a migrant worker or a member of his or her family, account should be taken of humanitarian considerations and of the length of time that the person concerned has already resided in the State of employment.

PART V: PROVISIONS APPLICABLE TO PARTICULAR CATEGORIES OF MIGRANT WORKERS AND OF THEIR FAMILIES

Article 57

The particular categories of migrant workers and members of their families specified in the present part of the Convention who are documented or in a regular situation shall enjoy the rights set forth in part III and, except as modified below, the rights set forth in part IV.

Article 58

1. Frontier workers, as defined in article 2, paragraph 2(a), of the present Convention, shall be entitled to the rights provided for in part IV that can be applied to them by reason of their presence and work in the territory of the State of employment, taking into account that they do not have their habitual residence in that State.

2. States of employment shall consider favourably granting frontier workers the right freely to choose their remunerated activity after a specified period of time. The granting of that right shall not affect their status as frontier workers.

Article 59

1. Seasonal workers, as defined in article 2, paragraph 2(b), of the present Convention, shall be entitled to the rights provided for in part IV that can be applied to them by reason of their presence and work in the territory of the State of employment and that are compatible with their status in that State as seasonal workers, taking into account the fact that they are present in that State for only part of the year.

2. The State of employment shall, subject to paragraph 1 of the present article, consider granting seasonal workers who have been employed in its territory for a significant period of time the possibility of taking up other remunerated activities and giving them priority over other workers who seek admission to that State, subject to applicable bilateral and multilateral agreements.

Article 60

Itinerant workers, as defined in article 2, paragraph 2(a), of the present Convention, shall be entitled to the rights provided for in part IV that can be granted to them by reason of their presence and work in the territory of the State of employment and that are compatible with their status as itinerant workers in that State.

Article 61

1. Project-tied workers, as defined in article 2, paragraph 2 (of the present Convention, and members of their families shall be entitled to the rights provided for in part IV except the provisions of article 43, paragraphs I(b) and (c), article 43, paragraph I(d), as it pertains to social housing schemes, article 45, paragraph I(b), and articles 52 to 55.

2. If a project-tied worker claims that the terms of his or her work contract have been violated by his or her employer, he or she shall have the right to address his or her case to the competent authorities of the State which has jurisdiction over that employer, on terms provided for in article 18, paragraph 1, of the present Convention.

3. Subject to bilateral or multilateral agreements in force for them, the States Parties concerned shall endeavour to enable project-tied workers to remain adequately protected by the social security systems of their States of origin or habitual residence during their engagement in the project. States Parties concerned shall take appropriate measures with the aim of avoiding any denial of rights or duplication of payments in this respect.

4. Without prejudice to the provisions of article 47 of the present Convention and to relevant bilateral or multilateral agreements, States Parties concerned shall permit payment of the earnings of project-tied workers in their State of origin or habitual residence.

Article 62

1. Specified-employment workers as defined in article 2, paragraph 2(g), of the present Convention, shall be entitled to the rights provided for in part IV, except the provisions of article 43, paragraphs I(b) and (c), article 43, paragraph I(d), as it pertains to social housing schemes, article 52, and article 54, paragraph 1(d).

2. Members of the families of specified-employment workers shall be entitled to the rights relating to family members of migrant workers provided for in part IV of the present Convention, except the provisions of article 53.

Article 63

1. Self-employed workers, as defined in article 2, paragraph 2(h), of the pre sent Convention, shall be entitled to the rights provided for in part IV with the exception of those

rights which are exclusively applicable to workers having a contract of employment.

2. Without prejudice to articles 52 and 79 of the present Convention, the termination of the economic activity of the self-employed workers shall not in itself imply the withdrawal of the authorization for them or for the members of their families to stay or to engage in a remunerated activity in the State of employment except where the authorization of residence is expressly dependent upon the specific remunerated activity for which they were admitted.

PART VI: PROMOTION OF SOUND, EQUITABLE, HUMANE AND LAWFUL CONDITIONS CONNECTION WITH INTERNATIONAL MIGRATION OF WORKERS AND MEMBERS OF THEIR FAMILIES

Article 64

1. Without prejudice to article 79 of the present Convention, the States Parties concerned shall as appropriate consult and co-operate with a view to promoting sound, equitable and humane conditions in connection with international migration of workers and members of their families.

2. In this respect, due regard shall be paid not only to labour needs and resources, but also to the social, economic, cultural and other needs of migrant workers and members of their families involved, as well as to the consequences of such migration for the communities concerned.

Article 65

1. States Parties shall maintain appropriate services to deal with questions concerning international migration of workers and members of their families. Their functions shall include, inter alia:

(a) The formulation and implementation of policies regarding such migration;

(b) An exchange of information. consultation and co-operation with the competent authorities of other States Parties involved in such migration;

(c) The provision of appropriate information, particularly to employers, workers and their organizations on policies, laws and regulations relating to migration and employment, on agreements concluded with other States concerning migration and on other relevant matters;

(d) The provision of information and appropriate assistance to migrant workers and members of their families regarding requisite authorizations and formalities and arrangements for departure, travel, arrival, stay, remunerated activities, exit and return, as well as on conditions of work and life in the State of employment and on customs, currency, tax and other relevant laws and regulations.

2. States Parties shall facilitate as appropriate the provision of adequate consular and other services that are necessary to meet the social, cultural and other needs of migrant workers and members of their families.

Article 66

1. Subject to paragraph 2 of the present article, the right to undertake operations with a view to the recruitment of workers for employment in another State shall be restricted to:

(a) Public services or bodies of the State in which such operations take place;

(b) Public services or bodies of the State of employment on the basis of agreement between the States concerned;

(c) A body established by virtue of a bilateral or multilateral agreement. 2. Subject to any authorization, approval and supervision by the public authorities of the States Parties concerned as may be established pursuant to the legislation and practice of those States, agencies, prospective employers or persons acting on their behalf may also be permitted to undertake the said operations.

Article 67

1. States Parties concerned shall co-operate as appropriate in the adoption of measures regarding the orderly return of migrant workers and members of their families to the State of origin when they decide to return or their authorization of residence or employment expires or when they are in the State of employment in an irregular situation.

2. Concerning migrant workers and members of their families in a regular situation, States Parties concerned shall co-operate as appropriate, on terms agreed upon by those States, with a view to promoting adequate economic conditions for their resettlement and to facilitating their durable social and cultural reintegration in the State of origin.

Article 68

1. States Parties, including States of transit, shall collaborate with a view to preventing and eliminating illegal or clandestine movements and employment of migrant workers in an irregular situation. The measures to be taken to this end within the jurisdiction of each State concerned shall include:

(a) Appropriate measures against the dissemination of misleading information relating to emigration and immigration;

(b) Measures to detect and eradicate illegal or clandestine movements of migrant workers and members of their families and to impose effective sanctions on persons, groups or entities which organize, operate or assist in organizing or operating such movements;

(c) Measures to impose effective sanctions on persons, groups or entities which use violence, threats or intimidation against migrant workers or members of their families in an irregular situation.

2. States of employment shall take all adequate and effective measures to eliminate employment in their territory of migrant workers in an irregular situation, including, whenever appropriate, sanctions on employers of such workers. The rights of migrant workers vis-a-vis their employer arising from employment shall not be impaired by these measures.

Article 69

1. States Parties shall, when there are migrant workers and members of their families within their territory in an irregular situation, take appropriate measures to ensure that such a situation does not persist.

2. Whenever States Parties concerned consider the possibility of regularizing the situation of such persons in accordance with applicable national legislation and bilateral or multilateral agreements, appropriate account shall be taken of the circumstances of their entry, the duration of their stay in the States of employment and other relevant considerations, in particular those relating to their family situation.

Article 70

States Parties shall take measures not less favourable than those applied to nationals to ensure that working and living conditions of migrant workers and members of their families in a regular situation are in keeping with the standards of fitness, safety, health and principles of human dignity.

Article 71

1. States Parties shall facilitate, whenever necessary, the repatriation to the State of origin of the bodies of deceased migrant workers or members of their families.

2. As regards compensation matters relating to the death of a migrant worker or a member of his or her family, States Parties shall, as appropriate, provide assistance to the persons concerned with a view to the prompt settlement of such matters. Settlement of these matters shall be carried out on the basis of applicable national law in accordance with the provisions of the present Convention and any relevant bilateral or multilateral agreements.

PART VII: APPLICATION OF THE CONVENTION

Article 72

1. (a) For the purpose of reviewing the application of the present Convention, there shall be established a Committee on the Protection of the Rights of All Migrant Workers and Members of Their Families (hereinafter referred to as 'the Committee');

(b) The Committee shall consist, at the time of entry into force of the present Convention, of ten and, after the entry into force of the Convention for the forty-first State Party, of fourteen experts of high moral standing, impartiality and recognized competence in the field covered by the Convention.

2. (a) Members of the Committee shall be elected by secret ballot by the States Parties from a list of persons nominated by the States Parties, due consideration being given to equitable geographical distribution, including both States of origin and States of employment, and to the representation of the principal legal system. Each State Party may nominate one person from among its own nationals;

(b) Members shall be elected and shall serve in their personal capacity.

3. The initial election shall be held no later than six months after the date of the entry into force of the present Convention and subsequent elections every second year. At least four months before the date of each election, the Secretary-General of the United Nations shall address a letter to all States Parties inviting them to submit their nominations within two months. The Secretary-General shall prepare a list in alphabetical order of all persons thus nominated, indicating the States Parties that have nominated them, and shall submit it to the States Parties not later than one month before the date of the corresponding election, together with the curricula vitae of the persons thus nominated.

4. Elections of members of the Committee shall be held at a meeting of States Parties convened by the Secretary-General at United Nations Headquarters. At that meeting, for which two thirds of the States Parties shall constitute a quorum, the persons elected to the Committee shall be those nominees who obtain the largest number of votes and an absolute majority of the votes of the States Parties present and voting.

5. (a) The members of the Committee shall serve for a term of four years. However, the terms of five of the members elected in the first election shall expire at the end of two years; immediately after the first election, the names of these five members shall be chosen by lot by the Chairman of the meeting of States Parties;

(b) The election of the four additional members of the Committee shall be held in accordance with the provisions of paragraphs 2, 3 and 4 of the present article, following the entry into force of the Convention for the forty-first State Party. The term of two of the additional members elected on this occasion shall expire at the end of two years; the names of these members shall be chosen by lot by the Chairman of the meeting of States Parties;

(c) The members of the Committee shall be eligible for re-election if renominated.

6. If a member of the Committee dies or resigns or declares that for any other cause he or she can no longer perform the duties of the Committee, the State Party that nominated the expert shall appoint another expert from among its own nationals for the remaining part of the term. The new appointment is subject to the approval of the Committee.

7. The Secretary-General of the United Nations shall provide the necessary staff and facilities for the effective performance of the functions of the Committee.

8. The members of the Committee shall receive emoluments from United Nations resources on such terms and conditions as the General Assembly may decide.

9. The members of the Committee shall be entitled to the facilities, privileges and immunities of experts on mission for the United Nations as laid down in the relevant sections of the Convention on the Privileges and Immunities of the United Nations.

Article 73

1. States Parties undertake to submit to the Secretary-General of the United Nations for consideration by the Committee a report on the legislative, judicial, administrative and other measures they have taken to give effect to the provisions of the present Convention:

(a) Within one year after the entry into force of the Convention for the State Party concerned;

(b) Thereafter every five years and whenever the Committee so requests.

2. Reports prepared under the present article shall also indicate factors and difficulties, if any, affecting the implementation of the Convention and shall include information on the characteristics of migration flows in which the State Party concerned is involved.

3. The Committee shall decide any further guidelines applicable to the content of the reports.

4. States Parties shall make their reports widely available to the public in their own countries.

Article 74

1. The Committee shall examine the reports submitted by each State Party and shall transmit such comments as it may consider appropriate to the State Party concerned. This State Party may submit to the Committee observations on any comment made by the Committee in accordance with the present article. The Committee may request supplementary information from States Parties when considering these reports.

2. The Secretary-General of the United Nations shall, in due time before the opening of each regular session of the Committee, transmit to the Director-General of the International Labour Office copies of the reports submitted by States Parties concerned and information relevant to the consideration of these reports, in order to enable the Office to assist the Committee with the expertise the Office may provide regarding those matters dealt with by the present Convention that fall within the sphere of competence of the International Labour Organisation. The Committee shall consider in its deliberations such comments and materials as the Office may provide.

3. The Secretary-General of the United Nations may also, after consultation with the Committee, transmit to other specialized agencies as well as to intergovernmental organizations, copies of such parts of these reports as may fall within their competence.

4. The Committee may invite the specialized agencies and organs of the United Nations, as well as intergovernmental organizations and other concerned bodies to submit, for consideration by the Committee, written information on such matters dealt with in the present Convention as fall within the scope of their activities.

5. The International Labour Office shall be invited by the Committee to appoint representatives to participate, in a consultative capacity, in the meetings of the Committee.

6. The Committee may invite representatives of other specialized agencies and organs of the United Nations, as well as of intergovernmental organizations, to be present and to be heard in its meetings whenever matters falling within their field of competence are considered.

7. The Committee shall present an annual report to the General Assembly of the United Nations on the implementation of the present Convention, containing its own considerations and recommendations, based, in particular, on the examination of the reports and any observations presented by States Parties.

8. The Secretary-General of the United Nations shall transmit the annual reports of the Committee to the States Parties to the present Convention, the Economic and Social Council, the Commission on Human Rights of the United Nations, the Director-General of the International Labour Office and other relevant organizations.

Article 75

1. The Committee shall adopt its own rules of procedure.

2. The Committee shall elect its officers for a term of two years.

3. The Committee shall normally meet annually.

4. The meetings of the Committee shall normally be held at United Nations Headquarters.

Article 76

1. A State Party to the present Convention may at any time declare under this article that it recognizes the competence of the Committee to receive and consider communications to the effect that a State Party claims that another State Party is not fulfilling its obligations under the present Convention. Communications under this article may be received and considered only if submitted by a State Party that has made a declaration recognizing in regard to itself the competence of the Committee. No communication shall be received by the Committee if it concerns a State Party which has not made such a declaration. Communications received under this article shall be dealt with in accordance with the following procedure:

(a) If a State Party to the present Convention considers that another State Party is not fulfilling its obligations under the present Convention, it may, by written communication, bring the matter to the attention of that State Party. The State Party may also inform the Committee of the matter. Within three months after the receipt of the communication the receiving State shall afford the State that sent the communication an explanation, or any other statement in writing clarifying the matter which should include, to the extent possible and pertinent, reference to domestic procedures and remedies taken, pending or available in the matter;

(b) If the matter is not adjusted to the satisfaction of both States Parties concerned within six months after the receipt by the receiving State of the initial communication, either

State shall have the right to refer the matter to the Committee, by notice given to the Committee and to the other State;

(c) The Committee shall deal with a matter referred to it only after it has ascertained that all available domestic remedies have been invoked and exhausted in the matter, in conformity with the generally recognized principles of international law. This shall not be the rule where, in the view of the Committee, the application of the remedies is unreasonably prolonged;

(d) Subject to the provisions of subparagraph (c) of the present paragraph, the Committee shall make available its good offices to the States Parties concerned with a view to a friendly solution of the matter on the basis of the respect for the obligations set forth in the present Convention;

(e) The Committee shall hold closed meetings when examining communications under the present article;

(f) In any matter referred to it in accordance with subparagraph (b) of the present paragraph, the Committee may call upon the States Parties concerned, referred to in subparagraph (b), to supply any relevant information;

(g) The States Parties concerned, referred to in subparagraph (b) of the present paragraph, shall have the right to be represented when the matter is being considered by the Committee and to make submissions orally and/or in writing;

(h) The Committee shall, within twelve months after the date of receipt of notice under subparagraph (b) of the present paragraph, submit a report, as follows:

(i) If a solution within the terms of subparagraph (d) of the present paragraph is reached, the Committee shall confine its report to a brief statement of the facts and of the solution reached;

(ii) If a solution within the terms of subparagraph (d) is not reached, the Committee shall, in its report, set forth the relevant facts concerning the issue between the States Parties concerned. The written submissions and record of the oral submissions made by the States Parties concerned shall be attached to the report. The Committee may also communicate only to the States Parties concerned any views that it may consider relevant to the issue between them. In every matter, the report shall be communicated to the States Parties concerned.

2. The provisions of the present article shall come into force when ten States Parties to the present Convention have made a declaration under paragraph I of the present article. Such declarations shall be deposited by the States Parties with the Secretary-General of the United Nations, who shall transmit copies thereof to the other States Parties. A declaration may be withdrawn at any time by notification to the Secretary-General. Such a withdrawal shall not prejudice the consideration of any matter that is the subject of a communication already transmitted under the present article; no further communication by any State Party shall be received under the present article after the notification of withdrawal of the declaration has been received by the Secretary-General, unless the State Party concerned has made a new declaration.

Article 77

1. A State Party to the present Convention may at any time declare under the present article that it recognizes the competence of the Committee to receive and consider communications from or on behalf of individuals subject to its jurisdiction who claim that their individual rights as established by the present Convention have been violated by that State

Party. No communication shall be received by the Committee if it concerns a State Party that has not made such a declaration.

2. The Committee shall consider inadmissible any communication under the present article which is anonymous or which it considers to be an abuse of the right of submission of such communications or to be incompatible with the provisions of the present Convention.

3. The Committee shall not consider any communication from an individual under the present article unless it has ascertained that:

(a) The same matter has not been, and is not being, examined under another procedure of international investigation or settlement;

(b) The individual has exhausted all available domestic remedies; this shall not be the rule where, in the view of the Committee, the application of the remedies is unreasonably prolonged or is unlikely to bring effective relief to that individual.

4. Subject to the provisions of paragraph 2 of the present article, the Committee shall bring any communications submitted to it under this article to the attention of the State Party to the present Convention that has made a declaration under paragraph 1 and is alleged to be violating any provisions of the Convention. Within six months, the receiving State shall submit to the Committee written explanations or statements clarifying the matter and the remedy, if any, that may have been taken by that State.

5. The Committee shall consider communications received under the present article in the light of all information made available to it by or on behalf of the individual and by the State Party concerned.

6. The Committee shall hold closed meetings when examining communications under the present article.

7. The Committee shall forward its views to the State Party concerned and to the individual.

8. The provisions of the present article shall come into force when ten States Parties to the present Convention have made declarations under paragraph 1 of the present article. Such declarations shall be deposited by the States Parties with the Secretary-General of the United Nations, who shall transmit copies thereof to the other States Parties. A declaration may be withdrawn at any time by notification to the Secretary-General. Such a withdrawal shall not prejudice the consideration of any matter that is the subject of a communication already transmitted under the present article; no further communication by or on behalf of an individual shall be received under the present article after the notification of withdrawal of the declaration has been received by the Secretary-General, unless the State Party has made a new declaration.

Article 78

The provisions of article 76 of the present Convention shall be applied without prejudice to any procedures for settling disputes or complaints in the field covered by the present Convention laid down in the constituent instruments of, or in conventions adopted by, the United Nations and the specialized agencies and shall not prevent the States Parties from having recourse to any procedures for settling a dispute in accordance with international agreements in force between them.

PART VIII: GENERAL PROVISIONS

Article 79
Nothing in the present Convention shall affect the right of each State Party to establish the criteria governing admission of migrant workers and members of their families. Concerning other matters related to their legal situation and treatment as migrant workers and members of their families, States Parties shall be subject to the limitations set forth in the present Convention.

Article 80
Nothing in the present Convention shall be interpreted as impairing the provisions of the Charter of the United Nations and of the constitutions of the specialized agencies which define the respective responsibilities of the various organs of the United Nations and of the specialized agencies in regard to the matters dealt with in the present Convention.

Article 81
1. Nothing in the present Convention shall affect more favourable rights or freedoms granted to migrant workers and members of their families by virtue of:
(a) The law or practice of a State Party; or
(b) Any bilateral or multilateral treaty in force for the State Party concerned.
2. Nothing in the present Convention may be interpreted as implying for any State, group or person any right to engage in any activity or perform any act that would impair any of the rights and freedoms as set forth in the present Convention.

Article 82
The rights of migrant workers and members of their families provided for in the present Convention may not be renounced. It shall not be permissible to exert any form of pressure upon migrant workers and members of their families with a view to their relinquishing or foregoing any of the said rights. It shall not be possible to derogate by contract from rights recognized in the present Convention. States Parties shall take appropriate measures to ensure that these principles are respected.

Article 83
Each State Party to the present Convention undertakes:
(a) To ensure that any person whose rights or freedoms as herein recognized are violated shall have an effective remedy, notwithstanding that the violation has been committed by persons acting in an official capacity;
(b) To ensure that any persons seeking such a remedy shall have his or her claim reviewed and decided by competent judicial, administrative or legislative authorities, or by any other competent authority provided for by the legal system of the State, and to develop the possibilities of judicial remedy;
(c) To ensure that the competent authorities shall enforce such remedies when granted.

Article 84
Each State Party undertakes to adopt the legislative and other measures that are necessary to implement the provisions of the present Convention.

PART IX: FINAL PROVISIONS

Article 85
The Secretary-General of the United Nations is designated as the depositary of the present Convention.

Article 86
1. The present Convention shall be open for signature by all States. It is subject to ratification.
2. The present Convention shall be open to accession by any State.
3. Instruments of ratification or accession shall be deposited with the Secretary-General of the United Nations.

Article 87
1. The present Convention shall enter into force on the first day of the month following a period of three months after the date of the deposit of the twentieth instrument of ratification or accession.
2. For each State ratifying or acceding to the present Convention after its entry into force, the Convention shall enter into force on the first day of the month following a period of three months after the date of the deposit of its own instrument of ratification or accession.

Article 88
A State ratifying or acceding to the present Convention may not exclude the application of any Part of it, or, without prejudice to article 3, exclude any particular category of migrant workers from its application.

Article 89
1. Any State Party may denounce the present Convention, not earlier than five years after the Convention has entered into force for the State concerned, by means of a notification writing addressed to the Secretary-General of the United Nations.
2. Such denunciation shall become effective on the first day of the month following the expiration of a period of twelve months after the date of the receipt of the notification by the Secretary-General of the United Nations.
3. Such a denunciation shall not have the effect of releasing the State Party from its obligations under the present Convention in regard to any act or omission which occurs prior to the date at which the denunciation becomes effective, nor shall denunciation prejudice in any way the continued consideration of any matter which is already under consideration by the Committee prior to the date at which the denunciation becomes effective.
4. Following the date at which the denunciation of a State Party becomes effective, the Committee shall not commence consideration of any new matter regarding that State.

Article 90
1. After five years from the entry into force of the Convention a request for the revision of the Convention may be made at any time by any State Party by means of a notification in writing addressed to the Secretary-General of the United Nations. The Secretary-General shall thereupon communicate any proposed amendments to the States Parties with a re-

quest that they notify him whether the favour a conference of States Parties for the purpose of considering and voting upon the proposals. In the event that within four months from the date of such communication at least one third of the States Parties favours such a conference, the Secretary-General shall convene the conference under the auspices of the United Nations. Any amendment adopted by a majority of the States Parties present and voting shall be submitted to the General Assembly for approval.

2. Amendments shall come into force when they have been approved by the General Assembly of the United Nations and accepted by a two-thirds majority of the States Parties in accordance with their respective constitutional processes.

3. When amendments come into force, they shall be binding on those States Parties that have accepted them, other States Parties still being bound by the provisions of the present Convention and any earlier amendment that they have accepted.

Article 91

1. The Secretary-General of the United Nations shall receive and circulate to all States the text of reservations made by States at the time of signature, ratification or accession.

2. A reservation incompatible with the object and purpose of the present Convention shall not be permitted.

3. Reservations may be withdrawn at any time by notification to this effect addressed to the Secretary-General of the United Nations, who shall then inform all States thereof. Such notification shall take effect on the date on which it is received.

Article 92

1. Any dispute between two or more States Parties concerning the interpretation or application of the present Convention that is not settled by negotiation shall, at the request of one of them, be submitted to arbitration. If within six months from the date of the request for arbitration the Parties are unable to agree on the organization of the arbitration, any one of those Parties may refer the dispute to the International Court of Justice by request in conformity with the Statute of the Court.

2. Each State Party may at the time of signature or ratification of the present Convention or accession thereto declare that it does not consider itself bound by paragraph 1 of the present article. The other States Parties shall not be bound by that paragraph with respect to any State Party that has made such a declaration.

3. Any State Party that has made a declaration in accordance with paragraph 2 of the present article may at any time withdraw that declaration by notification to the Secretary-General of the United Nations.

Article 93

1. The present Convention, of which the Arabic, Chinese, English, French, Russian and Spanish texts are equally authentic, shall be deposited with the Secretary-General of the United Nations.

2. The Secretary-General of the United Nations shall transmit certified copies of the present Convention to all States.

Vienna Declaration and Programme of Action, 1993

The World Conference on Human Rights[15], (...)

Determined to take new steps forward in the commitment of the international community
with a view to achieving substantial progress in human rights endeavours by an increased
and sustained effort of international cooperation and solidarity,
Solemnly adopts the Vienna Declaration and Programme of Action. (...)

I. 24. Great importance must be given to the promotion and protection of the human rights
of persons belonging to groups which have been rendered vulnerable, including migrant
workers, the elimination of all forms of discrimination against them, and the strengthening
and more effective implementation of existing human rights instruments. States have an
obligation to create and maintain adequate measures at the national level, in particular in
the fields of education, health and social support, for the promotion and protection of the
rights of persons in vulnerable sectors of their populations and to ensure the participation
of those among them who are interested in finding a solution to their own problems.

II A. Increased coordination on human rights within the United Nations system
II B. Equality, dignity and tolerance
2. Persons belonging to national or ethnic, religious and linguistic minorities (...)
Migrant workers
33. The World Conference on Human Rights urges all States to guarantee the protection
of the human rights of all migrant workers and their families.
34. The World Conference on Human Rights considers that the creation of conditions to
foster greater harmony and tolerance between migrant workers and the rest of the society
of the State in which they reside is of particular importance.
35. The World Conference on Human Rights invites States to consider the possibility of
signing and ratifying, at the earliest possible time, the International Convention on the
Rights of All Migrant Workers and Members of Their Families.

---

[15] General Assembly A/CONF.157/23, 12 July 1993. This Vienna Declaration and Programme of
Action was the result (unanimously adopted on 25 June 1993) of the World Conference on Human
Rights which took place in Vienna, 14-25 June 1993.

Cairo Resolutions on Population and Development[16] (excerpts)

The world population is currently estimated at 5.6 billion. While the rate of growth is on the decline, absolute increments have been increasing, currently exceeding 86 million persons per annum. Annual population increments are likely to remain above 86 million until the year 2015.

The two decades ahead are likely to produce a further shift of rural populations to urban areas as well as continued high levels of migration between countries. These migrations are an important part of the economic transformations occurring around the world, and they present serious new challenges. Therefore, these issues must be addressed with more emphasis within population and development policies. By the year 2015, nearly 56 per cent of the global population is expected to live in urban areas, compared to under 45 per cent in 1994. The most rapid rates of urbanization will occur in the developing countries. The urban population of the developing regions was just 26 per cent in 1975, but is projected to rise to 50 per cent by 2015. This change will place enormous strain on existing social services and infrastructure, much of which will not be able to expand at the same rate as that of urbanization.

Sustainable development as a means to ensure human well-being, equitably shared by all people today and in the future, requires that the interrelationships between population, resources, the environment and development should be fully recognized, properly managed and brought into harmonious, dynamic balance. To achieve sustainable development and a higher quality of life for all people, States should reduce and eliminate unsustainable patterns of production and consumption and promote appropriate policies, including population-related policies, in order to meet the needs of current generations without compromising the ability of future generations to meet their own needs. The family is the basic unit of society and as such should be strengthened. It is entitled to receive comprehensive protection and support. In different cultural, political and social systems, various forms of the family exist. Marriage must be entered into with the free consent of the intending spouses, and husband and wife should be equal partners. Countries receiving documented migrants should provide proper treatment and adequate social welfare services for them and their families, and should ensure their physical safety and security, bearing in mind the special circumstances and needs of countries, in particular developing countries, attempting to meet these objectives or requirements with regard to undocumented migrants, in conformity with the provisions of relevant conventions and international instruments and documents. Countries should guarantee to all migrants all basic human rights as included in the Universal Declaration of Human Rights.

---

[16] Cairo, 5-13 September 1994. A/CONF.171/13 18 October 1994 94-40486 (E) 091194.

CHAPTER V (THE FAMILY, ITS ROLES, RIGHTS, COMPOSITION AND STRUCTURE)

While various forms of the family exist in different social, cultural, legal and political systems, the family is the basic unit of society and as such is entitled to receive comprehensive protection and support. The process of rapid demographic and socio-economic change throughout the world has influenced patterns of family formation and family life, generating considerable change in family composition and structure. Traditional notions of gender-based division of parental and domestic functions and participation in the paid labour force do not reflect current realities and aspirations, as more and more women in all parts of the world take up paid employment outside the home. At the same time, widespread migration, forced shifts of population caused by violent conflicts and wars, urbanization, poverty, natural disasters and other causes of displacement have placed greater strains on the family, since assistance from extended family support networks is often no longer available. Parents are often more dependent on assistance from third parties than they used to be in order to reconcile work and family responsibilities. This is particularly the case when policies and programmes that affect the family ignore the existing diversity of family forms, or are insufficiently sensitive to the needs and rights of women and children.

The objectives are:
- to develop policies and laws that better support the family, contribute to its stability and take into account its plurality of forms, particularly the growing number of single-parent households;
- to establish social security measures that address the social, cultural and economic factors behind the increasing costs of child-rearing;
- to promote equality of opportunity for family members, especially the rights of women and children in the family.

Families are sensitive to strains induced by social and economic changes. It is essential to grant particular assistance to families in difficult life situations. Conditions have worsened for many families in recent years, owing to lack of gainful employment and measures taken by Governments seeking to balance their budget by reducing social expenditures. There are increasing numbers of vulnerable families, including single-parent families headed by women, poor families with elderly members or those with disabilities, refugee and displaced families, and families with members affected by AIDS or other terminal diseases, substance dependence, child abuse and domestic violence. Increased labour migrations and refugee movements are an additional source of family tension and disintegration and are contributing to increased responsibilities for women. In many urban environments, millions of children and youths are left to their own devices as family ties break down, and hence are increasingly exposed to risks such as dropping out of school, labour exploitation, sexual exploitation, unwanted pregnancies and sexually transmitted diseases.

CHAPTER IX (POPULATION DISTRIBUTION, URBANIZATION AND INTERNAL MIGRATION)

In the early 1990s, approximately half of the Governments in the world, mostly those of developing countries, considered the patterns of population distribution in their territories to be unsatisfactory and wished to modify them. key issue was the rapid growth of urban areas, which are expected to house more than half of the world population by 2005. Consequently, attention has mostly been paid to rural-urban migration, although rural-rural and urban- urban migration are in fact the dominant forms of spatial mobility in many countries.

The process of urbanization is an intrinsic dimension of economic and social development and, in consequence, both developed and developing countries are going through the process of shifting from predominantly rural to predominantly urban societies. For individuals, migration is often a rational and dynamic effort to seek new opportunities in life. Cities are centres of economic growth, providing the impetus for socio-economic innovation and change. However, migration is also prompted by push factors, such as inequitable allocation of development resources, adoption of inappropriate technologies and lack of access to available land.

The alarming consequences of urbanization visible in many countries are related to its rapid pace, to which Governments have been unable to respond with their current management capacities and practices. Even in developing countries, however, there are already signs of a changing pattern of population distribution, in the sense that the trend towards concentration in a few large cities is giving way to a more widespread distribution in medium-sized urban centres. This movement is also found in some developed countries, with people indicating preference for living in smaller places. Effective population distribution policies are those that, while respecting the right of individuals to live and work in the community of their choice, take into account the effects of development strategies on population distribution. Urbanization has profound implications for the livelihood, way of life and values of individuals. At the same time, migration has economic, social and environmental implications – both positive and negative – for the places of origin and destination.

The objectives are:
– to foster a more balanced spatial distribution of the population by promoting in an integrated manner the equitable and ecologically sustainable development of major sending and receiving areas, with particular emphasis on the promotion of economic, social and gender equity based on respect for human rights, especially the right to development;
– to reduce the role of the various push factors as they relate to migration flows.

Governments wishing to create alternatives to out-migration from rural areas should establish the preconditions for development in rural areas, actively support access to ownership or use of land and access to water resources, especially for family units, make and encourage investments to enhance rural productivity, improve rural infrastructure and social services and facilitate the establishment of credit, production and marketing cooperatives and other grass-roots organizations that give people greater control over resources and improve their livelihoods. Particular attention is needed to ensure that these opportunities are also made available to migrants' families remaining in the areas of origin.

Governments should pursue development strategies offering tangible benefits to investors in rural areas and to rural producers. Governments should also seek to reduce restrictions on international trade in agricultural products.

In many countries, the urban system is characterized by the overwhelming preponderance of a single major city or agglomeration.

The tendency towards population concentration, fostered by the concentration of public and private resources in some cities, has also contributed to the rising number and size of mega-cities. In 1992, there were 13 cities with at least 10 million inhabitants and their number is expected to double by 2010, when most mega-cities will be located in the developing countries. The continued concentration of population in primate cities, and in mega-cities in particular, poses specific economic, social and environmental challenges for Governments. Yet large agglomerations also represent the most dynamic centres of economic and cultural activity in many countries. It is therefore essential that the specific problems of large cities be analysed and addressed, in full awareness of the positive contribution that large cities make to national economic and social development. The challenges faced by cities are often exacerbated by weak management capacities at the local level to address the consequences of population concentration, socio-economic development, environmental impacts and their interrelations. The objective is to enhance the management of urban agglomerations through more participatory and resource-conscious planning and management, review and revise the policies and mechanisms that contribute to the excessive concentration of population in large cities, and improve the security and quality of life of both rural and urban low-income residents.

CHAPTER X (INTERNATIONAL MIGRATION)

International economic, political and cultural interrelations play an important role in the flow of people between countries, whether they are developing, developed or with economies in transition. In its diverse types, international migration is linked to such interrelations and both affects and is affected by the development process. International economic imbalances, poverty and environmental degradation, combined with the absence of peace and security, human rights violations and the varying degrees of development of judicial and democratic institutions are all factors affecting international migration. Although most international migration flows occur between neighbouring countries, interregional migration, particularly that directed to developed countries, has been growing. It is estimated that the number of international migrants in the world, including refugees, is in excess of 125 million, about half of them in the developing countries.

In recent years, the main receiving countries in the developed world registered a net migration intake of approximately 1.4 million persons annually, about two thirds of whom originated in developing countries. Orderly international migration can have positive impacts on both the communities of origin and the communities of destination, providing the former with remittances and the latter with needed human resources. International migration also has the potential of facilitating the transfer of skills and contributing to cultural enrichment. However, international migration entails the loss of human resources for many countries of origin and may give rise to political, economic or social tensions in countries of destination. To be effective, international migration policies need to take into account the economic constraints of the receiving country, the impact of migration on the host society and its effects on countries of origin. The long-term manageability of international migration hinges on making the option to remain in one's country a viable one for all people.

Sustainable economic growth with equity and development strategies consistent with this aim are a necessary means to that end. In addition, more effective use can be made of the potential contribution that expatriate nationals can make to the economic development of their countries of origin.

The objectives are:

- to address the root causes of migration, especially those related to poverty;
- to encourage more cooperation and dialogue between countries of origin and countries of destination in order to maximize the benefits of migration to those concerned and increase the likelihood that migration has positive consequences for the development of both sending and receiving countries;
- to facilitate the reintegration process of returning migrants.

Governments of countries of origin and of countries of destination should seek to make the option of remaining in one's country viable for all people. To that end, efforts to achieve sustainable economic and social development, ensuring a better economic balance between developed and developing countries and countries with economies in transition, should be strengthened. It is also necessary to increase efforts to defuse international and internal conflicts before they escalate; to ensure that the rights of persons belonging to ethnic, religious or linguistic minorities, and indigenous people are respected; and to respect the rule of law, promote good governance, strengthen democracy and promote human rights. Furthermore, greater support should be provided for the attainment of national and household food security, for education, nutrition, health and population-related programmes and to ensure effective environmental protection. Such efforts may require national and international financial assistance, reassessment of commercial and tariff relations, increased access to world markets and stepped-up efforts on the part of developing countries and countries with economies in transition to create a domestic framework for sustainable economic growth with an emphasis on job creation. The economic situation in those countries is likely to improve only gradually and, therefore, migration flows from those countries are likely to decline only in the long term; in the interim, the acute problems currently observed will cause migration flows to continue for the short-to-medium term, and Governments are accordingly urged to adopt transparent international migration policies and programmes to manage those flows.

Governments of countries of origin wishing to foster the inflow of remittances and their productive use for development should adopt sound exchange rate, monetary and economic policies, facilitate the provision of banking facilities that enable the safe and timely transfer of migrants' funds, and promote the conditions necessary to increase domestic savings and channel them into productive investment. Governments of countries of destination are invited to consider the use of certain forms of temporary migration, such as short-term and project-related migration, as a means of improving the skills of nationals of countries of origin, especially developing countries and countries with economies in transition. To that end, they should consider, as appropriate, entering into bilateral or multilateral agreements. Appropriate steps should be taken to safeguard the wages and working conditions of both migrant and native workers in the affected sectors. Governments of countries of origin are urged to facilitate the return of migrants and their reintegration into their home communities, and to devise ways of using their skills. Governments of countries of origin should consider collaborating with countries of destination and engaging the support of appropriate international organizations in promoting the return on a voluntary basis of qualified migrants who can play a crucial role in the transfer of knowledge, skills and technology. Countries of destination are encouraged to facilitate return migration by adopting flexible policies, such as the transferability of pensions and other work benefits.

Governments of countries affected by international migration are invited to cooperate, with a view to integrating the issue into their political and economic agendas and engaging in technical cooperation to aid developing countries and countries with economies in transition in addressing the impact of international migration. Governments are urged to exchange information regarding their international migration policies and the regulations governing the admission and stay of migrants in their territories. States that have not already done so are invited to consider ratifying the International Convention on the Protection of the Rights of All Migrant Workers and Members of Their Families.

Governments are encouraged to consider requests for migration from countries whose existence, according to available scientific evidence, is imminently threatened by global warming and climate change. In cooperation with international and non-governmental organizations and research institutions, Governments should support the gathering of data on flows and stocks of international migrants and on factors causing migration, as well as the monitoring of international migration. The identification of strategies to ensure that migration contributes to development and international relations should also be supported. The role of international organizations with mandates in the area of migration should be strengthened so that they can deliver adequate technical support to developing countries, advise in the management of international migration flows and promote intergovernmental cooperation through, inter alia, bilateral and multilateral negotiations, as appropriate.

Documented migrants

Documented migrants are those who satisfy all the legal requirements to enter, stay and, if applicable, hold employment in the country of destination. In some countries, many documented migrants have, over time, acquired the right to long-term residence. In such cases, the integration of documented migrants into the host society is generally desirable, and for that purpose it is important to extend to them the same social, economic and legal rights as those enjoyed by citizens, in accordance with national legislation. The family reunification of documented migrants is an important factor in international migration. It is also important to protect documented migrants and their families from racism, ethnocentrism and xenophobia, and to respect their physical integrity, dignity, religious beliefs and cultural values.

Documented migration is generally beneficial to the host country, since migrants are in general concentrated in the most productive ages and have skills needed by the receiving country, and their admission is congruent with the policies of the Government. The remittances of documented migrants to their countries of origin often constitute a very important source of foreign exchange and are instrumental in improving the well-being of relatives left behind.

The objectives are

– to ensure the social and economic integration of documented migrants, especially of those who have acquired the right to long-term residence in the country of destination, and their equal treatment before the law;
– to eliminate discriminatory practices against documented migrants, especially women, children and the elderly;
– to ensure protection against racism, ethnocentrism and xenophobia;
– to promote the welfare of documented migrants and members of their families;
– to ensure the respect of the cultural and religious values, beliefs and practices of documented migrants, in so far as they accord with national legislation and universally recognized human rights;
– to take into account the special needs and circumstances of temporary migrants.

Governments of receiving countries are urged to consider extending to documented migrants who meet appropriate length-of-stay requirements, and to members of their families whose stay in the receiving country is regular, treatment equal to that accorded their own nationals with regard to the enjoyment of basic human rights, including equality of opportunity and treatment in respect of religious practices, working conditions, social security, participation in trade unions, access to health, education, cultural and other social services, as well as equal access to the judicial system and equal treatment before the law. Governments of receiving countries are further urged to take appropriate steps to avoid all forms of discrimination against migrants, including eliminating discriminatory practices concerning their nationality and the nationality of their children, and to protect their rights and safety. Women and children who migrate as family members should be protected from abuse or denial of their human rights by their sponsors, and Governments are asked to consider extending their stay should the family relationship dissolve, within the limits of national legislation.

In order to promote the integration of documented migrants having the right to long-term residence, Governments of receiving countries are urged to consider giving them civil and political rights and responsibilities, as appropriate, and facilitating their naturalization. Special efforts should be made to enhance the integration of the children of long-term migrants by providing them with educational and training opportunities equal to those of nationals, allowing them to exercise an economic activity, and facilitating the naturalization of those who have been raised in the receiving country. Consistent with article 10 of the Convention on the Rights of the Child and all other relevant universally recognized human rights instruments, all Governments, particularly those of receiving countries, must recognize the vital importance of family reunification and promote its integration into their national legislation in order to ensure the protection of the unity of the families of documented migrants. Governments of receiving countries must ensure the protection of migrants and their families, giving priority to programmes and strategies that combat religious intolerance, racism, ethnocentrism, xenophobia and gender discrimination and that generate the necessary public sensitivity in that regard.

Governments of countries of destination should respect the basic human rights of documented migrants as those Governments assert their right to regulate access to their territory and adopt policies that respond to and shape immigration flows. With regard to the admission of migrants, Governments should avoid discriminating on the basis of race, religion, sex and disability, while taking into account health and other considerations relevant under national immigration regulations, particularly considering the special needs of the elderly and children. Governments are urged to promote, through family reunion, the normalization of the family life of legal migrants who have the right to long-term residence.

Governments should consider providing assistance and cooperation for programmes that would address the adverse social and economic consequences of forced migration.

Undocumented migrants

It is the right of every nation State to decide who can enter and stay in its territory and under what conditions. Such right, however, should be exercised taking care to avoid racist or xenophobic actions and policies. Undocumented or irregular migrants are persons who do not fulfil the requirements established by the country of destination to enter, stay or exercise an economic activity. Given that the pressures for migration are growing in a number of developing countries, especially since their labour force continues to increase, undocumented or irregular migration is expected to rise.

The objectives are:
- to address the root causes of undocumented migration;
- to reduce substantially the number of undocumented migrants, while ensuring that those in need of international protection receive it; to prevent the exploitation of undocumented migrants and to ensure that their basic human rights are protected;
- to prevent all international trafficking in migrants, especially for the purposes of prostitution;
- to ensure protection against racism, ethnocentrism and xenophobia.

Governments of countries of origin and countries of destination are urged to cooperate in reducing the causes of undocumented migration, safeguarding the basic human rights of undocumented migrants including the right to seek and to enjoy in other countries asylum from persecution, and preventing their exploitation.

Governments should identify the causes of undocumented migration and its economic, social and demographic impact as well as its implications for the formulation of social, economic and international migration policies.

Governments of both receiving countries and countries of origin should adopt effective sanctions against those who organize undocumented migration, exploit undocumented migrants or engage in trafficking in undocumented migrants, especially those who engage in any form of international traffic in women, youth and children.

Governments of countries of origin, where the activities of agents or other intermediaries in the migration process are legal, should regulate such activities in order to prevent abuses, especially exploitation, prostitution and coercive adoption.

Governments, with the assistance of appropriate international organizations, should deter undocumented migration by making potential migrants aware of the legal conditions for entry, stay and employment in host countries through information activities in the countries of origin.

Governments of countries of origin of undocumented migrants and persons whose asylum claims have been rejected have the responsibility to accept the return and reintegration of those persons, and should not penalize such persons on their return. In addition, Governments of countries of origin and countries of destination should try to find satisfactory solutions to the problems caused by undocumented migration through bilateral or multilateral negotiations on, *inter alia*, readmission agreements that protect the basic human rights of the persons involved in accordance with relevant international instruments.

General Assembly Resolution 1999 on the Protection of Migrants[17]

The General Assembly,

Considering that the Universal Declaration of Human Rights Resolution 217 A(III). proclaims that all human beings are born free and equal in dignity and rights and that everyone is entitled to all the rights and freedoms set out therein, without distinction of any kind, in particular as to race, colour or national origin,

Reaffirming the provisions concerning migrants adopted by the World Conference on Human Rights, See A/CONF.157/24(Part I), chap. III. the International Conference on Population and Development, See *Report of the International Conference on Population and Development, Cairo, 5-13 September 1994* (United Nations publication, Sales No. E.95.XIII.18), chap. I, resolution 1, annex. the World Summit for Social Development See *Report of the World Summit for Social Development, Copenhagen, 6-12 March 1995* (United Nations publication, Sales No. E.96.IV.8), chap. I, resolution 1, annexes I and II. and the Fourth World Conference on Women, See *Report of the Fourth World Conference on Women, Beijing, 4-15 September 1995* (United Nations publication, Sales No. E.96.IV.13), chap. I, resolution 1, annexes I and II.

Taking note of Commission on Human Rights resolution 1999/44 of 27 April 1999 on the human rights of migrants, *Official Records of the Economic and Social Council, 1999, Supplement No. 3* (E/1999/23), chap. II, sect. A. and of its decision to appoint a special rapporteur on the human rights of migrants,

Recalling its resolution 40/144 of 13 December 1985, by which it approved the Declaration on the Human Rights of Individuals Who are not Nationals of the Country in which They Live,

Bearing in mind the situation of vulnerability in which migrants frequently find themselves, owing, *inter alia*, to their absence from their State of origin and to the difficulties they encounter because of differences of language, custom and culture, as well as the economic and social difficulties and obstacles for the return to their States of origin of migrants who are non-documented or in an irregular situation,

Deeply concerned at the manifestations of violence, racism, xenophobia and other forms of discrimination and inhuman and degrading treatment against migrants, especially women and children, in different parts of the world,

Encouraged by the increasing interest of the international community in the effective and full protection of the human rights of all migrants, and underlining the need to make further efforts to ensure respect for the human rights and fundamental freedoms of all migrants,

Taking note with appreciation of the recommendations on strengthening the promotion, protection and implementation of the human rights of migrants of the working group of intergovernmental experts on the human rights of migrants E/CN.4/1999/80, paras. 102-124. established by the Commission on Human Rights,

---

[17] Fifty-fourth session, Agenda item 116(b); on the basis of the report of the Third Committee (A/54/605/Add.2), 17 December 1999.

Noting the efforts made by States to penalize the international trafficking of migrants and to protect the victims of this illegal activity,

Taking note of the decisions of the relevant international juridical bodies on questions relating to migrants, particularly advisory opinion OC-16/99, issued by the Inter-American Court of Human Rights on 1 October 1999, regarding the right to information about consular assistance within the framework of due process guarantees,

1. *Requests* all Member States, in conformity with their respective constitutional systems, effectively to promote and protect the human rights of all migrants, in conformity with the Universal Declaration of Human Rights[1] and the international instruments to which they are party, which may include the International Covenants on Human Rights, Resolution 2200 A(XXI), annex. the Convention against Torture and Other Cruel, Inhuman or Degrading Treatment or Punishment, Resolution 39/46, annex. the International Convention on the Elimination of All Forms of Racial Discrimination, Resolution 2106 A(XX), annex. the International Convention on the Protection of the Rights of All Migrant Workers and Members of Their Families, Resolution 45/158, annex. the Convention on the Elimination of All Forms of Discrimination against Women, Resolution 34/180, annex. the Convention on the Rights of the Child Resolution 44/25, annex. and other applicable international human rights instruments;

2. *Strongly condemns* all forms of racial discrimination and xenophobia with regard to access to employment, vocational training, housing, schooling, health services and social services, as well as services intended for use by the public, and welcomes the active role played by governmental and non-governmental organizations in combating racism and assisting individual victims of racist acts, including migrant victims;

3. *Calls upon* all States to review and, where necessary, revise immigration policies with a view to eliminating all discriminatory policies and practices against migrants and to provide specialized training for government policy-making and law enforcement, immigration and other concerned officials, thus underlining the importance of effective action to create conditions that foster greater harmony and tolerance within societies;

4. *Reiterates* the need for all States to protect fully the universally recognized human rights of migrants, especially women and children, regardless of their legal status, and to provide humane treatment, particularly with regard to assistance and protection, including those under the Vienna Convention on Consular Relations, United Nations, *Treaty Series*, vol. 596, No. 8638. regarding the right to receive consular assistance from the country of origin;

5. *Welcomes* the decision of the Commission on Human Rights to appoint a special rapporteur on the human rights of migrants to examine ways and means to overcome the obstacles existing to the full and effective protection of the human rights of this vulnerable group, including obstacles and difficulties for the return of migrants who are non-documented or in an irregular situation, with the following functions:

(a) To request and receive information from all relevant sources, including migrants themselves, on violations of the human rights of migrants and their families;

(b) To formulate appropriate recommendations to prevent and remedy violations of the human rights of migrants, wherever they may occur;

(c) To promote the effective application of relevant international norms and standards on the issue;

(d) To recommend actions and measures applicable at the national, regional and international levels to eliminate violations of the human rights of migrants;

(e) To take into account a gender perspective when requesting and analysing information, as well as to give special attention to the occurrence of multiple discrimination and violence against migrant women;

6. *Requests* all Governments to cooperate fully with the Special Rapporteur in the performance of the tasks and duties mandated and to furnish all information requested, including by reacting promptly to his/her urgent appeals;

7. *Encourages* Member States that have not yet done so to enact domestic criminal legislation to combat international trafficking of migrants, which should take into account, in particular, trafficking that endangers the lives of migrants or includes different forms of servitude or exploitation, such as any form of debt bondage, sexual or labour exploitation, and to strengthen international cooperation to combat such trafficking;

8. *Requests* the Secretary-General to submit to the General Assembly at its fifty-fifth session a report on the implementation of the present resolution under the sub-item entitled 'Human rights questions, including alternative approaches for improving the effective enjoyment of human rights and fundamental freedoms'.

4.5.6

General Assembly Resolution on International Migrants' Day: 18 December[18]

Calling attention to the need to protect the rights and dignity of people who migrate from their native lands, the United Nations will mark the first International Migrants' Day on Monday next, 18 December [2000]. It is hoped that the day, which will be observed worldwide, will help to ensure that the presence and contributions of migrants in the advancement of their host countries is recognized. It is estimated that between 120 and 130 million people live outside their countries of origin.

The Day will be launched at United Nations Headquarters in New York with a special event sponsored by the Office of the High Commissioner for Human Rights, the Interna-

---

[18] Press Release, PI/1315, HR/4509, 15 December 2000. See also the GA Resolution 55/92 declaring the 18th of December International Migrants'Day. Although not indicated in this Press release, it is recalled that the Resolution with which the Interernational Convention on the Protection of the Rights of All Migrant Workers and Members of Their Families (see Chapter 4.5.2) was adopted on 18 December 1990.

tional Labour Organization (ILO) and the International Non- governmental Organization (NGO) Committee on Human Rights. (...)

Migration is hardly a recent or localised phenomenon. Millions of men, women and even children have left their homelands in search of a better job or a better life in a different place. People have also left their own countries because of civil conflicts and insecurity or persecution. However, globalization has spurred a sharp increase in labour mobility. Almost every country has now become a country of origin, transit or destination of migrants.

The International Labour Organization estimates that there are between 70 and 80 million migrant workers, and the High Commissioner of Refugees reports that there are 21.5 million refugees and probably some 30 million displaced persons. In 1997, the ILO estimated that there were 20 million migrant workers in Africa; 17 million in North America; 12 million in Central and South America; 7 million in Asia; 9 million in the Middle East (Arab countries), and 30 million in Europe.

Along with this rise in migration, there has been an alarming upsurge in intolerance, discrimination, racism and xenophobia, that has been expressed in the form of outright violence against migrants in practically every region of the world in the last decade. Gareth Howell of the ILO points out that 'increasing restrictions on immigration leads to increased trafficking of migrants, often with tragic personal consequences'. Racism, discrimination and xenophobia may be aggravated by inequitable distribution of wealth, marginalization and social exclusion.

Mary Robinson, United Nations High Commissioner for Human Rights, recently expressed concern at the harsh treatment of children and families of migrants, and the incidence of fear and dislike of foreigners reflected in both the private and public sectors. She added, 'Such practices are of grave concern when they become institutionalized and reflect through the actions of the law enforcement officials or the judiciary'.

Women and children currently account for more than half of the refugees and internally displaced persons, and their proportion is rising among the ranks of other migrants as well. The ILO estimates that 96 per cent of children who work and sleep in the streets are migrants, most of them girls aged eight to fourteen. According to United Nations statistics on women, between 300,000 and 600,000 women are smuggled each year into the European and certain Central European countries. The problem is also widespread in Africa and Latin America.

Migrant women, who dominate the informal sector as domestic, industrial or agricultural labour or the service sector, undergo double discrimination, thus easily finding themselves in situations in which they are vulnerable to violence and abuse, both at home and at work. For example, migrant women are often forced to provide sexual favours for permission to transit, a common practice on some borders.

There is a growing number of children of mixed parentage and of children of migrants born in the destination/host country or to migrant women who have been raped. They are subjected to racial discrimination and are often stigmatized not only in host countries, but also in their home communities and countries.

There have been efforts by the international community to protect migrants. The ILO has put the protection of migrants workers' rights at the centre of its mandate and actions since its creation. The 1990 International Convention on the Protection of the Rights of Migrant Workers and Members of their Families has been ratified by 15 countries, but 10 years after its adoption, it still needs a handful of signatures to enter into force. The Human Rights High Commissioner, Ms. Robinson, issued a strong appeal to governments 'to ratify the Convention as soon as possible, so that its protective regime can be brought to bear upon the millions of migrant workers in different parts of the world'. Last year, the Commission on Human Rights, recognizing the increasing need for protection of the migrants, appointed a Special Rapporteur on Human Rights of Migrants.

More recently, in Palermo, Italy, the plight of migrants again attracted the attention of the international community, when more than a hundred countries signed the Convention against Transnational Organized Crime, and its accompanying protocols, to establish an international system to crack down on trafficking of women and children and the smuggling of migrants.

Racial discrimination against migrants is also at the centre of world-wide discussions leading to the World Conference against Racism, Racial Discrimination, Xenophobia and Related Intolerance, which will take place in Durban, South Africa from 31 August to 7 September [2001]. In a seminar to prepare for the World Conference, one expert observed that 'the elimination of prejudice towards the outsider in the society is going to be a much more difficult and long-term problem to resolve than legal and institutional forms of discrimination'. A call for educational programmes on immigration, which would result in the appreciation of diversity and the development of tolerance, was also made.

4.5.7

Report by the Special Rapporteur on the Human Rights of Migrants[19]

EXECUTIVE SUMMARY

In accordance with Commission on Human Rights resolution 1999/44, the Special Rapporteur on the human rights of migrants, Ms. Gabriela Rodríguez Pizarro, is submitting her first report. The first part of the text describes her activities under the mandate entrusted to her by the Commission. There follows a description of the context of the feminization of migration and the international community's growing interest in the phenomenon, which has led to various initiatives.

That description is followed by the first outline of the work programme itself, the main purpose of which is to collect information in order to be able to submit reports to the Commission at its fifty-seventh and fifty-eighth sessions, as well as to make recommenda-

---

[19] UNITED NATIONS, Economic and Social Council, E/CN.4/2000/82, 6 January 2000; COMMISSION ON HUMAN RIGHTS Fifty-sixth session; Item 14(a) of the provisional agenda; SPECIFIC GROUPS AND INDIVIDUALS; MIGRANT WORKERS, Human rights of migrants; Report of the Special Rapporteur, Ms. Gabriela Rodríguez Pizarro, Submitted pursuant to Commission on Human Rights Resolution 1999/44. The major parts of this report, probably the first of many, have been incorporated in this Handbook to provide an idea as to the methodology and impact of such reports. The footnotes, however, have been deleted to ensure easy access.

tions to the bodies concerned. This includes the preparatory process for the World Conference against Racism, Racial Discrimination, Xenophobia and Related Intolerance. Information will be collected from all sectors, including migrants themselves, and will take into account the gender perspective. The work programme should also include close monitoring of intergovernmental and intersectoral initiatives already under way to tackle the problem of migration, and observer missions to countries affected by the phenomenon.

The second part of the report is devoted to an initial examination of the international instruments available for the protection of the human rights of migrants and highlights the lack of a comprehensive definition of existing categories of migrants. This examination takes into account the net effects of the domestic laws and regional agreements regarded as critical for the defence of the human rights of migrants. Special emphasis if placed on the need to take into account the problem of trafficking in persons (not only for the purposes of prostitution) and the implications of returning undocumented migrants to their places of origin. In this chapter, the Special Rapporteur proposes that a working definition of the category of migrant should be formulated, and that the adoption of existing instruments covering the rights of one or more of the categories discussed should be recommended and encouraged.

Lastly, the report presents some comments by the Special Rapporteur on areas considered suitable for further research: the link between migration and the increase in racism, discrimination and intolerance, and a more detailed examination of the issues surrounding women migrants and their implications for a gender-based approach to the phenomenon of migration. This section is followed by observations on migration issues as they affect children.[20] Lastly, it is explained how, from this perspective, the concept of vulnerability applies to migrants and how considerations of the obstacles to the protection of their rights, which were noted by the working group of intergovernmental experts on the human rights of migrants, are taken up. The report concludes with chapters on preliminary conclusions and some recommendations.

I. INTRODUCTION

1. At its fifty-fifth session, the Commission on Human Rights adopted resolution 1999/44, by which it decided to appoint, for a three-year period, a special rapporteur on the human rights of migrants to examine ways and means to overcome the obstacles existing to the full and effective protection of the human rights of this vulnerable group, including obstacles and difficulties for the return of migrants who are undocumented or in an irregular situation. The Special Rapporteur should formulate strategies and recommendations for the promotion and implementation of policies to protect the human rights of migrants, and establish the criteria on which those policies should be based.

2. In the same resolution, the Commission invited the Special Rapporteur, in the performance of his/her functions, to request and receive information from all relevant sources, including migrants themselves, on violations of the human rights of migrants and their

---

[20] The parts specifically dealing with women and children had to be left out being too detailed for the purpose of this Handbook

families, to promote the effective application of relevant international norms and standards on the issue, and to recommend actions and measures applicable at the national, regional and international levels to eliminate violations of the human rights of migrants.

3. The Commission requested the Special Rapporteur to take into account a gender perspective when requesting and analysing information, a perspective that will also be taken into account when analysing existing legislation and making recommendations. It also recommended that special attention should be given to the occurrence of multiple forms of discrimination and violence against migrant women.

4. Pursuant to this resolution, on 6 August 1999, the Chairperson of the Commission on Human Rights at its fifty-fifth session, after consultation with the members of the Bureau, appointed Ms. Gabriela Rodríguez Pizarro (Costa Rica) as Special Rapporteur on the human rights of migrants.

5. The Economic and Social Council, in its decision 1999/239, endorsed Commission on Human Rights resolution 1999/44.

6. Aware of the weighty responsibility entrusted to her, as well as the amount of work involved and the need to seek the support and cooperation of all relevant bodies, in compliance with resolution 1999/44, the Special Rapporteur submits this report to the Commission on Human Rights for its consideration.

7. The report consists of eight chapters. Chapters II-V describe the recent activities of the Special Rapporteur, the background to her mandate, an outline of her plan of action and a first look at the existing legal framework of international instruments relating to the rights of migrants. Chapter VI contains observations on the aspects considered relevant to the design of a strategy for the human rights of migrants, including some of the main obstacles to the full protection of migrants' rights. The last part of the document consists of the preliminary conclusions and recommendations of the Special Rapporteur (chapters VII and VIII).

II. ACTIVITIES OF THE SPECIAL RAPPORTEUR

(...)
11. As a first step, and in compliance with the provisions of paragraph 5 of Commission on Human Rights resolution 1999/44, the Special Rapporteur sent out, on 27 September 1999, a letter to Governments, the specialized agencies of the United Nations, the chairpersons of treaty bodies, and NGOs, requesting information relevant to her mandate. She is especially interested in receiving information on measures being taken in response to the questions raised by the issue of the human rights of migrants, with a view to formulating suitable recommendations to the Commission.

12. The information provided in the replies to her letter is now being studied by the Special Rapporteur and will be reflected in her oral presentation of this report to the Commission at its fifty-sixth session.

III. BACKGROUND

13. The international community's growing interest in human rights issues has meant that migrants' rights have begun to receive special attention. In addition to the initiative taken by the Commission and the Vienna Declaration and Programme of Action adopted by the World Conference on Human Rights in 1993 (part II, paras. 33-35), the Programme of Action of the International Conference on Population and Development held at Cairo (chapter X), the Programme of Action of the World Summit for Social Development, held at Copenhagen (Programme of Action, chapter III), and the outcome of the Fourth World Conference on Women, held in Beijing (Platform for Action, chapter IV, section D), devote special attention to the issue of migrants' human rights.[21] The working group of intergovernmental experts on the human rights of migrants has made a considerable contribution to our knowledge of this phenomenon and to identifying the current obstacles to the full and effective exercise of their human rights by that 'vulnerable group'. Intergovernmental bodies have promoted a number of initiatives to establish a dialogue between Governments in regions that have to deal with the same migrant issues. A similar interest has been shown by sectors of civil society and has been brought to the attention of the general public all round the world by the news media. The news services tend to highlight the problems of trafficking in persons, particularly women and children, and the widespread abuse of undocumented workers in the informal economy.

14. The Special Rapporteur notes that migration occurs for a variety of reasons: people are unable to remain in their own countries mainly because of poverty and because they cannot earn a living for themselves or their family, and because of civil conflicts and insecurity or persecution for reasons of race, ethnic origin, religion, language or political views. The States whose citizens migrate for these reasons share these problems with the States which receive large numbers of migrants. Human rights violations hypothetically arise for the receiving or 'desired' State that rejects inflows of migrants. Such violations occur insofar as the national populations cannot be contained within their home countries. A common outcome of this phenomenon is that people become undocumented cross-border migrants.

15. Estimates of the different categories of migrant suggest that a total of between 120 and 130 million people are outside their countries of origin. The International Labour Organization (ILO) estimates that between 70 and 80 million of these are so-called 'migrant workers', while the Office of the United Nations High Commissioner for Refugees (UNHCR) reports that there are 21.5 million refugees and reckons that there are 30 million displaced persons. In 1997, ILO estimated that the number of migrant workers was as follows: Africa, 20 million; North America, 17 million; Central and South America, 12 million; Asia, 7 million; the Middle East (Arab countries), 9 million; and Europe, 30 million. There are massive movements of migrants towards the North, but there is more and more movement between the countries of the South. Women and children account for

---

[21] Ed.: In order to avoid repetition, only 'Vienna' and ' Cairo' have been included in this Handbook.

more than half of the refugees and internally displaced persons, and their proportion is increasing in the case of the other categories of migrants, including migrant workers.

IV. PLAN OF ACTION

16. The Special Rapporteur outlined a plan of action for the three-year period of her mandate. In this context, the Special Rapporteur considered that, in addition to the definition of the legal framework, which can be found in paragraph 25 and the following paragraphs and which should be broadened in the way described in that section, a survey of regional initiatives needs to be carried out so that the Governments of home countries and/or transit countries can enter into dialogue with those of countries that are traditionally seen as migrant destinations. Some of these initiatives, which are at varying stages of development, bear the name of the cities or regions where they were launched: the Puebla process, the Manila process, the Bangkok initiative (the Bangkok Declaration) and the Dakar, Mediterranean, Cairo, Lima and Commonwealth of Independent States (CIS) initiatives. (...)

19. She will also consult the Governments of countries in the African, Asian, American and European regions with a view to finding out about migration policies, in order to start a dialogue between Governments and civil society aimed at finding specific ways of dealing with the obstacles faced by migrant populations seeking recognition of their rights. A dialogue on policy measures and actual practice in this area is vital at the national and regional levels.

20. The Special Rapporteur believes it is crucial to support the campaign for the ratification of the International Convention on the Protection of the Rights of All Migrant Workers and Members of Their Families, as well as other international human rights instruments.

21. The Special Rapporteur acknowledges the important work on the ratification of the International Convention carried out by the Steering Committee of the Global Campaign for Ratification of the Convention through its secretariat in the International Migrants Rights Watch Committee.

22. The Special Rapporteur also acknowledges the important work carried out by the working group of intergovernmental experts on the human rights of migrants in giving an overall picture of the phenomenon of migration and in identifying the main obstacles to the full protection of the human rights of migrants.

23. As part of this process of documentation, the Special Rapporteur plans to examine relevant domestic policies and laws. This examination will be carried out with due regard for international norms and treaties, the case law of the international human rights treaty bodies, the recommendations and agreements adopted at international conferences, the measures and decisions taken by the United Nations and international organizations, and the case law and other measures of regional organizations.

24. With regard to the national contexts, the Special Rapporteur plans to compile a set of recommendations on measures to overcome the obstacles to the prevention of discrimina-

tion against migrants, basically with respect to: legislation and legal measures; administrative and governmental measures at the national, regional and local levels; the responsibilities of employers and entrepreneurs; the requirements for the dignified return of undocumented migrants; and actions by both civil society and States to take up all the issues relating to the human rights of migrants.

V. LEGAL FRAMEWORK: THE HUMAN RIGHTS OF MIGRANTS

25. If her work is to be effective, the Special Rapporteur believes a working definition of the concept of a migrant must be found. Since even the general term 'migrant' has not been defined in either international law or policy, a working definition needs to be found that will make it possible, in particular, to recognize and draw attention to situations in which the human rights of individuals can be protected by means of a legal, social and political framework.

26. Within the broad spectrum of international migrations there are some official definitions of certain categories of migrants, such as 'migrant worker' or 'migrant', which are defined in, respectively, the International Convention on the Protection of the Rights of All Migrant Workers and Members of Their Families and ILO Conventions Nos. 97 and 143. There is also a definition of a refugee in the Convention and Protocol relating to the Status of Refugees.

27. The above-mentioned instruments or the rules for their implementation include definitions of various subcategories, such as asylum-seekers, people in situations similar to those of refugees and various specific categories of migrant workers (frontier workers, seasonal workers, etc.). Work is being carried out in the context of the draft protocol on trafficking in persons to the draft convention against transnational organized crime on the definition of the persons who are the victims thereof (trafficking in persons). This definition should also be examined in the light of the concept of the migrant, which the Special Rapporteur intends to establish as part of the plan of action.

28. There is no commonly accepted generic or general legal concept of the migrant in international law. It is often said that, by definition, many international migrants are not refugees and a large number of them are not migrant workers either. This is especially true in the case of the many migrants who are undocumented or in an irregular situation, including the victims of trafficking in persons, who are the most vulnerable to potential or actual violations of their human rights.

29. The Commission on Human Rights tacitly acknowledged the limitations of the term 'migrant workers' when it established, first, the working group of intergovernmental experts on the human rights of migrants and, more recently, the post of Special Rapporteur on the human rights of migrants.

30. Definitions that are related to the reasons why people leave their countries of origin are perhaps the least suitable kind of definition, except to the extent that they give access to legal protection and status in the host country, as in the case of refugees. In the light of the political, social, economic and environmental situation of many countries, it is increasingly difficult, if not impossible, to make a clear distinction between migrants who leave

their countries because of political persecution, conflicts, economic problems, environmental degradation or a combination of these reasons and those who do so in search of conditions of survival or well-being that do not exist in their places of origin.

31. There is a gap in international human rights jurisprudence in this area. The virtually universal system of protection for refugees means that violations of their civil and political rights can be recognized and remedied, especially when they pose such a risk to persons' lives and security that they are forced to flee their country. However, there is no such recognition of violations of economic, social and cultural rights, which can also be serious enough to force people to flee their places of origin. Consequently, there is no recognition of the need to protect in any way people who do not want, or are unable, to return to situations in which the lack of fundamental economic, social and cultural rights makes it extremely difficult or impossible to survive.

32. People whose colour, physical appearance, dress, accent or religion are different from those of the majority in the host country are often subjected to physical violence and other violations of their rights, independently of their legal status. The choice of victim and the nature of the abuse do not depend on whether the persons are refugees, legal immigrants, members of national minorities or undocumented migrants.

33. Consequently, in order to give a definition of a migrant that is based on human rights, the first and most important step is to see whether or not the rights of those persons enjoy some form of legal, social and political protection.

34. Although the concept of vulnerability is useful for emphasizing the lack of protection of migrants, there is no reason to link it with the concept of weakness. It is also recognized that migrants in an irregular situation are in a particularly difficult position. The Special Rapporteur stresses that this consideration of vulnerability is the only one that makes it possible to protect migrants by empowering them.

35. On the basis of these considerations, an initial proposal for a basic definition of a migrant that takes into account his or her human rights would contain the elements given in the following paragraph.

36. For the purpose of studying and strengthening the protection of the human rights of migrants, the following can be considered as migrants:
(a) Persons who are outside the territory of the State of which they are nationals or citizens, are not subject to its legal protection and are in the territory of another State;
(b) Persons who do not enjoy the general legal recognition of rights which is inherent in the granting by the host State of the status of refugee, permanent resident or naturalized person or of similar status; and
(c) Persons who do not enjoy either general legal protection of their fundamental rights by virtue of diplomatic agreements, visas or other agreements.

37. Also for the purpose of studying and strengthening the protection of the human rights of migrants, attention should be given, as a matter of priority, to migrants in an irregular situation. The human rights of undocumented migrants are also a cause for concern, like the rights of the victims of trafficking. Another cause for concern is the rights of other

groups or categories of persons who are vulnerable to discrimination and the denial of their rights and who are legally, socially and politically the most disadvantaged in the places where they live.

38. A review of past practice shows that the Constitution of the Intergovernmental Committee for European Migration refers to migrants in its article 1, paragraph 1, subparagraph (a), on its purpose and functions. The term is understood as covering all cases of persons whose decision to migrate is taken freely, for reasons of personal convenience, and without intervention of an 'external compelling factor'. As far as the perceived reasons for migrating are concerned, the voluntary nature or otherwise of the move is a point that will need to be borne in mind and given priority in later discussions aimed at reaching a definition of the term 'migrant' that is closer to the reality of this complex phenomenon.

39. The term 'migrant worker' is defined in article 2 of the International Convention on the Protection of the Rights of All Migrant Workers and Members of Their Families as: '... a person who is to be engaged, is engaged or has been engaged in a remunerated activity in a State of which he or she is not a national ...'

40. This definition includes undocumented workers who enjoy certain rights recognized in part III ('Human rights of all migrant workers and members of their families') of the Convention. Article 2, paragraph 2, contains definitions of several specific categories of migrant workers, such as frontier workers, seasonal workers, seafarers, workers on offshore installations, itinerant workers, project-tied workers and self-employed workers. The definition in article 2 refers exclusively to migrant workers who are outside their own country. The Special Rapporteur expresses her concern at the shortcomings of a legal framework that disregards desperately poor migrants whose rights need to be protected by categorizing them as 'economic migrants'. In many of these cases, the departure has been prompted by violence and the conditions that lead to migration are similar to those that give rise to forced displacement or asylum-seeking.

41. Other categories of persons that ought to be mentioned are former refugees, persons who were once externally displaced, and demobilized soldiers. Several of these new kinds of migrant can be found in Central America. For example, once the peace agreements had been signed, those persons who had been resettled and reintegrated became classified as migrants in an irregular situation, and their problems were not resolved in a dignified way. Another important category is that of women who have been subjected to trafficking or forced into prostitution, and who have no status in the countries of destination, despite efforts to eradicate that practice.

42. The Special Rapporteur believes it is important to distinguish between 'migrant workers' and 'refugees and stateless persons', as the International Convention applies to the former but not the latter. On this point, the Convention differs from the four ILO conventions on migration, which apply to refugees and displaced persons as long as they are workers employed outside their home country. Similarly, the Constitution of the Intergovernmental Committee for European Migration (subsequently the International Organization for Migration (IOM)) stipulates that the Organization will deal with refugees, displaced persons and others forced to leave their home country who require international migration services.

43. The Special Rapporteur therefore believes that a provisional definition of a migrant that takes into account his or her human rights and the concepts already defined should be adopted in the near future, but the possibility must be left open of further refining the definition subsequently.

VI. OBSERVATIONS

A. Discrimination and intolerance

44. In the Third Decade to Combat Racism and Racial Discrimination, there has a been an alarming upsurge in intolerance, discrimination, racism and xenophobia in the form of outright violence against migrants in practically every region in the world.

45. As stated in working paper E/CN.4/AC.46/1998/5, 'One of the most relevant factors which led the Commission on Human Rights to create the working group on international migrations and human rights was: 'the increasing manifestations of racism, xenophobia and other forms of discrimination and inhuman and degrading treatment against migrants in different parts of the world' (resolution 1997/15).'

46. Racism, racial discrimination, xenophobia and related intolerance may be aggravated by, inter alia, inequitable distribution of wealth, marginalization and social exclusion. New communication technologies, including such computer networks as the Internet, are being used to disseminate racist and xenophobic propaganda. Racial discrimination against migrant workers continues to increase despite efforts undertaken by the international community to protect the human rights of migrant workers and members of their families (see General Assembly resolution 53/132).

47. The Special Rapporteur believes that the core of the problem lies in everyday customs, which is where the primary manifestations take place and where they are the most ingrained. Such customs are linked to a number of forms of behaviour that must be rooted out by taking specific and determined action to promote human rights and democracy.

48. A sense of alienation is part of being a migrant. Moreover, racial and ethnic conflicts were often at the origin of the great migrations of our era. Migrant populations who suffer from such violations do not necessarily have the status of a non-national and persons engaging in discriminatory acts are generally unaware of the migrant status of their victims.

49. Only in a few cases, where other more political and military considerations are involved, do such racial and ethnic conflicts lead to armed conflicts. Where that has not happened, migrant populations within and outside their own countries also suffer from discrimination and racism. This aspect of intolerance at the origin, in transit and at the destination of migrants is an important point where the issues related to racial discrimination and ethnic conflicts intersect with those related to movements of people.

50. The implications of this link between migration, racial discrimination and ethnic conflicts are even more disturbing when it comes to the problem of the return and reintegration of migrants who may have been sent back because they were undocumented in their 'desired' destinations. In addition to the issues raised by the right to development of these

people, they have to face the consequences of the cultural and psychological effects of returning.

51. Discrimination against migrant workers in the field of employment takes many forms, such as limitations or preferences with regard to the kind of work they can do. Some contracts deny migrants certain advantages and also apply rules on job security that differ from those applied to nationals; sometimes they are excluded from the regulations on working conditions and denied the right to take part in trade union activities. The ILO Migrant Workers (Supplementary Provisions) Convention, 1975 (No. 143) deals, in its part I, with migrations in abusive conditions and, in its part II, with equality of opportunity and treatment.

52. The incorporation of this complex set of issues into international standards is one of the features of the International Convention on the Protection of the Rights of All Migrant Workers and Members of Their Families, which has been ratified by 12 countries.

53. As regards the children of migrants, there is resistance in some States to registering or enrolling the children of immigrants in school for fear that the general educational level will fall. In dealing with this issue, it should be remembered that those children have to adapt to different customs and languages, unless special measures are taken to help them overcome their difficulties.

54. In many countries, there are laws and practices that discriminate against foreigners seeking work in a country that is not their own. The granting of visas on the basis of the applicant's country or continent of origin and labour market regulations based on discriminatory criteria, together with xenophobia in the name of national security, nationalism or national preferences, are some of the most common realities that migrant workers have to live with and that give the Special Rapporteur cause for concern.

B. Violence against women migrant workers

55. The Special Rapporteur believes it is very important to tackle the problem of violence against women migrant workers as a vulnerable group.

56. Due to their double marginalization as women and as migrants, women migrant workers may easily find themselves in situations in which they are vulnerable to violence and abuse, both at home and at work (see E/CN.4/1998/74/Add.1). Women migrant workers dominate the informal labour market of most countries, working as domestic, industrial or agricultural labour or in the service sector. When women, most of whom are heads of household, find themselves in social circumstances that make it difficult for them to find paid work, they are forced to migrate. The way in which gender roles are traditionally established and the fact that men often do not share the domestic chores, particularly looking after children on a daily basis, make it even more difficult for women to develop personally and professionally. That situation often discourages women from staying in their families and/or places of origin. Migrant women, like many other women who do not migrate but who work outside the home, often leave their children in the care of family members or someone else. In many cases, particularly when the father is mostly or com-

pletely absent, this leads to the loss of sources of affection and to family breakdown. Both women who have been the victims of trafficking and those who migrate voluntarily may end up in situations of exploitation, violence and abuse, all of which have their origin in a situation like the one described above. The exchange of sexual favours for permission to transit, which is common practice on some frontiers, is also a form of gender-based harassment to which migrant women are often subjected.

57. The situation of women migrant workers within most social structures is one of heightened marginalization, often exacerbated and implicitly condoned by the State (see E/CN.4/1997/47). (...)

64. According to the most recent estimates, there are today about 130 million international or 'non-national' migrants in the world. Women account for 50 per cent of this figure, although country statistics are regrettably scarce and take virtually no account of those without the necessary documentation. An estimated 30 million people come into the latter category, and women account for an increasing number of them.

65. The United Nations is concerned at the difficult situation of women migrant workers, as many of them have been the victims of gender-based violence. Migrant workers' lack of education, training and knowledge means they are easily deceived. The Fourth World Conference on Women, held in Beijing in September 1995, analysed the situation of migrant women and called on States to recognize the vulnerability of those women to violence and other forms of abuse. Particular attention was devoted to migrant women whose legal status in the host country depended on employers. The Platform for Action (chapter IV, section D) that came out of the Conference urged Governments to establish linguistically and culturally accessible services for migrant women and girls, including women migrant workers, who were victims of gender-based violence.

66. Although it is a research topic of growing interest, little attention has been paid to gender distribution in the various categories of migrants and its consequences for the families and communities in their places of origin.

C. **Situation of migrant children (...)**

D. **Vulnerability**

70. There are different perspectives on the vulnerability of migrants. Those perspectives vary according to whether the States concerned are countries of origin, transit or destination for migrants. Consequently, the differences between those perspectives becomes more pronounced with respect to problems stemming from the integration of migrants into the host society; social, religious and linguistic differences; the relationship between State sovereignty and undocumented migration; or problems stemming from the trafficking in migrants. 'An essential element in the understanding of vulnerability was the factor of powerlessness which, more often than not, characterized the migrant'.

71. In her address at the University of Oxford in 1997, the United Nations High Commissioner for Human Rights said that 'one lesson we need to learn, and to reflect in our ap-

proach, is that the essence of rights is that they are empowering'. Thus, vulnerability is understood as a condition of a lack of empowerment, a condition imposed on a person by the power structure of a country. There is a structural and cultural vulnerability ascribed to non-nationals, foreigners or immigrants by the 'nationals' of a given country. The structural nature derives from the existence of a power structure which shows that in any given national society, some have more power than others.

72. The cultural nature of vulnerability derives from the set of cultural elements (stereotypes, prejudices, racism, xenophobia, ignorance and institutional discrimination), with derogatory meanings which tend to justify the differences between 'nationals' and non-nationals or migrants.

73. The combination of (a) power differentials based on a structure where the immigrant is at a lower level than nationals, with (b) the set of cultural elements which justify it, results in various degrees of impunity in cases of the violation of the human rights of a migrant. This impunity then becomes an empirical indication of the powerlessness of the migrant, which is equal to his or her vulnerability. ' ''Impunity'' here is understood as the absence of economic, social or political costs for the violator of the human rights of a migrant' para. 30).

74. Vulnerability is not a condition that immigrants take with them to the country of destination, whether or not their entry into a given country is legal. It is not intrinsic to racial characteristics, or to a country or ethnic origin, or to the development conditions of the country or region of origin. What is intrinsic to the condition of every human being and thus to every migrant, wherever he or she may go, is the ability to transcend situations imposed against his or her will. In this commitment, the empowering function of human rights protection plays a fundamental role.

E. Obstacles to full protection

75. An important part of the mandate contained in resolution 1999/44 is to gather information on the obstacles to the full and effective protection of the human rights of migrants.

76. The obstacles identified by the working group of intergovernmental experts are categorized as institutional, social and economic; some of them deserve special attention.

77. One of the basic institutional obstacles is the absence or non-acceptance in domestic legislation of universal standards which explicitly recognize the human rights of migrants. Many countries have incorporated human rights standards into their domestic legal systems, although their application has, in the best of cases, been restricted to their own citizens. Another institutional obstacle is the failure to achieve widespread ratification of international instruments dealing with migrants' rights, such as ILO conventions No. 97 and No. 143 and the 1990 International Convention on the Protection of the Rights of All Migrant Workers and Members of Their Families.

78. The vulnerability of migrants is another significant obstacle: human rights abuses related to deportations and inadequate training of officials in human rights matters can be counted as institutional obstacles.

79. Among the social obstacles confronting migrants are social exclusion and the concentration of migrant households in disadvantaged urban areas, which make access to education, health care or employment more difficult. Even more seriously, the social obstacles include segregation and hostility, stereotyping, xenophobia and racism.

80. There are some groups of migrants who hover on the fringes of the documented and undocumented sectors. They include, in the first place, women used for pornography and prostitution; domestic workers, most of whom are women; and farm and seasonal workers, who seem to be particularly vulnerable to rights abuses because of their short-term employment, low educational level and labour legislation that favours agro-business.

81. A large number of countries are unwilling to ratify the human rights standards of the United Nations and ILO. This unwillingness is the result of real people defending real interests with the backing of real power bases – the very people who are often responsible for the obstacles to the full application of these human rights standards.

VII. PRELIMINARY CONCLUSIONS

82. Contemporary trends in migrant movements in the era of globalization pose a challenge to the protection of the human rights of that large sector of the world's population. The first challenge is to define a concept of migrant populations that will cover new situations and to translate that into definitions in the international instruments. The situations referred to are those in which a large number of persons find themselves after leaving their country of origin or even before they do so. Unlike refugees, these populations have no formal status that affords them international protection. In many cases, these same groups and individuals do not fit into the category of migrant worker. This shortcoming in terms of definitions is all the more serious if we bear in mind that well-founded field studies show that more and more of today's migrants are women on whom there are no data.

83. The phenomenon of women migrants is a sign of the growing participation of women in remunerated productive activities. The same phenomenon is also a manifestation of a change in the social fabric, the main feature of which is the increase in the number of households headed by women. In many cases, the new family situation arises when the father migrates or leaves his family.

84. Households in which the mother has to migrate in search of a better standard of living for its members, as well as households in which the mother stays behind while the father migrates, are becoming increasingly common, and will become a defining characteristic of societies in many countries in the twenty-first century.

85. The changes in lifestyle implied by these new roles also determine how individuals in these families are prepared for working life. Often, these households are the same as those in which the phenomenon of child migration is most common. In addition to all that, the

consequences of changing roles, particularly with regard to the use and control of resources and decision-making within the family, need to be dealt with. Often, these
changes in households find outward expression in alarming episodes of physical and psychological domestic violence.

86. As well as the question marks concerning definitions, the limitations of international
legislation have also to be considered. It is only the International Convention of 1990
which does not restrict itself exclusively to references to migrant workers but also includes members of their families. This Convention has not yet entered into force; if it
were to do so, it could be an important tool for the protection of the rights of migrants,
including those of undocumented migrants.

87. The documents relating to the Third Decade to Combat Racism and Racial Discrimination and, in particular, those relating to the Special Rapporteur on contemporary forms
of racism, racial discrimination, xenophobia and related intolerance also discuss discrimination against migrant workers (see E/CN.4/1998/78). The provisions of the international
conventions on migrant workers address discrimination in employment. Although the
Convention on the Elimination of All Forms of Discrimination against Women and the
Convention on the Rights of the Child cover migrant women and children, they do not
deal specifically with the rights of those persons who are in transit outside the borders of
their country. Those vulnerable groups receive special treatment in the analysis of the issue of trafficking in women and children. However, he issues of migrant women and children are not limited to the problem of trafficking.

88. Trafficking in persons is the aspect of migration about which the international community is particularly concerned. The concept of trafficking can be approached from various perspectives. The term should be distinguished from 'smuggling'. Whereas trafficking may include a complex organization of contacts, smuggling refers solely to unlawful
border-crossing services. Trafficking in persons in particular involves violations of a number of international conventions. This applies to persons who are victims at the moment of
departure, transit and arrival in the country of destination.

89. The Special Rapporteur believes that special emphasis should be laid on the problem
of the forms of intolerance that arise when the reinsertion of migrant populations is completed. Similar emphasis should be laid on dealing with the intolerance that impels these
groups to migrate.

90. The day-to-day problems faced by migrants, especially by women migrants who have
suffered from systematic gender-based violence and who have been unable to get a satisfactory response from the relevant authorities, are also a cause of deep concern and, as in
the case of the preliminary conclusions noted above, effective action must be taken to resolve them and to protect the rights of that sector of the population.

VIII. RECOMMENDATIONS

91. The Special Rapporteur makes the following recommendations:
(a) In order to allow the Special Rapporteur to carry out her mandate, an inter-agency task
force should be established to assist her and the Office of the High Commissioner for Hu-

man Rights in their work. The objectives of the task force would be: to contribute to research; to provide expert knowledge on how to deal with the topic in order to enhance the work of the Special Rapporteur; to collect and transmit systematically the data and information available on the situation of migrants in various countries; to facilitate the contacts the Special Rapporteur needs to make in order to fulfil her duties; and to help in the preparation of her reports to the Commission;

(b) Intersectoral cooperation should be promoted to collect and analyse specific casesto illustrate the emerging categories of migrants without protection;

(c) Existing standards and institutional arrangements for the full protection of migrants should be promoted, including the prevention of arbitrary expulsion, the return of undocumented migrants in dignified circumstances, and measures for the reinsertion of returnees, especially women who have been the victims of trafficking and persons belonging to national minorities;

(d) The forums for negotiation and discussion should be strengthened such as the Puebla process, the Manila process and the Bangkok, Dakar, Mediterranean, Cairo, Lima and Commonwealth of Independent States (CIS) initiatives, by finding ways to include the civil and academic sectors in that framework;

(e) Action should be taken to promote and lobby for the ratification of the International Convention on the Protection of the Rights of All Migrant Workers and Members of Their Families;

(f) Attention should be focused on the links between the topic of migration and the ongoing work of the Commission on Crime Prevention and Criminal Justice and, in particular, on the effects of trafficking and smuggling on migrants' rights;

(g) An intersectoral dialogue should be initiated to find ways and to develop specific policies to deal with migration issues and their implications for development, gender equity and the return and integration of repatriated migrants;

(h) The processes whereby multinational trading agreements are reached and country groupings formed should be monitored, with the aim of including in those processes a deeper analysis of the impact of globalization on the migration of people, thus averting situations in which the rights of migrants are violated;

(i) Action should be taken to strengthen technical advisory services and training in international human rights instruments for civil servants and migration officials at all levels, while incorporating the gender perspective into work with migrant populations;

(j) Cooperative action to draw up migration policies that prevent the recurrence of patterns of subordination, violence against women migrants and gender-based discrimination should be encouraged;

(k) Governments should be urged, in forums for negotiations and discussion, to take steps to prevent the trafficking in persons; and

(l) Close links should be established between the protection of migrants' rights and the work of the Preparatory Committee for the World Conference against Racism, Racial Discrimination, Xenophobia and Related Intolerance (to be held in 2001) as a way of documenting the cases of mass migrations caused by discrimination and by racial and ethnic conflicts. Of particular interest is the link between this phenomenon and factors that encourage people, especially women, to migrate.

The Human Rights Committee (ICCPR):
GENERAL COMMENT 15: The Position of Aliens under the Covenant (1986)[22]

1. Reports from States parties have often failed to take into account that each State party must ensure the rights in the Covenant to 'all individuals within its territory and subject to its jurisdiction' (art. 2, para. 1). In general, the rights set forth in the Covenant apply to everyone, irrespective of reciprocity, and irrespective of his or her nationality or stateless-ness.

2. Thus, the general rule is that each one of the rights of the Covenant must be guaranteed without discrimination between citizens and aliens. Aliens receive the benefit of the gen-eral requirement of non-discrimination in respect of the rights guaranteed in the Covenant, as provided for in article 2 thereof. This guarantee applies to aliens and citizens alike. Ex-ceptionally, some of the rights recognized in the Covenant are expressly applicable only to citizens (art. 25), while article 13 applies only to aliens. However, the Committee's ex-perience in examining reports shows that in a number of countries other rights that aliens should enjoy under the Covenant are denied to them or are subject to limitations that can-not always be justified under the Covenant.

3. A few constitutions provide for equality of aliens with citizens. Some constitutions adopted more recently carefully distinguish fundamental rights that apply to all and those granted to citizens only, and deal with each in detail. In many States, however, the consti-tutions are drafted in terms of citizens only when granting relevant rights. Legislation and case law may also play an important part in providing for the rights of aliens. The Com-mittee has been informed that in some States fundamental rights, though not guaranteed to aliens by the Constitution or other legislation, will also be extended to them as required by the Covenant. In certain cases, however, there has clearly been a failure to implement Covenant rights without discrimination in respect of aliens.

4. The Committee considers that in their reports States parties should give attention to the position of aliens, both under their law and in actual practice. The Covenant gives aliens all the protection regarding rights guaranteed therein, and its requirements should be ob-served by States parties in their legislation and in practice as appropriate. The position of aliens would thus be considerably improved. States parties should ensure that the provi-sions of the Covenant and the rights under it are made known to aliens within their juris-diction.

5. The Covenant does not recognize the right of aliens to enter or reside in the territory of a State party. It is in principle a matter for the State to decide who it will admit to its terri-tory. However, in certain circumstances an alien may enjoy the protection of the Covenant

---

[22] The Position of Aliens under the Covenant, (twenty-seventh session, 1986) 11 April 1986.

even in relation to entry or residence, for example, when considerations of non-discrimination, prohibition of inhuman treatment and respect for family life arise.

6. Consent for entry may be given subject to conditions relating, for example, to movement, residence and employment. A State may also impose general conditions upon an alien who is in transit. However, once aliens are allowed to enter the territory of a State party they are entitled to the rights set out in the Covenant.

7. Aliens thus have an inherent right to life, protected by law, and may not be arbitrarily deprived of life. They must not be subjected to torture or to cruel, inhuman or degrading treatment or punishment; nor may they be held in slavery or servitude. Aliens have the full right to liberty and security of the person. If lawfully deprived of their liberty, they shall be treated with humanity and with respect for the inherent dignity of their person. Aliens may not be imprisoned for failure to fulfil a contractual obligation. They have the right to liberty of movement and free choice of residence; they shall be free to leave the country. Aliens shall be equal before the courts and tribunals, and shall be entitled to a fair and public hearing by a competent, independent and impartial tribunal established by law in the determination of any criminal charge or of rights and obligations in a suit at law. Aliens shall not be subjected to retrospective penal legislation, and are entitled to recognition before the law. They may not be subjected to arbitrary or unlawful interference with their privacy, family, home or correspondence. They have the right to freedom of thought, conscience and religion, and the right to hold opinions and to express them. Aliens receive the benefit of the right of peaceful assembly and of freedom of association. They may marry when at marriageable age. Their children are entitled to those measures of protection required by their status as minors. In those cases where aliens constitute a minority within the meaning of article 27, they shall not be denied the right, in community with other members of their group, to enjoy their own culture, to profess and practise their own religion and to use their own language. Aliens are entitled to equal protection by the law. There shall be no discrimination between aliens and citizens in the application of these rights. These rights of aliens may be qualified only by such limitations as may be lawfully imposed under the Covenant.

8. Once an alien is lawfully within a territory, his freedom of movement within the territory and his right to leave that territory may only be restricted in accordance with article 12, paragraph 3. Differences in treatment in this regard between aliens and nationals, or between different categories of aliens, need to be justified under article 12, paragraph 3. Since such restrictions must, *inter alia*, be consistent with the other rights recognized in the Covenant, a State party cannot, by restraining an alien or deporting him to a third country, arbitrarily prevent his return to his own country (art. 12, para. 4).

9. Many reports have given insufficient information on matters relevant to article 13. That article is applicable to all procedures aimed at the obligatory departure of an alien, whether described in national law as expulsion or otherwise. If such procedures entail arrest, the safeguards of the Covenant relating to deprivation of liberty (arts. 9 and 10) may also be applicable. If the arrest is for the particular purpose of extradition, other provisions of national and international law may apply. Normally an alien who is expelled must be allowed to leave for any country that agrees to take him. The particular rights of article 13

only protect those aliens who are lawfully in the territory of a State party. This means that national law concerning the requirements for entry and stay must be taken into account in determining the scope of that protection, and that illegal entrants and aliens who have stayed longer than the law or their permits allow, in particular, are not covered by its provisions. However, if the legality of an alien's entry or stay is in dispute, any decision on this point leading to his expulsion or deportation ought to be taken in accordance with article 13. It is for the competent authorities of the State party, in good faith and in the exercise of their powers, to apply and interpret the domestic law, observing, however, such requirements under the Covenant as equality before the law (art. 26).

10. Article 13 directly regulates only the procedure and not the substantive grounds for expulsion. However, by allowing only those carried out 'in pursuance of a decision reached in accordance with law', its purpose is clearly to prevent arbitrary expulsions. On the other hand, it entitles each alien to a decision in his own case and, hence, article 13 would not be satisfied with laws or decisions providing for collective or mass expulsions. This understanding, in the opinion of the Committee, is confirmed by further provisions concerning the right to submit reasons against expulsion and to have the decision reviewed by and to be represented before the competent authority or someone designated by it. An alien must be given full facilities for pursuing his remedy against expulsion so that this right will in all the circumstances of his case be an effective one. The principles of article 13 relating to appeal against expulsion and the entitlement to review by a competent authority may only be departed from when 'compelling reasons of national security' so require. Discrimination may not be made between different categories of aliens in the application of article 13.

4.5.9

The Human Rights Committee (ICCPR): GENERAL COMMENT 27: Freedom of Movement (1999)[23]

1. Liberty of movement is an indispensable condition for the free development of a person. It interacts with several other rights enshrined in the Covenant, as is often shown in the Committee's practice in considering reports from States parties and communications from individuals. Moreover, the Committee in its general comment No. 15 ('The position of aliens under the Covenant', 1986) referred to the special link between articles 12 and 13.[24]

---

[23] Freedom of Movement (Art.12), 2 November 1999, CCPR/C/21/Rev.1/Add.9, CCPR General Comment 27(67).
[24] HRI/GEN/1/Rev.3, 15 August 1997, p. 20 (para. 8).

2. The permissible limitations which may be imposed on the rights protected under article 12 must not nullify the principle of liberty of movement, and are governed by the requirement of necessity provided for in article 12, paragraph 3, and by the need for consistency with the other rights recognized in the Covenant.

3. States parties should provide the Committee in their reports with the relevant domestic legal rules and administrative and judicial practices relating to the rights protected by article 12, taking into account the issues discussed in the present general comment. They must also include information on remedies available if these rights are restricted.

Liberty of movement and freedom to choose residence (para. 1)

4. Everyone lawfully within the territory of a State enjoys, within that territory, the right to move freely and to choose his or her place of residence. In principle, citizens of a State are always lawfully within the territory of that State. The question whether an alien is 'lawfully' within the territory of a State is a matter governed by domestic law, which may subject the entry of an alien to the territory of a State to restrictions, provided they are in compliance with the State's international obligations. In that connection, the Committee has held that an alien who entered the State illegally, but whose status has been regularized, must be considered to be lawfully within the territory for the purposes of article 12.[25] Once a person is lawfully within a State, any restrictions on his or her rights guaranteed by article 12, paragraphs 1 and 2, as well as any treatment different from that accorded to nationals, have to be justified under the rules provided for by article 12, paragraph 3.[26] It is, therefore, important that States parties indicate in their reports the circumstances in which they treat aliens differently from their nationals in this regard and how they justify this difference in treatment.

5. The right to move freely relates to the whole territory of a State, including all parts of federal States. According to article 12, paragraph 1, persons are entitled to move from one place to another and to establish themselves in a place of their choice. The enjoyment of this right must not be made dependent on any particular purpose or reason for the person wanting to move or to stay in a place. Any restrictions must be in conformity with paragraph 3.

6. The State party must ensure that the rights guaranteed in article 12 are protected not only from public but also from private interference. In the case of women, this obligation to protect is particularly pertinent. For example, it is incompatible with article 12, paragraph 1, that the right of a woman to move freely and to choose her residence be made subject, by law or practice, to the decision of another person, including a relative.

7. Subject to the provisions of article 12, paragraph 3, the right to reside in a place of one's choice within the territory includes protection against all forms of forced internal displacement. It also precludes preventing the entry or stay of persons in a defined part of

[25] Communication No. 456/1991, Celepli v. Sweden, para. 9.2.
[26] General comment No. 15, para. 8, in HRI/GEN/1/Rev.3, 15 August 1997, p. 20.

the territory. Lawful detention, however, affects more specifically the right to personal liberty and is covered by article 9 of the Covenant. In some circumstances, articles 12 and 9 may come into play together.[27]

Freedom to leave any country, including one's own (para. 2)

8. Freedom to leave the territory of a State may not be made dependent on any specific purpose or on the period of time the individual chooses to stay outside the country. Thus travelling abroad is covered, as well as departure for permanent emigration. Likewise, the right of the individual to determine the State of destination is part of the legal guarantee. As the scope of article 12, paragraph 2, is not restricted to persons lawfully within the territory of a State, an alien being legally expelled from the country is likewise entitled to elect the State of destination, subject to the agreement of that State.[28]

9. In order to enable the individual to enjoy the rights guaranteed by article 12, paragraph 2, obligations are imposed both on the State of residence and on the State of nationality. [29] Since international travel usually requires appropriate documents, in particular a passport, the right to leave a country must include the right to obtain the necessary travel documents. The issuing of passports is normally incumbent on the State of nationality of the individual. The refusal by a State to issue a passport or prolong its validity for a national residing abroad may deprive this person of the right to leave the country of residence and to travel elsewhere.[30] It is no justification for the State to claim that its national would be able to return to its territory without a passport.

10. The practice of States often shows that legal rules and administrative measures adversely affect the right to leave, in particular, a person's own country. It is therefore of the utmost importance that States parties report on all legal and practical restrictions on the right to leave which they apply both to nationals and to foreigners, in order to enable the Committee to assess the conformity of these rules and practices with article 12, paragraph 3. States parties should also include information in their reports on measures that impose sanctions on international carriers which bring to their territory persons without required documents, where those measures affect the right to leave another country.

Restrictions (para. 3)

11. Article 12, paragraph 3, provides for exceptional circumstances in which rights under paragraphs 1 and 2 may be restricted. This provision authorizes the State to restrict these rights only to protect national security, public order (*ordre public*), public health or mor-

---

[27] See, for example, communication No. 138/1983, *Mpandajila* v. *Zaire*, para. 10; communication No. 157/1983, *Mpaka-Nsusu* v. *Zaire*, para. 10; communication Nos. 241/1987 and 242/1987, *Birhashwirwa/Tshisekedi* v. *Zaire*, para. 13.

[28] See general comment No. 15, para. 9, in HRI/GEN/1/Rev.3, 15 August 1997, p. 21.

[29] See communication No. 106/1981, *Montero* v. *Uruguay*, para. 9.4; communication No. 57/1979, *Vidal Martins* v. *Uruguay*, para. 7; communication No. 77/1980, *Lichtensztejn* v. *Uruguay*, para. 6.1.

[30] See communication No. 57/1979, *Vidal Martins* v. *Uruguay*, para. 9.

als and the rights and freedoms of others. To be permissible, restrictions must be provided by law, must be necessary in a democratic society for the protection of these purposes and must be consistent with all other rights recognized in the Covenant (see para. 18 below).

12. The law itself has to establish the conditions under which the rights may be limited. State reports should therefore specify the legal norms upon which restrictions are founded. Restrictions which are not provided for in the law or are not in conformity with the requirements of article 12, paragraph 3, would violate the rights guaranteed by paragraphs 1 and 2.

13. In adopting laws providing for restrictions permitted by article 12, paragraph 3, States should always be guided by the principle that the restrictions must not impair the essence of the right (cf. art. 5, para. 1); the relation between right and restriction, between norm and exception, must not be reversed. The laws authorizing the application of restrictions should use precise criteria and may not confer unfettered discretion on those charged with their execution.

14. Article 12, paragraph 3, clearly indicates that it is not sufficient that the restrictions serve the permissible purposes; they must also be necessary to protect them. Restrictive measures must conform to the principle of proportionality; they must be appropriate to achieve their protective function; they must be the least intrusive instrument amongst those which might achieve the desired result; and they must be proportionate to the interest to be protected.

15. The principle of proportionality has to be respected not only in the law that frames the restrictions, but also by the administrative and judicial authorities in applying the law. States should ensure that any proceedings relating to the exercise or restriction of these rights are expeditious and that reasons for the application of restrictive measures are provided.

16. States have often failed to show that the application of their laws restricting the rights enshrined in article 12, paragraphs 1 and 2, are in conformity with all requirements referred to in article 12, paragraph 3. The application of restrictions in any individual case must be based on clear legal grounds and meet the test of necessity and the requirements of proportionality. These conditions would not be met, for example, if an individual were prevented from leaving a country merely on the ground that he or she is the holder of 'State secrets', or if an individual were prevented from travelling internally without a specific permit. On the other hand, the conditions could be met by restrictions on access to military zones on national security grounds, or limitations on the freedom to settle in areas inhabited by indigenous or minorities communities.[31]

17. A major source of concern is the manifold legal and bureaucratic barriers unnecessarily affecting the full enjoyment of the rights of the individuals to move freely, to leave a country, including their own, and to take up residence. Regarding the right to movement

---

[31] See general comment No. 23, para. 7, in HRI/GEN/1/Rev.3, 15 August 1997, p. 41.

within a country, the Committee has criticized provisions requiring individuals to apply for permission to change their residence or to seek the approval of the local authorities of the place of destination, as well as delays in processing such written applications. States' practice presents an even richer array of obstacles making it more difficult to leave the country, in particular for their own nationals. These rules and practices include, *inter alia*, lack of access for applicants to the competent authorities and lack of information regarding requirements; the requirement to apply for special forms through which the proper application documents for the issuance of a passport can be obtained; the need for supportive statements from employers or family members; exact description of the travel route; issuance of passports only on payment of high fees substantially exceeding the cost of the service rendered by the administration; unreasonable delays in the issuance of travel documents; restrictions on family members travelling together; requirement of a repatriation deposit or a return ticket; requirement of an invitation from the State of destination or from people living there; harassment of applicants, for example by physical intimidation, arrest, loss of employment or expulsion of their children from school or university; refusal to issue a passport because the applicant is said to harm the good name of the country. In the light of these practices, States parties should make sure that all restrictions imposed by them are in full compliance with article 12, paragraph 3.

18. The application of the restrictions permissible under article 12, paragraph 3, needs to be consistent with the other rights guaranteed in the Covenant and with the fundamental principles of equality and non-discrimination. Thus, it would be a clear violation of the Covenant if the rights enshrined in article 12, paragraphs 1 and 2, were restricted by making distinctions of any kind, such as on the basis of race, colour, sex, language, religion, political or other opinion, national or social origin, property, birth or other status. In examining State reports, the Committee has on several occasions found that measures preventing women from moving freely or from leaving the country by requiring them to have the consent or the escort of a male person constitute a violation of article 12.

The right to enter one's own country (para. 4)

19. The right of a person to enter his or her own country recognizes the special relationship of a person to that country. The right has various facets. It implies the right to remain in one's own country. It includes not only the right to return after having left one's own country; it may also entitle a person to come to the country for the first time if he or she was born outside the country (for example, if that country is the person's State of nationality). The right to return is of the utmost importance for refugees seeking voluntary repatriation. It also implies prohibition of enforced population transfers or mass expulsions to other countries.

20. The wording of article 12, paragraph 4, does not distinguish between nationals and aliens ('no one'). Thus, the persons entitled to exercise this right can be identified only by interpreting the meaning of the phrase 'his own country'.[32] The scope of 'his own country' is broader than the concept 'country of his nationality'. It is not limited to nationality

---

[32] See communication No. 538/1993, *Stewart* v. *Canada.*

in a formal sense, that is, nationality acquired at birth or by conferral; it embraces, at the very least, an individual who, because of his or her special ties to or claims in relation to a given country, cannot be considered to be a mere alien. This would be the case, for example, of nationals of a country who have there been stripped of their nationality in violation of international law, and of individuals whose country of nationality has been incorporated in or transferred to another national entity, whose nationality is being denied them. The language of article 12, paragraph 4, moreover, permits a broader interpretation that might embrace other categories of long-term residents, including but not limited to stateless persons arbitrarily deprived of the right to acquire the nationality of the country of such residence. Since other factors may in certain circumstances result in the establishment of close and enduring connections between a person and a country, States parties should include in their reports information on the rights of permanent residents to return to their country of residence.

21. In no case may a person be arbitrarily deprived of the right to enter his or her own country. The reference to the concept of arbitrariness in this context is intended to emphasize that it applies to all State action, legislative, administrative and judicial; it guarantees that even interference provided for by law should be in accordance with the provisions, aims and objectives of the Covenant and should be, in any event, reasonable in the particular circumstances. The Committee considers that there are few, if any, circumstances in which deprivation of the right to enter one's own country could be reasonable. A State party must not, by stripping a person of nationality or by expelling an individual to a third country, arbitrarily prevent this person from returning to his or her own country.

GLOSSARY[1]

adjudication	see 'determination'
adjudicator	A generic term to describe government officials who are authorized by law to issue determinations.
adjustment of status	see 'change of status'
administrative judge	A person who presides at an administrative hearing. In some States, administrative proceedings are conducted within the executive branch, rather than the judicial branch. In the U.S., for example, immigration matters are decided by administrative judges subordinate to the Attorney General (equivalent to Minister of Justice).
administrative law	The law governing the organization and operation of the executive branch of government and the relations of the executive with the legislature, the judiciary, and the public.
admission	In the migration context, the granting of entry into the State. An alien has been 'admitted' if he or she passed through a checkpoint (air, land or sea) and was permitted to enter by border control officials. In contrast, an alien who has entered clandestinely is not considered to have been admitted.
affidavit	Written testimony given under oath.
agreement	A mutual understanding (written or unwritten) between two or more persons regarding their relative rights and duties as to past/future conduct.
alias	A name which is not a person's natural name; an assumed or additional name.
alien	A person who is not a citizen of a given State.
amnesty	see 'regularization'
appeal	A proceeding undertaken to reverse a decision by bringing it to a higher authority; often the submission of a lower court's or agency's decision to a higher court for review and possible reversal.
applicant	In the migration context, one who formally requests some government action, such as the grant of refugee status, of a visa or work permit.
application	In the migration context, a request (usually written) submitted to the government by a person or organization seeking some government action.

[1] This Glossary relies heavily on a unofficial document prepared by Ms. Lisa Batey, IOM Vienna. The editor is grateful for her help. As will be noted, many of the terms are 'American' and will not be necessarily used in the EU-context. Yet, for the sake of easy communication, it has been decided to include these 'americanisms'.

arrival/departure card	A card which is filled out by an individual prior to or upon arrival in the country of destination and presented (along with passport and, if required, visa) to officials at the checkpoint. In some States, border officials collect the cards upon entry; in other States, the card or a portion of it is returned to the traveler and must be presented upon departure from the State. International standards for such cards are defined by ICAO in Annex 9 to the Convention on International Civil Aviation.
asset forfeiture	The governmental taking of property due to its, or its owner's, involvement in criminal activity, such as the impounding of a vehicle used for smuggling aliens into a State.
bilateral	Involving two parties or two States. Contrast 'multilateral'.
bill	In the legislative context, a bill is a proposed piece of legislation that has been submitted for consider-ation by the legislative body. If a bill passes and enters into force, it becomes a law.
birth certificate	An original document, usually issued under governmental or religious authority, stating when and where a person was born.
bona fide (Latin)	Made in good faith; without fraud; genuine. Contrasts '*mala fide*'.
***bona fide* applicant**	In the migration context, a person who: (a) genuinely intends to enter the State for a lawful purpose; and (b) who, in the opinion of a consular or immigration officer, (i) is not likely to remain unlawfully, and (ii) is not likely to breach the conditions of any permit granted.
bond	In the migration context, a bond means a monetary sum collected by the State as an assurance that a non-citizen will take some required action, usually leaving the State. Departure bonds might be collected upon visa issuance or entry, while another type of bond would be that paid in order to be released from detention. Funds held as a bond are typically refunded upon proof of departure, such as when the person visits the State's consulate in the person's home country.
border	The line separating two political or geographic areas, such as States or subparts thereof.
border control	A State's regulation of the entry of persons onto its territory, as an exercise of its sovereignty. Border control is a major element of migration manage-ment. The modern global economy and international standards require a balancing between facilitating the entry of legitimate travelers and intercepting the small minority of travelers entering for inappropriate reasons or with invalid documentation.
border control officials	A generic term to describe those officials whose primary task is to guard the border and enforce the immigration (and possibly customs) laws of the State – i.e. to identify

undocumented aliens, determine who may be a refugee, etc. In some States, there are 'border guards', in others 'border police' or 'aliens police'. Some States assign the functions of operating checkpoints and patrolling the border between checkpoints to two different government entities.

brain drain
Emigration of persons whose technical and professional skills are scarce in their home country.

burden of proof
A party's duty to prove a disputed assertion or charge. In the migration context, an alien seeking entry into foreign State generally bears the burden of proof; that is, the alien must prove that he or she is eligible to enter and not inadmissible under the laws of the State.

carbon dioxide sensors
Equipment (either stationary or portable) used to determine whether carbon dioxide is present in a closed container, such as a railway car or the back of a truck. Such sensors are used to determine whether persons are being smuggled together with cargo crossing state borders.

carrier
'Carrier' in relation to conveyance, means the owner or charterer of the conveyance. A 'carrier' usually refers to an airline, bus or rail company, or cruise line. But under the laws of some States, the term includes any owner of a conveyance (including conveyances intended for freight) which carries a person into the State.

carrier liability law
A law imposing fines upon carriers who bring in persons who do not have valid entry documents. International practice has shown that advanced administrative, procedural, and technological mechanisms must be in place in order for a fining regime to be effective.

certificate of identity
A certificate of identity is a document (other than a passport) issued by the government of any country to any person in order to facilitate that person's entry into or exit from any country. A certificate of identity: (i) establishes the identity but not the nationality of a person, and (ii) gives that person the right to enter the country whose government has issued the document. States recognize certificates of identity approved by the relevant Ministry, including travel documents issued by recognized international organizations. Example: United Nations travel documents are acceptable travel documents in nearly every State, even though they are not issued by a government.

change of status
Change of status procedures are those which define how an alien lawfully present in one immigration status may seek a different status. For example, a foreign student on a student visa who is offered a job upon completion of studies would typically need to seek a change of status, so that the student visa would be replaced by a work visa.

checkpoint
A location (on the land border or at an airport or seaport) where persons request admission from border control authorities in order to enter the State. Often referred to as 'passport control', which is a bit of a misnomer. In

	international practice, even where all documents are in order, someone may be denied entry if the border control official has reason to believe that the person falls within the grounds of inadmissibility or seeks entry for a purpose other than that stated.
citizenship	In international law, the legal bond between an individual and a State as recognized by operation of law. Citizenship (also often referred to as 'Nationality') is not limited by ethnic or religious characteristics. See also under 'nationality'.
civil law	1. One of the two prominent systems of jurisprudence in the Western world, originally administered in the Roman Empire and still in effect in continental Europe and Latin America, among other parts of the world. Contrast 'common law'. 2. Within a common law system, civil law is the branch of law relating to enforcement of non-criminal laws or protection of rights and interests of private parties. Some civil law actions involve only private individuals or firms; others involve government entities as either plaintiff or defendant. Civil law actions seek either payment of compensation (often called 'damages') or court order requiring or prohibiting a given action. They do not involve criminal liability or possibility of imprisonment.
claim	An assertion made to a government agency or court seeking an action or determination of a right or benefit, such as refugee status or the right to compensation or legal redress in civil proceedings. See also 'application'.
common law	One of the two prominent systems of jurisprudence in the Western World, where judicial interpretations form the body of law and are binding on later judges. Based on the English legal system, common law systems are found in most former British colonies, including the U.S. and Australia. Contrast 'civil law'.
complaint	A formal legal document filed by a plaintiff to initiate a civil suit or administrative proceedings. A complaint usually sets forth allegations that the defendant has engaged in conduct which breached the rights of the plaintiff, and may include multiple claims for legal redress.
consular officials	Government officials representing the State abroad concerning visa and residency issues. Consular officials are usually employees of the Ministry of Foreign Affairs, although in a few countries they come from a separate migration agency.
conveyance	Any form of aircraft, ship, train, automobile or other vehicle or vessel capable of being used to transport a person to or from a State.
craft	see 'conveyance'
credibility assessment	In the migration context, making a credibility assessment is a basic step in adjudicating any application for a visa, for

refugee or other immigration status. The essence of a credibility assessment is determining whether the information presented by the applicant (which might be on a written application, in an interview, or both) is consistent and believable.

credible   Believable on reasonable grounds.

criminal law   The branch of law relating to the punishment of crimes. The State brings before the court persons charged with violation of criminal statutes, usually seeking either imprisonment or fine (although increasing trend is toward alternative forms of punishment such as mandatory public service).

custody   The care and control of a thing or person for inspection, preservation, or security. In the case of a minor, a court might assign custody to a relative or other guardian. In the migration context, a person who is detained by authorities is 'in custody'.

customs   The agency or procedure for collecting duties (taxes) on imports or exports.

customs declaration A form which asks arriving persons for information about goods they are bringing into the country, designed to identify any illegal goods or goods on which a customs duty (tax) is owed.

data transfer   To cause factual information (data) to pass from one place to another. In modern usage, this often refers to information passing from one computer to another. Also referred to as 'data transmission'.

de facto (Latin)   Existing in fact; having effect even though not formally or legally recognized. Contrast '*de jure*'.

de facto partner   A growing number of States recognize not only spouses, but also certain relationships between unmarried adults, for purposes of granting permanent residence or other immigration status. For example, New Zealand defines 'de facto partner' as a partner in a heterosexual or same sex relationship who has been living with their partner in a genuine and stable relationship for at least 2 years immediately before their immigration application is filed.

de jure (Latin)   Existing by right or according to law. Contrast 'de facto'.

deadline   A time limit for the completion of an activity, such as the filing of an application for immigration status.

decision   A judicial or administrative determination after consideration of the facts and the law; a conclusion reached by a court or by an agency or other governmental authority.

defendant   A person required to answer a complaint filed in a civil suit. It can also refer to one accused of a crime in a criminal proceeding.

dependent   In general use, one who relies on another for support. In the migration context, a spouse and minor children are generally considered 'dependents', even if the spouse is not financially dependent.

deportation	The act of a State in the exercise of its sovereignty in removing an alien from its territory after refusal of admission or termination of permission to remain. Western practice generally is that deportation happens only upon order of a judge and after any appeal rights have been exhausted.
derivative applicant	A person, typically a spouse or minor child, who might receive immigration status on the basis of another's application. Contrast 'principal applicant'
detainee	A detainee is a person who is being held in detention.
detention	Restriction on freedom of movement, usually through enforced confinement, of persons by government authorities. In the migration context, in many States, an alien may be detained pending a decision on refugee status or on admission to or removal from the State. International practice is generally that detention in this and other non-criminal contexts is not intended to be punitive, and therefore that conditions in detention facilities should be better than those in prison facilities.
determination	In the migration context, the decision as to whether an applicant is qualified for the visa, refugee status, or other immigration status he or she seeks.
displaced person	A person who flees his/her State because of fear or dangers other that those which would make him/her a refugee. A displaced person is often forced to flee by internal conflict or natural or man-made disasters.
domicile	Permanent abode or place of residence.
due process	The conduct of legal proceedings according to generally-accepted rules and principles providing for the protection and enforcement of private rights, including notice and the right to a fair hearing before the court or administrative agency with the power to decide the case.
embarkation/ disembarkation card	see 'arrival/departure card'
emigration	The act of departing or exiting from one State in the hope of settling in another. International human rights norms provide that all persons should be free to leave any country, including their own, and that only in very limited circumstances may States impose restrictions on the individual's right to leave its territory.
entitlement	The legal right to something, particularly to monetary benefits paid by a State.
entry stamp	A mark made by a border official in a person's passport stating the date and place at which that person entered the State. Typically, entry stamps are made using rubber stamp and ink; increasingly, the rubber stamps are designed with features which (i) make it more difficult for the stamp to be counterfeited, and (ii) make it possible to identify which border official allowed the entry.
evidence	A perceptible thing that tends to establish or disprove a fact, including testimony, documents, photographs, and

exclusion	physical items relating to the crime or civil dispute at issue. In the migration context, the formal denial of an alien's entry into a State. In some States, border guards or other authorities have the power to exclude aliens; in other States, exclusion is ordered by an immigration judge after a hearing.
exclusion grounds	see 'grounds of inadmissibility'
expiration date	In the migration context, the date on which a visa or an immigration status ceases to be valid.
expulsion	see 'deportation'
extension	The continuation of something for a fixed period. In the migration context, a foreign businessman might apply for an extension of his visa or his immigration status, for example.
extradition	The formal surrender, generally based on treaty or other reciprocating arrangements, by one State to another of an individual accused or convicted of an offence outside its own territory and within the jurisdiction of the other, for the purpose of trial and punishment.
facilitation	In the migration context, facilitation is the fostering or encouraging of legitimate travelers by making travel easier and more convenient. Facilitation can include any number of measures, such as a streamlined visa application process, efficient and well-staffed passenger inspection procedures, etc.
family reunification	In the migration context, the movement of a member or members of a family to join those members of their family who already reside in the receiving country. Numerous international conventions promote family unity, which in many countries is a primary ground for receiving the right to residence.
filing an application	General practice is that an application for a visa or other immigration status is considered to be made, or filed, on the date upon which the application <u>with all required enclosures and necessary fees</u> is received by the appropriate State entity.
foreigner	A person belonging to or owing allegiance to another country. See also 'alien'.
fraud	A knowing misrepresentation of the truth or concealment of a material fact in order to obtain some benefit.
fraudulent documents	Passports, visas or other travel or identity documents which are either (i) altered, falsified, or counterfeited, or (ii) legitimate documents obtained using fraud, such as by pretending to be someone else.
genuine and stable marriage	In the migration context, a marriage that a consular or immigration officer determines: (i) is genuine, because it has been entered into with the intention of being maintained on a long term and exclusive basis, and (ii) is stable because it is likely to endure. In many States, if officers are unable to determine whether the marriage was

entered into with the intention of maintaining it on a long
term and exclusive basis, there is a presumption that it is
genuine, unless there is evidence to the contrary.

green border Term used to describe a State's border between
checkpoints. A water border (river or coastline) might also
be referred to as a 'blue border'.

grounds of inadmissibility Definitions, set forth in migration law or regulations, of
persons who are prohibited from entering the State. Even
where a person is otherwise eligible for a visa or other
immigration status, if he/she falls within a ground of
inadmissibility, the visa or other status will be denied (but
see 'waiver'). Grounds of inadmissibility are typically
designed to preclude entry of undesirable aliens, such as
persons without valid travel documents, persons with
criminal convictions, persons who are believed to be a
danger to public health or public safety, persons who have
been previously deported, etc.

guardian One who has the legal authority and duty to care for
another's person or property, usually because of the other's
incapacity, disability, or status as a minor.

guardianship The relationship between guardian and ward.

hearing The opportunity to be heard or to present one's side of a
case before a tribunal.

holding centres Centres gathering refugees as soon as they arrive in a
receiving country; their status is to be determined before
they are sent to refugee camps or back to their country.

illegal alien see 'undocumented alien'

immigration Movement of persons into a State. Some States define
immigration to include only those seeking permanent
residence, but common usage generally includes all non-
citizens entering the State, whether for a short visit or with
intent to remain permanently.

immunization A medical treatment, usually an injection, designed to
prevent certain diseases.

impostor One who pretends to be someone else in order to deceive
others, such as to receive immigration status or other
benefit.

influx A continuous coming in, especially of individuals in large
numbers.

information systems A generic term for collections of data; in modern usage, the
term implies automated or computerized collections of data.
In the migration context, typically includes lookout systems
and any system for collecting statistics and other
information regarding visa applicants, border crossers,
applicants for asylum and other immigration status.

injunction A court order commanding or preventing a specified action.

interview In the migration context, the process of questioning or
talking with a person in order to obtain information or
determine the personal qualities of the person. An interview

	is a common step in the adjudication of an application for refugee or other immigration status.
irregular migrant	see 'undocumented alien'
judgement	A court's final determination of the rights and obligations of the parties in a case.
jurisdiction	The legal power, right or authority to hear and determine a cause of action (legal or administrative). It can also refer to the limits or territory within which any particular power may be exercised.
jus sanguinis (Latin)	The rule (prevailing in most nations) that a child's nationality is determined by its parents' nationality, irrespective of the place of birth. Contrast '*jus soli*'.
jus soli (Latin)	The American rule that a child's nationality can be determined by its place of birth (although nationality can also be conveyed by the parents). Contrast '*jus sanguinis*'.
labour migration	Movement of persons from their home State to another State for the purpose of employment. Labour immigration is addressed by most States in their migration laws. In addition, some States take an active role in regulating outward labour migration and seeking opportunities for its citizens abroad.
legal proceedings	Any proceeding authorized by law and instituted in a court or administrative tribunal to acquire a right or enforce a remedy.
legalization	see 'regularization'
legitimate	In the migration context, something which is genuine, valid, or lawful (see also '*bona fide*'). For example, a legal migrant enters with a legitimate intent to comply with the migration laws, and presents legitimate travel documents. Contrast '*mala fide*'.
lodging an application	see 'filing an application'
lookout system	A State's official list, usually (but not necessarily) automated, of persons who should be prevented from entering the country or who should be arrested upon arrival. A lookout system is typically an inter-agency project, which receives input from all law enforcement, intelligence, and migration agencies. Whether on computer or in book form, the lookout list should be routinely checked by consular and border control officials when making decisions about granting a visa or allowing someone to enter the State.
machine-readable passport/machine-readable visa	A passport or visa from which common identified elements of information can be instantaneously retrieved using special equipment. International standards for machine-readable passports and visas have been established by ICAO.
mala fide (Latin)	In bad faith; with intent to deceive or defraud. Contrast '*bona fide*.'
migrant	The United Nations definition is an individual who has

resided in a foreign country for more than one year. Under such a definition, those traveling for shorter periods as tourists and businesspersons would not be considered migrants. However, common usage includes certain kinds of shorter-term migrants, such as seasonal farmworkers who travel for short periods to work planting or harvesting farm products. See also 'alien'.

migration
The movement of persons, usually between States. Migration can take many forms: immigration vs. emigration, permanent vs. temporary, voluntary vs. forced, etc. In general usage, migration can also refer to internal movement of persons within a State, but international practice suggests that regulation of such movement is not appropriate for migration laws and is not enforced by migration agencies.

migration management
This term is used to encompass numerous governmental functions and a national system of management for cross-border migration, particularly managing the entry and presence of foreign nationals within the borders of the State and the protection of refugees and others meriting protection.

minor
A person who, according to the law of the relevant country, is under the age of majority, i.e. is not yet entitled to exercise specific civil and political rights.

minority
A group that is different in some respect (such as race or religious belief) from the majority and that is sometimes treated differently as a result.

multilateral
Involving more than two parties or two States. Contrast 'bilateral'.

nationality
See: citizenship. Nationality was described by the International Court of Justice (Nootbohm case, 1957) as: '...a legal bond having as its basis a social fact of attachment, a genuine connection of existence, interests and sentiments, together with the existence of reciprocal rights and duties...'

naturalization
The conferring, by any means, of citizenship upon a person after birth.

oath
A solemn pledge of truthfulness, usually given force by being said in connection with something viewed as sacred (such as a god or gods) or something revered. In the legal context, making an oral or written statement under oath invokes a legal obligation to tell the truth. In most countries, one who does not tell the truth while under oath has committed a criminal offense.

overstay
To remain in a country beyond the period for which entry was granted. Also sometimes used as a noun, e.g., 'The undocumented alien population is evenly divided between overstays and those who entered illegally.'

passport
A government document identifying a person as a national of the issuing State, which is evidence of the holder's the right to return to that State. In Western traditions, passports

	have been used for foreign travel purposes, not as domestic identity documents.
penalty	Punishment. In the migration context, penalty usually means a fine, but could also be a prohibition on future entry. For example, in some States, a person who is deported ineligible to re-enter the State for a fixed number of years.
permanent residence	The right, granted by a State other than one's state of citizenship, to live and work on a permanent (unlimited) basis.
permit	Documentation, usually issued by a governmental authority, which allows something to exist or someone to perform certain acts or services. In the migration context, reference to residence permits or work permits is common.
plaintiff	A party who brings a civil suit (by filing a complaint) in a court of law.
point of entry	see 'checkpoint'
port of entry	see 'checkpoint'
prima facie (Latin)	On its face; true or valid on first impression. In the migration context, an application for refugee or other immigrant status might be undergo preliminary review to determine whether there is a prima facie showing of all the basic requirements (often as a condition for receiving financial assistance or a work permit).
primary inspection	In international practice, review of applicants for admission at checkpoints is divided into 'primary' and 'secondary' inspection. The vast majority of applicants for admission undergo only a short screening at primary inspection booths prior to admission. Any applicant about whom the migration official has doubts is referred to secondary inspection, where the applicant undergoes an interview or additional investigation. The use of this two-step approach is more efficient and minimizes delays for the majority of legitimate travelers.
principal applicant	In the migration context, the person who applies for refugee or other immigration status. General international practice is that dependents (usually a spouse and any minor children) would be considered derivative applicants and would receive the same status afforded to the principal applicant.
proof	The establishment or denial of a contested fact by evidence; the result of evidence.
quarantine	The temporary isolation of a person or animal afflicted with a contagious or infectious disease.
quota	A quantitative restriction. In the migration context, many countries establish quotas, or caps, on the number of migrants to be admitted each year.
readmission agreement	Agreements (usually bilateral) which address procedures for one State to return undocumented aliens to their home State or a State through which they passed on route to the

State which seeks to return them. In August 1999, IGC reported that the 220 of the 238 existing readmission agreements were concluded since 1990, and approximately 170 involved Central and East European countries.

reception centre see 'holding centres'

record The official report of the proceedings in a case or administrative matter, including all papers filed, any transcript or notes taken by the judge or tribunal, and any evidence presented.

regularization Any process by which a country allows undocumented aliens to obtain legal status in the country. Typical practices include the granting of an amnesty (also known as 'legalization') to aliens who have resided in the country for a given length of time and are not otherwise found inadmissible.

regulation A rule or order, having legal force, issued by an administrative agency or a local government. Regulations typically provide procedural and other detail necessary to implement legislation.

removal see 'deportation'

repatriation Return to the country of origin. Repatriation may be either voluntary or involuntary.

residence A temporary or permanent dwelling place or abode, or habitation to which one intends to return, as distinguished from a place of temporary stay or visit.

residence permit A document issued by a State to an alien, confirming that the alien has the right to live in the State.

retraction The act of withdrawing or taking back (such as a promise or a statement).

return In the migration context, a collective term to encompass the movement of an alien from a State which has found the alien's presence illegal to his homeland or country of prior residence. This includes deportation by the State as well as voluntary return either on an individual basis or under the auspices of an organization such as IOM.

Schengen Agreement An intergovernmental agreement signed in 1985 to create a European free-movement zone without controls at internal land, water and airport frontiers. In order to maintain internal security, a variety of measures have been taken, such as the coordination of visa controls at external borders of Member States through a common approach to visa policies and asylum procedures. Although the Schengen Agreement was concluded outside the context of the European Union, it has been brought into the realm of the EC/EU under the Amsterdam Treaty. States seeking accession to the EU must thus have border regimes which meet Schengen standards

screening The process of checking for a particular attribute or ability. In the migration context, a preliminary (often cursory) review to determine if a person is 'prima facie' eligible for

	the status requested.
secondary inspection	contrast 'primary inspection'
security features	In the migration context, attributes which make passports, visas or other documents more difficult to counterfeit. Typical security features include use of paper with special watermarks or fibers, use of microline or other special printing techniques, and use of laminates which become discolored upon tampering.
sensors	In the migration context, equipment designed to detect the movement or presence of persons. This includes motion sensors, carbon dioxide sensors, etc. Some sensors require a human operator, while others are fixed in remote places along the border and transmit information to a border control facility.
sentence	The judicial act which imposes punishment on a criminal wrongdoer after a determination of guilt.
smuggling	In the migration context, the facilitation of illegal border crossing, often (but not necessarily) for financial gain. Smuggling, in contrast with 'trafficking', does not require an element of exploitation or violation of human rights. Also: Smuggling is the service provided by intermediaries who organize illegal crossing of international borders.
sponsorship	The act of promising financial support for an alien seeking entry to the State. Some States require either sponsorship or proof of adequate income as a condition for certain categories of immigration status.
standard of proof	The degree or level of persuasiveness of the evidence required in a specific case. For example, in the refugee context, 'well-founded' is a standard of proof. In contrast, the US criminal standard, 'beyond a reasonable doubt', imposes a much higher standard of proof.
stateless	The status of a person without formal citizenship in any country .
suit	Any proceeding by a party or parties against another in a court.
summons	A notice requiring a person to appear in court or before an administrative agency to serve as a juror or witness.
suspect index	see 'lookout system'
suspend	To interrupt, postpone, or defer; to hold something such as a judgement in an undetermined state, waiting for fuller information.
technical cooperation	The sharing of information and expertise on a given subject, usually focused on public sector functions. Technical cooperation can include a vast array of elements, from the development of legislation and procedures to assistance on the design and implementation of infrastructure or technological enhancements.
testimony	A written or oral declaration made under oath by a witness in response to questioning by a lawyer or public official.
trafficking	In the migration context, the illicit engagement (through

recruitment, kidnapping, or other means) and movement of a person within or across international borders, during which process the trafficker[s] obtains economic or other profit by means of deception, coercion and/or other forms of exploitation under conditions that violate fundamental human rights. (Note the difference with 'smuggling'.)

transit A stopover, of varying length, while travelling between two or more countries, either incidental to continuous transportation or for the purposes of changing planes or joining an ongoing flight or other mode of transport.

transit passengers Many States define 'transit passengers ' as persons who: arrive in the State from another country while in transit to another (third country) destination; and throughout the whole period (up to a maximum of 24 hours from the time of arrival) during which they are in the State, remain: on board the craft they arrived on, or in a port or airport secure area, or in the custody of the police.

travel documents A generic term used to encompass all documents which are acceptable proof of identity for the purpose of entering another country. Passports and visas are the most widely-used forms of travel documents. Some States also accept certain identity cards or other documents described above under 'certificate of identity.'

treaty A formally signed and ratified agreement between States. A treaty is generally a bilateral agreement; multilateral agreements are more often called 'conventions' or 'covenants'.

unaccompanied minor Persons under the age of majority who are not accompanied by a parent, guardian, or other adult who by law or custom is responsible for them. Unaccompanied minors present special challenges for border control officials, because detention and other practices used with undocumented adult aliens may not be appropriate for minors.

undocumented alien An alien who enters a country at the wrong time or place, eludes an examination by officials, obtains entry by fraud, or enters into a sham marriage to evade immigration laws. This would include, among others, one: (a) who has no legal documentation to enter a country but manages to enter clandestinely, (b) who enters using fraudulent documentation, or (c) who, after entering using legal documentation, has stayed beyond the time authorized or otherwise violated the terms of entry and remained without authorization. Also: irregular or illegal alien.

unfounded Lacking a sound basis in reason or fact.

valid Legally acceptable; not having reached its expiration date.

visa An endorsement by a consular officer in a passport or a certificate of identity that indicates that the officer, at the time of issuance, believes the holder to fall within a category of aliens who can be admitted under the State's laws. International practice is moving more and more

	toward issuance of machine-readable visas which comport with ICAO standards, printed on labels with security features.
visitor	In the migration context, a person who seeks to enter for a temporary period (in contrast with one who seeks permanent resident status).
voluntary departure programme	A set of incentives to induce people to leave the receiving country and return to their home country.
waiver	A migration law might provide that certain legal requirements or grounds of inadmissibility not be applied in certain compelling cases, giving the appropriate agency the authority to exercise judgement as to whether the requirement should be 'waived' in a given case.
watchlist	see 'lookout system'
withdraw (an application)	To ask that an application previously filed be cancelled or returned, or to indicate to relevant officials that the person who filed it no longer seeks the benefit or status requested.
witness	Noun: One who has personal knowledge of certain events or facts by direct experience. In the legal context, a person with such knowledge who is legally qualified to present this knowledge in a court of law. Verb: To observe some event or action. In the legal context, to observe the execution of a written instrument, such as an agreement or contract.

T·M·C·ASSER PRESS
THE HAGUE — THE NETHERLANDS

THE ASYLUM ACQUIS HANDBOOK
The Foundation for a Common European Asylum Policy
Edited by Peter J. van Krieken

The *Asylum Acquis Handbook* is a unique and comprehensive tool for those who have a sincere interest in contributing to a sound, common European asylum policy.
Asylum has always been an intensively debated topic, and these days even more so than in the recent past. Virtually everyone has an opinion on the subject and the general consensus is that the European Union should strive for a common asylum policy. Yet, basic information is lacking: while there is talk on an 'acquis', talk on 'communitarization', the various discussions, so far, miss the firm foundation on which to build the common European asylum house.
The *Asylum Acquis Handbook* seeks to fill this gap and serves as an important reference book with in-depth information on asylum-related topics, including:
- an overview of the Acquis
- the texts of the various relevant instruments
- value-free commentaries
- informative contributions, especially written for this *Handbook* by leading experts, and
- additional information and sources.

Noteworthy is the *Preface* with relevant parts of a thought-provoking keynote address, delivered by António Vitorino, EU Commissioner for Justice and Home Affairs, at the 4th Metropolis Conference, Washington DC, December 1999.
The *Asylum Acquis Handbook* enhances accessibility and transparency and will become an important source for policy makers, the executive, the media, students and all others concerned with the issue of asylum.

Dr. Peter van Krieken's extensive UNHCR background, his role as special advisor on international affairs with the Netherlands Ministry of Justice/INS and his lecturing in international law and human rights at Webster University, Leiden, the Netherlands, made him the most suitable expert to compile and edit the *Asylum Acquis Handbook*. Dr. Van Krieken is actively involved in European asylum policy issues under CIREA, Phare assessment missions and related Twinning, Odysseus and Horizontal Programmes. He is also the editor of the book *Refugee law in Context: The Exclusion Clause*, which was recently published by T.M.C. ASSER PRESS.

ISBN 90-6704-122-X   Price NLG 165.00 / USD 87.50 / GBP 54.50   2000, pages: 360; hardbound

Distributed for T·M·C·ASSER PRESS by Kluwer Law International:

For USA, Canada, Central and South America:
Kluwer Law International, Order Department
675 Massachusetts Avenue
Cambridge, MA 02139, USA
Tel (617)354-0140. Fax (617)354-8595
Toll free in USA & Canada. 1-800-577-8118
email: sales@kluwerlaw.com

For Europe and Rest of World:
Kluwer Law International, Order Department
P.O.Box 322
3300 AH Dordrecht, The Netherlands
Tel +31 (0)78-6546454. Fax +31 (0)78-6546474
Freephone in the UK: 0800 963 955
email: sales@kli.wkap.nl

T·M·C·Asser Press

THE HAGUE — THE NETHERLANDS

Health, Migration and Return

A Handbook for a Multidisciplinary Approach

Edited by Peter J. van Krieken

What can and should be done if a rejectee or an illegal alien claims to suffer from a serious illness which can only be treated in the country where a residence permit has been sought and/or refused? Should health be considered and accepted as a ground for granting an alien access to a specific country and its health services?

A debate concerning these and other *health, migration and return* issues is much needed as answers to the challenging questions involved should be formulated. Various disciplines should take an active role in the discussion as fences need to be taken down: the legal experts and migration lawyers need to know the medical and societal implications, the ethics involved have to be clarified, the role played by the North-South relationship has to be determined and, finally, medical staff need to be informed of the human rights issues at stake.

This Handbook, with contributions by experts from WHO, IOM and academia, contains a wealth of relevant background documents, including an overview of praxis and of Strasbourg case-law. It offers a complete overview of theories from various disciplines. It will serve as a basis for a wider debate, covering:

– the right to health
– medical norm-setting
– ethics
– the right to migration
– the duty to return
– health and migration
– Strasbourg case law
– the need for information and harmonization.

Health, Migration and Return analyses the intricate relationship from a variety of perspectives. It will provide important tools to the legal and medical professions and will also become an indispensible source for policy makers, the executive, the media, students and all others interested in issues of migration.

The editor of *Health Migration and Return*, Dr. Peter van Krieken, is also the editor of *Refugee Law in Context: The Exclusion Clause* and *The Asylum Acquis Handbook*, which were recently published by T·M·C·Asser Press.

2001, ISBN 90-6704-128-9
464 pp., hardcover
Price EUR 99.00 / USD 86.00 / GBP 60.00

Distributed in all other countries by Kluwer Law International:

For North, Central and South America:
Kluwer Academic Publishers
101 Philip Drive, Norwell, MA 02061, USA
Toll free in the US 866-269-WKAP
all other customers: + 1 781-871-6600
Fax: + 1 781-681-9045
email: Kluwer@wkap.com

For all other countries:
Kluwer Law International, Order Department
P.O.Box 322
3300 AH Dordrecht, The Netherlands
Tel +31 (0)78-6546454. Fax +31 (0)78-6546474
Freephone in the UK: 0800 963 955
email: sales@kli.wkap.nl